To Tony

from

Mary + Peter + Nicki

For all your effort on the website.

Dec. 2004

'WELL AGAIN!
The Official History of Motherwell Football Club 1886 ~ 2004

By Graham Barnstaple & Keith Brown

Published by:
Yore Publications
12 The Furrows, Harefield,
Middx. UB9 6AT.

British Library Cataloguing-in-Publication Data.
A catalogue record for this book
is available from the British Library.

ISBN 0954783026

Printed and bound by:
The Cromwell Press, Trowbridge

Foreword

I was initially delighted to be asked to write the foreword to this book but then was overcome by a huge sense of responsibility! To many of you who are die-hard 'Well fans, you will probably (vaguely) remember me as the captain of Rangers, coming to Fir Park to do battle with your favourites, almost 20 years ago. Some of the reasons why I disliked playing at Fir Park (mainly due to a certain Mr. Arnott!) were because of the passion of the supporters and the extremely difficult games that always ensued. Nowadays, though, I am responsible for ensuring that visiting teams receive the same kind of hardship on the pitch, whilst your role remains the same, as always, off it.

My responsibility today is to try to maintain the standards of the Club at a level that is appreciated and enjoyed by yourselves. Whilst many might consider this task a difficult proposition, I really find it to be a pleasure and an enjoyable one. Motherwell, the town, has been dealt some severe blows recently and the football Club has suffered greatly too, but, through it all, both the community and the Club have emerged stronger and more united. At Fir Park everyone feels a big part of the Club; from the Chairman through to the groundsman. With this 'family' spirit the Club now has a strong future and I can fully understand why so many of you feel so passionately about your favourite team and Football Club.

Motherwell has overcome the odds; in football and as a community. It is a special place; it is a special club. It is special to work at Fir Park and to work in an environment that is enjoyable and exciting.

Enjoy the book and be proud to be part of a new future whilst looking back at those who helped shape the past. And Mr. Arnott? I wish I could have written his chapter!

Terry Butcher
October 2004

Acknowledgements

The authors would like to thank all of those who helped in putting this book together and in no particular order; James Reid and Ricky Mullen for help putting the player statistics together, Alex Smith for providing attendance information for the pre-war years, Derek Cox for his cover design, Terry Butcher for his foreword, all those who provided us with photographs to help illustrate the book, our wives (Christine and Carolyn) for their patience (!!) and support throughout, and the local newspapers for help with publicity.

We would also like to thank the club for its support in helping make this book possible, particularly Allen Robertson and his team.

We have tried to ensure that the information used is accurate. It has been compiled from the The Motherwell Database, which was compiled from information contained in back issues of the Motherwell Times and the Motherwell Standard. We have also made extensive use of the information contained in Motherwell Handbooks, Programmes and the Minute books of Board meetings.

In addition we have also taken information from other written sources, namely:

The First 100 years (The History of the Scottish Football League) – Bob Crampsey
The Men Who made Motherwell Football Club – Jim Jeffrey and Genge Fry
Motherwell, Champions of Scotland 1931/32 – Alex Smith
Motherwell Football Club, A history of the Steelmen 1886 – 1986 – John Swinburne
Steelopolis , The Making of Motherwell c 1750 – 1939 – Robert Duncan

The authors would also like to thank the former players, the families of former players and various supporters, plus Motherwell Football Club for permission to use many of the photographs in the book, and acknowledge the use of past and current newspapers for illustrations and photographs. Whilst every effort has been made to trace the ownership of illustrations, apologies are given should copyright have inadvertently been infringed.

The Authors:

Graham Barnstaple - started watching Motherwell back in the early sixties, and became a season ticket holder in 1971. During that time he has collected Motherwell programmes, home and away, then started writing for the original Motherwell fanzine, *'Waiting for the Great Leap Forward'*, in 1989. He took over as Matchday programme editor for the start of the 1999/2000 season, and now acts as official web site editor.

Keith Brown - is a fourth generation Motherwell fan who attended his first game in August 1968; he is being followed by his son and daughter who are both season ticket holders at Fir Park. Keith also sits on the board of the "Well Trust" which was formed in 2002, playing a big part in liaising between the club and it's fans. Many of the pictures and statistics in this publication came from his own personal collection of Motherwell memorabilia which is very extensive and varied, stretching back to the beginning of the last century when his Grandfather's brother (Craig Brown) played for the 'Well.

Contents:

Chapter 1 The Early Years

In the late 19th Century there was a conflict in Motherwell for the leisure pursuits of the working man between the UnGodly and Godly! The Church, which was a strong opinion former of the time, was constantly fighting against the attractions of the public house, gambling and street bookmakers. They, along with other working class organisations like the Co-op, would provide respectable entertainment and cultural evenings.

As the end of the century approached a number of new developments in leisure and entertainment were beginning to take hold in the ranks of the working class masses, and many of these had no connection with the Church or other like minded bodies, but still met with their approval.

Most notable amongst these pursuits were sport and recreation, particularly amongst the male population. Curling had been long established, the Dalziel club having been formed in 1820, but this was largely a pursuit for the local farmers and masons. Outdoor and indoor bowling was also being taken up by working men, initially at the High Rd. and Knowetop greens (both still thriving in the early 21st Century).

Organised cricket and football started to appear in the 1860s and 1870s but played initially by tradesman and artisans. In the early 1870s there were at least four cricket clubs mainly made up of English skilled workers but the popularity soon waned and by 1890 only one club remained, Dalziel Cricket Club which played within the grounds of Dalziel Estate until the late 20th Century.

From the 1870s there was a massive change as football took over as the mass sport for both players and spectators. The introduction of a Saturday half day holiday for many trades gave men the time to indulge in these pursuits. The first amateur teams in the area were mainly works teams in the 1870s.

The early teams in Motherwell were dominated by Glencairn who started up around 1877, named from John Glencairn Carter Hamilton of Dalziel. Initially they played their games on open ground in Craigneuk using a nearby school as their changing rooms, this park was known as the "foot of the knowe". They then moved to a pitch at Broomside near Kidstones Pit, in the area that is now North Lodge in the town, they then moved to the Meadows.

The Meadows was used within the town as a venue for the gala occasion of the annual athletic sports held there every July. Other football teams were also playing there, the most significant being Glencairn's rivals Alpha FC, the team that was to become Motherwell's most popular team and eventually the backbone of Motherwell FC.

Alpha were founded in 1881 by the workers in George Russell's Alpha Steam Crane and Engineering works which was based in Park St. They developed by playing against a host of other amateur teams that had sprung up in the area around Motherwell, Wishaw and Bellshill. Some of the names that were in existence at the time were; Dalziel Rovers, Milton Rovers, Motherwell North End, Motherwell Amateurs and Hamilton Park.

There were few organised competitions for teams to play in, but one that was founded in these formative times was the Lanarkshire Cup, but things were so chaotic that teams were often left waiting for opponents to arrive, or even to see if a full compliment of their own team would turn up. One Lanarkshire cup-tie in 1884 saw Alpha take on Hamilton Accies with only eight men but still run out 5-2 winners as late comers arrived to make up the numbers.

In 1886 a Motherwell Charity Cup was established to engage local teams in a tournament that was to be for the "benefit of the poor". Another event set up was for a friendly between Glasgow "Ancients, as the name suggest a selection of older players, to take on an Alpha and Glencairn select eleven. This was at a time when many were suggesting that the two top teams in the town should amalgamate and form one stronger team. This argument was done no harm when the select eleven overcame the Ancients by two goals to one in front of a large crowd.

On 6th May 1886 the Alpha met and decided that it was time to disband the club, as it was at that time, and re-form under a new constitution and set of rules but under the same name. Eleven days later representatives of both Glencairn and Alpha met in Baillie's Pub in Parkneuk and decided to form a completely new club, and to be named Motherwell FC. A committee was formed and was able to field a team, albeit an Alpha dominated one, to take on Hamilton Accies at Alpha's new ground at Roman Rd. The debut was a successful one as the newly formed Motherwell side emerged victors by three goals to two.

Motherwell's first goalscorers were A. Kemp with two and N. McMaster with the other.

At the time the Motherwell Times commented that the merger of the two sides could make *"Motherwell FC second to none in the West of Scotland as a country club"*. In the early years, life was still chaotic for the fledgling Motherwell FC with no regular competition to play in, although the Lanarkshire Cup was still seen as a prestigious tournament at this time. The new side reached their first final in 1888 where they lost to Airdrie. Not only was competition difficult to find but games would still start with players short, as they struggled to make the game after a shift in the local iron works.

Not only were there problems on the playing side, the ground at Roman Road was also causing difficulties with its muddy surface and the demands to build houses on the site. Despite looking at a site in Ladywell and one on Hamilton Road, the final decision was made to relocate to a site just off Airbles and Parkhead Streets, and although an original name of "Glencairn Park" had been suggested it was finally decided that the ground would be called Dalziel Park. The first game played at the new ground was played in March 1889 when Rangers were held to a 3-3 draw.

Many teams complained that the pitch was too narrow, in fact leading to a complaint from Campsie being upheld following a Scottish cup-tie in 1893. It was hardly surprising that the visitors had complained as they had lost 9-2 in the tie. Thankfully for Motherwell they still managed to win the tie 6-4 in the replayed match. Unfortunately Motherwell were knocked out 4-2 by Hearts in the Second Round.

At this time the Scottish Cup was played in a regional basis due to the high number of clubs wishing to take part, with only the final sixteen teams taking part in the tournament proper. In their first attempt at the trophy in the new club's first season they were to lose 6-1 away to Cambuslang in the first round. In the following years they only managed to reach the second round on three occasions before the 1893 season, although they did manage to reach this stage in the second season before losing out to Carfin Shamrock. The team bettered this with a run to the third round in 1888/89. Royal Albert were beaten in the first round after a replay following a 3-3 result in the first game, with Motherwell winning the replay 2-1 at Larkhall. The second round brought a visit from Hamilton Accies, and the home side won easily by five goals to one. The run ended abruptly with a 6-2 home defeat to Dumbarton.

Goals were never in short supply in these early Scottish Cup ties with the First Round in 1889/90 seeing a 6-5 win over Airdriehill being followed by another defeat at the hands of Carfin Shamrock, this time losing 6-2! In 1890/91 it was a return trip to take on Royal Albert, but this time Motherwell were defeated by four goals to five.

By this time things were not going all that well with players still failing to turn up and crowds falling away due a lack of on field success. To try to find consistent competition the club joined the Federation League in 1891, and despite a change in colours from the original blue and white to black and gold Motherwell finished bottom of the table. The second season was to see an improvement as they climbed to second in the table behind eventual Champions Royal Albert. Wins during the season had included a 16-1 victory over Clydebank, with the score being 10-0 at half time.

But in a move to push the club forward the AGM of 1893 saw a heated debate on the thorny issue of whether the club should turn professional or not, and in the end it was decided unanimously in favour of taking this positive step. This also meant an increase in gate prices with entry now costing 6d (2. 5p) and season tickets rising to 7/6 (37. 5p). The first professional game that the club played in was in August 1893 at Roman Road against Hamilton Accies, with Motherwell winning 3-2, with two goals for Kemp and one for McMaster.

Now that players were to be paid, Motherwell had to find better competition and rewards than that provided by the Federation League. They narrowly missed election to the Alliance League and as a result looked to form a Lanarkshire League, along with five other teams. But this was still not enough for the club who wanted to perform at an even higher level, and when the Scottish League was convinced the time was right to form a Second Division they were put forward for election.

The decision of the Scottish League to form the Second division allowed them to expand into geographical areas from which they were absent, those such as Tayside, Edinburgh and Industrial Lanarkshire. Motherwell were therefore duly elected along with nine other teams to form the Second Division for the start of the 1893/94 season. The other nine teams who joined them for this historic season were; Hibernian, Cowlairs, Clyde, Partick Thistle, Port Glasgow Athletic, Abercorn, Morton, Northern and Thistle. Motherwell's first game was a 4-1 win at home to Clyde, with the first profession Motherwell side striding out in maroon shirts and satin knickerbockers. Although the preferred colours throughout the period were to remain the original blue.

After this opening victory, Motherwell went on to win the next three games, against Abercorn, Cowlairs and Port Glasgow (who were beaten seven goals to two), before losing the next two games to Partick Thistle, home and away. But for all that the new League had been formed, there was still a deal of chaos in the game, with kick-off times being spasmodic, referees not turning up and teams still being short handed. In the end Motherwell finished fourth in that first season, having won eleven of their eighteen games, losing six and drawing once.

This first season in the League had the required effect of boosting income with the revenue rising from £521 to £1032. Sadly, despite a better League position the following season, due to a prolonged Miner's strike income was down. Season 1894/95 saw Motherwell finish second in the table, but were denied promotion as at this time there was no automatic promotion. Teams in the Second Division would put themselves for election into the First Division and it was up to the teams from the top League to vote in whoever they wished.

In that second season Motherwell won ten games, losing six and drawing two. In the second half of the season they only lost two of the nine games winning seven which pushed them into second place. The highest win of the season was a seven nil win over Abercorn in the early part of the season. There was no progress made in the Scottish Cup as Motherwell lost in the First Round by two goals to one to Mossend Swifts.

Two major events took place in 1895 with the Lanarkshire Cup finally being won when Albion Rovers were beaten 7-3 in the Final. Also at this stage the search was on for a new ground to replace the tight, muddy Dalziel Park. The last game to be played at the old ground was a benefit match against Royal Albert in May 1895. The first site chosen was at right angles to Hamilton Road, and a lease with the Duke of Hamilton had been prepared, but when it was discovered that the site was close to the County Hospital and no turf could be cut, the plan was abandoned and a new site had to be found.

As part of the existing Dalziel Park ground was also required for housing the search had to be stepped up. Lord Hamilton solved the problem by granting a lease on a piece of land at the Northern end of the Fir Park on his Dalziel Estate. The site was considered to be a little isolated being somewhat distant from the town itself, but at the same time it opened up new areas where people may be attracted to come to watch, with Flemington and Craigneuk only minutes walk away. The first game played at the new ground was watched by over 6000 spectators as Motherwell hosted a visit of Glasgow Celtic, but unfortunately the visitors were to spoil the party by winning 8-1.

Despite the move to the new ground the next three seasons were poor ones with the League positions dropping to eighth in 1895/96, then ninth the next season, and they finally ended bottom of the heap in 1897/98. Much of the blame for this performance was put down to the deteriorating finances of the club and the shambolic training regimes.

To help the financial side the SFA decided to grant the new Fir Park an international match in 1895 when Wales were to be the visitors. Much work was done to raise the capacity of the ground by increasing the size of the bankings around the pitch with clay and ashes carted in for the occasion. This helped raise the capacity to 15000, and a then record crowd of 7000 turned up to the game as Scotland won by five goals to two. Season 1897/98 saw Motherwell return to better on field performances as they finished fourth in the table once again. This was partly helped by playing more games as a new Lanarkshire League had been established, with Motherwell using this to fill in blanks in the fixture list where they had been knocked out of Cup competitions, and the confidence was boosted following their winning of that League.

The next three seasons saw continued improvements in the on-field performances as Motherwell showed a greater level of consistency, apart from season 1900/01 when they once again finished bottom of the table. But by 1903 things had progressed so well that they finished second in the table. A year earlier they won the Scottish Qualifying Cup, when they beat Stenhousemuir 2-1 at Ibrox in front of a 10000 crowd after a protested first game at Celtic Park.

The successful season of 1902/03 realised an income of £1973 and helped clear off all the existing debts. Also at this time, Dundee proposed that the First Division should be increased to fourteen clubs, primarily with a view to brining in a side from Aberdeen. This plan failed as the newly formed Aberdeen side was an amalgamation of three other sides, Aberdeen, Orion and Victoria and they failed to get enough votes to join the First Division. Motherwell were duly elected with eleven votes, with Airdrie gathering eight votes and the new Aberdeen FC managing only five.

Much work was required to bring Fir Park up to standard for the larger crowds expected for games in the top division. The pitch was upgraded, the bankings were improved, and extra land taken on at the Knowetop end where half a dozen turnstiles were installed. The team was also much changed from that which had gained promotion, but even then they still found the move up a division a tough mountain to climb.

The first season in the First Division, 1903/04, started with seven straight defeats as the new side struggled to find its feet. The first game in the top division was a 2-1 defeat to Lanarkshire rivals Airdrie at Fir Park, with the first win coming along in early October with a two nil victory over Partick Thistle at Fir Park once again. The first win away from Fir Park was gained at Morton's Cappielow ground when they won three-two, on Boxing Day 1903.

It was hardly surprising that the first season in Division One ended with a poor second from bottom finish in the table, having lost seventeen of the 26 games played, with only six wins and three draws. The Scottish Cup saw Motherwell reach the second round after beating Partick 2-1 in the first, but Leith Athletic proved too strong as they ran out 3-1 winners in the later tie.

With the move into the First Division it was hardly surprising that there was a proposal at the club's half yearly meeting, in December 1903, that the club was now too big to be undertaken by people running it in their spare time. It was therefore proposed to form the club into a Limited Liability Company, and it was hoped that at the same time that the revenue raised could go a long way to improving Fir Park and bring in new players. Rather than take a hasty decision at the December meeting the members decided to wait until the AGM planned for April 1904, where the vote was unanimous in favour of forming a company and appointing Directors to run the business of the club.

Season 1904/05 was still a difficult one with Motherwell finishing fourteenth in the fourteen team set up, winning only six of their games and once again losing seventeen. This League position left the club seeking re-election in the top Division. They were duly re-elected, along with Morton, but after a season of not having to play in the Scottish Qualifying Cup, they were once again forced to participate in that competition from season 1905/06.

The new Directors for the Limited Liability Company were finally appointed in January of 1905, along with the appointment of the first Secretary/Manager, when this post received the amazing total of 228 applicants in May 1904. The first person appointed to the post P. B. McDonald of Liverpool, who only lasted a few months (he left in October of 1904), to be replaced in January of 1905 by Alex F. McIntyre who filled the post until 1908 when it was put forward that retiring Director W. H. Barrie should take up the post.

In the years following this disastrous 14th place finish Motherwell established themselves as a solid middle of the table side during the following seasons, until a form slump saw them finishing second bottom of the table in 1910/11. During this spell Motherwell won their first ever game against Rangers, with a 1-0 home win at Fir Park on March 2 1907, and strangely in such a poor season also beat Celtic for the first time, with a 2-1 win at Fir Park on 4th February 1911.

Following the elevation to the top division, Motherwell players started to attract the attention of the International selectors, and goalkeeper Colin Hampton was chosen to play for the Scottish League. Outside left C. Robertson became the first Motherwell player to be selected for Scotland when he line-up against Wales at Kilmarnock on March 5th 1910, which resulted in a 1-0 win for the Scots. Also picked to represent his country was Murray who was picked to represent Ireland.

Season 1910/11 saw a decent run in the Scottish Cup, and after seeing off St. Johnstone (2-0) in the first round, and Airdrie (5-1) in the second, they were drawn to take on Hamilton at Douglas Park in the third round.

To cope with the interest amongst Motherwell supporters the Lanarkshire Tram Co was called upon to run a tram a minute over the Clyde to the game. The game attracted a crowd of 17000, but it did not prove a joyous occasion for the men from the Steel Town as their neighbours ran out 3-1 winners on the day.

After this game the Directors met in the Commercial Hotel in Hamilton, to resolve the important task of finding someone to manage the team. From an original list of 70 applicants a short list of twelve was drawn up and one of the most inspired decisions in the history of the club was taken when thirty-six year old John "Sailor" Hunter was appointed to the post of Team Manager.

Hunter had been born in Paisley and joined his first senior club, Abercorn, in 1897 where he made twenty appearances before moving south two years later to join Liverpool. He was part of the first Liverpool side to win the League Championship in 1901. He then returned north of the border, in 1902, when he joined Hearts as an inside left, but a year later moved south once again when he signed for Arsenal. He was at Arsenal for a year before moving on to Portsmouth before returning to Scotland for good when he joined Dundee.

At Dundee he won a Scottish Cup winners medal in 1910, also gaining his only Scottish Cap whilst there, when he lined up against Wales at Wrexham in 1909 with the Welsh winning 3-2.

The year after the Cup win Hunter moved on to Clyde as an amateur player and at the end of season 1910/11 he asked them for a free transfer to allow him to take over the post of Manager of Motherwell. Therefore for the start of season 1911/12 Motherwell had in place a man who was set to transform the fortunes of the club given his broad experience gained as a player which he was now ready to impart to others.

The start to his managerial career was an inauspicious one, opening the season with a draw versus Queen's Park at Hampden, followed by a defeat at the hands of one of his former clubs, Dundee, at Dens Park. His first win in charge came in his third game when Motherwell won the return game against Queen's Park 1-0 at Fir Park. This type of form summed up the season as a whole with results proving to be topsy turvy, and despite reaching the heights of seventh in the table at one point, a run of games that saw Celtic beaten 3-2 - their only defeat on the way to winning the Championship - Motherwell ended the season back in 14th place by the season's end, only four places from the bottom.

The Scottish Cup produced a good run in season 1911/12 with Motherwell making the Third Round for the second successive year.

The first two rounds saw Morton and Hamilton beaten before a trip to Cathkin Park to take on Third Lanark, where the home side proved too strong and Motherwell were beaten by three goals to one. There was one sign of what was to come under Hunter, for in his first season in charge the younger players under his tutelage won the Reserve League Championship for season 1911/12.

The following season was more successful, both on and off the pitch, with Motherwell finishing seventh in the table. Off the field the 'Well', as they were now becoming known in the local press, along with many other sides at the time were experiencing an upturn in the number of people attending games. An income of almost £6400 was generated during the season. Although the season had in fact started poorly with only one win in the first eleven games, but a strong finish which almost saw a complete reversal in fortunes with only two defeats in the last eleven games secured the respectable finish. The Scottish Cup was not quite as successful with 'Well losing to Hibs in the Second Round.

During the 1912/13 season club Secretary Mr. Barrie decided to move abroad and the club handed the duties to Mr. Hunter along with those that he already held as team Manager.

At the start of the next season, 1913/14, the club decided to change the colours form the Blue and White, that had been worn for the last twelve years, to the more distinctive Claret and Amber.

[FORM No. 6 L.]

No. of Certificate

"THE COMPANIES' ACTS, 1862 TO 1900."

FORM E

(As altered by the Board of Trade, by Notices in the London Gazette, pursuant to s. 71 of the Companies' Act, 1862, and s. 19 of the Companies' Act, 1900.

SUMMARY OF CAPITAL AND SHARES

of the ______ Company, Limited,

made up to the ______ day of ______ 19__

(being the fourteenth day succeeding the date of the First Ordinary General Meeting in the year).

Nominal Capital, £ 3000 divided into* 3000 Shares of £* 1 each.

Total Number of Shares taken up to the ______ day of ______ 19__ (which number must agree with the total shewn in the list, as held by existing members)* 874

Number to be paid for wholly in cash 619

Number issued as partly paid up to the extent of 15/ per Share otherwise than for cash 193

~~Number~~ issued as fully paid ~~up otherwise than for cash~~ ......

‡There has been called up on each of ______ Shares ...... £ 1

" " " ______ " ...... £

" " " ______ " ...... £

§Total amount of Calls received, including payments on application and allotment ...... £

Total amount (if any) agreed to be considered as paid on ______ Shares which have been issued as fully paid (otherwise than in cash) ...... £

Total amount (if any) agreed to be considered as paid on ______ Shares which have been issued as partly paid up to the extent of ______ per Share ...... £

Total amount of Calls unpaid ...... £

Total amount (if any) paid on || ______ Shares forfeited ...... £

Total amount of debt due from the Company in respect of mortgages and charges which require registration under the Companies' Act, 1900, at the date to which this Summary is made up ...... £

NOTE.—A list of the names and addresses of the Directors must follow the list of Members. Banking Companies must also add a list of all their places of business.

* *Where there are Shares of different kinds or amounts (e.g., Preference and Ordinary or £10 and £5) state numbers and nominal values separately.*

‡ *Where various amounts have been called, or there are Shares of different kinds, state them separately.*

§ *Include what has been received on forfeited, as well as on existing, Shares.*

|| *State the Aggregate number of Shares forfeited (if any).*

☞ The Return must be signed, at the End, by the Manager or Secretary of the Comp...

1913: 1st ever Share Issue, summary certificate

It was often thought that these were the racing colours of Lord Hamilton of Dalziel, but records show that in fact these have never been used by the family. It is more likely that the club were more influenced by the recent FA Cup success of Bradford City in England, and in a quest to find colours that would clash less often with other sides in the League they chose their distinctive Claret and Amber stripes.

The new colours were first worn in the opening fixture that season when Celtic were the visitors to Fir Park on 23rd August. In front of a crowd of 20000, producing gate receipts of almost £500, the sides fought out a 1-1 draw. Although when they travelled to play Hearts at Tynecastle in December they played, for one time only, in Chocolate brown tops to avoid clashing with Hearts maroon tops.

Colours prior to Claret and Amber

Period	Colours
1881 - 1886	Navy Blue shirts, white knickers and navy hose (Alpha's colours)
1886	Blue and white vertical stripes, blue knickers
1887 - 1889	Black and Gold shirts, dark blue knickers
1890	Blue and white
1891 - 1892	Black and Gold vertical stripes, blue knickers
1893	Maroon Shirts, sateen knickers
1894	Blue and white stripes
1895 - 1912	Pale blue shirts, white knickers
1913	Claret and Amber shirts, white knickers

The minutes of a board meeting on 24th November 1913 record a strange disciplinary hearing with player W. Loney being asked to explain his absence from training during that week. He explained that he had been so upset after the heavy defeat (0-5 to Clyde at Shawfield) that he had been very foolish and had been the worse for liquor for three days. He asked the Board for another chance, which he was given, but by the meeting of 10th March their patience had obviously run out with him and he was dismissed from the club for intemperance and breach of training regulations. He was eventually transferred to Partick Thistle for the princely sum of £40 in early May.

MOTHERWELL FOOTBALL & ATHLETIC CLUB, LTD.

GROUND:
FIR PARK, MOTHERWELL.

Date, January 1st 1914.

Hamilton Accies Club. League Match.

GATE RECEIPTS.

No. of Turnstile	Commencing No.	Finishing No.	No.	Rate.	Amount as per Stile.			Amount as per Collector.		
1	86144.	86884.	740.	6d	18	10.		18	9	6
2	61166.	61606.	440.	6d	11			10	19	6
3	13684.	14007.	323.	6d	8	1	6	8	1	
4	17081.	17427.	346.	6d	8	13		8	13	
5	70863	71461.	598.	6d	14	19		14	19.	
6	36768.	37969.	1201.	6d	30	-	6	30	1	
7	45228.	46273	1045.	6d	26	2	6	26	3	6
8	05371.	06515.	1144.	6d	28	12		28	12	
9	00058.	00893.	836.	6d	20	17	6	20	17	
10	74058.	74836.	778.	6d	19	19		19	8	6
11	31106.	31777.	671.	6d	16	16	6	16	14	6
12	24897.	25478.	581.	6d	14	10	6	14	10	6
13										
14	42368.	41774.	594.	3d	7	8	6	7	2	2.
15	24594.	25848.	1254.	3d	15	13	6	18	14	9.
16										
17										
18										
19										
20										
Certified				£	260	13	.	243	5	11

Stanley G. Baxter Secretary
Hamilton Accies Club.

STAND RECEIPTS.

21	27793.	28763.	970	6d	24	5		24	6	9
22	68920.	69410.	490	6d	12	5		12	6	
								£36	12	9

6/1/14

Directors.

TOTAL,	£ 277	8	-	£ 279	18	8

Gate receipts for match versus Accies

This season again proved to be a disappointment on the pitch as Motherwell once again finished in the lower regions of the table, eventually finishing the season in 16th spot. The Scottish Cup saw Motherwell reach the Quarter Final for the first time as they saw off Leith Athletic, after a replay, and Broxburn before finally succumbing 1-3 to Celtic at Fir Park.

The summer of 1914 saw the outbreak of World War I and unlike their English counterparts the SFA decided to carry on with League football but agreed to suspend the Scottish Cup competition. Very few people of the time felt that the War would last as long as a year. The desire to "do one's bit" for the country meant that there was no need to resort to conscription for the four years of the conflict. As a result it was left to the individual to respond to the decision as they saw fit, or based on the amount of moral pressure they were put under!

The result of this was that even in football the impact on clubs was uneven with some clubs, such as Hearts and Queen's Park and Hearts seeing their entire first team sign up en masse. Whereas others, such as Rangers and Celtic, saw their first eleven virtually untouched. There was an impact at Motherwell with players drifting in and out throughout the years as they returned home on leave.

There were a number of other impacts of War with crowds dwindling due to the high number men signing up for the conflict and being employed in the different battlefields of Europe. This led to clubs beginning to struggle financially, forcing calls for players to return to amateur status, but it was decided that players should still be paid but at a reduced level and look for additional jobs away from football. Many took up employment in munitions factories, this factor adding to fixture congestion, as games could only be played on Saturdays and holidays.

This led to clubs sometimes playing two games in one day, Motherwell taking on Ayr United and Celtic within hours of each other on the 15th of April 1916. The game against Ayr kicked off at 3:30 at Fir Park and Motherwell lost 3-0, they then kicked off again at 6:30, against Celtic, and lost 3-1, as darkness began to settle on Fir Park.

This was also Celtic's second game of the day and they proudly boasted that they won both, having beaten Raith Rovers at home earlier. One Motherwell player to make his debut on this strange day in April was goalkeeper Jock Rundell. The goalkeeping position had proved difficult to fill following the transfer of Hampton to Chelsea two years earlier. Rundell was to put an end to any uncertainty in this position as he went on to play over 270 games for the club, as Sailor Hunter started to build a side to challenge the monopoly of the Old Firm.

(Above) Craig Brown, capped for the Scottish League Select, and below, Willie Rankin

As many of the local men signed up for the forces, the club also made a number of goodwill gestures, agreeing to present a season ticket for three years to the first 300 natives or residents of the Parish of Dalziel who enlisted in the Army between 2nd and 16th September inclusive. Earlier, they agreed that Soldiers in uniform would pay half price at all home games and to reserve accommodation for wounded soldiers at Fir Park during 1914/15. Hunter continued his team building throughout the war years as he added three players who were to become amongst the most influential in the club's history. Firstly in August 1916 he moved to sign Hugh Ferguson from Parkhead Juniors to solve the problem centre forward position. The newcomer immediately scored two goals on his debut in the opening game of 1916/17 in a 2-2 draw with Raith Rovers, and followed this up with a hat trick two weeks later against Dundee in the 4-2 win.

During his time, Ferguson couldn't stop scoring, and in his nine years at the club he finished top of the club's scoring charts on each occasion. He also broke all records when he netted 42 goals in 1921/22. In total at Motherwell he managed a grand total of 282 League goals. Despite such a scoring record he never won a full cap for Scotland, although he was honoured by the Scottish League on a number of occasions. Ferguson eventually moved on to Cardiff City, where he made another name for himself by helping the Welsh side become the first (and only one) to take the FA Cup out of England, when they defeated Arsenal 1-0 in the Final of 1927, when he scored the only goal of the game. The next signing was Willie Rankine who also joined up from Parkhead Juniors, and played mostly as an inside right and acted principally as a provider for the prolific Ferguson. Hunter nurtured his talent and his cultured style was appreciated by the supporters of Motherwell. When Rankine left the club many thought he was the best player the club had ever had. Just as Ferguson never won a full Scotland Cap Rankine was treated in the same fashion and had to console himself with League honours instead.

A year later Hunter signed up outside left Bobby Ferrier from Petershill, in December 1917. Ferrier was to stay at the club for twenty-two seasons, playing in over 600 games, as he featured in one of the most successful spells in the club's history, appearing in Cup Finals, the League winning side as well as travelling the world with Motherwell. Like the two other significant signings he never managed to play for Scotland as he was born in Sheffield, but he also had the consolation of playing for the League's representative side.

With these changes on the playing side Hunter's side started to push their way up the League table finishing eighth in 1916/17 and then fifth a year later, as the manager's influence started to flow through the club at all levels. This fitted in well with the cessation of hostilities on the continent and once again the Miners and Steelworkers could once again get along to Fir Park after their shift on a Saturday, along with shopkeepers who could attend mid-week games thanks to their half day closing on Wednesday.

It took a couple of years after the War before things would fully return to normal. The initial seasons after the War saw the League operate with only one division of 22 clubs and the players were still to be kept on low wages while the clubs recovered from the financial constraints of the conflict. There was still a great deal of uncertainty surrounding football in Scotland, with the SFA not restarting the Scottish Cup until 1919/20, whilst the League was under pressure to re-instate a Second Division. Eventually the Second Division began from 1920/21 with automatic promotion and relegation for the first time, with three up and three down at the end of that first season.

Despite all this uncertainty, the foundations had been laid for a Motherwell side that would challenge for major honours and acts as ambassadors for the game across the world.

Chapter 2 The Nearly Twenties

Leage football probably got back to normal for Motherwell in 1920/21, just at a time when Industrial problems hit the area. There were major problems in the steel and iron industries with their main customer, the Clyde shipbuilders, cutting production due to a glut of German ships being snapped up by British shipping lines.

By the end of the season two of the major works would have ceased production with the Lanarkshire Steelworks and the Dalzell works suffering. This resulted in the number of unemployed in the town jumping from 1000 to 4500, which obviously had a knock on effect to the football club. This was compounded as there was also a slump in coalmining in the area.

Motherwell did provide a ray of sunshine in these dark Industrial times as they performed well in the League, finally finishing fifth in the table, with Ferguson netting 42 times and the club also reaching the Quarter Final of the Scottish Cup for the first time since the start of the War in 1914, when they lost to Celtic.

The League season started with a series of inconsistent results and saw Motherwell sitting mid-table at the halfway point. One of the highlights of the first half of the season came at Hampden against Queen's Park when Motherwell ran out six goals to nil winners and Ferguson continued the goal trail when he score four goals himself. He repeated the feat a few weeks later when this time the club rattled in eight goals, with Ferguson once again grabbing another four goal haul.

A run of 10 games without defeat saw Motherwell start to push up the table, the run included two back to back wins at the Christmas/New Year holiday period, with a 6-1 win over Ayr at Fir Park and 4-1 win over local rivals Hamilton Accies in games that saw Ferguson add another six goals to his already impressive tally for the season.

(Above) Bobby Lennie and (below) Hugh Ferguson

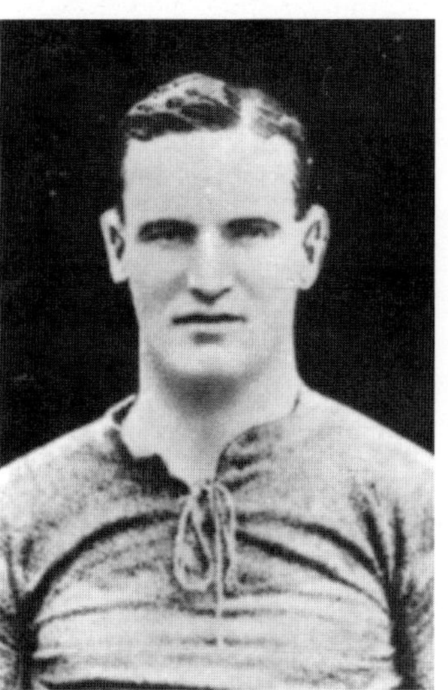

The Scottish Cup kicked off with Renton being the visitors to Fir Park at the start of February. Motherwell progressed with a comfortable 3-0 win despite regular 'keeper Rundell being absent due to the death of his father. The goals on the day were scored by Brown and two by Reid. The scoreline could have been even greater for Bell missed a penalty when the score line was 1-0.

The third round brought about a trip to play Ayr United at Somerset Park, and after beating the Honest Men 6-1 earlier in the season confidence was high. The game at Somerset Park ended in a 1-1 draw, as did the replay at Fir Park, which brought a third match at neutral Celtic Park. This time Motherwell ran out 3-1 winners, even though the first half had been a hard fought goalless affair. Ferguson put Motherwell in the lead early in the second half, only for Slade of Ayr to equalise. Motherwell progressed through goals from Rankine and a second for Ferguson.

The Quarter Final paired Motherwell with Partick Thistle at Fir Park, and the game was an exciting affair with the home side disappointed not to progress to the Semi Final. After taking the lead through Ferguson they were pulled back to level terms by a McFarlane goal. Ferguson had 'Well in the lead again before the interval and they looked like making it through to their first Cup Semi as they were in command until 'keeper Rundell misjudged a Salisbury shot to allow Thistle to force an equaliser. The replay at Firhill was another exciting affair with both teams having chances to win the game but they had to settle for a 0-0 draw that forced a second replay and played at Ibrox as the appointed neutral venue.

25000 fans turned up to see the third game, when once again Motherwell dominated much of the play and were denied time after time by Thistle's International 'keeper Campbell.

By the time the half time whistle was blown the tie was still level at 0-0. Thistle snatched a two goal lead early in the second half, which was enough to see them progress despite a penalty from Ferguson with two minutes left on the clock.

Following the defeat in the Scottish Cup Motherwell embarked on a run of ten games in which they only lost four games as they pushed up to fifth place in the League table. The game against Aberdeen on 16th April at Fir Park saw Ferguson break the record for the number of League goals scored in a season by one individual when he notched his fortieth of the season, scoring all four, in a four nil win. He then took his total to 42 when he scored two more goals the following week against Clydebank in a 2-1 win.

FOOTBALL CLUB RECORDS.
A SERIES OF 50.—No. 17

MOTHERWELL.

SCOTTISH LEAGUE, RECORD 1921-2.

	Home.	Away.
Aberdeen ..	W 3—0	L 0—2
Airdrieonians ..	L 1—2	L 0—2
Albion Rovers ..	D 1—1	D 0—0
Ayr United ..	W 2—1	L 1—2
Celtic ..	D 1—1	L 0—2
Clyde ..	W 2—0	L 0—1
Clydebank ..	W 5—2	L 0—2
Dumbarton ..	W 5—0	L 2—3
Dundee ..	W 2—1	D 1—1
Edin. Hibernians	W 4—1	L 0—2
Falkirk ..	L 0—1	L 0—1
Glasgow Rangers	W 2—0	L 1—2
Greenock Morton	W 2—0	D 0—0
Hamilton Acads.	W 2—1	L 1—3
H. of Midlothian	W 3—1	D 0—0
Kilmarnock ..	W 3—0	L 0—4
Partick Thistle..	W 2—1	W 2—0
Queen's Park ..	W 5—1	L 1—2
Raith Rovers ..	W 2—1	L 1—4
St. Mirren ..	D 1—1	L 1—2
Third Lanark ..	L 1—3	L 3—4

Total played, 42; W., 16; L., 19; D., 7. Goals for, 63; against, 58. Points, 39. Position 13th.

Issued by The Imperial Tobacco Co. (of Great Britain & Ireland), Limited.

1921/22

The new season was to prove disappointing after the previous season with only a 13th place League finish being achieved after the previous season's fifth, although the Scottish Cup did bring some more light relief again with another Quarter Final place being attained.

The first three games of the season gave the Motherwell fans a hint of what was to come as they made a promising start with a 0-0 draw in the opening game at Cappielow against Morton. They won their first game the following week with a 2-1 win over Raith Rovers, with Ferguson scoring another two goals at Fir Park. Then in the third game they went down 1-2 to Rangers at Ibrox. This was typical of the inconsistent results that Motherwell would string together throughout the League season.

The Scottish Cup was to prove the highlight of the season, the second round saw East Fife beaten 3-0 at Bayview Park in Methil. Ferguson had put Motherwell ahead after only fifteen minutes and then had to withstand a period of pressure from the home side, with Brown forced to clear an effort off the line, but Motherwell were two up before half time when Tennant scored. The victory was sealed in the second half when Ferguson added a third from the penalty spot.

This obviously inspired the players as a week later they produced a marvellous performance at Fir Park to beat Rangers by two goals to nil. Ferguson was on fine form and he had the 'Well a goal up in only fifteen minutes with a marvellous 20 yard shot. Lennie added a second when he headed home a Tennant corner.

Despite a Rangers rally, Motherwell held on comfortably for a fine win.

Motherwell made it a fantastic two weeks when they took on Hibs in the Scottish Cup and ran out 3-2 winners at Fir Park. Three quick goals setting the tie up nicely, Motherwell taking the lead through Ferguson, but Hibs equalise two minutes later through Young. But their opponents were only on level terms for just two minutes before Motherwell took the lead once again, Ferrier restoring the home side's lead. A Tennant goal gave Motherwell a two goal lead when he fired home an unstoppable shot following some fine work from Ferguson. Hibs did manage to pull one back in the second half but it wasn't enough to stop Motherwell progressing to the fourth round.

Alloa were the visitors to Fir Par in the fourth round, in a tie which attracted 20000 to see Motherwell advance to the Quarter Finals with a 1-0 win, and with a score line which flattered the visitors. Once again it was Ferguson who was the goalscorer as he smashed a left foot shot passed the visiting 'keeper.

After a scappy but competitive match Motherwell found themselves knocked out of the cup by a late goal that saw Morton go through to the next round. The Cappielow side went ahead just before the interval thanks to an error by Motherwell goalie Rundell. Instead of tipping a thirty yard effort over the bar he attempted to catch it but only succeeded in dropping the ball over the line.

The 'Well equalised in the second half when a Craig Brown header hit the crossbar and John Hart was on hand to score from the rebound, but with only a few minutes to go and the fans expecting a replay, French scored to give Morton the win and leave Motherwell still waiting on that first Semi Final place.

In June 1922 the Motherwell board were forced to consider an offer for Ferguson from Manchester City who had obviously been attracted by his scoring feats the previous season. The directors met to consider City's offer of £3500 which fell short of their valuation of £4000 for the player. They declined this offer, and Manchester City's representative Mr. Mangnall raised the offer to £3900 which the Board decided to accept. Unfortunately for Mr. Mangnall the player decided to turn down their personal terms, and as the minutes from the board meeting put it, *"the matter was left in abeyance"*.

A somewhat sparse Fir Park, in the 1920's

1922/23

The start of the season saw Motherwell line-up with two key players injured - Bobby Lennie missing due to illness, and Willie Rankine through an eye injury. Manager Hunter signed Royal Albert's Hart the night before the game and flung him straight into the action. The absence of these two players in the opening stages of the season was to prove difficult for Motherwell to cope with as they lost their first four games and found themselves at the foot of the table.

The run was halted with a 1-1 draw away to Alloa at Recreation Ground with Ferguson once again on target. It looked as though Motherwell would take both points from the game until Cochrane scored a solo goal to equalise with only nine minutes remaining. The first win was finally achieved in the sixth game of the season with an emphatic 4-0 home win against Ayr United.

Up until Christmas Motherwell were struggling to pull themselves clear of relegation as they struggled to turn draws into wins.

FIR PARK,
MOTHERWELL, 26*th May*, 1923.

THE MOTHERWELL FOOTBALL & ATHLETIC CLUB LIMITED

Notice is hereby given that an EXTRAORDINARY GENERAL MEETING of this Company will be held at FIR PARK, MOTHERWELL, on TUESDAY, 5th JUNE, 1923, at 8 o'clock P.M., for the purpose of considering, and, if deemed expedient, passing the following Extraordinary Resolution, vizt. :-

That the one thousand unissued Shares of the Company be offered to the Members as nearly as possible in proportion to the number of Shares already held by them, and that at par value; that such offer be made by notice specifying the number of unissued Shares to which each member is entitled, and limiting a time within which the offer, if not accepted, will be deemed to be declined; and, after the expiration of such time, or on receipt of an intimation from the member to whom such notice is given, that he declines to accept the Shares offered, the Directors may dispose of the same in such manner as they may think most beneficial to the Company."

By Order of the Directors.

JOHN HUNTER,
Secretary.

Notice calling the EGM in June 1923

However, even with Ferguson and Ferrier missing they did manage to pull off a couple of excellent wins over Falkirk and Morton that helped ease some of the relegation worries, just as the Scottish Cup campaign was about to kick in once again.

First round opponents were St. Johnstone at the Perth side's Muirton Park ground with 12000 people packed into the ground. The 'Well forged ahead in the 10th minute when Ferrier went up the the left wing and his cross was met by Ferguson who scored.

The Saints equalised soon after half time but the 'Well moved up a gear and went ahead with a controversial goal. Saints 'keeper Stewart made little attempt to stop a Rankin effort because he thought the Motherwell player was offside. Motherwell inside forward Wardrope, however, played to the whistle and as the referee waved play on he ran in to fire the ball home and send the Steelmen into the next round, where they would take on St. Mirren at Fir Park.

Once again it was to prove a close affair with Motherwell going ahead with two quick goals from Little and Lennie, the first hitting the bar with a 40 yard effort before striking the Saints 'keeper and rebounding over the line. Saints pulled one back in the 39th minute but in a tight second half the home side held out to win. The third round saw another home draw, with Falkirk coming to Fir Park, and being sent home again with a 3-0 defeat thanks to a hat trick from Motherwell hero Ferguson. Motherwell went ahead in the 8th minute when the prolific scorer headed home a Lennie cross. Just before half time Ferguson added a second from a Bobby Lennie run that left the visitors defence in ribbons, and then made Motherwell's win secure in the second half when he steered a Ferrier pass in to the net for his hat trick.

Bob Ferrier cigarette card

It was Bo'ness who stood between Motherwell and their first ever Semi Final, and they were swept aside with the Steelmen winning by four goals to two. Ferguson was once again instrumental in the victory with yet another hat trick, Reid adding the other, to send Motherwell through to their first ever Semi Final. The match was played at Ibrox against Celtic in front of a crowd of just over 70000 turning up for the tie, with nine special trains being laid on to take Motherwell fans through to Glasgow for this historic match. In the first minute a stumble by Motherwell centre half Craig Brown let Cassidy in and he made no mistake to put Celtic into the lead. The 'Well fought back and Ferguson, Reid, and Ferrier were all unlucky not to find the net with fine efforts. However, just when it looked like the Fir Park side might grab an equaliser a Mcattee shot struck 'Well full back Newbigging and flew into the net for Celtic's second. Motherwell tried hard to pull back the game, but the Celtic defence held firm and the Fir Park side went out of the competition losing 2-0.

A young George Stevenson, in 1924

Motherwell then only won three more games in the last ten games of the season as they ended up with a disappointing 13th place in the final League standings. In May 1923, Manager Hunter made one of his most significant signings for the club when he snapped up George Stevenson from Ayrshire Junior side Kilbirnie Laedside. Stevenson would go on to become a major member of the side that would go on to win the League less than ten years later.

1923/24

The League campaign started with two straight defeats against Rangers at Fir Park and Hamilton at Douglas Park. Things soon took a turn for the better with a string of eight games unbeaten seeing a League position of third being attained. In the middle of the eight game run, in a 0-0 draw at Ayr United, Willie McFadyen made his debut at outside right. But this was as high as they were to get in the table as disruption to team selection brought about a series of inconsistent results that saw them slide down the table to a mid table slot. Another significant League debut, thanks to the injuries, took place in December when George Stevenson lined up for the first team for his debut, replacing White at Inside left, against Third Lanark at Cathkin Park in a 2-1 defeat.

The Scottish Cup was not to prove as eventful this season as it had in the previous few years. Braedalbane were the visitors to Fir Park and Motherwell moved easily through to the next round of the Cup with a convincing win over their lowly opponents.

Two Hugh Ferguson goals saw Motherwell go in with a 2-0 lead at half time, and they completely dominated the second half as well. Ferguson notched his hat trick a few minutes after the interval with Bobby Stewart scoring the fourth. A rare goal from 'Well centre half Craig Brown completed the scoring.

A trip to Station Park, Forfar, was the reward for the first round victory, and they progressed to the next stage with another comfortable victory. Craig Brown headed home a Stewart corner to give the 'Well the lead but the home side replied with an equaliser from Gordon to send the teams in level at half time. In the second half Motherwell pressed home their superiority and Rankin scored with a thirty yard effort to make it 2-1 and then with eight minutes left on the clock Ferguson made it 3-1 from close in.

Lanarkshire rivals Airdrie were the opponents in the Third Round at Fir Park, and the visitors inflicted a heavy defeat on their hosts to see them crash out of the competition. The Diamonds, riding high in the league, were always in control of the match and McDougall put them ahead in the 33rd minute, then three minutes later Gallacher made it 2-0. Airdrie continued to dominate the second half, Russell added a third, and then a fourth and Gallacher notched the fifth to send the 'Well tumbling out of the cup.

Motherwell went on to secure a mid table finish of tenth in the League table when they lost only three more games during the remainder of the season.

1924/25

The start of the season was once again to prove a disappointment as Motherwell quickly found themselves in relegation trouble. Having only won two of their first eleven games they found themselves down at third bottom in the table and involved in a relegation dog fight.

There were a couple of significant changes at Fir Park in the month of September, one on the field and one off the field. On the field goalkeeper Alan McClory was snapped up from Ayr United, the newcomer replacing long serving stalwart Jock Rundell. Off the field the Evening Times were given approval to install a telephone line in the Main Stand to allow stories to be relayed much quicker using this modern technology.

Towards the end of November things on the field were getting worse as two heavy defeats away to St. Mirren (4-1) and at Fir Park to Airdrie (5-1) saw Motherwell hit the rock bottom of the table and in real danger of slipping out of the top division for the first time since being elected there. They did bounce back in their next two games, responding to the challenge as they ground out wins over Kilmarnock and Raith Rovers. By this stage of the season manager Hunter was being forced to tinker with the his defence and half back line almost every week due to injuries, but the results recovered as they pushed their way out of trouble.

Following the wins over Kilmarnock and Raith they only lost two games in the next seven as they desperately tried to hold on to their top flight status. They even managed to string together two four goal hauls in consecutive weeks, with a 4-1 win over Queen's Park at Fir Park on 3rd January and three days later they repeated the scoreline when Falkirk were the visitors.

The team followed this up with a fine 1-0 win over Celtic at Fir Park when they produced a fine performance to beat a Celtic team that finished the game with ten men after McGrogan was sent off. Ferguson scored the only goal of the game after great play by Bobby Ferrier. The Motherwell winger weaved his way through the Celtic defence and Shaw in the Parkhead goal could only parry his fierce drive to the feet of Hughie Ferguson who promptly scored. In the second half McGrogan was dismissed when he scythed down Hughie Ferguson with a vicious tackle.

The end of January meant that it was time for the Scottish Cup once again and Ayrshire side Galston were drawn to come to Fir Park in round one. Motherwell won the game by six goals to three with Hugh Ferguson having a field day as he rattled in five of the goals himself. The second round brought a visit from Arthurlie to Fir Park, with former 'Well 'keeper Jock Rundell in their line up, but he could do nothing to stop his former team mates from going through to the next round. The Barrhead team made a good start to the game but McGrath put Motherwell ahead when he curved a fine shot around Rundell. Stevenson added another to give the 'Well a 2-0 half time lead and complete the scoring.

Next up was a trip to Pittodrie to take on Aberdeen in the third round, and the homesters hosted a large crowd to watch this cup-tie but the fans left disappointed at the lack of goals. The Motherwell defence blocked out the menace of the Aberdeen forwards with McClory the Fir Park 'keeper in great form. Handicapped by injuries from the first game, Motherwell crashed out of the Scottish Cup at home in the replay. Disaster in the first 10 minutes saw Aberdeen take the lead, 'Well centre half Alan Craig trying to play the ball back to 'keeper McClory, but only succeeding in putting the ball into his own net. 10 minutes later it was 2-0 to the Dons when Jackson scored with a low shot. Ferguson reduced the arrears when he scored from a White corner but the 'Well couldn't find an equaliser and it was the Pittodrie team that went through to the next round.

The next three games after the Cup exit saw Motherwell slipping back into relegation trouble when they lost three consecutive games to Partick Thistle, Cowdenbeath and Dundee. But they bounced back with a result that went a long way to ensuring that Motherwell would stay up, not only for the two points gained but also for the improvement in their goal average when they beat Third Lanark 8-0. Stevenson sent the 'Well on their way with a shot that went into the net off the post, with Ferrier adding a second just after this opening goal. Ferguson netted the third from a Ferrier cross, and McGrath added two more to give the 'Well a 5-0 interval lead. The home side continued to dominate in the second half and goals from Ferguson, Stevenson, and Tennant completed the scoring. With only one more win after this game Motherwell closed the season with a 2-0 defeat at Aberdeen, a win which saw Aberdeen avoid relegation. Motherwell had amassed thirty points, the same as Ayr United and Third Lanark but thanks to that 8-0 win over Third Lanark their goal average was superior to the other two and Motherwell stayed up.

At the end of the season there was some startling news for the Motherwell supporters when Bobby Ferrier refused the terms offered by the board and he was placed on the transfer list with a fee of £100 being agreed after a long debate at board meetings. There were also stories that Hugh Ferguson was keen to move on and that teams were sniffing about desperate to snap up this free scoring centre forward.

Mid-1920's
George Stevenson & Opponent in the Tunnel

1925/26

The season opened with the two key forwards still in the line-up and a set of players who were looking to make sure that there would be no repeat of the last minute escape from relegation in the previous season. They only suffered one defeat in the first fifteen games of the season and were challenging for the title at the start of November.

It was at this time that the board agreed to sell Ferguson to Cardiff City as they had agreed to meet the terms for the transfer with a fee of £5000 being acceptable to both sides. Therefore, when Motherwell lined up against Raith Rovers at Fir Park on 7th November, all eyes were on Will McFadyen as he took Ferguson's place at centre forward, he responded well scoring a double in a five nil win. Ferguson moved to Cardiff having scored 362 goals in his nine years at the club and establishing a single season record of 42 goals in 1920/21. Overall a scoring record that is unlikely to be repeated by anyone in the future.

Despite the five nil win over Raith Rovers, Motherwell missed their star centre forward and slumped to five consecutive defeats to see them slip out of the Championship race and down to fifth in the table from second. They immediately bounced back with seven games unbeaten through mid December to the end of January, with two draws and five wins pushing them back into third in the table as they held on to a Championship challenge.

The news was not to be quite so good in the Scottish Cup, with the Cup run only lasting one game as a trip to Firhill to take on Partick Thistle saw Motherwell lose 3-0.

Bogey team Partick Thistle again had the hoodoo over Motherwell although their win was deserved. The visitors never reached the standard of football that they were capable of, and the defence in particular looked shaky.

The balance of the League campaign saw Motherwell winning five games of the twelve and losing the others, but a four game winning run at the end of the season saw the 'Well finally claim fifth in the table, which was probably disappointing given that second had been achieved at one point in the campaign.

One other interesting point to note was that after the Celtic game in March Bobby Ferrier took the gate money from this game as way of a benefit for his years of good service to the Club and was made captain for the day. This is probably the first time that a Motherwell player was awarded a benefit or testimonial of any kind. After a goalless first half, Motherwell took the lead when McFadyen was fouled outside the box. Dick Little stepped up and rattled the resultant free kick into the net. As Motherwell dominated Tennant took a Ferrier pass and fired home the second. The visitors scored late in the game but Motherwell never looked like losing a point.

By May 1926 things had deteriorated on the Industrial front when the Trade Unions called a general strike for ten days to support the Miners wage claim. The miners themselves were to be on strike for a further six months with all the collieries in the area being forced to close their doors. This also had a knock-on effect in the Iron and Steel works who ran short of this basic raw material. As a result money was extremely tight in the area, soup kitchens sprung up, and Motherwell themselves were hit by falling crowds as the working people could not afford to attend games.

The football club were in large part immune from the hardship in the area as they returned one of the best profits for a football club in the country, but this was mainly down to the transfer fee received for Hugh Ferguson a few months earlier.

1926/27

After the previous season's fifth place finish it was hoped that Motherwell could be the first team to break the Old Firm monopoly of the League title that they had established since Third Lanark won the title back before the First World War. The first four games went unbeaten with only one point dropped in a 1-1 draw with Falkirk at Brockville in the third game of the season.

This good start was followed by two straight defeats, by 2-0 to Rangers at Ibrox, and then a 5-2 reverse at Dens Park by Dundee. With Ferguson having departed, centre forward was still proving a difficult position to fill, with McSeveny, Tennant and Banks all having been tried in the position. They continued to take "turns" as both Banks and Tennant suffered injuries during the season. Despite this problem, the team embarked on a fine run of results that saw them string together a ten game unbeaten run, and they hit the top spot following a 3-1 win over Partick Thistle at Fir Park on November 27th. There was a temporary blip when they lost two games in a row losing to Celtic and St. Mirren which saw them drop off the top spot.

The drop to second was only for a week as they bounced back to the top of the table with a 1-0 win over Aberdeen at Fir Park in mid November, thanks to a McFadyen goal. There was now genuine belief that the Old Firm's grip on the League title could finally be broken.

Things got slightly worse the following week when they made a sharp exit from the Scottish Cup in the first round at Dens Park against Dundee. Almost 2000 Motherwell fans made the journey to Tayside to only to see their team perform poorly and to have little complaint about the three nil defeat. The Dens men repeated the feat a week later in the League when they defeated Motherwell for the third successive time at Dens Park.

After three successive reverses Motherwell returned to form with a 3-1 win over Hearts at Tynecastle to get their League challenge back on track. Three more games without defeat had pulled Motherwell back level with Rangers, until Lanarkshire neighbours Airdrie spoiled the Fir Park party with a five one win that allowed Rangers to pull two points clear. Motherwell kept plugging away and after a 2-1 win over Dunfermline at Fir Park in mid-March they were back to being only one point behind Rangers.

Then with four games to go they suffered a three nil defeat to bogey team Partick Thistle at Firhill and this virtually finished any hopes they had of winning the League title. The dream did finally end a week later at Celtic Park when they were beaten three two by Rangers' biggest rivals. They did secure second spot in the table on the second last Saturday of the season with a one nil win over St. Mirren at Fir Park.

Over the Christmas and New Year Period they maintained a two point lead over Rangers before the two title challengers met at Fir Park in mid-January. Unfortunately Motherwell produced a disappointing performance and slumped to defeat against Rangers with 32000 people there to witness a match that saw them knocked off top spot in the league with George Stevenson notching the only Motherwell goal in a four one defeat.

George Stevenson in training in 1927

During the season plans had been put in place to take part in a tour of Spain and it was finally agreed that a party of 16 players, the Manager, Trainer and a guide would make the trip that would provide the club with a guarantee of £1700 at the end of the season.

The tour lasted from May 11 to June 14 and proved an unqualified success, with only one defeat being suffered in the eight games played, that coming at the hands of Bilbao on May 29, when they ran out three one winners.

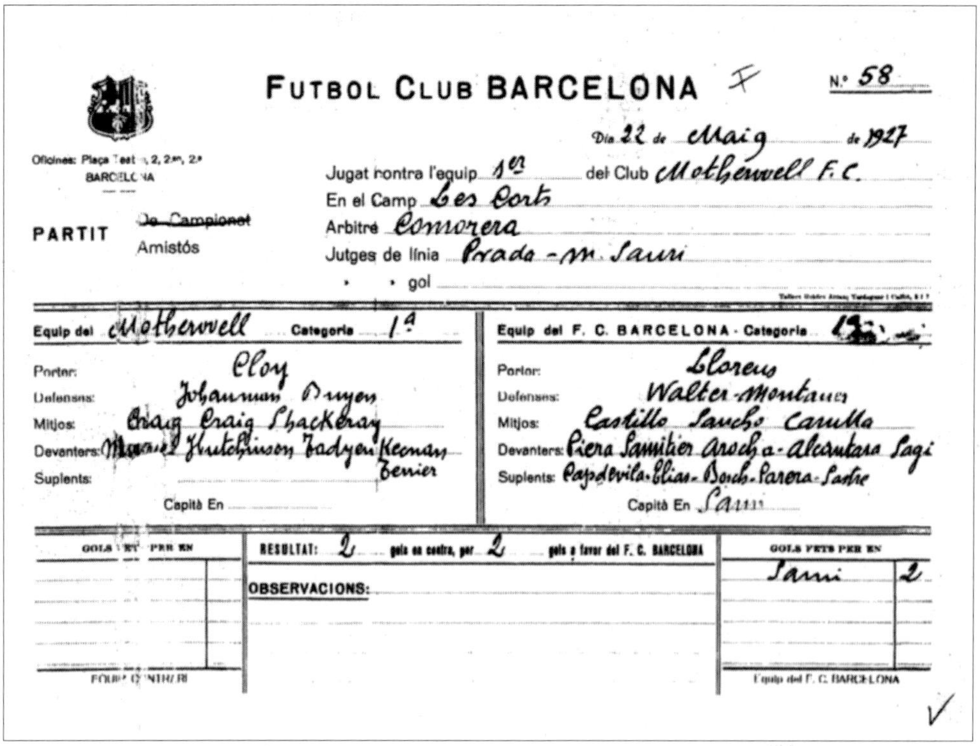

FUTBOL CLUB BARCELONA Nº 58

Oficines: Plaça ... BARCELONA

Dia 22 de Maig de 1927

PARTIT ~~De Campionat~~ Amistós

Jugat contra l'equip 1er del Club Motherwell F.C.

En el Camp Les Corts

Arbitre Comorera

Jutges de línia Prado - M. Sauri

• • gol

Equip del Motherwell Categoria 1a	Equip del F. C. BARCELONA - Categoria 1a
Porter: Cloy	Porter: Llorens
Defenses: Johnman Byers	Defenses: Walter - Montanes
Mitjos: Craig Craig Thackeray	Mitjos: Castillo Sancho Carulla
Devanters: McMurtrie Hutchinson Fadyen Keenan	Devanters: Piera Samitier Arocha - Alcantara Sagi
Suplents: Ferrier	Suplents: Papdevila - Elias - Bosch - Parera - Sastre
Capità En	Capità En Sauri

RESULTAT: 2 gols en contra, per 2 gols a favor del F. C. BARCELONA

OBSERVACIONS:

GOLS FETS PER EN: Sauri 2

1927: Team lines for the match versus Barcelona in the "King of Spain Cup"

Apart from that defeat Motherwell beat the might Real Madrid by three goals to one, with goals from Stevenson, McFadyen and Hutchison, in a game which saw the 'Well presented with the King of Spain's Cup. After beating touring Welsh side Swansea twice and drawing with Barcelona, they were then awarded the Barcelona Cup. This was at a time when Scots were feted for their football prowess and could teach players on the continent a thing or two.

The party that toured Spain in the summer consisted of: Manager Hunter, Trainer Walker, and Director James Taaggart with a playing pool of; McClory, Johnman, Frame, Byers, Livingstone, Arnot Craig, Alan Craig, Thackeray, Inglis, McMurtie, Hutchison, Keenan, McFadyen, Stevenson and skipper Ferrier. During the tour they played a total of eight games winning six, drawing one and losing one, scoring 23 goals for the loss of only 10.

Full results:

May 15	Swansea	- 4-3 (McFadyen 2, Thackeray, McMurtrie)
May 19	Real Madrid	- 3-1 (Hutchison, Ferrier, Thackeray)
May 22	Barcelona	- 2-2 (Alan Craig, Hutchison)
May 26	Swansea	- 1-0 (Ferrier)
May 29	Bilbao Select	- 1-3 (McMurtrie)
June 5	Vigo Celta	- 3-1 (Ferrier 2, McFadyen)
June 7	Vigo Celta	- 4-0 (Keenan, Stevenson, Thackeray, Ferrier)
June 12	Red Star Olympique	- 5-0 (In Paris) (Ferrier 3, McFadyen, Stevenson)

This successful tour combined with the excellent season that had preceded it had set Motherwell up for an unprecedented run of success over the next decade as they put up a sustained League challenge to the two Glasgow clubs who had dominated League football in Scotland since the game had turned professional in the late 18th Century.

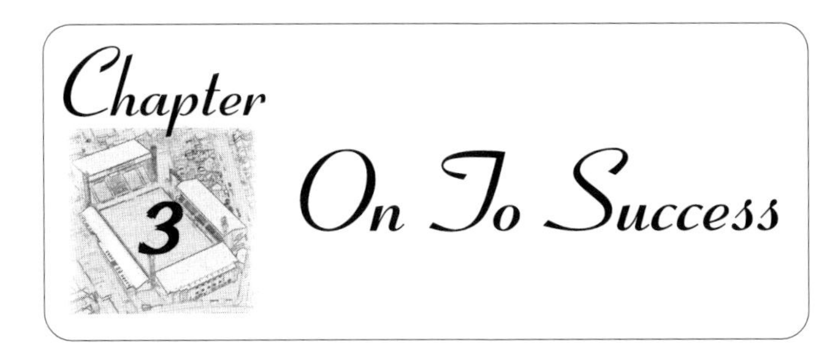

1927/28

Having just finished second, the Motherwell board did well to buck the trend of players going South to the rich pickings of the English League by retaining all the players from the previous season. This was demonstrated by the start they made to the season when the only lost one game in the opening five games (a 3-2 home defeat to Falkirk), that saw them sitting second in the table behind Celtic, with Rangers closing in with a game in hand.

This meant that there was a great deal of anticipation for the visit of Rangers to Fir Park on 24th September. The Secretary announced that he would be bringing *in "horses to cart ashes to extend the capacity of the ground "* As it turned out the game drew a crowd of 30000, who witnessed a dull 1-1 draw with Ferrier putting 'Well into the lead before McPhail equalised for Rangers from the penalty spot.

As well as the large paying crowd the game attracted the Leicester City manager to see the famous partnership of Stevenson and Ferrier but he was disappointed to go home empty handed after being told that the pair was not for sale at any price. This was not to be the last occasion that Motherwell were to receive offers for the left wing partnership. One offer from Arsenal's legendary manager Herbert Chapman would have broken the transfer record at the time as they offered £11000 for Stevenson alone; the record at the time stood at £10280.

The Falkirk defeat was to be the only one in the first eighteen games and put Motherwell in a position to be fighting for the title with the Old Firm. Over the busy holiday period at Christmas and New Year three impressive wins in four days had Motherwell top the table. On Christmas Eve they beat Dunfermline 5-0, then on Hogmanay they overcame Clyde 5-0 and rounded off the holiday games with another five goal haul against Hamilton on January 2nd. But sadly within a day they were off the top of the table when they lost to Falkirk again and Rangers returned to that position.

The Scottish Cup started at the end of January with a trip to the Highlands to take on Huntly. The game was still goalless at half time, but 'Well stepped up the pace in the second half and goals from Keenan and two from Cameron saw them safely through to the second round.

Before the second round tie Motherwell suffered a surprise loss to Queen's Park at Hampden, and this tied in with two draws prior to the Huntly game had put a dent in their League challenge. The Second Round of the Cup brought Raith Rovers to Fir Park, and it looked as though Motherwell were easing through to the third round comfortably when they took a two goal lead through Stevenson and Ferrier. But the visitors put up a tremendous fight back to force a replay through two second half goals from Turner. Motherwell did see the Kirkcaldy men off in the replay, with Cameron opening the scoring and despite an equaliser from Allison, a Keenan goal was enough to see 'Well progress to take on Hearts.

The next round, versus Hearts at Tynecastle, drew a crowd of over 40000 and Motherwell were one goal up at half time with Stevenson scoring on 37 minutes, and nine minutes after the break the same player doubled the lead. Despite a late goal from the home side Motherwell were safely through to another Quarter Final. Motherwell's performance at Fir Park against Celtic in the Quarter Final was a major disappointment and despite holding the Celts goalless at half time the crowd of over 20000 saw goals from Doyle and McGrory ensure Motherwell crashed out of the trophy.

Following the Scottish Cup exit, Motherwell won four of their last eight games, and it was the three draws and the defeat that saw them finally finish third in the table on goal average behind second place Celtic. This was despite beating Celtic 3-1 at Fir Park with three games left in the season. A Stevenson rocket and two goals from Tennant saw the 'Well take a three goal lead before losing a consolation goal to McLean.

Despite finishing a place lower in the table than in the previous season, they did manage to amass four points more than they had the previous season. Motherwell players finally received some International recognition with firstly George Stevenson being called up to play against Wales in October, before "Stevie" was joined by 'keeper Alan McClory to play against Ireland in February.

At the end of the season Motherwell set off on another overseas tour, this time they travelled to South American to undertake eleven games in Argentina and Brazil.

1928: Team photo in Rio stadium, versus Brazil

Cameron and Tennant in Agentina

Photograph of the Rio stadium in Brazil

The travelling party consisted of seventeen players, two trainers and Sailor Hunter. They only lost four games on the tour, the first three and the last one. The last game was played in Rio against Brazil and drew a crowd of 40000 to see the home side run out winners by five goals to nil. The game finished so late that the Motherwell party had to be taxied in their football gear to ensure they caught the boat back home!

The games on the tour were;

May 13	Buenos Aires Select	0-1
May 17	Provinces	1-2 (Ferrier)
May 20	Capitol	2-3 (McFadyen 2)
May 25	Rosario	4-3 (McFadyen 3, Stevenson)
Jun 2	Argentine Association	3-0 (McFadyen 2, Stevenson)
Jun 3	Argentina/ Uruguay	3-0 (McFadyen 2, Tennant)
Jun 5	Provinces	4-1 (Ferrier 2, McFadyen 2)
Jun 7	Rosario	3-2 (Stevenson,McFadyen, McMurtrie)
Jun 10	Penarol	1-0 (Tennant)
Jun 21	Brazil	1-1 (Ferrier)
Jun 24	Brazil Select	0-5

George Stevenson 're-united' many years later, with the cup won in Argentina on the 1928 tour

1928/29

Motherwell started the new season in high spirits and in a good financial position after the successful tour to South America. They had also retained all the players who had performed so well the previous season. This optimism was transferred to the start of the season when the team rattled off four straight wins to see them up amongst the Championship contenders once again for they topped the table at this early stage in the season. But this was before a loss at Somerset Park to Ayr United by two goals to nil in a game that saw centre forward Willie Tennant injured and out of the side until February. This misfortune was on top of losing forward Thackeray who moved for £3500 to Portsmouth. The board allowed the manager to pursue the signings of Murdoch from Airdrie and McMenemey from Celtic, and both were eventually signed up by the middle of October to help bolster the push for the title.

The newcomers helped string together three impressive results back to back in late October, starting with a three all draw with Celtic, followed by a magnificent comeback against local rivals Hamilton Accies. The Accies had stormed to a 3-1 lead, but goals from Ferrier, Watson and McFadyen secured the win for the Steelmen. The following week saw Falkirk hammered seven goals to nil at their own Brockville ground. Six of the goals came from new signing George Watson, with the other being added by Ferrier, as Motherwell joined Rangers at the top of the table with nineteen points. Disappointingly the next three games saw only one point picked up and the 'Well drop to fifth in the table. They then responded well, and only lost two games out of the next ten to get their Championship challenge back on course.

The Scottish Cup started in mid-January and Motherwell were drawn at home to Leith Athletic. 'Well produced a powerful first half performance to see off the challenge of their Second Division opponents and move through to the next round of the cup. Cameron gave them the lead after McMenemy had hit the post and Stevenson increased Motherwell's advantage with a fifteen yard drive. Cameron made it 3-0 before Murdoch added the fourth. Leith notched the visitor's consolation goal from the spot in the second half.

The second round brought a trip to St. Johnstone's Muirton Park, and Motherwell managed to progress by the odd goal in five, progressing by three goals to two. The 'Well goals came from McFadyen and Cameron netting two to see the team through to the third round. They managed to maintain their League form with two wins over Partick and Hibernian before Motherwell had to visit Broomfield to take on local rivals Airdrie in the Third Round of the Cup. The Broomfield surface was heavily sanded to cope with the heavy frost, and both sides were pleased to settle for a 1-1 draw, with the 'Well opening the scoring through Murdoch and Skinner equalising for the Diamonds. The replay at Fir Park saw Motherwell see off their local rivals by three goals to one, after racing into an early two goal lead, thanks to headers from Cameron and Murdoch.

This set up another Quarter Final against Celtic, and the game at Celtic Park was a hard fought 0-0 draw which forced a replay at Fir Park. Ferrier put the 'Well into the lead in the 20th minute. As the pressure mounted on the Celtic defence the ball reached the Motherwell winger and his shot flew past Thomson in the Celtic goal to put Motherwell one up. Connolly equalised for the visitors in the 30th minute with McGrory scoring the winner with just four minutes left. This game at Fir Park attracted a record crowd at the time of 34000.

With three League games to go Rangers were the visitors to Fir Park and their four two victory was enough to secure the title for the Ibrox side once again, Motherwell went on to finish third in the table, as they had done the previous season.

Throughout the season Motherwell had taken on a number of top English sides. They secured the Huddersfield Charity Cup when they beat the local First Division side by two goals to nil, and over the Easter period they recorded excellent wins over Everton (4-1), Doncaster Rovers (2-1), before a weakened side lost 2-1 to Blackpool.

1929/30

With Industrial conditions picking up in the local area there was great optimism going into another new season. There were also a number of other reasons for being upbeat, with an astute set of directors, a visionary manager, a much improved ground and a group of loyal and talented players who were seen as second to none in the country.

The ground improvements had seen over £1000 spent on a new concrete barrier wall around the pitch, an "elaborate" drainage system had been installed and the playing surface had been enlarged to 100 yards by 70 yards. The capacity of the ground was increased to 35000, with plans to move up to 40000 in the near future.

THE Standard SCORING CARD

MOTHERWELL'S

FOOTBALL FIXTURES

1929-30

Club Stationery
Circulars
Tickets
Cards
Posters
Handbills
Booklets
Accounts
Visiting and Business Cards
Holiday Fund and Club Cards
Membership Cards

f. a. Last Season.		LEAGUE FIXTURES.		f.-Goals	-a.	Pts.	GOAL-SCORERS.
2-4	Aug. 10	RANGERS	Home	0	2	0	—
1-1	,, 17	ABERDEEN	Away	2	2	1	Murdoch McMenemy
1-1	,, 24	DUNDEE	Home	3	0	2	Cameron (2) Ferrier
1-1	,, 31	CLYDE	Away	2	1	2	Stevenson, Ferrier
3-2	Sept. 7	HEARTS	Home	0	2	0	—
0-2	,, 14	AYR UNITED	Away	2	3	0	Stevenson Cameron.
4-2	,, 21	AIRDRIEONIANS	Home	2	0	2	Ferrier McMenemy.
3-2	,, 28	QUEEN'S PARK	Away	3	0	2	Stevenson McMenemy (2)
3-1	Oct. 5	HIBERNIAN	Home	3	0	2	Cameron, Ferrier (2)
3-1	,, 12	COWDENBEATH	Away	0	0	1	—
2-1	,, 19	FALKIRK	Home	4	3	2	McMenemy (2) Murdoch, Ferrier
3-0	,, 26	HAMILTON ACAS.	Away	3	2	2	Ferrier (2) Cameron
	Nov. 2	DUNDEE UNITED	Home	6	1	2	Dowall (2) Cameron (3) McMenemy
3-3	,, 9	CELTIC	Home	2	1	2	Dowall (2)
3-2	,, 16	ST. JOHNSTONE	Away	1	1	1	Dowall.
3-1	,, 23	PARTICK THISTLE	Away	1	6	0	Ferrier.
1-1	,, 30	ST. MIRREN	Home	3	0	2	Ferrier Dowall Murdoch
2-3	Dec. 7	KILMARNOCK	Home	2	0	2	Ferrier (2)
	,, 14	MORTON	Away	3	1	2	Cameron Murdoch Ferrier.
0-0	,, 21	RANGERS	Away	2	4	0	Stevenson, Cameron.
1-0	,, 28	ABERDEEN	Home	4	1	2	Ferrier Stevenson (2) Murdoch
4-3	Jan. 1	HAMILTON ACAS.	Home	5	1	2	Dowall (2) Murdoch (2) Stevenson
7-0	,, 2	FALKIRK	Away	1	4	0	Stevenson
0-3	,, 4	DUNDEE	Away	3	0	2	McMenemy Ferrier Dowall.
1-0	,, 11	CLYDE	Home	2	1	2	McMenemy Stevenson
1-5	25	HEARTS	Away	2	3	0	McMenemy Dowall
5-0	APR 26	AYR UNITED	Home	4	1	2	McMenemy (2) Stevenson Ferrier
1-0	FEB 8	AIRDRIEONIANS	Away	0	2	0	—
0-5	APR 2nd	QUEEN'S PARK	Home	9	0	2	Ferrier (4) Dowall (3) Murdoch (2)
1-1	FEB 22	HIBERNIAN	Away	1	1	1	Ferrier
5-1	Mar. 1	COWDENBEATH	Home	7	2	2	Stevenson Ferrier (3) Dowall (3)
	,, 8	DUNDEE UNITED	Away	1	1	1	Stevenson
0-2	,, 15	CELTIC	Away	4	0	2	McMenemy (2) Ferrier Dowall
1-1	,, 22	ST. JOHNSTONE	Home	5	0	2	Ferrier McFadyen (2) Dowall (2)
5-4	,, 29	PARTICK THISTLE	Home	4	0	2	Ferrier, Dowall, Stevenson, Murdoch
3-2	April 5	ST. MIRREN	Away	2	0	2	McFadyen Dowall
2-4	,, 12	KILMARNOCK	Away	3	2	2	Ferrier Stevenson, Dowall.
	,, 19	MORTON	Home	3	0	2	Ferrier (2) Dowall
		Total		104	48	55.	

1928-29 Played, 38: Won, 20: Lost 8: Drawn, 10: 50 Points. Goals Scored For, 85: Against, 66

Despite all the optimism the season started with only five points taken from the first five games. Although the significance of the defeat at home to Hearts on 7th September was not to be understood for a long time, as this in fact was to be the last home defeat for almost three years! League form was to prove consistent throughout the season, despite losing the sixth game they strung together a run of nine games unbeaten, including a 6-1 home win over Dundee United. This was followed by a 2-1 win over Celtic at Fir Park which had the Steelmen in the Championship running as they hauled themselves to within three points of Celtic at the top of the table.

In October Sailor Hunter once again stepped into the transfer market, this time snapping up Willie Telfer from Blantyre Celtic. A fortnight later the good run of form - nine games with out losing - was surprisingly ended by bogey team Partick Thistle at Firhill who beat the challengers by 6-1, with Motherwell collapsing in the second half. But this was to be a minor blip as Motherwell maintained their form after this defeat and maintained their title challenge, only dropping four points out of the next eighteen before the Scottish Cup commenced again.

But before the Cup campaign started the club received some bad news when they heard that legendary forward Hugh Ferguson, who had moved to Cardiff, tragically died, despite being still only a young man.

Motherwell's passage through the first round of the Scottish Cup was to be an easy won as they swept East Stirling aside by six goals to nil, with Dowalls grabbing a hat trick, Stevenson a double and Murdoch adding the sixth. In the next round Clyde were the visitors to Fir Park and once again Motherwell progressed comfortably once again, this time by three goals to nil, with two for Murdoch and one for Dowall.

Unfortunately at the same time as progressing in the Cup the team suffered a couple of League defeats either side of the Clyde game and as a result this put a dent in Motherwell's League title hopes. The third round of the Scottish Cup brought Rangers to Fir Park and Motherwell produced a disappointing performance to tumble out at the hands of the League leaders. Archibald put the light blues into a 7th minute lead, with McPhail adding another after 15. Fleming grabbed a third just after Alan McClory in the Motherwell goal saved from the spot, after Sandy Hunter was adjudged to have fouled Archibald. McPhail and then Fleming brought the score to 5-0. Just before the interval Stevenson ran through the Rangers defence to make it 5-1 with McFadyen notching the 'Well's second in the second half.

A one all draw with bottom side Hibs the week after the Scottish Cup defeat further dented the title challenge, then the team followed this up with a 7-2 win over Cowdenbeath at Fir Park with Stevenson scoring a hat trick. Two weeks later Motherwell went to Celtic Park and produced a stunning performance to overcome the Glasgow giants by four goals to nil, with goals from a Dowall hat trick and a Ferrier goal.

This saw 'Well start a run of seven straight wins to the end of the season, scoring 34 goals in these games, and losing only three in the process. The run ended on the last day of the season with an emphatic win by nine goals to nil over Queen's Park in a game that confirmed Motherwell to second place in the League table and the League's top scorers having rattled in 104 goals throughout the season. The proceeds of this last game went to Willie McFadyen for his services to the club.

1930/31

Once again the press were asking was it time for Motherwell to break the strangle hold of the Old Firm and wrestle the League title away from the Glasgow giants, given their recent runs in the League. Motherwell soon established themselves as League title challengers and they hit the top of the table by the end of September, having gone eight games unbeaten by this stage.

It was to be another four before the Fir Park men tasted defeat when they lost two-one at Dens Park, but they returned to the top of the table the following week when the challenge of Leith Athletic was easily swept aside, Motherwell scoring four with only one in reply.

During October Manager Sailor Hunter was given permission to take a deputation to look at a Welsh left back playing for Bangor in Northern Ireland, Ben Ellis. They were impressed and were given permission to sign him for a fee of £350 and a further £50 if he made 12 first team appearances (which he did comfortably). It took him until February to make his debut, and he was not removed from the side until the Second World War.

On Christmas Day 1930, Sailor Hunter decided to drop centre forward Dowdalls, replacing him with Willie McFadyen, this move putting in place the legendary forward line that contained, Murdoch, McMenemey, McFadyen, Stevenson and Ferrier for the first time.

The League challenge continued and Motherwell were constantly in touch right through until March when they suffered a massive blow, losing four one to Celtic at Parkhead, a defeat which knocked Motherwell off the top of the table.

Motherwell were by this time seeking success on two fronts as they had progressed through the Scottish Cup to the Semi Final stage after seeing off Bathgate (4-1), Albion Rover (4-1) and Hibs (3-0) in the early rounds. This brought a trip to Cowdenbeath in the Quarter Finals, when Motherwell scraped through thanks to a Murdoch goal.

The Semi Final, against St. Mirren, was played at neutral Ibrox and the 'Well fought through to their first ever Scottish Cup Final without touching the heights they had reached earlier in the season. The all important goal came around the 25 minute mark, when Ferrier switched play to Murdoch on the right wing. The winger sent the ball through to Stevenson, who raced into to take the return ball and send a diving header past goalkeeper Fortheringham and into the St. Mirren net.

The Final itself looked to be providing Motherwell with their first victory in the Cup, as within twenty minutes they were two goals up against Celtic, Stevenson scoring after only seven minutes and McMenemey doubling the lead on twenty. They held the lead until the 80th minute when McGrory pulled one back, but the Cup still looked to be heading for Motherwell. But disaster was to strike with only two minutes to go, Thomson of Celtic breaking down the wing and sending in a hopeful cross. As the ball came into the Motherwell box there was a shout *of "go for it Alan",* and centre half Alan Craig thought the shout was for him and he followed the instruction and the ball glanced off his head and into his own net.

Sadly the shout had been intended for goalkeeper Alan McClory who had also followed the same instruction and was left stranded by the header from Craig.

Unfortunately the replay did not go as well as the first game and the Celts ran out 4-2 winners in front of a crowd of 98588 fans. This was the only silver lining from Motherwell's first major final appearance when they collected £3917 as their share of the combined gate money from both games.

Things went even more 'pear-shaped' for Motherwell when three days after the Final they suffered a severe blow to their title hopes when they lost one-nil to Cowdenbaeth at Central Park. The season finished with a three-one win over St. Mirren at Fir Park that confirmed them in third place and once again the top scorers in the League with a grand total of 102 goals this time, This was arguably Motherwell's most successful season to date; third in League, runners up in the Scottish Cup and top goalscorers in the League Championship.

The club once again embarked on a tour to foreign shores, this time to South Africa where they spent two months spreading the values and traditions of Scottish football. On this tour they managed to fit in fifteen games, losing only one of the games, and that was against a side they had already been defeated 6-1 earlier in the tour. In the fifteen games they scored 57 goals, conceding only 10 in the process. The top scorer on the tour was Willie McFadyen who had a total of thirty goals, including six in one game against South Africa. Fifteen players made the trip along with Sailor Hunter, director William Duffy and trainer William Walker.

1931/32

Once again Motherwell had managed to retain all their star players for another season where it was hoped they could finally break the Old Firm monopoly, the only concern for Motherwell going into the new season was the impact that a down turn in trade and the likelihood of a depression hitting the region could have on the club. They made a great start to the season rattling off three straight wins, scoring twelve goals in the process as Queen's Park, Rangers and Ayr United were swept aside. The fourth game brought a one nil defeat at the hands of Kilmarnock at Rugby Park, but this was to be one of only two defeats in the season as Motherwell pushed to break that Old Firm stranglehold on the title.

Goals were certainly not hard to come by as Motherwell built their title challenge in the early part of the season, they scored four against Falkirk, six against Third Lanark, and poor Leith Athletic found themselves on the end of a seven goal hammering. By the time the season had reached mid-October wins over Dundee United and Hearts had the Steelmen three points clear at the top of the table.

1931: McFadyen and Stevenson en-route to South Africa

In the ten games leading up to the Hearts game centre forward Willie McFadyen was helping himself to goals galore as he chased the record of most goals in a season that was held by Jimmy McGrory, whose record was 49. During these ten games he helped himself to twenty goals, including two hat tricks, one four goal haul and five goals in a 6-0 win over Third Lanark.

The second and last defeat of the season came against Rangers on Boxing Day 1931 when Motherwell visited Ibrox to take on their nearest rivals. Rangers won the game 1-0 in front of 55000 supporters to cut the lead at the top of the table. The Glasgow side were ahead after 17 minutes through a goal from English, and Motherwell could find nothing to get back into the game, particularly in a poor second half.

Three straight wins after that defeat got the title charge back on track, this run of games included a derby win over Hamilton at Fir Park with McFadyen closing in on the goalscoring record by notching his 40th goal of the season in a three one win.

This set things up nicely for the Scottish Cup which started with a comfortable seven goals to two win over Stenhousemuir at Fir Park, McFadyen adding two Scottish Cup goals to his tally for the season. The next round did bring a trip to Hampden, but only to take on the amateurs of Queen's Park at their home ground. Goals from Stevenson and Moffat secured a two nil win to see Motherwell progress to the third round.

League Champions

Before they took on Celtic in the third round, bottom side Leith Athletic were beaten five nil at Portobello, and the Edinburgh side were no doubt delighted that McFadyen missed the game as the score could have been higher if he had been available!

The third round Cup-tie at Fir Park drew a record crowd of 36000 to see Motherwell take some revenge for the Cup Final defeat of the previous season when they won through two nil. Murdoch had put Motherwell one goal up in the first half, and on 30 minutes Jimmy McGrory left the field injured and failed to reappear. Motherwell made good use of the man advantage when Ferrier scored in the second half to seal the win.

Following the Cup victory Motherwell kept up their charge on the League Championship with three more straight wins, with McFadyen scoring four in a six one win at Tannadice against Dundee United as well as a hat trick in a 4-2 win over Morton, as he looked to break McGrory's record.

The Quarter Final of the Cup meant a trip to Ibrox to take on Rangers, but unfortunately for Motherwell the home side ran out two goal winners in front of 88000.

Despite early pressure and a couple of missed opportunities Motherwell found themselves a goal down when Murray put Rangers in the lead, and a further from McPhail with five minutes to go sealed the tie.

Following the Scottish Cup exit Motherwell responded with an excellent four-two win at Celtic Park to ensure there would be no slip up during the closing weeks of the season. In the 58th minute of the game McFadyen scored Motherwell's fourth goal on the day and at the same time equalled McGrory's record of forty nine League goals in the season, in front of his own fans.

With three games to go Motherwell travelled to Firhill looking to confirm themselves as Champions, and as a result the game attracted a crowd of 32000, including legendary Music Hall entertainer Harry Lauder. The game itself, as often happens on big occasions, was a major disappointment and despite recalling McFadyen to the starting line-up after resting him the previous week against Dundee it was the defence that took the plaudits in a 0-0 draw.

In the penultimate game of the season it looked as though Motherwell were set to be crowned Champions if they could beat Cowdenbeath at Fir Park. They duly obliged by winning the game three-nil, with goals from Ferrier, a Russell own goal and an historic 50th goal for McFadyen. The title was not mathematically yet secured as Rangers had built up a backlog of fixtures thanks to their cup exploits and if they won all their games and Motherwell lost the last game of the season against Clyde, Rangers could still make it six titles in a row.

McFadyen's record-breaking goal looked as though it would never come in the Cowdenbeath game. Throughout the season the trio of Stevenson, Ferrier and Telfer provided many of the goals for McFadyen and during the game the ball had been set up for him so many times by his team mates Stevenson and Ferrier, but they increasingly lost patience after he repeatedly missed the target. Stevenson finally gave up and hit a screamer for himself it crashed back off the bar and McFadyen threw himself at the ball to score a wonder goal to break the record.

A group of players in the tunnel at Fir Park during a break in training

But there was no need for concern about the threat from Rangers, as they dropped a point in a 1-1 draw the following Saturday and Motherwell's Championship was secured. This meant that there were no worries for Motherwell as they entertained Clyde in the last game of the season at Fir Park and they went on to win three nil with two more from McFadyen, to take his record to fifty two League goals in one season.

The Motherwell fans were not surprisingly ecstatic and they rushed on to the pitch at the end of the last match to salute their Championship heroes. The players, unused to winning titles, had already slipped into the bath. The crowd were "entertained" by Chairman Tom Ormiston who made a series of speeches, before he was replaced by Director Crystal who following some "witty" remarks managed to get the crowd to disperse.

The supporters merely moved from the inside of the ground to Fir Park Street where they waited for the players to emerge from the Stand. First to emerge was John McMenemey who was mobbed by the supporters, as were all his team mates with a particularly special reception given to record-breaker McFadyen. The last two to appear were the left wing pairing of Stevenson and Ferrier who were immediately hoisted shoulder high and carried through the street.

In the evening a commemorative dinner was held in the ballroom of the Grosvenor Hotel in Glasgow, with 200 guests present. Congratulations were read out from Lord Hamilton of Dalzell and Mr Livngstone French, president of the South African F.A. On behalf of the beaten Champions Rangers, Duncan Graham gave a brief review of Motherwell's history and acknowledged the key point that the Motherwell directors had refused to sell their players and eventually, as a result of this policy, they reaped the reward of their first League Title.

It was a truly remarkable season, for despite McFadyen's individual feat the team's tally of 119 was a new First Division record. They ended the season five points ahead of Rangers who were runners-up, and a remarkable eighteen in front of third place Celtic. The 66 points that they accumulated had only been bettered once since the top division had been made up to 20 teams, when Rangers gained 67 in 1928/29; in the same season Rangers only lost one game, the only other time that a team had bettered the two Motherwell suffered in 1931/32.

The League win was the first outside the Old Firm since Third Lanark had won the title back in 1904, and it was to be the only time that the League title was to be wrested from the big two in the years between the wars.

It was therefore as Champions that Motherwell travelled to Belgium and France for their latest foreign tour. Once again they impressed everyone as they went undefeated in the four games they played. In the first they swept aside Beerschot 5-0 in Antwerp, and followed this with a 4-2 win over Standard Liege in Brussells. After a well deserved week's holiday in Paris they took on Red Star Olympique who were beaten 3-1, and the next day they beat Racing Club five-nil, despite the French side boasting three French Internationalists.

Telegrams:
"EXECUTIVE, GLASGOW."

Telephone: 581 South.

48 CARLTON PLACE,
GLASGOW, C.5. *16th December, 1929.*

DEAR SIR,

CONTINENTAL TOURS.

Any club contemplating a tour must conform to the following procedure:—prior to entering into any contract or agreement, the sanction of this Association must be obtained. A form will be supplied, on which full details of all proposed matches must be given, at least **one month prior to date of departure**

Club matches only can be included in any proposed tour, and permission will not be granted for matches against representative teams or clubs specially reinforced for the occasion.

Yours truly,

Secretary

1932/33

All of the Championship winning side had been retained as Motherwell tried to retain the title they had won so handsomely the previous season. The opening game of the season was a gala occasion with the League Flag to be unfurled prior to the game. A special flagpole was erected for the occasion, one that was eight feet higher than the previous one on the ground. The flag was unfurled in front of a crowd of 12000 by the wife of the Chairman, Mrs Ormiston, as the Town Band played "See the Conquering Hero Comes".

The game itself matched the occasion with Killie giving the Champions a real test as they took a 2-1 lead in the first half, although the game was level at half time when Murdoch made it 2-2. The visitors took the lead again in the second half, but Motherwell fought back when Ferrier's goal gave the them a share of the points.

The first win of the season came at the third time of asking when Dundee were beaten three nil at Dens Park, with McFadyen scoring another two goals. On 10th September Motherwell lined up against the only other unbeaten side in the League when they hosted Lanarkshire rivals Hamilton Accies, with Motherwell keeping their run going by recording a 4-1 win.

The celebrations continued after the team's return home, when they were awarded a Civic Reception by the Town Council which was held in the Town Hall in June. It was on this occasion that the League Championship Medals were awarded to the players, despite Ellis, Stevenson and Ferrier being absent. The players awarded the medals were: McClory, Dowall, Ellis, Wales, Craig, Telfer, Murdoch, McMenemey, McFadyen, Stevenson, Ferrier, Moffat, Johnman, Walker, Donaldson, Walker, the Directors and the Manager John "Sailor" Hunter who had been the driving force behind the building of the side that had fulfilled both his and the dreams of his supportive board of directors.

Continental Tours were, surprisingly a somewhat controversial subject in the 1920's. In 1929 (above) The Scottish F.A. set out the rules quite strictly. (Below) In 1932, the club made their formal application to the F.A. for their proposed tour that year.

Motherwell Football & Athletic Club, Ltd.

JOHN HUNTER
Secretary-Manager

Office and Ground:
FIR PARK, MOTHERWELL

Telephones:
OFFICE, 129
HOUSE, 407

16th December 1932

Mr Geo.G.Graham
48 Carlton Place
Glasgow.

Dear Sir

Continental Tours

I have been instructed by my Board to make application to the Council for permission to play 5 matches in the Provinces of Denmark in May 1933.

We have been invited to play the following 4 matches.

1. Aarhus Town
2. Aalborg Pokalturnering
3. Odense Town
4. Jydsk Boldspil Union
5. Not yet fixed.

We understand both Hearts & 3rd Lanark have done this tour in recent years.

We trust this will meet with the Council's approval.

Yours faithfully

J.H.

Secy

In late September and early October, Motherwell once again showed Championship form as they notched seven goals in successive games at Fir Park with Morton and Queen's Park being the sides to suffer. Sandwiched between these two games was an excellent draw at Ibrox against title Challengers Rangers.

Cigarette cards from 1933: McMenemey and Ellis

Following these three excellent results the Championship challenge took a real dent as they not only suffered their first defeat of the season, a 2-0 Hearts, but they then slumped to three in a row. A 1-4 at Celtic Park saw Motherwell slide into sixth position and looking as if they were out of the running, particularly when this result was followed by a 1-2 reverse to Partick Thistle at Fir Park, the first home defeat in two and a half years.

This did not deter the 'Well as they bounced back and clawed their way back into contention when they win eight games in a row and were pushing Rangers and Celtic for the title. The resurgence was ended with a 3-2 defeat to Aberdeen, but this turned out to be no more than a blip, and four more wins on the bounce saw them back to the top of the table and ready to start another Scottish Cup campaign.

The first round saw Motherwell travel to Douglas Park to take on Hamilton Accies, when two first half goals from Stevenson and Ferrier were enough to see the visitors progress to the second round. Montrose were easily swept aside in the second round with Motherwell scoring seven goals with only one in response.

Before the third round, Motherwell had to take on Rangers at Fir Park in a vital League game. The game turned on a major off the ball incident when the score was tied at one goal apiece. Rangers forward Sam English deliberately charged into Motherwell goalkeeper Alan McClory as he rose to clear a free kick. McClory cleared the ball and as English ran past he clicked his heels. The referee didn't see the incident but the roar of the Rangers fans in the crowd brought it to his attention and after consulting his linesman McClory was sent off and a penalty awarded. Ferrier went in goal but was beaten by the penalty. With 19 minutes left the Ibrox team made sure of both points when Fleming scored.

The third round of the Scottish Cup saw Dundee's challenge being overcome with ease as they won the game 5-0 with the luxury of a missed penalty into the bargain. The following week Motherwell's title challenge suffered a massive blow as they lost 4-2 to Queen's Park at Hampden, a defeat that allowed Rangers to open up a four point lead at the top of the table.

The Quarter Final tie saw Motherwell line-up against Kilmarncok and they made a great start to the when McFadyen scored after two minutes from a Ferrier corner, but Killie equalised on 22 minutes. McFadyen again put Motherwell ahead but KIllie again equalised with 11 minutes to go. The Fir Park side pressed on and thought they had scored the winner when Ferrier headed home, but the Rugby Park side came back and Sneddon made it 3-3 with only five minutes left on the clock.

The replay was an entirely different affair as Motherwell stormed to a three goal half time lead thanks to a McFadyen hat trick. He added a fourth early in the second half before Killie managed to pull one back through Maxwell, but Murdoch soon had Motherwell four in front again. Killie scored two more goals, but Motherwell upped the pace and netted three more, Ferrier, McFadyen and Murdoch being the marksmen, and hence to win the tie by eight goals to three and advance to the Semi Finals.

Harry Lauder was once again in attendance as Motherwell took on Celtic ahead of the Semi Final, and the home team kept up their title challenge with a fine 4-2 win at Fir Park. This set the team up niceley to take on Clyde in the Cup at Ibrox. Motherwell won through thanks to outstanding performances from 'keeper McClory and Stevenson. McClory was in fact involved in a strange incident when he returned to the field after the half time break. He complained to referee Craigmyle that the goal line wasn't straight, and the line was repainted before the game was allowed to restart!

Motherwell made the vital break through with ten minutes left when McFadyen capitalised on a fumble by the Clyde 'keeper, and two minutes later the tie was sealed when Ferrier scored to send Motherwell into another Scottish Cup final.

In the run up to the Cup final, Motherwell plugged away in the chase for the title but they knew that they had to overcome a three point deficit on Rangers. They kept up their side of the bargain as they won the four games on the way to the Cup Final against Celtic, but sadly Rangers did the same!

Motherwell suffered defeat in this Scottish Cup Final but had only themselves to blame, when they conceded a poor goal. In the first minute Ben Ellis hammered in a free kick but Kennaway in the Celtic goal saved and then Stevenson weaved his magic past two defenders but his shot flew just wide of the post. Three minutes after the interval disaster struck the 'Well, when Ellis and McKenzie got in each others way trying to clear the ball and Celtic forward Bert Thomson sent the ball into the penalty area. Alan McClory in the Motherwell goal looked certain to collect but Jimmy McGrory nipped in front of him and sent the ball into the net. Motherwell fought back with Stevenson taking the ball around three defenders, but he failed to beat the 'keeper when clear through. On the final whistle Motherwell fans were left to reflect again on what might have been. After the anti climax of the final defeat, there was a crumb of comfort as Rangers had been held to a draw by Aberdeen on the day of the final. This meant if Motherwell could win their last three games and Rangers only gain one point from theirs against Queen's Park and Hamilton.

Motherwell kept the challenge going when they beat bottom of the table East Stirling by four goals to one, but Rangers had beaten Queen's Park which meant that the only way Motherwell could now win the title was on goal average if they won their last two games and Hamilton defeated Rangers.

In reality, it meant that the visit to Third Lanark for the penultimate game of the season was largely academic, and the 1-1 draw achieved on the day meant that Motherwell's spell as Champions of Scotland had been brought to an end. The win over Cowdenbeath in the final game of the season saw Motherwell finish the season as runners-up to Rangers who finished the with a 4-2 win over the Accies.

Once again McFadyen had been in prolific form scoring 45 goals in League games to once again finish top scorer by a mile, and adding his goals in the Scottish Cup, his grand total was 60, which was more than that in his record-breaking season the year before.

1933/34

There was little change in the playing squad for the new season with only Johnny Murdoch being given a free with the expectation that Duncan Ogilvie would step up and take his place. Motherwell started with three straight one nil wins over Clyde, St. Johnstone and Dundee, the latter who included Murdoch in their starting line up. There was a general concern that there was a problem in the scoring front with only three goals scored in the opening three games.

After the first three games there were only a trio of teams that were still unbeaten, Rangers, Queen's Park and Motherwell, with the Steelmen set to take on Queen of the South at Palmerston after the Dumfries side had beaten Celtic the week before. Fortunately Motherwell returned to goalscoring form by rattling five past the Doonhamers without losing a goal. The critics were also silenced with McFadyen scoring all five goals himself.

Not only had Motherwell won each of their opening four games, they had also yet to concede a goal as they moved quietly into second place in the table. The next game would test their Championship credibility when one of the other unbeaten sides, Rangers, were due to visit Fir Park. The game was goalless at half time, although Motherwell came close just before the break when Ferrier hit the post. Motherwell took the lead when McFadyen fairly charged 'keeper Dawson, four minutes into the second half. Rangers were the first side to score past McClory, Stevenson equalising with fifteen minutes left in the game. Motherwell were not to be denied and they forced a late winner with McFadyen scoring a second. The win put the Steelemen top of the table on the same points as Queen's Park but with a better goal average, and a point in front of Rangers.

By the time Motherwell were due to play Queen's Park in the ninth game of the season, they had still won all of their games and had pulled two points in front of the Queen's who were lying in second. Despite the Hampden side taking the lead Motherwell turned on an outstanding attacking performance and goals from McFadyen (2), Ogilvie (2) and a Ferrier rocket saw Motherwell run out five one winners.

The first point was dropped a week later when Motherwell had to travel to Aberdeen and despite taking the lead through Stevenson they could only take a point in a 1-1 draw. Even having dropped this point they were still three points in front of closest rivals Rangers at the top of the table.

Motherwell's fine form continued right through to the end of December by which time they were seven points clear of Rangers, but with the Glasgow side having two games in hand. Motherwell finally suffered their first defeat on the 23rd December after a run of 23 games unbeaten, when Clyde came to Fir Park. Motherwell were missing four key players going into the game in McClory, Crapnell, Ellis and Ferrier. Without this quartet Motherwell still dominated the game. but Clyde ran out 2-1 winners to put the first dent in the 'Well's title challenge.

Due to the injury to these key players, manager Hunter was forced to shuffle players around to cope, Dowall filling in for Ferrier, Wales moving to full back and McKenzie coming in at centre half. Despite this injury list they did manage to win their next three games but when Queen of the South visited Fir Park in early January they suffered their second defeat of the season with the Dumfries side winning 2-1. The title challenge was further damaged by a defeat to closest rivals Rangers the following week at Ibrox. This put Rangers only three points behind Motherwell with two games in hand, and 'Well had fallen from red hot favourites to joint favourites for the title with Rangers.

After the two successive defeats it was time for the Scottish Cup to kick-off once again, with non-League Gala Fairydean the visitors to Fir Park in the first round. Motherwell progressed with a four nil win, with all the goals coming from McFadyen once again. The following week they held their place at the top of the League with a three nil win over Queen's Park at Fir Park, before Partick Thistle were taken on in the second round of the Cup.

It took two games to separate the sides after a 3-3 draw at Firhill, with Thistle coming back from 3-0 down to force a replay at Fir Park. In the replay Thistle once again found themselves behind when they lost two quick goals to Stevenson and McFadyen, and this time there was no way back for them as they could only muster one in reply.

The third round of the Cup brought a visit from East Stirlingshire to Fir Park and the home side proved too strong for their visitors. McFadyen scored yet another hat trick before Ferrier added another two for a comfortable five nil win. The Cup wasn't getting in the way of the League challenge as a 2-0 win over Kilmarnock saw Motherwell move five points clear of Rangers, with the Ibrox side still having games in hand. In the Quarter Final of the Cup, Motherwell were drawn to take on Lanarkshire rivals Albion Rovers in Coatbridge. The game proved difficult for 'Well and despite taking a lead with 15 minutes to go through a goal from McFadyen the Wee Rovers equalised with eight minutes to go. The replay was to prove a totally different affair for the Rovers with Motherwell banging in six goals without reply, with yet another McFadyen hat trick included!

Following the Scottish Cup Quarter Final, the League form hit a bit of a minor slump, at a similar stage as in the previous season. This time they lost to Celtic at Celtic Park, then the following week another defeat, to Partick at Fir Park, saw Motherwell slide into second in the table, a point behind with one game more having been played than Rangers. The elusive second title win appeared to be slipping away from the Steelmen.

They did manage to bounce back with a League win over St.Mirren, only eleven days before playing the same team in the Scottish Cup Semi Final. The week before the Cup game Airdrie were almost certainly consigned to relegation when they were hammered 6-3 by their Lanarkshire neighbours.

McClory, Blair and Ferrier were all missing from the surprise Scottish Cup Semi Final defeat against St. Mirren. A hat trick from Saints' Knox saw them take a three goal lead, while Motherwell could only manage a McFadyen goal in consolation as they failed to lift the elusive Scottish Cup once again.

Relegation threatened Third Lanark held Motherwell to a 2-2 draw the following week making it almost impossible for Motherwell to make up the five points that they had fallen behind Rangers, with only three games left in the season. 'Well did everything right in the last three games as they won them all, but it was only good enough to secure another runners-up spot.

Rangers actually clinched the title with Motherwell already sailing to South Africa for another summer tour. On the way to the steamer they stopped off to take on London club Clapton Orient who they managed to overcome by six goals to four. The tour was an arduous one covering 25000 miles, and in their seven weeks in South Africa the players spent 21 nights on train journeys that made up 8000 miles of the trip.

They played sixteen games while on the tour without losing any of them, scoring 81 goals and only conceding 12. In the game against South Africa on June 16 there was a record crowd of over 20000 at the Kingsmead Stadium. The occasion was described in the South African Sporting News: *"It was a colourful scene and fully justified the optimism of the* (South African*) Football Association in bringing out such a famous combination."*

Results:

Date	Opponent	Score	Scorers
May 17	Eastern Province	10-1	(McFadyen 4, Stevenson 3, Ogilvie 2, McMenemey)
May 19	Frontier XI	6-2	(McFadyen 3, McMenemey 2, Ferrier)
May 23	Grigualand	9-0	(Crawley 3, Ogilvie 3, Johnstone 2, Ogilvie)
May 26	Southern Transvaal	7-1	(McFadyen 4, Ogilvie 2, Stevenson)
May 28	Orange Free State	3-1	(McMenemey 2, McFadyen)
May 31	Natal	7-1	(Ferrier 3, McFadyen 3, Ogilvie)
June 2	Transvaal	2-1	(McFadyen, McMenemey)
June 7	Matabeland	3-0	(Crawley 3)
June 9	Mashonaland	6-0	(McFadyen 5, Ogilvie)
June 13	Northern Transvaal	2-1	(McFadyen, Stewart)
June 16	South Africa (Test match)	5-2	(McFadyen 2, McMenemy 2, Stevenson)
June 20	Natal	5-0	(McFadyen 2, Crawley 2, Stevenson)
June 23	South Africa (Test match)	3-0	(Stevenson 2, Ogilvie)
June 30	Western Province	7-0	(McFadyen 3, Ogilvie 2 Wales, Crawley)
July 2	South Africa (Test match)	5-2	(McFadyen 3, McMenemey, Ogilvie).

Also during 1933/34 more 'Well players had been honoured at International level than at any other previous time in the club's history.

1934 request for SFA to tour South Africa granted

THE SCOTTISH FOOTBALL ASSOCIATION, LTD.

PATRON:
.H. THE DUKE OF YORK.

SECRETARY:
GEORGE G. GRAHAM.

TELEPHONE - SOUTH 581.
TELEGRAMS-"EXECUTIVE, GLASGOW"

48 CARLTON PLACE,
GLASGOW, C.5.

8th February, 1934.

Mr. J. Hunter,

Motherwell F.C.

Dear Sir,

I laid your application, in connection with South African Tour, before Council at their meeting yesterday, and I am instructed to inform you that permission cannot be granted for matches against teams selected by the National Association.

Permission has been granted for the tour on condition that only club matches, with regular club players, are played, or matches against teams selected by a District or Divisional Association, composed entirely of players belonging to clubs within the jurisdiction of such District or Divisional Association.

Yours truly,

Geo. G. Graham

SECY.

En route to South Africa

Tour
1934
PRICE 3D.
Souvenir
PROGRAMME
OF THE
Motherwell Association
Football Team's
Visit to Cape Town
1934
Three Cheers for Motherwell!
hip!
hip!!
hooray!!!
—and don't forget that
LION BEER
keeps Fatherwell
DURBAN'S MOST UP-TO-DATE SPORTS STORE
Hearty Welcome Extended to Motherwell Team
All the Latest Sports Goods in Stock
J. F. KING LTD. 345 WEST ST.
MOTHERWELL
VS.
NATAL
SOUVENIR
PROGRAMME
Price 6d.
1934
Leading Optician
Phone 2601
DURBAN
Southern Rhodesia Football Association.
ILLUSTRATED
Souvenir Programme
IN HONOUR OF THE VISIT OF THE
Motherwell Football Club,
Scotland,
To SOUTHERN RHODESIA.
Bulawayo: Thursday, 7th June, 1934,
Queen's Ground.
Salisbury: Saturday, 9th June, 1934,
Drill Hall Ground.
CONTAINING A BRIEF HISTORY OF THE GAME IN
SOUTHERN RHODESIA AND THE PROVINCES.
100% PURE SCOTCH
MOTHERWELL.
AND SO IS
Grants Whisky
QUALITY GUARANTEED and OVER 10 YEARS OLD.
STAND-FAST.
Chronicle, Byo.—6712
South Africa
Rhodesia

(Right)
Autographed South African Tour Dinner menu

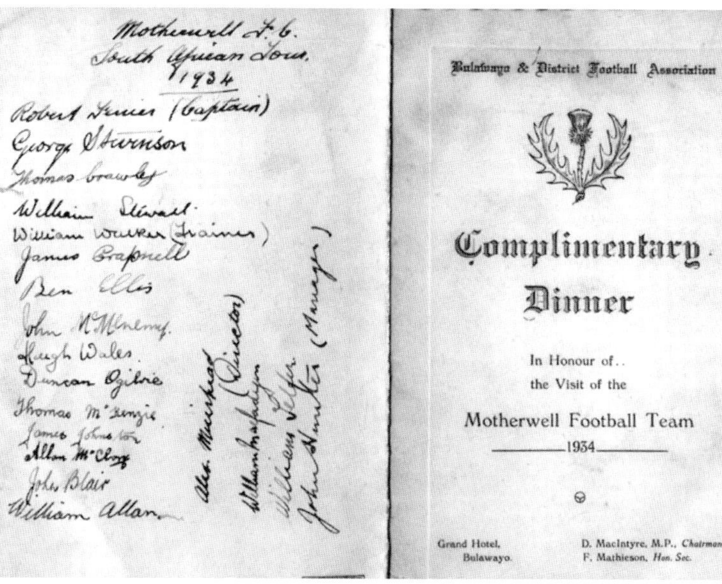

Motherwell F.C.
South African Tour.
1934

Robert Ferrier (Captain)
George Stevenson
Thomas Crawley
William Stewart
William Walker (Trainer)
James Crapnell
Ben Ellis
John McMenemy
Hugh Wales
Duncan Ogilvie
Thomas McKenzie
James Johnston
Allan McClory
John Blair
William Allan
Alex. Muirhead (Director)
William Macfadyen
William Telfer
John Hunter (Manager)

Bulawayo & District Football Association

Complimentary Dinner

In Honour of..
the Visit of the
Motherwell Football Team
1934

Grand Hotel,
Bulawayo.

D. MacIntyre, M.P., Chairman
F. Mathieson, Hon. Sec.

(Below)
Stevenson features in an action shot taken on the tour

Stevenson, McFadyen and McMenemey all picked up two caps during the season, while Blair, Telfer and Ogilvie were all capped for Scotland and Ben Ellis for Wales. Stevenson's Caps took his grand total of such honours to 21, made up of League Internationals and full international appearances. At this stage he had won eleven full caps, by adding one more against Ireland the following season, and set the record of most capped player for Motherwell up to this time with this twelfth appearance.

1934/35

All the major players in the squad were retained for the start of another season of championship chasing for Motherwell. The season started reasonably well with one defeat suffered in the first four games, a 0-1 reverse to Rangers at Ibrox. This was followed up by winning 1-0 over Celtic at Fir Park, despite missing the injured Ferrier who had picked up a knock in the pre-season trial match.

By mid September Motherwell were happy to sit fourth in the table, before a slump in form in September, when only six points were picked up in seven games. Things didn't get much better as the year progressed with only two points collected from four games in November, and the team dropped down the table to ninth. They did recover some form through December starting with a handsome 9-3 win over Dunfermline, and maintaining an excellent home record. This was despite the Pars going ahead twice, but hat tricks from Stevenson and McFadyen along with two from Ogilvie and a single from McMenemey saw Motherwell run riot over The Fifers.

A week later the team lost at Celtic Park with former Celtic winger John Thomson in the Motherwell line up. Motherwell did take the lead through McFadyen but they then fell three one down before Ellis scored with a late penalty to put a more respectable slant on the scoreline.

After a fine 2-2 draw with Rangers at Fir Park, Motherwell then turned in one of their worst performances of the season when they took on Hamilton Accies in the traditional Ne'erday fixture at Douglas Park. Motherwell were 1-0 down after just three minutes when McLaren scored. Injuries to Thomson and Stevenson saw Motherwell reduced to nine men at one point, but both players returned to the field. Accies continued their dominance and were 4-0 up by the time McFadyen scored for Motherwell to make the half time score 4-1.

Two further goals by Accies in the second half completed a miserable day for the Fir Park team. Ben Ellis and Hugh Wales were sent off in the closing stages of the match as the Motherwell players complained about the brutal tactics of their opponents and took retribution into their own hands.

They quickly wiped this horror show from their minds by seeing off one of the other Lanarkshire sides, Albion Rovers, by five goals to two. A fortnight later they lost their unbeaten home record when they lost by two goals to one to Aberdeen. Mills hit the bar for the visitors before they took the lead in the 27th minute through Armstrong. The Well stepped up the pressure, but it was the Dons who went two ahead when Conwell scored. Within three minutes of this second goal Ben Ellis scored from the spot after a penalty was awarded for handball against an Aberdeen defender.

The Scottish Cup looked as though it would provide some light relief with Dundee beaten 2-1 at Dens Park in the first round and Morton seen off comfortably when they were thrashed seven one at Fir Park. This set up a third round tie against Rangers at Fir Park, but four goals from Rangers' Jimmy Smith saw the Ibrox side cruise through to the next round. Telfer notched Motherwell's solitary reply. The only consolation that Motherwell could take from this game was their share of the gate money from the near 33,000 crowd.

This meant that Motherwell were left in the unusual position of being left with a string of meaningless games in the run-in towards the end of the season, given that they were in no danger of either winning the title or being relegated! In the end they finished the season in sixth place in the League table, their lowest since 1924/25. The explanation for such a poor run of form was the higher than normal number of players that Motherwell were forced to use during the season, with 25 in total.

Bos

Caricatures on cigarette cards: Jim Blair (top), Ben Ellis below

1935/36

For the first time in some years there were a number of changes in the playing side, with Crapnell and Thomson retiring, along with Crawley moving to Preston and Dowall to Bury. Coming in were Grant from Blackpool and Hutton Bremner from Queen's Park.

In the League they were not as consistent through this season as they had been during the early thirties and never really managed to mount any kind of challenge at all, although Celtic were the only side to beat them twice, as the Celts won the League for the first time since 1925/26.

Despite losing three games in the first twelve games, including one to Rangers and another to perpetual bogey team Partick Thistle, they climbed to fourth in the table with a four-two win over Hearts. Two weeks later Motherwell suffered their first defeat to Celtic as they lost 2-1 at Fir Park in a game that they should at least have taken a point from. A week later came a defeat to Third Lanark at Cathkin Park that sparked a three month League run without loss and saw them keep in touch with the League leaders without ever really mounting a serious challenge. The highlight of the run was probably the six-two win over Airdrie at Fir Park, with Ferrier scoring a hat trick. During this run, came the first sign of changing technologies, when the BBC carried out their first Radio commentary on 11 Jan 1936 in the match versus Clyde. The BBC commentary was carried out by Alan Breck of the Scottish Daily Express when the sides shared the points in a 1-1 draw.

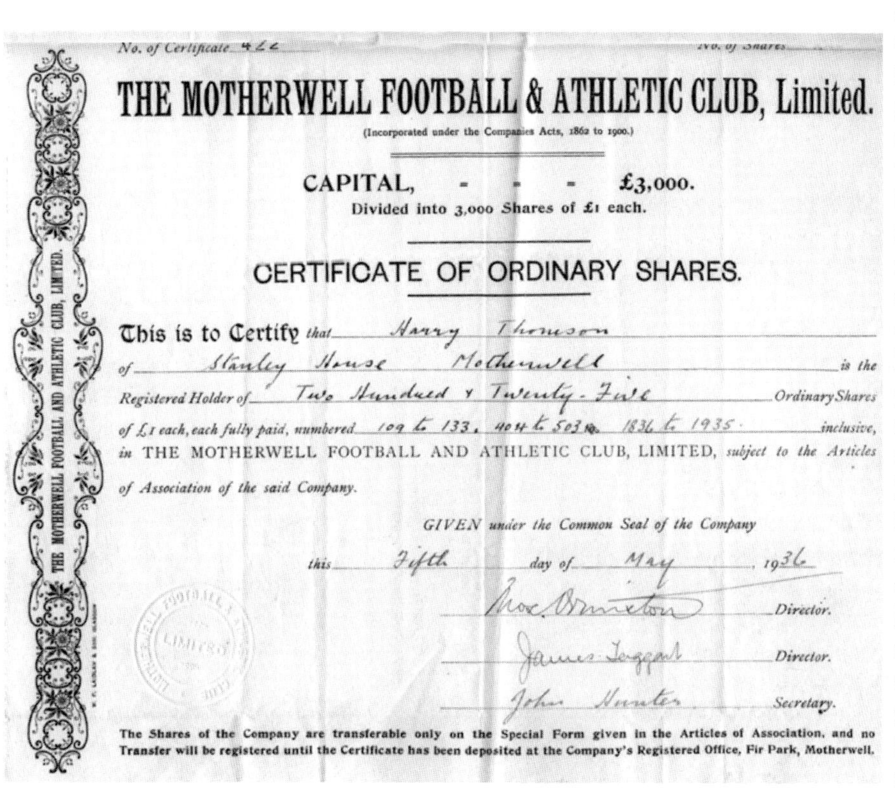
No. of Certificate 426

THE MOTHERWELL FOOTBALL & ATHLETIC CLUB, Limited.

(Incorporated under the Companies Acts, 1862 to 1900.)

CAPITAL, - - - £3,000.
Divided into 3,000 Shares of £1 each.

CERTIFICATE OF ORDINARY SHARES.

This is to Certify that Harry Thomson of Stanley House Motherwell is the Registered Holder of Two Hundred & Twenty-Five Ordinary Shares of £1 each, each fully paid, numbered 109 to 133, 404 to 503 & 1836 to 1935 inclusive, in THE MOTHERWELL FOOTBALL AND ATHLETIC CLUB, LIMITED, subject to the Articles of Association of the said Company.

GIVEN under the Common Seal of the Company this Fifth day of May 1936

Director.

James Taggart Director.

John Hunter Secretary.

The Shares of the Company are transferable only on the Special Form given in the Articles of Association, and no Transfer will be registered until the Certificate has been deposited at the Company's Registered Office, Fir Park, Motherwell.

The Scottish Cup started at the end of January with an away tie at Arbroath. The crowd stood silent for two minutes in memory of King George who had just died and after the match got underway Motherwell soon established their dominance. Ferrier put the 'Well ahead after 14 minutes and in the 69th, a cross from Ogilvie found Wylie who put the Fir Park side in to a 2-0 lead. Brand pulled one back for the Red Lichties but a last minute goal by Wylie ensured that Motherwell marched through to the next round.

The second round brought a visit from St. Bernard's of Edinburgh and a Geroge Stevenson hat trick was enough to secure a comfortable three nil win and raise hopes that the ever elusive Cup would at last be brought to Fir Park, particularly given the current run of form in the League. They had no problem getting past Cowdenbeath in the third round at Central Park, with goals from Wylie, Stevenson and an Ellis penalty being enough to secure a 3-1 win.

The Scottish Cup run ended at the Quarter Final stage, meaning the hopes of lifting the trophy were shelved for another year, when they fell to Clyde at Shawfield on a sodden pitch. Clyde kicked off in the wet and took the lead after seven minutes when Stewart shot past McClory. The Bully Wee extended their lead when McClory failed to gather and Cuthbert shot into an empty goal. In the 21st minute Motherwell pulled one back when a Stevenson pass found Wylie and he scored easily. The Fir Park side pressed hard and Ogilvie was unlucky when he almost headed home from a Ferrier cross. It looked like the 'Well must equalise, then Clyde scored a killer third when a mix up in the Motherwell defence allowed Rankine to net. Ogilvie notched Motherwell's second in the 79th minute from a Ferrier cross.

There was also much disappointment that in the club's Golden Jubilee Year no silverware could be picked up to help celebrate the milestone. The trend of holding on to the players as long as they possibly could was reversed when Duncan Ogilvie was allowed to move to Huddersfield for the sum of £2900. It could be said that this was in response to the falling numbers attending games, as more people left the Burgh and headed to Glasgow to watch either Rangers or Celtic.

The League campaign stuttered to a close with Motherwell introducing a number of new players in some of the meaningless games, with Rae, Hynds, Farmer and Stark all getting run-outs.

The final game of the season was a fine 3-0 win over Hearts at Fir Park that secured the fourth spot, which even in a disappointing season was three places better off than the season before. Ferrier ended up as the top scorer for the club, but with only 14 goals, as the club could only muster 77, the lowest total for ten years.

1936/37

This was to be a season of change at Fir Park as the side that won the title back in 1931/32 started to break up and Sailor Hunter was forced to rebuild once again. The first player to depart was forward John McMenemey who moved to Partick Thistle for £1000 after giving eight years service to the club after signing from Celtic.

The season started without Ferrier at outside left, William Stewart filling his berth alongside George Stevenson. This change did not prevent Motherwell starting the season well as they only dropped one point in the first six games under the captaincy of Ben Ellis. This started to build hopes that a title challenge could be mounted once again as Motherwell were sitting joint top with Aberdeen and Rangers.

The run was ended by Hearts, who won three-one at Fir Park, and the following week a three-two defeat at Ibrox saw them fall further behind Rangers in the table. It also signalled the end of another distinguished Motherwell career as Alan McClory was dropped to the reserves, after making a couple of errors to allow Rangers to win the game, and he was transferred at the end of the season.

Ferrier returned to the team in late October, but even he couldn't help the side overcome Arbroath at Gayfield in a game played in driving rain and high winds whipping in off the North Sea. It was hardly surprising given the conditions that neither side managed to muster a goal between them. By the end of December it was decided that Willie McFadyen could now be transferred and he moved South to Huddersfield with Duncan Ogilvie returning to Fir Park in exchange. McFadyen was one of the all-time greats with the highlight of his time at Motherwell being the 52 goals scored in securing the League title back in 1931/32. Motherwell immediately went on a five game unbeaten run after the transfer including a nine-one win over Albion Rovers at Fir Park; the goals coming from Stewart and McGillvray, both with hat tricks, a Stevenson double and an Ogilvie single.

With the League challenge having dwindled, once again all eyes were back on the Scottish Cup for hopes of glory. The first round brought Ayrshire side Galston to Fir Park and Motherwell eased themselves through to the next round, but their Ayrshire opponents put up stout resistance in front of a small crowd that saw gate receipts of only £39.

The Galston defence held the Motherwell forwards until just before break, then Alec Stewart who was running through on goal was impeded, and Ben Ellis scored to give the 'Well a 1-0 half time lead. Graham made it 2-0 when he headed home a McGillivray corner but 13 minutes later Galston scored from the spot to bring it back to 2-1. With only five minutes left Ogilvie netted for Motherwell to book their place in the next round.

The next round saw Motherwell travel to Brockville to take on Falkirk, and once again they scored three to progress to the third round. The visitors went ahead in the 7th minute when a splendid pass by Stevenson found Bremner and he scored from ten yards. The Bairns had the chance to equalise in the 65th minute when the referee awarded them a penalty, but Sneddon blasted wide. A minute later Stewart added to Falkirk's misery when he made it 2-0 heading home an Ogilvie cross, and the same combination saw Motherwell notching their third to march through to the next round.

Duns were next up and they moved the tie to Hearts' Tynecastle Park to accommodate the expected crowd, and once again Motherwell cruised through to the Quarter Final. Bremner put the Fir Park side ahead in the 15th minute, and the same player added a second in the 22nd minute. McCulloch notched a third to give the 'Well a commanding half time lead. Scott pulled one back for Duns in the 52nd minute, however, Ogilvie added a fourth for Motherwell to restore their clear lead. Duns kept plugging away and Walker scored their second but another from Ogilvie saw Motherwell qualify comfortably for the next round.

The Quarter Final paired Motherwell and Celtic, and they played out a marvellously entertaining cup-tie, but with a two goal lead at one point the 'Well should have gone through. Crum put the home side ahead but a great McCulloch run set Alec Stewart up to equalise. Crum added his second to give Celtic the lead for the second time, but again Motherwell fought back and Stewart rattled home from a Hugh Wales free kick. With the score at 2-2 the Fir Park side took command and two goals from Stevenson gave them a 4-2 lead. However, this time Celtic fought back and two goals gave them the draw.

In the replay Motherwell tumbled out of the Cup rueing the loss of a two goal lead in the first match a week earlier. Hugh Wales put Motherwell into the lead in the 28th minute when his shot from twenty five yards was misjudged by Celtic 'keeper Kennaway and the ball ended up in the net. Celtic looked stronger in the second half, however, and two goals saw them go through to the Semi Final.

As the season petered out with Motherwell heading for fourth in the table once again, they did manage to take some revenge over Celtic as they inflicted a record defeat on the Glasgow side when Motherwell ran out eight goals to nil winners at Fir Park in the last game of the season.

Motherwell played at the top of their form to win the game, although injuries to Celtic 'keeper Kennaway and Morrison helped, with the former having to leave the field, although by that stage Motherwell were already four goals up. In the first half, goals from Ogilvie, Stevenson and two from Stewart had the 'Well four up at half time. With Celtic shorthanded they went on to complete the rout with Stewart scoring another four to take his personal tally to six. The eight nil defeat still stands as Celtic's record defeat to date.

With the past transfer activity between Motherwell and Huddersfield, the clubs took advantage of this relationship to play a couple of benefit matches during the season. The first was played at Leeds Road, with Motherwell winning the game 3-1, which was staged to raise funds for Huddersfield Infirmary. The second match was played at Fir Park as a benefit for long serving left back Ben Ellis when a 1-1 draw ensued.

1937/38

The start of another new season saw the side contain a mix of new younger players and a core of the older heads. They set off well in the League losing only twice in the first twenty games, a 2-1 defeat at Ibrox and a similar reverse at Arbroath's Gayfield ground being the only blemishes on the Motherwell record. This run of form saw the 'Well sit top of the table after winning 3-2 against Falkirk at Brockville on 23rd October. They clung on to the top slot through the rest of October and most of November when a string of draws allowed Rangers to catch up, and then move ahead of 'Well on goal average at the end of the month.

The fine run of form was halted by Celtic at Fir Park when the Celts gained some degree of revenge for the previous season's eight goal hammering, running out two-one winners. This heralded a slump in form that saw only four points picked up from the next fourteen. One of the major contributions to the defeats was an injury that forced centre half John Blair to miss five games, and while he was absent the defence shipped thirteen goals.

This poor run effectively ended any hopes of challenging for the League title once again and it meant all hopes were pinned on Scottish Cup success, with all at the club desperate to bring the old trophy to the town. Clyde were beaten four one at Shawfield in the first round, with the goals coming from McCreadie, McGillvray and two from Bremner.

The second round was more difficult as they travelled to Stenhousemuir and escaped with a 1-1 draw thanks to a goal from Ogilvie. There were no such problems in the replay as Motherwell rattled six past the Warriors, with Ogilvie and McGillvray both bagging two with Bremner and an own goal rounding off the scoring.

A crowd of 22500 turned out to see local rivals Hamilton when they travelled to Fir Park in the third round. The 'Well went ahead in the 70th minute from an Ellis free kick which was headed against the post. Motherwell striker Alec Stewart reacted first to put his team ahead, and ten minutes later Stewart made sure that Motherwell's name would be in the hat for the next round when he fired home after a mix up in the Accies defence.

Sadly there was an ignominious defeat in the Quarter Finals, when Motherwell were asked to travel to Edinburgh to take on St. Bernards. There was controversy before the game when ticket prices were set at 2/- (10p) for the game, which led to many fans boycotting it, hence a crowd of only 3600 turned up to see one of the biggest days in St. Bernard's history.

The Fir Park side took the lead after 15 minutes through Ogilvie but Saints fought back and equalised through Flucker one minute later. Grant put the home side in to a 2-1 lead after McArthur in the Motherwell goal miskicked, then near the end Flucker scored a third for Saints to ruin Motherwell's Scottish Cup dream for another year.

Once again Motherwell were left with nothing to play for in the latter part of the season, and once again Sailor Hunter was in a position to experiment as he tried different players in different positions in the forward line, which even saw George Stevenson turn out in an unfamiliar outside right position.

The team eventually finished fifth, one place worse off than the previous season, with seven points less. The club could content itself that for ten years they had been the only side to mount a consistent challenge to the big two of Scottish Football, and in fact in that time had amassed an aggregate of 637 points, six more than Celtic in the same period.

1938/39

The season was the first for twenty years that the name of Bobby Ferrier would not appear amongst the list of retained players, as he had been promoted to take up the post of Motherwell's first assistant manager. As a result this meant the break up of one of the greatest wing partnerships the game had ever seen.

Much of Motherwell's success in the late twenties and thirties can be laid at the feet of the partnership of Stevenson and Ferrier, and the club's refusal to sell them on. This, despite the number of blank cheques offered by other clubs to remove the golden partnership from Fir Park.

As a result they played for almost fifteen years together, although Ferrier himself had joined the club twenty years earlier from junior side Petershill.

Although he had spent most of his life in Scotland, he was actually born in Sheffield and was therefore not available to play for the Scottish National side, depriving the nation of ever seeing the partners playing in the blue of Scotland together. Stevenson did become Motherwell's most capped Scottish Internationalist with twelve caps.

Ferrier did have the distinction of representing the Scottish League on seven occasions, two of them strangely against the Football League. During his years at Fir Park Ferrier played in 697 games scoring a grand total of 345 with 262 of them in League games. This solo contribution is on top of the goals he created for McFadyen and other great forwards at the time.

Despite the departure of such an outstanding player the season stared brightly enough with Motherwell wining the opening game by eight goals to five against Queen of the South, before a last minute equaliser denied them a win at Ibrox in the second, with the end result being two goals apiece.

Bizarrely the third game of the season was the return game with Queen of the South which saw the Doonhamers win by 4-3 this time, giving a combined total of eighteen goals across the two games. 'Well bounced back the following week to defeat Kilmarncok 5-2 at Fir Park with the win being secured largely on the back of a hat trick of penalties from Ben Ellis. A draw against Aberdeen meant that only one game had been lost in the opening six and things were looking bright once again.

This was followed by a run of three defeats, by Rangers, Hearts and Queen's Park, which saw Motherwell sitting as low as thirteenth in the table a long way behind the leaders. During the early stages of the season McGillvray moved to Dundee and was replaced by 19 year old Davie Mathie who joined up from Wishaw Juniors, and the centre forward made his mark right away as he scored in his debut in a 2-0 win against Queen's Park. This started a six game unbeaten run, that would ensure there would be no relegation worries, but without being in a position to push for the title.

The remainder of the League campaign was to prove as inconsistent as this opening spell and it was no surprise that Motherwell finished as low as 12th in the table, particularly as they started a cup run that would see them advance to the Final and look to bring that elusive Scottish Cup to the town for the first time. They were given what was, as expected, an easy tie to open the campaign being drawn to play Huntly away in the first round. Motherwell marched through to the next round of the Scottish Cup with a stroll over their Highland League opponents. Ogilvie set the 'Well on the road to victory with a goal in the first minute. McCulloch made it 2-0 after 15 minutes, with two from Ogilvie and another from McCulloch making it 5-0 at half time. Ogilvie, Stevenson and Mathie all notched goals for the Fir Park side in the second half with Stewart grabbing Huntly's solitary reply.

Motherwell travelled to Tannadice in the second round to take on Dundee United and won through amid great controversy surrounding their second goal. The referee appeared to blow for a George Stevenson handball, but the Motherwell forward played on and sent a long ball though to Davie Mathie who scored. After that, the United fans pelted the referee with stones and coins and a nasty atmosphere evolved. McCulloch scored first in the 30th minute and then came Mathie's, and Motherwell's second, controversial second. United fell apart after this and further goals from Ogilvie and McCulloch gave Motherwell a 4-0 interval lead. Nine minutes into the second half Ogilvie made it 5-0 with Ross grabbing a consolation goal for the Tannadice side.

The third round saw Motherwell emerge as emphatic winners by four goals to two over St. Mirren. Ogilvie put the 'Well ahead after five minutes, but four minutes later the Paisley Buddies drew level when Ferguson scored. Motherwell regained the lead after 22 minutes when a pass from Mathie found Ogilvie in space and he notched his own and Motherwell's second. The Fir Park side exerted further pressure on the Saints goal and it paid off in the 50th minute when Stevenson scored. The Saints reduced the leeway when Rankine fired home a penalty, but the 'Well were always in control and a fourth goal in the 63rd minute from Stevenson settled the issue.

The Quarter Final draw paired Motherwell with old rivals and Cup favourites Celtic at Fir Park. McCulloch put the team in front from a Stevenson pass and the same player made it 2-0 in the 28th minute when he seized on a fluffed clearance to fire home from a difficult angle. Delaney reduced the leeway with a Celtic goal after a mix up in the home defence. In the closing stages of the game Stevenson made sure it would be Motherwell who were going through to the Semi Finals. Standing with his back to goal he hooked a shot over his head and into the Celtic net.

It took two games to see off Aberdeen in the Semi Finals with the first game being drawn 1-1 at Ibrox in front of over 80000 fans. Warnock opened the scoring for the Dons before Mathie equalised half way through the second half to take the tie to a replay. The teams met four days later, at Ibrox once again, and this time Motherwell strode through comfortably to their third Scottish Cup final in nine years with goals from Mathie, McCulloch and Bremner scoring in a 3-1 win.

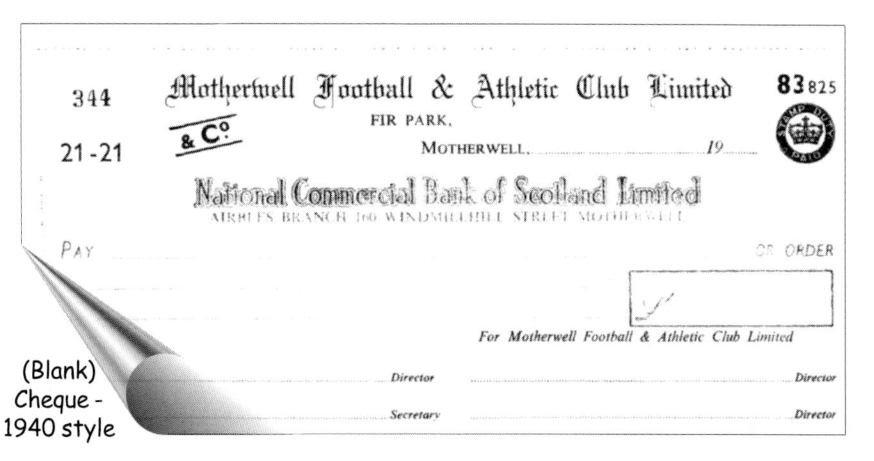
344

Motherwell Football & Athletic Club Limited

83825

& Co

21-21

FIR PARK,

MOTHERWELL, ... 19....

National Commercial Bank of Scotland Limited

PAY .... OR ORDER

For Motherwell Football & Athletic Club Limited

Director .... Director

Secretary .... Director

(Blank) Cheque - 1940 style

The other Semi Final was won by Clyde who overcame Rangers to set up a final that would not feature either of the Old Firm. The game still attracted 94000 to Hampden to see if Sailor Hunter's attractive football side could finally win the Cup. Sadly once again they were to return to Motherwell without the trophy. The Fir Park side started the game well with Ogilvie and McCulloch going close but it was Clyde who took the lead in the 30th minute against the run of play when Wallace scored with a fine drive. With five minutes of the second half gone Clyde struck again. Everyone thought Martin the Clyde forward was offside including Motherwell 'keeper Murray, but the referee played on and the Clyde player scored. Clyde scored a further two in the last six minutes to complete Motherwell's day of misery. Sadly the great Motherwell side built by Sailor Hunter will go into the record books as the best side never to have won the Scottish Cup.

1939/40

Preparations for a new season got underway with the possibility of a Second World War in the air. Motherwell started the season with all the players from the previous season intact, and opened the season with a 3-3 draw at Kilmarnock. The following week they picked up the first win with a 3-0 scoreline over Aberdeen. After taking both points in a 4-2 win over Kilmarnock at Fir Park, they subsequently lost the next two games to Alloa and Hearts.

It was after the fifth game, against Hearts, that the SFA decided that the Leagues would be suspended as war had officially been declared on the Germans only three days after they had invaded Poland. The SFA suspended the league as it was feared that football would be a target for bombing runs by the Luftwaffe and they were declared unsafe. As a consequence all players' contracts were declared void as the clubs would have no income to pay them, and it would also allow them to be called up if required.

This meant that a number of players had played their last official games for the club, with George Stevenson playing his last game against Alloa Athletic the week before war broke out. It was reported that he had been dropped from the side following the Kilmarnock draw as he was *"noticeably slow to strike form in the game"*, and he was dropped for the Aberdeen game to make way for the younger Turnbull.

"Stevie" had joined up from Ayrshire side Kilbirnie Leadside at the beginning of 1923/24, and made his debut at Cathkin Park against Third Lanark on 8th December 1923. In his time at Motherwell he played 511 League games scoring 170 goals; not bad for a player who was a provider rather than an out and out scorer. He won 22 representative caps, 12 full caps and 10 Scottish League Caps. His haul of twelve caps has been overtaken by 'Well players Tommy Coyne, Simo Valakari and Stuart Elliot, but all for other countries, as no other Motherwell player has yet matched Stevenson's haul while still at Fir Park. For his services to the club he was rewarded with a Life Membership of Motherwell football, which allowed him access to games without paying. He was also awarded the gift of 100 Savings Certificates!

Stevenson was not to break his ties with the club as he returned after the War to take over as manager when Sailor Hunter decided to concentrate on the role of Secretary. It was ironic that in 1952 he was to manage the side that finally brought the Scottish Cup to Fir Park, having missed out three times at the Final stage as a player.

The last game against Hearts saw five players from the title winning side still playing, but sadly this was also to be their last official games. The five were Blair, Ellis, Wales, Telfer and McKenzie, although despite injury at work during the war Ellis could not cut his ties with the club completely and returned as groundsman, assistant trainer and coach before leaving after 25 years to set up his own business in 1955.

Chapter 4 The War Years

After a few months the SFA decided that it was once again acceptable to play League Football once again. By October 1939 two Regional Leagues had been constituted under the auspices of the Scottish League, a West and an East League with 16 teams in each. Motherwell were to play in the West League, and they played out thirty games finishing fourth in the table. Even though League football resumed on this unofficial basis the SFA suspended the Scottish Cup competition.

The Geographical nature of the competition proved difficult particularly for the teams in the East who were denied the chance to play against the Glasgow giants and the income that came with their visits. It was agreed that change was needed, although the change still saw the League's played out on a geographical basis for the remainder of the war with the Country split North and South. But this now meant that the teams in the North, such as Aberdeen missed out on the money from playing against Rangers and Celtic.

Motherwell saw out the War years in the Southern League finishing as high as third in 1944/45 as the teams prepared for the ending of the conflict and the game was starting to return to near normality. They also secured a Summer Cup win in 1944 when they managed to gain revenge over Clyde for the Scottish Cup defeat in 1939 with 1-0 win at Hampden in front of a crowd of 40000.

During the war years players tended to turn out for the team nearest the Barracks where they had been stationed, this meant players like Gordon Bremner playing for Arsenal, and Davie Mathie guesting for Hibs.

Sailor Hunter was also busy during the War Years preparing a new team to replace the all conquering heroes of the thirties and it was during this period that a number of future stars were secured, and the first, in May 1941 was goalkeeper Johnny Johnstone. A year later in June 1942 Charlie Robertson and Archie Shaw were called up from Armadale Thistle and Wishaw respectively. In November 1942 after a successful trial Andy Paton was signed up. Paton played the trial match at centre half but was pencilled in at centre forward for his first game.

The Second World War was to act as a defining period in the history of Motherwell FC as it drew to an end the successful spell of challenging for the title, with a side that had stayed together for virtually ten years. By the time the war had ended the team had virtually ceased to exist and a new side had to be pulled together after the hostilities had ceased.

MOTHERWELL
FOOTBALL & ATHLETIC CLUB, Ltd.

SEASON TICKET

18

GROUND

Valid from 10th August, 1940, till 30th April, 1941.

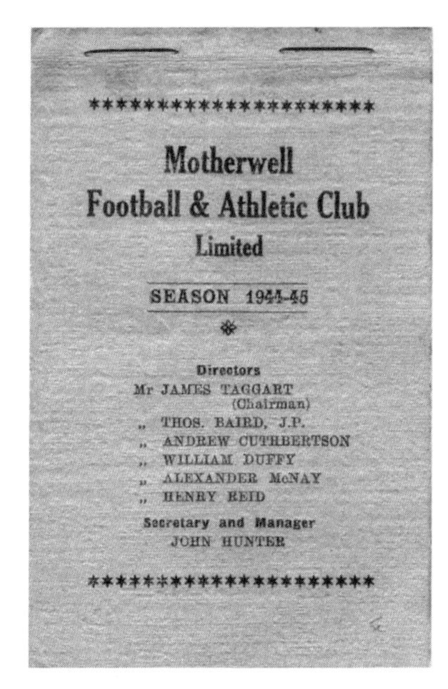

Motherwell
Football & Athletic Club
Limited

SEASON 1944-45

Directors
Mr JAMES TAGGART (Chairman)
" THOS. BAIRD, J.P.
" ANDREW CUTHBERTSON
" WILLIAM DUFFY
" ALEXANDER McNAY
" HENRY REID

Secretary and Manager
JOHN HUNTER

Play continued.
Season tickets from the 1940-41 season (left) and 1944-45 (above)

1945/46

With the conflict coming to an end the Scottish League were preparing for another war time season, even though Germany and Italy had surrendered in early May 1945 it was thought many of the servicemen no longer need in Europe would be diverted to take on Japan in the Pacific theatre of war.

The League was organised in two divisions but back under the control of the Scottish Football League, and to show that there was no resemblance with this set-up to that previously, the two divisions were named A and B rather than the traditional First and Second Division.

Motherwell were in Division A, and even though these divisions were meant to be temporary there was an almost immediate need for change given the sudden surrender of the Japanese only a few days into the season. This forced plans for a re-organisation of the Leagues and the teams for each division would have to be selected by the League authorities as relegation and promotion had not been in action during the war years. Therefore season 1945/46 was to be the last of the "unofficial" seasons.

This season saw Motherwell finish a creditable sixth having lost only ten of the 30 games played in what was a season of great change in Scottish football as it geared up for the first official post-War season.

1946/47

The season started with the planned re-organisation of the Leagues into three to try and accommodate all the teams who had filled in during the War years and also the sides that had previously been in the League but could not carry on during the war years. It was decided to hold on to the old division names of A, B and C, with the top division made up of six clubs including Motherwell.

The start of the season witnessed major changes both on and off the field at Fir Park. Firstly, off the field, long serving Manager John "Sailor" Hunter decided that he would step down and act as club secretary, he was to be replaced by League winning hero George Stevenson. On the field it was all change from the team who finished the last season prior to the War with Stevenson being the only connection between the two teams at Fir Park.

This saw the introduction of a number of players who were to become legends at Fir Park, including names such as Johnston, Kilmarnock, Shaw, Paton and Redpath.

In the opening ten games the side showed a degree of inconsistency winning only three. This included 6-1 at Palmerston against Queen of the South and at the other extreme a 5-2 defeat by Falkirk at Brockville. The opening game of the season was at home to Rangers, and although the game was lost four two, one of the 'Well goals came straight from a kick-off without a Rangers player touching the ball, with Bremner releasing Barclay and his cross being headed home by Brown. Ten points from ten games was not what was expected as the club moved into a break in the League campaign for the sectional stages of the League Cup.

The Scottish League also picked up the "ownership" of the League Cup in 1946/47, after it had initially been run as a War-time competition under the auspices of the Southern League which used the competition to help increase the number of fixtures, as there were only 16 teams in the League at the time. In the early War years Motherwell struggled to qualify from their group until 1944/45 when they finished top of their group containing Hearts, Dumbarton and St. Mirren. They then won a Semi-Final against Falkirk at Hampden thanks to a goal from McCulloch. The final was also played at Hampden, and this time it was Rangers in opposition. They ran out 2-1 winners to ensure they maintained their virtual monopoly of the early years of the trophy, winning four out of the first six competitions.

Season 1946/47 saw the tournament include all 30 League clubs rather than only the 16 Southern League Clubs of earlier. Motherwell were drawn with Aberdeen, Falkirk and Queen of the South in their qualifying group. Motherwell did not lose to Aberdeen in the group but dropped points against the other sides and were therefore eliminated with Aberdeen progressing to the Quarter Finals. The Dons progressed to the Final where they lost to Rangers.

When the League kicked off again after the League Cup, things looked to be picking up as three consecutive wins were secured against St. Mirren, Partick Thistle and Kilmarnock, showing how effective the full strength side could be.

The next five games showed the other side of the team as they all ended in defeat. One of them was against Rangers at Ibrox, and even then two refereeing decisions were to turn the game in the home side's favour, firstly a soft penalty when Duncanson appeared to lose the ball in the box and stumble over and a Brown equaliser ruled out for hand ball.

The inconsistent results continued until the end of the season, when the team finished with a record of 12 wins, 13 defeats and 5 draws, and a League position of eighth. Only twice all season did Motherwell fail to score away from home in all competitions.

The Scottish Cup did provide some light relief starting with a comfortable three nil win over Forfar at Fir Park in the first round, thanks to goals from Humphries, Johnston and Brown. February brought a trip to Brockville to take on Falkirk in the second round, and after a scoreless draw, the tie was replayed at Fir Park where Motherwell secured a one-nil win, on a heavily sanded Fir Park pitch, thanks to a Watson goal.

The third round brought a trip to Methil to take on East Fife and a comfortable two-nil win brought the reward of a Semi Final place against Hibs. The Hampden tie was played to a finish and turned into a marathon with the sides tied at 1-1 after the 90 minutes with Turnbull having put Hibs ahead and a Kimarnock equaliser bringing Motherwell back into the game. Motherwell then laid siege to the Hibs goal but disaster struck in the 142nd minute when Howie's long punt won the game for the Edinburgh side, and they progressed to the final.

One other major step taken in 1946 was the formation of the Motherwell Supporter's Association, which is still going today, helping fans travel to games by arranging coaches for those who either do not have a car or do not wish to travel on their own.

1947/48

At the end of the season the Club summed it up in the following way: *"Last season while failing to fulfil their early promise the club overall had reason for satisfaction. The gates both home and way reached record levels and had the form of the opening months been sustained then the financial return would have been of a phenomenal nature."*

In the League they picked up 14 points from eight games by the end of October, only dropping two points early that month, to Queen of the South, when Jimmy Watson was away on International duty. Also during this early season spell they went out of the League Cup, losing only one of six games in the Group Qualification stage. This defeat was to Aberdeen at Pittodrie by two goals to nil, and this was to prove costly as Aberdeen were to go on and win the group, but only by goal average. Both sides finished level on points and had conceded the same number of goals, but Aberdeen ended up scoring three more goals, sixteen against Motherwell's thirteen. The main reason for that was Aberdeen's thumping nine nil win over Queen of the South. It was during a home game against Queen of the South in the League Cup that Motherwell wore numbers on the back of their strips for the first time.

After this opening spell of the season injuries started to take their toll on the side and the level of performance with only 17 more points being secured in the remaining twenty three games. The main problem being goalscoring, for there were eleven of these seventeen games when the team failed to hit the net. For some part of the remainder of the season regulars such as Paton, Bremner, Watson, Shaw and Johnston were all missing at some time.

The Scottish Cup started with a home draw against local rivals Hamilton Accies, and in a exciting game the visitors were 1-0 up at half time through a goal from Timmins. With only ten minutes to go 'Well managed to equalise from a Humphries header but with only three more minutes gone the Accies took the lead again when Timmins got his second. With time running out Motherwell mounted a series of attacks which paid off with a Humphries equaliser in the 88th minute.

A week later at a rain swept Douglas Park, Motherwell eased through with a comfortable two-nil win, this time the goals coming from Reid and Barclay. The second round brought about a visit from Third Lanark to Fir Park, and they proved stiff opponents, but another Humphries cup goal was enough to see 'Well progress.

The third round draw paired Motherwell with Celtic at Celtic Park and again it took only one goal to decide the tie, with the opposition goal being hotly contested by the 'Well players, as Paton looked to be in an offside position when he scored.

The Directors were maybe not that dissatisfied with the season summing it up at the AGM by saying, *"While play disappointed after a brilliant start, we again experienced a gratifying financial return with a profit for the year of £4303 6s 6d with a dividend of 10%."* But they added, *"During the opening months of the season the play of the team was most satisfactory. Subsequently the injuries to players upset the rhythm of the team and the results were very disappointing."*

1948/49

Season 1948/49 was a tough one for Motherwell as they just managed to avoid relegation with only two games to go, when Morton were defeated 1-0 at the end of April, and it was the Greenock side who were left to look forward to a season in the B Division.

As stated in the Club handbook at the start of the next season, *"to lose half of the total of the League games was not in the Motherwell tradition. "* Even with the signings of Aitkenhead from Hibs and McCall from Newcastle (for a transfer fee of £5500) at the turn of the year injuries to key players saw a run of five defeats in a row through January. This was all hard to believe at the start of the season as the first seven League games brought only two defeats and produces seven points, with things looking set for a reasonable season.

This was up until the League Cup qualifying section cut in at the start of September 1948, when the 'Well were drawn along with Dundee, Falkirk and local rivals Albion Rovers. Two defeats, one each away to Falkirk and Dundee, was enough to see Motherwell finish second once again and go out of the tournament. There are two points worth noting from these six games, the first being that there 23000 in attendance for Dundee's 1-0 win at Den Park, and the second, an 8-3 win for Motherwell at home to Albion Rovers, with goals from Humphries (4), Watson (2), Johnston and Redpath.

Things started to take a turn for the worse when the League campaign kicked in once again with only one win from nine games in the run up to Christmas causing alarm bells to ring in the minds of the club directors. The Chairman, Alex McNay, was quoted as saying, *"the board realised that we would have difficulty in retaining our position in the A division of the League."*

The Directors reacted by going out and making the double signing of Aitkenhead and McCall in time for the game on New Year's day at Coatbridge against Albion Rovers, and both scored on their debut as the Wee Rovers were overcome by three goals to one. Interestingly the Rovers goal that day was scored by the legendary Celtic and Scotland manager Jock Stein.

This was followed by a run of five consecutive losses to Rangers, Queen of the South, Hearts, Falkirk and Clyde, that saw the club slip into relegation trouble, battling with injuries and with teams such as Partick, Aberdeen, Morton and Clyde. Players that missed out due to injury were the likes of, Humprhies, Paton, Goodall and McLeod.

In amongst these games the Scottish Cup kicked off and it brought about a victory at Fir Park when Stranraer were beaten three-nil with goals from Hunphries, Watson and Goodall.

But the run shuddered to an end when Rangers were drawn to visit Lanarkshire, this time it was Motherwell's turn to lost three nil, with all the goals coming in a fourteen minute spell in the second half.

After the League run of five losses there were only eight League games left in the season and thankfully Motherwell won four of them including the defeat of Morton in the third last game that ensured the 'Well stayed up and the Greenock men were consigned to the B division. The win over Morton was a tight one, being secured in the eighth minute by a McCall penalty.

The last two games of the campaign allowed the club to relax a little and only one further point was gained in the last game at home to Aberdeen, which was described at the time as being played with a *"lessening of the tempo"*. The club were also at pains to point out that due to the their poor form and the purchase of two costly players (Aitkenhead and McCall) to help get them out of trouble they posted a trading loss £1452 5s 3d. But they also pointed out that there was a silver lining at the club with the reserve side winning their League Cup when they beat Dundee 3-2 over two legs in the Final. On the way they beat Queen of the South, Morton, Rangers and Hibs.

During the season there were a couple of notable changes on the board at Fir Park, firstly in March the club's oldest and very highly respected Director William Duffy died. His long association with the club spanned forty years during which time he was Chairman on a number of occasions. At the end of the season James Taggart retired as the club's longest serving director, having been elected to the board in 1926. He had been involved through the successful times in the thirties, including the League Championship win, and had travelled as part of the party that went to South Africa and Spain where he met King Alfonoso. Neither of the two was replaced and it was decided that the board would remain at five in size.

It was also during season 1948/49 that saw the first programme issued for a Motherwell home game, that against Rangers on 14th August in a 1-1 draw.

1949/50

Once again the season opened with high hopes as it was felt the club had players of undoubted talent and as was stated in the club handbook, *"once that necessary penetrative power returns all will be 'Well with the 'Well"*. During the close season two new players had been added, outside right Jim Forrest who actually hailed from Newarthill, who was signed from Hearts, and Inside Forward Jacky Anderson who had scored fifty goals in his previous Junior season.

During the season history almost repeated itself as the club finished the season with almost exactly the same record as the previous one, with only the goals for and against showing any change. Disappointingly the number of wins draws and defeats were identical resulting in a similar disappointing points total of 25.

The season actually kicked off with the League Cup sections rather than this competition later interrupting the League campaign. Motherwell were in section C with Partick, Clyde and Dundee. They only lost one game out of the six, to Partick on the opening day, a defeat which was to prove costly. On the flip side they only managed to win two of the games and ended up finishing two points behind Thistle in second place and crashed out once again without reaching the Quarter Final stage.

It took until the sixth game of the season before the first win was registered in the League, as the club started the campaign with three draws and two defeats before finally overcoming Partick two nil at Fir Park. This was when it became apparent that the team were in for a relegation struggle again, as the next four games only managed to provide one point with a one all draw against Raith Rovers at home.

A much better spell from mid-November to the New Year eased the relegation pressure with some emphatic wins, including a 5-2 win over Clyde which saw the introduction of new centre forward Archie Kelly from Aberdeen who was signed, according to the Chairman *"at a considerable cost"*. This was followed up by a fine 4-0 win over eventual Champions Rangers, with Motherwell three goals up at half time. Then came a 4-2 win over Falkirk and a 4-0 victory against Third Lanark, again with the 'Well three up by half time.

The Rangers victory was without doubt the highlight of the season, celebrated under the Press headline, *"Rangers Outclassed by Motherwell: The defeats suffered by Rangers in their long, illustrious career have been comparatively few – so few indeed in proportion to their successes they fade into insignificance. Such a beating as they took at Fir Park on Saturday, however cannot be similarly dismissed , if only for the fact that in being defeated they were humiliated. I have never seen a Rangers eleven so outclassed in the arts and crafts of football, there were periods in the second half when Motherwell, admittedly confident in their big lead, toyed with them"*.

But as in recent times the season continued with its roller coaster progress, and the next four games through January, against St. Mirren, Dundee, Partick and Celtic, only produced a point from the first of them at Love St. 'Well were then given a tough draw in the Scottish Cup when they were drawn to play Rangers at home.

An all ticket crowd of 32000 packed into Fir Park for the tie amidst arctic conditions, which saw twelve people faint at the game. Motherwell could not re-produce the form of the previous week when they had beaten Raith Rovers 2-0, or of earlier in the season when they had beaten these opponents.

This time it was Rangers turn to be four goals up before Motherwell could find their feet in the tricky underfoot conditions and claw back two goals from an Aitkenhead penalty and a spectacular overhead kick from Kelly.

This left the last eight League games to ensure that there would be no repeat of the previous season's last minute heroics to steer clear of relegation. The week after the cup-tie brought another two points with a one-nil win over Queen of the South, but this was followed up by four defeats in a row, with Hibs, Clyde, Hearts and Rangers all taking two points from Motherwell.

Despite this the Division A fixtures for the following season were secured as Queen of the South and Stirling Albion had become detached at the bottom with three games to go, and both were already relegated. This allowed Motherwell to blood young Jim Forrest in the third last game of the season against Aberdeen and he was an instant hit with the 'Well fans. The Dons were defeated five-one, with Forrest helping to set up the goals, and Kelly netting a hat trick. They kept the fine form the following week with a four-one win over relegated Stirling Albion, before closing the season out with a four-three defeat to Cup finalists East Fife.

At the end of the season the Chairman expressed his disappointment saying, *"It was not long before we realised that we had not yet found the required strength in the forward line to the weight of the defence and get the necessary goals to bring victories."* Once again injuries were given as a reason for the poor performance in the League.

The club at this time were prepared to take a crumb of comfort from winning the Lanarkshire Cup, with Albion Rovers being beaten by four goals to nil in the final. Financially the club recorded its second loss in a row, this time by the princely sum of £641 2s 6. Despite players' expenses being down and gate receipts up, the problem was out down to increasing transfer fees again which were increased from £7065 the previous season to £8560.

At the AGM three new directors were elected to the board, James Collins a master baker in the town, John Marshall manager of the Broomside Boiler Works and also J Maxwell Muirhead head of the family joiners and building contractor's business who was to serve the club for many years, eventually being given the title of honorary Chairman.

1950/51

Looking forward to the season after the previous disappointing finish the side now had a nice blend of youth and experience. The hopes were high that the season would be one of the most successful in the club's history, and for once all associated with the club were not to be disappointed, particularly in the Cup competitions.

The season started with the now traditional League Cup qualifying section, this time the 'Well had been teamed up with Airdrie, Hearts and Partick Thistle (again!). The group games saw the 'Well win five out of six, losing four-one to Hearts at Tyne-castle. Hearts dropped one further point to Partick at Firhill, allowing Motherwell to progress to the Quarter Final stages for the first time since the War when the Cup was moved under the auspices of the Scottish Football League.

The draw brought a two legged tie with Celtic, with the first at Celtic Park. This tie brought a terrific result, with the 'Well winning by four goals to one, the goals coming from Watson, Forrest, Hunter and an own goal. The return leg ended in a 1-0 defeat but this was enough for a 4-2 win on aggregate and a Semi Final place. The draw saw Motherwell paired with Ayr United to be played at the neutral Ibrox Stadium.

In a close encounter Motherwell had to rely on two late goals in the last six minutes to claim their place in the Final. Goldie had put Ayr ahead as early as the third minute but the 'Well were soon two one up thanks to goals from Aitkenhead and Watson. Their opponents then fought back themselves and looked to be heading to the Final when they went three-two up thanks to goals from Crawford who scored two in a minute. With six minutes to go Aitkenhead pulled the tie level and a minute later it was Watson again who ensured that Motherwell progressed to the Final to take on Hibs at Hampden at the end of October.

Motherwell had all the answers in this League Cup Final success, the Fir Parkers' success was 'Well earned and the defence, which gained the Summer Cup in 1944 and took Motherwell to the League Cup Final of 1945, proved more than a match for the Hibernian forward power.

The game did not produce the skilful, pacey attacking game that many had expected when these two teams met, but this was probably down to the tactical preparation of the two sides. Both had lucky escapes as the confident Hibs forwards were thwarted by the well organised 'Well defence. As time wore on in the tie and with the Hibs attack blunted, Motherwell began to push forward themselves.

Eventually as the second half progressed Motherwell broke the deadlock with Kelly opening the scoring before Forrest made it two-nil within two minutes of the opener. The Cup was finally confirmed as Motherwell's, when Watter's goal near the finish sealed the victory. Five of the victorious players, Johnston, Kilmarnock, Shaw, Paton and Watson, had taken part in the earlier League Cup Final of 1945 when they lost 2-1 to Rangers.

The winning of the trophy was recognised by the Town Council with a Civic Reception held in the Town Hall on Monday January 8th. The Provost paid tribute to the club and its players past and present, after an enjoyable dinner served in the Large Hall.

The Club Chairman acknowledged the remarks of the Provost and thanked the Town Council for their hospitality. The occasion was set off by a telegram from the Chairman, directors and players of Hibs congratulating the club on their victory.

During all this, the players still had to concentrate on the League campaign and made a reasonable start after losing the first game against Third Lanark at Cathkin Park. This was followed up by three wins out of four in the run up to the League Cup Final, strangely the only defeat being at the hands of League Cup final opponents who triumphed six two at Fir Park.

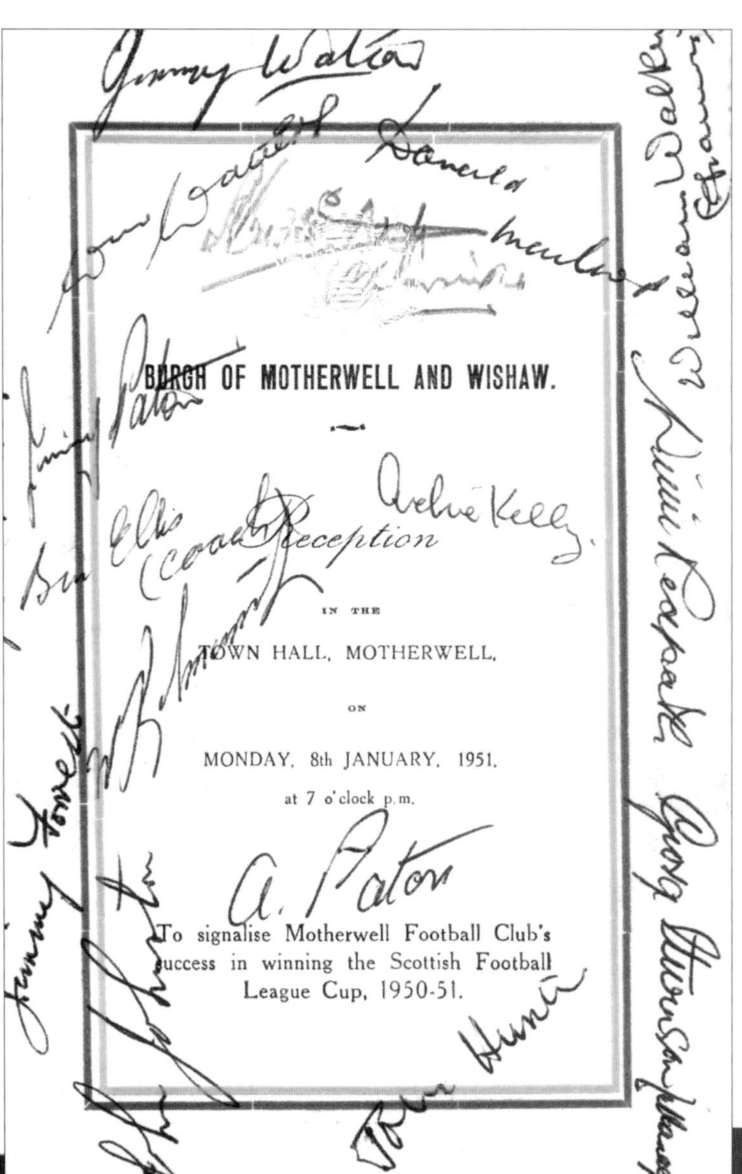

BURGH OF MOTHERWELL AND WISHAW.

Reception

IN THE

TOWN HALL, MOTHERWELL,

ON

MONDAY, 8th JANUARY, 1951,

at 7 o'clock p.m.

To signalise Motherwell Football Club's success in winning the Scottish Football League Cup, 1950-51.

The run to the League Cup Final had actually left Motherwell four games behind their League programme with all the Cup ties having been played on a Saturday. Therefore it was pleasing for all to get back into a run of League games before the Scottish Cup kicked in. Through the months of December to January the club only lost three of the eleven League games played, ensuring that there would be no need for any last minute heroics to avoid relegation this time round.

The Scottish Cup started with a second round trip to non-League Peterhead from the Highland League.

An autographed dinner card, and civic reception held at the Town Hall.

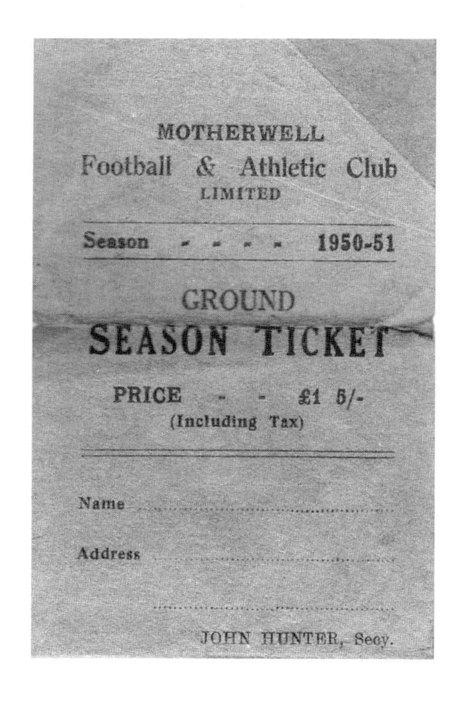
MOTHERWELL
Football & Athletic Club
LIMITED
Season - - - - 1950-51
GROUND
SEASON TICKET
PRICE - - £1 5/-
(Including Tax)
Name
Address
JOHN HUNTER, Secy.

Two momentoes from the 1950/51 season..... A season ticket, and a ticket stub from the Scottish Cup Final match.

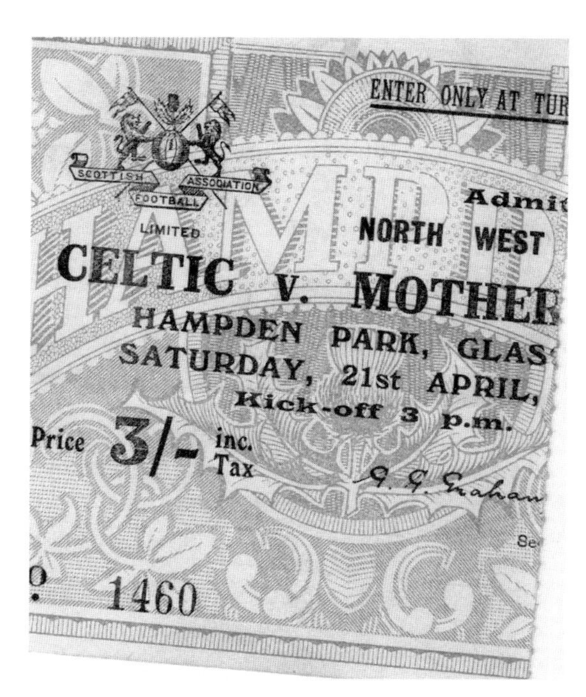

The goals in a four-nil win came from, Aitkenhead, Forrest (2) and Watson. The third round attracted a crowd of 18000 to witness the visit of Lanarkshire neighbours Hamilton Accies, and again this resulted in an easy win, this time by 4-1. Motherwell had the ball in the net twice in the first half only to have the goals disallowed, but they took control in the second period when they went two up through goals from Watters and Kelly. The Accies pulled one back through Todd but further goals from Forrest and Kelly sealed the tie.

The lure of the Cup brought further large crowds out when the draw paired Motherwell with Ayr United in the fourth round. A gate of just over 22000 was attracted to Somerset Park on 10th March to see the sides fight out a tough 2-2 draw, but Motherwell prevailed in the replay four days later progressing with a two-one win after extra time at Fir Park.

The Semi-Final paired old rivals Hibs and Motherwell for their fourth clash of the season, with Hibs having won both League games and Motherwell having the one victory in the League Cup Final at Hampden. The match was played at Hearts' Tynecastle Park and Motherwell were cheered on by an estimated 18000 their own fans in the crowd of 46000.

This was to prove another exciting clash between the two teams, with Kelly giving Motherwell the lead in only the first minute. Hibs then lost Ogilvie with a broken leg in the 15th minute and were therefore forced to persevere with only ten men, but rallied and found an equaliser on 39 minutes when Reilly converted a Smith cross. Two minutes later the 'Well were back in the lead, when after fine play by Humphries, on leave from the Army, Kelly was on hand to score his second.

The second half saw Motherwell score a third goal when McLeod beat two defenders to crash in an unstoppable shot in the 62nd minute. But within a minute Hibs had pulled a goal back, Reilly scoring his second of the game, but it wasn't enough and Motherwell progressed to their second Cup Final of the season, for the first time ever.

Once again the Final attracted a massive attendance at Hampden, for 131943 turned out to see the 'Well take on Celtic. After dominating much of the game and playing the better football Motherwell failed in their attempt to compete the Cup double. Celtic won the game thanks to a goal from McPhail, despite chances for Kelly, Humphries and Aitkenhead, the 'Well couldn't find the goals to clinch that Cup double. On reflection to have won the League Cup and qualified for the Scottish Cup Final was no mean feat and one that the club should look back on with a great deal of pride.

Motherwell, having fallen behind in the League campaign with the Cup runs, and combined with postponements, the club were forced to play 16 games in nine weeks from the beginning of March to the first week in May, playing almost every Saturday and midweek during that spell. Not surprisingly the League form faded and of the eleven League games played in that demanding period, only two were won and two drawn as fatigue took over. Having performed well in the early games of the season it meant that the poor run at the end of the season meant that a comfortable mid-table finish was achieved.

In April 1951, a remarkable anniversary was celebrated with John "Sailor" Hunter having achieved forty years service at Fir Park, having joined the club on the 11th of April 1911.

He started as secretary/manager with the aim of putting Motherwell on the football map, which he achieved with the clinching of the League Championship in 1931/32 and the League cup win in 1950. At this stage in his Motherwell career the only trophy that eluded him was the Scottish Cup.

1951/52

At the start of the new season the Club Chairman, Alex McNay, said in the club handbook, *"We look forward confidently to the advent of the new season and assure you we will spare no effort to see if we can get what we know you all want to see on the Fir Park sideboard – the Scottish Cup"*. The Chairman turned out to be a prophet as the players had duly delivered the trophy by the end of the season!

Fir Park itself opened the new season with a new look as it was turned into one of the finest provincial grounds of its time. The changes included a new frontage to the ground, new turnstiles, an extended boardroom, and separate rooms for the secretary and manager. In addition there was better accommodation for entertaining visitors, and the club was proud to announce that there was still money left in the bank.

The season started with Motherwell drawn to start the defence of the League Cup in a qualifying section with Partick Thistle, Hibernian (the previous season's beaten finalist) and Stirling Albion. Once again progress to the Quarter Finals was made with only one defeat in the group matches, ensuring that the group was won by two points from Partick Thistle in second place.

The draw paired St. Johnstone with the 'Well in a two legged affair that saw Motherwell progress easily with a seven-nil aggregate. The first leg at Muirton Park was won four nil with Motherwell going ahead through a Watson goal, but they had 'keeper Johnstone to thank on 16 minutes as he saved a penalty after a handling offence by Kilmarnock.

Two more goals from Forrest and Kelly before half time settled the tie. Aitkenhead added a fourth early in the second half to ensure that the second leg would indeed be a formality. Goals from Watson, Kelly and Redpath in the return at Fir Park made sure of a trip to the Semis.

The Semi-Final brought a tie with Dundee to be played at Ibrox Stadium, but sadly Motherwell's defence of their League Cup ended with a whimper as they crashed out when they lost by five goals to one. Dundee produced an excellent performance to beat the holders, their goals coming from a Flavell hat trick backed up by one each from Christie and Patillo, with Motherwell's consolation coming from Forrest.

The start to the League campaign had once again been disturbed by 'Well making it to the later stages of the League Cup competition, and only four League games had been completed by the start of October. In these games Motherwell suffered had gained five points from the eight available.

After their defeat in the League Cup Semi Final, things did not go quite so well with three games in a row lost against Stirling Albion, Morton and St. Mirren. The run was ended with a much needed win against Dundee at Fir Park when a degree of revenge was gained for the League Cup final defeat, the 'Well winning by two goals to one, with goals from Watson and Aitkenhead.

Despite this win by the end of November there were once again fears that relegation could become a reality. To try to halt the slide a number of the younger reserves were tried in the side but results did not improve, therefore the club decided to delve into the transfer market once again and they secured the transfer of Charlie Cox and Tommy Sloan from Hearts during December. The two new signings made an immediate impact with the League form improving with seven points gained from their first five games. The improvement in form was also timed perfectly for the start of the Scottish Cup campaign at the end January. It also meant the Cup campaign could be looked forward to knowing that the recent results had made relegation more unlikely.

The epic Cup campaign started in the unlikely surroundings of Station Park, Forfar, in the first round. The visitors received an early scare when Forfar went one up in eight minutes, Currie capitalising on defensive slackness. But by half time Motherwell were three one up, the equaliser came in the 23rd minute through McLeod, the lead on the half hour mark with Watson shooting home from 30 yards, and five minutes later a Sloan shot was deflected past the 'keeper. The second half started in a blizzard that created visibility problems for both players and spectators, but it didn't stop Kelly snatching Motherwell's fourth with fifteen minutes to go, before Forfar found a second consolation goal eleven minutes from time through Cunningham.

The second round brought another away tie, and this time it was a short trip to Paisley to take on St. Mirren at Love St. It looked as though the Cup run was about to be ended there and then as the home side went in at the half time break two goals up, having scored through Wilson and Gemmell. The lead was maybe a bit against the run of play as Motherwell had dominated the possession and had what looked like a good goal by Kelly ruled out for offside.

Motherwell started the second half in strong fashion, Redpath hitting the post and a Humphries header saved on the line.

The goal was only delayed until the 52nd minute when Sloan headed on from Watson to pick his spot to score. The 'Well equalised twenty minutes into the second half when Watson scored again, this time flicking a Sloan corner into the net. Two minutes later the comeback was complete when Humphries scored Motherwell's third and winning goal to keep the Cup dream alive.

The reward for beating St. Mirren was another away trip, this time to Dunfermline, where Motherwell earned a draw backed by a large number of visiting fans who had arrived in Fife on a "football special" train. The travelling support in the 22000 crowd was rewarded with an early lead when Watson headed home an Atkenhead cross in only the second minute. Despite creating numerous chances Motherwell couldn't find the crucial second goal and Dunfermline equalised through McGairy to force a replay at Fir Park.

The replay four days later saw Motherwell on top for most of the game but they couldn't force a goal in the first forty five minutes as Dunfermline showed terrific resistance, with Motherwell mounting wave after wave of attack. In the second half the Pars resistance was finally worn down as Motherwell took an early two goal lead with Humphries scoring in 52 minutes and three minutes later it was two when Aitkenhead netted from a Watson cross. Two more goals from Aitkenhead and Kelly in the last fifteen minutes finally ended any hopes Dunfermline had of progressing to the fourth round.

The Quarter Final brought another away draw, this time a trip to Ibrox to take on Rangers. Rangers took the lead in seven minutes when Thornton outpaced the Motherwell defence to shoot home. The equaliser was a long time coming despite incessant Motherwell pressure, the goal not arriving until only three minutes were left on the clock. Aitkenhead beat two defenders and sent the ball into Sloan who made no mistake to ensure the tie went to a well deserved replay for the visitors.

The replay at Fir Park is memorable for the fact that it produced a record home attendance for the 'Well with 35632 crammed into the ground, producing record gate receipts at the time of £2530. With recent changes to ground regulations and the vast reduction in the ground capacity, this is likely to be a Motherwell attendance record that will stand for all time.

The game itself started in similar fashion to the original tie with Thornton opening the scoring for the Gers and going into the break one goal up. It took a penalty in the second half to bring about the equaliser, with the ever efficient Aitkenhead making no mistake with the spot kick.

The Motherwell winner was another relatively late effort, with Humphries scoring with only ten minutes to go, to thus ensure a Semi Final berth.

Hearts were drawn as the opposition that were next in line to try to prevent Motherwell securing that Scottish Cup dream. It was to take three attempts to split the teams before Motherwell progressed to that much desired Final. The first tie ended one apiece with Hearts scoring the opening goal in five minutes through Conn, and Motherwell equalising in the 63rd minute when Watson's shot crashed into the net off the post.

Action from the Rangers match that produced the Fir Park record crowd - as acknowledged in the newspaper.

A Fir Park record

A CROWD of 35,632 paid for admission at Fir Park yesterday and, with season ticket-holders, the total crowd reached was 37,000.

This beats the previous Motherwell record of 36,800, set up against Celtic in 1937. Yesterday's gate money was £2560.

Just over a week later the two teams line-up at Hampden once again, and even after extra time the teams could not be separated.

This time it was Motherwell who got the early goal when Watson was on hand to put them ahead. But Hearts were on level terms only minutes later when Rutherford fired in an equaliser. Despite the extra thirty minutes the tie was forced into a second replay.

The game was played only two days after the initial replay, and at half time there had been no scoring despite both sides looking dangerous at various stages of the contest. The first goal arrived ten minutes into the second half when Motherwell took the lead, when Kelly was on hand to touch the ball over the line.

On the hour mark the lead had been doubled with Humphries making no mistake from 18 yards. Motherwell then made the mistake of falling back into defence to hold on to the two goal cushion and were punished in the 80th minute when Conn scored, but the seal was put on an epic 300 minutes of cup football when Repdpath scored in the final minute to send Motherwell through to meet Dundee in the Final at Hampden only ten days later.

Caricatures of the Cup-winning team, and a ticket stub from the match.

The final attracted the massive attendance of 136274 to see if Motherwell could finally win the Scottish Cup in their fifth final, having come so close on the four previous visits, including the 1-0 defeat to Celtic the previous season. The first half ended goalless, although Willie Kilmarnock was called upon to clear three Dundee efforts from his own goal line, but Motherwell had responded with a Watson effort hitting the Dundee cross bar with the 'keeper beaten.

With the wind at their back in the second half Motherwell swept forward and were rewarded with a goal in the 57th minute, a low shot from Watson putting them in the lead. Two minutes later the lead had been double when Redpath sent a 20 yard shot "shrieking" into the net. Motherwell were now in complete control and kept looking for more goals to ensure that nothing would prevent them from winning the Cup.

This pressure resulted in two more goals with Humphries scoring with six minutes to go, and the victory was rounded off with a fourth from Kelly two minutes later. Motherwell had finally secured the first Scottish Cup victory in their distinguished history to date, at the fifth attempt.

The Cup was indeed won the hard way, as they were never drawn at home in any round, and three of the ties went to replays, indeed the semi final took three attempts to complete. The ten ties it took to secure the Cup win were played out in front of a combined attendance of 564367 people, an average of over 56000 per game!

The scenes as the Cup was brought back to the town were unbelievable with the crowds lining the streets to see a glimpse of it being paraded on an open topped bus were almost enough to prevent the team reaching their destination at the cross, where they were to have a celebratory dinner.

It was difficult to remember in all this euphoria that there was still a League campaign going on and apart from the shaky spell in November the form in the League and a seventh place finish was achieved in what was described as a highly satisfactory season.

(Left) The Official Final programme, and below a "pirate" programme for the match

Action shots from the match

A further celebration after the historic Cup win, an "open top" bus that toured the town

1952/53

After the Cup successes of the previous two seasons hopes were high that either the Scottish Cup could be retained or that the League Cup could be regained. As the season kicked off there were a number of changes in the squad with Donald McLeod moving to Hearts as assistant trainer, he had been on the Fir Park books since first signing in 1938. Another player to leave was Joe Johnstone who had joined the year before McLeod, and he was "rewarded" with a free transfer for his long service and was immediately snapped up by Albion Rovers. One of the Cup winning heroes was also leaving the club, Jimmy Watson headed south to play for Huddersfield Town for a record fee of £10500. Also departing was reserve 'keeper Dick Hamilton who having signed in 1947 only managed seven first team appearances.

With four players going out, four were brought in with outside left Archie Williams joining from Hearts, Willie Stevenson an outside right from Kilsyth Rangers, versatile player George Dawson joining from Rutherglen Glencairn and finally back up 'keeper William White was snapped up from Alva Albion.

The League Cup campaign was over at the group stages as Motherwell finished third in their section behind Rangers and Hearts, despite losing only two games in the section. Rangers qualified as they managed to win one more game than both Motherwell and Hearts, with Aberdeen left floundering in fourth. Motherwell started with a five-two win over Aberdeen but followed this up with a two-nil defeat at Ibrox. 1-0 wins at Tynecastle and at Pittodrie brought hope that qualification could be achieved, but a draw with Rangers and a defeat at home to Hearts resulted in a final third place.

When the League got underway things weren't much better with only one win in the first six games, including a 7-3 hammering by Hibs at Fir Park at the end of September. Despite being virtually at full strength, the 'Well defence leaked like a sieve. At one stage, the 'Well were only 3-4 down, but three further goals late in the game saw the visitors complete the rout.

A win at Cathkin Park over Third Lanark two weeks later helped lift the gloom slightly, but this was followed by a six game run when only one point was picked up. This was in a draw with Raith Rovers at Stark's Park, with Aitkenhead scoring.

The dismal run was ended with the first home win of the season on December 13th when Falkirk visited Fir Park. The team made heavy weather of this victory after going two nil up, then Aitkenhead missed a rare penalty, before the Bairns broke up field to narrow the margin; but the 'Well held out. The following week they made it two wins in a row with another 2-1 win at Fir Park, this time over Dundee.

Much of the good work from this spell was undone when again only one point was taken in the next three games, including another hammering from Hibs, this time at their home ground at Easter Road. The result was seven goals to two, and once again it was another defensive nightmare. The following week the 'Well bounced back from this hammering by beating Celtic 4-2 at Fir Park, and then followed this up the next week with a 5-2 win at Love St against St. Mirren. These two wins were, as had been the pattern of the season, followed up by two more defeats that had the 'Well in a relegation dogfight, as they prepared to defend the Scottish Cup.

'Well entered the competition in the second round and were given a trip to Alloa's Recreation Ground to start their defence of their trophy. They were put under pressure from the start as they appeared to underestimate their lowly opponents, and it was against the run of play that the holders took the lead. Aitkenhead opened the scoring in the 22nd minutes and it took until the 81st to secure their place in the next round when Redpath shot home.

The third round brought about another away trip, this time to Aberdeen's Pittodrire Stadium. By half time Aberdeen were two goals up in a game which had produced six goals in the first forty five minutes. Kelly put Motherwell in the lead after only nine minutes but the Dons were level six minutes later when Buckley equalised. They then opened up a two goal lead thanks to goals from Yorston and Buckley's second. Aitkenhead pulled the lead back to one before Allister of Aberdeen scored from the spot to ensure a two goal lead for the home side at the break.

Motherwell were back in the tie on 67 minutes when they pulled a goal back, but Aberdeen were two up again after Allister scored another penalty. Two goals in the last ten minutes earned a replay, with Shaw scoring from 40 yards and then Cox heading the equaliser in the last minute to keep a tenuous hold on the Cup.

The replay was never as close as Motherwell were trounced by six goals to one by the visitors from the North, as rumours circulated that the 'Well players were below par as the result of a dispute over wages and bonuses with the Board of Directors. No matter the reason, the proud boast of all at Fir Park of being Scottish Cup holders had been shortlived.

This left seven games to ensure that they would be playing in Division A the following season. The first of the seven was a defeat at the hands Clyde at Shawfield but hope was re-kindled the following week with a win over relegation rivals Raith Rovers at Fir Park. A defeat at Ibrox against Championship challenger's Rangers in the next game was followed up by a win over another relegation rival Queen of the South, and 'Well's hopes were raised with three games to go.

Photograph from the period, of long-serving John Hunter, with Andy Paton, George Stevenson and Tommy McKenzie

Two of the games were against clubs in the relegation struggle and the final game against Rangers at Fir Park. The third last game resulted in a defeat at Falkirk meaning that full points were required from the last two games, and with this in mind the players went at Aberdeen from the kick-off and were three up by half time, before going on to win the game four nil.

The last game of the season saw Rangers run out with a deserve three nil win, this clinched the Championship for them and consigned Motherwell to at least one season in the B Division, only twelve short months after securing the elusive Scottish Cup win. In the final table Motherwell ended up one point behind local rivals Airdrie, Raith Rovers and Falkirk and went down along with Third Lanark.

1953/54

All at Fir Park were determined to do whatever was required to ensure that their stay in Division B would be as short as possible and that Motherwell should be quickly restored to their rightful place at the top table of Scottish football once again.

The season started with the League Cup section and being in the B Division it was felt that being drawn with Kilmarnock, Morton and Dundee United was a favourable draw. Motherwell only lost one game of the six, that being a 4-1 defeat at Rugby Park against Kilmarnock. This meant that both 'Well and Killie had only lost one game (to each other) and therefore gathered the same number of points. The Ayrshire side progressed to the Quarter Finals on goal average as their goal tally stood at 14 for and five against, while Motherwell's was 17 for and 7 against.

It was therefore time to concentrate on the job of getting back out of Division B and back into the top Division. The campaign started well with three straight wins, scoring 14 goals in the process against Forfar (5-0), Alloa (6-0) and Albion Rovers (3-2).

There was a bit of a set back when Ayr Utd visited Fir Park for the fourth game and went back down to Somerset Park with two lucky points. The game was tied at 3-3 in the last minute when Forrest of Motherwell hit the bar with a header, but Ayr broke away and scored a winner. The following week saw the defence leak more goals in another 4-3 defeat, this time at East End Park against Dunfermline. In this game the 'Well were 4-1 down before rallying to produce two goals, but couldn't completely pull the game back.

From the start of October to the end of January, before the start of the Scottish Cup campaign, only five points were dropped out of thirty six available. The side were also scoring freely, regularly rattling three goals or more on a regular basis. This culminated in an unbelievable 12 (twelve) goal to one win against Dundee United at Fir Park, Motherwell's record score to date.

This was a sparkling performance of attacking football rounded off by a six goal haul from Wilson Humphries. His own best goal was his second that was scored from fully

Training session on the Fir Park pitch in the early 1950's

20 yards, but one netted by Hunter was also brilliantly made by Humphries. The inside forward, now free from his Teacher Training studies, ran down the left wing and faced with three Dundee United defenders he swerved and beat all three before crossing for Hunter to score.

All the goals that Motherwell scored in the game came from Humphries and Hunter, with Hunter scoring two from the penalty spot having taken over the spot kick duties from Johnny Aitkenhead. The only regret in establishing this record victory was that it is was against a team managed by former 'Well great Willie McFadyen.

The following week saw the start of another Scottish Cup campaign with a trip to Love St. to take on First Division St. Mirren. Motherwell won comfortably by two goals to one thanks to goals from Aitkenhead and Sloan, with the Saints only scoring late in the game. This was to start off another run that almost took Motherwell to the final again.

It was another away trip in the second round, with a trip to East End Park to take on Dunfermline. The home side were 2-1 up at half time but Motherwell dominated the second half scoring four times to run out five two winners. The scorers at East End Park were Jim Forrest with a hat trick and Atikenhead with a brace.

Sandwiched in between this tie and the next round with Raith Rovers at Fir Park, was a loss in the League at the hands of Stenhousemuir at Ochilview, but this was a rare blip on the road to the First Division. The Raith Rovers cup-tie started with the Fifers trying to knock Motherwell out of their flowing style with a series of rough tackles early in the game.

But Motherwell ran out comfortable winners after visiting centre half Willie McNaught opened the scoring for Motherwell by knocking the ball past his own 'keeper. Motherwell went on to score a further three to run out 4-1 winners.

This win set up a Quarter Final tie with Partick Thistle at Firhill, which ended in a 1-1 draw with Motherwell scoring their deserved equaliser in the last 20 seconds when an Aitkenhead cross was converted by Hunter. In the replay Motherwell took the lead with Hunter scoring again, this time after only two minutes of the game. Thistle equalised by half time but 'Well deservedly progressed to the Semi Final when Humphries grabbed a second half winner.

The tie was against Motherwell's Scottish Cup bogey side Celtic, to be played at Hampden. By the time that the Semi Final had come around the relentless pursuit of a return to the top division was almost complete, and in the previous week debutant Willie McSeveney, who had signed from Dunfermline, secured a goal in the 1-1 draw with Third Lanark.

Motherwell took the lead in the Semi Final with Wilson Humphries managing to scramble the ball over the line, but Celtic were on level term within a minute when Mochan scored from 15 yards. Mochan netted again, in the second half, to put Celtic two one up, but Charlie Aitken, recently returned from his National Service, headed home a Kilmarncok free kick.

'Well could have made it to the Final in the dying seconds when Sloan was through on the Celtic goal but he could only lift his shot over the bar.

Celtic completed their ninth victory over Motherwell in the Scottish Cup when they won the replay by three goals to one, with Motherwell's consolation coming from Hunter. The two ties were played in front of a combined crowd of 195000 people who paid the princely sum of £15600 for the privilege.

Two days later Motherwell threw off the disappointment of their Scottish Cup exit by clinching promotion to the First Division, securing the Division B title with a 2-1 win over Arbroath at Fir Park. Willie McSeveny scored in the first half but after Arbroath had equalised it took a Redpath penalty to secure the win and the title along with it.

Returning to the top flight in only one season was celebrated as a great achievement, and with only six defeats - having scored 109 goals in thirty games - few could argue with this. It was also achieved without any damaging financial impact to the club, which reported a small profit of £33 7s 6d for the season.

1954/55

The new season back in the top League was looked forward to with a great deal of anticipation by the 'Well fans. The Directors decided to reward the supporters for standing by them when work on the building of a covered enclosure capable of holding 8000 to 10000 spectators was started. The squad had also been added to with the addition of Hastie Weir from Queens Park, along with three promising youngsters from the Junior ranks, W. Mason from Linlithgow Rose, Alex Harper from Douglas Water Thistle and finally Alex Bain from Cockenzie Star).

The season started brightly as 'Well progressed from a League Cup group containing St. Mirren, Kilmarnock and Raith Rovers. The first five games went undefeated including a draw and a win over nearest rivals St. Mirren, ensuring that the last game defeat to Raith meant nothing as the group had already been won by one point from the Saints. The form in the group sections followed, by a 3-2 aggregate win over Rangers in the Quarter Finals, and hopes rose for a repeat of the 1951 success in the same trophy.

The Semi Final saw Motherwell line-up against the holders of the trophy when they were drawn against East Fife. This was another trip to Hampden that ended in success for the 'Well, and it was thanks to a goal from Alec Bain who had scored seven goals in a reserve game against Kilmarnock earlier in the season. East Fife had actually taken the lead in the third minute, but this was equalised by a Willie Kilmarnock free kick from 25 yards that somehow found a gap in the Fifer's defensive wall. The winner from Bain was a gem when he headed home following excellent work from Cox and Hunter.

The final on 23rd October came at a time when there was a bit of an injury crisis at Fir Park which forced the omission of the influential Archie Shaw from the team line-up to face Hearts. Hearts produced an excellent performance to run out deserved and comfortable winners by four goals to two to ensure that Motherwell did not repeat the feat of the 1951 side. The 'Well goals, in a fighting performance, came from a Redpath penalty and the second from Semi- Final scorer Bain.

In the mean time things had actually started reasonably 'Well in the League Campaign, with only one defeat in the four games that had been played before the League Cup final. This meant that a satisfactory total of five points had been taken from these games.

The week after the League Cup final defeat was followed by a 3-2 win over Raith Rovers at Fir Park, thanks to goals from, Hunter, Aitken and Williams. This proved to be a rare victory as in the fourteen games between the League Cup and the Scottish Cup, there were only two more successes. This meant that once again Motherwell were facing a relegation fight square in the face. As seems to happen with all Motherwell sides, one of these rare victories was at home to Rangers, by 2-0 on 3rd January, and this gave 'Well fans something to cheer about, with the goals coming from McSeveney and Williams. This was to be a rare highlight in a depressing League season.

Motherwell's first game in the Scottish Cup bizzarely started in – the re-structured - round five against Highland League side Forres Mechanics at their Mosset Park. In truth the First Division side made heavy weather of seeing off their opponents by four goals to three. Motherwell were 3-1 up by half time despite going a goal down in the second minute, and after easing off at the start of the second half they found themselves hauled back to three goals apiece. Charlie Aitken did manage to put Motherwell back in the lead but it took a late penalty miss from Forres full back Hazle to allow 'Well to progress to the sixth round. Motherwell then enjoyed highland hospitality after the game as Forres hosted a Civic Reception in honour of the visit of the top division side in the Forres Town Hall.

The sixth round continued Motherwell's run of away draws when they visited Third Lanark's Cathkin Park. Thirds took the lead in through a goal from future Motherwell manager Ally McLeod. But three goals in the second half from Aitken, Sloan and Redpath secured the victory for the visitors from Lanarkshire.

This set up a home Quarter Final tie against Lanarkshire neighbours Airdrie and on the day it was the Diamonds who were too Strong from the 'Well as they powered to a four one win, with a consolation goal coming from Hunter.

The League form continued to cause concern as Motherwell slipped further into relegation trouble during the distraction of the Cup run. It didn't help that the four games following the Cup exit also ended in defeat, including a controversial reverse at the hands of Celtic. Celtic were one-nil up as the game headed into the last five minutes and a Motherwell effort on goal looked to have crossed the goal line for a deserved equaliser but, the referee waved play on as he considered that the ball had not actually crossed the line.

Three wins in a row helped raised hopes that relegation could be avoided once again, but subsequent dropped points to Hearts (twice) and Rangers in the last game of the season couldn't stop Motherwell finishing second bottom in the table, one point behind Raith Rovers, and facing a second season in Division B.

During the summer the Scottish Football League decided that something had to be done with the League structure, in response to some of the major clubs complaining about how reserve football was organised. Reserve teams at that time expected to compete in either of the C divisions, but this had not worked for some time. Eventually a number of sides indicated that they would not run reserve sides in the C divisions and at a recalled General Meeting on June 17 1955 the decision was taken to increase the top division to 18 teams and a lower League of 19, and return the titles to 'First' and 'Second' divisions.

To accommodate the increase in the top division it was decided, by 25 votes to 12, that the teams that finished in the relegation places, Motherwell and Stirling Albion, would stay in the First Division and be joined by the top two from the B division, Dunfermline and Airdrie, who were due to be promoted any way.

Therefore it was a highly relieved Motherwell who were to continue in the top flight for another season when the 1955/56 season kicked off.

But before the start there were to be three notable departures from Fir Park, as Manager George Stevenson stepped down, plus groundsman Ben Ellis and goalkeeper John Johnstone. Stevenson and Ellis had both played in the League winning campaign of 1931/32 before taking up their posts in the background. Stevenson had been manager for the previous nine years, taking over from his previous boss John "Sailor" Hunter. "Stevie" had been with the club since joining as a player from Kilbirnie Laedside in 1923. He handed in his resignation on returning form holiday on July 2nd and the Board accepted it with much regret, the club and the man parting on good terms.

Ben Ellis had joined the ground staff as the end of his playing days, after serving at left back after signing from his home town club of Bangor in 1930. He left to set up in business on his own as a masseur. Goalkeeper John Johnston's long service - at the close of the season he was the club's second longest player - was rewarded with a free transfer. He had joined Motherwell from Armadale Thistle in 1941 and had provided valuable and loyal service in his 14 years at Fir Park.

Prior to the start of season 1955/56 it was announced that the new manager would be Bobby Ancell, who was currently manage of Dunfermline, but would take up his role for the start of the season. This was the start of a new era at Motherwell as Ancell went on to produce an exciting young side.

Andy Paton, on a 'Soccer Heroes' card

Archie "Baldy" Shaw - depicted on a cigarette card

Chapter 6 Ancell Babes

1955/56

New Manager Bobby Ancell joined in the summer of 1955 after Dunfermline finally found a replacement for him. As a player Ancell had played as a left back for Queen of the South, St. Mirren, Newcastle United and Dundee. While at Newcastle he won two Scotland caps when he was selected to play against Wales and Northern Ireland in 1937. He left Dundee in 1950 to take up his first role as manager, at Berwick Rangers, and two years later he took over at Dunfermline, taking them to promotion to the First Division at the end of the 1954/55 season.

His first six games in charge saw Motherwell storm through their League Cup qualifying section, winning all six games, scoring 24 goals and conceding three in the process, as they brushed aside the challenge from Forfar, Dundee United and Albion Rovers. Thirteen of the goals came in the first two games, with seven at Forfar and six at home four days later against Albion Rovers.

Bobby Ancell,
in his playing days with Dundee

Ancell's first League game in charge was also to prove a highscoring success as East Fife were beaten by five goals to two at Fir Park. The goals scored by Aitkenhead - a hat trick - Bain and Billy Reid. Reid had been signed from Juvenile football on his 17th birthday in the previous January and while he is widely accepted as being one of the famous Ancell Babes, he was actually signed by previous manager George Stevenson.

In the League Cup Quarter Final, Motherwell were paired with St. Johnstone in a tie that would take place over two legs. In the first at the Perth side's home ground, Muirton Park, Motherwell won by the odd goal in three after Aitkenhead and Cox had put them two goals up.

The return leg at Fir Park was an exciting affair as Saints pulled a goal back in the first half and held on through the rest of the ninety minutes and extra time to force a third game.

The third game took place at Rangers' Ibrox Park, and Motherwell made no mistake this time as they swept aside the challenge of the Second Division side by two goals to nil. The Saints had held on until the 75th minute but their resistance was broken by an Aitken header and the result was given a fairer look by a last minute goal from Hunter.

Motherwell were to return to Ibrox for their Semi Final tie at the start of October to take on St. Mirren this time. The first game ended in a three all draw, once again forcing a replay, but this time it was to be played at Celtic Park. Motherwell struggled in the second encounter thanks to an injury to Wilson Humphries which upset the pattern of play, and the Buddies capitalised by scoring two goals through Gemmell and Brown to progress to the Final, and take on Aberdeen.

The League campaign saw Ancell start to make his mark on the initially side with Ian Gardiner coming on board from East Fife in October for the princely sum of £5100. The centre forward marked his debut against Celtic with a goal in a two all draw at Fir Park, with Charlie Atiken scoring the equaliser.

Results in the League campaign were mixed as Ancell tried to find his ideal team and this was highlighted with a seven goals to one thrashing at the hands of Hearts at Tynecastle in mid-November, and in the following week with a five one victory over Raith Rovers at Fir Park.

Another player who was brought in during the season was Pat Quinn who was signed up from Bridgeton Waverly after impressing the Manager and Director James Collins in a game for his club against St. Rochs in early December. Also joining in January were Wallace Rea a winger from Third Lanark and left back Charles Henderson from Blairgowrie.

The win against Raith Rovers sparked off a run of six games that saw only three points dropped, with just one defeat at Dens Park against Dundee, and a three nil win over local rivals Airdrie at Broomfield. The run was ended when another seven goals were lost in Edinburgh, this time to Hibs, when the home side ran out 7-0 winners, with 'keeper Hastie Weir, who it was reported kept the score down!

The next week saw the start of the Scottish Cup, with a home tie to the Amateurs of Queen's Park. Queen's deserved their win and Crampsey in their goal was outstanding. One particular save from an Aitken header even brought applause from the disgruntled home fans. Glen put the Queen's ahead from the penalty spot and Ormand put the tie out of Motherwell's reach. This was a tremendous disappointment to all at Motherwell and made a big impact in the club's finances for the season.

In the remaining fifteen games the club ensured a mid-table finish with only five defeats, two of them being in the last two games of the campaign. They gained thirty-three points with eleven wins, twelve draws and eleven defeats.

The poor Cup run, installation of floodlights and other ground improvements meant that the club made a loss for the first time in six years, amounting to £3657. The new floodlights were inaugurated during the season, with Wednesday 29th February a notable date in the clubs history when they were officially opened in a match against Preston North End.

The game finished with a win for the visitors by three goals to two, after dominating the game for most of the second half. England Internationalist Tom Finney scored the winning goal with 25 minutes to go. The 'Well goals came from a Docherty own goal and Brown, with Preston's others from Hatsell and Thomson.

1956/57

During the summer Motherwell started the implementation of their policy of no longer signing "ready made" seasoned pros and reverting to the previous policy of identifying promising youngsters who would be brought up in the Motherwell tradition. This policy produced League winners in Stevenson, Ferrier and McFadyen.

This saw four signings made in the close season to support this philosophy, with the following players brought in; inside right Bert McCann from Queen's Park, William Cowie a centre half from Kilsyth Rangers, left back Pat Holton from Hamilton and lastly a new 'keeper - Alan Wylie from Penicuik.

To make way for the new men, a number of players were freed to make way, this was on top of the release of Willie Redpath during the previous season which allowed him to move on to Third Lanark after ten years at Fir Park. One other major departure was Cup winner Wilson Humphries who had signed in 1945 when he left Dalziel High School, and he was immediately snapped up by St. Mirren. There were another seven players freed as Motherwell continued to make major changes to the squad.

The League Cup was a disappointment at the start of the season with only two wins in the six games meaning that they finished well behind Dundee United and Raith Rovers. The two wins were over old rivals Airdrie, with the home tie being won with an emphatic 6-1 result to go into the League campaign which was due to start with a trip to Firhill to take on Partick Thistle.

As disappointing as the League Cup campaign had been, the start to the League season was just the opposite with nine games passing before a game was lost. After only three games the team was proudly sitting on top of the First Division having beaten Thistle 3-2 on the opening day and following this up with a 2-2 draw with East Fife and a four one hammering of Airdrie at Broonfield.

A fantastic 1-0 win over Celtic at Fir Park was next, with a display of flowing football when Aitken, Paton, Forrest and Quinn were all prominent, Quinn scoring the winner. Motherwell confirmed their title ambitions during their magnificent to the start of the season with a seven nil win over Queen of the South at the end of October, the home side being five up by half time. Two weeks later they went to Ibrox and beat Rangers by three goals to two. They were three goals up by half time with the goals coming from Aitkenhead and two from Gardiner, they then eased off in the second half and allowed Rangers in with two goals. The good run was brought to an end with a visit to Starks Park where Raith Rovers ran out two nil winners in a game that was dominated by Motherwell, but they succumbed to two second half goals.

Ancell's "new" side continued to play impressive football as they lost only four games in the next twelve after the Raith defeat and continued to challenge for the title, being described as *"the most attractive footballing side in Scotland"*. During November and December, two more players were added to the squad with Billy Reid's brother Sammy being snapped up from Douglas Water to play on the right wing along with Gerry Baker from Chelsea.

The Scottish Cup kicked off in the Fifth Round at the start of February with the 'Well drawn away to Stirling Albion. It was a less than convincing performance from Motherwell that saw them squeeze through to the next round with a 2-1 win. They were two goals up through Brown and Hunter, but a last minute goal from the home side couldn't stop the 'Well progressing.

The next round brought a visit from Second Division Dumbarton to Fir Park, and a lack lustre display saw Motherwell crash out of the competition. A Gardiner goal gave Motherwell a one goal lead at half time, but second half goals from Gibson (2) and Cairns saw the visitors safely through to the next round.

Motherwell bounced back in the League the following week by defeating Ayr Utd 2-1 at Somerset Park. It was therefore hard to believe that they would then go on and lose the next eight games which saw them drop four places down the table and out of title contention. There was consolation in the last two games with a draw away to Queen of the South and a win at Falkirk in the last game of the season.

The disastrous run of eight games without a point cost the 'Well any chance of winning the title and saw them slip from challengers to finish seventh in the table 18 points off the leaders Rangers. Truly a case of what might have been....

1957/58

Ancell continued the change in his squad as three more great servants from the 1952 Cup-winning left the club, Willie Kilmarnock moving to Airdrie after serving since 1939, and Johnny Aitkenhead, a stalwart since joining in 1949 was also given a free transfer from that side, plus Tommy Sloan. These moves were instrumental in bringing the average age of the side down from 31 to 25.

Once again the League Cup was to prove fruitless as Motherwell failed to progress past the qualifying group, Aberdeen strolling through to the Quarter Finals unbeaten. Motherwell, in fact, finishing third one point behind Falkirk and only one ahead of Queen of the South. They amassed the grand total of four points with wins away to Falkirk and at home to Queen of the South.

The League campaign started with high hopes following the excellent form of the previous season, and also after a win at home to St. Mirren in the opening game. Motherwell had gone two down to the Paisley Saints before four headed goals shared between Hunter and Gardiner sealed it for 'Well. This was followed by a disappointing run which only produced one win in seven games - a four one win over Partick Thistle at Fir Park. Although they also managed to take a point away from title challenging Hearts at Tynecastle.

November marked the debut of Ian St. John who had been signed earlier in 1957 from Douglas Water Thistle. This coincided with two wins on the trot as Motherwell won against Kilmarnock at Rugby Park and at home to Queen of the South. But the season was marred by a number of injuries and a bout of flu that swept through the club and meant that consistent selection was made difficult. Players were therefore being asked to play in a number of positions, for example, Ian St. John was played in almost any of the five forward positions.

In January the problems led to another of Ancell's young signings making his debut, with John Martis lining up at centre half, to replace Andy Paton, against Hibs on 2nd January. The apprentice plumber had only joined the club from Royal Albert in November of 1957. Another debutant was Andy Weir who was called in to play at outside left after he had made the move from Junior side Arthurlie.

The Scottish Cup kicked off at the start of February with an away trip to face second division East Stirling at Firs Park. 'Well ran out comfortable seven goals to three winners. The goals were shared between Gardiner with four, Weir with two and a Kerr penalty. This victory brought a home tie against Partick in the third round and a controversial draw led to a replay. The first game saw Thistle awarded a disputed goal and Motherwell denied a penalty when Aitken had been barged in the box. Kerr and St. John's goals ensured that Motherwell would have a second chance at Firhill. Motherwell went on to win the replayed tie comfortably by four goals to one.

The next round saw Motherwell make a trip to the Highlands to take on Inverness Caledonian at Telford Park. The initial stages were a bit of a struggle for the First Division side, until the 40th minute when Forrest scored, and then Kerr added one to make it two before the break. Goals from Gardiner, Kerr, Weir, Forrest and St. John saw Motherwell score seven in the competition for the second time in the season.

Aberdeen were to be the visitors to Fir Park in the Quarter Final and Motherwell cruised through to the Semis with a 2-1 win. They took the lead in the first half through McSeveney, although Aberdeen had equalised through Davidson before the break. McSeveney had to be stretchered off ten minutes into the second half but it was ten man 'Well who progressed to the last four thanks to a St. John goal.

The Semi Final matches Motherwell against Clyde at Celtic Park at the start of April. Clyde were three nil up after 54 minutes, thanks to a hat trick from Coyle. But the 'Well fought back through goals from Quinn and St. John and were only denied a draw when in the dying seconds a McSeveney header crashed off the underside of the bar and bounced clear.

Back in the League Motherwell finished strongly in the last eight games when they lost only two of them and pushed themselves into a comfortable mid-table position. The major achievement of the campaign had been the introduction of a batch of new young players, including St. John, Weir, plus the two Reids, Rea and Martis.

This time saw the end of three illustrious careers at Fir Park when Archie Shaw, Andy Paton and Charlie Cox were awarded free transfers by Manager Ancell. Andy Paton move the short distance across the Clyde to become captain of neighbours Hamilton Accies, and Shaw was kept on at Fir Park in the role of assistant trainer. With the release of these three players all ties with the team that won the Scottish Cup back in 1952 had been broken, with none of the eleven left at the club.

At the end of the season it was also reported that once again a small loss was made of £764 9s 6d, thanks in part to the blowing down of a section of the Covered Enclosure and the floodlighting system that had to be repaired prior to the start of the following season.

1958/59

The only addition to the playing staff for the start of the new season was Robert McCallum, a local lad who was snapped up from Bellshill Athletic whom he had joined from the Motherwell Bridge Works team. This was the season that saw the emergence of the Ancell Babes in all their glory with the young players filling most of the positions in the side and being asked to put into practice the footballing beliefs of their manager. This was to produce a good footballing side, *"which concentrated on all out attack and a team would inevitably win providing they had the skill to sustain the constant pressure".*

The League Cup campaign would not see Motherwell progress past the group qualifying stages once again as they won three of the six games and finished second in the group to Partick Thistle, who strangely they overcame in the first League game which was sandwiched in the middle of the League Cup group matches.

In the League the 'Well went on to lose only one game out of the first sixteen, and many were starting to believe that this team could repeat the feat of the great side of the thirties and bring the League title back to Fir Park. To prove that the team was built in the image of attacking football that Ancell had prescribed, they won 5-1 at Airdrie 4-0 at Dunfermline and produced an 8-1 win at home to Third Lanark.

The Third Lanark game, in mid-October, showed what this young side could do as they tore the unfortunate Hi Hi apart, with Pat Quinn in particularly in fine form. The 'Well were five one up by half time with goals coming from Weir (2), Sammy Reid, Aitken and Quinn.

The second half was once again one way traffic and three more goals were added thanks to a St. John double, and Quinn rounded off the score with his second and the team's eighth.

It took until December 27th before Motherwell were to suffer a further defeat when they lost heavily by 4-0 to Partick Thistle at Firhill. They bounced back from this game, dropping only two points in the next six games before Third Lanark got some degree of revenge for the heavy defeat in October by winning 5-2 at their own patch in early February.

The next week saw the start of the Scottish Cup campaign and the second round brought a trip to play local rivals Airdrie at Broomfield. Once again the 'Well side produced a marvellous exhibition of attacking football and rattled in seven goals with Airdrie only able to reply with two. The game was a personal triumph for Ian St John as he bagged four of the goals to help his local side progress to take on St. Mirren at Love St in the next round.

Motherwell found themselves two goals down in 65 minutes before they woke up and a brace from Quinn had them back on level terms, but the Saints progressed when Bryceland score a winner late in the game. The only consolation from this defeat was the fact that the Paisley Buddies went on to win the trophy later in the season.

Following the Third Lanark defeat and squeezed between the ties were two further reverses, away to Clyde, and St Mirren on the Saturday before the Cup. The week after the cup-tie a fourth consecutive League defeat was suffered as injuries to key players started to take their toll on the side, this time to Raith Rovers at Stark's Park.

This run of four consecutive defeats were to prove decisive in the push for the title as Motherwell dropped out of contention behind Rangers and Hearts. In the run-in third place was secured with only one defeat - to Champions Rangers - in the last six games. The season was rounded off in fine style with an emphatic five nil win away to Queen of the South with Andy Weir grabbing a second half hat trick, one of them being scored direct from a corner, following a first half opener from Sammy Reid.

Another interesting feature of the season was the appearance of floodlit friendlies which proved to be extremely popular with the Motherwell supporters. Leeds United were the first visitors and they were thumped by seven goals to nil. Swedish side Djugardens were next up and they were also defeated this by only the odd goal in three. Celtic also played in a benefit match in aid of the Lanarkshire Spastics association, with the game ending in a 1-1 draw. The popular appeal of these games was demonstrated by the fact that crowds of 20000 turned up for each of them.

Although there was to be no silverware on the Fir Park sideboard at the end of the season there were a few memorable highlights to be celebrated with Ian St. John being the top goalscorer in the First Division with 24, and he also added seven in Cup competitions and six in friendlies to give an overall total of 37 for the season.

There were also plenty of International honours, with on one occasion three Motherwell players, Bert McCann, Ian St. John and Andy Weir representing Scotland in a match against Germany, the latter chipping in with a goal. There were also Scottish League honours for Aitken and Hunter, and Pat Quinn played for the Scotland Under 23s. Allied with Martis and Sammy Reid being in the reserve squads the Ancell "babes" were certainly gaining a great deal of recognition for their style of attacking football.

One major change during the season was behind the scenes with long serving doyen of Motherwell John "Sailor" Hunter deciding to retire from the post of Secretary due to illness and advancing years, on 25th March, after 48 years service at the club. He had joined as Manager in April 1911 after a playing career that saw him play for Liverpool (where he won a League title) Arsenal and Portsmouth in England and Hearts and Dundee in Scotland.

He would always be remembered for his winning of the League title and the foreign tours he took the team on. During his time as Manager he was never lured away even though he was approached by some of the biggest names in the game, including Manchester United. When he gave up the position of manager, he handed the mantle on to prodigy George Stevenson, and became full time Secretary for the club.

The Board decided to recognise his major contribution in making Motherwell the club it had become by awarding him a pension of £10 per week and they also presented him with a substantial cheque in tribute to his loyal service. His wife was also recognised with the gift of a gold wristlet watch.

It is hard to put in context the role that Mr Hunter played in the cementing of Motherwell FC over the 48 years that he was involved with the club, but its probably safe to say that the club's standing as a major force in Scottish football was due mainly to his efforts and subsequent generations were to benefit from his wisdom and vision.

1959/60

The season started with hopes following the highlights of the previous season, and also with the work carried out off the park to improve the ground. The covered enclosure and part of the terracing had been fitted with concrete steps giving increased and *"more comfortable"* viewing for spectators and increasing the ground capacity to 40000.

There was also a planned improvement in training facilities as Motherwell took out a lease on Motherwell Stadium to help protect the pitch at Fir Park to keep it in top condition, instigated by Ancell's football ideals.

During the previous months three players had been transferred with Gerry Baker moving to St. Mirren, where he went on to win a Cup winners medal, Ian Gardiner who moved to Raith Rovers and Pat Holton who travelled South to join Chelsea. During the season the squad had been bolstered by the addition of centre half Pat Delaney, son of Celtic legend Jimmy.

The League Cup qualifying campaign saw Motherwell progress to the Quarter Finals from a group containing League Champions Rangers, Hibs and Dundee. Rangers were beaten both home and away but the highlight was reserved for the trip to Hibernian. Motherwell won the game by three goals to one, all three being scored by Ian St. John in the record time of two and a half minutes.

Hibs actually took the lead in 71 minutes when Fox opened the scoring. Within nine minutes they were three one down thanks to St. John. He scored his first in 78 minutes from a Reid cross, his second came two minutes later when he capitalised on a goalkeeping error to prod the ball over the line. Thirty seconds later he completed his whirlwind hat trick when he headed home a Reid cross.

The Quarter Final first leg at Fir Park produced another St. John goal in a 1-1 draw with Hearts at Fir Park. This wasn't enough to help the side progress as in the second leg Hearts ran out comfortable six two winners at Tynecastle in front of 42000 fans.

Once again Ancell's team delighted people the length and breadth of the country with their excellent style of football but still didn't manage to win any of the major trophies. The club's standing was probably still higher than for many years with the team recognised by the press as the "team of the year" with a large number of the players represented at International level.

The League campaign actually saw the team finish two places lower than the previous season, when they came in fifth. The opening set of results didn't get the side off to the best possible start losing three of the first four games before hitting form again by the end of September, when a draw at Dundee got them back on the rails.

The excellent form of centre forward Ian St. John was starting to attract attention from clubs in England, and in October the club showed some ambition when they rejected a £25000 offer from Newcastle United. One player who did move on was Sammy Reid who moved south to join Liverpool in February of 1960.

Results were mixed throughout the season, including two five goal defeats at the hands of Celtic and St. Mirren as well as convincing victories over Third Lanark and Hearts. This run of form meant that the club was comfortable in the top half of the table but without really producing a challenge for the title.

1959/60: Hunter, Weir, Martis and St.John - Scotland Under23 v England

This brought about a trip to Kilmarnock in the next round, but they tumbled out 2-0. The first goal was a 'comic-cuts' affair, when Motherwell 'keeper Joe Mackin's attempted clearance bounced off Billy Reid for a disastrous own goal. Jackie McInally added a second to allow Killie to progress to the fourth round.

The League game against Hibs at Fir Park on 6th February was the first time that BBC cameras had covered a Motherwell home game, with Hibs winning 4-3 in a match billed as a great advert for Scottish football.

The Scottish Cup second round in February brought a visit from Highland League side Keith, but Motherwell proved too wrong for their visitors and ran out comfortable winners by six goals to nil.

In the last nine games Motherwell only lost two, to secure the fifth place finish, closing the season with a 2-0 win over Rangers at Ibrox and a 6-0 win over Arbroath at Fir Park. In the last game both St. John and Quinn bagged hat tricks, with the latter even missing a penalty.

As with the previous season one of the highlights of the year was the floodlit friendlies that were played at Fir Park, which once again thrilled people from Motherwell and beyond. At the beginning of the season Winterthur of Switzerland were the visitors and Motherwell ran out 3-0 winners, this was followed by a visit from Gothenburg of Sweden who were also beaten, but only by a 2-1 scoreline.

These were to act as mere appetisers for the major visitors later in the season, when in two weeks in April, Athletico Bilbao of Spain and Flamengo of Brazil were to visit Fir Park. April 13 saw 18000 people turn up to see the locals take on the Spanish side on a night of torrential rain.

Ian St.John in action, and scoring against (above) Flamenco of Brazil, and (right) Bilbao from Spain

The conditions did not impair the feast of football served up to the crowd, with Motherwell going two goals up in the first twenty five minutes, but Bilbao had levelled before half time. An Ian St John goal two minutes into the second half gave the home side a well deserved 3-2 win.

On the 26th April it was the turn of Flamengo to take on Ancell's babes in front of 25000 expectant fans, this time the perfect conditions allowed the 'Well players to turn in what was recognised as one of their best ever displays. In the early stages it looked as though the game would actually go the other way with Flamengo opening the scoring after only six minutes, but a wonderful goal by Willlie Hunter levelled things up and seemed to inspire the Motherwell side. Ian St. John netted two goals to give the Fir Parkers a two one lead at half time.

If the supporters were delighted with the display in the first half they were left ecstatic by the marvellous second forty five minutes period. A Quinn penalty followed by St John's hat trick goal and a second Hunter goal saw Motherwell 6-1 up before the visitors added a second. Motherwell only turned on the style even more and St. John went on to complete a sensational double hat trick with a further three goals in the last ten minutes, to see the final score turn out as a win for the home side by 9-2.

1960/61

A major change at Fir Park at the start of this campaign was the upgrading of the floodlighting system which saw pylons sprout from the four corners of the ground, replacing the lamps that were on top of the stand and enclosure roofs.

At the end of the previous season the club had decided to free one of its longest serving players when Jim Forrest moved on. Forrest had signed in 1949 from Newarthill Hearts as a winger but played with distinction in many positions and won a Scotland cap in 1958 when he lined up against England. One other significant change in the playing squad was the arrival of left back Matt Thomson who signed on from Ardeer Thistle. He was to prove a valuable asset to Ancell's side in the coming years, but as a centre half rather than a full back.

The League Cup did not live up to expectations with Motherwell failing to progress beyond the qualifying group, finishing on six points, one point behind Hearts and Clyde, the Edinburgh side progressing to the Quarter Finals. The League season was a bit of a disappointment, for despite finishing fifth for the second season in a row, they were a long way behind champions Rangers who were 13 points ahead.

The season was marred by injuries to three key players, with Ian St. John missing the start of the season after undergoing a close season cartilage operation. Charlie Aitken only appeared in one of the first twenty one games and just as he returned Andy Weir was stretchered off in a game against Third Lanark, and was ruled out for the remainder of the season.

As a result League results were inconsistent with no real run of form established with the side, who struggled to string more than a couple of results together at a time. It was left to the Scottish Cup to provide the season's major highlight.

The run started with a tie against Cowdenbeath at Central Park which resulted in a comfortable win by four goals to one, with goals from McSeveney, St. John, Lindsay and Quinn. This meant a visit to Fir Park from Champions Rangers in the next round, when the tie resulted in a 2-2 draw that thrilled the 32000 fans.

Rangers were 2-0 up thanks to two goals from Murray, but a St. John goal before half time reduced the lead. Both teams made further chances but it was Bert McCann who found an equaliser to take the tie to a replay.

Ian St. John
Pat Quinn
Willie Hunter
Sammy Reid
Andy Weir

Motherwell's 'Famous Five'

MOTHERWELL'S INTERNATIONALISTS

Ian St. John

Bert McCann

Andy Weir

John Martis

Willie Hunter

Ibrox was sold out for the game which provided one of the best results and performances in the Motherwell's history. 'Well took the lead after 10 minutes when a Quinn pass released McPhee to score. Rangers responded and goals from McMillan and Wilson had the home side in front by two goals to one.

Motherwell then took charge of the game and turned on the style to overpower the Ibrox men. Pat Delaney scored the equaliser with a great free kick from just outside the Rangers penalty area, and in the 59th minute Motherwell took the lead when Roberts prodded a Hunter pass past keeper Niven.

Jim Forrest in action

The massive Rangers crowd were stunned as Motherwell went on to score two more goals through St. John and Roberts to complete a five two thrashing of the League Champions.

It was therefore a massive disappointment when the club crashed out at the Quarter Final stage to local rivals Airdrie. Motherwell had the bulk of possession and created numerous chances but couldn't beat the outstanding Leslie in the Airdrie goal, and the Broomfield men ran out one-nil winners.

Once again the Motherwell fans were treated to a number of floodlit friendlies during the season. In fact the visit of Brazilian side Bahia in September was used to open the new tower floodlighting system. Motherwell kept up their excellent record of never having lost to a foreign side at Fir Park winning the game by three goals to nil, these coming from Young, Hunter and St. John.

The other foreign visitors to Fir Park, were French side Toulouse as part of an Anglo-French-Scottish tournament called the Friendship Cup.

The game was played over two ties, with the first taking place preseason in Toulouse, when the 'Well ran out 2-1 winners with Bobby Roberts bagging both goals. The return leg was played at Fir Park in mid-October and once again the 'Well were successful, this time by a more comfortable four goals to one, the scorers being Roberts, McSeveney (2) and Quinn.

It was once again another season that brought a great number of International honours for Motherwell players, including four players being called up to play in three World Cup Qualifying matches for the 1962 competition.

The players were McCann, St. John, Quinn and Hunter. The first three also had the distinction of lining up in the same Scotland team to face "Auld Enemy" England, but will probably not want to be reminded of the final scoreline of 9-3 to England.

At the end of the season the club had received a couple off offers for forward Ian St John and at the beginning of May, rejecting a £20000 bid from Norwich but accepting a bid of £37500 from Bill Shankly's Liverpool.

St. John had been keen to move to England for some time and had submitted a transfer request in the middle of the season, but withdrew this when Andy Weir suffered his injury.

The money received would be used to help complete the building of the new Main Stand although the clubs was at pains to stress that these plans had been well in hand before the transfer of their prize asset.

1961/62

With the success of Ancell's side the board had started to look at how to extend and improve the ground once again and proposals were being reviewed how to enlarge the Main Stand to hold 5000 people and raise the capacity of the ground to 45000. A quotation for the steelwork and cladding was received in October 1960 from Tubewrights Limited for £30000. This was updated in January 1961 to £32738 which the board accepted, and plans were put in place for this major ground improvement to be ready for the start of the 1962/63 season.

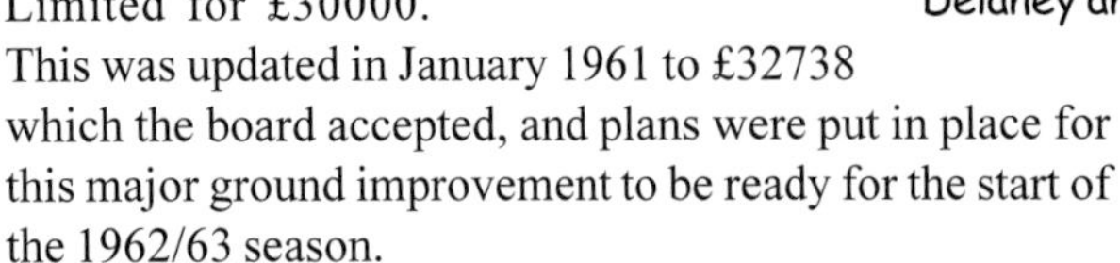

Delaney and McPhee

The League Cup section matches resulted in only one defeat, this in the sixth game at East End Park against Dunfermline, with qualification for the Quarter Finals secured, and Dundee United plus Aberdeen also knocked out. The first brought about a bit of a shock result as St. Johnstone visited Fir Park and left with a 3-2 lead to take back to Muirton Park and the Perth side completed their progress with a 1-1 draw in the second game. Although the Perth Saints had been playing well at this early stage of the season they were eventually relegated.

The League season was to prove immensely disappointing with League points being dropped on a regular basis. As in the previous season the side found it difficult to string a run of victories together, apart from a four match spell in December, including a first round Cup win over Dundee United. As throughout Motherwell's history it was the Cup that was to prove the highlight of the season, and Motherwell progressed by four goals to nil at Fir Park, with goals from Young, Hunter and two from McPhee.

The second round brought a chance for revenge against League Cup conquerors St. Johnstone, and this was achieved comfortably with another convincing four nil win at Fir Park. The goals came from two doubles by Hunter and Roberts, Motherwell progressing to take on Stranraer at Stair Park in the third round. The tie was level at 0-0 at half time, but Motherwell stepped up the pace in the second half and went ahead in the 70th minute when McSeveney scored at the second attempt. Stranraer did manage an equaliser through Hanlon but further goals from McSeveney and Hunter kept up hopes that Motherwell could once again bring the old trophy back to Fir Park. The crowd of 5583 that took in the Stranraer tie was their largest for fourteen years.

Pat Quinn

Next up, at the Quarter Final stage, was Stirling Albion at their own Annfield ground. Once again, the 'Well marched into the Semi Final in a convincing fashion, with a six goal win. The half time score was only 1-0 with Stevenson scoring, but a Delaney hat trick, his third in thirteen games as a centre forward, and a Quinn double, ensured safe passage to the next stage.

The semi final was against old Cup rivals Rangers at Hampden Park, but Motherwell's chances disappeared when Bert McCann was injured in the first half and, with no substitutes, he was a virtual passenger on the right wing. Rangers capitalised on Motherwell's misfortune scoring two quick goals through Murray as half time approached. Motherwell did pull one back through Roberts in the seventh minute of the second half through Bobby Roberts, and despite a brave performance Rangers added a third late on, much to their relief, to move on to the Final.

The season ended in disappointing fashion, with seven straight defeats, including the Cup match and a Friendship Cup defeat. This poor run saw Motherwell slipped to ninth in the table, their lowest League position since 1955.

Once again the club entertained foreign sides during the season with a friendly match against Elfsborg of Sweden continuing the good run against foreign visitors, as goals from Young and Aitken secured a 2-1 win.

Sadly the run of impressive victories against sides from the continent came to an end when French League Leaders, Nimes, visited Fir Park on 4th April. The game ended in a 2-1 defeat with Jones scoring for 'Well, albeit the game was played in the middle of a busy fixture list. Motherwell had played against Rangers in the Scottish Cup on the Saturday, then lined up against Hearts on the Monday, losing 2-1 at Fir Park before entertaining the French side two days later. The third game in five days in the end proving too much for 'Well. Some pride was restored with a 3-3 draw in the return game in France, along with a win over Marseilles as part of the same trip.

The season saw the departure of two Motherwell stalwarts, with Billy Reid moving to Lanarkshire neighbours Airdrie in October, and he helped steer them clear of relegation. Billy had signed for his home town club in 1955 straight from school and served with distinction in a number of positions. Also moving on was popular 'keeper Hastie Weir who was forced to leave the club in mid-February, having to take up a business appointment in India which would have seen him away for at least two years.

Rather than look at signing major players in the transfer market, Manager Bobby Ancell continued to ensure that the club's future was in good hands as he continued to rear his own young players in readiness for first team action. This was achieved either through the reserve side of being "farmed" out to local junior teams. The transfer market was also being made more difficult with the abolition of the minimum wage in English football making a move south more attractive for many players.

1962/63

The major talking point at the start of this season was the magnificent newly extended Main Stand running along the Western side of the ground, with its capacity of 3500 providing greater comfort and capacity for supporters. The Stand should have had a capacity for 5000, but the residents of Fir Park Street put a stop to that as they complained about the lack of light they would have if the Stand ran its full course to the Southern end of the ground. This meant that a proportion of the Stand was never built and the steel frame was left exposed, even into the 21st Century.

The first competitive game in front of the new stand seemed to inspire the players as they took on Falkirk in the League Cup qualifying section in the season opener. 'Well made a whirlwind beginning, and were unbelievably nine nil up by half time. The scoring started in the fifth minute from Russell, and by half time he had added another four to his tally, whilst Pat Quinn also helped himself to a personal haul of four, all in the first 32 minutes. Being nine down at half time Falkirk fought a brave rearguard action in the second forty-five minute period, and conceded no further goals, in fact grabbing a consolation to make the final score 9-1.

Unfortunately this was not a taster of what was to come, despite this magnificent opening game, for Motherwell could only finish third in their group in a three cornered fight with Aberdeen and Partick Thistle, with the Glasgow side progressing to the Quarter Final stage. Early League results proved to be little better with only one win in the first thirteen games, and hence seeing the side in the relegation zone. Anxieties weren't helped by a severe injury, a compound fracture of the forearm, to Willie Hunter in October, and then the transfer of Pat Quinn to Blackpool in November. Motherwell had found it impossible to hold on to Quinn who had professed his interest in playing in England for some time, having submitted a number of previous transfer requests that were repeatedly turned down. He moved south for the princely sum of £34000.

To help bolster the forward line Bobby Ancell was forced into the transfer market for the first time in six years, when he paid Partick Thistle £5000 for their centre forward Joe McBride. McBride was originally brought to Fir Park to solve a centre forward problem but with the departure of Quinn he was moved to inside forward, where his enthusiasm brought a bit of life back into the team.

From the start of December to mid-January, 'Well then went on a seven game unbeaten run which pushed them back up the table and out of the relegation zone. Just as 'Well's form picked up severe winter weather kicked in and they played their last game on January 6th, before resuming again on March 6 with a Scottish cup-tie away to East Stirling.

The cup-tie was to prove another major disappointment in a season that was full of them. After being considered as dark horses to lift the Cup given their good form in December and January, Motherwell slumped to a one goal defeat at Firs Park missing out on the opportunity of another crack at Rangers if they had made it through.

The last thirteen games were played in a compressed time scale thanks to the two months lost in January and February. During this time results were mixed, although a greater spirit was shown by the side as they hoisted themselves into a mid-table position that was only one place worse off than the previous season, and with only point less gained.

For the first time in a number of seasons Motherwell did not play any games against foreign opposition. It was proving difficult to find spaces in the fixture calendar to fit these games in, and the club also felt that at the times when games could have been arranged, they were not playing sufficiently well to do themselves justice.

At the end of the season the lure of bigger money in England was making life difficult for the Manager as he tried to sign up players. Although almost all of the players were re-signed for the start of the new season, planning was being wrecked by the number of transfer requests being received from players wanting to move south. On the plus side, was the fact that it allowed other younger players to shine through, with players such as Bobby McCallum and Alan Wylie making great progress in the first team through the 1962/63 season, with McCallum being voted player of the year.

1963/64

The season started with high hopes once again fuelled by an excellent run in the League Cup qualifying campaign. In the six games against Partick Thistle, Hearts and Falkirk, they only dropped one point in a goalless draw with Hearts at Tynecastle. The team to really suffer once again were Falkirk, who conceded ten goals in the two games this time, with 6-0 and 4-0 defeats. The Quarter Final draw paired Motherwell with Second Division Greenock Morton, and in the first game at Fir Park they put up an excellent fight and Alan Wylie in the 'Well goal had to be in top form to keep the scores level at 0-0. Even with the Greenock side down to ten men after the sending off of Adamson they still looked likely to be the only side to score. Morton ran out 2-0 winners in the return leg at Cappielow, scoring in the fifth minute, capitalising on a poor Delaney pass back, before adding to this in the second half.

The League campaign was nothing to write home about with no threat of relegation and no chance of pushing for the title, this was mainly down to a poor start after the defeat in the League Cup. Early in the season the side suffered the loss of another player to the lure of English football when centre forward Bobby Roberts left to join Leicester City.

With the League campaign going nowhere, it was once again left to the Scottish Cup to lift the gloom. The second round draw brought Dumbarton to Fir Park, and prior to the game centre forward Joe McBride prophesied that he would score a hat trick and he duly did! His first came in 16 minutes with a great free kick that flew into the roof of the net, the second arrived three minutes later when he outjumped the Sons' defence, and the third on the 29th minute when he seized on a defensive error to ram the ball home. Robertson made it four before Delaney scored a consolation own goal for the visitors.

The third round tie with Hearts took two games to complete after a 3-3 draw at Fir Park in the first match. Another McBride hat trick had Motherwell 3-1 up early in the second half and looking likely to be heading into the Quarter Final, but goals in the 65th and 79th minutes helped Hearts force a replay at their own Tynecastle Park. Motherwell were soon two goals up in the replay, Aitken scoring in six minutes before on form McBride added another in the 16th. White pulled a goal back for the home side in the 50th minute but Motherwell ran out winners to face Dundee in the Quarter Final.

The replay crowd of 32403 was Hearts highest attendance of the season and produced gate receipts of £4370.

Motherwell maintained their six year unbeaten run at Dens Park when they snatched an equaliser with only seconds remaining, after Cameron had put the Dark Blues in front on the 56th minute mark. With time running out McCann was bundled over at the edge of the box, and it looked as though Weir was about to take the kick, but he ran over the ball and McBride smashed the ball past the helpless Dens keeper to earn a replay.

Motherwell's biggest crowd of the season took in the replay, with 26280 in attendance to see the visitors run out 4-2 winners. Motherwell had taken the lead through Murray and despite McBride scoring his 32nd goal of the season to break Ian St John's record the Dee ran out deserved winners.

The rest of the season seemed to hold little attraction for players and fans alike as it fizzled out in front of dropping attendances. The only bright spot was that Bobby Ancell was in a position to blood even more young players, with Coakley, Baillie, Murdoch and Willie McCallum all making appearances in the last few games.

An innovation at the end of the season was the introduction of the Summer Cup to be competed for by First Division clubs only, who were divided in to four groups of four as in the League Cup, with the winners moving forward to the Semi Finals. In the first competition Motherwell were drawn in the same group as Kilmanock, Airdrie and Queen of the South and in this inaugural competition they finished as runners up to Kilmarnock in the group, therefore the Ayrshire men progressed through to the Semi Final.

1964/65

There was one major departure from the club with Willie McSeveney being given a free transfer, after serving the club for more than 10 years, having first signed in 1954 from Dunfermline. The previous season he played mainly in the reserve side where his experience proved a massive help to the young players on the staff.

The League Cup once again saw the club fail to progress to the Quarter Finals as only two wins and a draw from six games was only enough to finish third in the section behind the two Dundee clubs, five points behind United.

The League campaign started in a slightly better fashion with only three defeats in the first ten games, with Joe McBride in fine goalscoring form, including a late equaliser against Third Lanark in a 3-3 draw at Fir Park and a vital winner in a 1-0 win over Aberdeen at Pittodrie, when the ball rebounded off him and trundled over the line.

After the opening 10 games the form dipped with only two wins in the next 12 games, almost a complete mirror image of the opening matches of the season. The two victories that were gained were emphatic with four goals being put past both Morton and St. Mirren at Fir Park.

This famous magazine featured action from the Hearts match, Wylie and Thomson being the two prominent 'Well players

As with many seasons at Fir Park the Scottish Cup came along at the right time in the season to help lift the club once again. The first round saw a tricky tie against Stenhousemuir negotiated with a 3-2 win at Fir Park. Initially it looked as though Motherwell would sail through as goals from Weir and McBride had the home side 2-0 up. The Warriors pulled it back to 2-2 and only a late second goal from Weir was enough to see the 'Well progress.

The second round a week later was against St. Johnstone at Fir Park and once again it was a tight tie, despite Motherwell dominating. It took a 57th minute goal from Joe McBride that allowed 'Well through to the Quarter Final. The next game brought another home tie, against Hearts, at the start of March, and once again it took only one goal to seal it in favour of the 'Well. The goal came in the seventh minute when Carlyle finished off a move between Hunter and McBride. The win set up a Semi Final place against Glasgow giants Celtic at Hampden.

Before the Semi Final came around Motherwell were under new management as Bobby Ancell had accepted the manager's position at Dundee FC at the end of February. The board did not stand in his way and expressed their gratitude for his service to Motherwell by presenting him with a gold watch.

There was a great deal of interest in the vacant position with four of the applicants being interviewed for the post. The appicants were Messrs Howitt, Husband, Prentice and Pearson, and after careful consideration the position was offered to Bobby Howitt, a former captain of Stoke City, who had been coaching at Morton. Howitt took charge of his first game against Kimarnock at Fir Park on 13th March 1965 in the middle of what turned out to be a five League game losing run; this being broken by the Scottish Cup ties against Celtic.

The Semi Final saw Motherwell take the lead when McBride got on to the end of an outstanding McCann's pass. Celtic equalised, but 'Well were back in front before half when McBride scored his second goal. Celtic pulled back to 2-2 in the second half when Auld was fouled in the box, and he stepped up to convert the penalty himself.

The replay proved the old adage that you can never give the Old Firm a second chance, as 'Well were soundly thumped 3-0, and left regretting the missed chances in the first game. Celtic dominated the tie with their goals coming from Chalmers, Hughes and Lennox, with Motherwell missing the influential Hunter.

In a season of change it was hardly surprising that the League form dipped, and the final League position of 14 out of 18 reflected this as relegation was eventually avoided. This also led to transfer requests coming in from Joe McBride and Willie Hunter. The end of the season saw the second Summer Cup competition and this time Motherwell made it through to the Semi Finals, where they were drawn to play Hibs with the first leg in Edinburgh. The home side won 2-0, and it looked as though 'Well would crash out, but they stormed back in the Fir Park leg to win the tie 6-4 on aggregate after extra time. The final was also a two legged affair against Dundee United, and Motherwell's thirteen year run without a trophy was brought to an end with a 3-2 aggregate win. All the goals had been scored in the first leg at Fir Park and a 0-0 draw at Tannadice clinched the capture of the trophy. Almost immediately after this victory Joe McBride was transferred to Celtic.

Four Faces Of Charlie

Charlie Aitken

Captain, Delaney, proudly holds aloft the Summer Cup

It was the end of an era at the club when Manager Ancell decided to move on, and he will always be fondly remembered for the style of football that he brought to Motherwell as he tried to attack at all times while at the same time encouraging local talent rather than plundering the transfer market.

This can be seen by the number of players who graduated from Boys' Brigade football into their works side, and then into the Motherwell first team. Ian St. John probably being the most famous example on this route, moving from minor football to the Motherwell Bridge side, and then after a short spell with Junior side Douglas Water Thistle, into the 'Well team.

It was also the end of sustained stability at the club, for after only three different managers in fifty-four years, the next twenty were to see eight men fill the hot seat as the club struggled to find a firm hold on to its top flight status.

Chapter 7 Disappointing Years Ahead

Following the success of the Summer Cup win in 1965 the future looked good for 'Well once again, but the following seasons were to prove disappointing and ended with one in the Second Division.

1965/66

New manager Howitt's first League Cup campaign was to prove unsuccessful at the group stages, when the 'Well lined up in a section with Celtic, Dundee and Dundee United. Motherwell finished second in the group behind Celtic, winning three of the six ties and losing the other three. Celtic ultimately went on to win the trophy beating Rangers 2-1 in the Final.

The side was once again in what could best be called a transitional phase as the Ancell Babes had mainly started to move on, with only Charlie Aitken, John Martis, Matt Thomson, Bobby McCallum and Pat Delaney appearing on a regular basis. Peter McCloy had established himself as first choice goalkeeper after joining from Crosshill Thistle in 1963. The giant 'keeper had been a major factor in the Summer Cup win earlier in the year.

In the forward line Howitt struggled to find a settled line up, and consistency of selection eluded him, and results of on the field reflected this. After taking six points out of twelve in the first six games, with emphatic wins over Hamilton and St. Johnstone, the next six saw Motherwell plunge into relegation trouble as they were all lost. Indeed the last five of these saw Motherwell's opponents score fourteen goals without Motherwell finding anything in reply.

The slide was arrested with two home wins in a row as firstly St. Mirren were beaten four one at Fir Park and then the following week Aberdeen were beaten 1-0 thanks to a last minute penalty from Bobby McCallum. After a ne'erday win at Douglas Park over Hamilton, another four game losing streak ensured that relegation was a real possibility. The fourth defeat saw Joe McBride come back to haunt his former employers by scoring the only goal for Celtic in a one nil win at Celtic Park.

The start of February saw the Scottish Cup start off once again, and the 'Well were drawn to visit Firs Park to take on East Stirling in the first round.

A poor game resulted in a goalless draw despite good chances for Hunter, Thomson, Campbell and Cairney. The replay five days later saw Motherwell eventually win comfortably by four goals to one. 'Well were one nil up at half time through Cairney, and early in the second half they were three up through Thomson and another Cairney goal. The Shire pulled one back but a further goal from Thomson.

A week later the second round brought an unsuccessful trip to Rugby Park, Kilmarnock as the home side ran out five nil winners. The goals for Killie came from Queen, McIlroy, McInally, Black and a Willie McCallum own goal. McCallum was playing one of his first games for the club after signing in 1959 and having to be patient as understudy to John Martis.

Results remained inconsistent after the Cup exit and it took until three games to the end of the League campaign before First Division status was secured with a two one win over Aberdeen at Pittodrie at the end of April. The last game of the season brought a visit from Celtic and a goal from Lennox in the final minute clinched their first Championship under Jock Stein. Motherwell finally finished in thirteenth place with a points total of 28 from the 34 games played.

Earlier in the season, in an effort to find a replacement for Joe McBride, Howitt made his first signing when he paid the modest sum of £100 for John Deans from Neilston Juniors. Deans had been nicknamed Dixie during his spell in the Junior ranks as his scoring exploits with the Junior side were compared to the Everton legend Dixie Dean. This followed his sixty goals in one season, Motherwell pipping Newcastle Untied for his signature, in October. He made his debut against Kilmarnock on 12th March in a League game at Fir Park, although it took until the following season to establish himself as a goalscorer.

As one player sought to establish himself, another decided that after seventeen years it was time to retire, with Charlie Aitken hanging up his boots. Aitken was the only Ancell "Babe" who played his complete career at Fir Park. Despite being one of the most skilful players of his time, noted for his heading and tackling abilities, he was never selected for Scotland at full International level having to settle for two B international caps and two appearances for the Scottish League side.

Gentleman Charlie was awarded a testimonial match and in an emotional game against Rangers at Fir Park on 24 May 1967, Ian St. John and Scotland legend Dave McKay turned out in a 1-1 draw. It was McKay who scored for 'Well with a penalty, the Rangers goal coming from Roger Hynd. The Motherwell side that night was, McCloy, Whiteford, Thomson, McKay (Tottenham), Martis, Stevenson (Liverpool), Hogg (ex-Hibs), Hunter, St. John (Liverpool), S. Reid (Berwick Rangers), Weir. Reserves Willie McCallum and 'Dixie' Deans.

When Aitken retired from the game he was to be lost to football forever, never getting involved in coaching, and the undoubted talent and ability he had was surely a great loss to the game as whole. Without doubt Charlie Aitken will go down in Motherwell's history as one of their greatest, and one of the best uncapped players of all time.

1966/67

For the second year in a row Motherwell were to finish second in their League Cup section, this time finishing one point behind Dunfermline. The opening game against Dunfermline saw the first occurrence of one of the most significant innovations in Scottish Football, with Gus Moffat being the first substitute to appear in a game, when he replaced Murray at half time. Not settling for that unique distinction he went on to become the first competitive match substitute to score, when he netted Motherwell's goal in the 70th minute in a 2-1 defeat.

The League Cup section games also saw the first goals from Dixie Deans, with two clutches of two goals, one pair against Partick and the other versus Dunfermline, the latter in a 4-3 win at Fir Park. The goals weren't enough to see the team progress but were the sign of things to come.

The League season was nothing to write home about with only a tenth placed finish ensuring that there was no threat of relegation but equally at the other end there was no push for the title. Results were inconsistent throughout the season, and there was no real run of form established at all. The longest winning sequence of three came in the last games of the season, when there was nothing at stake in the table.

Despite this the club were forced to see off a bid from Stoke City for manager Bobby Howitt. The Potteries club had been looking to take their former player back south, but Motherwell responded by offering him a five year contract which was readily accepted.

There were some individual games of note throughout the season, starting with a five nil win over St. Mirren at Love St. , which was secured on the back of a marvellous performance by Bobby Campbell. Campbell scored all five goals, his first coming after 40 minutes, to give Motherwell a 1-0 half time lead.

He scored a second on the hour mark and then remarkably he netted his other three in a four minute burst to give Motherwell their first win of the season. Another significant debutant during the season was that of right back Davie Whiteford who first appeared on November 5th against Rangers at Ibrox in a five one defeat. Whiteford had joined in 1965 from Jordanhill College with an eye to eventually replacing Matt Thomson in the right back position.

Towards the end of November Dunfermline visited Fir Park and were defeated 6-2, with Dixie Deans netting his first hat trick for the club. Motherwell were four goals up at half time with goals from Hunter and Murray, then the first two of Deans' hat trick. His feat was completed two minutes into the second half, and Hunter added to the scoring, before Paton and Edwards bagged two consolation goals for the Pars.

Deans showed the other side of his character two weeks later when he was sent off for the first time in his Motherwell career in a game against Celtic at Celtic Park. He was dismissed in the 65th minute for flattening Jimmy Johnstone; sadly this was not to be Deans' last run-in with the authorities.

On Christmas Eve the game against Falkirk at Fir Park was forced to be abandoned after 72 minutes when one set of floodlights on the South Stand side of the ground failed. Motherwell were 3-1 up at the time, and unfortunately when the game was replayed in April Falkirk ran out 2-1 winners!

At the end of January the club made an ignominious exit from the Scottish Cup losing 1-0 to East Fife at Fir Park in the third round. However, lady luck did not shine on Motherwell that day as they hit the woodwork on four occasions, through Campbell twice, Hunter and Whiteford. They were made to pay for these missed chances in 73rd minute when Gardner scored the winner.

The season duly ran its course, the third last being a 4-0 at Fir Park over St. Mirren, which consigned the Paisley men to Second Division football. The season was completed with two single goal victories over Falkirk and Hearts.

1967/68

This was to prove to be a tumultuous season for the club as they ended up relegated for the first time since 1952/53, slumped into the Second Division at the end of what was one of the worst in the club's history.

The season started with a poor League Cup performance, finishing third behind Dundee and Hibs after only winning one game out of the six played. The third place was only secured on a better goal average than Clyde who finished on the same three points total. The only victory gained was a two win over Hibs at Fir Park, thanks to goals from Campbell and Lindsay.

The League campaign started badly with only one draw in the first five games before picking up the first win in the sixth game, with a 3-1 home win over Stirling Albion. Following this a run of ten games without a victory, and only three draws to show from these games saw Motherwell firmly entrenched in relegation trouble.

It is fair to say that during this run of poor results good fortune was not shining on the team, including Kilmarnock scoring a last minute winner at Fir Park. But the League position wasn't helped by some disastrous on-field performances that had nothing to do with luck. Against Falkirk at Brockville, Willie McCallum was sent off and the Bairns then punished the ten men by scoring the winner.

Two possible victories were turned into draws in early December, firstly a poor second half performance against Raith Rovers allowed them to come back from 2-0 down to leave with a share of the points and the following week two own goals allowed Partick Thistle to claim a share of the spoils in a 2-2 draw at Firhill.

The draw at Firhill was followed by a defeat at Fir Park to a Colin Stein goal for Hibs. The disappointing run of results was halted with a four game unbeaten run over the Christmas and New Year holiday period. The first by 3-2 over Clyde at Shawfield, with 'Well three up at half time thanks to goals from Wilson, McCall and Deans in a blistering first half performance.

This was followed up by a 2-1 home win over St. Johnstone in the last game of 1967. Once again they stormed into a lead with Wilson opening the scoring again and McInally adding the second. New Year's Day brought a trip to local rivals Airdrie's Broomfield ground for the traditional holiday fixture. Drew Jarvie gave the home side the lead in the first half but Dixie Deans had pulled 'Well level by half time. It looked as though Deans volleyed second goal was enough to have taken both points, but Jarvie also got his second a minute later to ensure both sides were left with a share of the points.

Deans was in sparkling form only a day later when Morton were the first visitors to Fir Park in 1968. He opened the scoring in the 34th minute latching on to a McCall pass to prod home, but Morton were level before the break through Stevenson. But 'Well kept up their good run when Deans was on hand to net after a Whiteford shot had hit the post.

Sadly this was to be an end to the good run, and results were poor for the rest of the season with only two more victories and two draws in the last fourteen games confirming relegation to the Second Division. Relegation was hardly a surprise given that of thirty four League games a grand total of twenty one of them were lost, with only six wins.

The frustrating thing throughout the season was that most of the lost games were by one goal, and very often after taking the lead. But boss Howitt was left to re-build and ensure that the stay in the Second Division would be a short one.

Even the Scottish Cup could provide little cheer in 1967/68, as they stumbled out of the competition after two games against Lanarkshire rivals Airdrie in the third round. The first game at Fir Park saw Airdrie take the lead in 15 minutes through Phillips, and it took Motherwell until the 60th minute to find an equaliser when McCall was on hand to sweep a Deans knock down into the net from six yards out.

The replay four days later saw the team tumble out of the competition. They managed to hold the eager Airdrie forwards at bay throughout a first half that had seen them play into a gale force wind. But despite the 'Well then having the same wind at their back in the second half, the Diamonds clinched the tie in the 59th minute when Jarvie waltzed through the defence to set up Ramsay to score.

1968/69

There was one major change to the squad for the new season with Joe Wark being signed from Irvine Meadow and making his debut in a pre-season friendly against Tranmere Rovers at Fir Park. This was to prove a dramatic debut for Joe with 'keeper Keith MacRae picking up an injury after only three minutes forcing Joe to take over between the sticks, and remarkably he went on to keep a clean sheet in a 2-0 home win.

Also joining the club in the summer was wing half Tom Donnelly who signed up after being freed by Rangers. Also breaking through was Jim "Jumbo" Muir a 19 year old who had played three games at the end of the previous season. The season also saw the introduction of another stalwart, Tom Forsyth making his breakthrough after signing up from his local side Stonehouse Violet. This meant that boss Howitt had a fresh look to the squad as they tried to return to the top division at the first attempt.

Having said that the League Cup campaign did not point to a successful return, as they stumbled out of the tournament at the group stage winning only one game out of six. The win though was an emphatic one, as it was a six nil win over promoted St. Mirren at Fir Park. The goals were shared out with Forsyth getting two and the others coming from Deans, Muir, McInally and Wilson. This was the only ray of light in a dull competition, which saw Montrose complete the double over 'Well and local rivals Hamilton remaining undefeated in the two games.

The League campaign opened in the middle of the League Cup with a home game against Albion Rovers and Motherwell brought their tally to thirteen goals in two games as they rattled in seven only four days after scoring against six against St. Mirren in the League Cup.

In early September, following the League Cup matches, the second League game of the season brought a trip to Station Park Forfar, and the 'Well left with a one nil defeat thanks to a hotly disputed penalty in the 83rd minute. A decision that saw centre half Willie McCallum sent off for taking his protests too far.

This was to be the last League defeat the side suffered until early February as they stormed through the League being in top spot for most of the campaign. There were a great number of highlights along the way with a number of convincing victories. The first large margin was a 4-1 win over Ayr United at Fir Park, this being achieved being even though they were 1-0 down at half time. Second half goals from Deans with a couple, a Whiteford penalty and a rare Joe Wark goal. This match was followed by a 6-1 win away to Stenhousemuir, this time there was no early slip up as by half time 'Well were already leading 5-1. This time the goals came from another brace from Deans, McInally, Forsyth, Donnelly and Wark.

From-mid October, 'Well went on a run of seven games without conceding a goal and rattled in 25 at the other end, the games in question being, Alloa away 2-0, East Fife at home 4-0, Stirling away 4-0, Berwick at home 7-0, Clydebank away 4-0, Montrose away 2-0 and finally a 2-0 win at home to Brechin. This also rounded off a run of twelve consecutive wins since losing to Forfar in the second game of the season. The run was ended with a 2-2 draw at home to Queen of the South, Deans having put 'Well 1-0 ahead at half time, but two goals from Law and Lindsay had the Doonhamers looking like unlikely winners. Thankfully a late scrambled goal from John Godthorpe brought about an equaliser to keep the unbeaten run going.

The only other dropped point before the turn of the year was another home draw, this time against Dumbarton. Once again the visitors held the lead but a Deans goal secured the draw for the Fir Parkers. The New Year derby fixture against Hamilton on 2nd January was to prove quite a match which saw two players sent off and four more booked. The game was played in a constant downpour and despite Motherwell's best efforts it looked as though the game was going to end up goalless.

Then with four minutes to go the game turned on its head completely, Dixie Deans burst into the box and as Hamilton 'keeper Lamont came out to challenge, the striker seemed to trip over his own feet. The ref pointed to the spot much to the disgust of the Accies 'keeper who squared up to the Deans, and both were sent off after a scuffle ensued. Davie Whiteford remained calm through this melee and calmly slotted the ball home from the spot to secure a 1-0 win.

Two more games prior to the start of the Scottish Cup saw ten more goals scored with only one in reply, as Queen's Park were defeated 5-1 and then Cowdenbeath were thumped 5-0.

The Scottish Cup brought a visit from First Division Clyde to Fir Park and a controversial game ended in a 1-1 draw. The first major incident was in the 11th minute when the Bully Wee were awarded a penalty, but McCloy pulled off a magnificent save to keep the scoreline blank. Clyde however still took the lead when Quinn netted in the 31st minute. Four minutes into the second half the same player was sent off after aiming a vicious kick at Jimmy Wilson. The home side were back on level terms in 63 minutes when Deans lashed a volley home. Two minutes later Clyde were reduced to nine men when Mulheron was also sent off, but they held out for a replay at Shawfield.

In another marvellous cup-tie Motherwell were unlucky to lose to a last gasp Clyde winner. Motherwell took the lead in two minutes when Bryson reacted quickly to score after his initial shot had rebounded off the post. In 38 minutes Clyde equalised when an attempted punch from McCloy rebounded off Burns and into the net.

The game was on a knife edge until the last minute when Anderson scored the winner with the last kick of the ball. One of the highlights of the game was the performance of reserve 'keeper Keith MacRae who turned out in a midfield role just to show his versatility in the squad.

After a 4-0 home win over Alloa, East Fife inflicted the second and last League defeat of the season when they won 3-1 at an icy Bayview Park. The game was tied 0-0 at half time but two early second half goals gave East Fife a comfortable lead, a Jumbo Muir goal could not bring 'Well back into the game as a Guild penalty secured the points for the home side.

In the remaining thirteen games only two more points were dropped with draws away to Brechin and Ayr United. Promotion was secured on 12th April with five games left, when Dumbarton were beaten 4-2 at Boghead. Then the following week the League Championship was tied up at Fir Park with a 7-1 win over Stenhousemuir, and this result took their goals tally to over 100 for the season.

When Stirling Albion were beaten 3-0 in the last home game, it meant that 'Well had gone the whole season without losing at Fir Park, and with only single points dropped to Queen of the South and Dumbarton. There was great relief that the stay in the Second Division was a short one with an immediate return to the top flight secured, although it was felt that the side that was promoted would not be strong enough to stay up.

1969/70

Despite the grim foreboding, there was only one real change to the squad for the start of the new season, with defender John Muir signing from Rotherham to help bolster the back line, given that he was comfortable at right back or centre half.

Motherwell stormed through their League Cup group dropping only one point in the qualifiers which included East Fife, Montrose and Albion Rovers. The draw was away to East Fife, but this point in the fifth game was enough to ensure that Motherwell progressed to the Quarter Final stage. The first leg of the Quarter Final against Morton was played in early September at Cappielow Park.

Two goals from Ton striker Joe Harper and an own goal from 'Well centre half Willie McCallum looked to have out the tie out of the Fir Park men's reach. The second leg was played a fortnight later at Fir Park, only four days after losing a League match 1-0 at Cappielow.

In an epic second leg Motherwell survived an early scare when 'keeper McCloy was forced to save well from striker Harper once again. 'Well then fought back and goals from McInally and Jumbo Muir had them back in touch with their opponents from Greenock. The team capped a marvellous performance from a Forsyth equaliser with only sixteen minutes left. The tie then went into extra time but with no further goals, this brought about a replay at neutral Ibrox Stadium.

Well were forced to play up and coming goalkeeper Keith MacRae at right back for the replay at the end of September. The game turned into a titanic struggle which saw Donnelly and Deans come close for 'Well. It looked as though the tie would be heading for extra time again as a Deans header hit the bar, but with only four minutes left Jumbo Muir was on hand to poke the ball over the line for a fantastic victory.

A week later 'Well lined up against St. Johnstone at Hampden Park, and were installed as favourites to progress to the Final having beaten the Perth Saints comfortably, by four goals to one, in mid-September. Sadly the Semi Final did not turn out as easy for 'Well and after the Saints took the lead through McGarry they dominated the tie and added a second through Aitken to deny Motherwell a Final place against Celtic.

Following the successful League Cup qualifying campaign, Motherwell took the same form into the opening League games, winning the first four in a row, seeing off Kilmarnock, Dundee, Clyde and St. Johnstone, before losing their 100% record to Morton four days prior to the second leg of the League Cup Quarter Final.

After the disappointment of the League Cup defeat, the team responded well by going on a five game unbeaten run, although this did include four draws and only one win. One of the draws was an excellent 2-2 result at home to Rangers, with the visitors being two nil ahead at half time thanks to both goals from Colin Stein. After the interval Motherwell dominated proceedings and despite pulling a goal back with nine minutes remaining through McInally, it looked as thought their efforts would end up in defeat. Three minutes later they conjured up a deserved equaliser when former Ranger Tom Donnelly was sent through to round 'keeper Neef and slot the ball into the empty net.

The next eight games failed to bring about a win, with four draws and four defeats but by this stage there was little fear of relegation, and the focus could turn to finishing as high up the table as possible, and qualify for the new British Cup which would be introduced the following season.

The end of January saw the start of the Scottish Cup with a home tie against League Cup conquerors St. Johnstone, who had also won a League game at Muirton 4-3 the previous week. This time it was the 'Well's turn to progress with a 2-1 win, despite Henry Hall giving the visitors a second minute lead in the tie. First half goals from McInally and Deans were enough to see 'Well through to the fourth round.

Inverness Caledonian were the next opponents at Fir Park, and the First Division side were to prove too strong for their Highland League opponents. The final scoreline of 3-1 could have been much greater if the Steelmen had taken all their chances. As it was, a double from Deans set 'Well on their way, but they were set back slightly when Johnston netted for the visitors.. In the end a McInally penalty sealed the tie and set up a home Quarter Final against Kilmarnock.

The tie against Kilmarnock drew a crowd of more than 16000 with the bulk hoping that Motherwell could progress to their second Semi Final of the season. For long spells it looked as though this would be the case but the 'Well attack were constantly denied by Sandy McLaughlin in the visitors goal. The team was punished for not converting any of their chances when Motherwell born Ross Mathie headed home spectacularly in the 67th minute to put Killie through to the semi final.

League form slumped after this with only four wins in the last thirteen games, but the eleventh place finish was higher than expected at the start of the season and it made sure that Motherwell had qualified to play in the inaugural British Cup the following season. Although in truth if they had converted a number of the ten draws into wins it could've been European competition for the first time rather than the "consolation" of the British Cup.

During the season 'keeper Peter McCloy was transferred to Rangers, after serving seven years at the club and winning a Summer Cup medal in 1965. He had become unsettled after the outstanding form of young reserve 'keeper Keith MacRae who had forced his way into the first team on a regular basis. As part of the same transfer deal Motherwell received two players in return, with midfield player Bobby Watson and Striker Brian Heron moving to Fir Park. Both made an immediate impact after making their debuts against Raith Rovers in March, with Watson being installed as team captain.

Also during the season the club lost one of its longest serving employees when PA announcer James Adams handed in his resignation in January 1970 having filled the role since 1949. The board rewarded this long service by awarding Mr Adams a honorarium along with a Complimentary Stand season ticket for life.

1970/71

There were two significant changes to the squad for the start of the new season with Jimmy Wilson heading up to Dundee in exchange for Northern Ireland international winger Billy Campbell. Also coming in was veteran Rangers 'keeper Billy Ritchie, having been asked to fill in for the injured Keith MacRae, who had undergone a close season bone graft operation on his wrist.

Dixie Deans scoring against Kilmarnock in the opening league match

Motherwell made an impressive start to the League Cup qualifying campaign winning two of the first three games. In the opener Morton were beaten 4-1 at Cappielow with an impressive Motherwell performance, despite missing Dixie Deans through suspension. The next game saw them lose 2-0 to Rangers at Fir Park, but they bounced back in the third game with an emphatic 3-0 win over Dunfermline, also at Fir Park. They then only took one point from the next three games to end up finishing third in the group behind Rangers and Morton. The crucial games were consecutive 2-0 defeats to Rangers and Morton in the second half of the group stages.

The League campaign started reasonably well with two wins out of the first three games, at home to Kilmarnock and Clyde either side of a defeat away to Airdrie at Broomfield. Most of the attention was not focussed on the League but on the start of the first British Cup competition that was to be sponsored by Texaco Petroleum. The competition was to include teams from England, Scotland and Northern Ireland, that hadn't qualified for any of the European competitions.

Motherwell were drawn to play against Stoke City in the first round, with a side that included England's World Cup winning 'keeper Gordon Banks in their ranks. The first leg was played at Fir Park in mid-September, and it took a magnificent performance from Banks to keep to the scoreline down. Motherwell did manage to take a 1-0 lead into the Second Leg thanks to a Goldthorpe goal. At the end of 90 minutes in the second leg the teams were tied at 2-2 with the home side winning the game 2-1. No more goals were scored in the thirty additional minutes and Keith MacRae was to be the hero in the penalty shoot-out saving two of the Stoke spot kicks, to set up a tie with Tottenham Hotspur in the second round.

Before taking on Tottenham another two games were won out of three, with the only defeat coming at the hands of Rangers at Ibrox.

The first leg of the Tottenham match was played at White Hart Lane and many had dismissed Motherwell's chances against a side packed full of Internationals, including Jennings, Mullery, Peters, Chivers and Gilzean. It was therefore a pleasant surprise when Motherwell returned from London only one goal down after suffering a three two defeat, with goals from Donnelly and Watson.

Before the return leg Motherwell saw off Cowdenbeath at Central Park before being hammered five nil by Celtic on a sodden Fir Park pitch only three days before the big Texaco Cup tie. In the early stages of the second leg against Tottenham it looked as though the tie had been put beyond Motherwell when Chivers opened the scoring to give 'Spurs a two goal overall lead.

This setback seemed only to inspire the 'Well players and a Heron goal just before half time brought Motherwell back within one goal and in with a chance once again. In a storming second half Keith MacRae produced a fantastic save from Gilzean to keep the tie in the balance before outstanding goals from Watson and Donnelly secured an unlikely win for Motherwell.

League form stuttered after these games with only one win in six leading up to the Semi Final Texaco first leg against Scottish rivals Hearts, and the team settled into a comfortable mid-table position. The first leg produced a 1-1 draw at Tynecastle in mid-December and this looked to have set Motherwell up for a final place with the second leg due at Fir Park in early March.

In the lead up to the Scottish Cup third round confidence was high as the tie at Stirling came on the back of a five game unbeaten run, with three draws against Dundee, Kilmarnock and Airdrie being followed by wins over St. Johnstone and Morton. It was therefore a major shock when Motherwell turned in an abysmal performance to crash out of the Scottish Cup at the first attempt to Second Division Stirling Albion. The home side ran out three one winners and the only consolation for the visitors was a Davie Whiteford penalty after Deans had been bundled in the box.

The second leg of the Texaco Cup Semi Final was to prove to be a thrilling affair with the teams tied at 1-1 and the game looking as though it was heading for extra time. Then deep into stoppage time up popped Hearts striker Donald Ford to force the ball home and clinch the tie for the Gorgie men as they qualified to take on Wolves in the first ever Final.

The run in to the season saw Motherwell pick up nine points out of a total of eighteen as they struggled to find the net to turn draws into wins once again, only managing to score eight goals in those nine games. The final league position of 10th was one better than the previous season and at least set up a crack at the Texaco Cup once again.

1971/72

During the previous season Manager Howitt had started to introduce a number of younger players - Davie Main, Alex Martin and Kirkie Lawson - into the side and it was to some of these young players that he was to turn to in this season to try to solve the goalscoring problems.

A season that was to promise much but deliver little started in disastrous fashion with 'Well finishing bottom of their League Cup qualifying campaign with only three points from six games. The only win coming at Fir Park, with a Bobby Watson double providing the goals for a 2-0 win over Kilmarnock. In general Hibs, Dundee United, and Killie were to prove too strong and Hibs swept into the Quarter Finals dropping only one point on the way. The 'Well selection problems were not helped with the absence of Deans and Forsyth through injury.

The League season also got off to a miserable start and by the turn of the year relegation once again looked a real possibility with only four wins in the first half of the fixture

Pre-season training at the Dalziel Estate in 1971

list giving real cause for concern. There was also to be no repeat of the Texaco Cup heroics of the previous season with Stoke City once again providing the first round opposition, this time the English side one both legs and progressed to the second round with an aggregate score of 5-1, winning 1-0 at Fir Park and 4-0 at the Victoria Ground. One of the reasons for the poor run of goalscoring form could have been the departure of centre forward Dixie Deans who was snapped up by Jock Stein for the princely sum of £30000.

There was one bright spot in the League campaign in early November when Hearts were the visitors to Fir Park, and in an end to end match the teams produced an eight goal thriller with Motherwell winning by five goals to three. Brian Heron was without doubt the man of the match on the day, with three blistering goals that set the foundation for the win, with the others being added by Jumbo Muir and John Goldthorpe.

Rather than spark a revival in fortune this result started another run of poor results, culminating in an embarrassing eight three defeat to Partick Thistle at Firhill. Thistle had beaten Celtic four one in the League Cup final only two months earlier so it was maybe no surprise. For the record the Motherwell scorers on the day were McCabe, Heron and Brown.

Tam Forsyth

A turn in fortunes did arrive, starting with a 2-0 win away to Airdrie in the traditional New Year's Day derby. This was followed up two days later with a fine four one victory at home to Clyde, including a bizarre own goal from McHugh who hit a pass back to his ill-prepared goalie and the ball trundled over the line. A defeat at Rugby Park was to prove only a temporary blip with three more excellent wins over Dunfermline, Hibs and St. Johnstone pushing 'Well clear of relegation and setting things up for the Scottish Cup campaign.

The third round draw brought about a home tie against Second Division Montrose and they were truly despatched thanks to second half goals from Lawson and Campbell. The good run continued the following week with a fine win over Rangers at Fir Park with goals from Heron early in the first half as he nipped between Jardine, and former 'Well 'keeper McCloy. The tall stopper was also at fault for the second as failed to deal with a cross and Jumbo Muir was on hand to capitalise.

The next round of the Cup brought a trip to Ayr United's Somerset Park, and in an iratable game peppered with free kicks, neither side could find the back of the net and a replay was required at Fir Park the following Wednesday. There were a couple of problems in the lead up to the game one footballwise and one off the field.

On the field regular 'keeper Keith MacRae had picked up an injury in the first game that would keep him out of the replay, and 'Well signed Celtic goalie John Fallon as cover, but were told he could not play in the replay as he was not registered for the first game, this meant a rare appearance for youngster Timmy Burns.

The off-field problem resolved round the timing of the kick off, as the country at the time was in the middle of industrial conflict with a miners strike causing power cuts and a three day working week. Rather than take any chances with the floodlighting, it was decided that the game should take place at three o'clock on the Wednesday afternoon. This did not prevent over 11000 people turn up to see an absorbing Cup tie, with the winners rewarded with a home tie against Rangers.

Ayr took the lead in the third minute through an Ingram effort and they held the lead up until the break despite some concerted attacking from the home side. The second half saw Motherwell come close on a number of occasions before Lawson was fouled in the box on 59 minutes, and Heron fired the spot kick high past 'keeper Stewart for a deserved equaliser. The winner finally arrived for 'Well with only eight minutes left when Lawson headed home a Whiteford free kick.

The home game against Rangers in the next round was another pulsating tie with both teams going for goals and the lead changing hands before both sides had to settle for a 2-2 draw and a replay at Ibrox. McDonald had put Rangers in the lead before Heron found a 'Well equaliser, then with 17 minutes left the homesters took the lead through Campbell, but a late Stein goal set up the replay. The game had lived up to the pre-match hype which had seen demand for tickets at an all time high and eventually saw over 28000 crammed into Fir Park. In the replay, Lawson put Motherwell ahead in only ninety seconds, but two controversial goals put Rangers in front, and despite another equaliser from Lawson 'Well were dumped out by two more late goals from Colin Stein.

Once again after being knocked out of the Cup the season stuttered to a close with only one more win in the remaining six games, 2-1 win over Partick Thistle, which at least gained a little revenge for the earlier hammering. Once again a 10th place finish had been secured, and given the early season troubles no one could complain about that, and set up a third chance to play in the Texaco Cup.

'Goalkeeper' Joe Wark

During the season one of the problem positions proved to be that of goalkeeper, with no fewer than six players taking on the role. The season started with veteran Billy Ritchie called out of retirement to fill in for the injured Keith MacRae, who was considered to be the number one, along with young Tommy Burns as his number two.

When Ritchie broke his leg and MacRae was injured at Ayr, Burns was pitched into the replay despite the signing of John Fallon. These four were at least recognised goalkeepers, the other two were normally left backs! When Ritchie broke his leg against St. Johnstone in late January, Joe Wark had to leave his left back position to take over, and in more than forty five minutes he played he kept a clean sheet in a 2-0 win.

Davie Main also had to move, from left back, to take over in a match with Dundee United, and he did so well that he held down the goalkeeping spot in the reserves for several weeks after!

There were International honours for two 'Well players at Scotland Under 23 level, with both Keith MacRae and Tom Forsyth turning out for the side.

1972/73

Once again as a new season loomed the management were looking for the young players to stake a claim and the side to find some consistency and push for honours. There was also one experienced addition to the squad, with Peter Miller moving from Dunfermline to his home town team, and he was seen as a player who could add depth to the playing squad as he could play in a number of positions in defence and midfield.

The format for the League Cup campaign changed slightly with the top two from the Qualifying groups going through to the next stage. With nine groups a supplementary round was required to whittle the qualifiers down to the last sixteen. This was just as well as Motherwell managed to finish second in their group with only six points, six behind Dundee who didn't drop a point.

John Goldthorpe scoring 1972

In the supplementary round Motherwell were drawn to play another Lanarkshire side, Albion Rovers, with the winners going forward to another Lanarkshire derby against Airdrie. Rovers were comfortably beaten eight one on aggregate, with a 4-1 win at home followed by a 4-0 win at Cliftonhill.

Motherwell went into the first leg against Airdrie at Fir Park with a degree of confidence having beaten their rivals in a League match only a matter of weeks earlier. Despite applying much of the pressure in the first leg they could not find a way to goal and Airdrie took an unlikely 1-0 lead back to Broomfield, thanks to a Mallon goal with 20 minutes left. This left a tricky second leg to come, but things started well when Lawson put 'Well ahead just before half time, but a late thunderbolt from Derek Whiteford punished Motherwell for their failings in the first leg.

It was hard for Motherwell to string any kind of consistency in the League with the early stages being littered with Cup ties in not only the League Cup but also the start of another Texaco Cup campaign. The first round paired Motherwell with Coventry and after a thrilling 3-3 draw at Highfield Road, Motherwell progressed thanks to a 1-0 win at Fir Park.

To illustrate the poor League form one only needed to look at one result, which was a seven two defeat at Aberdeen's Pittodrie stadium at the end of September. A rapid fire assault in the first twenty minutes saw 'Well five nil down, with a Harper hat trick being added to by others. 'Well pulled one back through a McClymont penalty before half time, but even though Gray scored another, the game was over as a contest when Goldthorpe was sent off, and Aberdeen added additional goals from Harper and Murray.

The start of October saw a flurry of transfer activity with defender Tom Forsyth moving to Rangers for a reported fee of £40000, and he was immediately replaced with the signing of Sam Goodwin from Crystal Palace for £23000. Goodwin had made his name as an Airdrie player before clinching his move to full time football at Crystal Palace, but neither he nor his wife settled in London and he jumped at the chance to return home. Strangely both players made their debuts for their respective clubs in the same game with Rangers being the visitors only three days after Forsyth's move to Ibrox. It was Forsyth who was to have the last laugh with Rangers winning thanks to goals from Young and Parlane.

Willie McCallum

Inconsistent results continued, with the only relief being a 4-2 aggregate win over Hearts in the Texaco Cup, after being two nil down at half time in the second leg. Despite this boost, the 'Well fans were becoming increasingly impatient and were starting to chant for the head of Manager Bobby Howitt, with the club being forced to acknowledge a petition from supporters in early February.

The fans were even more upset with a poor run in the Scottish Cup after seeing off Raith Rovers at Fir Park in the third round the team was soundly hammered five nil by Celtic in the next, with two of the Celts goals coming from former 'Well man Dixie Deans. After losing 2-0 in the first leg of the Texaco Cup Semi Final to Norwich at Carrow Road, Mr. Howitt advised the board of his intention to resign, and this was accepted. Howitt agreed to fill in as Assistant Manager until a new manager was appointed.

It took a further three weeks before the new man was appointed, in the meantime Motherwell had once again failed to reach the Texaco Cup Final, losing four three on aggregate despite a fine 3-2 win at home. The eventual managerial appointment proved to be a popular one with former 'Well centre forward Ian St. John being given the job. St. John had gone on to be a major success at Liverpool, winning two championship medals and an FA Cup winners medal after scoring the winner in the final against Leeds.

Two wins in his three games in charge saw Motherwell finish eighth in the table, which despite the inconsistent form that had led to the sacking of the manager, was the highest League placing since 1960/61 when the much vaunted Ancell babes finished fifth. The eighth place finish once again ensured another tilt at the Texaco Cup.

The season saw a couple of other changes in the 'Well line up, apart from the transfer of Forsyth. Popular winger Brian Heron moved to Dumbarton in mid-March for a reported transfer fee of £40000. Also leaving was veteran midfielder Jackie McInally who was awarded a free transfer at the end of the season, Jackie served six years at Fir Park after initially being signed as a stop-gap player.

One significant, if slightly less publicised, signing was that of striker Willie Pettigrew, who joined up in April 1974 from East Kilbride Thistle. Pettigrew was a local lad who had been a prolific scorer with Dalziel High School, who had secured the Scottish Schools Under 18 shield in 1969/70 and 1971/72, the youngster scoring 40 goals in 20 appearances in the competition.

1973/74

The League Cup qualifying group was to prove a nail-biter with three teams, Motherwell, Aberdeen and Dundee United, all ending up with seven points, 'Well progressing to the next round as section winners on goal difference. This was mainly down to three emphatic wins of 5-0 against East Fife, plus 4-0 and 3-0 over Dundee United. The Quarter Final draw paired Motherwell with Celtic over two legs with the first to be played at Fir Park in mid-September.

Before that match, 'Well had gone through the opening two League games without defeat opening with a draw against Aberdeen at Fir Park and a 2-0 win at Arbroath which marked the debut of striker Bobby Graham. Graham had played at Liverpool at the same time as manager St. John, but had then moved to Coventry for £80000.

The first leg of the League cup-tie with Celtic at Fir Park was a hard fought match. Celtic were two up at half time with Dalglish and Murray the scorers, but the 'Well fought hard in the second half and secured a goal from Goldthorpe. Things could have been better for the home side if Goldthorpe's late effort had gone in rather than strike the underside of the bar and bounce to safety.

The second leg in mid-October was to prove to be a historic one for Motherwell as they secured their first win at Celtic Park for twenty three years, as well as the first win of any sort against the Celts in fourteen years. The match was memorable for other reasons, firstly the debut of Centre half Willie Watson who had only just been signed from Manchester United. The winning goal in the 38th minute was also notable, when Goldthorpe picked the ball up on the half way line and swept past McNeill and Brogan before unleashing an unstoppable shot from 18 yards. Finally, in the 68th minute MacRae produced a stunning save from a Connolly penalty to secure a replay.

MacRae only played one more game for 'Well as he was transferred to Manchester City, after months of speculation, for a fee of around £100000. His space was filled when Ian St John snapped up Falkirk reserve 'keeper Stuart Rennie. Rennie made his debut in a 1-0 defeat away to Ayr, with the goal coming from Alex Ferguson.

Keith MacRae, who moved on to Manchester City

The Texaco Cup had also kicked off during the same spell of the season, and once again Motherwell were drawn to play Coventry, this time they managed to get through with a 4-2 aggregate win. The next round saw Norwich drawn to play against 'Well again, and once more they were successful, winning four nil over the two legs.

There was also the small matter of the League Cup replay against Celtic which was to be played at Celtic Park at the end of October. There was to be no repeat of the second leg heroics, Murray gave Celtic an early lead, but McLymont equalised early in the second half. Deans restored the Celts lead before Motherwell found a second equaliser through Graham. As the game looked to be heading for extra time a controversial winner in the dying seconds when Jimmy Johnstone scored from what looked like an offside position.

Amidst all this Cup football Motherwell were going through a terrible League run, losing five games in a row which finally ended with a 1-1 draw at home to Hibs. This then sparked a run of only two defeats in 10 games that ensured there was no need to worry about relegation, and a push could be made to gain either a European or a British Cup place.

It was Scottish Cup time again at the end of January with a home tie against Brechin City. The tie ended in a comfortable two nil win, with both goals being scored by Alex Martin. The following week brought a second win of the season against Celtic with a 3-2 result at home, in the League this time. Celtic were 2-0 up thanks to goals from Dalglish and Murray but 'Well rallied and Martin pulled them back in it before two late goals from Graham and Goldthorpe clinched the two points.

The next round brought a trip to the North Sea coast at Arbroath's Gayfield Ground. A Goldthorpe hat trick was enough to provide a convincing win despite a late Sellars consolation for the home side. This set up another cup-tie against Celtic in the Quarter Finals at Parkhead this time. The game was to prove to be another titanic struggle as both teams went all out for victory. Motherwell went ahead when Bobby Graham latched onto a Jumbo Muir clearance, then Celtic were on level terms when Hood was on hand to score. 'Well were back in the lead before half time, Kennedy heading home a Martin cross, but Celtic scored a second equaliser when Hood was on target for his second, when Motherwell failed to clear.

(Above) A dressing room team group in 1974, and below, Willie Pettigrew in action

Sadly Celtic went on to win the replay at Fir Park with a goal from former 'Well man Dixie Deans, which was enough to see his team through. League form to the end of the season was to remain patchy but the game allowed St. John to blood some youngsters, such as Pettigrew and Leishman. The safe mid-table position of ninth had been secured but was not enough to qualify for the new Anglo Scottish Cup, which had been introduced to replace the Texaco Cup which had been struggling following the withdrawal of top English sides, and travelling to Northern Ireland was proving difficult with the troubles in the province.

In the last game of the season, against Dundee, Ian St John was able to introduce another new signing. This time it was winger Ian Taylor who had been snapped up from Aberdeen even though he had been signed by them only a month or so earlier. He had missed the official transfer deadline and was therefore only eligible to play in the last game of the season.

The season saw the departure of a long serving player, when Willie McCallum moved to St. Mirren, after serving the club for over 15 years following his signing as a schoolboy. He was a faithful player, patiently waiting on John Martis moving on before establishing himself as a first team regular. Also leaving was Irish winger Billy Campbell who returned to Northern Ireland as player/manager of Glenavon.

1974/75

During the summer of 1974 the authorities in charge of the Scottish game at the SFA and the SFL finally agreed, after severe lobbying from a number of top clubs (Rangers, Hearts, Hibs, Dundee and Dundee United), that change was needed to re-invigorate interest in Senior football. In recent years attendances had continued to fall for a number of reasons, one being the uncompetitive nature of the League, with Celtic having run away with the last nine titles.

It was finally decided by the League's member clubs to a radical shake-up of the League structure and they proposed a top League (the Premier Division) of 10 teams, and two further Leagues of 14 (the First and Second Divisions), that would be formed for the start of season 1975/76.

Therefore during this season the clubs found themselves competing to enter one of these higher divisions for the forthcoming season. At the end of 1974/75, the top ten teams in the old First Division would make up the Premier Division, the remaining eight and the top six from the old Second Division would make up the new First Division, and the remaining fourteen clubs in the Second Division would constitute the new Second Division.

It was hoped that with just the top ten, this would become more competitive with two up two down relegation still in operation, and all the clubs being full time would also help. Therefore a tense season was ahead as all clubs jockeyed for a high position in their respective divisions.

The League Cup was to prove difficult with Motherwell in a section along with Celtic, Dundee United and Ayr United. Despite only suffering two defeats in these games Motherwell could still only finish second in the table, three points behind top placed Celtic. One feature of these League Cup games was the beginning of what was to prove a fruitful goalscoring partnership between Willie Pettigrew and Bobby Graham. Between they managed to score five of Motherwell's eleven goals in the six games.

In the League, things started poorly with the first two games being lost heavily, a 5-0 defeat to Dundee United at Tannadice being followed up with a 3-1 defeat at home to Airdrie. It was at this time that stories started to appear that Manager Ian St. John was wanted by Portsmouth to take over their vacant position. Following a fine 4-0 win away to Ayr, in which a young Gregor Stevens made his debut, St. John resigned and accepted the post as Portsmouth Manager.

A week later managerless Motherwell lost by two goals to one to Celtic, with 'keeper Graeme Lloyd, a St. John signing from Liverpool, conceding two penalties on his debut. By the time of the next game a new manager had been appointed with Willie McLean taking over. It took time for the side to adapt to the new manager's style, and by the half way mark in the League campaign, Motherwell had only won two games at home and were struggling to make the top ten, and the Premier League for the following season.

The form started to turn round in December and January with six points out of ten picked up before the start of the Scottish Cup campaign at the end of January. One of the main factors for the change in fortunes was the goalscoring form of Willie Pettigrew alongside Bobby Graham. This culminated in Pettigrew scoring four in one game in a five one win over Ayr at Somerset Park.

With this good run of form, confidence was once again high going into the Scottish Cup campaign, kicking off with a third round tie at home to Partick Thistle. The game started in explosive fashion with Sam Goodwin retaliating to a tackle from John Hansen in the first minute and being sent off. He was so upset he was actually back home before the second half started! Midway through the second period, Willie Pettigrew and Thistle 'keeper John Arrol challenged for a through ball, which resulted in the visitors 'keeper having to leave the field with a broken leg.

He was replaced by right half Campbell who was never troubled by a shot-shy 'Well. The 'Well fans got a bit of a shock at Firhill for the replay when their favourites were unrecognisable in an Inter Milan style strip of black and blue stripes. Unfortunately they did not play in a style similar to the Italian giants, but a long range effort from right back Willie Watson with eight minutes to go was enough to see the 'Well through.

It was a visit from Queen's Park in the fourth round, and with Graham and Pettigrew cementing their partnership an easy four nil win saw 'Well progress. Both Pettigrew and Graham netted in the tie along with McIlwraith and Goldthorpe. This victory brought a trip to Pittodrie to take on Aberdeen in the Quarter Finals, where a Bobby Graham effort just before half time was enough to see the 'Well through. Although on the day the Dons were unlucky not to at least force a replay as they hit the woodwork twice during the game.

The Semi Final draw brought out a Lanarkshire Derby when Motherwell were drawn to play old rivals Airdrie at Hampden Park. The first game looked to be heading in Motherwell's favour when Pettigrew opened the scoring with only twenty minutes left. Sadly disaster struck with 10 minutes left when Stuart McLaren headed through his own goal past 'keeper Stuart Rennie, which took the game to a replay.

This mirrored the incident in 1931 when Alan Craig headed past his own goalkeeper, Alan McClory, in the Final, which also forced a replay. It was said at the time that Motherwell should never again field a team where the centre half and goalkeeper had the same first name to avoid any confusion in the box!

The replay was to prove an even bigger disaster for Motherwell. The game was a poor affair with neither side looking dangerous, and with time running out Stuart Rennie was adjudged to have broken the four step rule as he cleared the ball. From the resultant free kick, the ball was tapped to John Lapsley who drilled a low shot past Rennie to take the Diamonds through to the Final against Celtic.

League form remained as inconsistent as ever and for long spells it looked as though Premier Division football would be beyond Motherwell. Going into the last game of the season at home to Dumbarton, Motherwell needed to take one point to be assured of a place in the top ten in the following season. For once they did it the easy way, with a convincing three one win, with goals from Graham, a Miller penalty and McIlwraith making sure that they took their place in the historic first season of the ten team league.

Chapter 8 A Brave New Dawn

1975/76

In preparation for the start of the first Premier League Season Motherwell made a number of major moves in the summer transfer market. First to sign up, for a then record transfer fee of £35000 - £50000, was Colin McAdam who moved from Dumbarton with a reputation as a goalscoring midfielder. Next to join was midfielder Vic Davidson who had been one Celtic's "Quality Street" kids, alongside players such as Kenny Dalglish and Danny McGrain, but he never quite managed to establish himself in their first team. The third signing was centre half Willie McVie who moved from Clyde on the eve of pre-season training. The only player heading out the door was Sam Goodwin after four years sterling service. With these additions to the squad and the emergence of Pettigrew and Graham's partnership gave everybody confidence going into this historic season in Scottish Football.

Joe Wark gets his player of the year award from team mates Leishman, MacLaren, Watson, Rennie, Miller, Wark, Graham

The season started with the re-vamped British Cup, now called the Anglo-Scottish Cup, as it now only featured teams from the English and Scottish Leagues. The first phase of the competition was a qualifying round held on a regional basis, and Motherwell progressed to the full knock-out stage with an aggregate 2-1 win over Dundee.

This was followed by the League Cup qualifying campaign in which Motherwell's section included Rangers, Airdrie and Clyde, and it was a defeat in the second game to Airdrie that was enough to knock them out of the competition. This was despite drawing twice with eventual trophy winners Rangers, but the Airdrie reverse resulted in a finish two points behind the Ibrox men.

The League campaign started in a slightly frustrating fashion with a run of five draws in the first five games. The first ever Premier League game was played at Fir Park against Ayr United, and it was the Honest Men who took the lead through a Johnny Graham penalty. Five minutes into the second half Motherwell's first goal in the new competition was scored by defender Gregor Stevens.

The next four games saw Motherwell draw with Aberdeen, Celtic, Dundee United and Hearts before turning in a poor performance at Muirton Park where they lost 2-1 to St. Johnstone. It took until October 11th for 'Well to register their first win in the new League set-up, when Hibs were the victims at Fir Park in a 2-1 win for the home side, with goals from Pettigrew and Stevens, as they were forced to fight back from 1-0 down.

This was the start of a rich vein of form for Willie McLean could pick a settled side. The next encounter was a home win over Rangers, and once again they had to come from one nil down, Derek Johnstone putting Rangers ahead after only eight minutes, but goals in the last fifteen minutes from Pettigrew and Davidson sealed a win and pushed Motherwell into the top three in the table. The next week Pettigrew almost single-handedly secured a win at Dens Park when he scored four goals in the 6-3 win over Dundee; 'Well's other two goals came from Ian Taylor.

By this time 'Well had crashed out of the Anglos Scottish Cup, despite a fine 2-1 aggregate win over Blackburn Rovers, and holding a Bobby Moore inspired Fulham 1-1 at Craven Cottage.

Despite this result, the Londoners were too strong for Motherwell at Fir Park and won the second leg 3-2 and once again, the club was left pondering on what might have been in this competition.

After a 3-2 defeat to Ayr at Somerset Park a five game unbeaten run saw Motherwell cement their place at third in the table and they started to think about a potential European place for the first time in the club's history. To help the push for that European slot Willie McLean once again dipped into the transfer market, this time adding former Hibs and Arsenal winger Peter Marinello to the squad which allowed him to move away from a troubled spell at Portsmouth.

Two consecutive defeats to Hibs and Rangers pushed Motherwell out of contention as one of the main title challengers, but they rebounded well, and by the end of January they were in high spirits once again for the visit of Celtic to Fir Park for a Scottish Cup third round tie. Celtic were two goals up at half time and were well on top. In truth 'Well could have been out of the competition by the break if the visitors had taken their chances with former Motherwell man Deans being culpable on a number of occasions. McLean made a change at half time introducing Ian Taylor into the game and things slowly turned in favour of the home side. Bobby Graham pulled one back with a diving header at the back post before Taylor equalised from a direct free kick. It was left to Willie Pettigrew to score the winner picking up a long ball just outside the box and turning on a burst of pace to take him clear of defenders before crashing a low shot past the 'keeper for a memorable win.

The next round brought a tricky trip to Fife to take on Cowdenbeath at Central Park, but despite struggling for a spell Motherwell finally broke down their resistance to record a 2-0 win. About this time Scottish football was hit with a flu bug, and this game saw the first Motherwell player to be struck down, with Joe Wark forced to miss out. Next up in the Scottish Cup was a home tie with Hibs in a tie which caught the imagination of the Lanarkshire public when over 20000 squeezed into Fir Park for the game. Motherwell looked to be coasting to the Semi Final as they were two goals up through Pettigrew and a Marinello penalty but Hibs fought back and took the tie to a replay with a last gasp equaliser.

Free-scoring
Willie Pettigrew

The replay at Easter Rd was another exciting affair and once again Motherwell had taken the lead, this time Pettigrew was the provider for his strike partner Bobby Graham who headed the opening goal. But once again Hibs were to proved doughty Cup fighters and forced an equaliser to take the tie into extra time. No more goals were added, and the game was forced into a third game to be played at neutral Ibrox.

The match took place amidst a deal of controversy as Motherwell tried to get the game postponed due to the number of players at the club who were suffering from the flu bug. The SFA decreed that the game should go ahead and manager Willie McLean was forced to field a patched up side. The weakened team managed to find enough energy to clinch a Semi Final place with a fine 2-1 win thanks to goals from Taylor and a Marinello penalty.

The Semi was against Rangers, and in many quarters it was billed as the "final before the final" with both sides going so well in the League. Motherwell were resplendent in new white away tops as they took to the Hampden turf, and they turned in a fantastic first half performance to be two goals up at half time. McLaren scored first, after he managed to squeeze a ball low past McCloy, and then Pettigrew doubled the lead, leaving the 'Well fans looking forward to taking on Hearts in the Final.

As the second half wore on Rangers looked to have run out of ideas and confidence was growing even further amongst the Claret and Amber hordes. With twenty minutes to go Rangers were awarded a hotly disputed penalty when Stuart Rennie was alleged to have pulled down Derek Johnstone. It looked to many in the ground that referee John Gordon, at least 30 yards behind play, was awarding a free kick on the edge of the box, but he was in fact pointing to the penalty spot.

Rangers scored from the penalty and the game was completely turned on its head, and with their large support behind them the Gers could smell victory. Two minutes after the penalty they were on level terms and with seconds left Derek Johnstone snatched a cruel winner, which had the Motherwell fans shaking their heads as they left Hampden wondering just how the Cup Final spot had been snatched away from them in such a controversial manner.

Willie McVie & Colin McAdam prevent a goal being scored at Ibrox in 1975

In the League game following the Scottish Cup exit 'Well found themselves up against a rampant Celtic side who swept them aside 4-0 at Celtic Park. Successive wins over Dundee United, Hearts and St. Johnstone had pushed Motherwell back into third spot. But a defeat to nearest Euro challengers Hibs pushed them back, and two more defeats to Rangers and Dundee meant the European dream was over, despite finishing a creditable fourth in the debut season of the Premier League. The consolation was that there would be another crack at the Anglo Scottish cup.

The remarkable success story of the season had been the scoring rate of young striker Willie Pettigrew who scored 30 goals in 47 appearances in the three domestic competitions, and he also managed to add two more in the Anglo Scottish Cup. This led to him gaining five Scotland Under 23 caps, making his International debut against Switzerland in a Friendly, in which he scored. He won two further "full" Caps in the Home Internationals against Northern Ireland and Wales, scoring again in the Welsh match. But this wasn't enough to see him start against England as he was consigned to the bench as Scotland went on to clinch the Championship.

Willie was not the only Motherwell player to be recognised at International level during the season. Left Back Joe Wark gained overdue recognition when he was selected to play for the Scottish League against the Football League. He would have been joined in that game by team mate Bobby Graham but the striker was forced to withdraw due to an injury. Centre half Willie McVie was selected to play for the Scotland under 23s against Wales and Holland, before being selected for the full squad to play Switzerland.

1976/77

During the close season the club under took a trip to Mexico, Haiti and Columbia. The tour started in the Azteca Stadim in Mexico city where Ian Taylor scored in a 2-1 defeat to Toluca. In the second game, in Haiti, Isaac Farrell scored the winner in a victory over Voilet. The third match was against Racing of Haiti, when Ian Kennedy was the scorer in the 2-1 defeat. The final game saw Willie Pettigrew net the solitary Motherwell goal in a 2-1 defeat to Santa Fe of Columbia. Sadly, despite it being deemed a success at the time, it was felt that the tour played a part in the poor form shown at the start of the season, as some of the players were still suffering from the effects of the travelling when the season began.

There were more changes to the squad before the start of another season, with goalkeeper Ally Hunter being signed up from Celtic just before the end of season transfer deadline. Hunter had previously played for Kilmarnock and played a number of times for Scotland. Another significant signing was that of centre forward Jim O'Rourke who moved from St. Johnstone after starring at Hibs.

Heading the other way was one major surprise with club skipper Bobby Watson deciding that he wanted to retire from the game to concentrate on his steel stockholding business. Towards the end of the previous season 'Well's longest serving player moved on with John Goldthorpe moving to Morton to try to help keep them in the First Division. During the summer, winger Ian Taylor moved to St. Johnstone and Jim McIlwraith was also transferred during the season when he joined English side Bury.

The season's Anglo Scottish Cup campaign was over almost before it began as Kilmarncok knocked Motherwell out in the Scottish preliminary round. The League Cup campaign was a complete disaster as Motherwell finished bottom of their group having only managed to pick up two points from draws with Partick Thistle and Dundee. There was little to cheer apart from this with Hearts doing the double over the 'Well and Thistle and Dundee also taking two points from their victories over them.

After the excitement of the fist Premier League season hopes were high as Motherwell head into the League Campaign, but there was never any consistency at any time with few performances that hinted at what could have been. As in the previous season the first couple of League games were drawn, away to Kilmarnock and at home to Hibs. The first win came in the fourth game against Ayr United, following a defeat at Firhill. The Ayr game resulted in a 4-1 victory with a fine attacking performance proving too much for the visitors. This game saw Pettigrew open his account for the season with two goals.

Bobby Graham

Results did not improve through October with only one more win in five games, albeit this was a 3-1 triumph over Rangers at Fir Park. Motherwell did go one behind in the 8th minute but goals from Wark and two from Pettigrew sealed the game for a well deserved victory.

November started with a dramatic win over Kilmarnock at Fir Park in a nine goal thriller. The visitors were two nil up at half time, but a hat trick by Jim O'Rourke within 13 minutes of the second half put 'Well in front. This was added to by Pettigrew and Davidson before Kilmarnock once again fought back, but Motherwell held out to win one of the most dramatic games seen at Fir Park.

The next two games saw Motherwell complete a couple of back to back wins against Thistle and Hibs. But sadly this run of results was not maintained and the next six games produced only two draws with Kilmarnock and Hibs. During this spell the weather hit the Scottish game badly and the game was almost frozen out for several weeks from the end of November to late December.

By the end of January it was time for the Scottish Cup again and hopes were high, following the run to the Semi Final the previous season, that this could be repeated, or even lead to a stage further. The third round brought a comfortable 3-0 win over Kilmarnock, Motherwell taking the lead in 26 seconds through Pettigrew when he hit a 20 yarder past the 'keeper without a Killie player even touching the ball. The tie was sealed with a Davidson goal and a second Pettigrew effort.

The fourth round saw Motherwell drawn to play Alex Ferguson's high flying First Dvision leaders St. Mirren at Fir Park. The tie attracted a massive crowd of over 26000 to witness a tense, tough affair. The streetwise experience of the Motherwell side was to prove too much for the fine young side that Ferguson had built. Davidson scored first for 'Well before McGarvey found an equaliser but a Willie Pettigrew penalty was enough to see the Steelmen progress to the Quarter Final stage once again.

The Quarter Final was a repeat of the previous season's Semi against Rangers, and was part of a double header against the Ibrox side. The first was a League game at Fir Park which was comfortably won 2-0 by Rangers. The cup-tie was played at Ibrox and was a major disappointment for Motherwell as Rangers went ahead after only five minutes through a Bobby McKean goal, and the visitors never really got in the game. A Kenny Watson goal in the last minute sealed victory for the home side. The remainder of the season continued on the same inconsistent path as the early part of the season, with games coming thick and fast to make up for fixtures lost due to the poor weather and the run in the Scottish Cup, with Motherwell forced to play eight games in April alone.

There was one major highlight in the later period, when Celtic came to call in mid-April, knowing that a win at Fir Park would be enough to clinch the league title. Unfortunately for them Motherwell hadn't been given the same script, and at half time they were one goal up thanks to Ian Kennedy when he slammed home a Bobby Graham cross. The second half was to prove a personal disaster for Celtic left back Andy Lynch as he scored two own goals in the dying minutes to secure an improbable victory for the 'Well, and put his own side's title celebrations on hold for a little while longer.

This win was followed up with a 4-0 victory over Dundee United the following week in a game played on a Sunday, something that was rare at the time. The win ended any fears of relegation for another year and this allowed the side to relax in the remaining five games, in which only two draws were achieved. The final game was a 2-2 result at home to Celtic, which left Motherwell unbeaten against them at Fir Park over the season. The visitors had paraded the Scottish Cup they had won a week earlier.

Motherwell closed the season out with a glamour Friendly against former European Cup winners from Holland, Ajax of Amsterdam, and much to everyone's surprise ran out 4-2 winners against a side peppered with Dutch Internationals who had contested the 1974 World Cup Final and would feature the following year in Argentina.

1977/78

At the start of another season all at the club were looking for a greater degree of consistency compared to the previous season, and to be in a position for a UEFA Cup qualifying slot. Veteran forward Bobby Graham had moved on in the summer when he joined Hamilton Accies for the princely sum of £15000, his role as Pettrigrew's strike partner was handed over to Jim O'Rourke.

The curtain went up on the season with the Scottish qualifying round of the Anglo Scottish Cup against Alloa Athletic, and Motherwell went on a bit of a scoring spree. The first leg at Fir Park was won by seven goals to nil, with Vic Davidson bagging five, including one directly from a corner. The second leg at Recreation Park was to prove a formality with 'Well winning 4-1, hence giving an 11-1 aggregate over the two legs. The run in the competition was to be short with two poor performances against Notts County, which saw Motherwell crash out 1-2 on aggregate.

The season started with the League Cup campaign with the preliminary sections being scrapped, as it was felt that people had lost interest in the long drawn out early stage and the low crowds, even at the knock-out stage. The first five games in the League Cup campaign saw Motherwell lose only one game, at home to St. Mirren, and moving into third place. One of the early wins came at Celtic Park with former Celt Vic Davidson scoring a long range screamer to give 'Well the win with the only goal.

This result set things up nicely for the second round tie in the new two leg knock-out format. Things looked good for 'Well as they held the Celts to a 0-0 draw in the first leg at Celtic Park. The closest to a goal in the game came when Celtic were awarded a penalty, but Glavin smashed his kick-off the post. In the second leg Celtic powered to a 3-0 lead before two goals from Vic Davidson looked to have brought 'Well back into the game, but one more goal late on from Joe Craig sealed the tie for the visitors. This defeat, along with the defeat to Notts County in the Anglo Scottish Cup led to a run of poor results, with only one win, 1-0 at home to Hibs in mid-October, in the next twelve League games. This meant a slide down the table and a perilously close position to the relegation zone. The run of poor results saw the club take the now traditional route to solve the problem, when they parted company with manager Willie McLean in November.

Despite doing well in his first season, taking his team to the Scottish Cup Semi Final, he suffered after a run of poor results as many managers do, and was asked to leave. His assistant John Haggart took over as caretaker-manager until former Rangers centre half Roger Hynd took over at the helm on Boxing Day. This appointment seemed to act as an immediate spur for the side with full points being collected in four consecutive games, and without conceding a goal, leading up to the Scottish Cup third round tie with Arbroath at Gayfield.

The Scottish cup-tie was to provide a comfortable passage to the fourth round as Motherwell rattled in four goals without reply. They were three up at half time with goals from Marinello, O'Rourke and McLaren putting them well in commandt. Another Marinello goal in the second half rounded off the scoring as 'Well progressed to a home tie against Queen's Park.

The week following the Arbroath cup-tie Motherwell had entertained Aberdeen at Fir Park, and prior to the game introduced new Honorary Director, Scots Entertainer, Christioan to the crowd. His prime role was to add influence and style to the club's commercial, publicity and fund-raising ventures. The game itself was an entertaining 0-0 draw which saw visiting 'keeper Bobby Clark in fine form.

The week after was to serve up one of the most talked about games in the club's history when Rangers were the visitors at Fir Park. Motherwell had stormed into an early two nil lead through goals from O'Rourke and Davidson. Upset with the flow of the game a section of the large visiting support in the 20000 crowd invaded the pitch and refused to leave, and the game was halted whilst the players were forced to leave the pitch.

The disruption changed the atmosphere, both on and off the pitch, which upset the early form of the 'Well side and a Derek Johnstone inspired Rangers rattled five goals past Rennie to win the game comfortably. The incident was investigated by the SFA but the result was allowed to stand and Rangers managed to go on and win the title.

The Queen's Park cup-tie was to prove disastrous for 'Well when they put in a poor performance and crashed out of the competition losing by three goals to one, with the Spiders centre half Alan Mackin impressing so much that Motherwell signed him up only a few months later.

The introduction of young players such as Steve Mungall, Jimmy Lindsay, Ian Sommerville and Ian McLeod saw results improve and an outside chance of a European place was still on. But this was ended once and for all with a disastrous run of games in the last month of the season when all four games were lost without the scoring of a single goal; Rangers clinched the title in the last game of the season with a 2-0 win at Ibrox.

This meant that Motherwell had to settle for another sixth placed finish and rather than that first tilt at Europe they had to contend themselves with another attempt at the Anglo Scottish Cup.

1978/79

As Roger Hynd started his first full season in charge he added three players to his squad with goalkeeper Dave Latchford moving north from Birmingham. He was joined by Alan Mackin from Queen's Park, the centre half who had performed so well for his side in the Scottish Cup in the previous season. The third player to sign on was young forward John Clifford from Celtic. It was felt that with these additions to the existing squad the elusive consistency would be found and success would not be far away for the squad. The players were also joined by former Clydebank striker Mike Larnach who had struggled to settle at Newcastle United. As it turned out things actually went from bad to worse, followed with another change of manager, and eventually another relegation plus a complete change in the playing squad!

Before the season started Motherwell entertained English First Division side West Bromwich Albion in a match as part of long serving left back Joe Wark's testimonial season. Joe was only the second player to be awarded a benefit match in the club's history, following in the footsteps of Charlie Aitken. This was real reward for ten years outstanding service during which time he had become one of the most popular players at the club with his consistent performances.

The match was only a small part of his benefit season, with other events including a Dinner Dance, Cabaret, Boxing show and amateur golf tournament. Sadly, the game itself provided Motherwell with a real hammering and a 8-1 result, with Gregor Steven scoring the first two goals in the game! The real entertainment was to come from West Brom's exciting duo of Regis and Cunningham who ripped Motherwell apart with their pace and striking ability.

Once again the Anglo Scottish Cup campaign was over before it really began, after St. Mirren won 3-1 on aggregate despite Motherwell winning the first leg 1-0 at Fir Park. The League started with a defeat at home to Partick Thistle followed by a win at Anglo Scottish Cup conquerors St. Mirren. This was followed by a run of six straight League defeats, only interrupted by 4-3 aggregate win over Clyde in the League Cup, despite being 1-3 down from the first leg at Shawfield.

The third round of the League Cup brought another clash with Celtic and once again it looked as though Motherwell had a great chance to progress when a Willie Pettigrew goal gave them a 1-0 lead going into the home leg. As in the previous season Celtic turned the tie round at Fir Park when they scored four times to win 4-2 on aggregate.

A win at Cappielow over Morton was followed by two defeats to Partick and St. Mirren with Roger Hynd upsetting the 'Well fans prior to the Thistle game when he dropped star striker Willie Pettigrew following a disagreement between the two. Sadly his striking prowess was missed as Motherwell drew a blank at Firhill. Pettirgrew was restored to the starting eleven the following week and even though he was on the scoresheet he couldn't prevent Motherwell from losing 2-1.

Following the St. Mirren defeat and with Motherwell struggling against relegation, manager Roger Hynd handed in his resignation on 1st November and once again assistant manger John Hagart was left in charge on a caretaker basis. Hynd had only been in charge for ten months, and after his original success, which pushed the side up the table the previous season, results became consistently poor, and relegation was looking a real possibility.

Hagart was left in charge for six games while a new boss was found and he started with a 2-1 win over Celtic at Celtic Park as goals from Stevens and McLaren saw 'Well come back from a one goal deficit to take two valuable points. The next week saw Motherwell pick up their first home point of the season with a 1-1 draw against Aberdeen, 'Well's goal coming from Paul Wilson.

A new manager was finally appointed on December 12th when former Scotland boss Ally McLeod was enticed away from the same role at Ayr United to take over and try to stave off the looming relegation. McLeod had previously been successful with Ayr United and Aberdeen before leading Scotland to their disastrous World Cup campaign in Argentina in 1978. He had re-joined Ayr as part of his recovery from the traumatic time he had spent in South America.

His enthusiasm immediately saw the team string together a three game unbeaten run, starting with a 1-1 draw with Morton at Fir Park thanks to a Willie Pettigrew goal. This was followed by another one all draw, with Partick at home once again, Peter Miller scoring from the spot. The game also saw the debut of one of Ally McLeod's first signings, defender Joe Smith, who moved south from McLeod's former club Aberdeen. The next week, 20th January 1979, saw Motherwell finally secure their first home win of the season when Hearts were the visitors. A Pettigrew goal had Motherwell level 1-1 at half time, then goals from Steven and Clinging were enough to ensure a narrow 3-2 win.

As with the other cup competitions in 1978/79 the Scottish Cup campaign was short with an early exit for Motherwell, in the third round at Ibrox to Rangers, in an uninspiring performance that produced a 3-1 defeat.

Two further League defeats to Hibs and St. Mirren saw McLeod's patience snap with the established first team squad, and for the match with Partick Thistle at the start of March he selected five teenagers and two others under 21 years.

The young side battled hard to secure a scoreless draw, despite Gregor Stevens getting himself sent off late in the game. McLeod stuck with the young players as they slumped to nine defeats in a row, many of them heavy losses. The run started with 4-0 at Tannadice against Dundee United, but this was nothing to compare with the 6-0 defeat at Cappielow to Morton and then 8-0 at Pittodrie; to date this is still Motherwell's heaviest defeat in the Premier League.

The relegation that had been hanging over the club for most of the season was confirmed on April 7th with a 3-0 defeat to Hearts at Tynecastle. There was good news two weeks later when the losing run was ended at Fir Park with a 2-0 win over Rangers, with goals from Pettigrew and Donnelly sealing the points. A season that started with such high hopes saw Motherwell relegated for only the third time in their history, another change in manager and a massive turnaround in the playing squad.

Heading out the door during the season had been Peter Marinello who joined Fulham in time to play for them in a Boxing Day fixture. The clearout continued when Stewart McLaren and Peter Miller left to join newly promoted Dundee, and hence were able to continue their Premier League career. Centre half pairing Willie McVie and Gregor Stevens also moved on, with the former being freed to take up a move to the United States, and the latter joining Leicester for a reported £150000 transfer fee. Two players moved to Ayr United with 'keeper Stuart Rennie being swapped for Ayr's colourful goalkeeper Hugh Sproat, also heading to the coast was striker Jimmy Lindsay. Finally two players who had joined early in the season left with Dave Latchford heading south again to join Barnsley, and Jim Boyd who had joined from Clyde heading back to Shawfield. There was also a clear out of young players as McLeod attempted to make the squad his own, which resulted another 10 players leaving.

Heading in the other direction, he had already added Joe Smith from Aberdeen, and then in March McLeod made a double swoop to pick up striker Willie Irvine and midfielder Bobby Carberry from Alloa Athletic. April saw left back Tommy O'Rourke move from Meadowbank Thistle and in the same month prolific scorer Bruce Clelland from Albion Rovers was snapped up. The newcomers were joined in the close season with another of McLeod's former players from Aberdeen in experienced full back Chic McLelland.

1979/80

With all these changes to the playing squad it was hardly surprising that the team got off to a poor start in the League campaign with no wins in the first seven games, which saw them sitting second bottom of the table. In that spell Motherwell had managed to accumulate three points with draws against Clydebank, Arbroath and Berwick Rangers.

In the same spell they also crashed out of the League Cup, once again losing to the Spiders from Queen's Park. Motherwell slumped to a 4-1 defeat at Fir Park in the first leg, the tie being level at half time with Motherwell forcing an equaliser through Ian Clinging. The visiting Glasgow side were dominant in the second period and rattled in three goals that looked to have sealed the tie.

Motherwell responded well in the second leg at Hampden only four days later when they won the game 2-0, dominating the game but not making a breakthrough until they went down to ten men with centre back Alan Mackin being sent off. Two goals in the last fifteen minutes from Irvine and Clinging weren't enough to make any progress in the competition.

The League form did pick up in late September with four straight wins at least pushing Motherwell as high as ninth in the fourteen team table. The first victory of the season came at Fir Park against Hearts when goals from Soutat, McLaughlin, Clinging and Larnach sealed a 4-2 win. This was followed up by wins over Clyde, Dumbarton and St. Johnstone.

Brian McLaughlin who had scored two goals in this run had only recently been signed for £100000 from Ayr United. McLaughlin had been a promising young player whose career had looked to have ended when he suffered a severe leg break. He had spent a season at Ayr Utd and was First Division Player of the Year in 1978/79. Ally McLeod had tried to sign him for some time after working with him at Ayr United, and eventually the Honest Men caved in with a £100000 cheque dangled in front of them.

McLaughlin's promptings seemed to lift Motherwell, although after the four straight wins another run of defeats saw the side slip back down the table, leaving 'Well fans frustrated with the form of the side in a division that they were expected to win easily. From the start of November things did start to look a little brighter, with only two defeats in 12 games up until the end of January when the Scottish Cup started.

The major problem was the high number of draws in the run meaning that instead of a real promotion push being made the sequence only ensured that relegation was out of the question.

Around the Christmas period Manager Ally McLeod once again dipped into the transfer market when he snapped up two players from Arbroath to bolster the defence and midfield. Midfielder Albert Kidd and centre half Joe Carson were snapped up for a combined fee of £100000. Another popular signing at the time was that of winger John Gahagan who was called up from Shettleston Juniors after impressing in a Junior Cup Final held at Fir Park.

The Scottish Cup provided no light relief in a season that was turning out to be one of the most disappointing in the club's history. Motherwell were paired with Queen of the South away at Palmerston and they turned in another poor performance, with only Joe Wark getting pass marks in a tie that Motherwell deservedly lost. The game was a disaster for Motherwell with McLaughlin missing a penalty, Joe Carson carried off injured and Ian McLeod sent off in the two-nil defeat. McCall and Mitchell were to be the heroes for the Doonhamers on the day as they deservedly progressed to the fourth round. This was the second time in the season that Motherwell had lost to a Second Division side in a Cup tie, the other being Queen's Park.

Willie Irvine scoring against Hamilton Accies during the 1979/80 season

The poor form continued immediately after the Cup defeat with a 2-1 reverse to St. Johnstone, with former 'Well man John Goldthorpe scoring the winning goal for the Perth Saints. This was followed by a run of eight games without defeat, with only one of these being a draw this time, and 'Well were on the periphery of the promotion chase with an outside chance of actually making an immediate return to the Premier League.

With four games left Motherwell lost 1-0 to Dumbarton at Boghead and realistically put an end to Motherwell's hopes of a return to the top League. Despite a win over Clyde at Shawfield, the season ended on a flat note with a defeat at Broomfield and a draw with Dunfermline. Motherwell slipped to sixth, although given the early part of the season this final position was met with a great deal of relief.

1980/81

There was only one major change in the squad during the summer in preparation for the second season in the First Division, with striker Steve McLelland moving from Ay United after a successful campaign at Somerset Park. As it turned out he was soon to be transformed into a centre half and went on to become a fans favourite with his wholehearted defensive performances. He was joined at the club by another towering Centre half when Graeme Forbes joined up from Tayside junior club Lochee United.

Once again optimism was high going into the season, particularly as Motherwell had looked impressive in pre-season with the highlight being a win in the Lanarkshire Cup. Newly promoted Airdrie were beaten 2-1 in the final at Douglas Park leading to hopes that this would be the last season in the lower League.

As in the previous season the first few games brought a sequence of poor results and once again Motherwell were sitting just out of the relegation positions after six games, with only one win in the opening fixtures. That victory came by 3-0 at home to Falkirk with Steve McLelland opening his scoring account, and additional goals from young striker John McKeever and midfielder Albert Kidd.

The League Cup also got off to a poor start with a 0-0 draw at Stenhousemuir's Ochilview ground in the second round first leg, in a game where the home side largely resorted to defensive tactics to frustrate the visitors. The second leg was an altogether different affair, particularly after Clinging opened the scoring and Motherwell settled and scored five more to run out 6-1 winners. Clinging scored a second goal, McLaughlin netted a hat trick and a single was scored by Albert Kidd.

The third round saw Premier Division Dundee United drawn to visit Fir Park in the first leg, and Motherwell secured a creditable 2-1 win, with two quick goals, after going down to an Addison goal, from McKeever and Clinging.

By the time of the second leg Motherwell had secured their second League win of the season, coming back from two goals down against Dundee at Fir Park to win three two, the winning goal coming from McKeever with only five minutes left. 'Well did not fare so well in the second leg of the League Cup tie, despite keeping United to a 2-2 scoreline in ninety minutes they could not hold out in extra time and were dumped out of the competition following two more United goals. Dundee United went on to win the competition beating city rivals Dundee in the final at Dens Park.

Two more wins, this time over Dumbarton and Dunfermline, at last saw 'Well push up the table, but a not unusual inconsistency of results in a run which saw the side struggle to string two wins together meant that a real promotion push was unlikely once again. Although by the time of the New Year fixture against local rivals Hamilton Accies, at Fir Park, they had climbed into the lofty position of sixth.

John Gahagan

The Ne'erday game was to prove a bit of a disaster for 'Well as they suffered their first home defeat of the season. It started badly with a poor pass back from Kidd letting former 'Well winger Mick McManus in to score the opener. Even when Brian McLaughlin restored parity, 'Well were back to a goal behind within a couple of minutes when Brian Wright's header restored the Accies lead.

Worse was to follow in the dying minutes, with Motherwell pushing for the equaliser they won a corner and threw every outfield player forward with 'keeper Hugh Sproat on the half way line to pick up any clearance. The Accies did manage to clear the ball and unfortunately Hugh Sproat failed to deal with it leaving Neil Howie the easy task of scoring and securing the points for the Hamilton side.

Motherwell made amends the following week by beating Ayr United three two at Fir Park. This result actually launched Motherwell off on a 15 game unbeaten League run until the end of the season but given the start they had given the other sides they could only pull themselves into fifth and consign themselves to another season in the First Division.

The Scottish Cup once again proved eventful, with Motherwell once again drawn to play away to Stenhousemuir, just as they had been in the League Cup earlier in the season. After a jittery start, when the home side could have been two up, a Joe Carson goal seemed to have settled the nerves. With thirteen minutes to go 'Well paid for not finding that killer second goal and Jack scored an equaliser for the home side to take the tie to a replay.

The replay was not to prove as easy as the second leg of the League cup-tie had been. Even with Motherwell going two goals up through McLelland and Gahagan they were made to sweat in the last twenty minutes. Muir pulled one back, but 'Well did hold on and had a Quarter Final trip to take on Dundee United, also for the second time in a Cup competition that season.

Motherwell won the three League games leading up to the Dundee United clash, and as a result a large travelling support of around 3000 headed to Tannadice with high expectations. As on many occasions in the club's history they were to be disappointed as United won with a devastating seven minute spell in the first half which had pushed them out of 'Well's reach. They opened the scoring in the seventh minute through Dodds, and by the time the same player complete his hat trick in the seventeenth minute they were four goals up.

Motherwell did manage to pull a goal back through Gordon Soutar, but further goals from Kirkwood and Narey meant an unhappy trip home for the many 'Well fans in the crowd. To rub salt in Motherwell's wounds, United manager Jim McLean fined his team for not playing well enough - despite rattling in six goals!

At the end of the season Manager Ally McLeod was under pressure from sections of the supporters, as the club reluctantly looked forward to a third season away from the top flight. The board decided that there had been enough shown in the last fifteen games to give him another chance of trying to secure that top flight berth once again.

1981/82

McLeod tinkered with his squad in preparation for his third tilt at promotion, with Mackin, Larnach and Donnelly leaving. He brought in a mixture of experience and youth to replace them. Alfie Conn was snapped up from Blackpool having served both sides of the Old Firm, as well as a spell at Tottenham Hotspur. He was joined by Tommy O'Hara who was returning from a period playing in the United States, where he starred alongside Dutch superstar Johan Cruyff for the Washington Diplomats. The youth was provided by Aston Villa's Brian McClair and Brian Coyne who was snapped up from Shrewsbury.

The League Cup had reverted to a pre-season qualifying section once again after the trial period of playing it as a knock-out tournament. Motherwell were drawn in the same group as Partick, Ayr and Dundee United, and opened with five straight defeats which saw Ally McLeod depart the scene before the League campaign could get under way.

It was often thought that McLeod had never recovered from the psychological scars of the disastrous Scotland Argentina 1978 campaign, and he never recovered his spark and enthusiasm for the game. After leaving Motherwell he moved back to his beloved Ayr United for a third spell as manager at the club.

Motherwell moved quickly to appoint former Celtic and Chelsea star Davie Hay as manager, promoting him from the position of McLeod's assistant. Hay had been a talented midfielder who played in Germany in 1974 for Scotland and had starred in a 0-0 draw with Brazil. It was hoped that this drive and ambition would restore the club to the Premier Division at his first attempt.

Alfie Conn

Things looked as though they were heading the same way as the previous two seasons when after three games only one win and a draw had been picked up, the club sitting eighth in the table. After the fourth game, when Hay had obviously set out his expectations, there was no looking back as they hit the top of the table following three consecutive wins over St. Johnstone, Falkirk and Dumbarton. The Dumbarton game showed the transformation that Hay had managed without changing the playing squad, the side demolishing the homesters 6-0 with Clelland grabbing a hat trick.

This started a run of games that didn't see a League defeat again until 13th February, in a period highlighted with great moments. In early October Alfie Conn scored a memorable goal in a 3-0 demolition of East Stirling at Fir Park, when he picked the ball up mid way in his own half, then waltzed through the 'Shire side before chipping a delightful effort over the 'keeper from 18 yards. Two weeks later Clydebank were swept aside by this irrepressible Motherwell side as the Kilbowie team were torn apart by 7-1 in a vintage display of attacking football. At the end of November they even managed to score six times in back to back games, with Dunfermline suffering at Fir Park and East Stirling on the wrong end at Firs Park.

With this kind of irrepressible form under their belts 'Well fans were once again looking forward to the Scottish Cup, and there was real optimism that high flying Aberdeen could be beaten at Fir Park in the third round. A little bit of history was created on the day, with Aberdeen scoring the quickest ever Scottish Cup goal, when Hewitt latched on to an Ian McLeod error to sweep the ball home from close range after only twelve seconds. Motherwell battled hard to come back from this early set back but could not break down a defence including the partnership of McLeish and Miller, and failed to get the draw that their pressure deserved.

This Cup defeat did not halt the unrelenting march back to the Premier Division, and the following week they knocked three past promotion contenders Hearts at Tynecastle. Hearts had looked more likely to score early on, and former 'Well men Pettrigrew and Marinello came closest for the Jambos, but Sproat was in magnificent form as he kept them at bay. Goals from Irvine, Coyne and Clinging secured a great away win for 'Well.

Albert Kidd scores from the penalty spot.

The nineteen game unbeaten run came to an end at Douglas Park the home of Lanarkshire rivals Hamilton Accies. Motherwell turned in a lack lustre performance and in all truth probably deserved to lose to the 83rd minute goal from Donnelly. This was only a minor blip, along with the only other defeat, at Ayr in mid April, on the way to the promotion and the title. Promotion was clinched on 17th April with a 3-1 win at Brockville over Falkirk, when Forbes scored two and McClair the other.

One week later the title was clinched in one of the dullest home performances of the season, a scoreless draw with Clydebank, which was played out in front of the BBC TV cameras. The result did not dampen the enthusiasm of the 'Well fans who ran on to the field to mob their heroes and celebrate the end of their top division exile.

There was still time left for more excitement in the season, with the last game at Tynecastle proving vital for Hearts as they tried to return to the Premier League along with their opponents. Before heading to Tyencastle, Davie Hay took the opportunity to blood one of 'Well's promising youngsters, with midfielder Gary McAllister making his first appearances for the club.

As the season headed into that last game Hearts needed to win and hope that Kilmarnock lost to have any hopes of finishing second. Motherwell scored through Willie Irvine as early as the seventh minute, and with Killie comfortably ahead at half time, things looked bleak for the Jambos. Things looked even bleaker as their fans in the shed started to fight amongst themselves and club Chairman Wallace Mercer had to act as peacemaker to allow the game to continue.

In the end 'Well saw the game out and consigned their great Edinburgh rivals to a second season in the First Division.

The season had been a triumph for Davie Hay as he saw his side romp away with the title, scoring 92 to create a First Divison record for the number of goals Three players had netted 56 goals between them, with McLaughlin and Irvine claiming 20 each and Clelland chipping in with 16.

It was therefore no surprise that Hay was attracting interest from others looking to hire a top coach, and it was a great disappointment when Hay announced he would not take the side into the Premier Division as he had accepted a coaching post in the US and planned to move his family out there in the summer.

There was one other period during the season when two games were played in the one weekend in October. On Saturday 10th October Motherwell drew 1-1 with Ayr, Johnny Gahagan's goal clinching the point. The next day, Sunday 11th October, they played a friendly at home to North American Soccer League side San Jose Earthquake's, the visitors. one major drawing power for the US side was that they included ex-Manchester United legend George Best in their line up. In fact Best played a half for both sides, giving 'Well fans the opportunity to boast that the great man played for their favourites. On the day Motherwell were to prove too strong for the Americans as they ran out five-two winners.

1982/83

With Davie Hay deciding that his future lay elsewhere, Motherwell were left looking for another new manager, the fifth in five years. The board were showing a great degree of ambition when they finally decided that there choice would be former Rangers manager Jock Wallace who recently had been in charge of Leicester City. Wallace had been successful in his time at Rangers, where he was in charge for two treble winning seasons.

By the time the League Cup campaign got under way Wallace had added experienced full back Alex Forsyth to the squad. Forsyth had started this career at Partick Thistle before a successful spell at Manchester United where he was picked for Scotland on a regular basis.

Optimism was high once again and an opening day win over Hearts did little to dampen this, Brian Coyne opened the scoring with Alfie Conn adding a second. Hearts did pull one goal back but the victory remained at Fir Park. Sadly the next two games did not see the 'Well build upon the excellent start with two disappointing draws away to Clyde and then at home to Forfar.

A young Gary McAllister in 1982

They were back in contention for a Quarter Final place with a fine 3-1 win over Clyde at Fir Park, with Brian McClair coming on as a substitute for Ian Clinging, and he immediately set about claiming a hat trick to clinch the win. This set up a group decider against nearest rivals Hearts at Tynecastle, but 'Well turned in a poor performance that saw them lose 1-0 to an Alex McDonald goal, and it was the Jambos who progressed to the next round.

Another new face was in place for the start of the League campaign, with another experienced internationalist joining the squad, this time it was Icelandic star Johannes "Shuggy" Edvaldsson. He had spent a successful spell at Celtic before finally being released and being snapped up by Wallace, to add some experience and depth to the squad, particularly as the player could turn out at either centre forward or centre half.

As very often happens in football the fixture computer set up a first League game against Wallace's former side Rangers at Fir Park.

It was indeed strange to see Motherwell's new manager receive a rapturous welcome from the visiting support, and acknowledge them more than the small band of 'Well fans in the crowd. The game itself was an exciting affair with Rangers taking a two goal lead, but Motherwell fought back and managed to take a point thanks to goals from Bruce Clelland and Joe Carson.

In the weeks following this opening day draw there was little to celebrate, with the next game away at Dens Park being lost 3-1 and then a humiliation at home to Celtic. Wallace left two of the previous season's top scorers, McLaughlin and Clelland, on the bench and Willie Irvine out of the picture completely. He also shuffled the defence about with Joe Wark taking on the unfamiliar role as a sweeper behind centre half Joe Carson. Celtic exploited these unfamiliar changes to the full by rattling in seven goals without reply, with Charlie Nicholas in sparkling form throughout the game.

The following week at Cappielow for a game against Morton, Wallace once again shuffled the pack with Joe Wark dropped, Edvaldson moved to centre back and Bruce Clelland restored up front. The end result was much the same with another loss being inflicted upon the hapless 'Well side. A trip to Pittodrie the following week, and another defeat confirmed that another relegation dogfight was on the cards.

The run was ended with a two nil win at home to St. Mirren, when Edvaldsson was outstanding, and goals coming from a rare Ian McLeod strike and then a debut goal from new signing Bobby Flavell who scored from 35 yards. Flavell had arrived from Hibs, with fans' favourite Willie Irvine heading in the opposite direction. The victory against St. Mirren was followed by two more defeats, at Hibs and at home to Dundee United, and this saw Motherwell hit the bottom of the table. It was to be a short stay as a 4-1 win over Kilmarnock hauled them back off the bottom but still deep in relegation trouble.

By this time Wallace was beginning to model the side to his own design, with Steve McLelland back as a striker, Flavell in for Irvine, Ally Mauchlen in midfield after signing up from Kilmarnock and Edvaldsson as his skipper at centre back.

Following a defeat at Ibrox, a win over Dundee briefly relieved Motherwell from the bottom of the League, for a 3-1 defeat at Celtic Park saw them back at the bottom again the following week. But once again they rose one week later after a 3-1 win over Morton, and when this rare victory was followed by four straight defeats, this still saw them firmly in relegation trouble.

Just in time for the fixture away to Kilmarnock at Rugby Park, Wallace manage to sign up two new players with right back Andy Dornan and striker Andy Harrow moving from Aberdeen. Both were immediately pitched in to the fray at Rugby Park and their presence had an immediate effect as Motherwell ran out winners by two goals to nil, with goals from Flavell and Mauchlen, the first away win of the season. Two days later an even more unlikely win was achieved when Rangers were the first visitors to Fir Park in 1983. Motherwell ran out three nil victors with Brian McClair scoring all three. The following week they failed to make it two away wins in a row when they lost 3-1 at Dens Park against Dundee.

As Motherwell prepared to take on Celtic at Fir Park, Wallace once again dipped in to the transfer market, this time to bring in goalkeeper Nicky Walker from Leicester City to replace the enigmatic Hugh Sproat. The newcomer was left helpless on 23 minutes when a Murdo McLeod thunderbolt gave the visitors the lead. In the second half Motherwell worked their way back into the game when McClair continued his one man demolition of the Old Firm by equalising from the penalty spot after O'Hara had been tripped. The young striker then managed to get himself noticed when he scored the winner late in the game, which was tapped home from close range after Bonnar has misjudged a Mauchlen cross.

The following week brought a trip to Shawfield to take on Clyde in the Scottish Cup and following the run of good form in the rest of January there were high hopes of a good run. After the game at Shawfield, Motherwell were lucky to be still in the competition as Nicky Walker was forced to pull off a string of fine saves to deny a Pat Nevin inspired home side.

The replay at Fir Park was a real roller coaster affair which took extra time to separate the sides. This looked unlikely in the early stages as Motherwell were two goals up thanks to strikes from McClair and Harrow. Despite Pat Nevin pulling a goal back, Forbes soon restored Motherwell's two goal lead. Clyde stormed back and goals from Evans and Dempsey took the tie into extra time. In the end it was a bizarre own goal from Bobby Flavell eleven minutes into the extra period that won the game for the Bully Wee. He attempted to head away a near post corner but only managed to send the ball spinning high over Walker and in off the far post.

This meant that every one at Fir Park could concentrate on steering clear of relegation and despite more inconsistent results they confirmed their Premier League place with a 2-0 win over Hibs in the third last game of the season. This was a relief to all as the last two games were away from home, including a trip to Tannadice to take on Champions elect Dundee United.

Wallace had managed to achieve his first objective in keeping Motherwell in the Premier League for another season despite having to transform the squad at the same time.

1983/84

Wallace added one more player to his squad for the start of the season, when he brought in striker Jim Gillespie who had recently been plying his trade in Belgian football. Heading out of the door in the summer was Brian McClair who moved to Celtic for a fee of £75000, a reward for his scoring exploits against the Old Firm in January. With the League Cup being re-vamped once again, the season started with a visit to Tannadice for the opening League fixture, and the game ended in a four-nil defeat, just as the game at the end of the previous season had finished.

After this opening day hammering, Motherwell were faced with a two legged League cup-tie against Berwick Rangers to determine who went forward to the group stages. Motherwell progressed comfortably enough winning the tie by four goals to nil over the two legs. This meant a series of sectional matches that were to be intermingled with the League games from the end of August right through until late November.

The first group match was at home to Morton, and Motherwell secured a 3-0 win despite a brave effort from the home side. Motherwell were 2-0 up thanks to goals from Edvaldsson and Gillespie before former Ton legend Andy Ritchie, who had signed for 'Well after a successful trial spell, scored the third to seal the win. The second League game brought an away draw at Love St., with Edvaldsson once again on target, and another League cup-tie was squeezed in the midweek following the trip to Paisley, with two Jim Gillespie goals securing a 2-1 win away to Alloa.

The League Cup was put on hold for four games, allowing the clubs to focus on the League campaign. Motherwell did secure a draw at home to Aberdeen, but followed this up with three straight defeats to Celtic, Hibs and Dundee, ensuring another relegation battle was on the cards. This was followed by another hammering by Dundee United, who managed to score four for the third time in a row against the Steelmen, after they ran out 4-2 winners at Fir Park in the League Cup.

Andy Dornan & Andy Harrow head for goal in 1983

Wallace's departure seemed to unsettle things further at the club with two away defeats at Celtic and Dundee following his exit, and the club appointed popular former player Bobby Watson as manager after these two games. Watson had been popular in his playing days at Fir Park, but had retired from playing to look after his Steel Stockholding business. However he couldn't stay away from the game and he was soon attending matches at his home town club Airdrie. His attachment to the club saw him take over as Manager, and after serving his time at Broomfield he was lured back to Fir Park to try to steer Motherwell clear of relegation.

The League started up again with three games before Alloa visited in the League Cup The first of the three was a 0-0 draw away to newly promoted Hearts, followed by a defeat at Fir Park against St. Johnstone. Given that they hadn't won a League match all season, it was hardly expected that a trip to Ibrox would yield anything, but it did when Motherwell fought back from a goal down to secure their first victory. McCoist has put Rangers 1-0 up, but 'Well equalised in the second half when Ritchie scored from the spot after Rafferty had been fouled. The win was secured when Junior Burns trundled the ball home with only nine minutes left, and they held on despite Ian McLeod being shown a red card with two minutes to go. The result was to have major implications for Motherwell in the long run, as this was the final straw for the Rangers fans and their board, for manager John Greig was forced to leave the club, and the favourite to take his place was former boss and Jock Wallace.

After the Ibrox victory normal service was resumed as Motherwell took on Alloa at Fir Park and only managed to secure a 2-2 draw. Then in typical fashion they followed that up with a surprise 2-2 draw against Champions Dundee United, and a scoreless draw at Fir Park against St. Mirren, which included a missed penalty.

The League Cup campaign kicked in once again with a trip to Greenock to take on Morton in what was to prove Jock Wallace's last game in charge as the lure of a return to Ibrox proved too strong for him. Sadly for Wallace this was not one to remember as his side found themselves 3-0 down early in the game, then despite goals from Ritchie and Harrow they were soundly beaten 2-4 by their hosts.

There weren't many tears for the departure of Wallace as there was always a feeling that his heart was never in the job. Results were never great either as he constantly tinkered with the team selection, despite inheriting a squad that had stormed through the First Division the previous season.

Despite the appointment of the new manager there was no immediate improvement in results with Hibs winning in Watson's first game, and Dundee United the 3-0 victors at Fir Park in the final League Cup section game as Motherwell crashed out of the competition.

A dismal run through December and January saw Motherwell firmly rooted at the bottom of the table and looking favourites for the drop to Division One. In this sequence of eight games, Motherwell only managed to secure two points in draws against Hearts and a surprising point taken from Celtic. This was despite the addition of two new players in the middle of the run when Kenny Black and Kenny Lyall moved from Rangers to boost Watson's squad. These changes were was part of the deal that saw Nicky Walker move to Ibrox to team up with former boss Jock Wallace once again.

It was no surprise that the Scottish Cup was welcomed with a sigh of relief as a break from the rigours of the Premier League battle. The third round brought a visit from Queens Park to Fir Park and the release of the pressures of the League seemed to help the home side as they ran out three nil winners thanks to an Andy Harrow hat trick.

A defeat to Aberdeen at Fir Park kept the poor League form going before Clydebank were the next visitors to Lanarkshire in the fourth round of the Cup. Once again the break from League action seemed to help Motherwell as they romped to a convincing 3-1 win to set up a Quarter Final tie against Celtic.

The week after the Clydebank cup-tie Watson's side managed to secure the first win in his charge, with a 1-0 victory at home to St. Johnstone, with Andy Harrow's goal enough to clinch the two points. Two weeks later they claimed a surprise two points when they beat Hibs 2-1 at Easter Rd, a result that sparked outrageous celebrations from the manager as he rushed down the touchline to greet the departing 'Well fans.

By this time Watson was trying to freshen up the side as he introduced Jim Dobbin, Bernie Grant and Derek Weldon. But all three only managed a handful of appearances as Watson's team selections became stranger and stranger, as he tried anything he could to prevent the almost inevitable slide into the First Division.

The next match after the victory at Easter Rd was the Scottish Cup Quarter Final against Celtic at Fir Park. The game proved to be too much for some of the inexperienced 'Well men, for the Celts hammered in six goals without reply. Motherwell even had the ignominy of missing a penalty with seven minutes to go.

Two consecutive League defeats following the Scottish Cup exit sealed Motherwell's relegation fate with seven games still left in the season. In those remaining games they only managed to win one match, 1-0 at home to St. Mirren, as Watson blooded even more youngsters - Maxwell, Wishart, McAllister, Boyd and Kennedy all getting valuable first team experience.

This was a difficult time for the club as the turmoil of so many managers in a short space of time and the constant turnover of players had started to take its toll on the clubs finances. One of the ways to combat this was one of the lasting testaments to the reign of Wallace and his assistant Frank Connor and that is their formation of a structured youth policy.

This policy had started to pay off even by the end of this season with the number of "home grown" youngsters who had broken into the first eleven. Not only did the playing side benefit for the addition of a clutch of excellent young players, they were also to prove a valuable asset in helping the club's finances with the transfer fees some of them would attract in the coming years.

Local character and Groundsman
Andy Russell and his dog Tizer -
1970's to 1990's

Chapter 9 The McLean Years

After the turbulent management years of McLeod, Hay, Wallace and Watson and the perilous financial state of the club, and the need to get back out of the First Division, the board decided that a coach with a proven record was needed to steady the ship. Watson resigned after the last game of the 1983/84 season, as he believed that the club was not the one he had played at and it was time for him to move on.

The club were linked with a number of candidates, including Tommy McLean, Peter Cormack, Benny Rooney and former assistant manager Frank Connor. The board decided upon the partnership of Tommy McLean and Tom Forsyth, who had just steered Morton out of the First Division. Little did they know where this was about to lead the club....

McLean was a former Kilmarnock and Rangers winger who was one of the finest crossers of a ball who set up many a goal for his team mates. As a youngster at Kilmarnock he was a League winner back in 1964/65, when Killie pipped Hearts on goal difference in the very last game of the season. As a result he was quickly on his way to Rangers where he won every domestic honour as well as a European Cup Winners Cup medal when Moscow Dynamo were defeated 3-2 in Barcelona.

He was joined at Rangers by Forsyth in 1972 when he moved to Ibrox after starting his career at Motherwell whom he joined from his hometown team Stonehouse Violet. Forsyth was a versatile player at Fir Park who could just as easily play in midfield or as a Centre Half. His consistency of performance soon had Rangers knocking at his door and he went on to establish himself as one of the top defenders in the country. He was a regular for the Scotland side in the late seventies and was "lucky" enough to travel to Argentina with Ally McLeod's ill fated squad.

The two players struck up a great friendship at Ibrox with both of them travelling together from the same part of Lanarkshire. When Tommy McLean gave up the playing side of the game he was quickly appointed to the Rangers coaching staff serving under Rangers legend John Grieg. Unfortunately for the two of them this was one of the toughest spells in the Ibrox club's history, and indeed a victory for a Jock Wallace managed Motherwell was enough to see Grieg given the sack and McLean was put in temporary charge During season 1983/84 the two joined up as the coaching team at Morton who were trying to get themselves out of the First Division, after Tommy McLean had initially served a short spell as assistant to Alex Miller before his former team mate moved to St. Mirren. They did such a great job that when in the summer of 1984 Motherwell were looking for a management team to restore them back to the Premier League there was no real decision to be taken and the two of them were on their way to Fir Park.

Their task was simple, get Motherwell back to Premier League and keep them there. The years that were to follow were more successful than anyone could've imagined.

1984/85

Ironically they started the season at McLean's first club with a game against Kilmarnock at Fir Park. It was a great start for the duo as the team won the game 2-0 with only three players in the side who weren't available the previous season, with Derek Murray filling in at left back after joining from McLean's brother Jim's side Dundee united, Ian McDonald from Partick Thistle and striker Rab Stewart from Dunfermline. To help fund his rebuilding plans he was forced to sell on two of the experienced players in the squad with Stuart Rafferty moving to Dundee and Kenny Black moving to Hearts. Murray was signed from United for £50000, with the balance of the £50000 received for Black still available to the new manager.

The first game was won 2-0 with goals from Gary McAllister and Andy Harrow ensuring the first hurdle between Motherwell and the Premier League was overcome easily. The following week they travelled to near neighbours Hamilton for the first local derby of the season, but the momentum that fans thought had been established in week one was soon halted as the Accies won 2-0 on the day. This at least helped temper the expectations that the journey to the Premier League was going to be a stroll. This was further reinforced by a defeat at Ayr's Somerset Park in the League Cup which saw the club crash out of the tournament at the first time of asking.

The next four games fuelled the expectation of a quick return as Motherwell hit the top of the League after four games unbeaten, with wins against Partick, Forfar and Falkirk and a draw at home to League Cup conquerors Ayr United.

The stay at the top was short lived and by Christmas the table saw the 'Well sitting in sixth and promotion back to the top flight looking a long way off.

Ally Mauchlen scores versus Forfar in 1984

This spell was characterised by a catastrophic first visit to Meadowbank Stadium to take on Meadowbank Thistle, with the game ending in a shambolic 4-2 defeat. The game was played to a crowd on only side of the ground and a bring and buy sale under the Stand which saw visiting fans having to use turnstile behind the goal to gain access to the Stand, climbing walls and crossing the running track to reach their seats.

The game itself saw Andy Dornan miss a penalty, a Forbes own goal and two goals lost in the last five minutes to ensure we made an interesting debut at the former Commonwealth Stadium. Things were to get even more entertaining as the frustration of both fans and players boiled over with goalkeeper John Gardner offering his gloves to fans if they thought they could do better!

Things picked up after Christmas, following a 3-0 derby win against Hamilton on 2nd January, the team went on a 10 match unbeaten League run that saw them catapulted back to the top of the table by the middle of March. During the same timescale they had managed to negotiate a route to the Scottish Cup semi final, beating Dumbarton, Meadowbank and Forfar in the process.

Making the Cup semi acted as a bit of a distraction as two successive defeats at the hands of Clyde and Meadowbank almost blew the promotion charge off course. The Cup semi final took place on a sunny early April Saturday afternoon and Motherwell came out of the traps quickly and rocked their illustrious opponents by taking the lead in front of just over 30000 fans.

A Raymond Blair cutback in only the thirteenth minute was met superbly by Gary McAllister to fire home. Celtic fought back to equalise through Tommy Burns but the underdog 'Well side continued to push forward and created the best chances in the remainder of the game. Particularly a Graeme Forbes header that had the 'Well fans celebrating before it slipped harmlessly past the post.

In the replay the following Tuesday, the old cliché of not giving an Old Firm side a second chance proved to be true, when Celtic ran out comfortable winners scoring three unanswered goals in the last fifteen minutes to progress through to the Final.

Six games unbeaten between the semi final defeat and the end of the season saw 'Well fans celebrating in Forfar as promotion back to the Premier League was settled with a 0-0 draw at Station Park, even though promotion had been clinched some weeks earlier with a 1-0 win at Firhill against Partick Thistle. Tommy McLean's first objective had been achieved, he had stabilised the ship and returned it to the top level of Scottish Football where it belonged.

As a footnote to this season, the club decided the Joe Wark's service to the club should be rewarded with a second Testimonial game. This time the game was played mid season frozen January Sunday afternoon with a Motherwell select taking on an Old Firm select. The visitors won the game 3-1, with Joe Jordan being the scorer for Motherwell on the afternoon.

During the summer McLean was frustrated on two fronts as he prepared for the Premier League campaign. He had been given no money to help add to the squad, and three experienced players, Mauchlen, Forbes and Dornan, had all refused new contract terms. Throughout the summer there had been constant speculation over the future of midfielder Muachlen, with a bid of £100000 from Birmingham being rejected as it did not match the club's valuation of £150000 for the player.

Just as the season was about to get underway it was also announced that Chairman Bill Dickie would stand down from that position and a new Chairman appointed at the club's AGM in August. When the AGM was held later in August it was decided that the position should be held on a rotational basis for two years at a time, with Ian Livingston filling the position for the first two years. Although the club had been through turbulent financial times Dickie left the role of Chairman with club announcing a small profit and the club back on a reasonably sound financial footing.

Prior to the first game of season 1985/86 against fellow promoted club Clydebank, Motherwell were presented with the First Division Championship trophy and the accompanying Championship flag was unfurled. But the game itself was largely uninspiring as the teams fought out a dull 0-0 draw. But 'Well fans were shocked after the game when it was announced that two of their top players were being transferred.

1985/86

After only one game back at the top level of Scottish football the club accepted a combined offer of a reported £350000 offer from Leicester City for two key midfielders Ally Mauchlen and Gary McAllister. The money would at least ensure that the club was once again on a sound financial footing but many wondered how severely weakened the playing side of the club would be.

McLean then set about rebuilding the squad, with the first signing from the Leicester money bringing in John Reilly from Dundee United and Brian Wright signed from local rivals Hamilton Accies.

The season was a frustrating one as the team stayed in the bottom two for the whole season and setting the unenviable record of never winning away from home in the process. It took seven games before a win was secured, at home to Hearts who were to be narrowly tipped for the title by the end of the season.

As in more recent times Manager Tommy McLean was forced to rely on a number of home grown youngsters breaking into the squad, with three future regulars making their first tentative steps in the first team during 85/86, with Tom Boyd, Chris McCart, Jim Griffin and Fraser Wishart all appearing on a regular basis. New faces such as Crawford Baptie signed from Falkirk, who grabbed a double in his debut against Dundee, and Jim Clark from Kilmarnock brought some depth of experience to the squad.

One strange incident during the season was a bomb scare at the home game against Hearts in September. A call had been received in the Vice Presidents Club and the police ordered the Covered Enclosure to be evacuated. No device was found and the second half started eleven minutes late, with little effect to Motherwell performance as they went on and 2-1.

Even the Cups couldn't brighten up another wise desperate season, the League Cup did see Partick Thistle overcome in the first round, but this was followed by a 6-1 hiding at Easter Rd as Hibs went on the rampage after Motherwell had taken the lead. In the Scottish Cup it took three attempts to see off Brechin in the Third round, with the replay and a second replay played on consecutive nights. Despite seeing off Alloa in the fourth round, the Cup run was brought to an end by Dundee United when they won 1-0 at Fir Park in the Quarter Final.

As the season dragged to an end it was pretty clear that Motherwell were destined to finish in the bottom two places and facing the prospect of returning to the First Division after only one season. But there was a mood for change in the Scottish game and League reconstruction was on the cards with a proposal in place by the top flight clubs to move to a one up-one down promotion and relegation system to ease the tension provided by 20% of the League being relegated each season.

Not surprisingly the Motherwell board at the time jumped on this suggestion as they sensed an escape route and ensure Premier League survival for another year. Although there was a lot of ill feeling from other SFL clubs at the time as they felt that the proposed changes were mainly being put together to ensure that Motherwell were not relegated. Particularly as they had been saved from a similar fate by a similar re-organisation back in 1955.

It was finally agreed by the member clubs that the no one would be relegated at the end of season 1985/86 and that two clubs would be promoted from the First Division to give a top League of 12. With Motherwell ending the season in ninth and relegation looming, this latest re-structuring of the Scottish Leagues secured Premier League football for another year.

This reprieve gave the management team the breathing space they needed to build their team without having a further financially debilitating season in the First Division. It also meant that the Centenary season of 1986/87 was spent in the top flight.

There were a number of new signings to augment the existing squad as Tommy McLean slowly transformed the side into one that could compete in the Premier League survive on merit rather than rely on outside factors. Players who arrived included; Paul Smith from Raith Rovers, Gordon Mair from Lincoln City, Stevie Kirk from East Fife, John Philliben from Doncaster, Ray Farningham from Forfar and Dougie Arnott from Junior side Pollok.

Also added to the ranks were two former Old Firm Centre Backs who were brought in to ensure that the goals against tally was kept down, Tom McAdam formerly of Celtic joined from Hamilton and Craig Paterson signed up from Rangers. The were also probably more significantly brought in to give youngsters like McCart and Boyd time to develop and learn good habits from these senior pros.

To accommodate these arrivals there were two significant departures, with Graeme Forbes and Andy Dornan moving south to join Wallsall in the English Second Division. The two of them had been excellent servants to the club and proved to be reliable and consistent performers which prompted the interest from down south.

1986/87

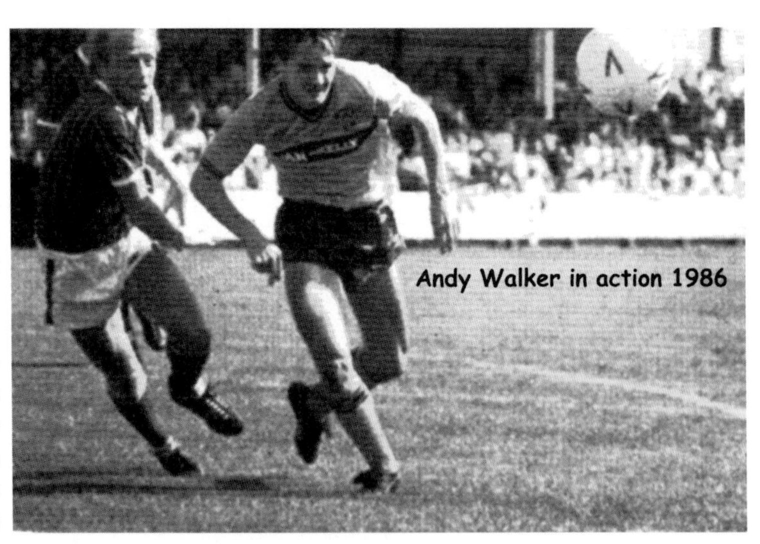
Andy Walker in action 1986

Again it was a topsy turvy season as the club strived for consistency of performance, but at least this time there was no need for League reconstruction to help keep Motherwell in the top League as they finished a comfortable eighth in the table. With possibly the most significant result of the season was a victory at Ibrox.

Tommy McLean's sides had been regularly criticised for defending deeply and in numbers when travelling to play the Old Firm in Glasgow. The game at Ibrox in November 1986 proved to be one of those days when Motherwell couldn't break out of their own half against Graeme Souness' all conquering Rangers side. That was until the 87th minute when a well placed diving header from midfielder Ray Farningham flew past Chris Woods in the home goal to give the visitors an unlikely victory.

The close on 31000 crowd were soon pouring out of the stadium as the small band of travelling 'Well fans were left to jump for joy in the dark corner of the Main Stand that they had been allocated that day.

The Cups were once again, in typical Motherwell fashion, were to provide a mix of excitement and frustration. In the League Cup a semi final place at Hampden against Celtic was the reward for seeing off Arbroath, Clydebank and Forfar in the earlier rounds.

In the semi final Celtic were two up through goals from former Fir Park favourite Brian McClair, but the 'Well side fought back and goals from Andy Walker and Paul Smith brought the sides level. Extra time was goalless which brought about a penalty shoot out but John Philliben's effort smacked off the old square cross bar at Hampden and rebounded out. This was to be the only miss of the shoot out and Celtic progressed to the Final with a 5-4 penalty victory.

The Scottish Cup saw regulation victories over Partick and local rivals Hamilton setting up a Quarter Final trip to play Hearts at Tynecastle. Motherwell took the lead through Andy Walker but were pegged back to 1-1, allowing Hearts to force a replay at Fir Park four days later. 'Well were favourites on a wild, windy night but a freak goal allowed Hearts to progress to the semi final stage of the tournament. A harmless cross from the right was palmed on to his own cross bar by 'keeper John Gardiner to allow Hearts winger John Colquhoun to latch on to the rebound to score the only goal of the game.

One of the highlights of the 1986/87 season was the visit of Liverpool to Fir Park in a match held to celebrate the Centenary of the club.

Over 10000 turned up to witness a game played in great spirit between a team of household names, including Kenny Dalglish, Allan Hansen, Ian Rush, Jan Mjolby, and a workmanlike Motherwell side.

A well known Motherwell name, Wark albeit this time it was John and not Joe, opened the scoring for Liverpool in the 24th minute following a superb pass from Dalglish. Throughout the first half Liverpool looked as though they could've repeated the scoreline from their League game on the previous Saturday when they put six past Norwich City. As Liverpool slipped back a gear Motherwell's hard graft was rewarded with an equaliser with fourteen minutes to go, when Kirk smashed the ball high into the net when an Alex Kennedy header had rebounded off the post.

This was a match fit to celebrate the Centenary of the club, given that Liverpool put out a full strength side and provided a high level of entertainment, but the home side also showed a determination not to be over run and fought hard for their equaliser.

The night was also marked by many former players returning from different eras in the club history including members of the 1952 Cup winning side and a number of the Ancell Babes also in attendance, including Ian St. John who had played for both clubs during his career.

One other significant off the field event took place during the season when the lease allowing the Fir Park Club to use the facilities under the stand came to an end. They moved their premises to the former Squash Club building in Edward Street and Motherwell could use the vacated space for offices, and additional hospitality space to generate additional income for the club.

The summer of 1987 was again a busy one for the management team as they shuffled the pack once again, young striker Andy Walker following a succession of Motherwell strikers as he joined Celtic for £375000.

Fraser Wishart v
Terry Butcher
in 1987

But joining up were Paul Kinnaird a winger from Dundee United, Striker Stevie Cowan from Hibs along with midfielder Jamie Fairlie from Clydebank.

Although the most significant signing of the summer was probably that of midfielder Bobby Russell from Rangers who brought a much need touch of class and creativity to the side. He introduced himself to the 'Well faithful with a debut goal in the first game of the season at home to St. Mirren.

1987/88

Having said that the team still found goals difficult to come by throughout the season, scoring only 37 in 44 League games, but despite this a secure eighth place finish was secured again, built on a solid defence that only lost 56 goals.

League highlights were hard to come by and it was once again left to one of the Cups to provide some excitement. For the second season in a row there was a visit to Hampden for a League Cup semi final against one of the Old Firm, this time the opposition was Rangers.

The route to the semi final had been relatively trouble free despite being drawn to play two Lanarkshire derbies in the first two rounds. The first round saw 'Well drawn at home to Airdrie where goals from Mair, Fairlie and Boyd secured a 3-1 win. An even more comfortable 4-0 victory was secured in the next round when Albion Rovers were the visitors to Fir Park, the scores this time were Kirk, Russell with two and an own goal.

A tougher tie was to follow in the Quarter Final when Hibs were drawn to visit Lanarkshire, and it took a Jamie Fairlie strike to secure a semi final berth. In the semi final an early goal from Paul Smith gave Motherwell an unlikely lead, but a mad two minutes before the break gave Rangers a half time lead. Firstly in 38 minutes Stevie Kirk headed a Davie Copper free kick past his own 'keeper, then two minutes later a poor passback allowed Fleck in to score. Rangers went on to clinch victory with another goal in the dying minutes from Mark Falco.

Sadly the Scottish Cup provided no relief from the second half of the League season, despite seeing off Kilmarnock after two games in the third round.

A trip to play Dundee at Dens Park was the reward, and a large, expectant Motherwell crowd were let down when the home side were quickly two up and their own side could offer little in return, apart from a Griffin strike that rattled the cross bar.

The season that followed saw another massive turnaround in the squad as McLean continued to strive for that blend that could push the club further up the table and restore them to their former glories. Out went Paul Smith and Ray Farningham who both joined Dunfermline, while Dave McCabe moved to Morton and Alex Kennedy joined Partick Thistle. A typical piece of Tommy McLean transfer dealing was that of Paul Kinnaird who was bought for £20000 from Dundee United, and the sold on to St. Mirren for £80000.

The significant incomer in this season was that of Colin O'Neill from Portadown of Northern Ireland. He played 19 games that season and his aggressive midfield style immediately endeared him to the 'Well fans. With the regular break through of younger players such as McCart and Boyd there were signs that the squad was beginning to take the shape the management team was looking for.

Season 1988/89 therefore kicked off with a degree of optimism but despite all that a ninth place finish was secured, that at least maintained the Premier League run. Again it was goal scoring that proved to be the problem with only 35 goals scored in 36 games, and again it was the goals against, only 44, that kept them up. The League was much tighter again as the League reconstruction started two seasons earlier was completed and the Premier League was back at 10 with only one up one down.

Contained within the seven League wins were two memorable wins over the Old Firm. Firstly a two one win over Rangers at Fir Park with the winner being an own goal by Rangers defender Richard Gough. Then a 2-1 victory at Celtic Park after being pegged back to 1-1 after Gahagan had put 'Well in front.

Goalscorer Stevie Kirk

It was then that Bobby Russell provided a magical moment when he weaved his past three or four Celtic defenders to crash the ball high into the roof of the net.

The Cups were a major disappointment as we crashed out at the second time of asking in both. The League Cup saw 'Well scrape by Airdrie by 1-0 at Broomfield before losing with an insipid performance at East End Park as the home side moved into the Quarter Finals with a 2- win. The Scottish Cup was no better, it took two games to beat Falkirk in the Third Round but again an uninspiring performance at Easter Rd against Hibs once again saw Motherwell knocked out by a two to one margin.

1989/90

Season 1989/90 was a major step forward for the club as the rebuilding process took effect. In came striker Nick Cusack from Peterborough and experienced full back George Burley from Ipswich. Out went Fraser Wishart who moved on to St. Mirren, and veteran defender Tom McAdam moved on to Airdrie as a player coach.

But the biggest transfer coup of McLean's spell as manager as Motherwell when he managed to convince Rangers winger Davie Cooper that he would be better playing regular first team football at Motherwell rather than sitting on the bench or in the reserves at Ibrox. Cooper joined up for a reported fee of the ridiculous bargain price of £50000.

Cooper's debut at Kilmarnock in the League Cup gave early glimpses of what we were about to see over the next four years. His pinpoint crosses helped new signing Nick Cusack to two goals in this game and his ability to help others find space proving a joy to watch.

As a result goals were easier to come by with 43 goals in the 36 League games seeing the winning record move to eleven for the season. This helped push the club to its highest League placing of sixth which was last achieved in 1977/78.

The Cups were major disappointments, despite beating Kilmarnock 4-1 in Cooper's debut game at Rugby Park, a trip to Love St proved to be eventful in defeat. The score line was a disappointed 1-0 defeat, but the game will be remembered for a red card incident which saw David Winnie and Dougie Arnott sent off for a bout of fisticuffs.

The other disappointment on the night was that former 'Well man Paul Kinnaird scored the winning goal despite never managing a goal in his time at Fir Park.

The highlight of the Scottish Cup was in the Third Round when Clyde were the visitors to Fir Park. The result was 7-0, and the record created that night was the goals came from seven different scorers; McCart, Cooper, Arnott, Russell, Bryce, Kirk and Gahagan. But once again a disappointing performance in the next round saw the team humbled at Tynecastle with Hearts running out 4-0 winners.

The season ended with a testimonial for one of the most popular 'Well players, John Gahagan, who had decided it was time to move on after over ten years service, when he elected to join Morton. The long time Motherwell fan signed for his favourite club in December 1989 when manager Ally McLeod had been impressed by his performance in a Junior Cup Final at Fir Park earlier that season.

His performances on the wing made him a popular player with the 'Well fans throughout his time at the club. Although he holds one record that he would surely like to see broken, he has made the most appearances from the subs bench, 93 times no less. He was awarded a testimonial year, which included a gala dinner at Motherwell Civic Centre and a benefit match against an All Star XI made up of players from the Premier League.

This brings to a point the season when all the hard work paid off, with more key signings, Dutch defender Luc Nijholt from Swiss side Old Boys of Basle, along with Scots Ian Angus from Dundee, Joe McLeod from Dundee United and Ian Ferguson from Hearts. Two of these signings were to make a major mark on club history before the season had finished. The only major departure was that of George Burley who joined Ayr United in a coaching capacity.

1990/91

Davie Cooper, seen here being presented with his Scotland "Man of the match" award

The season actually started with a minor record broken as Moscow Torpedo became the first team from foreign shores to win a game at Fir Park when they won a pre-season friendly 1-0. But this was soon forgotten as Celtic were beaten 2-0 in the League opener at Fir Park with the goals coming from Russell and Arnott. Winning three home games out of the first five saw the lofty League position of third attained but the early form was not maintained and a more consistent 7th or 8th was sustained for the bulk of the season.

The League Cup in the early part of the season was a bit of a disappointment after seeing off Morton and Clyde at home, a trip to Tannadice to play Dundee United in the quarter finals ended in a two nil defeat. But revenge was to be sweet later in the season when the two sides met in the Scottish Cup.

The League season had shown an improvement from previous seasons with relegation not really in the picture and convincing home victories over Hibs (4-1), St. Johnstone (4-1) and St. Mirren (3-1), along with a second victory of season over Celtic with a 2-1 at Celtic Park.

But it was the Scottish Cup that proved to be the highlight of the season. When the third round paired Motherwell away to holders Aberdeen at Pittodrie at the end of January it as generally felt that the Cup run would e short. As a result a large contingent of 'Well fans made the journey north thinking that this would be the only tie they would get to see.

The tie looked to have started badly with Alex McLeish forcing the ball over the line from close range but the linesman had his flag up for offside. Aberdeen continued to force the game in the first half without managing to score, mainly thanks to the efforts of the defensive trio of 'keeper Ally Maxwell and his centre backs McCart and Paterson. As the game wore on the promptings of Davie Cooperstarted to find openings and an Ian Angus header almost beat Schnelders in the home goal. Then came one of Tommy McLean's most inspired substitutions, Stevie Kirk was sent on for the tiring Ian Ferguson as Cooper lined up to take a free kick some 25 yards out. Kirk ran on and with his first touch he blasted a left foot shot wide of the despairing dive of Schnelders and the 'Well had claimed an unlikely victory.

The fourth round saw First Division Falkirk drawn to visit Fir Park, and with the visitors pushing for promotion out of that division and therefore a tight tie was in prospect. 'Well did start the game well as they went ahead when a right footed cross from Cooper was tapped in by Cusack. The Bairns fought back and were level before half time when McGivern scored after collecting a long ball over the top. The teams then traded goals in the second half with McLeod scoring for the Steelmen and Taylor scoring for Falkirk. Then it was the turn of Super Sub Kirk again to come on to scrape the ball over the line to score a third with the win being sealed late on when Cusack netted a fourth, with his second of the game.

The Quarter Final saw another First Division side picked out of the hat to travel to Fir Park, this time it was the turn of Morton. This was another hard fought tie against a First Division side with Morton probably deserving to win the tie at Fir Park. The replay was no easier even though Motherwell took the lead with a rare goal from Tom Boyd although it's debatable if he knew much about it at the time, as the ball hit him rather than the other way about! But Morton were undaunted and pushed forward for an equaliser, and as happens in Cup ties it was a former 'Well hero who equalised, Gahagan smashing home after Maxwell had beaten out a shot. The teams couldn't be separated even after extra time. Therefore it was on to penalties and five of the coolest penalties you'll ever see, taken by – Cooper, Ferguson, Kirk, Russell and O'Neill saw Motherwell through to the Semi Final, with Morton missing one of theirs. O'Neill celebrated the wining penalty by doing one of the best sambas ever seen in Greenock.

(Left) Dougie Arnott scores in the 1991 Scottish Cup semi-final versus Celtic

John Philliben celebrates 'Kirkies' goal in the semi-final

(Right) Angus, Boyd & Arnott celebrate the win - "We're in the Final"

(Left) Luc Nijholt in action versus Rangers

With St. Johnstone, Dundee United and Celtic also through it was hoped that the tie against Celtic could be avoided, but this was not to be the case and it was a trip to Hampden on a wet and windy April evening. Two classic ties, the first was a tale of Motherwell defending with Nijholt and Maxwell outstanding. But in the end they left disappointed after a Ferguson shot had rattled the bar, and what appeared a stone wall penalty denied, but nonetheless the tie ended goalless.

As usual it was believed that the chance to progress was gone as you don't get a second chance against the Old Firm were told that there were no second chances against the Old Firm! Celtic looked to have taken a first minute lead but Elliot's goal was disallowed. They did score with a scrappy Boyd own goal within two minutes to put the 'Well on the backfoot. The tie was brought back to level terms when a rare left shot from Arnott flew past Bonnar. But by half time it was 2-1 to Celtic with Rogan scoring just before the break, with no one predicting what would happen in the second half. Firstly Arnott levelled with a header from 12 yards that Bonnar only saw on the way out. Then the two goals that sealed it, a Colin O'Neill 40 yarder that was unbelievable then Kirk's sub goal that rattled the stanchion before coming out, a Cup Final place had been achieved after many years of waiting.

Before the final itself a sixth place League position had been assured, and the home League campaign was climaxed with a 3-0 win over Rangers who, if they had won, would have clinched the title that day. A thundering volley from Philliben opened the scoring, and a double by Angus made the victory the more emphatic.

Two weeks later it was another trip to Hampden to take on Dundee United who had seen off St. Johnstone in the other semi final. May 18th 1991 and it turned out to be a roller coaster of emotions for the close on 30000 Motherwell fans in the crowd that day. This was the final billed as the Family Final partly due to the Brothers Jim and Tommy McLean managing the two teams (despite their father dying early in the same week) but mainly to fact that no Old Firm team was involved and a large number of families were able to attend.

In the early minutes United looked the more likely with a Hamish French goal disallowed for offside and a Van Der Hoorn effort striking the post and bouncing clear. But a Ferguson header had Motherwell in the lead half way through the first half, and this was to be the half time score.

Things were made more difficult as Clark of United barged into Maxwell in the home goal and the 'Well stopper had to limp his way through the remainder of the game and Bowman then equalised. The cause was helped when a two goal lead was established through an O'Donnell header and an Angus drive from the edge of the box.

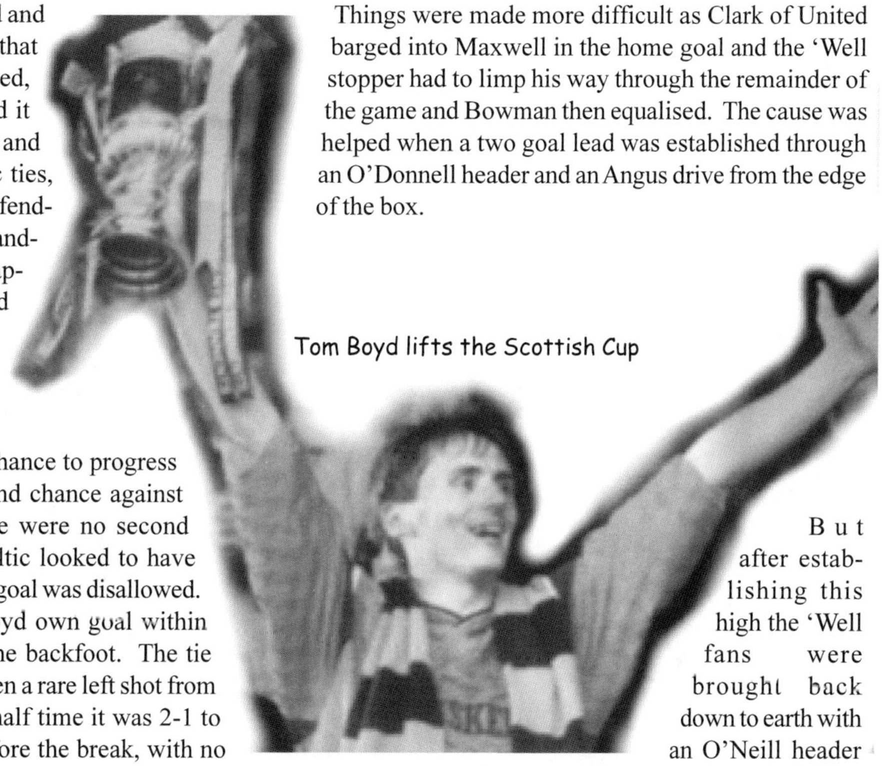

Tom Boyd lifts the Scottish Cup

But after establishing this high the 'Well fans were brought back down to earth with an O'Neill header bringing United back into the game, before suffering the heart break of a last minute equaliser when Jackson beat the onrushing Maxwell to head into an unguarded net.

Into extra time and Cup talisman Stevie Kirk has been introduced into the fray, but 30 more minutes seemed an eternity to survive with a goal 'keeper who could hardly walk. But within minutes of the restart Kirk was on hand at the back post to head past Alan Main for what proved to be the winner, despite some late scares as United pushed for the winner, with the injured 'keeper Maxwell making a heroic save in the dying seconds when he pushed a Malpas shot over the bar.

Tommy Boyd was therefore the first Motherwell to receive a major piece of silverware for over 40 years, it also ensured that the club qualified for European competition for the first time in their history and would play in the European Cup Winners Cup in 1991/92 season.

On the Sunday after the game the town turned out in its tens of thousands to see the Cup heroes parade the trophy through the streets on board an open top double-decker bus. This summed up the feeling of the Family Final from the previous days with people off all ages thronging the streets of Motherwell and Wishaw.

It was also seen as an opportunity to forget the desperate Industrial times that the town was experiencing at the time. The Cup run had taken people's minds off the closure of the massive British Steel complex at Ravenscraig, a move which saw many Motherwell fans losing their jobs.

The open top bus tour through the town

The players mentioned on a number of occasions during the Cup run that this was part of the driving force behind their determination to win the trophy.

Sadly the same eleven that picked up the trophy would never play together as a unit again, with Tommy Boyd sold to Chelsea for £800000 and Craig Paterson moved on after contract talks failed between him and the club. Goalkeeper Ally Maxwell also failed to appear again, after being frozen out for a year by manager McLean as he too refused new contract terms.

Experienced 'keeper Billy Thomson was signed from Dundee United to take over from Maxwell, and he was joined by giant Dutch 'keeper Sieb Dykstra who cam in from Roda JC in Holland. To plug the gap left by the departure of Paterson Dutch centre half Rob Maskaant also joined up, along with Dutch midfielder Bart Verheul. McLean also looked to add some experience to the midfield when he picked up former Aberdeen Cup Winners Cup winner Neil Simpson who had been released by Newcastle.

Not only had the squad change during the summer but Fir Park itself saw the first steps made on the way to complying with the Taylor Report and its requirements for 10000 all seater stadia which was introduced following the Hillsborough Disaster in Sheffield a few years earlier. The old "Shed" Terracing had plastic seats installed and was officially named as the "East Stand".

1991/92

After all the excitement generated by the Cup win it was back to reality with a trip to Brockville to take on Falkirk on the opening day of the League campaign. The Cup was paraded before the game and this seemed to inspire the home side more than it did the visitors from Lanarkshire. Falkirk took the lead through Simon Stainrod and it took a Nijholt penalty to secure a point for the Cup holders.

This was symptomatic of the start of the season when it took until the eighth game of the League season before a League win was secured when Dunfermline were beaten three nil thanks to goals from Philliben, Dolan and Russell. Things were even worse in the League Cup when a trip to Starks Park to take on Raith Rovers ended in a 4-1 defeat. This was Dykstra's first game in goal and he had no chance with the opener from McKenzie, but things appeared to be back to normal when Kirk equalised just after half time but three more goals, one from Nelson and two from Brewster, saw 'Well crash out at the first hurdle and brought everybody back to earth with a bump.

But the main focus of the early part of the season was the prospect of playing in Europe when the European Cup Winners Cup draw pulled out GKS Katowice of Poland to play Motherwell, with the first leg in Poland. Katowice were experienced campaigners who had lost narrowly to Bayer Leverkeusen the previous season, and had qualified for the Cup Winners Cup by beating Legia Warsaw 1-0 in the Polish Cup Final.

Just over 500 'Well fans travelled, by whatever manner possible to see the European debut for the club. The official party flew from Glasgow to Krakow airport, along with a number of fans paying for the privilege of filling the remainder of the plane. The journey itself was not without mishap with a lengthy wait of almost four and a half hours before take off at Glasgow, as Polish authorities had demanded a $10000 as additional landing fees due to troubles in Yugoslavia at the time. Katowice was not the glamour location that many would have hoped for but both the players and the fans made the best of the conditions in this deprived area of Europe.

Match ticket for the club's first European tie.

The game itself was a disappointment with the home side running out 2-0 winners, almost effectively putting the tie out of reach. The flow of the game was reflected in Motherwell's man of the match being new 'keeper Billy Thomson, but credit at the time was given to all players in Claret and Amber who gave their all to make the first European expedition a successful one.

One of the strangest stories of this tie were the fans who travelled over land by coach, with one coach load only seeing 30 minutes of the game and the other only seeing the last 10 minutes after being held up in roadworks in Germany after being on the road for two days, before turning to head for home.

The home tie was played two weeks later at Fir Park with over 10000 expectant 'Well fans getting behind the home side in their efforts to pull back the two goal advantage. 'Well were deservedly ahead in the first half when Kirk scored following a pass from Cooper. But Katowice looked to have put the tie out of reach early in the second half when Rzezniczek scored on the break. Two late goals helped raise expectations for a miracle as Cusack scored in 86 minutes and Kirk scored his second in injury time.

The League season remained solid rather spectacular with the League placing never dropping below seventh or eighth until a run of poor results in the last seven games which only yielded three goals in seven straight defeats and this saw the final position end up as 10th out of a League of 12.

The defence of the Scottish Cup started with a trip to Somerset Park to take on Ayr United in the Third Round. Despite taking a second half lead through Brian Martin the home side managed to come up with a deserved late equaliser when George snatched a late goal.

The replay at Fir Park was a different matter entirely as Ayr's resistance was swept aside in a terrific first half performance which saw a four goal lead established thanks to strikes from, Niholt, Arnott, Kirk and Ferguson. The fourth round threw up a trip to Ibrox to take on Rangers with optimism high that a victory could be achieved.

In the early stages of the first half this looked likely as chances were missed by Kirk and Arnott, before O'Donnell shot home for a well deserved lead. Unfortunately this type of form could not be maintained in the second half and two goals from Michaelachenko saw the defence of the Cup last only two rounds.

1992/93

Season 1992/93 saw the start, and eventually completion, of the next phase of the transformation of Fir Park when the terracing at the Southern end of the ground, backing on to Fir Park School was flattened. This was to make way for the construction of the South Stand, the opening of which was marked by a challenge match in April against Coventry which saw the home side win 2-1 with goals from Graham and Kirk.

The first competitive game played in front of the new Stand had been played some months earlier in early January when Rangers were visitors in the Scottish Cup, in a game that ended in a disappointing 2-0 defeat in the Third Round.

For long spells of the season relegation looked a real possibility with the League position bouncing between eleventh and twelfth. Part of the problem was consistency of team selection due to disappointing performances from new signings including Dutch defender Elroy Kromheer, Striker Paul Baker signed from Hartlepool and former Aberdeen midfielder Neil Simpson.

Eventually a settled back five of Nijholt, Philliben, McCart, Martin and McKinnon brought a solid base to build a side on. It took until 6th February when a goalless draw with Airdrie, who included debutant Justin Fashanu in their ranks, provided a point that lifted the League position to tenth.

It took until the second last game of the season before top flight football was secured for another year when a 2-1 win against Falkirk at Fir Park sealed the place, and consigned the visitors to relegation along with Airdrie.

This was followed by a 2-1 win at Airdrie in the lat game of the season and provided a slightly flattering final league placing of ninth.

1993/94

The League Cup early in the season proved to be a major disappointment once again despite winning the opening tie 4-2 against Clyde at Fir Park, with the highlight being a hat trick from striker Ian Ferguson. Within a week this particular cup run was over as Falkirk ran out 1-0 winners at Fir Park. Despite the disappointing nature of this season it proved to be a springboard for the following season where the same team formation and a couple of key additions saw a dramatic change in League fortunes.

Luc Nijholt decided it was time to move on to the greener pastures of the English Premiership to join newly promoted Swindon Town, and Tommy McLean moved quickly to bring in a player he had been eyeing up for some time, Rab Shannon. He also brought in cultured defender Miodrag Krivocapic. In midfield McLean took the gamble of singing Paul Lambert from St. Mirren even though it looked as though his career was drifting after winning a number of Under 21 caps in his time at Love St along with a Scottish Cup winners medal in 1987.

The new side set about the League campaign with a real vigour, starting with an exciting 2-2 draw at home to Celtic on the opening day of the season, with goals from Arnott and home grown youngster Alex Burns. After losing only one game in the first six, the sixth of which was a 2-0 home win against Hearts in which Paul Lambert made his debut, the team were sitting top of the Premier League.

Once again the League Cup campaign had been a short one, despite starting it off so well with a 6-0 win away to Ayr United at Somerset Park. The second round brought a trip to Pittodrie to take on Aberdeen, the visitors dominated much of the game but after 90 minutes the score line was level at 2-2, with Aberdeen equalising through Miller with only 11 minutes to go. Aberdeen punished the visitors by piling on the misery with three goals in extra time to run out five three winners on the night.

In the League things did hit a bit of a snag as goals proved hard to come by for a short spell, with only one game of the next five yielding any kind of goal return. On the plus side this was a two nil win at Ibrox against Rangers, with Dougie Arnott scoring both goals. But having only scored these two goals in five games the League table saw Motherwell having slipped to fourth, which was to prove the lowest League position of the season.

Things soon picked up as the backbone of the side picked itself with Dykstra commanding his six yard box, Shannon and McKinnon rampaging up and down as wing backs in a back five.

The central defensive trio of Krivocapic, McCart and Martin were almost unbeatable with a fine mix of hard tackling and an ability to push forward to pick people out and start attacks from the back.

A regular midfield of Lambert, Dolan and O'Donnell was soon in place as the new signing from St. Mirren slotted in beside the two home gown players. The missing link was in the striking department, but this space was filled with the signing of Tommy Coyne from Tranmere, as the former Celt was keen to return north after the tragic death of his wife. His partnership with 'Well favourite Dougie Arnott was to prove a profitable one over the next couple of seasons. This side was backed up well by stalwarts such as Kirk, McGrillen and Philliben.

One major change to the squad in the early part of the season was the decision of Davie Cooper to stop playing at the top level and return to his first senior club Clydebank to help extend his playing career. Many had assumed that Cooper's move to Fir Park would see him treating the move as a form of early retirement. But Cooper proved that he was bigger and better than that by not only winning a Scottish Cup winners medal with Motherwell, he also revived his Scotland career winning two more caps during his time at the club. In fact if not for injury he would have travelled with Scotland to the World Cup Finals in Italy in 1990.

The settled side went on a run of six games undefeated, climaxed with a 2-0 win against Dundee United meant a return to the top of the League. But in true Motherwell tradition this was followed by a three defeats in four including a 2-0 defeat by both Rangers and Celtic. This saw their League position drop to fourth, but with Coyne on board and getting on the score sheet for the first time in the third defeat against Hibs at Easter Rd things were about to start looking up again.

There were to be only four more defeats in the last 24 games of the season, with the third being on the last day of the season against St. Johnstone, who had proved to be a bit of a bogey side throughout that season. The season was full of games to remember, with a 2-1 win at Tannadice against Dundee United thanks to own goals from Bowman and Van Der Hoorn of the home side. A 1-1 draw at home to Aberdeen with a late equaliser thanks to another own goal, this time courtesy of Scotland centre back Alex McLeish.

There was also an outstanding win against Hibs at Easter Road, the lead was established through a Coyne penalty early in the game. The highlight was to be kept until late in the game when Motherwell broke upfield from a corner with the move ending with Miodrag Krivocapic heading home a cross from Tommy Coyne for his only goal for the club.

This was met with an ecstatic reception from the 'Well fans who had grown to respect the skilful defender during his time at the club.

The following week Rangers were defeated at Fir Park with Coyne converting another penalty and Philliben crashing home the other. This brought thoughts of a chance of catching Rangers at the top of the League into the thoughts of all connected with the club. But two defeats in the last three games saw the season end with a disappointing third place finish, but this did ensure that Motherwell had qualified for European place through their League position for the first time ever, and would play in the UEFA Cup the following season.

The Scottish Cup was not to prove as fruitful as could have been hoped for given the League form at the time. These expectations were fuelled with a 1-0 home against Celtic on the third round. The game was played in a swirling wind and could've gone either way as both teams pushed for the goal that would've won the game. The goal was to prove a sweet one for Tommy Coyne as his effort knocked out his former club.

In the early 1990's work got underway to improve and redevelop Fir Park....

...... A few years later and the work was complete

The fourth round brought a trip to Tannadice to take on Dundee United in a repeat of the 1991 Cup Final, and the game was to prove just as exciting. 'Well took the lead through Kirk after dominating the early passages of play. But the home side responded well and were in front through two goals from Craig Brewster. These goals looked to have clinched the tie particularly when Tommy Coyne missed a penalty after McGrillen had been brought down. But the visitors kept plugging away and forced a replay with an injury time equaliser when Philliben crashed a shot high into the net when the United defence had failed to cope with a corner.

The replay was played at Fir Park three weeks later, and just over 13000 were inside Fir Park that night looking for the home side to progress. The game never hit the heights of the first tie, and was settled by one goal in the second half, this time it was Motherwell who failed to clear a corner and United defender Brian Walsh was on hand to send the Tangerine hoards home happy with a powerful shot past Dykstra and 'Well were left with nothing in what was an outstanding season.

The summer of 1994 was to prove an eventful one, starting with Tommy Coyne travelling to the USA with the Republic of Ireland for the World Cup Finals. His appearance in Ireland's 1-0 win over Italy in New York made him the first ever Motherwell player to appear in a World Cup Finals tournament. He also turned out for Ireland against Mexico in Orlando and also Holland in the second stages also in Orlando, only missing out on their first round match against Norway.

In fact Coyne's thirteen caps for Ireland while playing for Motherwell saw him pass George Stevenson's record of twelve for Scotland to make him the club's most capped player.

After the defeat against Dundee United in May, which effectively handed the title to Rangers with only two games to go, stories started to appear that McLean was unsettled at Fir Park and had still not accepted a new contract that had been offered to him at the end of the previous season. After this game he told the local press that there were no issues and he was happy to work under his existing contract,It was therefore a surprise when in mid June the news broke that McLean had resigned following a disagreement with the rest of the board. He felt that the rest of the board wanted to take the club in a different direction from the one that he wanted to take it. It was harder to take for both the fans and the club when within a matter of weeks he was announced as the new manager of Hearts to replace the sacked Sandy Clark.

It was frustrating for 'Well fans at the time that the man who had re-established the club in the higher reaches of the Scottish game had decided to leave at a time when it was felt that the job was only half finished. The move was even harder to take when the move he was making was perceived as a sideways move at best.

There is no doubt that despite the ups and downs during his ten years in charge the McLean years will always be looked upon as one of the most successful periods in Motherwell's history, with a third place finish in the League and a Scottish Cup win leading to European qualification for the first time.

In the early days the style of football was not always the prettiest to watch as he concentrated on ensuring that teams would score few goals against Motherwell, making the point that if you don't lose goals you don't lost matches. But as the team matured and better players were brought in thanks to some excellent wheeling and dealing in the bottom end of the transfer market McLean could allow his teams to be more expansive and start to attack teams, both home and away. The season that McLean brought Motherwell back into the Premier League saw them score only 33 goals in 36 games, but in his last season 58 goals were scored with 45 lost compared to 66.

In his time at Fir Park McLean bought just over 60 players, with almost as many heading in the opposite direction as he searched for the blend that would make a successful side. Many of the players were bought for the short term and were moved on quickly after their specific role had been fulfilled. Two of the best examples being Tom McAdam and George Burley who were brought in at the tail end of their careers to help bring along youngsters in the side and were allowed to leave to take on coaching roles when McLean felt the youngsters were ready for top flight football.

Many also remember the headline signings of players such as Cooper, Russell and Coyne, but he also introduced a complete team of home grown players, including; Maxwell, Griffin, Boyd, McCart, Dolan, O'Donnell, McGrillen, Burns. He also left a longer legacy with a youth policy that would go on and produce players for many years to come.

It is also fair to say that McLean was also backed to the hilt by the clubs Chairman and board throughout this period. John Chapman, the Chairman, left McLean to look after the football side, but within very clear financial constraints. He understood what he had to spend in the transfer market and cleverly managed this by bringing in a player at £40000 and selling him a year or so later for £60000 which allowed him to push the quality of player each time.

When looking back on Tommy McLean's time at Motherwell many look back and wonder what if he had stayed, where could he have taken the set of players that he spent ten years so patiently putting together. As always in football we'll never know and a new chapter in the clubs history was about to be opened.

Chapter 10 McLeish and on....

When Tommy McLean decided to resign the board were left in the lurch as no obvious replacement was lined up to takeover as the manager at that time. The post was advertised and there was a flood of applications which were reported to include names such as Dutch coach Guus Hiddink, and former England International Peter Reid. But despite this the board pulled a rabbit from the hat and appointed Aberdeen and Scotland defender Alex McLeish as player/manager.

There is no doubt that McLeish was one of the most respected players of his generation, having signed for Aberdeen in 1977 after being spotted playing in his home city for Glasgow United. Ironically he was signed by former Motherwell manager Ally McLeod, but his major success came when Alex Ferguson took over at Pittodrie.

When Ferguson took over and his partnership with Willie Miller had been established the Dons dominated Scottish Football for over a decade. They won all the major, domestic honours on a regular basis and also stunned the great Real Madrid in the European Cup Winners Cup Final in Gothenburg in 1983 when they won the final 2-1, the following season they became the only Scottish side to win the European Super Cup. McLeish's partnership with Miller had played a major part in all of these triumphs.

It was no surprise in 1980 when he was finally awarded his first Scotland cap, lining up against Portugal in a 4-1 win at Hampden. He managed to accumulate 77 caps in his time with Scotland, with 48 of them alongside club team mate Willie Miller. It was therefore widely accepted that he had all the credentials to be one of Scotland's brightest coaches, particularly as he had been encouraged by his boss and mentor Alex Ferguson to take all his coaching certificates in preparation for the end of his playing days.

1994/95

McLeish arrived to face an interesting challenge as soon as he took over, as the club had no goalkeepers, with Sieb Dykstra having moved to Queen's Park Rangers in the summer and Billy Thomson deciding that the grass was greener at Ibrox for he joined up with Glasgow Rangers. The Manager quickly moved to snap up Stevie Woods from Preston for £75000, a 'keeper who had put up the shutters for Clydebank in a Cup replay against his old club Aberdeen.

He also signed veteran goalkeeper Ray Allan as cover for Woods as the club was about to make its debut in the UEFA Cup against the Faroe Islands side Havnar Boltfelag, before the Premier League season began.

The first leg was played at Fir Park and was comfortably won 3-0 with goals from Tommy Coyne, on his return from his World Cup exploits with Ireland, youngster Paul McGrillen and Stevie Kirk. The result was surely enough to make sure that the return leg would be a formality a fortnight later, given that the journey to Toftir would be an interesting one involving plane and ferry trips!

Jamie Dolan, in action here against Havnor. He is the only player to have appeared in all eight of 'Wells' European ties.

The second leg was another comfortable win, this time by four goals to one with goals coming from Billy Davies, Alex Burns and two more from Stevie Kirk. Sadly the goal that was the first that a Scottish side had conceded to a side from these remote Islands, but that didn't detract from the fact that Mothewell had moved through to the first round proper with a comfortable 7-1 aggregate. The draw for the next round brought a great deal of excitement and anticipation that one of the major sides in Europe could end up visiting Fir Park, and nobody was disappointed when the draw pulled out Bundesliga side Borussia Dortmund to face Motherwell.

This meant that every one involved at Fir Park had something to look forward to as the League season kicked off. McLeish had made no change to the side McLean had built, apart from Woods in goal who had been joined by former Clyde and Norwich 'keeper Scott Howie.

Tommy Coyne, Motherwell's only player to have played at the World Cup Finals, USA '94

The first four League games were disappointing, as if minds were on the UEFA Cup rather than points. In the run up to the games against Dortmund only one brought full points, a 1-0 victory at Rugby Park against Kilmarnock, and the League table showed Motherwell 6th in the Premier League as they headed to Germany to take play in the Westfalon Stadion for the first leg of the Cup tie.

In the early stages the home side powered forward and looked as thought they would make sure that all per-match predictions came true, But they were kept at bay by excellent defending from the back three of McCart, Philliben and Martin, with some fine saves from Woods. The longer the game stayed at 0-0 the more Motherwell got foothold in the game and created a number of chances through the midfield promptings of Davies and Lambert, and the running of Coyne and Arnott up front. One of the best chances fell to Tommy Coyne but his shot shaved the wrong side of the post.

The Germans proved their quality in the second half when a well created move allowed Moeller to shoot across Woods and high into the net. The icing was taken off the cake when, with just minutes to go, substitute Paul McGrillen was sent off. It was widely accepted that Motherwell had given the Germans a major fright and were still in the tie with the second leg to come at Fir Park two weeks later.

The League Cup also got in the way of the build up to the UEFA Cup ties, the first round seeing Clydebank beaten 3-1 at Fir Park. The second round brought local rivals Airdrie to Fir Park and they left having won 2-1 after extra time, despite a late equaliser from Chris McCart, but the Diamonds scored through Boyle in extra time to secure they represented Lanarkshire in the next round. All this had happened between August and early September, but now the waiting for the big UEFA tie was over. Although there was still time for controversy before the party left for Germany. Celtic were looking to add to their midfield and had targeted Phil O'Don-nell as the man the needed to complete that picture. Just before the Dortmund tie they came in with a bid of £1.75 million pounds, and this was just too much for the Motherwell board to turn down, even with the prospect of one of the biggest games in the club's history looming.

It was widely believed that the tie would be over in the first leg as the Germans would be too powerful for this Motherwell side as they had internationals in most positions including Riedle , Freund, Kholer and Moeller of Germany, plus Chapuisat of Switzerland.

The second leg was moved to a Wednesday afternoon kick-off to accommodate live German television coverage. It was to end as a major disappointment for all connected with Motherwell as the visitors had learned not to take the Scots lightly after the fright they had been given in the first leg. This meant that there was a far more "professional" approach to the game. The Germans ran out 2-0 winners but won no friends with their diving and play acting. The game was spoiled as a contest as the ref flashed red cards to two Motherwell players, Shannon and Arnott getting the early bath.

Despite this disappointment the fact that the side had competed with a major European side over two legs provided a huge confidence boost and from the start of October results improved as did the League position into a challenging second position.

UEFA Cup action at Fir Park versus Borussia Dortmund in 1994....and Paul Lambert who went on to win a UEFA Champions League medal with the German club.

The run of games after the Dortmund defeat started with a 1-1 draw at home to Celtic, and the team remained unbeaten until December when Aberdeen won 1-0 at Fir Park. During this run Motherwell played some of the most exciting football that many had ever seen.

The highlight for many was a home performance against Partick Thistle in late November. The game was won 3-1, but it was not the scoreline that lives in the memory but the style with which it was achieved. It was 3-0 at half time, in a forty five minute spell of almost perfect football from the men in Claret and Amber which saw the visiting Jags barely touch the ball.

The goals were scored by Coyne, Davies and Arnott, Thistle replied in the second half through Cameron, but when Watson was sent off there was only one winner. Many 'Well fans left that night believing they had witnessed the best side to play in Claret and Amber since the one that won the League in the 1930s.

Unfortunately the smiles were soon to be wiped off the faces of those fans, as the next five games only produced one win. The run included a defeat at home to fellow title challengers Rangers, and this pushed Motherwell back to third. But there was worse to come, on the 21st January at Tannadice, when the wheels completely came off the push for the title. Things looked good as Tommy Coyne gave Motherwell the lead, but Dundee United responded with six goals of their own.

Thankfully for McLeish there was the distraction of the Scottish Cup to look forward to with an away tie at Falkirk in the third round. Even this didn't go as planned, for the original game planned for the Saturday was postponed and then rearranged for the Tuesday night. The game started with the usual passion and excitement of a cup-tie at Falkirk's tight Brockville ground. As it went into the second half scoreless, the ground was plunged into darkness after only seven minutes. The floodlights had failed and despite the best attempts to restore the lighting system the game was abandoned. Thankfully when the tie was replayed in early February two Alex Burns goals were enough to secure a 2-0 win and set up a fourth round tie against Hibs at Easter Rd.

Sandwiched between the two Cup ties was a League visit from Celtic, which did produce a 1-0 victory thanks to a McKinnon penalty, after McGrillen had been fouled in the box. The Cup trip to Easter Rd was to end in disappointment as the home side won 2-0 against a 'Well side missing McCart and Coyne, and reduced to ten men when Brian Martin was sent off after protesting the second goal. It was at this stage that McLeish decided that the squad needed freshening up, despite having already added winger Andy Roddie from Aberdeen and midfielder Shaun McSkimming from Kilmarnock.

He targeted Eddie May who was playing for Falkirk and his offer of £100000 along with Stevie Kirk and Paul McGrillen was too tempting for the Bairns to resist.

This was a major disappointment for many 'Well fans, for whom Kirk had become a bit of a legend during his time at Fir Park. Thanks to his goalscoring exploits, including four in one game against St. Mirren in 1989, his goals in the winning Cup run of 1991, and his exploits in Europe where he amassed five goals, and is still Motherwell's top scorer in European competition. He was also remembered for his goalkeeping heroics in a match at Tynecastle in 1988, when he took over from Cammy Duncan who collided with a post after only two minutes. He saved a John Colquhoun penalty as he inspired a comeback from two down, to secure a draw through goals from Farningham and Paterson.

As often happens on these occasions two games later Falkirk visited Fir Park and both May and Kirk were on the scoresheet for their new clubs in a 2-2 draw. By this time the League challenge was back on, with 'Well sitting in second place and pushing Rangers for top spot. But there was to be one major piece of news that put all of this in the background for the fans one Wednesday afternoon, as they headed for a game against Hibs.

The news had broken the previous day that former 'Well winger Davie Cooper had collapsed while training kids at Clyde's Broadwood Stadium. As the players and fans headed to Easter Road, which was under reconstruction hence the afternoon kick off, it was confirmed that he had in fact passed away that morning. Given the impact that Cooper had made during his time at Fir Park this seemed to have a major impact on both players and fans and neither seemed capable of raising themselves for the game, with Hibs running out 2-0 winners.

The run-in to the end of season from then on proved to be a bit of a damp squib despite a win at Ibrox with three games to go against the eventual Champions Rangers that did keep hope flickering. In the end second spot was secured the following week with a 2-0 win over Kilmarnock at Fir Park. This was the club's highest League finish since the 1930's and apart from the poor run in December and January who knows what might have happened. The second place finish ensured that there would be European football at Fir Park for the second successive season and given that the appetite had already been whetted, this was something that everyone was looking forward to.

1995 was also the year that Fir Park celebrated its centenary after the club had moved there in 1895, when their Roman Road ground was deemed not suitable for League football. It was probably most significant that the redevelopments forced on clubs by the Taylor report had been concluded and the old ground was transformed into a 13500 all-seater stadium.

The Main Stand still gives a hint of the character of the old ground, with the unfinished portion to the southern end. But the rest of the ground would be unrecognisable to the first committee who took up Lord Hamilton's offer of land on his estate.

1995/96

The draw for the UEFA Cup preliminary round paired Motherwell with the relatively unknown Finnish side Mypa-47. As a result expectations were high when they were due to meet prior to the League season beginning, with the first leg due up at Fir Park. Prior to this match, Manager McLeish did have a bit of a striker crisis with Arnott suspended after his red card against Dortmund. He moved quickly to snap up Tottenham striker John Hendry to fill the gap.

The first game started well with Shaun McSkimming heading home a Coyne cross in only the ninth minute, and the 'Well fans sat back waiting on a deluge of goals that would almost guarantee a passage to the first round. They soon followed but unfortunately they were all at the wrong end, as the Finns capitalised on some sloppy defending to score three times to take a 3-1 lead home with them.

The next game was a League cup-tie which almost ended in disaster as Motherwell struggled to overcome Clydebank at Kilbowie Park. This time Motherwell had to come back from behind after losing a goal in only three minutes, when Robertson volleyed a shot past Howie in the 'Well goal. It took until the second half before Arnott equalised to push the tie into extra time. Poised at 1-1, and both outfield substitutes already committed, defender Mitchell Van Der Gaag picked up an injury, and this caused a deal of scurrying on the visitor's bench as substitute goalkeeper Stevie Woods scrambled for an outfield jersey to take his place. Woods filled in wide on the right of midfield, and one of his crosses almost led to a winner, but his efforts were in vain and the game was decided on a penalty shootout. Motherwell held their nerve to win the tie 4-1 on penalties, and hence move into the next round.

Before the League season got underway there was still the return leg of the Mypa UEFA cup-tie to be decided. Only about a hundred of so fans travelled to Finland, maybe reflecting the way many felt about the state of the tie, and feeling it was beyond Motherwell. Winger Andy Roddie had the ball in the net early in the first half only to be ruled offside. But the opener was only delayed until the 28th minute, when Roddie's cross allowed Burns to score. Motherwell continued to push forward and a second half goal from Dougie Arnott pulled the scores level, but the Finns were still ahead on the 'away goals rule'. The 'Well were cruelly denied the opportunity to progress when in the last minute of the tie young Lee McCulloch's shot struck a post and rebounded to safety. Once again Motherwell were knocked out of Europe on the 'away goals rule' with the damage done in the first leg at Fir Park.

Before August was finished Dundee United had been beaten 2-1 at Tannadice in the League Cup and the opening League game had finally been played with a creditable 1-1 draw at Tynecastle against Hearts, with Dougie Arnott scoring his third competitive goal of the season in only the first League game.

The start of the League campaign gave no indication of the troubles to follow. Three further games were drawn after the opening day draw at Hearts, including a 1-1 at Celtic Park. When Kilmarnock were beaten 3-0 at Fir Park at the end of September, Motherwell were still unbeaten and sitting mid-table in fifth position, and looking ready to push for a European place once again. Despite this reasonable start to the League campaign the League Cup run soon came to an end in mid-September, when Aberdeen visited Fir Park, and despite taking the lead through an Arnott goal, the Dons scored an equaliser which took the tie into extra time. During the additional period John Inglis struck a fortunate winner for the visitors and hopes of silverware were dashed again.

October started with a visit to Ibrox to take on title-chasing Rangers, and it took a late goal from Ally McCoist to give the home side a 2-1 victory, and end Motherwell's unbeaten run to the start of the season. Despite beating Aberdeen by two goals to one in the next home game, the club were about to embark on one of the worst runs in their history. The Aberdeen victory was the only one in a run of 18 games that saw the League position slump from 5th to bottom. The other major issue was an inability to score goals, with only six goals being scored in that run, culminating with a sequence of seven games without a goal. This was only ended by a Joe McLaughlin own goal at Brockville, when Falkirk were beaten 1-0 on 24th January, a full three months since the last victory against Aberdeen in October.

The Scottish Cup did not manage to provide any light relief with Aberdeen completing a cup double at Fir Park by winning 2-0. Goals from Windass and Shearer were enough for the Dons to deservedly progress to the fourth round at the expense of their hosts.

The Falkirk victory in the League proved to be one of two major turning points in the season, along with the signing of striker Willie Falconer from Celtic. The much travelled striker, who had previously seen service with Aberdeen, Sheffield United, Watford and Middlesbrough, brought a depth and experience to the front line that was definitely needed to stave off the threat of relegation.

This experience up front was allied to a tightening up of the defence which coincided with the return from injury of Dutch defender Mitchell Van Der Gaag. The week after the Brockville victory brought a trip to Ibrox which ended with a 3-2 defeat, but the confidence taken from the performance boosted the side for the run-in.

The next seven games were unbeaten, with the first four ending 1-0, and culminating in a 0-0 draw against Celtic at Fir Park. These were then followed up by more convincing wins against Partick and Hibs which resulted in a much healthier sixth place League position being attained, and ensured that the clubs in relegation trouble would be Partick Thistle and Falkirk and not Motherwell. In fact the run of victories in March earned manager Alex McLeish the title of Manager of the Month.

Having secured top flight football for another season the remaining games were a major source of disappointment as only one point was gained from four games, which saw a League placing of eighth achieved, a major disappointment given what had been attained in the two previous seasons. The year would be looked back on as unlucky given the side's inability to score goals to turn draws into wins during the middle part of the season, due in part to Tommy Coyne being missing for most of the time due to a knee injury.

1996/97

Season 1996/97 saw the first major impact of the Bosman ruling which allowed players to move between clubs at the end of their contract without a transfer free being required. In the summer of 1996 three Motherwell players had refused to sign new contracts and were looking to move on. The three were midfielder Paul Lambert, full back Rob McKinnon and striker Alex Burns. Lambert initially struggled to find a club but after a trial with German side Borussia Dortmund, whose coach Otmar Hitzfield had remembered Lambert's performance for Motherwell in the UEFA Cup only 18 months before. He secured a two year deal with the German Champions. McKinnon moved to Holland to join Twente Enschede, after giving five years of excellent service at left back.

Miodrag Krivocapic also left the club towards the end of the previous season when he decided to join Raith Rovers as a Player/Coach. The elegant defender was a fans favourite for his desire to play football at all times and his coolness under pressure.

This forced McLeish into calling up youngsters Steven McMillan, Greg Denham and Lee McCulloch into his squad on a regular basis. As often happened the League Cup ended quickly with an embarrassing defeat at home to lowly Alloa , the tie being goalless at the end of normal and extra time. Alloa progressed four-two after a penalty shoot out, the only successful marksmen being McSkimming and Martin.

The League season started with two draws against newly promoted Dundee United and Aberdeen, before a 3-0 win was secured away to Raith Rovers. Once again goalscoring was to prove a problem with only eleven being scored in the next fourteen games.

This included four at Rugby Park in a 4-2 win, which included a hat trick from Tommy Coyne. This run of games also included an excellent 2-1 win at home to Celtic, made all the more remarkable for the fact that much of the second half was played with midfielder Jamie Dolan playing in goal, after regular 'keeper Scott Howie was injured in a clash with Celtic's East German striker Andy Thom. The winner was scored by Ian Ross as he bundled the ball over the line from close range, with time running out.

But this win did not hide the fact that Motherwell were once again facing a relegation struggle, sitting ninth in the table, which would've meant becoming involved in a play-off against the team sitting second top of the First Division.

To help solve the goalscoring problems, McLeish moved to snap up another much travelled striker, just as he had done the season before, with Willie Falconer, and this time it was Owen Coyle from Dundee United. The striker joined for a reported fee of £350000 which also included the transfer of Jamie Dolan to United.

This move gave the side an immediate lift and seven points from twelve between the end of January and the start of February helped lift the League position to seventh. But the inconsistency of the season continued with another run of five games with only one point secured and only one goal scored which meant that the club was back in the play off position with only four games to go.

The first of the four was at home to relegated Raith Rovers and a much needed victory was achieved by five goals to nil, which also gave a boost to the goal difference. The following Saturday saw Dundee United visit Fir Park and the sides fought out a 1-1 draw which left Motherwell still sitting ninth in the table, and back in touch with the rest of the pack. But it still looked as though it would take a minimum of four points from six from the last two games, away to Rangers and at home to Dunfermline.

The Rangers game had been moved to the May Day Bank holiday for live TV coverage of what was meant to be the home team's celebration party for clinching their ninth successive League title, always assuming they won on the day. The Motherwell side obviously hadn't read the script, or were inspired by the party atmosphere, for they went on to win by two goals to nil. Motherwell stunned the large, expectant home crowd by taking the lead in only the eighth minute when Coyle was on hand to score.

Motherwell then played football that belied their League position as they outplayed the Champions elect, the only surprise being how long it took to seal all three points. The second goal not arriving until four minutes to go when Coyle scored his own second from the penalty spot, after Mickey Weir had been fouled by Ian Durrant.

This moved Motherwell into seventh spot moving into the last Saturday of the season. Dunfermline were the visitors in what turned out to be a very taught afternoon. Nearest rivals Hibs, who were on the same 37 points total as Motherwell but with a six goal inferior goal difference, and Kilmarnock (on 38 points) were also both at home on the last day. Hibs task looked the easier as they were to take on relegated Raith Rovers while Kilmarnock met Aberdeen.

Owen Coyle scoring in a victory over Rangers at Ibrox in the 1996/97 season... and Coyle empties Ibrox!

Motherwell took the lead through a Coyne penalty but two goals from the visitors had the 'Well fans sweating as other results at that stage meant that a play-off spot was on the cards. With fifteen minutes to go 'Well were awarded a free kick just outside the box, and centre back Mitchell Van Der Gaag fired an unstoppable shot from 25 yards to bring huge sighs of relief from the Fir Park stands as the draw ensure the safety of eighth spot.

This place was only achieved on goal difference as Hibs only managed to draw with Raith Rovers and it was thanks mainly to heavy victories over relegated this team that 'Well's Premier League survival was achieved. The combined result of 13-2 in the four games was the difference between Motherwell and their nearest rivals Hibs whose goal difference ended up six goals poorer than Motherwell's.

The Scottish Cup of 1996/97 provided its usual mixture of hope and desperation, starting out with a comfortable 2-0 win over Patick Thistle at Firhill in the third round.

The fourth round paired the team with local rivals Hamilton Accies at Fir Park, the end result of 1-1 flattering Motherwell who had been tormented by Accies winger Jose Quitongo throughout the 90 minutes. The replay at Clyde's Broadwood Stadium also proved to be a struggle, but at least ended with a 2-0 victory thanks to two goals from Owen Coyle. The prize for this victory was a trip to Tannadice to take on Dundee United, and in one of the worst performances of the season the cup run ended with a 4-1 defeat at the hands of the home side.

1997/98

At the start of the following season Alex McLeish set out to strengthen his squad further to ensure that there was to be no repeat of the last day heroics this time rounds. His first move was to secure the longer term future of Finnish International Simo Valakari who had been signed on a short term deal midway through the previous season.

He also looked to add two experienced Austrians to his squad, striker Mario Dorner who was an Austrian Under 21 and Olympic International and defender Franz

Mitchell van der Gaag scores to keep 'Well in the top flight

Resch who had won five full Caps for Austria. Both were signed from VFB Modling in Austria, who claimed that they were still registered with them and were therefore not available to play for Motherwell who had been led to believe that the players were out of contract. The contract wrangle held up the players ability to play in Friendlies, but both were available to play in the first game of the season at Dunfermline, which was won by two goals to one with both goals scored by Tommy Coyne.

Another colourful character who was added to the squad was Namibian International Eliphus Shivute, who had been released from Namibian side Eleven Arrows, but he had also had experience of playing in the lower Leagues in Germany. He was also courted by Hearts but chose Motherwell as he was looked after much better by them during his initial trial period. He immediately became a fans favourite with his strong running and desire to shoot even if both were generally a bit wayward. He did leave behind him the delight of scoring at Ibrox in a 2-2 draw, and becoming the first Namibian to score in the Premier League!

Sadly for all three of these signings their tenure at Fir Park was of short duration, with the two Austrians being released to join Darlington after only a matter of months, and Shivute dropped out of the first team half way through the season, before being finally released in October 1998.

There was some early excitement in the season when the club reached the Quarter Finals of the League Cup. In the second round, the recently created Inverness Caledonian Thistle paid their first visit to Fir Park for a competitive match. The match ended two goals apiece, with Falconer and Coyle netting for 'Well, after normal time, and forcing an extra thirty minutes. The only major incident of note in extra time was Motherwell being reduced to nine men, with Davies and Martin both seeing red as frustration built up in home ranks. The tie was won 4-1 on penalties and it was on to a home tie to Morton. This game was a more straight forward affair with an Owen Coyle hat trick being enough to secure a three-nil victory. The run came to a swift end with a trip to Celtic Park in the next round with the home side progressing by one goal to nil.

A good start to the League season with the early run of results ensured a top half place in the table. Results from the start of October until mid-December were not quite so positive with only one win in ten games ensuring that another relegation battle was back on the agenda for yet another season. That win was a surprise victory, as it was by 2-0 over Celtic - away from home - the goals coming from Coyle and Weir.

A home double-header in mid-December brought some relief as wins were secured against Dundee United and Dunfermline, therefore putting some distance between 'Well and the bottom side Hibs.

Once again another miserable run through January saw more pressure put back on the League position with only one point taken from a total of twelve available. Again a point was taken was at the hands of Celtic, this time in a one all draw at Fir Park, even though Motherwell took the lead early in the second half through ex-Celtic Willie Falconer, it was former Motherwell man Paul Lambert who hit a sensational equaliser for the visitors.

January also saw the Scottish Cup kick-off for another season, and 'Well were drawn away to Dumbarton in the third round. As has happened so many times in the club's history what should have proved an easy task turned into a major struggle. The game at Boghead was dominated by Motherwell, but spirited defending by the home side reduced the scoring opportunities to a minimum. Motherwell finally took the lead early in the second half thanks to a Shaun McSkimming goal. The Sons did push for an equaliser and were awarded a penalty with 14 minutes to go, when recent signing Rob Newman conceded a penalty from which they scored. This lifted their spirits and they looked the more likely to score, and only a wonder save from Stevie Woods in the dying minutes saw the tie head to a replay.

The replay itself saw Dumbarton dictate much of the play at Fir Park and the home side were lucky to be on level terms at half time. Even a Dougie Arnott goal in the 73rd minute couldn't settle the nerves and it took another superb save from Stevie Woods for the 'Well to progress to a fourth round tie against Rangers.

Before this tie was played there was still time for a major victory over Hibs in the relegation battle and for Alex McLeish to be linked with the Hibs managerial vacancy after they had parted company with Alex Miller. The Hibs game was played against the background that McLeish was favourite to replace Miller at Easter Road, and this factor added even more spice to what was already a crucial match.

Hibs were quickly two goals up with goals from Lavety and Cameron in the first seven minutes, but Motherwell managed to claw one back within two minutes through Dougie Arnott and were level in 23 minutes when former Hibee, Mickey Weir, scored. By half time Motherwell were a goal ahead with Garcin capitalising after Welsh's foul on the edge of the box had earned him a red card, and the Frenchman bent an unstoppable free kick high into the roof of the net. The game was sealed in the second half with two goals from McCulloch and one from Tommy Coyne.

Within days McLeish was announced as the new manager of Hibs, taking up his appointment immediately, and the Motherwell team affairs would be looked after by his assistant Andy Watson until a full time replacement was appointed.

This was hardly ideal preparation for the upcoming cup-tie against Rangers at Fir Park, nevertheless the performance on the day turned out to be one of the best of the season. 'Well took the lead in the first half when Coyne turned an Arnott cut back over the line. Rangers were level by half time when Negri was on hand to tap in the rebound after woods had saved from Albertz. It looked as though the home side had won the tie when Richard Gough headed past his own 'keeper with only 12 minutes to go. But a terrible blunder by 'Well 'keeper Stevie Woods handed the Gers a lifeline. Rather than fire a pass back into the stand he chose to try to pick out a team mate but only picked out Rangers' Gordon Durie who duly slipped the ball into the empty net.

Sadly for 'Well, the replay at Ibrox three days later was to prove a whole lot easier for the home side. They were two goals up by half time thanks to goals from Durie and Albertz and despite a brave showing by Motherwell in the second half another Albertz goal made it three-nil and the Scottish Cup was over for another year.

Brian McClair after returning to his first club

By the time Motherwell played St. Johnstone at home at the end of February, a new manager was in place and the man chosen came as a shock to Motherwell fans as well as almost everyone in the Scottish game. The man that the board appointed was the Finn, Harri Kampmann, who had been the brains behind Mypa 47's UEFA Cup win over Motherwell a couple of seasons earlier.

He was also famous as the man who discovered the legendary Finnish International player Jari Litmannen, and there were constant reports suggesting that they would team up at Fir Park; unfortunately this proved totally unfounded. To help Kampmann's introduction to the Scottish club, former 'Well favourite Jim Griffen was appointed as his assistant.

Kampmann's first game in charge against St. Johnstone was a successful one with the game being won 2-1 thanks to a double from Tommy Coyne. With ten games to go and no real threat of relegation the new manager had time to assess the squad he had inherited as he looked forward to his first full campaign. There would only be one more win in this run in, 1-0 at home to Dundee United, and a couple of draws, one secured by a goal from Kampmann's first signing Swedish Internationalist Stefan Lindquist. By the end of the season a ninth place finish had been secured but once again this was viewed as a disappointment.

Around this time John Chapman decided that the day to day running of a top flight football club was becoming too demanding and he decided to put the club up for sale.

1998/99

As the season started there was still much speculation about the ownership of the club, with local business man John Boyle being linked with the task of taking the club forward, two years since John Chapman first indicated that he wanted to sell out. He had the cash as he had just sold up his stake in the travel agency business he had helped found, Direct Holidays, a transaction that was said to have netted him £42million.

The season started with a new look to the side with many established faces moving, such as Dougie Arnott who retired, and Tommy Coyne who returned to Dundee. Harri Kampmann therefore was forced to look at re-building the side and he went about this by bringing in nine of his own men to put his own stamp on the squad. There were Scots, Brian McClair, returning from Manchester United, plus Jered Stirling, and Gregg Miller, Englishmen, Stephen Halliday and Shaun Teale, Dutchmen, Michel Doesburg, Jan Michels and Ron Matthaei, along with German Central defender Holm Kraska. These players were also joined by Jamie McGowan from St. Mirren and Finnish 'keeper Miko Kavan, which meant a much changed line-up on the opening day of the season.

Seven players made their debut in the starting line-up for the opening day game at Fir Park against St. Johnstone. The new side got off to a good start as they won the match 1-0 with a thundering free kick from one of the new men, Jered Stirling. The following Saturday saw the start of the League Cup campaign against 'Well legend Stevie Kirk's East Fife. Another 1-0 win, this time after extra time, ensured a third round berth. The third game for the new side was a trip to Ibrox in the League which ended in a 2-1 defeat and saw the debut of another striker when Finn, Kai Nyssonen, made his first appearance.

It was after this game that it was finally announced that John Boyle would be taking the club over, and he quickly revealed his big plans for the club. His intention was to invest heavily and attract the floating football supporter in the Lanarkshire area by promoting Motherwell as the 'Third Way' in Scottish football, an alternative to the 'Old Firm' and all that was associated with them. The plan was to grow the season ticket base by 1000 per year for the following three years.

His first move was to introduce a "Football for a Fiver" scheme for the first two home games under his charge.

It almost looked as though his vision was going to be fulfilled extremely quickly as 9858 turned up for the 0-0 draw with Dunfermline, and 11201 for the Dundee United game the following Sunday. This was a remarkable achievement given that the game was live on Sky TV and that the previous week there had been poor fare. This time the fans left cheering a victory as a scrambled Nyssonen goal secured a 1-0 win.

Two draws in the next two games, 1-1 at Aberdeen and 0-0 at home to Kilmarnock, looked to have got the season off to a good start as the 'Well were now sitting in third spot. But the results and League placing could not hide a couple of basic flaws; the team could not score and the football was terrible to watch. Three defeats in the next three gave Boyle and his new Chief Executive, Pat Nevin who had also joined as a player from Kilmarnock, the opportunity to remove Kampmann from the post of manager.

The man that they had their eye on was former player Billy Davies who had taken over as a youth coach at the club. This move surprised many as it was widely believed that Kampmann, odds on to be sacked as soon as Nevin and Boyle took over, would be replaced by Brian McClair, but Davies became the man to turn Motherwell into the Third Way.

The task ahead for the new man was made apparent in his first game in charge which ended in a 5-0 humiliation at St. Johnstone, with goals raining in from all directions, including an O'Boyle lob from the half way line. This led to great deal of trepidation as the team headed into the next home game against Rangers, 11 days after this debacle.

This gave Davies and Nevin the opportunity to change the squad around, as well as Nevin, the club had also snapped up prolific scorer Derek Adams from Ross County. Prior to the Rangers game the duo used their contacts to sign up Nevin's former team mate at Tranmere, Ged Brannan, and Davies' brother-in-law John Spencer on loan. The two combined for Spencer to make an instant impact by scoring the only goal in a 1-0 win.

The new men: (Top) Bill Davies was appointed manager by John Boyle, and (below) Pat Nevin who became the Chief Executive

These two games almost sum up the entire history of Motherwell with a transformation from the ridiculous to the sublime in two games.

The next major signing that surprised everybody was a replacement 'keeper for the erratic Kavan, the surprise wasn't that a replacement was needed but that the replacement would be former Rangers' legend Andy Goram who had been without a club since being released at the end of the previous season. The Fir Park front door almost had to be replaced with a revolving door as players came and went, as another side was being built in Davies' image. Out went McClair, Michels and Stirling and in came Tony Thomas a defender who had played alongside Nevin at Tranmere, and Tottenham youngster Mark Gower who joined on loan.

By mid-January there was a major panic as John Spencer's loan period from Everton came to an end, but there was a demand from all sides that the diminutive striker should be retained at all costs. Everton were also keen to have him return, but Boyle and Nevin finally came up with a package that satisfied both Everton and Spencer and he was retained for a further two years.

Not surprisingly, given this amount of change in the squad, results were never consistent, with a mixture of good wins and embarrassing defeats, such as a home 7-1 demolition to Celtic at Fir Park which was televised live on Sky. Once again the Scottish Cup looked as though it would provide much needed relief. Round three saw Goram make his debut in a 3-1 victory at home to Hearts, followed by a 2-0 win in the next round against a stubborn Stirling Albion side. The Stirling side contained a floppy haired youngster who tormented the 'Well defence, and Steven Nicholas was soon to be snapped up by Davies as one for the future. The Quarter Finals brought a home tie against St. Johnstone, but as with the League form, a surprisingly poor performance allowed the Saints to progress with a two nil victory.

As April approached Premier League football had still not been assured, but a 3-0 win over Dundee United at Tannadice helped ease the worries, in a game that marked the debut of another new signing, this time striker Don Goodman. Relegation was finally put out of everybody's mind with four games to go when Kilmarnock were beaten by one goal to nil at Rugby Park.

1999/2000

This was a pivotal season in the club's history with a change in ownership and ambition, and almost a complete change in the playing squad. It would be true to say that no real progress was made during the season as another mid-table seventh place finish was achieved. Expectations were raised for the seasons ahead given the investment prospects and the new hopes set for 'Well fans.

Davies used the summer to stregthen his squad again, this time snapping up two wingers, with Kevin Twaddle joining from Morton and Derek Townsley of Queen of the South. He also added two midfielders with his brother John arriving from Ayr United and Paul Harvey who also signed from Queen of the South.

Club chairman & owner John Boyle

The start of the season was fairly inauspicious with one win in the seven games, but with four draws also in the same spell, seven points in seven games was deemed as acceptable. Then in the middle of October Aberdeen arrived at Fir Park pointless, but no one was prepared for what was about to happen that night as one of the greatest games at Fir Park was about to unfold.

The Dons were two up in only eight minutes with goals from Dow and Winters, but 'Well pulled one back in 19 minutes through John Spencer. It was actually getting to the stage that every time either side attacked a goal was expected. There were to be another three before half time, with Aberdeen going four one up, Winters getting his second and Eoin Jess adding to the total. A Don Goodman goal in 44 minutes gave Motherwell fans hope that they could come back and take something from the game.

Sadly Aberdeen made it five-two when Winters bagged his hat trick, then Spencer scored his second to bring the lead back to only two goals. Three minutes after that Aberdeen were three in front again when Bernard scored, and it looked as though the game was well beyond Motherwell. But the 'Well side just kept plugging away and John Spencer scored his third goal for the second hat-trick of the match, and the lead was back down to two. With eleven minutes to go a Shaun Teale penalty brought the lead back to only one, and in a mad last ten minutes there were chances at both ends, but the scoreline ended up 6-5, for a night that those who were there will never forget.

Prior to the Aberdeen game the first two rounds of the League Cup had been successfully negotiated, although it took penalties at Stark's Park to see off Raith Rovers after the ninety minutes had finished 2-2. Then a rather dour struggle up at Inverness against Caledonian Thistle saw progression to the next round secured with a one-nil victory thanks to a Lee McCulloch goal.

This set up a Quarter Final tie with Dundee United a couple of months later at Tannadice.

The game against Aberdeen seemed to have a galvanising effect on the squad as they embarked on a nine game unbeaten run in the League which saw the League position rise from ninth to third and talk started regarding UEFA Cup qualification. This run included two wins over Celtic, the first by 1-0 at Celtic Park, when a Kevin Twaddle breakaway allowed 10 man 'Well to win after Shaun Teale had been red carded for a professional foul. At the end of the run was a terrific 3-2 victory at Fir Park, with goals this time from Brannan, Townsley and Goodman.

With this good League form it was hoped that the trip to Tannadice would afford a comfortable win and the chance to move to a Cup Semi Final. The team was two goals down by half time, and major changes were made at half time. This produced an an excellent fight back and was topped off by an equalising penalty from Teale. At this stage there looked to be only one winner, but United had other ideas and Thomson scored a third for the home side on the break to seal the tie.

This season the Scottish Premier League introduced a winter break, and the last game before was a thumping five-one defeat to Rangers. For the return to football, the first game planned was a Scottish cup-tie away to Arbroath. But the day of the game saw Scotland battered by gale forced winds, and given that Gayfield is on the North Sea coast it was hardly surprising that the game was abandoned at half time, considering the ball was being blown off course at every kick.

The game was finally played at the start of February and as often happens in these circumstances ended as a draw, thus forcing another game into the calendar. The tie was delayed even further when the original date set aside for the replay saw Fir Park waterlogged after torrential rain, with the game being called off at the eleventh hour. The match was finally completed almost a month after the original tie was due to be played, with Motherwell progressing to play Ayr United in the next round.

This was to prove a hectic spell in the season with games being played midweek and Saturdays through January and February. As a result there was an impact on the League results with only one win in six League games allowing Hearts to close in on third place and the coveted European qualification place. Also by the end of February the Scottish Cup run was over, a major blow as there should've been a free run to the Semi Final if Ayr United could've been overcome at Fir Park, for only Second Division Partick were between Motherwell and a trip to the Semis.

John Spencer tussles with Maurice Malpas

Being Motherwell this is not how the plan worked out at all, with Ayr United being 3-1 up by half time and withstanding strong Motherwell pressure in the second half to run out winners by four goals to three. This at least meant that as the football cliché goes, all energies could be focussed on the League campaign.

However, the results remained inconsistent, and with only five games to go it looked unlikely that Hearts could be caught in third place. Aberdeeen were beaten towards the end of April, followed by a draw with Celtic, and with Hearts stuttering there was a glimmer of hope that if all three games on the run-in yielded three points they could be caught, particularly as Hearts had to play Rangers and local rivals Hibs in their last three games. 'Well's first was successful with a 2-0 win over Hibs, then a 2-1 win at Tannadice, and with Hearts drawing with St. Johnston and losing to Rangers it meant that a win over Rangers on the final day, and a defeat for Hearts would see Motherwell clinch third place and qualify for the UEFA Cup.

The atmosphere was electric at Fir Park as the game kicked off with a real belief that it could be won, by both players and fans. Goals from Twaddle and Spencer indeed won the game two-nil, but unfortunately Hearts didn't live up to their side of the bargain as they also won, by two goals to one against Hibs, ensuring that Motherwell would have to settle for a fourth place finish only two points behind Hearts and hence miss out on Europe. This was a major disappointment, as the run of poor results after the winter break that cost the club the European place could have helped to take them to a higher level.

2000/01

The next season, 2000/01, started with only one new signing to add to the squad, with winger Stuart Elliot moving from Northern Ireland club Glentoran. Not long after the start of the season Scott Leitch joined from Swindon, the former Fir Park Boys Club player was seen as a replacement for Simo Valakari who had left to join English Premiership side Derby County.

The League season therefore started with a similar side to the one that finished the previous one on a high against Rangers. It was therefore disappointing that the first six games of the season only provided two points with only four goals, and after this sequence the side was sitting at the bottom of the table.

The League Cup had proved difficult as well, with an away trip to Queen's Park that did eventually see Motherwell win 3-0. The game was marred by the abuse thrown at some of the players and even the families of some of them sitting in the Stand from fans who let their frustration get the better of them. The next round brought a trip to East End Park to take on Dunfermline, and a much changed side tamely succumbed to a 2-0 defeat.

The first League win finally came in the seventh game with by 1-0 at Love Street against St. Mirren with Lee McCulloch providing the goal, but the next three games added three more defeats without scoring the scoring of a goal. But the table position was improved as a five game unbeaten run from mid-October to mid-November saw a major jump to seventh in the table, and hopes that another push for a European place could start.

Unfortunately the results from then until the League split at the start of January left Motherwell in ninth place, and a long way from any chance of making the European place. The first game back after the break was an awkward trip to Love St in the Scottish Cup, but despite seeing both Goodman and Strong sent off Motherwell won the tie by two goals to one, thanks to goals from McCulloch and Spencer.

League results were still inconsistent and the week before taking on Dundee United in the Scottish Cup, midfielder Ged Brannan was transferred to Wigan for a reported fee of £175000. This was to turn out to be the start of a major turn round in the squad as John Boyle looked to trim the outgoings, for the plan to increase gates by 1000 per season was falling short. This was due to a number of reasons, not least the poor performances that were served up at home, and equally an inability to attract people away from Glasgow and the attractions of Celtic and Rangers.

Two weeks after Ged Brannan had headed down the M6 to Wigan he was joined by team mates Steven McMillan and Lee McCulloch who moved for a combined fee of over £1000000 in the continuing move to reduce the wage bill. By the middle of March John Spencer had also left as he headed to the USA to play in Major League Soccer for Colorado Rapids, and Andy Goram headed to Manchester United on loan for the rest of the season. Before the end of the season Don Goodman had also joined the exodus through when he left to join Walsall.

The squad was supplemented by two African Internationals, Nigerian centre back James Okoli and Moroccan midfielder Said Chiba, who were brought in on loan for the rest of the season. Once again with all this change in the side results were inconsistent, and in the twelve games after the exodus only three were won and a disappointing eighth place League finish was the end result.

The transfer of Brannan and a host of injuries meant that Motherwell went into the second Scottish cup-tie of the season with a makeshift side, including a back three of full backs, with Corrigan and Hammell lined up alongside winger Derek Townsley who was to act as a makeshift centre half. Not surprisingly the game ended up two-nil to the visitors, but on the plus side there was the first appearances of a clutch of youngsters, such as Keith Lasley, James McFadden, Dougie Ramsay and Brian Dempsie, who were joined later in the season by Stephen Pearson.

On their way... Top, Andy Goram, and below, Don Goodman

2001/02

With so many players heading out of the club towards the end of the season, including Okoli and Chiba who were not retained after their loan spell, it was another summer that meant that the squad required a major piece of restructuring. Billy Davies picked up seven players in the summer as he built a squad that he hoped would push for that European place that everybody wanted, since John Boyle took over as Chairman.

The players coming in were goalkeeper Mark Brown who had been released by Rangers, defenders Karl Ready from Queens Park Rangers and Eddie Forrest from Airdrie, midfielders Andy Dow from Aberdeen, Steven Cosgrove from Manchester United, plus Roberto Martinez from Wigan and finally experienced striker David Kelly from Sheffield United.

Stephen McMillan, shrugs off an opponent

Five of the seven were in the starting line-up in the opening day line as they took on Dunfermline at East End Park. There was a large travelling 'Well support to welcome them as hopes were high for a successful season. The game itself was a disaster, for despite being level at half time and looking every bit as good as the Pars, the roof fell in during the second half as the home side ran out comfortable 5-2 winners.

Of the next five games four were at home and it was expected a good haul of points from these games would set the team up for the season ahead. The first two against Dundee United and Kilmarnock were drawn and the performances were a disappointment, but a new side against tricky opponents were given a second chance by the fans.

Another heavy defeat at Pittodrie, where Motherwell lost 4-2 to Aberdeen, despite scoring one of the best free kick goals seen, when Andy Dow flipped the ball over the wall for Kelly to score. The next two home games against Livingston and Hibs saw only one point gathered, only a single goal scored, and by this time the fans were getting restless as the team were settling into the wrong end of the table.

The next match was a trip along the M8 to Ibrox and a comprehensive 3-0 defeat was enough to end the reign of Billy Davies as manager. Seven games into the season, only three points had been gained, and they were stuck close to the bottom of the table. No replacement was available to take over immediately therefore coaches John Philliben and Miodrag Krivocapic were installed as caretaker managers. Their four games in charge ended with a 50% record, winning two games and losing two. One of the two defeats was an embarrassing one in the League Cup to near neighbours Aidrie who ran out 2-1 winners.

With the game looking as though it was heading to extra time the Motherwell defence struggled to deal with a long throw and midfielder Keith Lasley lashed the ball into his own net to put the seal on a miserable night.

On the plus side Krivocapic and Philliben did breathe life back into the League campaign with wins at home to Hearts and away at St. Johnnstone. Sadly this level of performance was not good enough for the popular duo to secure the job on a more permanent basis, and in a matter of days after they had been in charge for the defeat at home to Celtic, it was announced that the new management team would consist of Eric Black as manager, Terry Butcher as his assistant, along with Chris McCart as youth coach and George Adams as Head of Youth Development.

All four men came with excellent credentials for the post that they had been selected to fill. Black, like previous manager Alex McLeish, had been part of the all-conquering Aberdeen side managed by Alex Ferguson, he even managed to score the first goal in their epic Cup Winners Cup triumph over Real Madrid. He then moved to France to play for Metz, but his playing career was brought to a premature end due to a knee injury. He joined the SFA coaching staff and worked with the Under 21 team and other young sides, and his work was recognised by Celtic who took him on as one of their youth coaches. During his time there his abilities as a coach were recognised, but he left Celtic after their shambolic defeat to Inverness in the Scottish Cup.

He was out of the game for a short period until being asked to take on the Motherwell job, although he had set up a scouting agency in partnership with another player who had dropped out of top line coaching, Terry Butcher. Butcher had played all of his career at the top level, firstly in England with Bobby Robson's outstanding Ipswich side before he was attracted North of the Border to join Graeme Souness' revolution at Ibrox.

When Butcher left Rangers, after winning every major domestic trophy available, he moved south to take over as player-manager at Coventry City, but this move was unsuccessful and he was soon moving north to take over as manager at Sunderland, where once again his inexperience saw him quickly move on again. He returned north to Scotland where he had spells coaching at youth level with Raith Rovers and Dundee United before he entered into business with Eric Black.

Chris McCart had been a Motherwell stalwart from the late eighties, when he broke into the first team as a teenager and was involved as part of the Cup Winning team in 1991, before the successful team of the mid nineties. He finally left Motherwell in 1997 and after two seasons at Falkirk he joined Celtic as a youth team coach, where he was highly regarded, thus explaining why Eric Black was keen to have him as part of his team.

Before joining Motherwell, George Adams had been a little more low profile than the other members of the team but he was one of the key people, as his job was to look at how the whole youth development programme was to be run. His reputation was built on as a successful scout for Celtic, based in his native North East, where he spotted Scotland Under 21 International Shaun Maloney, the reasoning behind Eric Black saw him as the final piece in his management jigsaw.

This team then set about rebuilding the squad with a number of players coming in. The first to sign up was French defender Eric Deloumeaux, who was bought from Second Division French club Le Havre for a fee of £100,000.

The next signings were Francois Dubordeau, Yon Soloy and David Ferrere who were to complement the emergence of youngsters like Stephen Pearson and James McFadden. McFadden burst on to the scene on a regular basis at the turn of the year when he scored five goals in a run of seven games. January also saw the departure of David Kelly after a reported dust up in the dressing room following a flat performance at East End Park had made sure that the Scottish Cup run would be short, when Dunfermline ran out 3-1 winners. Ten days later it was announced that Kelly's contract had been terminated by mutual consent.

Another season of constant change ensured that results would yet again be inconsistent. As the season rolled into March another French defender was signed up when Frank Bernhard moved from Strasbourg, and moving in the other direction Paul Harvey joined up at Stenhousemuir.

Relegation was averted when St. Johnsotne were beaten at the start of March and another point taken from them in early April. One other positive piece of news from the club at this time was Stuart Elliot becoming Motherwell's most capped player when he picked up his 14th cap for Northern Ireland, playing in the defeat to Spain.

This was to be the last piece of good news for some time as John Boyle announced on 24th April decided that he would put the club up for sale and at the same time seek a court order to put the club into interim administration. The announcement secured the short term future of the club and ensured that they could continue to trade on a day to day basis. With two games left it ensured that the fixtures for the remainder of the season would be fulfilled.

The initial announcement also advised that there would be a financial restructuring of the club and that redundancies would be necessary in both playing and non-playing staff. John Boyle decided on this course of action as otherwise the club was would become insolvent, for they were haemorrhaging money and would continue to pile up heavy losses for the foreseeable future.

Reasons for the financial position were complex but in his press release at the time John Boyle said, *"Dwindling gates, loss of sponsorship, reduced corporate support and the continuing uncertainty over TV income mean that, on its present cost base, the club is not financially viable. The issue of television rights has been particularly difficult for us. The failure to agree a deal with Sky TV last year and the collapse of plans for SPL TV, which we wholeheartedly supported, were bitterly disappointing and extremely bad news for us financially. That said, even with the most optimistic estimates of any television income indicate we will receive less from TV rights than before".*

He added, *"There has been interest from potential buyers previously and hopefully there will be further interest in view of the decisions taken today. The board would look favourably on handing over control of the club to the community in some form and a number of measures to encourage such a community-based bid could be put in place".*

During the period of interim administration, the club's financial affairs would effectively be frozen with the function of the administrator to preserve the club as a going concern and to seek a new buyer.

Chief Executive Pat Nevin and Manager Eric Black did not agree with the course of action and announced that they would resign from their posts, but would help the administrator until the end of the season. Both felt that with more cash injected that the corner could be turned and that the original aims of becoming the third force could be achieved, but they were outvoted by the rest of the board. Terry Butcher was handed the position of team manager until the end of the season.

Following the announcement, a joint venture between club and fans was established to help raise funds to help the club's plight which became known as *'Well Worth Saving.*

The initial drive was to mobilise the fan base to turn up for a fundraising match against Serie A side Chievo and the final League game at Fir Park against Dundee.

Before any of this could take place Terry Butcher had to take the side down to Rugby Park for an League fixture against Kilmarnock. This was a very emotional occasion for the players were uncertain of their futures as the announcement of redundancies was planned for the early part of the following week. Supporters turned out in large numbers and gave the players a rousing welcome, which seemed to inspire the team, and they went on to outplay Kilmarnock and win by four goals to one.

On the Monday after the game, the announcement came confirming the names of the players being made redundant and another list who were being released from their contracts with immediate effect. The announcement was made by the court appointed administrator, Brian Jackson of financial consultants PKF.

The nine players made redundant were: Mark Brown, Stephen Cosgrove, Andy Dow, Eddie Forrest, Roberto Martinez, Brian Macdonald, Karl Ready, Greg Strong and Kevin Twaddle. The ten players released were: Franck Bernhard, Billy Brawley, John Fallon, David Ferrere, Liam Fleming, Steven Nicholas, Ange Oueifio, Yan Soloy, Scott Wilson and Martin Wood. Also affected were three non-playing staff who were also made redundant.

The club also offered revised contracts to four players. The club captain, Scott Leitch and Derek Adams accepted new reduced terms while Dirk Lehmann and Eric Deloumeaux were prepared to consider other offers before committing themselves to Motheerwell.

"'Well Worth Saving" held its first public meeting on 2nd May, with the original plan being that the meeting would take place in the Davie Cooper Suite within the that Stand, but due to higher numbers than anticipated the meeting had to be held in the seated area of the stand itself, with over 500 in attendance.

The main drive of the meeting was a two pronged attack, with the hastily formed committee looking for ideas to raise money while at the same time urging as many people as possible to pay through the gate at the final two home games of the season, as this money would be vital to see the club through the summer period. The meeting also introduced the idea of setting up a Supporters Trust which would look to purchase shares in the club and hopefully gain a greater influence in the running of it. Those present at the meeting were fully supportive of this idea.

Teenager James McFadden

On 7th May it was back to football matters as Chievo visited Fir Park for a Friendly match which attracted a bumper crowd that witnessed a fiery match with McFadden scoring a late equaliser for Motherwell in a one-all draw. This was followed five days later by the last home League game of the season versus Dundee. The game saw three young 'Well players making their debuts, Willie Kinniburgh, Paul Quinn and David Clarke, and following in the footsteps of David Clarkson and Shaun Fagan who had done likewise in the previous game at Kilmarnock.

Once again the players produced an emotional response and won the game by two goals to one, thanks to goals from Dirk Lehmann and Stuart Elliot. The final league position of ninth seemed almost irrelevant with the future of the club at this stage in so much doubt, but the key thing was that the club was still in the top flight and as such would be an attractive proposition for a prospective buyer.

The end of the season also coincided with the end of one of the longest running shirt sponsorship deals in Scotland when Motorola decided that they would no longer be in a position to carry on with the deal that had run from the start of the 1991/92 season. The club were fortunate that just as the new season was about to start a new sponsor was found in the shape of local DIY store 'The Untouchables' who agreed a two year deal.

The end of the season also saw the announcement that French defender Eric Deloumaux was not prepared to accept the revised terms offered by the administrator and was looking for Motherwell to honour his existing deal. As a result of this decision the player was placed on the transfer list, and in July his £50000 move to Aberdeen was concluded. Also on the move in the summer months was striker Stuart Elliot who moved to Hull City for a reported fee of £230000.

Despite the financial constraints at the club, Terry Butcher was in a position to add three players to his young squad with the acquisition of defender David Partridge from Dundee United, Algerian striker Khaled Khemas who had been with Dundee the previous season and German defender Daniel Sengewald. Also on the plus side, striker Dirk Lehmann had decided to stay on at the club with the revised terms offered to him.

2002/03

The squad that prepared for the start of season 2002/03 was probably the youngest ever that Motherwell had put together, with only eleven of the thirty five players registered being over 21. The jewel in the crown being James McFadden who was preparing for his first full season with the senior squad after picking up his initial Scotland Cap in the summer when he was used as a substitute against South Africa on a tour to Hong Kong.

As the new season loomed it was announced that two of the new signings would miss the big kick-off with Sengewald and Khemas both carrying injuries. This, along with a suspension for Derek Adams, meant that the first team of the season contained three players under 21 when they lined up at Almondvale Stadium to take on Livingston. The home side were 3-0 up just after the half time break, but the young 'Well side showed its teeth for the first time as they fought back to end up losing 3-2.

This was to prove to be only one of two defeats in the first six games that then saw Motherwell sitting fourth in the table. When Celtic were beaten 2-1 in the sixth game things looked bright, as youngsters like McFadden, Fagan, Hammell and Pearson lit up the SPL.

Stevie Woods who had seen off eight goalkeepers in his time at Fir Park

By this time Butcher had also added two more players to the squad with defender David Cowan joining from Newcastle and striker Steven Ferguson joining on loan from Tottenham Hotspur.

Little did anyone realise that this was the end of the good times and things were about to head in a disastrous downward spiral. In the next eleven League games only one solitary point was picked up as the League position slumped from fourth to twelfth.

The League Cup did not provide much light relief, the second round saw an away struggle against East Fife, although a two nil win ensure progression to the next round. The third round brought a trip to Pittodrie to take on Aberdeen, and despite a spectacular free kick goal from Derek Adams the 'Well slipped out of the tournament with a whimper as they eventually went down by three goals to one.

One of the other major disruptions to team selection was the number of suspensions that were being picked up due to silly bookings and red cards. This Culminated in a horror show at Easter Rd in November, when three players saw red at Easter Road, with Sengewald, Pearson and Partridge all getting the early bath.

Remarkably this awful run was ended with a spectacular destruction of Hearts at Fir Park as they were torn apart primarily by McFadden, Hammell and Pearson on the Motherwell left. The game was won by the unbelievable scoreline of six goals to one with McFadden and Pearson scoring three of the goals along with Adams, Corrigan and Ferguson. The remaining five games before the winter shut down brought only one defeat and included another win against the Old Firm, this time one nil over Rangers.

These results meant that the League position looked a deal better as it had improved to eleventh and out of the relegation position. The winter break also coincided with the opening of the transfer window and not surprisingly there were a number of stories linking clubs with a move for James McFadden, including confirmed bids from Preston and Everton. Both were rejected by the club as not matching their valuation of the player, and this was followed by a warning to all clubs that there would be no "fire sale" of young players as the club was breaking even financially.

Confirmed moves did take place with Steven Ferguson's loan period ending and the player returning to White Hart Lane. The first player snapped up was former Falkirk striker Steven Craig after a couple of appearances in the Under 21 side, who was signed as cover for the injured Dirk Lehmann. Two more players were signed on loan just as the transfer window closed, with Nottingham Forest defender Tony Vaughan and Newcastle winger Richard Offiong moving north.

In February there were also changes behind the scenes, with George Adams being lured to Ibrox, Terry Butcher beefed up his back room staff by appointing former Dundee United man Maurice Malpas as his assistant manager with Chris McCart being promoted to the position of Head of Youth Development.

Two wins at home to Hibs and Dunfermline briefly lifted the club off the bottom of the table to eleventh. But another dramatic decline in results saw a further run of 10 games without a win, ensuring a 12th place finish. It looked for a long time as though this could mean relegation to the First Division.

Falkirk were sitting top of the First Division and had asked the SPL board at their March board meeting to consider a possible ground share with Airdrie to give them time to come up with a new 10000 seater stadium of their own to replace the decrepit Brockville. The board decided that Falkirk needed more time to prepare their case and prove that they would have first call on the stadium over Airdrie for their SPL fixtures.

This distraction did not help during the ten game run without a win, but everyone breathed a huge sigh of relief when the day before the last round of fixtures it was announced that Falkirk's appeal had been rejected and that Motherwell would indeed be a Premier League side in the 2003/04 season. This seemed to ease all the pressure from the Motherwell players and the following day they had a field day against UEFA Cup qualifiers Livingston and thrashed them 6-2, including a magnificent hat trick from McFadden.

The sighs of relief that had been breathed prior to the Livingston game were to be shortlived as Falkirk announced that they would appeal the decision, and the SPL said that the meeting to hear if the appeal could be heard would be held on 19th June. On that night it was decided that Falkirk could indeed appeal to the full SPL board and that it would be heard by 25th June, only a matter of weeks before the new season started.

This delay in the appeal had started to pay havoc with the fixture lists, with the Scottish Football League releasing their fixtures with Club X listed rather than Motherwell or Falkirk. It also meant that Motherwell were drawn in the first round of the Bell's Challenge Cup, a competition for those clubs playing outside the SPL. Even when the 25th of June did come round there was no decision made and everyone was left to sweat for another 24 hours before it was announced that Falkirk's appeal had been rejected and that Motherwell would indeed line-up in the SPL once again the following season.

Despite the threat of relegation, the players seemed to enjoy the distraction of the Scottish Cup and embarked on a good run. The third round draw brought a visit to Rugby Park on the weekend after the SPL winter break, and on a very wet day a James McFadden penalty was enough to see Motherwell progress to the fourth round.

The next round brought about a trip to near neighbours Clyde at Broadwood Stadium. Despite being an SPL side, Motherwell were not the favourites as Clyde had shown excellent home form in the First Division and the tie was one that was predicted by many pundits to be the shock of the round. Two individual goals from McFadden were to prove the difference between the teams as the Premier League side progressed with a degree of comfort. The Quarter Finals brought about yet another away tie, this time to the South West of the country to visit Stair Park in Stranraer. After a shaky start it took an unfortunate own goal by the home side to settle the 'Well's nerves, who in the end ran out comfortable four nil winners.

As always seems to be the way Motherwell were drawn to play Rangers at Hampden in the Semi Final. They went into the game as underdogs but not overawed, having beaten Rangers earlier in the season. The game got off to the worst possible start with Konterman opening the scoring in the second minute. But this only seemed to fire up the Motherwell players and they pushed forward and looked to take the game to Rangers at every opportunity. Goals from Craig and McFadden gave the underdogs the lead at half time and provided optimism to all the fans wearing Claret and Amber.

Rangers started the second half the stronger side and were quickly four goals to two in front, from Mols, Amoruso and an own goal. This looked to have put the tie out of reach, but the young 'Well side just kept going and a late goal from Adams gave hopes of a replay, but only for a few seconds, for it wasn't to be.

The season had been one of the most ill-disciplined in the clubs history with eleven red cards being shown along with 99 yellows. As a result the SFA had warned the club during the season that if there was no improvement a financial penalty would be imposed on the club. Not surprisingly on the eve of the new season it was reported that the SFA had imposed a £10000 fine as well as warning the club that it had to show an improvement in discipline.

In the close season Terry Butcher took the opportunity to re-shape his squad for the coming season, when he initially released Dougie Ramsey, Dirk Lehmann, David Clarke, Darren Jack and Iain Russell. Richard Offiong and Tony Vaughan also returned to their clubs south of the border. Stevie Woods decided after nine years it was time to move on, and the other 'keeper, Francois Dubordeau, was also not offered a new contract.

Left back Steven Hammell shields the ball

Butcher also managed to secure the signature of three experienced players that he believed would help his young squad. He managed to prise former 'Well men Stephen Craigan and Alex Burns away from Partick Thistle after the duo had rejected terms at Firhill. He also snapped up experienced goalkeeper Gordon Marshall who had been released by Kilmarnock at the end of the previous season.

2003/04

The season started with constant rumours surrounding the future of young stars James McFadden and Stephen Pearson, as a new story seemed to appear in the press every day. Pearson was the subject of a bid from English Premiership side Leicester City but this was rejected as it did not come close to the club's valuation of the player.

Supporters hopes for the season were pegged at survival in the SPL, coming out of administration and being able to focus on the longer term future.

The start to the season was disappointing with McFadden missing the first two games through injury and Adams absent as well due to suspension. The games, at home to Dundee and away at Livingston, were lost without a goal being scored by the 'Well.

McFadden and Adams returned for the second home game of the season, against Kilmarnock, and despite dominating for long spells it took a late goal from Pearson to produce the first win of the season. The following week against Partick, it was billed as a grudge match with Craigan and Burns lining up against their former side. It was a hard fought affair which ended two all and included two stunning goals from James McFadden.

As it turned out these were to be his parting gifts to the 'Well faithful, with the end of August seeing the transfer window close until January. Everton moved in with a bid for the young starlet, and to the relief of 'Well fans the initial bid was rejected, but Everton were not to be put off and just as the deadline loomed they came back in with a £1.25 million offer that Motherwell could not refuse. Terry Butcher was only allowed to bring in one player to add to the squad following McFadden's departure, with Jason Dair coming in from Dunfermline after previous spells with Raith Rovers and Millwall.

Suprisingly, after the departure of McFadden, there was a significant improvement in form with only one defeat in six games, a 3-0 reverse at Celtic Park. The game after McFadden left there was a trip to Easter Rd to take on Hibs, and Motherwell produced one of their finest away performances for many a year and returned with a well deserved two nil win.

The excellent run of form was made easier with Terry Butcher having no difficult selection decisions to make, with the team remaining the same for 10 games in a row. This was helped by a marked improvement in on field discipline with no red cards (although Pearson had been sent of against Thistle, the red card was rescinded on appeal) and a reduced number of yellow ones.

The only setback was a defeat in the League Cup away to Second Division Forfar Atheltic. Despite making a good start with a goal from Craig in the fourth minute, Forfar were level by half time. Early in the second half the home side scored two quick goals to set the Premier League side on their heels. But this 'Well side rolled up their sleeves and clawed their way back into the tie through goals from Lasley and Pearson. But the tie was eventually forced into extra time and then into a penalty shoot-out. Forfar won the shoot out four-two, with only Dair and Wright being on target for 'Well.

Phil O'Donnell returned after over a decade away

The excellent run of results ended in a 2-0 defeat at Rugby Park against Kilmarnock, this signalled a run of five games without scoring a goal. This sequence was ended with a fine three-one win at Fir Park over Dundee United, a game which saw David Clarkson score a second half hat trick to seal the win. This maintained a top six spot at the half way stage, and despite modest early season hopes of finishing eleventh, there was now talk of qualifying for a UEFA Cup slot.

During the run up to the transfer window opening in January there was once again a constant stream of rumours that Steven Pearson had already joined Celtic. These were strenuously denied by the club, but sadly he moved in early January when this club came in with an offer of £350000. There were also three players coming into the club in the same period, as Butcher tried to add some depth and experience. His first move was to offer terms to Cup winning hero Phil O'Donnell who had been without a club since being released by Sheffield Wednesday at the end of the previous season. He had been training with the club for the previous two months and the manager saw enough to offer him an 18 month deal.

Also joining up in January were experienced defender Gary Bollan, who had just been released by Dundee United, and Australian Under 20 skipper, Scott McDonald, the 20 year old striker having just been released by Wimbledon after a previous spell at Southampton.

The Scottish Cup draw had been relatively kind with an away trip to First Division promotion challengers St. Johnstone. This resulted in a comfortable 3-0 win, with two goals from Clarkson and one from Australian debutant Scott McDonald. The fourth round produced a home tie against another promotion challenger, Queen of the South, and again this looked like a formality when three first half goals seemed to have put the tie beyond the visitors. But they rallied in the second half to score two themselves and give Motherwell a fright, but in the end the three-two win saw Motherwell through to the Quarter Finals for the second year in a row.

By the time of the Quarter Final, against yet another promotion challenger, Inverness Caledonian Thistle, came round it was in a spell of four games in a row at home that looked as though they would define the season. The games against Kilmarnock, Aberdeen and Partick were all won without losing a goal, and this cemented a fifth place position in the table and hence made a final top six place more likely.

The cup-tie was to prove a disappointment as Inverness progressed by an early Barry Wilson effort from 40 yards. Motherwell struggled to cope with Inverness as they sat in to defend the early goal, and they stumbled out of the competition.

League form did stutter a bit after this, although a 1-1 draw at Celtic Park was the first points that the Champions elect had dropped at home during the season. The month of March did not produce a League win as along with that against Celtic, a further draw was ground out at Easter Road versus Hibs, followed by a defeat to Dundee United at Tannadice. This meant that everyone was left waiting tentatively to see whether a top six place could be achieved. There were nine more games to play, the first four were at home to the teams sitting 2nd (Rangers), 3rd (Hearts) and 4th (Dunfermline), plus a trip to take on Aberdeen at Pittodrie.

These games were negotiated well with a defeat against Rangers, a draw with Hearts and two wins over Dunfermline and Aberdeen, and a top six finish was secured for the first time since the SPL had introduced the League split.

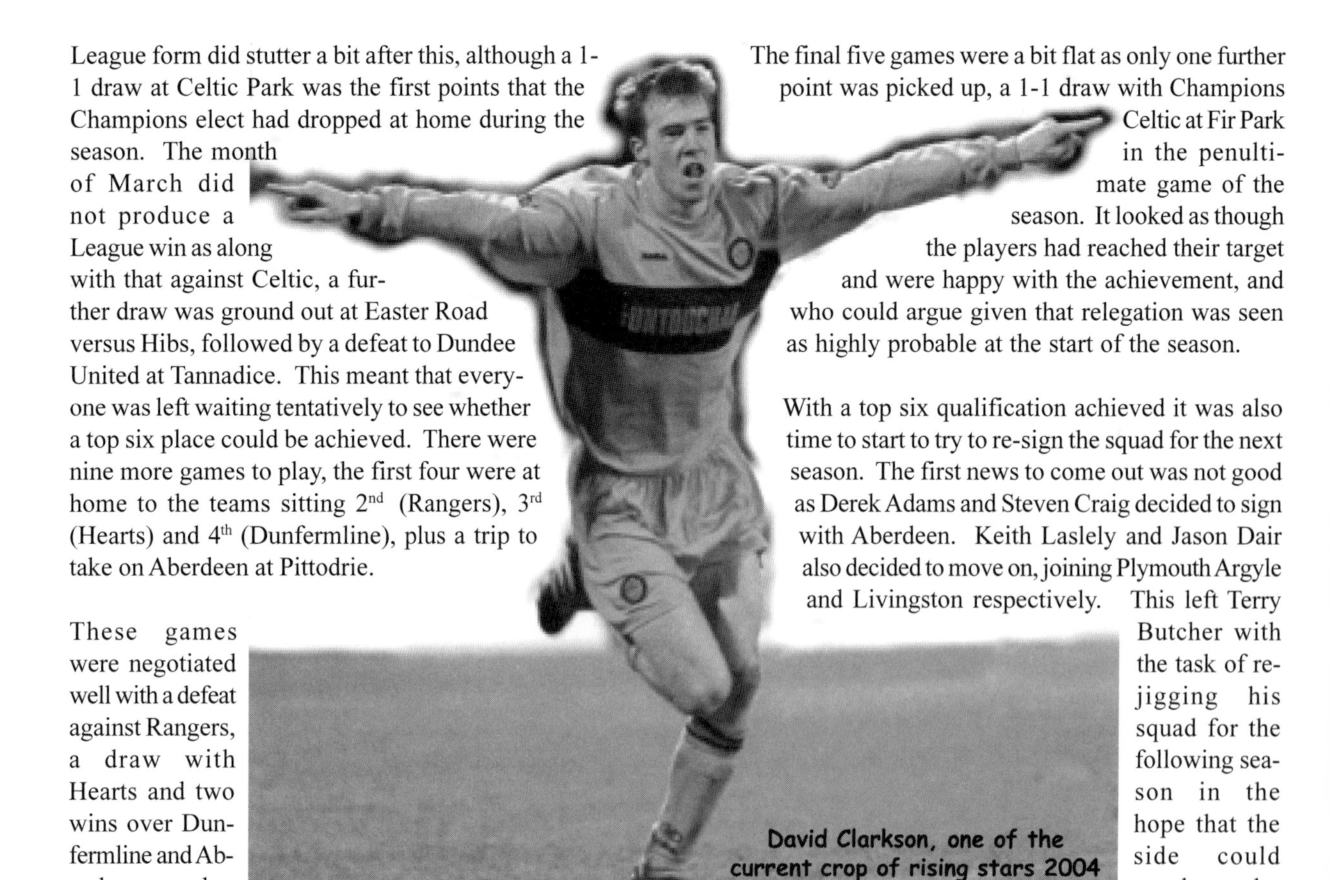

David Clarkson, one of the current crop of rising stars 2004

The final five games were a bit flat as only one further point was picked up, a 1-1 draw with Champions Celtic at Fir Park in the penultimate game of the season. It looked as though the players had reached their target and were happy with the achievement, and who could argue given that relegation was seen as highly probable at the start of the season.

With a top six qualification achieved it was also time to start to try to re-sign the squad for the next season. The first news to come out was not good as Derek Adams and Steven Craig decided to sign with Aberdeen. Keith Laslely and Jason Dair also decided to move on, joining Plymouth Argyle and Livingston respectively. This left Terry Butcher with the task of re-jigging his squad for the following season in the hope that the side could emulate the top six finish.

In Conclusion

Throughout the 2003/04 season administrator Bryan Jackson had been working to come up with a deal to pay a dividend to the creditors that would bring the club out of interim administration. At a press conference at Fir Park, on 17th September, administrator Bryan Jackson said that improved financial stability and the sale of James McFadden to Everton were the primary reasons the club could now begin the process of coming out of administration. It was also made possible by Chairman John Boyle being prepared to write off the debt that he was owed. He also announced at the same time that he would be standing down as Chairman, and that his share-holding was still up for sale, and that if a creditable buyer came forward with the interests of Motherwell at heart he would be happy to sell.

In a statement the day after the announcement, the outgoing Chairman said, *"There has been a lot talked about the pain of the players but it has been extremely painful to me. To lose and write off £10million, I can assure you, is not a pleasant experience by any stretch of the imagination. There are things that, perhaps, one shouldn't have done but I do not regret getting involved in the football club.*

This is my home town and I wanted to support Motherwell. I will continue to support Motherwell and I don't look over my shoulder too much. I would rather have not lost £10m but I made the decision, nobody pushed me.

"There were mistakes and I acknowledge my part in those mistakes, but we were investing at a time that was cataclysmic for football, where the whole environment changed within a two-year period. "I was ambitious for the club and some of those ambitions have not come to fruition, I can't deny or dispute that. But I hope I will be perceived as giving it my best shot, which I definitely did, and as having the best interests of the club at heart. Obviously we had a very difficult and painful task of bringing the club into administration. It had to be done to ensure the long-term survival of the club. It has been a very difficult 17 months and there have been victims of the administration - and we sympathise with all of them. However, the objective that I had, and the board had, was to ensure the long-term survival of Motherwell.

"The vast substantive part of my debt to the club will be eliminated. I will not take part in any of the proceeds of

the distribution which is perhaps going to take place in January. The vast majority of the money I am owed will have been written off. The club will not be saddled with any substantial long-term debt."

At the club's AGM on 27th October Boyle officially stood down and local Architect Bill Dickie took over for his third stint as Chairman of the club. It was also confirmed that Martin Rose, Chairman of the newly formed Motherwell Supporters Trust, had been asked to join the board and that he was delighted to accept.

Towards the end of January there was as slight hiccup as the court of session directed that the Inland Revenue and HM Customs and Excise were preferred creditors who should be paid ahead of ordinary creditors in the proposal that was being prepared by the administrators and directors of the club. However, a spokesman for the club said, *"This decision will not delay Motherwell emerging from interim administration. That will happen before the end of the season.*

"We had to wait until we received the decision from the Court of Session on the status of the Inland Revenue and Customs and Excise before we could put a proposal to creditors but the administrator and directors are now exploring every way to maximise the dividend to creditors as a matter of urgency."

It was in early March that Bryan Jackson announced that he had sent a proposed settlement to creditors of the club. He and the directors of the club had agreed the proposal, and a meeting of creditors was called for March 17 when it would be explained in further detail and voted upon. The meeting in Glasgow on that date actually saw the creditors vote unanimously to accept what turned out to be an offer of 20p in the £1.

Bryan Jackson, the administrator, said after the meeting: *"We have been able to pay creditors a dividend, which other clubs in administration have not been in a position to do.*

Manager Terry Butcher

"We have only been able to pay this level of dividend because the major creditor, John Boyle, agreed to waive his rights to this distribution of funds. We had expected to pay a dividend of 15p in the £ but were able to increase it to 20p, because the Inland Revenue has agreed to be treated as an ordinary creditor, something the club has been fighting hard for, for sometime."

Then finally, on 20th April 2004, The Court of Session in Edinburgh approved an application from the club to discharge its administrators and, in accordance with insolvency legislation, resume trading normally as a limited company. Motherwell chairman Bill Dickie said: *"We are delighted and relieved to be passing this very important milestone for the club.*

"The last two years have been very hard for everyone involved with the club but we are now looking forward with one of the best young teams in Scotland"

John Boyle, Motherwell's majority shareholder, added: *"I would like to thank the administrators for the valuable assistance they have given the club. Motherwell is emerging from administration on a sound financial footing and can meet the challenges ahead with confidence."*

Bryan Jackson, the administrator appointed by the Court of Session, said: *"Over the last two years it has been a privilege to work with people at a club who were totally committed to ensuring the survival of the club and always had its interests at heart.*

"The directors have done a remarkable job in very difficult circumstances and working together we have proved that a period of administration can be run successfully. The club can look to the future in a very positive frame of mind. I would also like to thank the staff, players and in particular the manager Terry Butcher for their help."

The Left Backs

Throughout its history Motherwell has had a fine tradition of producing outstanding left backs who have represented their club, and on many occasions their country, with great distinction. Many of them have been "home grown" and brought through the ranks, or plucked from lower level football and have consequently saved the club a great deal of money over the years.

From 1931 to 1984, a period of 53 years, there were just three players who filled the position for almost 40 of those years. Starting with Welshman **Ben Ellis** who was the left back from 1931 to the start of the War in 1938, and therefore played in this position in the Championship winning side of 1931/32.

Ellis was signed from Northern Ireland side Bangor in 1930 and quickly fitted into Sailor Hunter's side as he tried to find the eleven that would finally break the Old Firm monopoly of the Scottish League title. He played a major role in the side that did break that monopoly in 1931/32 as he played throughout that season and was an inspiration to his team mates.

While he did help bring the League championship to Motherwell he never quite managed to bring the Scottish Cup home despite playing in two finals in 1933 and 1939. He did capture one other major honour, but not in football, as he won the Scottish Professional Snooker Championship in 1941. Ellis' was honoured for his country when he made six appearances for his native Wales between 1932 and 1937, with three of them coming against England and the other trio against his adopted homeland Scotland. On retiring from the playing side Ellis maintained his ties with the club as groundsman and then as trainer before setting up his own business in the town.

Ben was followed by **Archie "Baldy" Shaw** who took over following the Second World War, after signing for the club in 1942, and filled the position until 1957, when he moved on after winning Cup winners medals in both the Scottish and the League Cups.

Archie was a local lad who was born in Netherton, and graduated through local football, starting our in Boys brigade football with Craigneuk Belhaven's Co, before moving to Motherwell Miners and finally at Wishaw Juniors, where the story goes he *was "kept under wraps"* until Ben Ellis decided to call it a day. He joined Motherwell after playing only seventeen games for the Juniors before taking his place at left back alongside Willie Kilmarnock in a summer Cup Semi Final against Celtic. This started the longest running full back partnership in the club's history.

Shaw is always described as being a strong tackling full back whose timing in the tackle was accomplished to perfection. He was a two-footed player who was also comfortable in the air and was always committed to do his best for his club.

In the early fifties he was part of the successful Cup winning sides that brought both the League Cup and Scottish Cup back to Fir Park in 1951 and 1952. He was very often the driving force behind the side as he raised spirits if at anytime he saw his team mates flagging.

Having won these two major trophies you would have thought that these would be the highlights of Baldy's Motherwell career, but they were matched in his last season when he captained the reserves to a win in the 2nd XI Cup with a victory over Celtic in the final at Celtic Park. This was after he had scored a rare goal in the Semi win over Hearts; his cross aimed for Humphries sailed high over the 'keeper and dropped into the net!

Baldy was another in a long line of outstanding Motherwell players who never managed to win a full Scotland cap, having to settle for a couple of appearances for the Scottish League side against the League of Ireland and the Irish League, the latter saw him line-up against future Northern Ireland manager Billy Bingham. Shaw found it hard to cut his links with the club and served in a number of roles for many later years , among them he acted as coach, groundsman and finally in a fund raising-role with the FPDA.

The next in line, after a short gap when the position was never really filled by any long-serving regular, was **Joe Wark** who joined up in 1968 before retiring in 1984 after receiving two benefit matches from the club.

Joe was born in Glasgow on 9th October 1947 and signed for Motherwell from Ayrshire Junior side Irvine Vics in 1968, making his debut in a pre-season friendly that year against Tranmere Rovers. It was to prove a strange debut, for after only three minutes 'keeper Keith MacRae was injured and Joe filled in for him for the remainder of the game during which he kept a clean sheet in a 2-0 win. In his first season, Joe actually played as an inside forward, when he helped Motherwell surge to the Second Division title in the 1968/69 season. During that year, he managed to score eight goals, including a hat trick in a four one win over Montrose.

On the 'Wells return to the First Division he moved to the left back berth and immediately became a fans favourite as he showed an impeccable timing in the tackle, and. He also appeared to have "rubber legs", with his ability to hook the ball away from attackers when it looked as though they had evaded him.

In the changing role as a full back, Joe also proved useful as an overlapping marauder down the flank with the ability to deliver a perfect ball into the box. At the other end he was calmness personified in his own box, where on numerous occasions he would calmly kill the ball on his chest to allow his goalkeeper the vital seconds he needed to pick the it up and clear any danger.

The Second Division winners medal that Joe won in 1968/69 was the only actual "winners" medal that he picked up in his career at Motherwell, although he was part of a promotion winning season, in 1981/82, when once again he played in the team that ran away with the title. In his time at the club he did reach two Scottish Cup Semi Finals, but both were lost to Airdrie in 1975 and the following year to Rangers.

The best League campaign that Joe was part of was the first season of the newly former Premier League in 1975/76, when the side finished fourth in the table and narrowly missed out on a UEFA Cup slot for the first time.

Something of a travesty for Joe was the fact that he was considered the best uncapped left back of all time. Wark's career coincided with that of two of Scotland's legendary full backs, Sandy Jardine of Rangers and Danny McGrain of Celtic, and as a result he never got a look in at full International level. He did manage one consolation appearance for the Scottish League in a fixture against the Football League in 1976.

Only two players in the history of the club have played more games for Motherwell than Joe Wark and that was the pair in the legendary partnership of George Stevenson and Bobby Ferrier. Joe made 469 appearances in League games for the club, which is still a post War record that will be difficult to break, given the amount of movement in the game these days.

To mark this level of loyalty Joe was given the honour of having two benefit matches arranged for him. The first in 1978 marked his tenth year at the club, and was played pre-season against West Bromwich Albion, who included Laurie Cunnigham and Cyrille Regis in their ranks. They proved far too strong for the 'Well and ran out 8-1 winners to take the edge off Joe's night. His second benefit match was held on a frosty January Sunday in 1985 to mark his retirement, and this time a Motherwell select lost narrowly by 2-1 against an Old Firm select, with Scotland legend Joe Jordan scoring as a guest for Motherwell.

The more recent generations have also been lucky to see four fine left backs hold up the tradition, although not with the same longevity.

Tom Boyd joined the club in 1983 as a YTS Trainee before establishing himself as first choice left back in the late 80's, where he linked up with the legendary Davie Cooper. Boyd started his career at Fir Park as a central defender but his pace and ability to get up and down the pitch saw him moved to left back.

Boyd captained the side to the Scottish Cup success of 1991 in his last game, before an £800000 move to Chelsea, where unfortunately he never really settled. It was no surprise that he quickly returned to Scotland, and played for Celtic, where he won the bulk of his 72 caps for Scotland to be "enshrined" in the SFA's Hall of Fame.

It took Tommy McLean just six months to find the ideal replacement for Boyd when he snapped up Rob McKinnon from English side Hartlepool in January 1992. McKinnon quickly became a favourite with the fans, thanks to his strong tacking and impressive overlapping runs in the Motherwell side that finished third and second in the mid-1990's. After tasting European football with Motherwell, McKinnon decide to move on and in the summer of 1996 he moved to Twente Enchede of Holland on a Bosman type free transfer.

McKinnon won Scotland honours during his time at Motherwell when he picked up a total of three caps, two on a Japanese tour against Japan and Finland in 1995, after making his debut the previous year against Malta.

Hot on the heels of McKinnon was another home grown talent in Stephen McMillan who served in the side from 1996 through to 2001 before making a big money move to Wigan Athetic, along with Lee McCulloch. During his time at Motherwell McMillan picked up four Scotland under 21 caps thanks to his impressive performances.

One of the reasons that McMillan was allowed to leave for Wigan was the form of another up and coming youngster, Steven Hammell, who took over in 2000 and is still filling the position to date. Hammell came into the side as an eighteen year, and as has been the way over the years, he quickly made the number three jersey his, and is continuing the club's fine tradition of filling in this position.

Hammell played a major role for Scotland Under 21s, scoring in a sensational comeback in a European Qualifying match against Lithuania, when the Scots come back from three down to draw and progress to a play-off for the finals. Sadly they lost this game and Hammell can only hope he does not suffer the same fate as some of his predecessors, and never make the jump to senior level.

Motherwell Managers

In this section we pay a brief tribute (or not in some cases!) to the men who have been in charge of team selection throughout the history of the club. Although, in the early days, the team was picked by committee and not by a single individual, until John "Sailor" Hunter changed all that......................................

John "Sailor" Hunter – April 1911 to May 1946. After playing at Abercorn, Liverpool, Portsmouth and Dundee he joined Clyde as an amateur to start his coaching career before being enticed to Motherwell, initially as Secretary/Manager. During his time in charge he built a team that would be one of the best ever in Scotland, culminating with a League win in 1931/32. Even when he gave up the position of manager he continued as club secretary!

George Stevenson – April 1946 – May 1955. Stevenson had been a mainstay of the League winning side having joined Motherwell in the twenties. He took over when Hunter decided to concentrate on the role of secretary full time. He managed to achieve something his mentor had never quite achieved when he won the League and Scottish Cups in successive seasons.

Bobby Ancell – July 1955 – June 1965. Ancell moved from Dunfermline to take over Motherwell in 1955 and he immediately took on the task of rebuilding the side, using mainly home grown players, with the side becoming known as the 'Ancell Babes'. Despite playing some of the best football of any Motherwell side they never managed to win a major trophy.

Bobby Howitt – March 1965 – July 1973. A former Stoke player who moved from his coaching role there to take over from Ancell. He was in charge when the side was relegated in 1967/68, only to bounce back as Second Division champions the following season.

Ian St John – June 1973 – Sept 1974. A popular choice to take over when Howitt resigned, being a former Ancell Babe and local hero. He did galvanise the side and had crowds returning to Fir Park before being lured south with the promise of money to spend at Portsmouth.

Willie McLean – Sept 1974 – Dec 1977. He joined after a spell managing Queen of the South, and steered Motherwell into the first ever season of the Premier League as well as two Scottish Cup semi final appearances. When he left the club he took up the post as a Community Coach.

Roger Hynd – Dec 1977 – Nov 1978. The former Rangers and Birmingham centre half had a brief spell in charge, but never set the heather on fire and left to take up various PE teaching posts.

Ally McLeod – Dec 1978 – Aug 1981. McLeod had been recovering from his traumatic Argentina 1978 experience with Scotland at his beloved Ayr United when the Motherwell board decided that he was the man to restore Premier League football to Motherwell. Despite signing some fine young players, he could never find the right blend to bring them back up.

Davie Hay – Aug 1981 – May 1982. The former Celtic and Chelsea star had been McLeod's assistant, and with the same squad of players took the side straight to the top of the First Division table with some fine attacking football. He left at the end of the season for an abortive job in the USA.

Jock Wallace – June 1982 – November 1983. He returned to Scotland from Seville to take over at Motherwell, but didn't stay too long and was off back to Ibrox as soon as his old employers came calling!

Bobby Watson – November 1983 – May 1984. Returned to football to manage Airdrie after a spell out of the game and he was a popular choice when he was picked to take over at Fir Park. But he never really took to the job and left at the end of the season, with the side relegated to the First Division once again.

Tommy McLean – June1984 – July 1994. McLean had steered Morton to the First Division title the year before joining Motherwell, and repeated the feat in his first season at Motherwell. He then slowly set about building a side to challenge the best in Scotland. This saw his side pick up the Scottish Cup in 1991 and reach third in the League in 1993/94.

Alex McLeish – July 1994 – Feb 1998. He was a surprise choice as Player/Manager after spending all of his playing career with Aberdeen. Basically took Tommy McLean's side to second, but struggled in later seasons as he was forced to build his own side, before moving to Hibernian.

Harri Kampan – Feb 1998 – Oct 1998. He was the successful manager of Mypa 47 when they beat Motherwell in the UEFA Cup, and as a result was appointed to take the club forward. He was never given the chance to finish the job he started as he was an early casualty following the change of ownership.

Billy Davies – Oct 1998 – Oct 2001. Moved up from Youth team coach after a successful spell as a player at Motherwell. Despite being given money to spend the side never reached the heights that were expected from the new regime.

Eric Black – Oct 2001 – April 2002. Black, along with Terry Butcher, was convinced to move back into coaching from that of his agents role. Moved on when the club was placed in administration, and found a coaching role at Coventry City with former 'Well player Gary McAllister.

Terry Butcher – Aprill 2002 – Present. Was forced into the Manager's role when Black left along with Pat Nevin and after a traumatic first season steered his young side into a top six slot in 2003/04.

The Managers

1911 - To Date

1: John Hunter
1911 -1945

2: George Stevenson
1946 - 1955

3: Bobby Ancell
1955 -1965

4: Bobby Howitt
1965 - 1973

5: Ian St John
1973 -1974

6: Willie McLean
1974 -1977

7: Roger Hynd
1977 -1978

8: Ally McLeod
1978 - 1981

9: Davie Hay
1981 - 1982

10: Jock Wallace
1982 - 1983

11: Bobby Watson
1983 - 1984

12: Tommy McLean
1984 - 1994

13: Alex McLeish
1994 - 1998

14: Harri Kampman
1998

15: Billy Davies
1998 - 2001

16: Eric Black
2001 - 2002

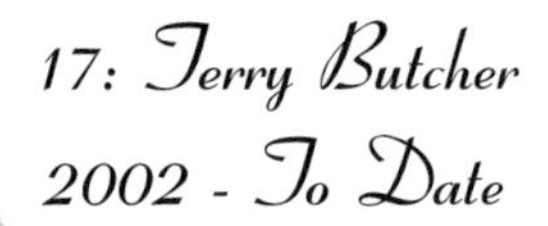

17: Terry Butcher
2002 - To Date

~ Club Handbooks Through The Years ~

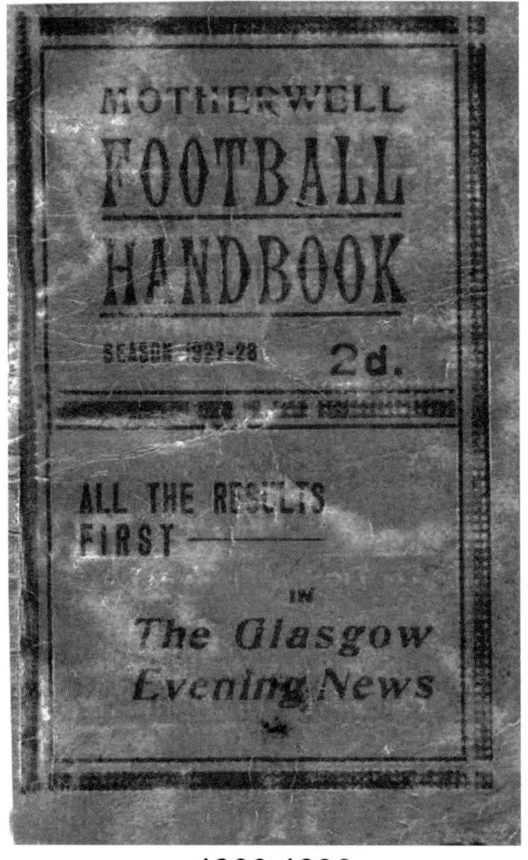

1922-1933

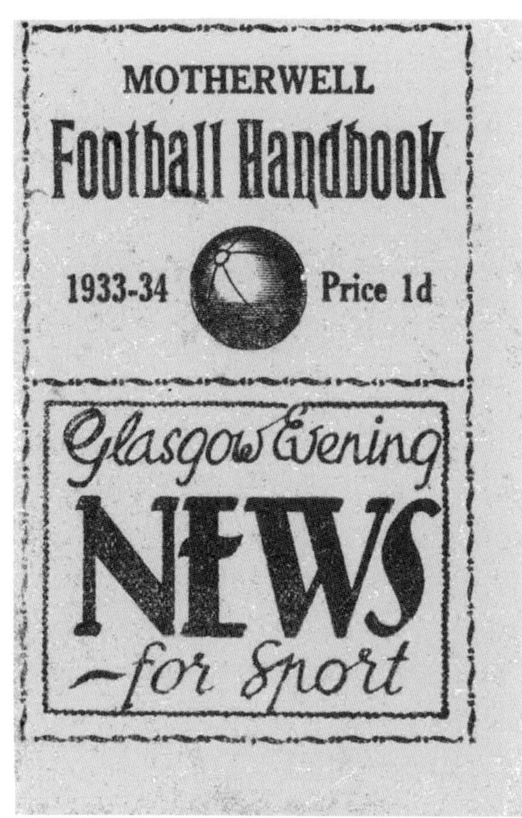

1933-1935

1935-1938

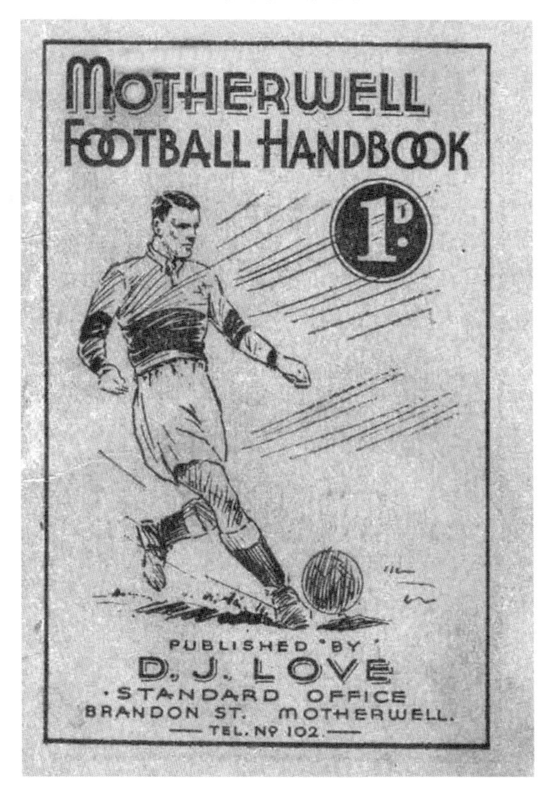

1938-1940

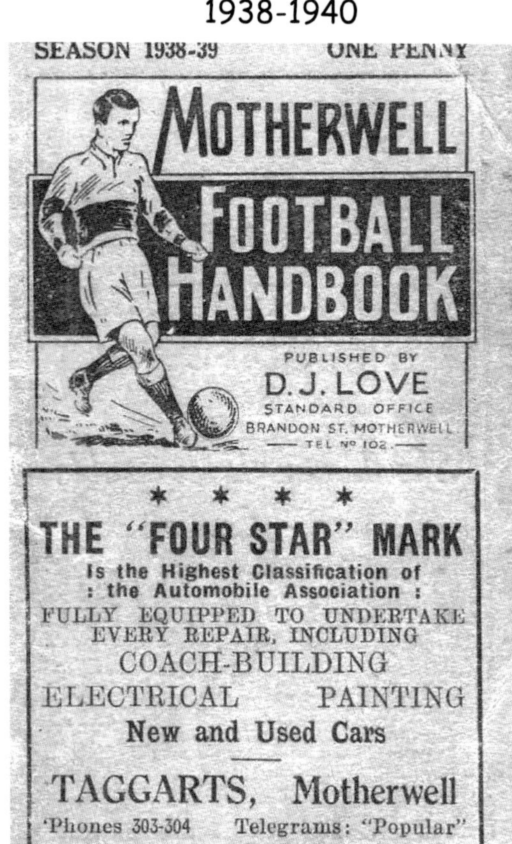

1948-1952

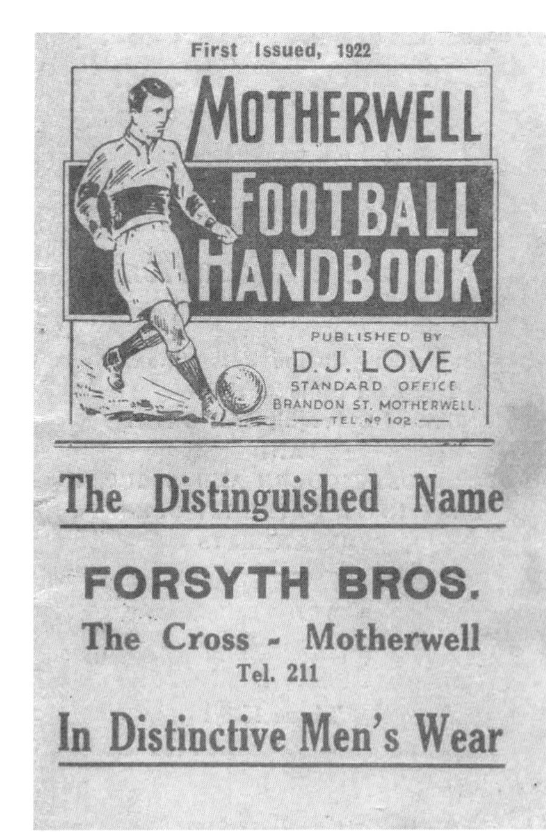

1952-1965

1969-1971

1972-1981

1982/83

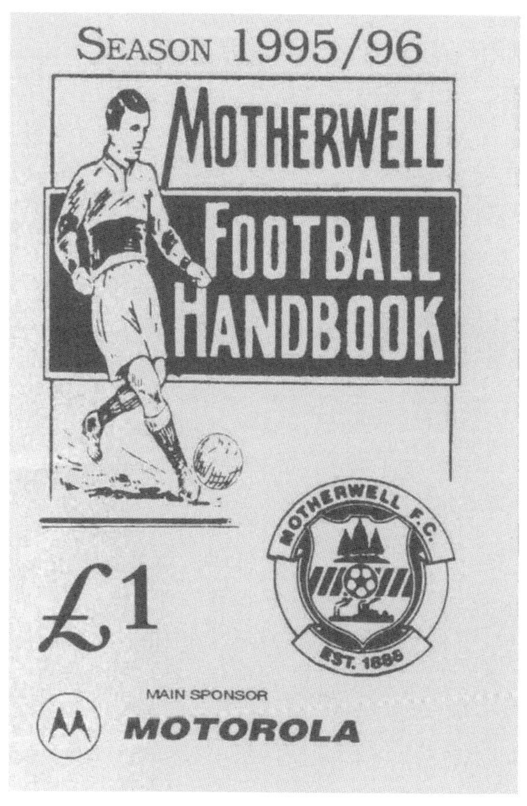

1995-1998

2000/01

These illustrations show the front covers and represent the change in style over the years from the first - in 1922, to the most recent. As can be seen, a Handbook has not been issued for every season

~ Matchday Programmes Through The Years ~

1964-1969
OFFICIAL PROGRAMME
First Published, August 1948
Motherwell F.C.
SEASON 1964-65
No 607
£5 Given Away
(See Inside)
FIR PARK, MOTHERWELL
SCOTTISH LEAGUE CUP—SECTION 4
Motherwell v
United
On SATURDAY
Kick-off 3 p.m.
1971/72
MOTHERWELL F.C.
OFFICIAL PROGRAMME
FIR PARK NEWS
5p
002362
WELL
VERSUS
HIBERNIAN
ON SATURDAY, AUGUST 14, 1971, at 3 P.M.
3rd Issue, No 2.
MOTHERWELL F.C.
OFFICIAL PROGRAMME
League champions, 1932.
Runners-up 1927, '30, '33, '34.
Scottish Cup winners, 1952.
Runners-up 1931, '33, '39, '51.
Summer Cup winners, 1944, '65.
League Cup winners, 1951.
Runners-up 1953.
Division II Champions, 1955, '69.
Second XI Cup, 1943, '50, '57.
Lanarkshire Cup holders.
FIR PARK NEWS
'WELL
VERSUS
3648
DUNFERMLINE
on Saturday, August, 15th 1970
2nd Issue No. 3.
1970/71
1969/70
Fir Park NEWS
No 0747
(INCORPORATING OFFICIAL PROGRAMME)
£5 Given Away
(See Inside)
1/-
JIM MUIR
Motherwell F.C.
Versus:—EAST FIFE
SCOTTISH LEAGUE CUP
ON SATURDAY, 9th AUGUST, 1969 AT 3 p.m.
1972/73
FIR PARK NEWS
INCORPORATING OFFICIAL PROGRAMME AND PRE-MATCH REVIEW SEASON 1972-73
'WELL
V
ALBION ROVERS
SCOTTISH LEAGUE CUP
MONDAY, SEPTEMBER 4, 1972
KICK-OFF 7.30 p.m.
Vol. 3 No. 6
5p

1973/74
SEASON 1973-74
FIR PARK NEWS
NEWS, VIEWS and PHOTOGRAPHS of the FIR PARK SCENE
price 5p
'Well
VERSUS
DUNDEE UNITED
on
Saturday, August 18th, 1973
1976/77
OFFICIAL MOTHERWELL FC MATCHDAY MAGAZINE
Fir Park NEWS
1976
10p
Anglo-Scottish Cup first round, first leg
MOTHERWELL
v
KILMARNOCK
1977
Vol 9 No 1
FIR PARK SCENE
FIR PARK NEWS
4th AUG '75
MOTHERWELL v DUNDEE
ANGLO-SCOTTISH CUP
MOTHERWELL F.C. OFFICIAL PROGRAMME
VOL 7 Nº2
PRICE 10p
1975/76
1974/75
'74- SPECIAL WEMBLEY OFFER: See page 4 -'75
Motherwell F.C. official matchday programme
FIRPARK NEWS
'WELL v CELTIC
8p
Scottish League Cup
Wednesday, 28th August, 1974
Vol. 6 Issue No. 3
News views and photographs
1977/78
MOTHERWELL
V
CELTIC
SCOTTISH LEAGUE CUP
2nd ROUND (2nd LEG)
Saturday, September 3, 1977
Kick-off 3 p.m.
OFFICIAL MATCH DAY PROGRAMME
No. 2
12p

1978/79
MOTHERWELL
V
ST. MIRREN
Sunday, August 6, 1978
Kick-off 3 p.m.
ANGLO-SCOTTISH CUP
No. 1
12p
OFFICIAL MATCH DAY
1982/83
MOTHERWELL
v. FORFAR ATH.
SCOTTISH LEAGUE CUP
QUALIFYING TIE
OFFICIAL PROGRAMME
40p
№ 830
ISSUE NO. 2
FIR PARK GUIDE
THE OFFICIAL PUBLICATION OF MOTHERWELL F.C.
'WELL Vs.
STENHOUSEMUIR
Saturday August 30 1980
BELL'S LEAGUE CUP
2nd ROUND, 2nd LEG
1980-81
20p
1980 -1982
1979/80
SEASON 1979-80
No. 2
FIR PARK
football guide
The Official Motherwell F.C. Match day Magazine
15p
MOTHERWELL
MOTHERWELL
V
QUEEN'S PARK
WEDNESDAY, AUGUST 29, 1979
1983-1987
Firpark Guide
MOTHERWELL
SCOTTISH LEAGUE CUP
2nd Round – 1st Leg
V.
BERWICK RANGERS
Wednesday
24th August
1983
KICK-OFF
7.30 p.m.
Official Programme 40p
MOTHERWELL

1987/88

1990/91

1988/89

1989/90

1991/92

1992/93
MOTHERWELL FC
OFFICIAL PROGRAMME
Price £1.00
'Well
v
DUNDEE UNITED
Scottish Premier Division
Saturday, 1st August, 1992
Kick-off 3.00 p.m.
Match sponsor
MOTOROLA
MAIN CLUB SPONSOR
MOTOROLA
EST. 1886
Health Education
1995/96
Motherwell
Football Club
Fir Park Centenary Year 1895-1995
v. KILMARNOCK
MOTOROLA
£1
Bell's Scottish League - Premier Division
OFF 3.00 PM
Motorola
MOTOROLA
Coca-Cola Cup — Second Round
MOTHERWELL v.
CLYDEBANK
Tonight's Match Sponsored by Coca-Cola
OFFICIAL PROGRAMME Price £1
TUESDAY, 16th AUGUST, 1994
Kick-off 6.30 p.m
PONY
EST. 1886
Health Education Board for Sco
1994/95
1993/94
MOTOROLA
MOTHERWELL F.C.
EST. 1886
The 'WELL
OFFICIAL MATCHDAY MAGAZINE £1
MOTHERWELL F.C.
V. CELTIC
PREMIER LEAGUE
SATURDAY, 7th AUGUST, 1993 Kick-off 3.00 p.m
MATCH SPONSOR
MOTOROLA
Health Education Board for Scotland
1996/97
MOTHERWELL
SEASON 1996/97
The Health Education
Board For Scotland
AND IF MY OLD ABERDEEN FANS SLAG ME, VANS THE MAN TO GAG EM
Bells Premier Division
August 17th, 1996. Kick Off 3.00pm
Motherwell v Aberdeen
Today's Match is sponsored by
WATSON DUNNE & CO. -
THE CRAWFORD GROUP - D & W NIMMO -
and EQUIBRITE
OFFICIAL
£1
PROGRAMME
MOTOROLA

1997/98

2000/01

1998/99

1999/2000

2001/02

2002/03

Motherwell never issued programmes until the 1948/49 season. This has been a selection through the seasons, showing the various changing styles over the years.

2003/04

2004/05

Players' Who's Who: 1946 - 2004

Name	First	Last			Appearances				Goals			
	Season	Season	Previous Club	Next Club	League	SC	LC	Other	League	SC	LC	Other
Adams, Derek	1998/99	2003/04	Ross County	Aberdeen	124 (20)	11(2)	5 (1)	0	19	2	1	0
Ainslie, Christopher	1989/90	1990/91	Nottingham Forest	Brechin City	Never Played	0	0	0	0	0	0	0
Aitken, Charlie	1949/50	1966/67	Arniston Rangers		314	32	69	0	38	4	10	0
Aitkenhead, Jack	1948/49	1951/52	Stoneyburn	Cowdenbeath	9	1	2	0	0	0	0	0
Aitkenhead, Johnny	1948/49	1956/57	Hibernian	Hamilton	170	32	54	0	50	13	20	0
Alexander, Ian	1983/84	1984/85	Rotherham	Morton	19 (5)	0	3	0	2	0	1	0
Alexander, James	1956/57	1957/58	Camelon		Never Played	0	0	0	0	0	0	0
Allan, Gerard	1985/86	1986/87	Wishaw	East Stirling	Never Played	0	0	0	0	0	0	0
Allan, Ray	1994/95	1994/95	Brechin City	Raith Rovers	0	0	0	1	0	0	0	0
Allan, Stuart	1965/66	1968/69	Netherton Hearts		Never Played	0	0	0	0	0	0	0
Anderson, Jim	1965/66	1967/68		East Stirling	Never Played	0	0	0	0	0	0	0
Anderson, Tom	1946/47	1949/50	Newarthill Hearts	Albion Rovers	3	0	0	0	0	0	0	0
Angus, Ian	1990/91	1993/94	Dundee	Clyde	70 (17)	8 (1)	4 (1)	1	8	1	1	0
Arnott, Dougie	1986/87	1997/98	Pollok Juniors		199 (41)	17 (2)	13 (2)	3	58	4	7	1
Bacque, Herve	1998/99	1998/99	Free		0 (1)	0	0	0	0	0	0	0
Baillie, Craig	1963/64	1964/65	Brighton	Distillery	6	0	0	2	3	0	0	0
Bain, Alex	1954/55	1956/57	Cockenzie Star	Huddersfield	23	2	12	0	10	0	11	0
Baker, Paul	1992/93	1992/93	Hartlepool United	Gillingham	5 (4)	0	1	0	1	0	0	0
Baker, Gerry	1956/57	1958/59	Chelsea	St Mirren	11	0	1	0	4	0	0	0
Ballantyne, Ross	2002/03	2003/04	Motherwell Youth		0 (1)	0	0	0	0	0	0	0
Baptie, Crawford	1985/86	1986/87	Falkirk	Falkirk	20 (13)	0	0	0	3	0	0	0
Barclay, Willie	1946/47	1948/49	Larkhall Thistle	Bury	55	4	10	0	6	1	0	0
Barkey, Kevin	2002/03				Never Played	0	0	0	0	0	0	0
Barrowman, Cliff	1973/74	1976/77	Royal Albert	Berwick Rangers	Never Played	0	0	0	0	0	0	0
Bartholomew, Henry	1946/47				Never Played	0	0	0	0	0	0	0
Beaton, Jim	1967/68	1968/69	Carluke Rovers		4	0	0	0	0	0	0	0
Bell, Andrew	2000/01		S Form		Never Played	0	0	0	0	0	0	0
Bell, David	1997/98	1998/99	Bearsden BC	Stirling Albion	Never Played	0	0	0	0	0	0	0
Berhnard, Franck	2001/02	2001/02	Free		2 (1)	0	0	0	0	0	0	0
Black, Kenny	1983/84	1983/84	Rangers	Hearts	17	1	0	0	0	0	0	0
Blair, Ian	1963/64	1963/64		Stranraer	2	0	0	0	0	0	0	0
Blair, Ray	1984/85	1985/86	St Johnstone	East Fife	38 (14)	0 (1)	1 (1)	0	8	1	0	0
Bollan, Gary	2003/04	2003/04	Dundee Utd	Clyde	1 (2)	0 (1)	0	0	0	0	0	0
Boyd, Jim	1978/79	1978/79	Clyde	Clyde	9 (2)	1	3	0	0	0	0	0
Boyd, John	1967/68	1967/68	Clydebank	Clyde	2	0	0	0	0	0	0	0
Boyd, Tom	1983/84	1990/91	S Form	Chelsea	246 (6)	31	18	0	6	0	1	0
Brannan, Ged	1998/99	200/01	Manchester City	Wigan Athletic	81	7	3 (1)	0	16	2	0	0
Brawley, Billy	2002/03				Never Played	0	0	0	0	0	0	0
Bremner, Gordon	1946/47	1950/51	Arsenal		99	9	14	0	17	0	3	0
Brims, Donald	1956/57	1957/58	Arniston Rangers	Bradford PA	11	0	0	0	0	0	0	0
Brown, Billy	1970/71	1972/73	Hull City	Raith Rovers	9	0	5 (3)	2	1	0	0	0
Brown, Gary	1987/88		St Columbas B C		Never Played	0	0	0	0	0	0	0
Brown, James	1946/47	1946/47	Kello Rovers	Chesterfield	18	5	6	0	16	2	6	0
Brown, James	1990/91	1993/94	M/well B C	Stranraer	Never Played	0	0	0	0	0	0	0
Brown, James	1955/56	1957/58	Bathgate	Free	Never Played	0	0	0	0	0	0	0
Brown, Mark	2001/02	2001/02	Rangers	Inverness CT	19	0	1	0	0	0	0	0
Brown, Michael	1999/00	2000/01	Manchester City	Partick Thistle	Never Played	0	0	0	0	0	0	0
Brown, Robert	1951/52	1955/56	Polkemmet Juniors	Workington	3	3	0	0	0	0	0	0
Brown, Stuart	1955/56	1958/59	Beith	Stranraer	25	1	5	0	0	1	0	0
Bryce, Stevie	1987/88	1992/92	Motherwell BC	Ayr	7 (15)	0 (3)	0	0	1	2	0	0
Bryden, John	1951/52	1954/55	Motherwell Juniors	East Stirling	4	0	1	0	0	0	0	0
Bryson, Ramsay	1967/68	1969/70	Dalziel HS		7	1	0	0	1	1	0	0
Buchan, George	1975/76	1975/76	Bury	Bury	Never Played	0	0	0	0	0	0	0
Buchanan, Steve	1976/77		Drumchapel		Never Played	0	0	0	0	0	0	0
Buchanan, William	1946/47	1948/49		Carlisle	0	0	1	0	0	0	0	0
Burke, John	1979/80	1980/81	Fir Park B C	Sheffield United	Never Played	0	0	0	0	0	0	0
Burke, Paul	1990/91	1992/93	X Form	Ayr United	Never Played	0	0	0	0	0	0	0
Burley, George	1989/90	1990/91	Gillingham	Ayr	54	0	5	0	0	2	1	0
Burley, George	1993/94	1993/94	Falkirk	Colchester	3 (2)	0	0	0	0	0	0	0
Burns, Alex	1991/92	1997/98	Shotts Bon Accord	Den Bosch	39 (37)	6 (1)	5 (1)	2 (1)	8	2	1	2
Burns, Alex	2003/04		Partick Thistle		29 (4)	3	0	0	2	2	0	0
Burns, James	1982/83	1983/84	Fir Park BC		4 (6)	0	1 (1)	0	1	0	0	0
Burns, John	1982/83	1983/84	Fir Park BC		Never Played	0	0	0	0	0	0	0
Burns, Tom	1969/70	1973/74	Springboig YM		2	1	4	0	0	0	0	0
Bury, John	1951/52	1952/53	Glenafton		Never Played	0	0	0	0	0	0	0
Cadden, Stephen	1986/87	1987/88	Wishaw	Albion Rovers	Never Played	0	0	0	0	0	0	0
Cairney, Benny	1965/66	1967/68	Leicester	Wigan	41 (2)	0	11	0	7	0	4	0
Cairney, Jim	1973/74		Royal Albert		Never Played	0	0	0	0	0	0	0
Calder, Douglas	2003/04		Hamilton		Never Played	0	0	0	0	0	0	0
Callachan, Craig	1999/00		X Form		Never Played	0	0	0	0	0	0	0
Cameron, Johnny	1954/55	1955/56	Gourock Juniors	Bradford PA	6	0	0	0	0	0	0	0
Cameron, Mark	2003/04		S Form		Never Played	0	0	0	0	0	0	0
Campbell, Bobby	1965/66	1970/71	Morton	Stranraer	160 (1)	11	24 (1)	0	36	0	10	0
Campbell, John	1954/55	1958/59	Rob Roy	Chesterfield	3	0	3	0	0	0	0	0
Campbell, William	1970/71	1973/74	Dundee	Glenavon	71 (5)	8	19	7	6	2	3	2
Candlish, Neil	1984/85	1990/91	Bellfield BC	Glentoran	8 (3)	0	0	0	1	0	0	0
Capaldi, John	1978/79	1979/80	Aston Villa		3 (8)	0	0	0	0	0	0	0
Carberry, Bobby	1978/79	1980/81	Alloa	Falkirk	33 (2)	0	2	0	1	0	0	0
Carlyle, Walter	1963/64	1965/66	Dundee United	St Johnstone	26	2	2	0	7	1	1	0
Carr, Peter	1978/79	1978/79	Carlisle		6 (1)	0	1	0	0	0	0	0
Carson, Joe	1979/80	1983/84	Arbroath	Dumbarton	127	8	23	0	8	1	1	0
Cattenach, Tiny	1958/59	1959/60	Annbank		Never Played	0	0	0	0	0	0	0

Name	First	Last			Appearances				Goals			
	Season	Season	Previous Club	Next Club	League	SC	LC	Other	League	SC	LC	Other
Caughey, Mark	1987/88	1987/88	Hamilton	Ards	9 (6)	0	0	0	0	0	0	0
Chiba, Said	200/01	2000/01	Free		7	0	0	0	0	0	0	0
Christie, Kevin	1996/97	1998/99	East Fife	Falkirk	27 (6)	2	3	0	0	0	0	0
Clark, Billy	1964/65		Renfrew		Never Played	0	0	0	0	0	0	0
Clark, Jim	1985/86	1985/86	Kilmarnock	Meadowbank	5	0	1	0	0	0	0	0
Clark, John	1968/69	1969/70	Irvine Vics		0 (1)	0	0	0	0	0	0	0
Clark, Robert	1984/85	1986/87	Kilmarnock	Kilmarnock	9 (3)	1 (1)	0	0	1	0	0	0
Clarke, David	1999/2000	2002/03	S-Form		0 (2)	0	0	0	0	0	0	0
Clarkson, David	2001/02		Motherwell Youth		45 (13)	5 (2)	1	0	15	2	0	0
Cleland, Peter	1950/51	1955/56	Newarthill Hearts	Norwich	1	0	0	0	0	0	0	0
Clelland, Bruce	1978/79	1982/83	Albion Rovers	Ayr	50 (16)	4 (1)	9 (1)	0	25	0	1	0
Clifford, James	1965/66	1967/68	Holytown	Hamilton Accies	Never Played	0	0	0	0	0	0	0
Clifford, John	1977/78	1978/79	Celtic	Fredrikshavn (den)	Never Played	0	0	0	0	0	0	0
Clinging, Ian	1977/78	1982/82	Carluke Rovers	Morton	92 (22)	2	15 (2)	2	21	1	8	0
Clinton, William	1986/87	1987/88	Wishaw	Sligo Rvs	Never Played	0	0	0	0	0	0	0
Coakley, Tommy	1963/64	1965/66	Bellshill Athletic	Arsenal	23	2	4	4	1	0	0	1
Conlin, Bobby	1955/56	1956/57	Grangemouth United	Hamilton Accies	Never Played	0	0	0	0	0	0	0
Conn, Alfie	1981/82	1983/84	Blackpool		21 (6)	0	8 (1)	0	3	0	2	0
Connolly, Jon	2000/01	2001/02	Thorniewood United	Motherwell	2	0	0	0	0	0	0	0
Connolly, Kenneth	2003/04		Youths		Never Played	0	0	0	0	0	0	0
Constable, John	1999/00		X Form		Never Played	0	0	0	0	0	0	0
Cook, John	1959/60	1960/61	Whitburn	Hearts	Never Played	0	0	0	0	0	0	0
Cook, Malcolm	1961/62	1963/64	St Rochs	Bradford P A	Never Played	0	0	0	0	0	0	0
Cooper, Davie	1989/90	1993/94	Rangers	Clydebank	147 (10	10	6 (1)	2	17	1	0	0
Cormack, Mike	1982/83	1984/85	Deveronvale	Kilmarnock	6 (11)	0 (1)	3	0	1	0	0	0
Corr, Barry John	2003/04		Celtic		5	0	0	0	0	0	0	0
Corrigan, Martyn	1999/2000		Falkirk		151 (9)	10	6	0	3	0	0	0
Cosgrove, Stephen	2001/02	2001/02	Man Utd	Clyde	0 (2)	0	0 (1)	0	0	0	0	0
Cowan, David	2002/03		Newcastle Utd		15 (2)	0 (3)	0	0	0	0	0	0
Cowan, Stevie	1987/88	1989/90	Hibs	Albion Rovers	44 (7)	3	2	0	11	1	0	0
Cowie, Willie	1956/57	1958/59	Kilsyth Rangers	QoS	10	0	6	0	0	0	0	0
Cox, Charlie	1951/52	1957/58	Hearts		88	19	24	0	4	1	4	0
Coyle, Owen	1996/97	1998/99	Dundee Utd	Dunfermline	75 (2)	10	4	0	23	5	4	0
Coyne, Brian	1980/81	1982/83	Shrewsbury Town	Falkirk	26 (8)	0 (1)	4 (1)	0	2	0	1	0
Coyne, Tommy	1993/94	1997/98	Tranmere Rovers	Dundee	122 (10)	11	7	0	59	2	1	0
Craig, Steven	2002/03	2003/04	Falkirk	Aberdeen	24 (13)	2	1	0	5	1	1	0
Craigan, Stephen	1995/96	1999/2000	Blantyre Vics	Partick Thistle	18 (22)	1 (1)	0 (2)	0	0	0	0	0
Craigan, Stephen	2003/04		Partick Thistle		36	3	1	0	0	0	0	0
Crawley, John	2001/02	2002/03	S Form		Never Played	0	0	0	0	0	0	0
Creany, John	1972/73	1974/75	Schools		Never Played	0	0	0	0	0	0	0
Cumming, Richard	1949/50	1951/52	Killermont Amateurs	Dumbarton	2	0	0	0	0	0	0	0
Cunningham, Denis	1960/61	1961/62	Hearts	Berwick	1	0	0	0	0	0	0	0
Curcic, Sasa	1999/2000	1999/2000	Free		3 (3)	0	0	0	0	0	0	0
Currie, Derek	1968/69	1969/70	Cumnock		Never Played	0	0	0	0	0	0	0
Cusack, Nick	1989/90	1991/92	Peterborough	Darlington	68 (9)	3 (1)	5	0	17	2	4	0
Dair, Jason	2003/04	2003/04	Dunfermline	Livingston	19 (10)	2	0 (1)	0	2	0	0	0
Davidson, Vic	1975/76	1977/78	Celtic	Blackpool	88 (7)	7 (2)	12 (2)	10	19	2	6	8
Davies, John	1999/2000	2000/01	Ayr Utd	Ayr Utd	9 (1)	1 (1)	1 (1)	0	0	0	0	0
Davies, Billy	1993/94	1999/2000	Dunfermline		95 (21)	4 (3)	5 (3)	4 (2)	9	1	0	1
Dawson, George	1952/53	1954/55	Glencairn	QPR	16	1	1	0	2	0	0	0
Deans, John 'Dixie'	1965/66	1971/72	Neilston Juniors	Celtic	150	9	32	7	79	4	6	0
Delaney, Pat	1958/59	1966/67	Douglas Water Thistle	Dunfermline	164	23	29	13	22	4	5	9
Deloumeaux, Eric	2001/02	2001/02	Le Havre	Aberdeen	22 (1)	1	0	0	0	0	0	0
Dempsey, Jim	1978/79	1979/80	Fir Park BC	Clyde	20	0	1	0	0	0	0	0
Dempsie, Brian	1999/2000	2002/03	Motherwell BC		1	0 (1)	0	0	0	0	0	0
Denham, Greig	1993/94	1999/2000	Cumbernauld United	Falkirk	40 (7)	5 (2)	5	0	0	0	0	0
Dickson, Billy	1973/74	1975/76	Kilmarnock	Hamilton	10 (2)	2	5 (1)	0	0	0	0	0
Dickson, Mark	1990/91	1992/93	X Form		Never Played	0	0	0	0	0	0	0
Dijkstra, Sieb	1991/92	1993/94	Roda JC	QPR	80	4	3	0	0	0	0	0
Diver, Danny	1985/86	1985/86	K I F		Never Played	0	0	0	0	0	0	0
Dobbin, Jim	1983/84	1983/84	Celtic	Celtic	1	0	0	0	0	0	0	0
Doesburg, Michel	1998/99	1999/2000	AZ Alkmaar	Dunfermline	46 (3)	6	4	0	0	0	0	0
Doherty, David	1999/00		M/well B C		Never Played	0	0	0	0	0	0	0
Dolan, Jamie	1987/88	1996/97	Motherwell BC	Dundee Utd	160 (34)	7 (4)	7 (3)	8	5	0	1	0
Donnachie, Frank	1964/65	1966/67	Shotts BA	Stenhousemuir	9 (1)	0	0	0	1	0	0	0
Donnelly, John	1978/79	1980/81	Notts Co	Dumbarton	21 (4)	0 (1)	1	0	2	0	0	0
Donnelly, Robert	2003/04		Youths		Never Played	0	0	0	0	0	0	0
Donnelly, Tom	1968/69	1970/71	Rangers	East Stirling	72 (2)	5	17 (1)	3	10	0	1	2
Dornan, Andy	1982/83	1985/86	Aberdeen	Walsall	88 (4)	8 (2)	10	0	3	0	0	0
Dorner, Mario	1997/98	1997/98	Vfb Modling	Darlington	1 (1)	0	0 (2)	0	0	0	0	0
Dow, Andy	2001/02	2001/02	Aberdeen	St Mirren	7 (2)	1	0	0	1	0	0	0
Dow, John Paul	1998/99		Celtic		Never Played	0	0	0	0	0	0	0
Downie, Henry	1951/52	1952/53	Schools	Montrose	Never Played	0	0	0	0	0	0	0
Doyle, Jamie	1984/85	1986/87	Partick Thistle	Partick Thistle	34 (2)	6	4	0	1	1	1	0
Doyle, John Paul	1992/93	1992/93	M/well B C		Never Played	0	0	0	0	0	0	0
DuPlessis, Charles	1959/60				Never Played	0	0	0	0	0	0	0
Dubourdeau, Francois	2001/02	2002/03	Free	Kilmarnock	26	0	0	0	0	4	0	0
Duncan, Cammy	1987/88	1989/90	Sunderland	Partick Thistle	60	3	6	0	0	0	0	0
Duncan, David	1982/83		Fir Park B C		Never Played	0	0	0	0	0	0	0
Duncan, Frank	1957/58	1961/62	Newtongrange Star	Berwick Rangers	Never Played	0	0	0	0	0	0	0
Duncan, Tom	1972/73		Dalziel H S		Never Played	0	0	0	0	0	0	0
Ebner, David	1975/76		Airdrie		Never Played	0	0	0	0	0	0	0

Name	First Season	Last Season	Previous Club	Next Club	Appearances League	SC	LC	Other	Goals League	SC	LC	Other
Edvaldsson, Johannes	1982/83	1983/84	Hannover 96		54	3	8	0	6	0	0	0
Elliott, Stuart	2000/02	20001/02	Glentoran	Hull City	50 (20)	1 (1)	2 (1)	0	20	1	0	0
Erwin, Henry	1976/77	1978/79	M/well B C	Airdrie	Never Played	0	0	0	0	0	0	0
Essandoh, Roy	1995/96	1996/97	Cumbernauld Utd	East Fife	0 (5)	0	0	0 (1)	0	0	0	0
Ewing, Christopher	1996/97	1997/98	Cumbernauld	Stranraer	Never Played	0	0	0	0	0	0	0
Ewings, Jamie	2001/02		Hibs		Never Played	0	0	0	0	0	0	0
Fagan, Shaun	2000/01		Motherwell Youth		18 (16)	2 (3)	0	0	2	0	0	0
Fairlie, Jamie	1987/88	1987/88	Clydebank	Hamilton	8 (4)	0	3 (1)	0	1	0	3	0
Falconer, Neil	1959/60	1960/61	Morgan Acadamy		Never Played	0	0	0	0	0	0	0
Falconer, Willie	1995/96	1997/98	Celtic	Dundee	57 (1)	7	4	0	10	0	1	0
Fallon, John	1971/72	1971/72	Celtic	Morton	10	2	0	0	0	0	0	0
Fallon, John	1999/00	2002/03	Calderbraes B C	Stranraer	Never Played	0	0	0	0	0	0	0
Farningham, Ray	1986/87	1988/89	Forfar	Dunfermline	69(7)	6	4	0	12	1	1	0
Farrell, Isaac	1975/76	1976/77	Rangers		1	0	2 (1)	0	0	0	0	0
Ferguson, Iain	1990/91	1993/94	Hearts	Airdrie	34 (17)	6 (5)	1 (3)	0 (1)	10	2	4	0
Ferguson, Paul	1993/94	1995/96	Stoneyburn United		1	0	0	0	0	0	0	0
Ferguson, Steven	2002/03	2002/03	Tottenham (loan)		8 (11)	0	1 (1)	0	2	0	0	0
Ferrere, David	2001/02	2001/02		Louhans-Cuiseaux	7 (2)	0	0	0	3	0	0	0
Fitzgerald, Gerald	1979/80	1980/81	Shamrock B C		Never Played	0	0	0	0	0	0	0
Fitzpatrick, Mark	2003/04		Motherwell Youths		1 (1)	0	0	0	0	0	0	0
Fitzpatrick, John Patrick	1998/99		Celtic B C		Never Played	0	0	0	0	0	0	0
Flavell, Bobby	1982/83	1983/84	Hibs	Dundee Utd	27 (5)	2	1 (1)	0	6	0	0	0
Fleming, Liam	2000/01	2002/03	S Form	Clyde	Never Played	0	0	0	0	0	0	0
Forbes, Graeme	1980/81	1986/87	Lochee United	Walsall	170 (16)	19	19 (1)	0	16	2	2	0
Fordyce, John	1953/54		Hearts		Never Played	0	0	0	0	0	0	0
Forrest, Eddie	2001/02	2001/02	Airdrie	Berwick	9 (5)	1	1	0	0	0	0	0
Forrest, Jim	1949/50	1959/60	Newarthill Hearts	Stenhousemuir	214	23	70	2	57	10	24	0
Forrest, Maxwell	1948/49	1949/50	Burnbank Ath	Alloa	Never Played	0	0	0	0	0	0	0
Forsyth, Alex	1982/83	1982/83	Rangers	Hamilton	18 (1)	0 (2)	5	0	0	0	0	0
Forsyth, Tom	1967/68	1972/73	Stonehouse Thistle	Rangers	147 (4)	13	32	10	17	0	6	0
Frame, Bobby	1962/63		North Motherwell B C		Never Played	0	0	0	0	0	0	0
Fraser, Gary	1986/87	1988/89	Queens Park	QoS	10 (13)	1	0	0	0	0	0	0
French, John	1969/70		Dalziel H S		Never Played	0	0	0	0	0	0	0
Friar, John Paul	1983/84	1983/84	Rotherham (loan)		1 (1)	0	0	0	0	0	0	0
Gahagan, John	1979/80	1990/91	Shettleston Jnrs	Morton	191 (93)	13 (11)	20 (9)	0	35	4	4	0
Gallacher, Willie	1961/62	1964/65	Larkhall Vic	Stranraer	4	0	0	0	2	0	0	0
Garcin, Eric	1997/98	1997/98		Dundee	7 (4)	2	0	0	1	0	0	0
Gardiner, Ian	1955/56	1958/59	East Fife	Raith	95	7	17	0	48	7	9	0
Gardiner, John	1984/85	1986/87	Dundee Utd	Montrose	78	14	6	0	0	0	0	0
Gardner, Jim	1988/89	1992/93	Queens Park	St Mirren	8 (8)	0 (1)	0	0	0	0	0	0
Gardner, Pat	1974/75	1975/76	Dundee Utd	Arbroath	29 (5)	9 (1)	4	2 (1)	5	0	0	0
Geddes, Jim	1952/53	1954/55	Forth Wanderers		1	0	5	0	0	0	0	0
Gibson, Alex	1946/47	1946/47			8	0	1	0	2	0	0	0
Gibson, James	1946/47				Never Played	0	0	0	0	0	0	0
Gilchrist, Robert	1956/57	1957/58	Aldershot	Cambridge City	10	0	4	0	0	0	0	0
Gillespie, Eric	1971/72	1971/72	Kilmarnock	Hamilton	11	0	0	1	0	0	0	0
Gillespie, Jim	1983/84	1983/84	Standard Wettern	Morton	12 (3)	2 (1)	4 (1)	0	0	1	4	0
Goldie, David	1960/61	1963/64	Kilsyth Rangers	Stranraer	7 (1)	0	2	0	0	0	0	0
Goldthorpe, John	1967/68	1975/76	Lesmahagow	Morton	142 (21)	12 (3)	23 (1)	8 (2)	44	5	6	2
Goodall, Ian	1947/48	1949/50	Kilsyth Rangers	Third Lanark	16	2	2	0	2	1	0	0
Goodman, Don	1998/99	2000/01	Hiroshima	Walsall	39 (16)	4	4 (1)	0	9	3	0	0
Goodwin, John	1961/62	1964/65	Carluke Rovers		7	0	0	0	1	0	0	0
Goodwin, Sam	1972/73	1974/75	Crystal Palace	Clydebank	61 (3)	5 (2)	7	7	2	0	0	0
Goram, Andy	1998/99	2000/01	Sheffield United	Manchester Utd	57	8	4	0	0	0	0	0
Gormely, Edward Joseph	1988/89		Spurs		Never Played	0	0	0	0	0	0	0
Gourlay, Archie	1991/92	1993/94	Newcastle	Hartlepool	0 (3)	0	0	0	0	0	0	0
Gow, Garry	1994/95	1998/99	Yoker	Stirling Albion	Never Played	0	0	0	0	0	0	0
Gower, Mark	1998/99	1998/99	Tottenham (loan)		8 (1)	0	0	0	1	0	0	0
Graham, Ally	1992/93	1993/94	Ayr Utd	Raith Rovers	6 (3)	0	0 (1)	0	1	0	1	0
Graham, Bobby	1973/74	1976/77	Coventry	Hamilton	126 (6)	17	18	11 (1)	37	6	3	2
Graham, Thomas	1982/83	1982/83	Doncaster	Scunthorpe	0 (1)	0 (1)	0	0	0	0	0	0
Graham, Tommy	1982/83	1982/83	Arthurlie	Scunthorpe	Never Played	0	0	0	0	0	0	0
Grant, Bernie	1983/84	1984/85	East Kilbride Dynamo	Stirling	5 (1)	1	0	0	0	0	0	0
Grant, Ryan	2003/04		Schools	Freed	Never Played	0	0	0	0	0	0	0
Grant, William	1958/59	1959/60	Douglas		Never Played	0	0	0	0	0	0	0
Gray, Harry	1977/78	1978/79	Celtic	St Johnstone	Never Played	0	0	0	0	0	0	0
Gray, Jim	1966/67	1968/69	Maryhill Harp		0 (1)	0	0	0	0	0	0	0
Gray, John	1970/71	1975/76	Cumbernauld Utd	Ayr	22 (3)	0	6	4	2	0	1	0
Griffin, Jim	1985/86	1994/95	Fir Park BC		81 (11)	6	1 (1)	2	6	0	0	0
Grozier, James	1951/52	1952/53	Glenafton	Distillery	3	0	0	0	1	0	0	0
Grzybowski, George	1963/64		Norton House B C		Never Played	0	0	0	0	0	0	0
Halliday, Stephen	1998/99	1999/2000	Hartlepool		3 (6)	0	3 (2)	0	0	0	2	0
Halpin, John	1989/90	1990/91	M/well B C	Clyde	Never Played	0	0	0	0	0	0	0
Hamill, John	1946/47	1948/49	Arbroath	Kilmarnock	Never Played	0	0	0	0	0	0	0
Hamilton, Bob	1974/75	1975/76	Baillieston		6 (1)	2	0	0	0	0	0	0
Hamilton, Brian	1974/75	1974/75	Baillieston		Never Played	0	0	0	0	0	0	0
Hamilton, James	1946/47	1947/48	Cowdenbeith		Never Played	0	0	0	0	0	0	0
Hamilton, Richard	1946/47	1951/52	Wishaw Juniors		36	3	9	0	0	0	0	0
Hamilton, Willie	1967/68	1970/71	Alva Rovers		1 (2)	0	0	0	0	0	0	0
Hammell, Steven	1999/2000		X Form		146 (4)	10	6	0	2	0	0	0
Hare, Billy	1977/78	1979/80	Fir Park BC		1	0	0	0	0	0	0	0
Harper, Alex	1954/55	1955/56	Douglas Water Thistle	Northampton	0	0	1	0	0	0	0	0

Name	First	Last			Appearances				Goals			
	Season	Season	Previous Club	Next Club	League	SC	LC	Other	League	SC	LC	Other
Harrow, Andy	1982/82	1985/86	Aberdeen	Raith	94 (9)	13 (1)	8	0	19	8	2	0
Harvey, Paul	1999/2000	2001/02	QotS	Stenhousemuir	16 (10)	0	0 (1)	0	0	0	1	0
Healey, Des	1981/82	1982/83	Fir Park B C		Never Played	0	0	0	0	0	0	0
Henderson, Billy	1970/71	1970/71	St Mirren		Never Played	0	0	0	0	0	0	0
Henderson, Chas	1956/57				Never Played	0	0	0	0	0	0	0
Henderson, James	1946/47	1946/47		Forfar	1	0	0	0	0	0	0	0
Henderson, Tom	1985/86		Queens Park		Never Played	0	0	0	0	0	0	0
Hendry, John	1995/96	1997/98	Tottenham	Stirling	23 (12)	0 (1)	0	1	3	0	0	0
Heron, Brian	1969/70	1972/73	Rangers	Dumbarton	76	6	16	8 (1)	19	2	6	3
Higgins, Charlie	1949/50	1954/55	Airdrie	Albion Rovers	30	3	6	0	0	0	0	0
Higgins, Chris	2003/04				Never Played	0	0	0	0	0	0	0
Hogg, Bobby	1967/68	1967/68	Hibs		5(2)	0	4	0	2	0	0	0
Holton, Pat	1956/57	1958/59	Hamilton	Chelsea	69	10	9	0	0	0	0	0
Hood, Andrew	1970/71	1971/72	Annbank	Stranraer	Never Played	0	0	0	0	0	0	0
Hood, Harry	1976/77	1976/77	Celtic	QoS	6 (9)	1	2 (1)	0	0	0	1	0
Hood, Willie	1973/74	1975/76		Hamilton Accies	Never Played	0	0	0	0	0	0	0
Hope, Douglas	1963/4		Dalziel HS		Never Played	0	0	0	0	0	0	0
Howie, Scott	1994/95	1997/98	Norwich	Reading	69	5	4	1	0	0	0	0
Howieson, Bert	1965/66	1965/66	Dundee Utd		3	0	4	0	0	0	2	0
Hume, Ronnie	1964/65	1964/95	Partick Thistle		5	0	0	0	0	0	0	0
Humphries, Wilson	1946/47	1955/56	Dalziel HS	St Mirren	199	32	51	2	68	14	21	2
Hunter, Ally	1975/76	1977/78	Celtic	St Mirren	8	0	4	0	0	0	0	0
Hunter, Jim	1956/57		Edina Hearts		Never Played	0	0	0	0	0	0	0
Hunter, Jackie	1948/49	1957/58	Tranent	Poole Town	106	9	22	2	59	6	11	0
Hunter, Robert	1950/51	1959/60	Hamilton		2	0	1	0	1	0	1	0
Hunter, William	1957/58	1966/67	Edinburgh Norton	Detroit Cougars	228	19	48	6	43	6	15	0
Innes, Alexander	1982/83	1983/84	Buckie Thistle	Buckie Thistle	Never Played	0	0	0	0	0	0	0
Irvine, Willie	1978/79	1982/83	Alloa	Hibs	117 (3)	6	7 (5)	0	49	0	2	0
Irving, James	1946/47	1946/47	Petershill	St Johnstone	2	0	0	0	0	0	0	0
Jack, Darren	2001/02	2002/03	Ross County		(3)	0	0	0	0	0	0	0
Johnston, Joe	1946/47	1952/53	Renfew	Albion Rovers	32	1	1	0	7	1	1	0
Johnstone, John	1946/47	1955/56	Armadale	Hamilton	205	35	46	0	0	0	0	0
Jones, Alex	1991/92	1992/93	Rochdale		12	0	1	0	1	0	0	0
Jones, Bobby	1962/63	1962/63	Larkhall Th	Montrose	2	0	0	0	0	0	0	0
Jones, Sandy	1961/62	1962/63	Coltness utd	Ayr utd	1	0	0	0	0	0	0	0
Jonsson, Gunnlaugar	1997/98	19997/98	Icelandic		2	0	0	0	0	0	0	0
Joyce, John	1973/74	1974/75	Livingston Utd		(2)	(1)	0	0	0	0	0	0
Kane Tony	1977/78	1980/81	Lanark United		11	1	0	0	0	0	0	0
Kaven, Mikko	1998/99	1998/99	HJK Helsinki		16	0	1	0	0	0	0	0
Kelly, Archibald	1949/50	1953/54	Aberdeen	Stirling	104	20	28	0	65	11	18	0
Kelly, David	2001/02	2001/02	Sheffield United		19	1	1	0	6	0	1	0
Kelly, Frank	1977/78	1979/80	Bargeddie Amateurs		1	0	1	0	0	0	0	0
Kelly, Jim	1976/77	1976/77	Motherwell BC		Never Played	0	0	0	0	0	0	0
Kemas, Khaled	2002/03	2002/03	Dundee		4 (2)	0	1	0	2	0	0	0
Kemble, Benito	1999/00	2000/01	PSV Eindhoven	St. Johnstone	48	1	1	0	1	0	0	0
Kemp, Daniel	1998/99	1998/99	Bearsden BC		Never Played	0	0	0	0	0	0	0
Kennedy, Alex	1982/83	1988/89	Craigmark Bruntonians	Partick Thistle	68 (8)	4	6 (1)	0	4	1	1	0
Kennedy, Ian	1973/74	1978/79	East Klbride Th	Odball (Nor)	45 (19)	4 (1)	9 (4)	3	2	2	1	1
Keogh, David	2003/04		Youths		Never Played	0	0	0	0	0	0	0
Kerr, Archie	1953/54	1959/60	Camelon		31	4	4	0	6	3	0	0
Kerr, Jerry	1947/48	1947/48			2	0	0	0	0	0	0	0
Kerr, John	1946/47	1946/47			2	0	0	0	0	0	0	0
Kesley, James	1946/47	1946/47		Cowdenbeath	Never Played	0	0	0	0	0	0	0
Kidd, Albert	1979/80	1981/82	Arbroath	Dundee	53	3	4	0	18	0	1	0
Kilmarnock, Willie	1946/47	1956/57	Irvine Meadow	Airdrie	296	42	80	0	11	1	4	0
Kinnaird, Paul	1987/88	1988/89	Dundee United	St. Mirren	34	3	2	0	0	0	0	0
Kinniburgh, Willie	2000/01		Motherwell BC		12 (5)	1	0	0	1	0	0	0
Kinross, Scott	1991/92	1992/93	Motherwell BC	Stirling Albion	(1)	0	1	0	0	0	0	0
Kirk, Stephen	1987/88	1994/95	East Fife	Falkirk	196 (70)	4 (9)	4 (2)	3 (1)	53	10	6	5
Kraska, Holm	1998/99	1998/99	Delmenhorst		Never Played	0	0	0	0	0	0	0
Krivokapic, Miodrag	1993/94	1995/96	Dundee United	Raith Rovers	71	5	2	0	1	0	0	0
Kromheer, Elroy	1992/93	1993/94	FC Volendam		11 (1)	1	1	0	0	0	0	0
Laird, Jim	1959/60	1961/62	Burnbank Ath	Berwick R	Never Played	0	0	0	0	0	0	0
Lambe, Christopher	1989/90	1989/90	Motherwell BC		Never Played	0	0	0	0	0	0	0
Lambert, Paul	1993/94	1995/96	St. Mirren	Borussia Dortmund	101 (2)	6	5	5	6	0	1	0
Larnach, Michael	1978/79	1980/81	Newcastle	Ayr United	49 (9)	1	8	0	9	0	1	0
Lasley, Keith	1999/00	2003/04	Gleniffer Th	Plymouth Argyle	85 (12)	7 (1)	4	0	9	0	1	0
Latchford, David	1978/79	1978/79	Birmingham	Barnsley	4	0	0	2	0	0	0	0
Lawson, Kirkland	1969/70	1973/74	Blantyre Vics	Falkirk	51 (11)	7	18 (2)	0	15	4	0	6
Lehmann, Dirk	2001/02	2002/03	Brighton		37 (6)	1 (2)	2	0	9	0	1	0
Lehtonen, Joni	1996/97	1996/97	FC Ilves (Finland)		4 (2)	0	0	0	0	0	0	0
Leishman, Willie	1969/70	1976/77	Dalziel High School	Albion Rovers	4	0	1 (1)	0	0	0	0	0
Leitch, Scott	2000/01		Swindon Town		95 (3)	6	5	0	1	0	0	0
Leitch, William	1946/47	1948/49	Wishaw High School	Dumbarton	5	0	0	0	0	0	0	0
Lemon, John	1979/80	1979/80	Kilbryde KV		0	0	(1)	0	0	0	0	0
Leonard. Peter	1978/79	1978/79	St. Mirren		2 (4)	0	0	0	0	0	0	0
Lindqvist, Stefan	1997/98	1997/98	Neuchatel Xamax		5 (1)	0	0	0	1	0	0	0
Lindsay, George	1960/61	1967/68	Carluke Rovers	Queen of the South	157 (2)	17	31	0	29	1	5	0
Lindsay, Jimmy	1976/77	1978/79	Fir Park BC	Notts County	11 (10)	0	3	2	1	0	0	0
Lloyd, Graham	1974/75	1974/75	Liverpool	Portsmouth	9	0	0	0	0	0	0	0
Logan, Bert	1965/66	1966/67	Tranent	Berwick R	1	0	1	0	0	0	0	0
Lonie, Jim	1962/63	1963/64	Grangemouth United		1	0	1	0	1	0	1	0

Name	First	Last			Appearances				Goals			
	Season	Season	Previous Club	Next Club	League	SC	LC	Other	League	SC	LC	Other
Lyall, Kenny	1983/84	1984/85	Rangers	St. Johnstone	18 (1)	2	0	0	2	0	0	0
Maaskant, Robert	91/2	91/92	SC Club Emmen		12	0	0	0	0	0	0	0
MacCabe, David A R	88/89	89/90	Airdrie	Kilmarnock	12 (2)	1	0	0	0	0	0	0
Macdonald, Kevin G	00/01	2003/4	Glennifer Thistle	Stirling Albion	5 (8)	0	0 (1)	0	0	0	0	0
Mackay, John	79/80	82/83	Crookston Castle School		17 (1)	0	0	0	0	0	0	0
Mackin, Alan Jams	78/79	80/81	Queen's Park	Falkirk	15 (2)	0	3	0	0	0	0	0
Mackin, Joe	58/59	59/60	Ayr United	Freed	19	2	0	0	0	0	0	0
MacLeod, Ian Murdo	78/79	86/8	Claremont Amateurs	Falkirk	235 (7)	19 (1)	24 (3)	0	3	0	0	0
MacRae, Keith Alexander	67/68	73/74	Lanark GS	Manchester City	124 (2)	9	20 (1)	14	1	0	1	0
Macguire, Stephen	2003/04		Motherwell Youths		Never Played	0	0	0	0	0	0	0
Main, Dave	69/70	73/74	Wishaw HS	Albion Rovers	15 (2)	0	10 (1)	1	2	0	0	0
Mair, Gordon	85/86	90/91	Lincoln City	Clydebank	49 (24)	4 (3)	6 (4)	0	2	1	1	0
Mair, Joseph	68/9	68/69	Youth	Freed 30/4/69	Never Played	0	0	0	0	0	0	0
Mann, Andrew R	61/62	61/62	Clyde	Hamilton Academical	1	0	0	0	0	0	0	0
Marinello, Peter	75/76	78/79	Portsmouth	Fulham	77 (12)	9 (2)	8 (2)	7	12	5	3	1
Marshall, David	53/54	53/54	Rangers		Never Played	0	0	0	0	0	0	0
Marshall, Gordon Banks	2003/04		Kilmarnock		33	3	1	0	0	0	0	0
Martin, Alec	70/71	74/75	Hull City		60 (16)	4	16	5	8	2	4	1
Martin, Brian	91/92	97/98	Saint Mirren	Stirling Albion	236 (1)	17	13	0	10	1	0	0
Martin, John	58/59		Blantyre Victoria	Morton	Never Played	0	0	0	0	0	0	0
Martin, Johnny	51/52		Queen of the South	Arbroath	Never Played	0	0	0	0	0	0	0
Martin, Robert	77/78	78/79	Lanark United		0	0	0	0	0	0	0	0
Martinez, Roberto	2001/2	2001/2	Wigan Athletic	Swansea City	8 (8)	0	0	0	0	0	0	0
Martis, John	57/58	68/69	Royal Albert	Hellenic (South Africa)	295 (2)	30	59	14	2	0	0	0
Mason, William A	54/55	55/56	Linlithgow Rose	Hamilton Academical	26	3	0	0	0	0	0	0
Mathie, David	47/48	50/51	Partik Thistle	Llanelly	30	1	11	0	15	0	1	0
Mathie, Graeme Ross	2002/3	2003/4	Bournemouth		Never Played	0	0	0	0	0	0	0
Mathie, Ross C	75/76	75/76	Dumbarton	Berwick Rangers	Never Played	0	0	0	0	0	0	0
Matthei, Rob	98/99	2000/01	Volendam	Dunfermline Athletic	16 (4)	0 (1)	1 (1)	0	0	0	0	0
Mauchlen, Alister Henry	82/83	85/86	Kilmarnock	Leicester City	75 (1)	6	6	0	4	0	1	0
Maxwell, Alastair Espie	82/83	91/92	Fir Park BC	Rangers	135	12	6	0	0	0	0	0
May, Edward Skillion	94/95	99/00	Falkirk	Dunfermline Athletic	102 (7)	8 (1)	8	2	5	0	0	0
McAdam, Colin C	74/75	77/78	Dumbarton	Partick Thistle	48 (14)	5 (2)	5	9	3	0	0	0
McAdam, Thomas Ian	86/87	89/90	Hamilton Academical	Aidrieonians	98 (1)	10	4	0	3	0	0	0
McAllister, Gary	81/82	85/86	Fir Park BC	Leicester City	52 (7)	7	3 (1)	0	6	2	0	0
McAndie, Brian James	2003/4		Motherwell Youths		Never Played	0	0	0	0	0	0	0
McAnenay, Michael Samuel	87/88	88/89	Shettleston Juniors	Albion Rovers	Never Played	0	0	0	0	0	0	0
McArthur, Peter	79/80	79/80	Fir Park BC	Clyde	Never Played	0	0	0	0	0	0	0
McBride, Joe	62/63	64/65	Partick Thistle	Celtic	90	11	14	16	56	13	9	10
McBride, Martin Joseph	85/86	90/91	Wishaw Juniors	East Stirlingshire	16 (15)	3 (1)	1 (2)	0	1	0	0	0
McBride, Stephen	83/84	83/84	Linfield		0 (4)	0 (1)	0	0	0	0	0	0
McCabe, James	69/70	74/75	Bargeddie Amateurs	Stranraer	66 (4)	8	13	6	13	1	6	4
McCall, Alex	66/67	67/68	Arsenal	Partick Thistle	21 (2)	2	2 (2)	0	3	1	0	0
McCall, Billy	48/49	50/51	Newcastle United	Third Lanark	28	3	6	0	4	0	0	0
McCall, Ian Holland	82/83	82/83	Dumfries Academy	Queen's Park	Never Played	0	0	0	0	0	0	0
McCallum, Bobby	57/58	67/68	Motherwell YC		163	17	29	16	11	0	1	2
McCallum, David John	96/97	97/98	Bearsden BC	Stirling Albion	Never Played	0	0	0	0	0	0	0
McCallum, William	59/60	73/74	Douglas Water Thistle	Saint Mirren	271 (1)	22	44 (1)	13	1	0	0	0
McCann, Robert Johnston	55/56	65/66	Queen's Park	Hamilton Academical	247	28	53	3	22	1	4	0
McCart, Christopher	84/85	96/97	Fir Park B.C.	Falkirk	259 (8)	17 (1)	12	8	6	1	1	0
McClair, Brian John	81/82	82/83	Aston Villa	Celtic	33 (6)	2	9 (1)	0	15	1	5	0
McClen, Jamie	2000/01	2000/01	Newcastle United	Newcastle United	1 (2)	0	0	0	0	0	0	0
McCloy, Peter	63/64	69/70	Crosshill Thistle	Rangers	137	8	29	10	0	0	0	0
McClymont, Willie	71/72	74/75	Cumbernauld United	Stranraer	38 (5)	3	14 (3)	4	8	0	2	2
McColl, Bobby	2003/4		Aberdeen		Never Played	0	0	0	0	0	0	0
McCorriston, Bobby	80/81	81/82	Kilmarnock A		Never Played	0	0	0	0	0	0	0
McCoy, John	53/54	53/54	Southampton		Never Played	0	0	0	0	0	0	0
McCulloch, Lee Henry	94/95	2000/01	Carluke Roers	Wigan Athletic	75 (47)	11 (2)	5 (2)	0 (1)	22	3	2	0
McCaid, Jim	66/67	66/67	Shotts BA	Freed	2	0	0	0	0	0	0	0
McDonald, Ian	84/85	84/85	Partick Thistle	Partick Thistle	10 (3)	0	0	0	4	0	0	0
McDonald, Paul	81/82	81/82	Fir Park BC		Never Played	0	0	0	0	0	0	0
McDonald, Scott	2003/04		Milton Keynes Dons		10 (5)	1 (2)	0	0	1	1	0	0
McFadden, James	99/00	2003/4	Motherwell BC	Everton	52 (11)	5	1	0	26	5	1	0
McFadden, Paul	83/84	85/86	Duntocher BC	Marleta Eagles	12 (10)	2	1 (2)	0	4	0	0	0
McFadyen, Ian	54/55	58/59	Dundee United	Dundee United	39	2	3	0	0	0	0	0
McFarlane, Fraser	66/67	68/69	North Motherwell	Airdrieonians	0	0	1	0	0	0	0	0
McGhee, Alex J	74/75	74/75	Morton	Hibernian	Never Played	0	0	0	0	0	0	0
McGoldrick, John	84/85	84/85	Leeds United	Leeds United	Never Played	0	0	0	0	0	0	0
McGowan, Jamie	98/99	99/00	Falkirk	Saint Mirren	42 (3)	4	1	0	1	0	0	0
McGowan, Samuel	46/47	46/47	Morton	Saint Johnstone	1	0	0	0	0	0	0	0
McGrillen, Paul Alexander	90/91	94/95	Motherwell BC	Falkirk	39 (48)	1 (3)	1 (1)	2 (1)	13	0	2	1
McGuinness, Robert F	72/73	74/75	Lesmahagow	Portsmouth	3 (4)	0	0	0	0	0	0	0
McGuire, Gordon	79/80	79/80	Falkirk		Never Played	0	0	0	0	0	0	0
Mcllwraith, Jim	73/74	75/76	Kilwinning Rangers	Bury	21 (7)	5	0	0	6	1	0	0
Mclnally, John Whitfield	67/68	73/74	Kilmarnock	Hamilton Academical	130 (4)	11 (1)	28 (1)	8 (1)	38	2	12	2
Mcintyre, Jim	53/54	55/56	Forth Wanderers	Albion Rovers	17	3	0	0	0	0	0	0
McKay, Allan	67/68	68/69	Third Lanark	Dumbarton	37 (2)	2	2 (2)	0	0	0	0	0
McKay, Kevin	84/85	84/85	Netherdale		Never Played	0	0	0	0	0	0	0
Mckeeer, John	80/81	81/82	Old Kilpatrick		14 (8)	0	4	0	7	0	1	0
McKeown, Kevin	84/85	90/91	Celtic BC	Ayr United	3	0	0	0	0	0	0	0
McKinnon, Robert	91/92	95/96	Hartlepool United	FC Twente Enschede	152	10	8	5	8	0	0	0
McLardie, Jim	64/65	64/65	North Motherwell	Saint Mirren	Never Played	0	0	0	0	0	0	0

Name	First	Last			Appearances				Goals			
	Season	Season	Previous Club	Next Club	League	SC	LC	Other	League	SC	LC	Other
McLaren, Stewart	74/75	78/79	West Bromwich Albion	Dundee	117(6)	17	11	7 (1)	5	2	0	0
McLaughlin, John	65/66	65/66	Dunfermline Athletic	Dunfermline Athletic	18	2	2	0	4	0	0	0
McLaughlin, Brian	79/80	82/83	Ayr United	Hamilton Academical	108 (6)	6	9	0	37	1	4	0
McLaughlin, Kevin	99/00	99/00	Cathkin United BC		Never Played	0	0	0	0	0	0	0
McLean, Alistair	80/81	80/81	Partick		1	0	0	0	0	0	0	0
McLean, James	84/85	85/86	Fir Park BC		Never Played	0	0	0	0	0	0	0
McLean, Paul	89/90	90/91	Queen's Park	Ayr United	0 (3)	0	0	0	0	0	0	0
McLeish, Alexander	94/95	96/97	Aberdeen	Hibernian	3	0	1	1	0	0	0	0
McLelland, Charles	79/80	80/81	Aberdeen	Dundee	49 (2)	1	5	0	1	0	0	0
McLelland, Stephen J	80/81	82/83	Ayr United	Hamilton Academical	78 (1)	5	16 (1)	0	7	1	1	0
McLeod, Donald A	46/47	52/53	Whitburn		143	18	35	2	2	2	1	0
McLeod, Joseph	90/91	92/93	Dundee United	Stirling Albion	23 (23)	1	1	1	1	1	0	0
McManus, Michael Q	75/76	76/7	Ashfield	Hamilton Academical	1 (2)	0	0	0	0	0	0	0
McMillan, James C	46/47	49/50	Dalziel HS	Dougals Water	Never Played	0	0	0	0	0	0	0
McMillan, John David	94/95	94/95	Carluke Roers	Saint Mirren	Never Played	0	0	0	0	0	0	0
McMillan, Stephen	93/94	2000/01	Troon	Wigan Athletic	144 (8)	13 (1)	9	0	6	0	0	0
McNair, Colin	89/90	89/90	Falkirk	Dumbarton	1 (1)	0	0	0	0	0	0	0
McNeil, John	53/54	54/55	Albion Rovers	Airdrieonians	5	2	0	0	0	0	0	0
McPhee, John	56/57	61/62	North Motherwell	Blackpool	74	11	10	0	16	6	4	0
McQueen, Tom	46/47	46/47	Juniors	Leith Athletic	Never Played	0	0	0	0	0	0	0
McRoberts, William	46/47	47/48		Saint Johnstone	5	0	0	0	2	0	0	0
McSeveney, William	53/54	63/64	Dunfermline Athletic	Freed	196	24	36	0	20	4	4	0
McSherry, Paul	93/94		Cumbernauld United		Never Played	0	0	0	0	0	0	0
McSkimming, Shaun Peter	94/95	97/98	Kilmarnock	Dundee	57 (7)	5 (1)	4	1	7	2	0	1
McStay, John	83/84	86/87	Gartcosh United	Raith Rovers	11 (10)	0 (1)	1 (1)	0	1	0	0	0
McStay, John [1]	2003/04		Celtic Youth		Never Played	0	0	0	0	0	0	0
McVie, Willie	75/76		Clyde	Toronto Blizzard	85 (2)	8	15	12	2	0	0	0
Nelson, Charles	69/70	69/70	Dalzell HS		Never Played	0	0	0	0	0	0	0
Nelson, Maxwell	55/56	56/57	Northpark Athletic	Greenock Morton	1	0	0	0	0	0	0	0
Nelson, Richard	52/53	52/53	Larkhall Thistle		Never Played	0	0	0	0	0	0	0
Neville, Barry Robert	2003/04		Motherwell Youths		Never Played	0	0	0	0	0	0	0
Nevin, Patrick Kevin Francis	98/99	99/00	Kilmarnock		20 (38)	2 (3)	2 (1)	0	2	0	0	0
Newman, Robert Nigel	97/98	97/98	Norwich City		11	4	0	0	0	0	0	0
Nicholas, Steven Arthur	98/99	2001/02	Stirling Albion	Stirling Albion	13 (49)	0 (3)	1 (1)	0	5	0	0	0
Nijholt, Luc	90/91	92/93	Basle Old Boys	Swindon Town	91 (5)	9	6	2	5	1	0	0
Nyyssonen, Kai Juhani	98/99	98/99	CD Cordoba	Finland	3	0	1	0	1	0	0	0
O'Donnell, Philip	90/91	1994/95	Schools	Celtic	130 (3)	12 (2)	6	2	15	2	0	0
Offiong, Richard	2002/03	2002/03	Newastle United	Newcastle United	0 (9)	0 (1)	0	0	0	0	0	0
Ogilivie, Duncan Henderson	31/32	31/32	Alva Albion Rangers		Never Played	0	0	0	0	0	0	0
O'Hara, Tommy	81/82	82/83	Jacksonville Teamen	Falkirk	47 (6)	3	6	0	0	0	0	0
O'Hare, James	84/85	86/87	Fir Park BC	Freed	Never Played	0	0	0	0	0	0	0
Okoli, James	2000/01	2000/01		Freed	6	0	0	0	0	0	0	0
O'Neill, Colin	88/89	93/94	Portadown	Retired	64	9 (1)	5	0	4	1	2	0
O'Neill, Thomas	73/74	77/78	Shotts Bon Accord	Clyde	5 (7)	0	0 (2)	3	1	0	0	2
O'Rourke, Jimmy	76/77	80/81	Saint Johnstone		47 (14)	4 (2)	4 (2)	2	14	2	0	0
O'Rourke, Tom L	78/79	80/81	Meadowbank Thistle	Forfar Athletic	10	0	4	0	0	0	0	0
Oueifio, Ange	2000/01	2001/02	Denderleeun	Freed	14 (3)	1	2	0	0	0	0	0
Partridge, David William	2002/03		Dundee United		47	4	2 (1)	0	1	0	0	0
Paterson, Craig Stewart	86/87	91/92	Rangers	Kilmarnock	154 (4)	17	8	0	8	0	0	0
Paterson, Robert	59/60	59/60			1	0	0	0	0	0	0	0
Paterson, Robin	60/61	60/61	Glenafton Athletic	Freed	Never Played	0	0	0	0	0	0	0
Paton, Andrew	46/47	57/58	Kello Rovers	Hamilton Academical	302	37	79	2	0	0	1	0
Paton, Ian	61/62	63/64	North Motherwell	Carluke Rovers	Never Played	0	0	0	0	0	0	0
Payon, William J	46/47	51/52	Bo'ness United	Freed	11	0	1	0	1	0	0	0
Pearce, Brian	77/78	78/79	Fir Park BC	Airdrie	Never Played	0	0	0	0	0	0	0
Pearson, Stephen Paul	2000/01	2003/04	Our Lady's High School	Celtic	68 (12)	4 (1)	3	0	12	0	1	0
Peolsi, John	73/74	74/75	Aston Villa	Saint Johnstone	Never Played	0	0	0	0	0	0	0
Pettigrew, William H	72/73	78/79	East Kilbride Thistle	Dundee United	157 (9)	18	18	13 (1)	80	8	11	3
Philliben, John	86/8	97/98	Doncaster Rovers	Stirling Albion	264 (38)	21 (3)	10 (3)	5 (1)	7	1	0	0
Phillips, John	68/69	69/70	Aidrieonians		0	0	2	0	0	0	0	0
Picken, James	91/92	92/93	Motherwell BC		Never Played	0	0	0	0	0	0	0
Pithie, Charles	65/66		Morton		Never Played	0	0	0	0	0	0	0
Pollock, Stewart	55/56	55/56	Partick Thistle	Gillingham	2	0	0	0	0	0	0	0
Porteous, John Roberts	46/47	47/48		Alloa Athletic	Never Played	0	0	0	0	0	0	0
Purdie, Ian	77/78	77/78	Dundee	Wigan Athletic	11 (5)	0	2	3 (1)	3	0	0	1
Quinn, Mark James	2003/04		Motherwell Youths		0	0	0	0	0	0	0	0
Quinn, Pat	55/56	62/63	Albion Rovers	Blackpool	196	16	39	0	86	7	26	0
Quinn, Paul Charles	2002/03		Motherwell Youths		27 (3)	0	0	0	1	0	0	0
Rae, Derek Parlane	95/96	95/96	Rangers	East Stirlingshire	Never Played	0	0	0	0	0	0	0
Rafferty, Stuart	78/79	83/84	Port Glasgow BC	Dundee	71 (18)	6 (2)	6 (7)	0	1	1	0	0
Ramsay, Bobby	62/63	64/65	North Motherwell	Airdrieonians	5	0	2	1	0	0	0	0
Ramsay, Douglas	97/98	2002/03	Bearsden BC	Ayr United	21 (18)	1	1 (1)	0	2	0	0	0
Rathmell, Ian	66/67	66/67		Freed	0	0	0	0	0	0	0	0
Rea, Wallace	55/56	59/60	Third Lanark	Bradford City	14	1	0	0	3	0	0	0
Ready, Karl	2001/02	2001/02	Queens Park Rangers	Freed	35 (1)	0	1	0	3	0	0	0
Redpath, William Yates	46/47	55/56	Polkemmet		227	39	70	1	15	4	7	0
Reid, Andrew	2003/04	2003/04	Nottingham Forest	Hibernian	Never Played	0	0	0	0	0	0	0
Reid, Billy	54/55	61/62	Wishaw HS	Airdrieonians	56	3	14	0	9	0	2	0
Reid, Ian	49/50		Kilsyth Rangers	Cowdenbeath	4	0	0	0	0	0	0	0
Reid, Joseph HB	46/47	48/49	Polkemmet	Freed	4	2	0	0	0	1	0	0
Reid, Phillip	2003/04		Celtic Youth		Never Played	0	0	0	0	0	0	0
Reid, Ricky	65/66	66/67	Dalziel High	Freed	Never Played	0	0	0	0	0	0	0

Name	First	Last			Appearances				Goals			
	Season	Season	Previous Club	Next Club	League	SC	LC	Other	League	SC	LC	Other
Reid, Sammy	56/57	59/60	Douglas Water Thistle	Liverpool	60	4	10	0	19	0	5	0
Reilly, James Alfred	2003/04		Youths		Never Played	0	0	0	0	0	0	0
Reilly, John Paul	85/86	88/89	Dundee United	Dunfermline Athletic	42 (14)	6 (1)	4	0	12	2	3	0
Reilly, Mark Francis	86/87	90/91	Wishaw	Kilmarnock	3 (1)	0	0	0	0	0	0	0
Rennie, Stuart	73/74	78/79	Falkirk	Ayr United	174	22	14	12	0	0	0	0
Resch, Franz	97/98	97/98	Rapid Vienna	Darlington	3	0	2	0	0	0	0	0
Richardson, Ronnie	66/67	66/67	Troon	Freed	Never Played	0	0	0	0	0	0	0
Ritchie, Andrew	83/84	83/84	Greenock Morton	Clydebank	6 (2)	0	7 (1)	0	1	0	3	0
Ritchie, Billy	70/71	73/74	Partick Thistle	Stranraer	13	0	14	2	0	0	0	0
Ritchie, Ian	66/67	66/67	Shettleston	Freed	Never Played	0	0	0	0	0	0	0
Ritchie, Innes	92/93	96/97	Motherwell BC		6 (5)	0	0 (1)	0	0	0	0	0
Roarty, David Francis	95/96		Motherwell BC		Never Played	0	0	0	0	0	0	0
Roberts, Bobby	58/59	63/64	Edinburgh Norton	Leicester City	91	9	28	0	27	4	11	0
Roberts, Gordon	76/77		Hull City BC		Never Played	0	0	0	0	0	0	0
Robertson, Charles R	46/47	49/50	Armadale Thistle	Freed	17	2	4	0	6	0	2	0
Robertson, David	62/63	62/63	Baillieston	Crewe	Never Played	0	0	0	0	0	0	0
Robertson, James T	76/77	77/78	East Kilbride Thistle	Stranraer	5	0	0	0	0	0	0	0
Robertson, Jimmy	63/64	64/65	Bath City	Freed	24	2	8	0	2	1	2	0
Robertson, Russell	69/70	69/70	Edinburgh Juv		Never Played	0	0	0	0	0	0	0
Robinson, Gordon	51/52	52/53	Army	Bury	7	2	0	0	3	0	0	0
Roddie, Andrew Robert	93/94	96/97	Aberdeen	Saint Mirren	24 (31)	0 (1)	2 (2)	1	0	0	0	0
Ross, Alex	73/74	73/74	Whitburn School		Never Played	0	0	0	0	0	0	0
Ross, Ian	93/94	98/99	Bathgate Thistle	Saint Mirren	46 (19)	4 (1)	0 (3)	0	3	0	0	0
Ross, Jim	76/77	77/78	Eastercraigs	Airdrieonians	Never Played	0	0	0	0	0	0	0
Ross, Samuel Y	46/47	46/47	Falkirk	Dundee United	Never Played	0	0	0	0	0	0	0
Ruane, Brian	79/0	79/0	Lesmahagow		1 (1)	0	0	0	0	0	0	0
Russell, Bobby F	62/63	63/64	Darvel	Arbroath	18	0	3	0	9	0	5	0
Russell, Iain Thomas	2002/03	2002/03	Rangers	Dumbarton	0 (5)	0	0 (1)	0	0	0	0	0
Russell, John	46/47	50/51	Pollok Juniors	Kilmarnock	38	2	13	1	1	0	0	0
Russell, Robert	87/88	91/92	Shettleston Juniors	Ayr United	110 (21)	5 (2)	10 (2)	2	15	1	2	0
Russell, Ryan	2003/04		Motherwell Youths		Never Played	0	0	0	0	0	0	0
Sammeroff, Howard	81/82	81/82	Kilsyth Rangers	Hamilton Academical	4	0	0	0	0	0	0	0
Scotland, Alex	52/53	52/53	Whitburn	Freed	Never Played	0	0	0	0	0	0	0
Scott, Ian	46/47	48/49		Freed	Never Played	0	0	0	0	0	0	0
Scott, Robert Andrew	2002/03		Motherwell Youths		0 (1)	0	0	0	0	0	0	0
Seath, Jim	62/63	63/64	Hill o'Beath Juveniles	Freed	1	0	0	0	0	0	0	0
Sengewald, Daniel	2002/03	2002/03	SC Ven		6 (1)	0	0	0	0	0	0	0
Shanks, David Thow	87/88	89/90	Clydebank	Alloa Athletic	8 (3)	2	0	0	0	0	0	0
Shanks, John R Mark	78/79	78/79	Blackburn		10 (1)	0	1	2	0	0	0	0
Shannon, Robert	93/94	94/95	Dunfermline Athletic	Dundee United	64 (4)	3	3	4	3	0	1	0
Shaw, Archibald	46/47	58/59	Wishaw	Freed	256	39	65	2	0	3	0	0
Shaw, Robert McL	83/84	83/84	Leicester City	Freed	0 (2)	0	0	0	0	0	0	0
Shepherd, Anthony	91/92	92/93	Carlisle United	Portadown	3 (7)	0	0	0	0	0	0	0
Shepstone, Paul	92/93	93/94	Blackburn Rovers		1	0	0 (1)	0	0	0	0	0
Shields, Alan	95/96	95/96	Cumbernauld United		Never Played	0	0	0	0	0	0	0
Shivute, Eliphas	97/98	98/99	Eleven Arrows	Shinzan	12 (12)	0	0 (2)	0	3	0	0	0
Simpson, Neil	91/92	92/93	Newcastle United		32 (1)	2 (1)	2	0	1	0	0	0
Sinclair, Andrew	46/47	49/50	Armadale Thistle	Cowdenbeath	11	0	1	0	0	0	0	0
Slaven, John M	46/47	47/48		Freed	0	0	1	0	0	0	1	0
Sloan, Thomas	51/52	56/57	Heart of Midlothian	Gloucester City	112	23	25	0	35	6	13	0
Smith, Joe F	78/79	81/82	Aberdeen		55 (2)	3	3	0	0	0	0	0
Smith, Paul McKinnon	86/87	88/89	Raith Rovers	Dunfermline Athletic	70 (8)	7	9	0	13	1	2	0
Smith, Ricky	65/66	66/67	Royston Roseberry	Freed	Never Played	0	0	0	0	0	0	0
Smyth, Pat	72/73	72/73	Petershill		Never Played	0	0	0	0	0	0	0
Sneddon, Alan	92/93	92/93	Hibernian	East Fife	16	2	1	0	0	0	0	0
Sneddon, Willie	50/51	51/52	Hulford United	Freed	1	0	0	0	1	0	0	0
Soloy, Yan	2001/02	2001/02	Le Harve		11 (1)	1	0	0	1	0	0	0
Somerville, Jim T	77/78	78/79	Fir Park BC	Fredrikshaven	3 (5)	0	0	0	0	0	0	0
Soutar, Gordon	79/00	81/82	Falkirk	East Stirlingshire	52 (3)	3	3 (2)	0	10	1	0	0
Spark, Alexander	76/77	76/77	Preston North End	Bradford City	0	0	2	1 (1)	0	0	0	0
Spencer, John	98/99	2000/01	Everton	Colorado Rapids	66 (5)	5 (1)	3 (1)	0	20	1	0	0
Sproat, John	79/80	83/84	Ayr United	Ayr United	145	9	19	0	0	0	0	0
Saint John, Ian	56/57	60/61	Douglas Water Thistle	Liverpool	113	14	17	0	79	13	13	0
Stenhouse, Alan S	57/58	61/62	Edina Hearts	Cowdenbeath	5	0	0	0	1	0	0	0
Stevens, Gregor McK	73/74	84/85	Eastercraig Amateurs	Leicester City	144 (3)	10	19	12 (1)	19	0	0	0
Stevenson, Morris John	59/60	61/62	Musselburgh W	Hibernian	12	1	3	0	3	1	3	0
Stevenson, Wilie	52/53	52/53	Kilsyth Rangers	Freed	Never Played	0	0	0	0	0	0	0
Stewart, Alan	65/66	65/66	Netherton Hearts	Freed	Never Played	0	0	0	0	0	0	0
Stewart, John	62/63	62/63		Freed	Never Played	0	0	0	0	0	0	0
Stewart, John	58/59	60/61	Strathclyde	Greenock Morton	1	0	0	0	0	0	0	0
Stewart, Robert	83/84	85/86	Whitburn Bluebells	Falkirk	25 (8)	5	0 (1)	0	10	2	0	0
Stirling, Jered	98/99	98/99	Partick Thistle	Partick Thistle	4 (1)	0	1 (1)	0	1	0	0	0
Strachan, Hugh Mair	57/58	62/63	Cumnock Juniors	Greenock Morton	26	0	5	0	4	0	1	0
Strong, Greg	99/00	2001/02	Bolton Wanderers		72 (2)	2	1	0	3	0	1	0
Struthers, William	70/71	72/73	Stonehouse Violet	Albion Rovers	21 (4)	2 (1)	8	0	1	0	1	0
Tannock,Ross	89/00	90/91	Bellfield BC	Ayr Unitd	Never Played	0	0	0	0	0	0	0
Tarrant,Neil Nenneth	2001/02	2001/02	Aston Villa	Ross County	2 (3)	0	0 (1)	0	0	0	0	0
Taylor, Ian Wishart	73/74	75/76	Aberdeen	Saint Johnstone	38 (10)	5 (3)	11 (1)	3	5	2	3	0
Teale, Shaun	98/99	99/00	Happy Valley	Southend United	45	3	4	0	3	0	1	0
Telford, John	49/50	50/51	Third Lanark	Ayr United	7	0	0	0	0	0	0	0
Thomas, Tony	98/99	2000/01	Everton		16	1	2	0	0	1	0	0
Thomson, Andrew	98/99				Never Played	0	0	0	0	0	0	0

Name	First Season	Last Season	Previous Club	Next Club	Appearances League	Appearances SC	Appearances LC	Appearances Other	Goals League	Goals SC	Goals LC	Goals Other
Thomson, Brian Fraser	87/88	88/89	Fraserburgh	Arbroath	Never Played	0	0	0	0	0	0	0
Thomson, Ian	62/63	67/68	Musselburgh Windsor		52	3	11 (1)	14	11	2	1	1
Thomson, Matt	59/60	68/69	Ardeer Thistle	Freed	170 (3)	14	37	14	0	0	0	0
Thomson, Scott Yuill	97/98	97/98	Hull City	Airdrieonians	1	0	0	0	0	0	0	0
Thomson, William Marshall	91/92	93/94	Dundee United	Rangers	52	3	2	2	0	0	0	0
Todd, Thomas Bell	46/47	48/49	Burnbank Athletic	Airdrieonians	Never Played	0	0	0	0	0	0	0
Toner, Jimmy	55/56	55/56	Leeds United	Forfar Athletic	1	0	0	0	0	0	0	0
Townsley, Derek	99/00	2000/01	Queen Of The South	Hibernian	38 (17)	4 (1)	5	0	7	0	1	0
Trcey, Paul	83/84	84/85	Fir Park BC	Clyde	0 (3)	0	0	0	0	0	0	0
Tulloch, Barry	2000/01	2000/01	Lenzie BC	Cowdenbeath	Never Played	0	0	0	0	0	0	0
Twaddle, Kevin	99/00	2001/02	Greenock Morton	Heart of Midlothian	45 (17)	3 (2)	1	0	7	0	0	0
Valarkari, Simo	96/97	99/00	Finn Pa	Derby County	98 (6)	7 (2)	4 (1)	0	0	0	0	0
Van Der Gaag, Michael	94/95	96/97	PSV Eindhoven	FC Utrecht	40	4	1	1	7	1	0	0
Vaughan, Anthony John	2002/03	2002/03	Nottingham Forest	Nottingham Forest	12	3	0	0	1	0	0	0
Verhuel, Bart	91/92	92/93	Go Ahead Eagles Deventer	Freed	1 (3)	0	0	0	0	0	0	0
Walker, Andrew Francis	84/84	86/87	Ballieston Juniors	Celtic	65 (11)	9 (1)	3 (3)	0	17	2	1	0
Walker, Joseph Nicol	82/83	83/84	Leicester City	Rangers	31	2	7	0	0	0	0	0
Wallace, Ian	53/54	54/55	Grange Rovers	Freed	0	0	0	0	0	0	0	0
Wallace, William	62/63	63/64	Muirkirk	Clydebank	2	0	1	0	1	0	0	0
Wark, joe	67/68	83/84	Irvine Victoria		459 (5)	37	7 (2)	29	14	0	3	1
Watson, Bobby	69/70	76/77	Rangers		179 (3)	23 (1)	31	19	3	0	3	2
Watson, James	46/47	51/52	Armdale Thistle	Huddersfield Town	147	26	42	2	48	8	17	2
Watson, Willie	73/74	77/78	Manchester United	Dundee	122 (5)	18	15 (1)	12	2	1	0	0
Watt, Graham	82/83	82/83	Celtic	Freed	Never Played	0	0	0	0	0	0	0
Watters, Willie	47/48	50/51	Bonnyrigg Rose	Dunfermline Athletic	61	8	13	0	12	1	3	0
Weir, Andrew Best	57/58	67/68	Arthurlie		200 (2)	21	49	13	44	9	5	3
Weir, Ian	59/60	61/62	Clyde	Stirling Albion	22	0	5	0	0	0	0	0
Weir, James	1985/86	1986/87	Hamilton Academical	KSV Hessen Kasselin	7 (1)	1	2 (1)	0	0	0	0	0
Weir, Michael Graham	96/97	97/98	Hibernian		18 (5)	2	3	0	6	0	0	0
Weir, S Hastie	54/55	64/65	Queen's Park	Partick Thistle	196	16	58	0	0	0	0	0
Weldon, Derek	83/84	84/85	Shotts BA	Freed	1 (1)	0	0	0	0	0	0	0
Welsh, Jimmy	59/60	60/61	Sunderland	Freed	Never Played	0	0	0	0	0	0	0
White, David William	98/99	98/99	Ipswich town	Cowdenbeath	Never Played	0	0	0	0	0	0	0
White, George	76/77	77/78	Eastercraigs	Freed	Never Played	0	0	0	0	0	0	0
White, Willie	52/53	52/53	Alva Albion R	Accrington	Never Played	0	0	0	0	0	0	0
Whiteford, David	66/67	73/74	Jordanhill College	Falkirk	197	12	36	13 (1)	13	1	2	0
Williams, Archibald	51/52	55/56	Heart of midlothian	Dunfermline Athletic	36	1	10	0	12	1	0	0
Williams, Derek	80/81	81/82	Fir Park BC		1	0	0	0	0	0	0	0
Williams, Lawrence	80/81	80/81	Dumbarton	Dumbarton	4	0	0	0	0	0	0	0
Williamson, David Francis	95/96	95/96	Irvine Victoria	Cambridge United	Never Played	0	0	0	0	0	0	0
Williamson, Jim	55/56	55/56		Freed	Never Played	0	0	0	0	0	0	0
Wilson, Jack	50/51	50/51	Liverpool	Arbroath	Never Played	0	0	0	0	0	0	0
Wilson, Jimmy	67/68	69/70	Aberdeen	Dundee	83	5	16	0	11	0	4	0
Wilson, Paul	78/79	78/79	Celtic	Partick Thistle	18 (3)	1	0	0	1	0	0	0
Wilson, Scott william	99/00	2001/02	Ayr United	Airdrieonians	Never Played	0	0	0	0	0	0	0
Wishart, Fraser	83/84	96/97	Pollok Juniors	Clydebank	168 (4)	12 (1)	10 (1)	0	5	0	1	0
Wood, Gary	84/85	84/85	Elgin BC		Never Played	0	0	0	0	0	0	0
Wood, Martin	2000/01	2001/02	Rothes County	Ross County	3 (5)	0	0 (1)	0	0	0	0	0
Woods, Stephen Gerard	94/95	2002/03	Preston North End	Saint Mirren	126 (3)	7	9 (1)	5	0	0	0	0
Wright, Brain Vincent	85/86	87/88	Hamilton Academical	Clydebank	67 (7)	6	3 (3)	0	6	1	0	0
Wright, Kenneth Thomas	2002/03		Motherwell Youth		2 (13)	0 (1)	0 (1)	0	0	0	0	0
Wylie, Alan	56/57	68/69	Penicuik Athletic	Cowdenbeath	132	16	24	6	0	0	0	0
Young, Bobby	59/60	61/62	Neilston W	Saint Johnstone	26	2	4	0	7	2	0	0
Young, Robert B	46/47	48/49		Dundee United	Never Played	0	0	0	0	0	0	0

Statistical Sections key and notes

Who's Who

Every player known to have been registered with the club who either played or never played a post-Second World War first team competitive match (from the 1946/47 to the 2003/04 season) is included. In the first column, the surname is followed by first christian/given name (full or as popularly known). A blank third column for recent seasons indicates the player may still be registered with the club. The player's previous and next clubs are shown where applicable/where known (4th and 5th columns). Number of substitute appearances are included and are shown in brackets (in the 6th to 9th columns).

Match Statistics

Matches from 1886 to 1893 (Scottish Cup only) and from 1893 (Scottish League and Scottish Cup) are included; from 1946/47 to 2003/04 seasons, all competitive and friendly matches have been included Whilst the total number of appearances (League and Scottish Cup) for the pre-Second World War seasons are generally known - and included - the actual line-ups for individual matches are not complete and are therefore not included. In all cases details are shown where known.

Pre-war seasons: The first column shows the League match number (these have been shown in the chronological order of their original dates, but where these dates have been changed, 'p' indicates the match was postponed to the date that follows, i.e. day/month in figures. Scottish Cup round (Q = qualifying round, S/F = Semi-final, F = Final, P/O = Play-off, R or rep = replay. AET = after extra time) The second column gives the date of the match (a blank indicates date unknown and a question mark indicates records show conflicting dates and has not been included). The third column shows the opposition (upper case - capitals - home games, lower case - away games). The fourth column shows the result (Motherwell score first), the fifth column the goalscorers (number of goals scored in brackets and OG indicates an 'own goal') and the sixth column the attendance.

Post-War seasons: All generally as above, for the pre-War seasons (with additional tables for other cup games and recognised first team friendly matches), with extra columns (6th onwards) providing the match line-ups. It has not always been possible to define a player's actual playing position/role in the team (especially in recent seasons), and therefore a player in the starting line-up is shown as an 'x', and a used substitute shown as 's'.

1882-83 Season

First ever Motherwell team who played and won 3-2 against Hamilton Academicals.
The goalscorers were A.Kemp (2) and N.McMaster.
The first ever supporters' player of the year award was given to "Big Drew" of Motherwell.
Team consisted of : Goalkeeper. Sneddon & Sharp, Backs. : Murray & D Kemp. Half backs : Anderson, McKillop, Anderson. Forwards : Moodie, W Charteris, McPherson, Thomson, A Kemp, Cowie.

The Statistical Record
Part 1: 1886 - 1946

1885-86 Season

Sneddon, Gray, R.Sharp, Murray, Irvine, Watson, T.Charteris, T.Sharp, Moodie, W.Charteris

Pre League: Scottish Qualifying Cup ties

1886

1	11-Sep	Cambuslang	1	6

1887

1	3-Sep	Drumpellier	3	2
1r	10-Sep	DRUMPELLIER	2	0
2	24-Sep	Carfin Shamrock	1	3

1888

1	1-Sep	ROYAL ALBERT	3	3
1r	8-Sep	Royal Albert	2	1
2	22-Sep	HAMILTON ACCIES	5	1
3	13-Oct	DUMBARTON	2	6

1889

1	7-Sep	Airdriehill	6	5
2	28-Sep	Carfin Shamrock	2	6

1890

1	6-Sep	Royal Albert	4	5

1891

1	5-Sep	COWDENBEATH	1	4

1892

1	26-Nov	CAMPSIE	9	2
1r	17-Dec	CAMPSIE	6	4
2	24-Dec	HEARTS	2	4

1893 - 94 Season
Second Division

1	12-Aug	CLYDE	4	1	Phillips (2), Gray, Galloway	2000
2	19-Aug	Abercorn	3	2	Gray, Lambie, Denholm	1000
3	26-Aug	COWLAIRS	3	2	Denholm (2), Collins	
4	30-Sep	PORT GLASGOW	7	2	Galloway (4), Govan, Brand, OG	
5	7-Oct	Partick Thistle	2	4	Allan, Lambie	
6	4-Nov	PARTICK THISTLE	2	3	Watson, Lambie	
7	11-Nov	Greenock Morton	3	2	Cowan, Allan, Lambie	1500
8	25-Nov	Hibernian	2	8	Lambie (2)	2000
9	2-Dec	Northern	2	2	Cowan (2)	
10	16-Dec	GLASGOW THISTLE	6	2	Lightbody (2),Cowan,Henderson, ?, ?	
11	17-Feb	ABERCORN	5	3	Ostler (2), Galloway, Cowan, Govan	
12	24-Mar	Glasgow Thistle	8	1	Galloway(4),Watson(2),Lambie,Ostler	
13	14-Apr	HIBERNIAN	2	1	McLuskie, Allan	5000
14	21-Apr	Clyde	2	3	Leighton, Cowan	
15	28-Apr	Port Glasgow	3	5	Leighton, Cowan, Steel	
16	5-May	Cowlairs	1	4	Galloway	
17	19-May	NORTHERN	2	0	Cowan, Steel	
18	26-May	GREENOCK MORTON	4	1	Cowan (2), Steel, Wright	
Sqc						
Q1	2-Sep	Airdriehill	5	0	Tait, Cowan,Lambie,Galloway,Denholm	
Q2	23-Sep	BURNBANK SWIFTS	6	1	Denholm (3), Galloway (2), Allan	
Q3	14-Oct	Kilmarnock	3	3	Cowan, Denholm, Mathie	
Q3r	21-Oct	KILMARNOCK	1	3	Denholm	

1894 Div. 2

		Pl.	Home					Away					F.	A.	Pts.
			W.	D.	L.	F.	A.	W.	D.	L.	F	A.	(Total)		
1	Hibernian	18	8	0	1	57	15	5	3	1	26	14	83	29	29
2	Cowlairs	18	8	0	1	46	13	5	1	3	26	19	72	32	27
3	Clyde	18	6	2	1	27	17	5	0	4	24	19	51	36	24
4	MOTHERWELL	18	8	0	1	35	15	3	1	5	26	31	61	46	23
5	Partick Thistle	18	6	0	3	37	26	4	0	5	19	32	56	58	20
6	Pt. Glasgow A.	18	6	1	2	39	23	3	1	5	12	29	51	52	13*
7	Abercorn	18	3	1	5	18	22	2	1	6	24	37	42	59	12
8	Morton	18	3	1	5	18	16	1	0	8	18	46	36	62	9
8	Northern	18	3	3	3	21	25	0	0	9	8	41	29	66	9
10	Thistle	18	2	1	6	16	26	0	2	7	15	46	31	72	7

1894 - 95 Season
Second Division

1	11-Aug	AIRDRIEONIANS	4	2	Cowan (2), Edgar, Galloway	
2	18-Aug	Port Glasgow	1	3	Cowan	
3	25-Aug	Dundee Wanderers	2	2	Gourlay, Dunn	
4	8-Sep	ABERCORN	7	0	Gray (4), Cowan, Dunn, Goldie	
5	15-Sep	Renton	4	3	Goldie (2), Cowan, ?	100
6	29-Sep	Cowlairs	3	4	Goldie (2), Mullen	
7	6-Oct	HIBERNIAN	2	0	Cowan (2)	5000
8	17-Nov	Partick Thistle	3	5	Steel (2), ?	
9	1-Dec	RENTON	0	2		
10	29-Dec	Airdrieonians	2	2	Goldie, Edgar	
11	2-Feb	Hibernian	0	5		1000
12	9-Mar	GREENOCK MORTON	6	4	Easson (2), Galloway, Edgar, Goldie, Cowan	
13	16-Mar	Greenock Morton	5	3	Easson, Cowan, ?, ?, ?	
14	30-Mar	DUNDEE WANDERERS	5	0	Goldie (2), Cowan (2), ?	
15	6-Apr	PARTICK THISTLE	3	0	Henderson (2), Edgar	
16	20-Apr	PORT GLASGOW	2	0	Goldie, Edgar	
17	4-May	Abercorn	3	4	Cowan (2), Goldie	
18	18-May	COWLAIRS	4	0	Gray (2), Allan, Cowan	
Sqc						
Q1	22-Sep	Airdriehill	3	1	Cowan, Goldie, ?	
Q2	13-Oct	Paisley Accies	7	3	Cowan (3), Dunn, Docherty, ?, ?	
Sc						
1	24-Nov	MOSSEND SWIFTS	1	2	Goldie	
	31-May	ROYAL ALBERT	5	0	Last Game Played At Dalziel Park	

1893-94

Player	Appearances (Total)
Henderson J	22
Collins	21
Tait	21
Govan	20
Allan	18
Galloway	18
Lambie	16
Cowan	15
Watson	15
Denholm	11
Brand	8
Wright	7
McLuskie	6
Ostler	6
Steel	6
Mathie	5
Phillips	5
Gray	3
Henderson G	3
Leighton	3

1894-95

Player	Appearances (Total)
Goldie	21
Mullen	21
Cowan	20
McCall	20
Collins	19
Harding	19
Daly	17
Govan	15
Edgar	13
Galloway	11
Steel	9
Dunn	8
Easson	8
Gray	5
McLuskie	5
Docherty	3
Wallace	3
Clifford	2
Henderson G	2
Smith	2

1895 Div. 2

		Pl.	Home					Away					F.	A.	Pts.
			W.	D.	L.	F.	A.	W.	D.	L.	F	A.	(Total)		
1	Hibernian	18	8	1	0	54	15	6	1	2	38	13	92	28	30
2	MOTHERWELL	18	8	0	1	33	8	2	2	5	23	31	56	39	22
3	Pt. Glasgow A.	18	8	1	0	45	19	0	3	6	17	37	62	56	20
3	Renton	17	6	0	2	27	15	4	0	5	19	29	46	44	20+
5	Morton	18	7	0	2	38	23	2	1	6	21	40	59	63	19
6	Airdrieonians	18	7	1	1	50	14	1	1	7	18	31	68	45	18
6	Abercorn	18	6	2	1	34	22	1	2	6	17	43	51	65	18
8	Partick Thistle	18	5	2	2	30	22	2	1	6	20	40	50	62	17
9	Dundee Wands	17	3	1	5	31	29	0	0	8	13	57	44	86	9+
10	Cowlairs	18	2	3	4	23	33	0	0	9	14	44	37	77	7

Renton and Dundee W. - only 1 game, Dundee awarded points.

1895 - 96 Season
Second Division

	Date	Opponent	F	A	Scorers	Att
1	10-Aug	PORT GLASGOW	2	1	Edgar, Galloway	2500
2	17-Aug	RENTON	1	0	Gray	3000
3	24-Aug	Kilmarnock	1	7	Edgar	
4	21-Sep	Abercorn	0	1		
5	5-Oct	Greenock Morton	1	4	Smith	
6	12-Oct	LINTHOUSE	1	3	Goldie	
7	19-Oct	Airdrieonians	0	0		
8	26-Oct	Linthouse	3	0	Daly, Thomas, Ferguson	500
9	16-Nov	KILMARNOCK	2	4	Edgar (2)	
10	30-Nov	Partick Thistle	2	1	Edgar, ?	
11	21-Dec	Port Glasgow	4	3	Galloway, Goldie, Ostler, ?	
12	11-Jan	PARTICK THISTLE	3	3	Edgar, Gray, Ferguson	
13	18-Jan	Renton	2	3	Edgar, Cairns	
14	25-Jan	LEITH ATHLETIC	2	4	Gray, Summers	
15	15-Feb	Leith Athletic	1	6	Smith	
16	22-Feb	GREENOCK MORTON	2	2	Edgar (2)	
17	14-Mar	AIRDRIEONIANS	3	6	Peden, Edgar, Cherry	
18	28-Mar	ABERCORN	1	4	?	
Sqc						
Q1	31-Aug	Royal Albert	1	0	Galloway	750
Q2	14-Sep	ABERCORN	2	3	Smith, Edgar	3500
	3-Aug	GLASGOW CELTIC	1	8	First Game att Fir Park, Reciepts £82	5500

Player Appearances

	(Total)
Collins	20
Goldie	19
Edgar	19
Ostler	15
Steel	15
Daly	14
Galloway	11
Palmer	10
Smith T	10
Thomas	10
Gray	9
Ferguson	9
Haddow	8
Brown	8
Lynch	5
Cairns	5
Tennant	4
Summers	3
Easson	3
Paterson	2

1896 Div. 2

		Pl.	Home					Away					F.	A.	Pts.
			W.	D.	L.	F.	A.	W.	D.	L.	F	A.		(Total)	
1	Abercorn	18	8	0	1	29	12	4	3	2	26	19	55	31	27
2	Leith Athletic	18	8	0	1	36	12	3	1	5	19	25	55	37	23
3	Renton	18	6	2	1	23	11	3	1	5	17	17	40	28	21
3	Kilmarnock	18	7	0	2	32	18	3	1	5	18	27	50	45	21
5	Airdrieonians	18	5	3	1	26	17	2	1	6	22	27	48	44	18
5	Partick Thistle	18	4	1	4	20	22	4	1	4	24	32	44	54	18
7	Pt. Glasgow A.	18	5	2	2	28	17	1	2	6	12	24	40	41	16
8	MOTHERWELL	18	2	2	5	17	27	3	1	5	14	25	31	52	13
9	Morton	18	3	3	3	22	15	1	1	7	10	25	32	40	12
10	Linthouse	18	3	0	6	12	24	2	1	6	13	24	25	48	11

1896 - 97 Season
Second Division

	Date	Opponent	F	A	Scorers	Att
1	15-Aug	LEITH ATHLETIC	2	4	Miller, Stewart	
2	22-Aug	Linthouse	1	2	?	
3	5-Sep	AIRDRIEONIANS	2	3	Miller, Edgar	
4	19-Sep	Renton	0	2		
5	3-Oct	PORT GLASGOW	3	3	Miller, Edgar, Stewart	
6	31-Oct	GREENOCK MORTON	1	0	Maxwell	
7	13-Feb	PARTICK THISTLE	0	6		2000
8	20-Feb	Partick Thistle	2	6	Logan, Edgar	2000
9	27-Feb	RENTON	4	2	Logan (3), Edgar	
10	6-Mar	Leith Athletic	3	6	Neil, Stewart, Law	1500
11	13-Mar	LINTHOUSE	4	5	Stewart, Goldie, ?, ?	
12	20-Mar	Airdrieonians	5	3	Stewart (2), Goldie, Thomas, OG	
13	3-Apr	Port Glasgow	2	0	Law, ?	800
14	17-Apr	DUMBARTON	5	1	Logan, Edgar, OG, ?, ?	
15	1-May	KILMARNOCK	1	2	Thomas	3000
16	6-May	Kilmarnock	0	2		
17	8-May	Greenock Morton	4	3	Neil, Logan, Stewart, ?	
18	15-May	Dumbarton	1	3	?	
Sqc						
Q1	12-Sep	AIRDRIEONIANS	4	2	Ostler, McFarlane, Maxwell, Miller	4000
Q2	26-Sep	Wishaw Thistle	5	3	Miller (3), Maxwell, Edgar	2500
Q3	24-Oct	JOHNSTONE	3	0	Thomas, Ostler, Miller	1500
Q4	7-Nov	Orion*	3	1	Goldie, Galloway, ?	3500
QSf	28-Nov	Falkirk	4	2	Edgar (2), OG, ?	3000
Qf	5-Dec	Kilmarnock **	1	4	Edgar	4500
		* Played at Aberdeen			** Played at Second Hampden	
Sc						
1	9-Jan	KILMARNOCK	3	3	Maxwell, Goldie, Logan	
1r	16-Jan	Kilmarnock	2	5	Thomson, ?	5000

Player Appearances

(Total)	
Edgar	26
Neil	26
Maxwell	23
Goldie	21
Stewart W	21
Thomas	20
Daly	15
Galloway	14
Gordon	12
Ostler	12
Stewart G	12
Clark	11
Logan	11
Gourlay	10
Leitch	10
Miller	10
Law	5
MacFarlane	4
Thomson	4
Cherry	2

1897 Div. 2

		Pl.	Home					Away					F.	A.	Pts.
			W.	D.	L.	F.	A.	W.	D.	L.	F	A.		(Total)	
1	Partick Thistle	18	8	1	0	34	12	6	2	1	27	16	61	28	31
2	Leith Athletic	18	9	0	0	40	10	4	1	4	15	17	55	27	27
3	Kilmarnock	18	6	0	3	21	12	4	1	4	21	21	42	33	21
3	Airdrieonians	18	6	0	3	26	17	4	1	4	23	22	49	39	21
5	Morton	18	5	1	3	22	15	2	1	6	16	25	38	40	16
6	Linthouse	18	4	2	3	23	23	4	0	5	21	30	44	53	14*
6	Renton	18	4	1	4	22	15	2	1	6	12	26	34	41	14
8	Pt. Glasgow A.	18	4	3	2	26	20	0	2	7	12	30	38	50	13
8	MOTHERWELL	18	3	1	5	22	26	3	0	6	18	27	40	53	13
10	Dumbarton	18	2	1	6	16	26	0	1	8	11	38	27	64	6

***1895**: An unnamed Team Group*

***1899**: An unnamed Team Group*

1897 - 98 Season
Second Division

	Date	Opponent	F	A	Scorers	Att
1	4-Sep	KILMARNOCK	1	2	Kyle	
2	18-Sep	Renton	4	1	Calderwood (3), Logan	
3	2-Oct	ABERCORN	3	2	Calderwood, Logan, McGregor	2000
4	6-Nov	LEITH ATHLETIC	2	4	Slavin, Fraser	
5	20-Nov	LINTHOUSE	1	1	Slavin	
6	4-Dec	GREENOCK MORTON	1	3	Smellie	
7	18-Dec	Kilmarnock	2	6	Slavin, ?	
8	25-Dec	HAMILTON ACCIES	3	3	?,?,?	
9	15-Jan	Greenock Morton	1	6	Law	3000
10	22-Jan	Port Glasgow	3	4	Lawson, Law, Fraser	
11	29-Jan	Ayr United	3	3	Lawson, Stewart, ?	
12	5-Feb	AYR UNITED	2	3	Law (2)	
13	12-Feb	Leith Athletic	0	1		
14	19-Feb	Abercorn	1	0	Stewart	
15	5-Mar	Linthouse	0	4		
16	9-Apr	AIRDRIEONIANS	2	2	Stewart, ?	
17	16-Apr	PORT GLASGOW	0	4		
18	30-Apr	Airdrieonians	2	7	?, ?	
Sqc						
Q1	11-Sep	Hamilton Accies	4	3	Calderwood, Logan, Fraser, ?	2000
Q2	25-Sep	Renton	3	0	Logan (2), Cowan	1000
Q3	9-Oct	VALE OF LEVEN	4	0	Neil, Gray, Calderwood, McGregor	1000
Q4	23-Oct	PORT GLASGOW	2	2	Cowan, OG	3000
Q4r	30-Oct	Port Glasgow	2	3	Fraser (2)	4000
Sc						
1	8-Jan	Greenock Morton	1	7	Fraser	3000

Player Appearances

	(Total)
Neale J	21
Kerr	20
Russell	20
Stewart W	18
Cowan	17
Daly	13
Gardiner	13
Fraser	12
Slavin	12
Johnston	11
Clark	10
Calderwood	9
Logan	9
Grant	8
Law	8
Morrison	7
McGregor	6
Smith	6
Lawson	5
Campbell	4

1897 Div. 2

		Pl.	Home					Away					F.	A.	Pts.
			W.	D.	L.	F.	A.	W.	D.	L.	F.	A.	(Total)		
1	Kilmarnock	18	9	0	0	43	11	5	1	3	21	18	64	29	29
2	Pt. Glasgow A.	18	9	0	0	47	12	3	1	5	19	24	66	36	25
3	Morton	18	5	2	2	25	12	4	2	3	22	26	47	38	22
4	Leith Athletic	18	7	2	0	24	11	2	0	7	16	28	40	39	20
5	Linthouse	18	5	1	3	26	17	1	3	5	12	22	38	39	16
5	Ayr F.C.	18	5	1	3	27	18	2	1	6	9	25	36	43	16
5	Abercorn	18	4	2	3	19	14	2	2	5	14	27	33	41	16
8	Airdrieonians	18	6	1	2	29	16	0	1	8	16	40	45	56	14
9	Hamilton Acad.	18	4	1	4	20	18	1	1	7	8	33	28	51	12
10	MOTHERWELL	18	1	3	5	15	24	2	1	6	16	32	31	56	10

1898 - 99 Season
Second Division

	Date	Opponent	F	A	Scorers	Att
1	20-Aug	Port Glasgow	0	2		3000
2	27-Aug	HAMILTON ACCIES	1	1	Cowan	
3	3-Sep	Ayr United	0	1		
4	17-Sep	Leith Athletic	0	5		
5	1-Oct	Greenock Morton	2	2	Smith, ?	
6	8-Oct	Linthouse	4	2	Wales (2), Smith, Russell	
7	22-Oct	LEITH ATHLETIC	2	2	McNeill, Russell	
8	29-Oct	ABERCORN	3	2	Smith (2), Duffin	
9	5-Nov	Greenock Morton	4	2	Mount, Duffin, Smith, OG	
10	19-Nov	PORT GLASGOW	4	3	Duffin, Gourlay, ?, ?	1500
11	3-Dec	AYR UNITED	3	1	M Smith, Gourlay, Smith	
12	10-Dec	LINTHOUSE	6	1	Wales (4), Duffin, ?	300
13	24-Dec	Airdrieonians	2	2	Smith (2)	
14	31-Dec	Abercorn	5	1	Smith (2), Wales, Mount, Russell	
15	7-Jan	AIRDRIEONIANS	1	1	Wales	100
16	21-Jan	Hamilton Accies	1	4	Smith	2000
17	18-Mar	KILMARNOCK	3	3	Russell, Duffin, Smith	
18	22-Apr	Kilmarnock	0	5		
Sqc						
Q1	10-Sep	Wishaw Thistle	1	3	McNeil	

Player Appearances

	(Total)
Watt	19
Smith	19
Cowan	19
Kerr	17
Russell	16
Neale	15
Wales	15
Duffin	14
Grant	13
Mount	13
Smith M	13
Gourlay	9
McNeil	6
Meechin	4
McGinn	3
Barrowman	3
Lawson	2
Downs	2
Woodlock	2
Johnson	2
Law	2
McGonnigle	1
Daly	1
Murdoch	1

1899 Div. 2

		Pl.	Home					Away					F.	A.	Pts.
			W.	D.	L.	F.	A.	W.	D.	L.	F.	A.	(Total)		
1	Kilmarnock	18	9	0	0	44	6	5	4	0	29	18	73	24	32
2	Leith Athletic	18	8	1	0	36	12	4	2	3	27	26	63	38	27
3	Pt. Glasgow A.	18	8	0	1	49	20	4	1	4	26	31	75	51	25
4	MOTHERWELL	18	4	5	0	25	16	3	1	5	16	24	41	40	20
5	Hamilton Acad.	18	7	0	2	40	24	0	1	8	8	34	48	58	15
5	Airdrieonians	18	5	2	2	26	14	1	1	7	10	32	36	46	15
7	Morton	18	4	0	5	23	21	2	1	6	13	21	36	42	13
7	Ayr F.C.	18	5	2	2	21	10	0	1	8	14	41	35	51	13
9	Linthouse	18	4	1	4	22	20	1	0	8	7	42	29	62	11
10	Abercorn	18	4	1	4	25	23	0	0	9	16	42	41	65	9

1899 - 1900 Season
Second Division

	Date	Opponent	F	A	Scorers	Att
1	19-Aug	PARTICK THISTLE	1	3	Cowan	
2	26-Aug	Port Glasgow	1	3	McNeil	
3	2-Sep	LEITH ATHLETIC	2	1	Duffin, Wilson	
4	4-Nov	AYR UNITED	4	2	M Smith (2), Wilson, Miller	
5	25-Nov	GREENOCK MORTON	4	3	Duffin, Wilson, Grant, M Smith	
6	2-Dec	PORT GLASGOW	4	2	M Smith (2), Steen, Duffin	
7	9-Dec	Airdrieonians	3	1	M Smith, ?, ?	
8	23-Dec	LINTHOUSE	4	0	Duffin, Steen, Miller, ?	
9	30-Dec	Leith Athletic	1	0	M Smith	
10	6-Jan	AIRDRIEONIANS	4	2	Duffin (2), Wilson, McNeil	
11	20-Jan	HAMILTON ACCIES	1	2	Duffin	2500
12	3-Feb	Partick Thistle	2	1	Steen, ?	
13	17-Feb	Ayr United	1	2	McCabe	
14	3-Mar	Hamilton Accies	2	4	Duffin, M Smith	2000
15	10-Mar	Linthouse	2	2	Wilson, M Smith	
16	17-Mar	Abercorn	2	1	Duffin, Cowan	1100
17	31-Mar	ABERCORN	1	3	Smith	1500
18	7-Apr	Greenock Morton	0	3		2000
Sqc						
Q1	9-Sep	LINTHOUSE	5	1	Wilson (2), M Smith, ?, ?	
Q2	23-Sep	Carfin Emmett	1	1	Smith	2500
Q2r	30-Sep	CARFIN EMMETT	3	3	Cowan, Duffin, ?	
Q2/2r	7-Oct	Carfin Emmett*	3	2	M Smith, Miller, Wilson	3500
Q3	14-Oct	Kilbarchan	5	2	M Smith, Miller, Wilson, Wales, ?	
Q4	28-Oct	HAMILTON ACCIES	2	4	Miller, M Smith	3000
Sc						
1	13-Jan	Forfar Athletic	4	3	M Smith (2), McFarlane, ?, ?	
2	27-Jan	Third Lanark	1	2	Wilson	

* played at Hamilton

Player Appearances

	(Total)
Watt	26
Grant	26
Cowan	26
Kerr	25
McNeil	25
Wilson	25
Duffin	23
Smith M	22
Earl	21
Miller	18
Smith	9
Wales	9
Steen	8
Russell	4
McCabe	4
Aitken	4
Littlejohn	3
McFarlane	2
Lang	1
Barrowman	1
Beveridge	1

1900 Div. 2

		Pl.	Home W.	D.	L.	F.	A.	Away W.	D.	L.	F.	A.	F. (Total)	A.	Pts.
1	Partick Thistle	18	9	0	0	33	10	5	1	3	22	16	55	26	29
2	Morton	18	8	0	1	36	7	6	0	3	30	18	66	25	28
3	Pt. Glasgow A.	18	8	0	1	37	20	2	0	7	13	21	50	41	20
4	MOTHERWELL	18	6	0	3	25	18	3	1	5	13	18	38	36	19
4	Leith Athletic	18	7	0	2	23	10	2	1	6	9	27	32	37	19
6	Abercorn	18	4	2	3	25	15	3	0	6	21	24	46	39	16
7	Hamilton Acad.	18	5	1	3	24	18	2	0	7	9	27	33	45	15
8	Ayr F.C.	18	4	0	5	15	18	2	2	5	24	30	39	48	14
9	Airdrieonians	18	4	2	3	17	20	0	1	8	10	29	27	49	11
10	Linthouse	18	0	3	6	10	33	2	2	5	18	35	28	68	9

1900 - 01 Season
Second Division

	Date	Opponent	F	A	Scorers	Att
1	18-Aug	Abercorn	2	2	Reid, Rose	900
2	25-Aug	EAST STIRLINGSHIRE	0	3		
3	1-Sep	Hamilton Accies	1	1	Aitken	1500
4	29-Sep	LEITH ATHLETIC	0	2		
5	13-Oct	HAMILTON ACCIES	4	2	Miller, Duffin, Chambers, ?	1000
6	20-Oct	Airdrieonians	0	2		2000
7	27-Oct	Port Glasgow	0	5		
8	3-Nov	CLYDE	2	3	Watt (2)	
9	10-Nov	PORT GLASGOW	5	1	Watt (2), Wilson (2), Aitken	
10	17-Nov	Leith Athletic	2	1	Watt, Duffin	1500
11	24-Nov	St. Bernards	3	4	Chambers, Aitken, ?	
12	1-Dec	AIRDRIEONIANS	0	2		
13	8-Dec	Ayr United	1	3	Reid	600
14	15-Dec	ST. BERNARDS	2	2	Wilson (2)	750
15	22-Dec	East Stirlingshire	1	2	Wilson	
16	29-Dec	Cylde	0	4		
17	12-Jan	ABERCORN	1	2	Duffin	
18	19-Mar	AYR UNITED	2	1	Cowan, Wilson	
Sqc						
Q1	8-Sep	WISHAW UNITED	1	1	Cowan	
Q1r	15-Sep	Wishaw United	1	1	Duffin	2500
Q1/2r	22-Sep	Wishaw United*	3	1	Robertson (2), Duffin	3200
Q2		BYE				
Q3	6-Oct	Royal Albert	2	3	Aitkin, Duffin	2000

* Played at Hamilton

Player Appearances

	(Total)
Reid	22
Connor	21
McGregor	19
Cowan	18
Duffin	18
Earl	17
Aitken	17
Kerr	15
Robertson	10
Rose	10
Wilson	10
Watt	10
Mitchell	9
Chambers	8
Miller	8
McBride	5
Chalmers	3
McNeil	3
Shields	3
Tullis	1
Watson	1

1901 Div. 2

		Pl.	Home W.	D.	L.	F.	A.	Away W.	D.	L.	F.	A.	F. (Total)	A.	Pts.
1	St. Bernards	18	8	1	0	28	11	3	3	3	14	15	42	26	26
2	Airdrieonians	18	7	1	1	28	13	4	0	5	15	19	43	32	23
3	Abercorn	18	6	3	0	27	11	3	0	6	10	22	37	33	21
4	Clyde	18	5	1	3	22	14	4	1	4	21	21	43	35	20
4	Pt. Glasgow A.	18	7	0	2	31	16	3	0	6	14	27	45	43	20
6	Ayr F.C.	18	9	0	0	22	8	0	0	9	10	26	32	34	18
7	East Stirling.	18	5	2	2	20	14	2	1	6	14	25	34	39	17
8	Hamilton Acad.	18	3	2	4	22	16	1	2	6	19	33	41	49	12
9	Leith Athletic	18	4	0	5	14	14	1	2	6	8	18	22	32	12
10	MOTHERWELL	18	3	1	5	16	18	1	2	6	10	24	26	42	11

1901 - 02 Season
Second Division

No.	Date	Opponent	F	A	Scorers	Att.
1	17-Aug	ARTHURLIE	2	2	Wilson, Sommen	
2	24-Aug	East Stirling	3	1	Cowan, Sommen, ?	
3	31-Aug	Abercorn	3	0	McFarlane, Sommen, McAllister	
4	14-Sep	AIRDRIEONIANS	1	2	Sommen	4500
5	28-Sep	Leith Athletic	0	3		
6	12-Oct	HAMILTON ACCIES	3	0	Forrest (3)	2000
7	26-Oct	ABERCORN	3	1	Forrest , ?, ?	
8	2-Nov	ST. BERNARDS	0	4		
9	9-Nov	Airdrieonians	3	0	Duffin (2), Sommen	
10	30-Nov	PARTICK THISTLE	3	2	Kerr, Forrest, ?	3000
11	7-Dec	Port Glasgow	1	8	Forrest	
12	21-Dec	Partick Thistle	1	4	Sommen	
13	4-Jan	Cylde	4	0	Cowan, Kerr, Sommen, Forrest	
14	25-Jan	EAST STIRLING	2	3	Wales, McAllister	
15	1-Mar	arthurlie	1	2	Cowan	
16	8-Mar	LEITH ATHLETIC	4	2	Sommen (2), Cowan, Chapple	
17	15-Mar	CLYDE	6	2	Forrest (2), Sommen (2), Wales, McAllister	
18	22-Mar	St. Bernards	2	1	Crainey, Kerr	
19	29-Mar	PORT GLASGOW	4	2	Cowan (2), Forrest, McAllister	
20	5-Apr	Ayr United	2	2	Forrest, Kerr	
21	12-Apr	Hamilton Accies	0	2		3000
22	19-Apr	AYR UNITED	2	1	Forrest, Reid	
Sc						
1	11-Jan	St. Bernards	0	1		

Player Appearances

	(Total)
Sommen	23
McAllister	23
Paterson	23
Forrest	23
Cowan	23
McBride	23
W Reid	20
Crainey	20
Wales	20
Connor	16
Duffin	12
Adams	8
Earl	6
Kerr	4
Chapple	4
McFarlane	3
McPherson	3
D Reid	2
Wilson	1
McGregor	1
McIntosh	1

1902 Div. 2

		Pl.	Home W.	D.	L.	F.	A.	Away W.	D.	L.	F.	A.	F. (Total)	A.	Pts.
1	Pt. Glasgow A.	22	10	1	0	51	11	4	3	4	24	20	75	31	32
2	Partick Thistle	22	10	0	1	31	12	3	4	4	19	17	50	29	30
3	MOTHERWELL	22	7	2	2	32	19	5	0	6	18	25	50	44	26
4	Airdrieonians	22	8	0	3	25	14	2	5	4	16	18	41	32	25
4	Hamilton Acad.	22	7	2	2	29	15	4	1	6	16	25	45	40	25
6	St. Bernards	22	8	1	2	23	8	2	1	8	7	23	30	31	22
7	Leith Athletic	22	7	3	1	24	9	2	0	9	10	29	34	38	21
7	Ayr F.C.	22	6	3	2	16	8	2	2	7	11	25	27	33	21
9	East Stirling.	22	4	2	5	19	20	4	1	6	19	26	38	46	19
10	Arthurlie	22	5	2	4	20	20	1	3	7	12	22	32	42	17
11	Clyde	22	4	2	5	8	12	1	1	9	13	33	21	45	13
11	Abercorn	22	4	4	3	22	22	0	1	10	5	37	27	59	13

1902 - 03 Season
Second Division

No.	Date	Opponent	F	A	Scorers	Att.
1	16-Aug	HAMILTON ACCIES	1	0	Sharp	
2	23-Aug	Abercorn	1	0	Sommen	
3	30-Aug	ARTHURLIE	2	2	Fotheringham, Sharp	
4	13-Sep	Hamilton Accies	1	0	Sharp	3000
5	27-Sep	Airdrieonians	2	4	Sharp, Sommen	
6	4-Oct	LEITH ATHLETIC	3	3	Sharp (2), ?	2500
7	11-Oct	East Stirlingshire	1	2	Paterson	
8	25-Oct	ST. BERNARDS	4	3	McAllister (2), McNab, OG	
9	8-Nov	FALKIRK	2	2	Hamilton (2)	
10	22-Nov	ABERCORN	1	0	Sharp	
11	29-Nov	St. Bernards	2	1	Hamilton (2)	
12	20-Dec	Leith Athletic	3	4	McAllister, Lynn, Crainey	
13	3-Jan	Cylde	2	1	McKenna, OG	
14	14-Feb	CLYDE	3	0	Sharp, McKillop, Hamilton	
15	21-Feb	Arthurlie	2	0	Sharp (2), ?	
16	28-Feb	Ayr United	0	1		
17	7-Mar	RAITH ROVERS	2	1	Sharp, Crainey	
18	14-Mar	AIRDRIEONIANS	1	3	Wales	
19	21-Mar	Raith Rovers	5	2	Hamilton (3), Lynn, ?	
20	28-Mar	AYR UNITED	2	0	Hamilton (2)	
21	11-Apr	Falkirk	2	4	Sommen, Sharp	1200
22	18-Apr	East Stirlingshire	2	2	Sommen, OG	
Sc						
1	24-Jan	Queens Park	2	1	Sommen, Lynn	5000
2	31-Jan	PARTICK THISTLE	0	2		5000

Player Appearances

	(League)
McNab	22
Sharp	22
Pritchard	21
Crainey	20
Wylie	20
Adams	19
Wales	19
Chappell	18
Sommen	15
McAllister	12
Hamilton	12
Murphy	9
Paterson	8
Lynn	7
McKillop	5
Fotheringham	3
Fletcher	3
McFarlane	2
Reid	2
McCourt	2
Webster	1
McKenna	1

1903 Div. 2

		Pl.	Home W.	D.	L.	F.	A.	Away W.	D.	L.	F.	A.	F. (Total)	A.	Pts.
1	Airdrieonians	22	9	2	0	27	8	6	3	2	16	11	43	19	35
2	MOTHERWELL	22	6	4	1	23	16	6	0	5	21	19	44	35	28
3	Ayr F.C.	22	10	0	1	23	3	2	3	6	11	21	34	24	27
3	Leith Athletic	22	8	2	1	28	15	3	3	5	15	27	43	42	27
5	St. Bernards	22	6	2	3	26	13	6	0	5	19	19	45	32	26
6	Hamilton Acad.	22	8	0	3	29	13	3	1	7	16	22	45	35	23
7	Falkirk	22	5	4	2	23	14	3	3	5	16	23	39	37	23
8	East Stirling.	22	7	1	3	32	21	2	2	7	14	20	46	41	21
9	Arthurlie	22	3	4	4	19	22	3	4	4	15	24	34	46	20
10	Abercorn	22	3	1	7	15	26	2	1	8	20	32	35	58	12
11	Raith Rovers	22	3	3	5	20	21	0	2	9	14	34	34	55	11
11	Clyde	22	1	3	7	8	19	1	4	6	14	21	22	40	11

1900-01 Season

Motherwell football team and Committee (winners of the Lanarkshire Challenge Cup Season 1900-01).

1906-07 Season

Back: Barrie (Sec), Quirk (Dir), McLean, Sneddon, White (Dir), McDonald, McCallum, Flemin(Treas), Rattray, McLaughlan (Chair), Waugh (Asst. Train)
Front: Reid, Richmond, Nicol, McNeil, Donaldson, Robertson

1903 - 04 Season
First Division

1	15-Aug	AIRDRIEONIANS	1	2	Menzies	
2	22-Aug	Hibernian	1	2	Sommen	
3	29-Aug	QUEENS PARK	2	4	Hamilton (2)	
4	5-Sep	RANGERS	2	5	Menzies, OG	6000
5	12-Sep	Hearts	0	5		5000
6	19-Sep	DUNDEE	1	3	Menzies	4500
7	26-Sep	Airdrieonians	1	2	Sharp	
8	3-Oct	PARTICK THISTLE	2	0	Sharp, Main	4500
9	10-Oct	Port Glasgow	3	4	McNab, Neillis, Crainey	
10	17-Oct	GREENOCK MORTON	0	0		4000
11	20-Oct	KILMARNOCK	2	0	Sommen, Main	3000
12	31-Oct	PORT GLASGOW	1	0	Walker A	3000
13	14-Nov	ST. MIRREN	1	0	Ford	
14	21-Nov	Queens Park	0	1		
15	28-Nov	HEARTS	0	4		4000
16	5-Dec	Dundee	1	7	Sommen	
17	12-Dec	Rangers	0	3		
18	19-Dec	THIRD LANARK	0	2		
19	26-Dec	Greenock Morton	3	2	McMurray, Sharp, Main	3000
20	2-Jan	St. Mirren	0	0		
21	9-Jan	Kilmarnock	1	2	Sharp	
22	16-Jan	Celtic	0	6		
23	30-Jan	HIBERNIAN	1	0	Russell	5000
24	5-Mar	Partick Thistle	2	2	McMurray, Sharp	
25	12-Mar	Third Lanark	0	3		3000
26	26-Mar	CELTIC	1	2	Sharp	6500
Sc						
1	23-Jan	PARTICK THISTLE	2	1	McMurray	4000
2	6-Feb	Leith Athletic	1	3	Russell	3000

Player Appearances (League)

Pritchard	26
Dickson	24
R Walker	21
McNab	20
Crainey	19
Sommen	18
A Walker	18
Leiper	18
Main	18
Sharp	17
Diamond	16
Ford	16
McMurray	13
Russell	12
Neillis	10
Paterson	6
Hamilton	6
Menzies	5
Chapple	5
Wylie	4
Adams	2
Baird	1

1904 Div. 1

		Pl.	Home					Away					F.	A.	Pts.
			W.	D.	L.	F.	A.	W.	D.	L.	F.	A	(Total)		
1	Third Lanark	26	10	2	1	28	10	10	1	2	33	16	61	26	43
2	Heart of Mid.	26	13	0	0	41	9	5	3	5	22	26	63	35	39
3	Celtic	26	11	1	1	44	12	7	1	5	25	16	69	28	38
3	Rangers	26	10	3	0	47	10	6	3	4	33	23	80	33	38
5	Dundee	26	10	1	2	39	12	3	1	9	16	34	55	46	28
6	St. Mirren	26	10	1	2	34	13	1	4	8	11	25	45	38	27
6	Partick Thistle	26	7	4	2	28	17	3	3	7	15	23	43	40	27
8	Queen's Park	26	4	7	2	17	19	2	2	9	11	28	28	47	21
9	Pt. Glasgow A.	26	6	3	4	23	17	2	1	10	10	32	33	49	20
10	Hibernian	26	5	3	5	22	19	2	2	9	9	23	31	42	19
11	Morton	26	5	1	7	19	23	2	3	8	12	28	31	51	18
11	Airdrieonians	26	5	1	7	18	25	2	3	8	14	37	32	62	18
13	MOTHERWELL	26	5	1	7	14	22	1	2	10	12	39	26	61	15
14	Kilmarnock	26	3	3	7	15	27	1	2	10	12	39	27	66	13

1904 - 05 Season
First Division

1	20-Aug	Airdrieonians	2	3	Findlay (20)	7000
2	27-Aug	Kilmarnock	2	0	McMurray, Burton	
3	3-Sep	Greenock Morton	0	1		
4	10-Sep	Third Lanark	3	4	Haxton (2), Findlay	
5	17-Sep	HEARTS	2	4	Haxton (2)	6000
6	24-Sep	Port Glasgow	1	2	White	4000
7	1-Oct	DUNDEE	0	2		
8	8-Oct	GREENOCK MORTON	0	3		2000
9	15-Oct	Hibernian	0	2		2500
10	29-Oct	AIRDRIEONIANS	1	0	Haxton	7000
11	5-Nov	Partick Thistle	0	1		5000
12	12-Nov	QUEENS PARK	1	1	Joyce	
13	19-Nov	KILMARNOCK	2	1	Burton (2)	3500
14	3-Dec	Celtic	2	4	Cowan, Joyce	5000
15	10-Dec	RANGERS	0	2		
16	17-Dec	HIBERNIAN	1	2	Haxton	
17	24-Dec	Queens Park	0	2		3000
18	31-Dec	Hearts	1	4	Joyce	
19	2-Jan	St. Mirren	2	1	Hopkins (2)	
20	14-Jan	Rangers	2	3	Paton, Nicol	
21	7-Jan	Dundee	0	0		
22	21-Jan	PORT GLASGOW	0	2		
23	4-Mar	CELTIC	2	6	Haxton (2)	8000
24	18-Mar	THIRD LANARK	0	1		
25	25-Mar	ST. MIRREN	3	2	Nicol, Haxton, Clifford	
26	8-Apr	PARTICK THISTLE	1	0	Haxton	
Sc						
1	28-Jan	Arthurlie	0	0		2500
1r	4-Feb	ARTHURLIE	1	0	Haxton	4500
2	11-Feb	THIRD LANARK	0	1		9000

Player Appearances (League)

Haxton	26
Anderson	26
McNeill	23
Burton	22
McLean	19
McNab	19
Montgomery	18
Clifford	17
Nicol	17
Crainey	17
Cowan	16
Boyle	15
Atherton	15
Dickson	13
Paton	13
Joyce	11
McMurray	9
Findlay	7
Caie	6
Hopkins	6
White	5
Stalker	2

1905 Div. 1

		Pl.	Home					Away					F.	A.	Pts.
			W.	D.	L.	F.	A.	W.	D.	L.	F.	A.	(Total)		
1	Celtic	26	8	4	1	31	15	10	1	2	37	16	68	31	41
1	Rangers	26	10	1	2	49	17	9	2	2	34	11	83	28	41
3	Third Lanark	26	11	1	1	48	12	3	6	4	12	16	60	28	35
4	Airdrieonians	26	6	4	3	23	18	5	1	7	15	27	38	45	27
5	Hibernian	26	7	5	1	27	11	2	3	8	12	28	39	39	26
5	Partick Thistle	26	8	0	5	20	20	4	2	7	16	36	36	56	26
7	Dundee	26	8	2	3	26	8	2	3	8	12	24	38	32	25
7	Heart of Mid.	26	10	0	3	30	13	1	3	9	13	31	43	44	25
9	Kilmarnock	26	8	2	3	16	17	1	3	9	13	28	29	45	23
10	St. Mirren	26	4	4	5	17	15	5	0	8	16	21	33	36	22
11	Pt. Glasgow A.	26	6	3	4	23	20	2	2	9	7	28	30	48	21
12	Queen's Park	26	5	3	5	18	19	1	5	7	10	26	28	45	20
13	Morton	26	6	3	4	16	12	1	1	11	11	38	27	50	18
14	MOTHERWELL	26	4	1	8	13	26	2	1	10	15	27	28	53	14

1905 - 06 Season
First Division

1	19-Aug	Celtic	1	3	Findlay R	5000
2	26-Aug	PORT GLASGOW	2	0	Findlay R (2)	
3	2-Sep	Hearts	0	4		7000
4	9-Sep	Third Lanark	1	6	Findlay T	
5	16-Sep	DUNDEE	4	1	Findlay T (2), Richmond, Galbraith	
6	23-Sep	FALKIRK	2	3	Galbraith, Richmond	4000
7	30-Sep	Kilmarnock	0	1		
8	7-Oct	QUEENS PARK	4	2	McNeil, Galbraith, Richmond, Findlay T	4000
9	14-Oct	Greenock Morton	1	1	Wood	5000
10	21-Oct	ST. MIRREN	1	1	Findlay T	5000
11	28-Oct	Partick Thistle	2	2	Cowan (2)	3000
12	4-Nov	AIRDRIEONIANS	2	1	Findlay R, Galbraith	8000
13	18-Nov	RANGERS	3	3	Findlay T, Findlay R, Galbraith	5500
14	25-Nov	HIBERNIAN	0	2		4500
15	2-Dec	Falkirk	1	6	Galbraith	4000
16	9-Dec	St. Mirren	1	1	Galbraith	
17	16-Dec	CELTIC	0	4		8500
18	23-Dec	Rangers	1	2	Galbraith	6000
19	30-Dec	HEARTS	2	1	Nicol, Wood	5000
20	1-Jan	PARTICK THISTLE	2	3	Galbraith, Bell	4500
21	6-Jan	Queens Park	1	2	Millar	4500
22	13-Jan	ABERDEEN	3	3	Findlay T, Cowan, Nicol	3500
23	20-Jan	Dundee	0	2		4000
24	3-Feb	Hibernian	3	2	Nicol, Findlay T, Findlay R	4000
25	17-Feb	GREENOCK MORTON	1	1	Galbraith	
26	24-Feb	Aberdeen	2	2	Findlay R (2)	
27	3-Mar	THIRD LANARK	2	1	Findlay T, Nicol	3500
28	10-Mar	KILMARNOCK	5	1	Findlay T(2),Findlay R,Nicol,Richmond	3000
29	17-Mar	Airdrieonians	1	2	Findlay T	
30	7-Apr	Port Glasgow	2	1	Findlay T, Findlay R	
Sc						
1	27-Jan	HAMILTON ACCIES	2	3	Findlay R (2)	6500

Player Appearances (Total)

Montgomery	31
McNeill	31
T Findlay	30
Richmond	30
Coleman	29
Sneddon	28
Nicol	28
Galbraith	27
McCallum	24
R Findlay	23
McLean	22
Armstrong	10
Wood	9
Miller	5
Pritchard	4
Thorburn	3
Anderson	3
Cowan	2
Bell	2

1906 Div. 1

		Pl.	Home W.	D.	L.	F.	A.	Away W.	D.	L.	F.	A.	F. (Total)	A. (Total)	Pts.
1	Celtic	30	13	0	2	36	8	11	1	3	40	11	76	19	49
2	Heart of Mid.	30	12	3	0	35	8	6	4	5	29	19	64	27	43
3	Airdrieonians	30	8	4	3	31	18	7	4	4	22	13	53	31	38
4	Rangers	30	9	2	4	27	23	6	5	4	31	25	58	48	37
5	Partick Thistle	30	9	3	3	25	18	6	3	6	19	22	44	40	36
6	Third Lanark	30	10	0	5	35	15	6	2	7	27	23	62	38	34
6	Dundee	30	8	6	1	26	9	3	6	6	14	24	40	33	34
8	St. Mirren	30	10	2	3	29	16	3	3	9	12	21	41	37	31
9	MOTHERWELL	30	7	4	4	33	27	2	4	9	17	37	50	64	26
9	Morton	30	5	5	5	17	20	5	1	9	18	34	35	54	26
11	Hibernian	30	7	1	7	23	22	3	4	8	12	18	35	40	25
12	Aberdeen	30	7	4	4	23	16	1	4	10	13	32	36	48	24
13	Falkirk	30	7	5	3	36	28	2	0	13	16	40	52	68	23
14	Kilmarnock	30	8	3	4	32	22	0	1	14	14	46	46	68	20
14	Pt. Glasgow A.	30	4	3	8	23	33	2	5	8	15	35	38	68	20
16	Queen's Park	30	4	3	8	21	36	1	1	13	20	52	41	88	14

1906 - 07 Season
First Division

1	18-Aug	CELTIC	0	6	12000	
2	25-Aug	Queens Park	1	2	Richmond	5500
3	1-Sep	AIRDRIEONIANS	1	1	Robertson	7000
4	8-Sep	Falkirk	1	2	Reid	5000
5	15-Sep	Partick Thistle	2	3	Reid (2)	
6	22-Sep	ST. MIRREN	1	2	Sneddon	
7	29-Sep	ABERDEEN	3	2	Reid (2), Robertson	4000
8	6-Oct	Hamilton Accies	3	0	Nicol, Donaldson, Reid	5000
9	13-Oct	DUNDEE	0	3		5000
10	20-Oct	Hibernian	1	1	Donaldson	3000
11	27-Oct	CLYDE	0	1		
12	3-Nov	Port Glasgow	1	0	Miller	2000
13	10-Nov	KILMARNOCK	3	0	Miller (2), Robertson	3500
14	17-Nov	GREENOCK MORTON	4	1	Miller, Donaldson, McCallum, McAlpine	3000
15	24-Nov	THIRD LANARK	3	2	Miller (3)	3000
16	1-Dec	St. Mirren	0	1		4500
17	8-Dec	HEARTS	2	0	Miller, McAlpine	
18	15-Dec	Rangers	1	0	Reid	
19	22-Dec	HAMILTON ACCIES	0	2		5000
20	29-Dec	HIBERNIAN	0	0		
21	31-Dec	Third Lanark	3	2	Reid (2), Nicol	
22	5-Jan	Airdrieonians	0	0		4500
23	12-Jan	PARTICK THISTLE	2	2	McNeil, Reid	3000
24	19-Jan	Dundee	0	1		7000
25	16-Feb	QUEENS PARK	0	5		4000
26	23-Feb	Aberdeen	2	2	Robertson, Reid	
27	2-Mar	RANGERS	1	0	Donaldson	4500
28	9-Mar	FALKIRK	4	0	Reid (3), Nicol	3500
29	16-Mar	Greenock Morton	1	1	Nicol	
30	23-Mar	Kilmarnock	2	3	Miller (2)	2500
31	30-Mar	Cylde	0	1		
32	6-Apr	Hearts	1	1	Nicol	1000
33	13-Apr	PORT GLASGOW	1	0	Reid	
34	15-May	Celtic	1	1	Reid	
Sc						
##	2-Feb	Galston	2	2	Match Abandoned, Snow	
##	9-Feb	Galston	1	2	McAlpine	

Player Appearances (Total)

Nicol	34
Donaldson	33
McNeill	32
Robertson	32
McLean	31
McCallum	30
Reid	29
Rattray	28
Sneddon	27
Miller	20
McAlpine	14
Coleman	12
Montgomery	11
McDonald	9
Stewart	5
McConnell	4
McMillan	3
Richmond	2
Findlay	2
Laughlin	1

1907 Div. 1

		Pl.	Home W.	D.	L.	F.	A.	Away W.	D.	L.	F.	A.	F. (Total)	A. (Total)	Pts.
1	Celtic	34	13	4	0	40	14	10	5	2	40	16	80	30	55
2	Dundee	34	10	5	2	24	10	8	7	2	29	16	53	26	48
3	Rangers	34	9	5	3	35	16	10	2	5	34	17	69	33	45
4	Airdrieonians	34	12	1	4	36	20	6	5	6	23	24	59	44	42
5	Falkirk	34	12	4	1	45	23	5	3	9	28	35	73	58	41
6	Third Lanark	34	8	5	4	34	26	7	4	6	23	22	57	48	39
7	St. Mirren	34	6	8	3	23	19	6	5	6	27	25	50	44	37
8	Clyde	34	9	3	5	27	22	6	3	8	20	30	47	52	36
9	Heart of Mid.	34	7	7	3	27	16	4	6	7	19	27	46	43	35
10	MOTHERWELL	34	8	3	6	25	27	4	6	7	20	21	45	48	33
11	Aberdeen	34	7	6	4	24	20	3	4	10	24	35	48	55	30
11	Hibernian	34	7	5	5	22	20	3	5	9	18	29	40	49	30
13	Morton	34	9	4	4	26	15	2	2	13	15	35	41	50	28
14	Partick Thistle	34	7	3	7	22	22	2	5	10	18	38	40	60	26
15	Queen's Park	34	7	1	9	27	29	2	5	10	24	37	51	66	24
16	Hamilton Acad.	34	5	1	11	27	37	3	4	10	13	27	40	64	21
16	Kilmarnock	34	7	3	7	29	33	1	2	14	11	39	40	72	21
16	Pt. Glasgow A.	34	4	6	7	20	27	3	1	13	10	40	30	67	21

1907 - 08 Season
First Division

	Date	Opponent			Scorers	Att.
1	15-Aug	ST. MIRREN	2	3	McCallum, Reid	2000
2	17-Aug	Celtic	0	3		12000
3	24-Aug	PORT GLASGOW	6	0	Donaldson (2), Reid (2), Stewart, Nicol	3000
4	31-Aug	Third Lanark	3	1	Donaldson, Reid, Sneddon	
5	7-Sep	QUEENS PARK	6	1	Nicol (3), Robertson, Stewart, Donaldson	5000
6	14-Sep	FALKIRK	1	5	Reid	8000
7	21-Sep	Hibernian	1	1	Reid	4000
8	28-Sep	HIBERNIAN	0	0		5500
9	12-Oct	St. Mirren	1	2	Stewart	
10	15-Oct	DUNDEE	0	1		6000
11	19-Oct	Greenock Morton	1	1	McNeil	5000
12	26-Oct	Airdrieonians	1	1	Reid	
13	2-Nov	KILMARNOCK	1	2	Stewart	4000
14	9-Nov	Hamilton Accies	3	2	Reid (3)	6000
15	16-Nov	ABERDEEN	2	3	Donaldson, OG	4000
16	23-Nov	GREENOCK MORTON	4	0	Reid (2), Stewart, Donaldson	3000
17	30-Nov	HEARTS	3	0	Richmond, Donaldson, Reid	6000
18	7-Dec	Falkirk	1	2	Nicol	5000
19	10-Dec	HEARTS	2	0	?,?	
20	14-Dec	Rangers	2	4	Donaldson, Robertson	10000
21	21-Dec	THIRD LANARK	2	1	Stewart, Reid	3500
22	28-Dec	Kilmarnock	0	2		
23	1-Jan	CLYDE	3	0	Reid (2), Stewart	
24	2-Jan	AIRDRIEONIANS	2	0	Reid, Richmond	6000
25	11-Jan	HAMILTON ACCIES	2	1	Robertson J, McConnell	6000
26	18-Jan	CELTIC	2	2	Stewart, Robertson J	10000
27	1-Feb	Dundee	0	0		
28	16-Feb	QUEENS PARK	0	5		
29	29-Feb	PARTICK THISTLE	3	4	Donaldson, Robertson J, Stewart	
30	7-Mar	Aberdeen	1	2	Nicol	5000
31	14-Mar	Hearts	3	0	Nicol, Johnstone, McConnell	5000
32	21-Mar	Port Glasgow	2	2	Reid, Stewart	
33	28-Mar	Cylde	0	2		3000
34	4-Apr	RANGERS	1	2	Donaldson	3000
35	18-Apr	Partick Thistle	0	2		2000
36	25-Apr	Queens Park	2	1	Johnstone, Reid	3500
S c						
1	25-Jan	Dumfries	4	0	Reid (2), Johnstone, Robertson J	3000
2	8-Feb	ST. MIRREN	2	2	Stewart, Reid	12000
2r	15-Feb	St. Mirren	0	2		15000

Player Appearances

	(Total)
McDonald	38
Robertson	36
Nicol	35
Reid	35
McNeill	34
Stewart	33
Rattray	32
McConnell	32
Donaldson	32
McLean	29
G Robertson	18
McCallum	15
Johnstone	13
Sneddon	12
Richmond	7
Walker	6
Dick	3
Ballantyne	1

1908 Div. 1

		Pl.	Home W.	D.	L.	F.	A.	Away W.	D.	L.	F.	A.	F.	A.	Pts. (Total)
1	Celtic	34	15	2	0	57	11	9	5	3	29	16	86	27	55
2	Falkirk	34	13	2	2	58	17	9	5	3	45	25	103	42	51
3	Rangers	34	10	5	2	35	16	11	3	3	39	24	74	40	50
4	Dundee	34	12	3	2	43	10	8	5	4	28	18	71	28	48
5	Hibernian	34	10	1	6	35	24	7	7	3	20	18	55	42	42
6	Airdrieonians	34	10	3	4	37	16	8	2	7	21	25	58	41	41
7	St. Mirren	34	6	6	5	24	24	7	4	6	26	35	50	59	36
8	Aberdeen	34	9	5	3	25	14	4	4	9	20	30	45	44	35
9	Third Lanark	34	8	3	6	31	29	5	4	8	14	21	45	50	33
10	MOTHERWELL	34	8	2	7	40	25	4	5	8	21	28	61	53	31
11	Hamilton Acad.	34	7	6	4	32	25	3	2	12	23	40	55	65	28
11	Heart of Mid.	34	9	1	7	33	24	2	5	10	17	38	50	62	28
13	Morton	34	5	6	6	24	27	4	3	10	19	39	43	66	27
14	Partick Thistle	34	3	7	7	19	30	5	2	10	24	39	43	69	25
14	Kilmarnock	34	5	7	5	22	22	1	6	10	16	39	38	61	25
16	Queen's Park	34	5	5	7	28	29	2	3	12	26	55	54	84	22
17	Clyde	34	4	4	9	21	34	1	4	12	15	41	36	75	18
18	Pt. Glasgow A.	34	3	4	10	21	44	2	3	12	18	54	39	98	17

1908 - 09 Season
First Division

	Date	Opponent			Scorers	Att.
1	15-Aug	THIRD LANARK	1	0	Tait	4000
2	22-Aug	Falkirk	1	4	Stewart	3500
3	29-Sep	PORT GLASGOW	1	0	Robertson	1200
4	5-Sep	Airdrieonians	0	3		2500
5	12-Sep	HEARTS	1	6	Stewart	5000
6	19-Sep	Kilmarnock	1	4	Tait	
7	26-Sep	HIBERNIAN	3	0	Stewart (2), Tait	
8	3-Oct	Queens Park	1	0	Johnstone	6000
9	10-Oct	GREENOCK MORTON	2	1	Johnstone, Stewart	4000
10	17-Oct	Rangers	1	3	Tait	12000
11	24-Oct	CLYDE	0	1		3500
12	31-Oct	Dundee	1	3	Stewart	
13	7-Nov	HAMILTON ACCIES	2	2	Stewart, OG	5000
14	14-Nov	St. Mirren	1	3	Robertson	4000
15	21-Nov	QUEENS PARK	3	3	Johnstone, Stewart, Robertson	7000
16	28-Nov	Aberdeen	3	1	Stewart (2), Hill	
17	5-Dec	CELTIC	1	2	Stewart	7000
18	12-Dec	Partick Thistle	2	0	Stewart, Hill	
19	19-Dec	Hibernian	0	3		
20	26-Dec	FALKIRK	3	1	Hill, Robertson, Johnstone	4000
21	1-Jan	AIRDRIEONIANS	2	4	Johnstone, Tait	10000
22	2-Jan	DUNDEE	1	4	Johnstone	
23	9-Jan	Third Lanark	1	3	Stewart	4000
24	16-Jan	Hearts	2	3	McArthur, OG	
25	30-Jan	RANGERS	2	5	Robertson, Hill	7000
26	13-Feb	Cylde	1	1	Stewart	
27	20-Feb	PARTICK THISTLE	3	3	Hill (2), Johnstone	2000
28	27-Feb	ABERDEEN	3	2	Stewart (2), Robertson	3000
29	6-Mar	Hamilton Accies	0	2		1000
30	13-Mar	Greenock Morton	1	1	Stewart	3000
31	20-Mar	ST. MIRREN	1	0	Hill	3000
32	27-Mar	KILMARNOCK	2	1	Hill (2)	
33	3-Apr	Port Glasgow	0	0		
34	26-Apr	Celtic	0	4		
S c						
1	23-Jan	ELGIN CITY	6	1	Hill (3), Stewart (2), Nicol	3000
2	6-Feb	FALKIRK	1	3	Stewart	9500

Player Appearances

	(Total)
Stewart	35
Robertson	35
McLean	33
Johnstone	33
Sneddon	32
Tait	32
Young	30
Rattray	30
Buttery	22
Hill	21
Nicol	19
Jones	18
McNeil	17
McArthur	15
McFarlane	5
Breslin	4
Sharp	2
Wakeman	1
Stevenson	1
Tennant	1

1909 Div. 1

		Pl.	Home W.	D.	L.	F.	A.	Away W.	D.	L.	F.	A.	F.	A.	Pts. (Total)
1	Celtic	34	11	3	3	36	10	12	2	3	35	14	71	24	51
2	Dundee	34	14	2	1	44	12	8	4	5	26	20	70	32	50
3	Clyde	34	12	2	3	32	16	9	4	4	29	21	61	37	48
4	Rangers	34	10	5	2	48	18	9	2	6	43	20	91	38	45
5	Airdrieonians	34	8	5	4	38	28	8	4	5	29	18	67	46	41
6	Hibernian	34	12	3	2	28	9	4	4	9	12	23	40	32	39
7	St. Mirren	34	11	2	4	35	16	4	4	9	18	29	53	45	36
7	Aberdeen	34	11	2	4	39	22	4	4	9	22	31	61	53	36
9	Falkirk	34	10	4	3	37	18	3	3	11	21	38	58	56	33
9	Kilmarnock	34	11	2	4	32	24	2	5	10	15	37	47	61	33
11	Third Lanark	34	9	4	4	36	19	2	6	9	20	30	56	49	32
11	Heart of Mid.	34	8	5	4	26	17	4	3	10	28	32	54	49	32
13	Pt. Glasgow A.	34	6	5	6	20	19	4	3	10	19	33	39	52	28
13	MOTHERWELL	34	8	3	6	31	35	3	3	11	16	38	47	73	28
15	Queen's Park	34	2	6	9	18	31	4	7	6	24	34	42	65	25
16	Hamilton Acad.	34	4	7	6	23	29	2	5	10	19	43	42	72	24
17	Morton	34	5	6	6	24	32	3	1	13	15	58	39	90	23
18	Partick Thistle	34	2	1	14	21	53	0	3	14	17	49	38	102	8

1909 - 10 Season
First Division

	Date	Opponent	F	A	Scorers	Att.
1	16-Aug	Cylde	1	3	Gray	5000
2	21-Aug	Dundee	0	2		
3	28-Aug	PARTICK THISTLE	2	2	Taylor, Murray	
4	4-Sep	Celtic	2	2	Murray (2)	6000
5	11-Sep	AIRDRIEONIANS	0	1		8000
6	18-Sep	THIRD LANARK	1	3	Johnstone	5000
7	25-Sep	Falkirk	1	3	Lawson	7000
8	2-Oct	HIBERNIAN	3	1	Murray (2), Lawson	6000
9	9-Oct	Kilmarnock	1	2	Murray	4000
10	16-Oct	ST. MIRREN	5	2	Murray (3), Robertson (2)	4000
11	23-Oct	Aberdeen	2	2	Robertson, Johnstone	6000
12	30-Oct	Hamilton Accies	1	3	Robertson	6000
13	6-Nov	FALKIRK	2	2	Johnstone, Murray	6000
14	13-Nov	Port Glasgow	1	0	Murray	2000
15	20-Nov	CLYDE	0	0		4000
16	27-Nov	Rangers	1	4	Murray	6000
17	4-Dec	QUEENS PARK	3	0	Murray (2), Robertson	2000
18	11-Dec	Hearts	1	5	Gray	2000
19	18-Dec	CELTIC	1	3	Taylor	8000
20	25-Dec	GREENOCK MORTON	5	0	Murray, Nicol, Duff, Atkinson, Robertson	5000
21	1-Jan	HAMILTON ACCIES	2	2	Murray, Atkinson	8000
22	3-Jan	KILMARNOCK	3	1	Brand, Taylor, ?	6000
23	8-Jan	ABERDEEN	2	1	Murray, Robertson	
24	15-Jan	Queens Park	1	3	Murray	3000
25	29-Jan	RANGERS	2	3	Murray, Robertson	8000
26	12-Feb	Partick Thistle	1	2	Hill5000	
27	5-Mar	PORT GLASGOW	6	3	Gray (2), Tennant (2), Johnstone, OG	2000
28	12-Mar	Airdrieonians	2	2	Nicol, Robertson	4000
29	19-Mar	Greenock Morton	1	0	Brand	4000
30	26-Mar	Third Lanark	2	0	Brand, Gray	3000
31	9-Apr	HEARTS	1	0	Taylor	
32	16-Apr	St. Mirren	2	1	Gray, OG	2000
33	23-Apr	Hibernian	0	1		2000
34	25-Apr	DUNDEE	1	1	Brand	2500
Sc						
1	22-Jan	FORFAR ATHLETIC	1	0	Gray	2000
2	5-Feb	GREENOCK MORTON	3	0	Robertson (2), Murray	6000
3	26-Feb	DUNDEE	1	3	Robertson	18000

Player Appearances (Total)

Player	Apps
Taylor	37
Gray	36
McDonald	33
Johnstone	33
McNeill	33
Nicol	31
Robertson	30
Gillespie	30
Murray	25
Davidson	19
Duff	18
Johnston	14
Rattray	11
Atkinson	11
McLean	10
Brand	9
Lawson	8
Hill	7
Downie	7
Tennant	7
Hampton	4
Sneddon	3
Sharp	2
Kelly	1

1910 Div. 1

		Pl.	Home W.	D.	L.	F.	A.	Away W.	D.	L.	F.	A.	F. (Total)	A.	Pts.
1	Celtic	34	13	4	0	38	9	11	2	4	25	13	63	22	54
2	Falkirk	34	14	3	0	44	10	8	5	4	27	18	71	28	52
3	Rangers	34	14	2	1	39	9	6	4	7	31	26	70	35	46
4	Aberdeen	34	10	4	3	25	11	6	4	7	19	18	44	29	40
5	Clyde	34	10	4	3	24	11	4	5	8	23	29	47	40	37
6	Dundee	34	12	5	0	37	12	2	3	12	15	32	52	44	36
7	Third Lanark	34	10	2	5	44	19	3	6	8	18	25	62	44	34
7	Hibernian	34	10	4	3	20	12	4	2	11	13	28	33	40	34
9	Airdrieonians	34	7	5	5	28	26	5	4	8	18	31	46	57	33
10	MOTHERWELL	34	8	5	4	39	25	4	3	10	20	35	59	60	32
10	Kilmarnock	34	10	3	4	35	19	2	5	10	18	40	53	59	32
12	Heart of Mid.	34	9	3	5	37	19	3	4	10	22	31	59	50	31
12	St. Mirren	34	11	0	6	31	28	2	5	10	17	30	48	58	31
14	Queen's Park	34	8	5	4	37	25	4	1	12	17	49	54	74	30
15	Hamilton Acad.	34	9	4	4	35	34	2	2	13	15	33	50	67	28
16	Partick Thistle	34	6	6	5	24	22	2	4	11	21	37	45	59	26
17	Morton	34	9	1	7	22	18	2	2	13	16	42	38	60	25
18	Pt. Glasgow A.	34	2	3	12	15	36	1	2	14	10	57	25	93	11

1910 - 11 Season
First Division

	Date	Opponent	F	A	Scorers	Att.
1	15-Aug	Third Lanark	4	2	Brand, Tennant, Johnstone, McConnell	3500
2	20-Aug	DUNDEE	3	0	Nicol, Robertson, Brand	
3	27-Aug	Partick Thistle	1	2	Tennant	10000
4	3-Sep	HEARTS	3	2	Robertson (2), Tennant	8000
5	10-Sep	Airdrieonians	1	1	Nicol	8000
6	17-Sep	HAMILTON ACCIES	2	2	Johnstone, Main	10000
7	24-Sep	St. Mirren	1	4	Brand	6000
8	1-Oct	RANGERS	1	2	Wilson	12000
9	8-Oct	Aberdeen	0	3		9000
10	15-Oct	CLYDE	0	2		7000
11	22-Oct	Kilmarnock	0	1		4000
12	29-Oct	Greenock Morton	0	3		
13	5-Nov	THIRD LANARK	0	1		
14	12-Nov	Raith Rovers	1	0	Robertson	
15	19-Nov	HIBERNIAN	1	2	Robertson	5000
16	26-Nov	Rangers	1	7	Robertson	8000
17	3-Dec	Celtic	0	3		
18	10-Dec	QUEENS PARK	3	3	Robertson, Davidson, Butler	3000
19	17-Dec	Falkirk	1	3	Davidson	
20	24-Dec	PARTICK THISTLE	2	3	Davidson, Butler	
21	31-Dec	GREENOCK MORTON	3	2	Butler (3)	3000
22	2-Jan	AIRDRIEONIANS	2	2	Butler , ?	10000
23	7-Jan	Hearts	0	1		5000
24	14-Jan	Cylde	0	2		
25	21-Jan	ABERDEEN	0	1		5500
26	4-Feb	CELTIC	2	1	Brand (2)	9000
27	25-Feb	Hibernian	1	2	Butler	
28	11-Mar	FALKIRK	0	3		2000
29	18-Mar	RAITH ROVERS	0	1		
30	25-Mar	Queens Park	0	1		
31	1-Apr	KILMARNOCK	1	0	Robertson	
32	8-Apr	ST. MIRREN	2	0	Brand, McConnell	2000
33	15-Apr	Dundee	1	3	Johnstone	
34	22-Apr	Hamilton Accies	0	1		
Sc						
1	28-Jan	Annbank	5	0	Blair (2), Brand (2), Donaldson	4000
2	11-Feb	NITHSDALE WANDERERS	0	0		5000
2r	18-Feb	NITHSDALE WANDERERS	1	0	Davidson	3000
3	4-Mar	Hamilton Accies	1	2	Brand	18000

Player Appearances (Total)

Player	Apps
Kelly	38
McNeill	37
Hampton	36
Nicol	36
Robertson	32
John Johnstone	31
Gray	26
McConnell	25
James Johnston	22
A Davidson	20
Brand	18
Tennant	17
Butler	13
Hanson	12
Wilson	9
Hill	5
Blair	5
Main	4
Downie	3
E Davidson	3
Ewart	2
Welsh	2
Maxwell	1

1911 Div. 1

		Pl.	Home W.	D.	L.	F.	A.	Away W.	D.	L.	F.	A.	F. (Total)	A.	Pts.
1	Rangers	34	12	2	3	53	18	11	4	2	37	16	90	34	52
2	Aberdeen	34	12	5	0	31	11	7	5	5	22	17	53	28	48
3	Falkirk	34	12	4	1	41	18	5	6	6	24	24	65	42	44
4	Partick Thistle	34	13	4	0	30	12	4	4	9	20	29	50	41	42
5	Celtic	34	11	4	2	31	3	4	7	6	17	15	48	18	41
5	Dundee	34	13	2	2	36	13	5	3	9	18	29	54	42	41
7	Clyde	34	8	6	3	21	8	6	5	6	24	28	45	36	39
7	Third Lanark	34	8	5	4	30	28	8	2	7	29	25	59	53	39
9	Hibernian	34	11	2	4	27	19	4	4	9	17	29	44	48	36
10	Kilmarnock	34	9	3	5	29	22	3	7	7	13	23	42	45	34
11	Airdrieonians	34	9	4	4	36	24	3	5	9	13	29	49	53	33
12	St. Mirren	34	11	2	4	30	17	1	5	11	16	40	46	57	31
13	Morton	34	4	8	5	24	22	5	3	9	25	29	49	51	29
14	Heart of Mid.	34	7	6	4	27	18	1	2	14	15	41	42	59	24
14	Raith Rovers	34	6	6	5	26	22	1	4	12	10	33	36	55	24
16	Hamilton Acad.	34	7	3	7	22	24	1	2	14	9	36	31	60	21
17	MOTHERWELL	34	6	3	8	25	27	2	1	14	12	39	37	66	20
18	Queen's Park	34	5	2	10	15	28	0	2	15	13	52	28	80	14

1909-10 Season

Back: Barrie (Sec), Gilmour (Dir), Duffy (Dir), Quirk (Chair), , Baillie (Dir)
Middle: Hill, John Johnston, Taylor, McDonald, Rattray, Downie, McNeil, Bowman (Dir)
Front: Sharp, James Johnston, Gray, Murray, Lawson, Robertson, Miller (Train)

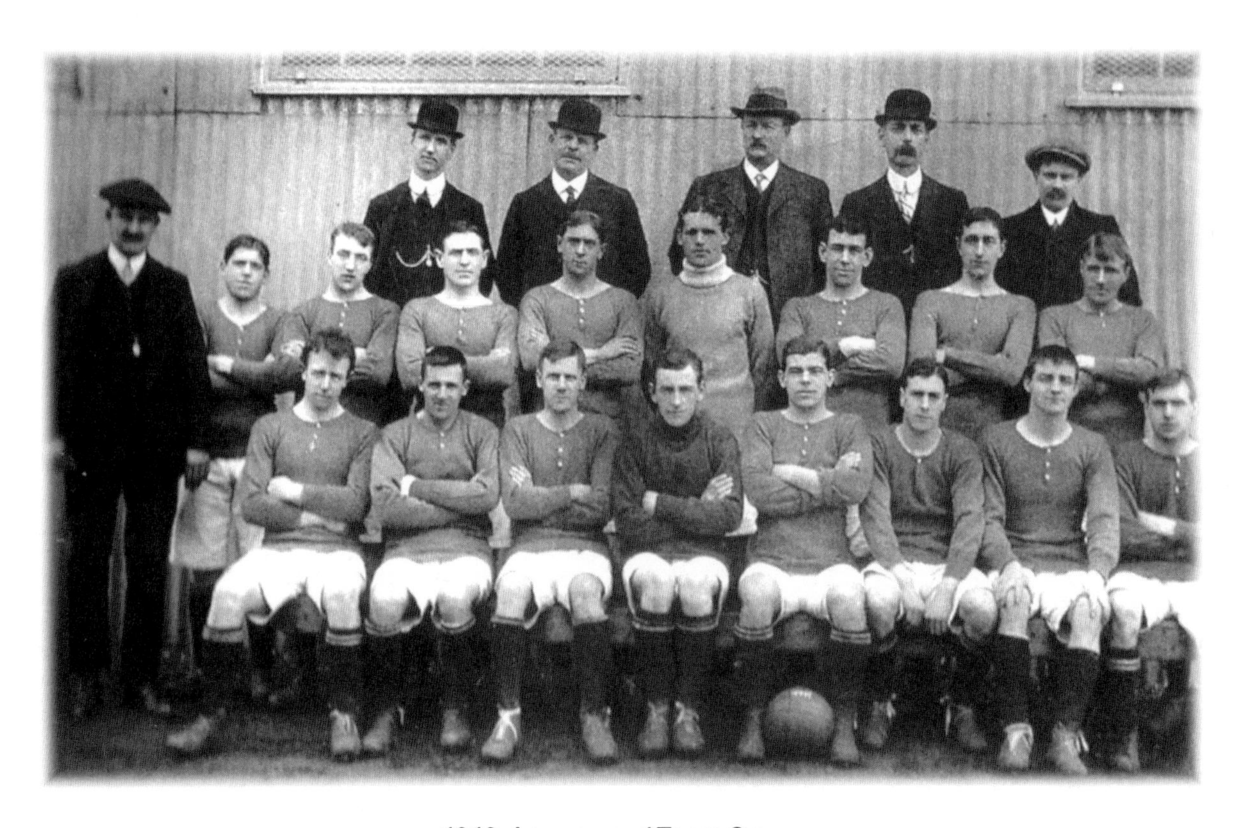

***1912**: An unnamed Team Group*

1911 - 12 Season
First Division

	Date	Opponent	F	A	Scorers	Att.
1	16-Aug	Queens Park	1	1	Lindley	5500
2	19-Aug	Dundee	1	3	Gray	
3	23-Aug	QUEENS PARK	1	0	Hall	3000
4	26-Aug	PARTICK THISTLE	1	2	Watson	3000
5	9-Sep	THIRD LANARK	2	1	Gilchrist, Robertson	8000
6	23-Sep	ST. MIRREN	3	2	Robertson, Gray, Lindley	6000
7	7-Oct	Hibernian	0	1		6000
8	14-Oct	CLYDE	2	3	Nicol, Gilchrist	8000
9	21-Oct	Falkirk	3	1	Gilchrist (2), Robertson	
10	28-Oct	KILMARNOCK	0	1		
11	4-Nov	Hamilton Accies	0	1		7000
12	11-Nov	RANGERS	1	2	Nicol, Gilchrist	15000
13	18-Nov	Cylde	2	1	Gilchrist, Gray	4000
14	25-Nov	CELTIC	3	2	McStey, Watson, Lindley	10000
15	2-Dec	Aberdeen	1	0	Lindley	7000
16	9-Dec	AIRDRIEONIANS	0	0		6000
17	16-Dec	Raith Rovers	0	3		
18	23-Dec	HEARTS	0	3		6000
19	30-Dec	GREENOCK MORTON	0	1		5000
20	1-Jan	Airdrieonians	0	1		6000
21	6-Jan	DUNDEE	0	0		6000
22	13-Jan	Celtic	0	2		
23	20-Jan	FALKIRK	2	0	Robertson, Nicol	5000
24	3-Feb	Greenock Morton	2	0	Robertson (2)	
25	17-Feb	HAMILTON ACCIES	0	2		8000
26	2-Mar	St. Mirren	0	1		6000
27	9-Mar	Kilmarnock	1	1	McNeil	3000
28	16-Mar	RAITH ROVERS	3	0	Robertson (3)	
29	23-Mar	HIBERNIAN	0	2		2000
30	6-Apr	Third Lanark	1	1	Kelly (2), Gilchrist (2), Robertson	
31	13-Apr	ABERDEEN	2	0	Gilchrist (2), Robertson	5000
32	20-Apr	Partick Thistle	0	1		
33	22-Apr	Hearts	1	2	Mair	
34	27-Apr	Rangers	1	3	Gray	
Sqc						
Q1	2-Sep	Johnstone	2	1	Gilchrist, Lindley	2000
Q2	16-Sep	QUEENS PARK	5	1	Lindley (2), Robertson, Nicol, Buchan	12000
Q3	30-Sep	HURLFORD	3	1	Gilchrist, Robertson, Watson	5000
Q4	14-Oct	Abercorn	1	0	Gray	3000
Q5	4-Nov	clachnacuddin	1	1	?	
Q5r	11-Nov	CLACHNACUDDIN	2	1	Watson, Gray	
Q Sf	18-Nov	Dunfermline	2	4	Main, Watson	4000
Sc						
1	27-Jan	St. Johnstone	2	0	McStey, Watson	6000
2	10-Feb	AIRDRIEONIANS	5	1	Kelly (2), Gilchrist (2), Robertson	15000
3	24-Feb	Third Lanark	1	3	Gray	24500

Player Appearances

	(Total)
Wilson	39
Pat Kelly	39
Hampton	38
Gilchrist	36
McStey	35
McNeill	33
Gray	29
Nicol	28
Mair	27
Lindley	26
Robertson	25
Watson	22
Buchan	17
Hall	11
H Kelly	11
Rae	7
Dixon	6
Mitchell	2
Cameron	1
Murray	1
Roxburgh	1

1912 Div. 1

		Pl.	Home W.	D.	L.	F.	A.	Away W.	D.	L.	F.	A.	F. (Total)	A.	Pts.
1	Rangers	34	16	0	1	60	10	8	3	6	26	24	86	34	51
2	Celtic	34	14	3	0	38	11	3	8	6	20	22	58	33	45
3	Clyde	34	10	1	6	25	14	9	3	5	31	18	56	32	42
4	Heart of Mid.	34	11	2	4	28	16	5	6	6	26	24	54	40	40
4	Partick Thistle	34	7	8	2	24	14	9	0	8	23	26	47	40	40
6	Morton	34	10	3	4	27	19	4	6	7	17	25	44	44	37
7	Falkirk	34	10	3	4	30	17	5	3	9	16	26	46	43	36
8	Dundee	34	11	4	2	40	18	2	5	10	12	23	52	41	35
8	Aberdeen	34	9	4	4	26	14	5	3	9	18	30	44	44	35
10	Airdrieonians	34	8	5	4	25	14	4	3	10	15	27	40	41	32
11	Third Lanark	34	10	1	6	26	19	2	6	9	14	38	40	57	31
12	Hamilton Acad.	34	7	5	5	21	16	4	3	10	11	28	32	44	30
13	Hibernian	34	10	3	4	32	15	2	2	13	12	32	44	47	29
14	MOTHERWELL	34	7	2	8	20	21	4	3	10	14	23	34	44	27
14	Raith Rovers	34	6	6	5	25	22	3	3	11	14	37	39	59	27
16	Kilmarnock	34	7	3	7	22	22	4	1	12	16	38	38	60	26
17	Queen's Park	34	6	6	5	18	22	2	3	12	11	31	29	53	25
18	St. Mirren	34	5	6	6	19	25	2	4	11	13	34	32	59	24

1912 - 13 Season
First Division

	Date	Opponent	F	A	Scorers	Att.
1	17-Aug	DUNDEE	0	0		8000
2	24-Aug	Partick Thistle	1	1	Robertson	11000
3	31-Aug	HEARTS	1	2	Watson	10000
4	7-Sep	Third Lanark	1	0	Hunter	6000
5	14-Sep	RANGERS	1	2	Gilchrist	20000
6	21-Sep	RAITH ROVERS	1	1	Bellamy	5000
7	28-Sep	Airdrieonians	1	1	Gray	
8	5-Oct	CLYDE	0	1		6000
9	12-Oct	St. Mirren	1	2	Keith	
10	19-Oct	HAMILTON ACCIES	0	0		8000
11	26-Oct	Queens Park	1	1	Kelly	
12	2-Nov	HIBERNIAN	5	1	Gray (2), Kelly, Gilchrist, Hunter	
13	9-Nov	Greenock Morton	2	2	Nicol, Hunter	6000
14	16-Nov	FALKIRK	1	4	Watson	6000
15	23-Nov	Celtic	2	1	Gray, Kelly	
16	30-Nov	ABERDEEN	1	1	Kelly (2)	5000
17	7-Dec	QUEENS PARK	6	3	Robertson (2), Nicol (2), Gilchrist, Gray	5000
18	14-Dec	Kilmarnock	1	0	Nicol	
19	21-Dec	GREENOCK MORTON	2	0	Nicol, Robertson	
20	28-Dec	Cylde	2	3	Kelly (2)	
21	1-Jan	Hamilton Accies	0	0		14000
22	4-Jan	ST. MIRREN	3	1	Finlayson (2), Kelly	6000
23	11-Jan	Rangers	1	3	Gilchrist	
24	18-Jan	THIRD LANARK	0	0		
25	25-Jan	PARTICK THISTLE	4	1	Watson (2), Gray, Kelly	
26	1-Mar	Dundee	0	0		
27	8-Mar	Hibernian	2	1	Nicol, Finlayson	4000
28	15-Mar	CELTIC	1	0	Gray	15000
29	22-Mar	Raith Rovers	0	2		5000
30	29-Mar	Aberdeen	2	2	Nicol, Gray	
31	5-Apr	AIRDRIEONIANS	2	1	Nicol, Finlayson	6000
32	12-Apr	KILMARNOCK	0	1		
33	16-Apr	Falkirk	1	1	Gilchrist	3000
34	26-Apr	Hearts	1	0	Finlayson	6000
Sc						
1		BYE				
2	8-Feb	HIBERNIAN	1	1	Watson	12000
2r	15-Feb	Hibernian	0	0		21000
2/2r	19-Feb	Hibernian*	1	2	Gilchrist	20000

* Played at Celtic

Player Appearances

	(Total)
Pat Kelly	36
Mair	35
Gray	35
Hampton	34
McStey	34
Watson	30
Gilchrist	29
H Kelly	29
Nicol	29
Wilson	25
McNeill	25
Hunter	11
Robertson	11
Finlayson	10
Bellamy	7
Prentice	7
Dixon	3
Mitchell	3
Keith	2
Crichton	1
Clark	1

1913 Div. 1

		Pl.	Home W.	D.	L.	F.	A.	Away W.	D.	L.	F.	A.	F. (Total)	A.	Pts.
1	Rangers	34	13	2	2	46	22	11	3	3	30	19	76	41	53
2	Celtic	34	13	2	2	32	12	9	3	5	21	16	53	28	49
3	Heart of Mid.	34	10	4	3	42	18	7	3	7	29	25	71	43	41
3	Airdrieonians	34	10	4	3	39	22	5	7	5	25	24	64	46	41
5	Falkirk	34	9	4	4	29	14	5	8	4	27	24	56	38	40
6	MOTHERWELL	34	7	5	5	28	19	5	8	4	19	20	47	39	37
6	Aberdeen	34	9	4	4	31	14	5	5	7	16	26	47	40	37
6	Hibernian	34	9	3	5	34	22	7	2	8	29	32	63	54	37
9	Clyde	34	6	8	3	18	12	7	1	9	23	32	41	44	35
10	Hamilton Acad.	34	10	3	4	29	14	2	5	10	15	33	44	47	32
11	Kilmarnock	34	8	4	5	27	22	2	7	8	10	32	37	54	31
12	St. Mirren	34	9	4	4	32	26	1	6	10	18	34	50	60	30
13	Morton	34	8	3	6	28	23	3	4	10	22	36	50	59	29
13	Dundee	34	7	7	3	19	14	1	6	10	14	32	33	46	29
15	Third Lanark	34	4	7	6	11	14	4	5	8	20	27	31	41	28
16	Raith Rovers	34	5	7	5	33	28	3	3	11	13	32	46	60	26
17	Partick Thistle	34	9	3	5	33	24	1	1	15	7	31	40	55	24
18	Queen's Park	34	4	3	10	20	32	1	0	16	14	56	34	88	13

1913 - 14 Season
First Division

No.	Date	Opponent	F	A	Scorers	Att.
1	16-Aug	Partick Thistle	1	2	Gilchrist	15000
2	23-Aug	CELTIC	1	1	Spiers	20000
3	30-Aug	Third Lanark	1	0	Gilchrist	8000
4	6-Sep	DUNDEE	0	1		10000
5	13-Sep	Raith Rovers	3	0	Kelly, McStey, ?	3000
6	20-Sep	ABERDEEN	3	2	Finlayson, Gilchrist, McStey	9000
7	27-Sep	Dumbarton	1	1	Finlayson	5000
8	4-Oct	St. Mirren	0	4		8000
9	11-Oct	AIRDRIEONIANS	0	1		10000
10	18-Oct	Ayr United	0	4		7000
11	25-Oct	HIBERNIAN	2	3	Finlayson, Drummond	8000
12	1-Nov	Greenock Morton	1	3	Og	5000
13	8-Nov	KILMARNOCK	4	0	Gilchrist (2), Gray, Nicol	6000
14	15-Nov	Cylde	0	5		
15	22-Nov	RANGERS	1	0	Gilchrist	18000
16	29-Nov	FALKIRK	1	2	McStey	5000
17	6-Dec	Hearts	1	2	Nicol	10000
18	13-Dec	QUEENS PARK	1	3	Finlayson	7000
19	20-Dec	Celtic	0	0		10000
20	27-Dec	ST. MIRREN	3	0	Gilchrist, Loney, Nicol	3000
21	1-Jan	HAMILTON ACCIES	3	1	Whitehead (2), Gilchrist	12000
22	3-Jan	Airdrieonians	1	3	Whitehead	8000
23	10-Jan	CLYDE	2	1	Gilchrist, Nicol	8000
24	17-Jan	Rangers	0	0		25000
25	24-Jan	GREENOCK MORTON	2	3	Gilchrist, Whitehead	4000
26	31-Jan	THIRD LANARK	1	2	Gray (2), Mair, Hillhouse	
27	28-Feb	DUMBARTON	4	3	Gray (2), Mair, Hillhouse	5000
28	14-Mar	RAITH ROVERS	3	2	Whitehead (3)	
29	21-Mar	PARTICK THISTLE	1	1	Whitehead	5000
30	23-Mar	Queens Park	2	4	Whitehead, Watson	5000
31	28-Mar	AYR UNITED	2	0	Whitehead, Robertson	5500
32	1-Apr	HEARTS	0	2		5000
33	4-Apr	Dundee	1	2	Whitehead	6000
34	11-Apr	Aberdeen	0	0		6000
35	15-Apr	Hamilton Accies	0	1		4000
36	22-Apr	Falkirk	0	2		
37	25-Apr	Kilmarnock	0	2		4000
38	28-Apr	Hibernian	0	2		500

S c

No.	Date	Opponent	F	A	Scorers	Att.
1		BYE				
2	7-Feb	Leith Athletic	1	1	Whitehead	3500
2r	14-Feb	LEITH ATHLETIC	5	2	Nicol (2), Whitehead (2), Gilchrist	8000
3	21-Feb	Broxburn	2	0	Young, Whitehead	5000
Qf	7-Mar	CELTIC	1	3	Whitehead	18000

Player Appearances

Player	(Total)
Pat Kelly	42
Gray	41
McStey	40
Hampton	39
Wilson	34
Gilchrist	34
Mair	29
Whitehead	22
Finlayson	21
Nicol	20
Hillhouse	19
H Kelly	17
Loney	16
McNeill	13
Drummond	10
Watson	10
J M Young	10
Dixon	5
Spiers	4
W Brown	4
Murray	3
Denoon	3
Knowles	2
Sneddon	1
Coleman	1
Dunn	1
Robertson	1

1914 Div. 1

		Pl.	Home					Away					F.	A.	Pts.
			W.	D.	L.	F.	A.	W.	D.	L.	F.	A.	(Total)		
1	Celtic	38	15	3	1	45	6	15	2	2	36	8	81	14	65
2	Rangers	38	14	3	2	40	15	13	2	4	39	16	79	31	59
3	Heart of Mid.	38	17	1	1	43	7	6	7	6	27	22	70	29	54
3	Morton	38	16	0	3	45	17	10	2	7	31	34	76	51	54
5	Falkirk	38	14	4	1	44	18	6	5	8	25	33	69	51	49
6	Airdrieonians	38	10	7	2	46	24	8	5	6	26	19	72	43	48
7	Dundee	38	13	2	4	41	19	6	3	10	23	34	64	53	43
8	Third Lanark	38	10	4	5	30	22	3	6	10	12	29	42	51	36
9	Clyde	38	8	5	6	27	17	3	6	10	17	27	44	44	33
9	Ayr United	38	8	3	8	26	30	5	4	10	30	42	56	72	33
11	Raith Rovers	38	9	4	6	38	22	4	2	13	18	35	56	57	32
12	Kilmarnock	38	8	3	8	34	29	3	6	10	14	39	48	68	31
13	Hibernian	38	6	2	11	27	36	6	4	9	31	39	58	75	30
13	Aberdeen	38	5	8	6	21	18	5	2	12	17	37	38	55	30
15	Partick Thistle	38	9	4	6	25	23	1	5	13	12	28	37	51	29
15	Queen's Park	38	7	6	6	29	33	3	3	13	23	51	52	84	29
17	Hamilton Acad.	38	8	4	7	31	21	3	2	14	18	45	49	66	28
17	MOTHERWELL	38	9	2	8	34	28	2	4	13	12	37	46	65	28
19	Dumbarton	38	7	4	8	24	35	3	3	13	21	52	45	87	27
20	St. Mirren	38	6	5	8	22	28	2	1	16	16	45	38	73	22

1914 - 15 Season
First Division

No.	Date	Opponent	F	A	Scorers	Att.
1	15-Aug	RAITH ROVERS	1	2	Waugh	6000
2	22-Aug	Celtic	0	1		
3	29-Aug	HIBERNIAN	3	0	Waugh, Nicol, Whitehead	6000
4	5-Sep	Partick Thistle	1	4	Gray	10000
5	12-Sep	KILMARNOCK	3	2	Waugh, Finlayson, McStey	2000
6	19-Sep	Aberdeen	1	3	Nicol	7000
7	26-Sep	DUMBARTON	2	3	Waugh, Bond	5000
8	3-Oct	THIRD LANARK	3	2	Nicol (2), Gray	5000
9	10-Oct	Hearts	0	2		12000
P 12/12	12-Oct	FALKIRK	4	1	Waugh (3), McStey	5000
11	17-Oct	GREENOCK MORTON	1	1	Gray	5000
12	24-Oct	St. Mirren	1	1	Archibald	6000
13	31-Oct	CLYDE	0	2		5000
14	7-Nov	Airdrieonians	1	4	Bond	4000
15	14-Nov	Dundee	0	1		5000
16	21-Nov	QUEENS PARK	1	0	Bond	4000
17	28-Nov	Falkirk	1	5	Waugh	
18	5-Dec	HAMILTON ACCIES	2	4	Archibald (2)	3000
19	19-Dec	Rangers	0	5		
20	26-Dec	ABERDEEN	1	1	Archibald	
21	1-Jan	Hamilton Accies	3	0	Fairgray (2), Gray	
22	2-Jan	AIRDRIEONIANS	4	2	Archibald (2), Gray, Nicol	
23	9-Jan	Third Lanark	0	1		500
24	16-Jan	AYR UNITED	1	1	Archibald	4000
25	23-Jan	Hibernian	2	1	Whitehead, Waugh	5000
26	30-Jan	DUNDEE	1	1	Fairgray	3000
27	6-Feb	Raith Rovers	1	2	Waugh	
28	13-Feb	HEARTS	0	1		8000
29	20-Feb	Queens Park	3	0	Waugh, McLean, Nicol	
30	27-Feb	RANGERS	2	4	Waugh, McLean	7000
31	6-Mar	Kilmarnock	2	2	Waugh (2)	4000
32	13-Mar	Ayr United	1	1	Gray	4500
33	20-Mar	Greenock Morton	0	2		2000
34	27-Mar	ST. MIRREN	0	2		4000
35	3-Apr	Cylde	0	0		
36	10-Apr	Dumbarton	1	1	Nicol	3000
37	17-Apr	PARTICK THISTLE	1	0	Gray	
38	24-Apr	CELTIC	1	1	Archibald	10000

S c Postponed due to 1st World War

Player Appearances

Player	(Total)
Allan	38
Findlayson	37
McStey	36
Gray	36
Waugh	35
Penman	35
Pat Kelly	33
Fairgray	33
Nicol	22
McGlade	21
Archibald	14
Bond	13
Whitehead	10
Eglington	9
Murray	7
Hillhouse	6
McLean	6
Watson	3
McDonald	2
Spiers	2
Calderhead	1
Hunter	1
Neil	1

1915 Div. 1 (Division 'A')

		Pl.	Home					Away					F.	A.	Pts.
			W.	D.	L.	F.	A.	W.	D.	L.	F.	A.	(Total)		
1	Celtic	38	18	1	0	56	10	12	4	3	35	15	91	25	65
2	Heart of Mid.	38	17	1	1	50	13	10	6	3	33	19	83	32	61
3	Rangers	38	11	1	7	37	23	12	3	4	37	24	74	47	50
4	Morton	38	13	4	2	43	17	5	8	6	31	31	74	48	48
4	Ayr United	38	13	3	3	29	12	7	5	7	26	28	55	40	48
6	Falkirk	38	10	5	4	31	19	6	2	11	17	29	48	48	39
7	Hamilton Acad.	38	9	5	5	37	26	7	1	11	23	29	60	55	38
7	Partick Thistle	38	10	3	6	36	22	5	5	9	20	36	56	58	38
9	St. Mirren	38	9	4	6	31	25	5	4	10	25	40	56	65	36
10	Airdrieonians	38	9	4	6	35	28	5	3	11	19	32	54	60	35
10	Hibernian	38	9	5	5	36	27	3	6	10	23	39	59	66	35
12	Kilmarnock	38	12	2	5	39	24	3	2	14	16	35	55	59	34
12	Dumbarton	38	9	3	7	29	30	4	5	10	22	36	51	66	34
14	Aberdeen	38	7	7	5	21	14	4	4	11	18	38	39	52	33
14	Dundee	38	8	4	7	24	21	4	5	10	19	40	43	61	33
16	Third Lanark	38	7	8	4	32	22	3	4	12	19	35	51	57	32
17	Clyde	38	8	4	7	27	24	4	2	13	17	35	44	59	30
17	MOTHERWELL	38	7	5	7	31	30	3	5	11	18	36	49	66	30
19	Raith Rovers	38	5	8	6	31	27	4	2	13	22	41	53	68	28
20	Queen's Park	38	3	2	14	14	39	1	3	15	13	51	27	90	13

1915 - 16 Season
First Division

No.	Date	Opponent	F	A	Scorers	Att.
1	21-Aug	Celtic	1	3	Waugh	6000
2	28-Aug	PARTICK THISTLE	2	2	Waugh, Neil	3000
3	4-Sep	Dundee	3	1	Neil (3)	5000
4	11-Sep	DUMBARTON	4	2	Neil (2), Gray, Waugh	3000
5	18-Sep	Kilmarnock	0	1		
6	25-Sep	ST. MIRREN	3	1	Archibald (3)	3000
7	2-Oct	Queens Park	4	1	Finlayson (3), Kelly	
8	9-Oct	AIRDRIEONIANS	3	2	Archibald (3)	
9	16-Oct	Ayr United	2	3	Waugh, Murray	4000
10	23-Oct	CLYDE	2	2	Kelly, Finlayson	3000
11	30-Oct	HEARTS	1	3	Kelly	6000
12	6-Nov	Hibernian	2	1	Neil (2),	
13	13-Nov	FALKIRK	1	1	Waugh	3000
14	20-Nov	Hamilton Accies	1	3	Waugh	3000
15	27-Nov	ABERDEEN	2	2	Waugh, Archibald	3000
16	4-Dec	Third Lanark	3	1	Neil, McNeil, Kelly	
17	11-Dec	DUNDEE	3	0	Waugh, Kelly, McNeil	
18	18-Dec	Hearts	0	4		6000
P 15/4	23-Dec	CELTIC	1	3	Robertson	8500
20	25-Dec	Dumbarton	0	0		2000
21	31-Dec	Falkirk	1	0	Neil	
22	1-Jan	HAMILTON ACCIES	0	3		4000
23	8-Jan	Rangers	1	1	McNeil	9000
24	15-Jan	RAITH ROVERS	1	4	Waugh	4000
25	22-Jan	Cylde	2	1	Kelly (2)	
26	29-Jan	RANGERS	2	2	Waugh, Young	9500
27	5-Feb	THIRD LANARK	3	4	Archibald (2), Kelly	5000
28	12-Feb	Airdrieonians	0	4		
29	19-Feb	GREENOCK MORTON	2	3	Finlayson (2)	6000
30	26-Feb	Partick Thistle	1	3	Finlayson	8000
31	4-Mar	HIBERNIAN	1	1	Bennett	3000
32	11-Mar	KILMARNOCK	1	1	Finlayson	
33	18-Mar	Raith Rovers	0	1		4000
34	1-Apr	Aberdeen	0	5		
35	8-Apr	St. Mirren	0	5		
36	15-Apr	AYR UNITED	0	3		4000
37	22-Apr	QUEENS PARK	2	1	Neil, Kelly	
38	30-Apr	Greenock Morton	0	1		5000

Player Appearances

	(Total)
Penman	36
F Kelly	36
Gray	33
Waugh	32
Finlayson	31
McStey	29
Pat Kelly	27
Archibald	25
Bennett	23
Collins	22
T Sneddon	21
Neill	20
Murray	19
Robertson	12
D McNeill	12
McSkimming	11
Young	6
Rundell	4
R McNeill	4
J Sneddon	3
Allan	1

1916 Div. 1

		Pl.	Home					Away					F.	A.	Pts.
			W.	D.	L.	F.	A.	W.	D.	L.	F.	A.	(Total)		
1	Celtic	38	15	3	1	64	13	17	0	2	52	10	116	23	67
2	Rangers	38	15	2	2	55	17	10	4	5	32	22	87	39	56
3	Morton	37	15	0	3	58	9	7	7	5	28	26	86	35	51
4	Ayr United	38	12	4	3	39	19	8	4	7	33	26	72	45	48
5	Partick Thistle	38	13	2	4	48	20	6	6	7	17	21	65	41	46
5	Heart of Mid.	37	12	1	6	35	23	8	5	5	31	22	66	45	46
7	Hamilton Acad.	38	13	2	4	49	28	6	1	12	19	48	68	76	41
8	Dundee	38	13	2	4	37	14	5	2	12	19	35	56	49	40
9	Dumbarton	38	9	6	4	33	22	4	5	10	21	42	54	64	37
10	Kilmarnock	38	9	5	5	34	17	3	6	10	12	32	46	49	35
11	Aberdeen	38	8	8	3	31	20	3	4	12	20	44	51	64	34
12	Falkirk	38	8	6	5	21	19	4	3	12	24	42	45	61	33
13	St. Mirren	38	11	1	7	37	26	2	3	14	13	41	50	67	30
13	MOTHERWELL	38	5	7	7	34	40	6	1	12	21	42	55	82	30
13	Airdrieonians	38	8	6	5	25	19	3	2	14	19	55	44	74	30
16	Third Lanark	38	6	5	8	26	23	3	6	10	14	33	40	56	29
16	Clyde	38	7	2	10	30	34	4	5	10	19	37	49	71	29
18	Queen's Park	38	7	5	7	30	34	4	1	14	23	66	53	100	28
19	Hibernian	38	7	2	10	21	28	2	5	12	23	43	44	71	25
20	Raith Rovers	38	8	3	8	21	24	1	2	16	9	41	30	65	23

1916 - 17 Season
First Division

No.	Date	Opponent	F	A	Scorers	Att.
1	19-Aug	RAITH ROVERS	2	2	Ferguson (2)	6000
2	26-Aug	Airdrieonians	1	3	King	
3	2-Sep	DUNDEE	4	2	Ferguson (3), Stewart	
4	9-Sep	St. Mirren	1	3	Ferguson	
5	16-Sep	CELTIC	0	4		
6	23-Sep	Dumbarton	1	3	Finlayson	3000
7	30-Sep	KILMARNOCK	0	1		3000
8	7-Oct	HAMILTON ACCIES	2	2	Brown (2)	
9	14-Oct	Rangers	1	2	Brown	
10	21-Oct	QUEENS PARK	4	1	Ferguson (2), Browell, Ramsey	4000
11	28-Oct	Greenock Morton	1	2	Stewart	
12	4-Nov	HIBERNIAN	1	1	Browell	
13	11-Nov	ABERDEEN	1	2	Stewart	
14	18-Nov	Falkirk	1	3	Gray	
15	25-Nov	CLYDE	3	3	Ferguson (2), Archibald	
16	2-Dec	Aberdeen	1	0	Ferguson	
17	9-Dec	HEARTS	2	0	Kelly (2)	
18	16-Dec	Third Lanark	1	2	Ferguson	
19	23-Dec	RANGERS	2	1	Kelly, Morgan	
20	30-Dec	PARTICK THISTLE	2	3	Ferguson, Morgan	
21	1-Jan	Hamilton Accies	4	2	Ferguson, Morgan, Kelly, Brown	
22	2-Jan	AIRDRIEONIANS	1	0	Ferguson	
23	6-Jan	Celtic	0	1		
24	13-Jan	Ayr United	2	1	Finlayson (2)	
25	20-Jan	ST. MIRREN	2	1	Brown, Kelly	
26	27-Jan	AYR UNITED	2	1	Kelly, Gray	
27	3-Feb	Queens Park	0	0		
28	10-Feb	DUMBARTON	3	0	Ferguson (3)	
29	17-Feb	Hibernian	3	2	Ferguson (2), Stewart	
30	24-Feb	Hearts	3	1	Ferguson, King, Morgan	
31	3-Mar	FALKIRK	1	0	Ferguson	
32	10-Mar	Kilmarnock	0	3		
33	17-Mar	Partick Thistle	1	1	Kelly	5000
34	24-Mar	THIRD LANARK	0	2		
35	31-Mar	Raith Rovers	1	2	Morgan	2000
36	7-Apr	Cylde	1	0	Ferguson	3000
37	14-Apr	Dundee	2	0	Ferguson (2)	5000
38	21-Apr	Greenock Morton	0	2		

Player Appearances

	(Total)
Rundell	38
McStey	36
Kelly	35
Gray	34
Stewart	32
Craig Brown	30
McSkimming	29
Ferguson	29
King	29
Stewart	29
Morgan	25
Finlayson	16
Ramsay	14
Murray	14
Penman	11
Dunsmuir	8
Gilloghley	7
Archibald	5
Browell	3
Reid	1

1917 Div. 1

		Pl.	Home					Away					F.	A.	Pts.
			W.	D.	L.	F.	A.	W.	D.	L.	F.	A.	(Total)		
1	Celtic	38	13	5	1	38	8	14	5	0	41	9	79	17	64
2	Morton	38	16	1	2	44	16	8	5	6	28	23	72	39	54
3	Rangers	38	16	1	2	40	9	8	4	7	28	23	68	32	53
4	Airdrieonians	38	16	1	2	47	17	5	7	7	24	21	71	38	50
5	Third Lanark	38	11	7	1	32	15	8	4	7	21	22	53	37	49
6	Kilmarnock	38	12	2	5	48	22	6	5	8	21	24	69	46	43
7	St. Mirren	38	8	7	4	25	15	7	3	9	24	28	49	43	40
8	MOTHERWELL	38	9	4	6	32	28	7	2	10	25	31	57	59	38
9	Partick Thistle	38	9	5	5	28	11	5	2	12	16	32	44	43	35
9	Dumbarton	38	8	6	5	35	31	4	5	10	21	42	56	73	35
9	Hamilton Acad.	38	11	3	5	35	24	2	6	11	19	49	54	73	35
12	Falkirk	38	7	5	7	29	24	5	5	9	29	33	58	57	34
12	Clyde	38	6	7	6	21	24	4	7	8	20	29	41	53	34
14	Heart of Mid.	38	9	1	9	25	30	5	3	11	19	29	44	59	32
15	Ayr United	38	6	6	7	21	24	6	1	12	26	35	47	59	31
16	Dundee	38	9	2	8	37	28	4	2	13	21	43	58	71	30
16	Hibernian	38	6	6	7	33	34	4	4	11	24	38	57	72	30
18	Queen's Park	38	7	5	7	34	37	4	2	13	22	44	56	81	29
19	Raith Rovers	38	6	2	11	22	41	2	5	12	20	50	42	91	23
20	Aberdeen	38	6	4	9	24	23	1	3	15	12	45	36	68	21

1917 - 18 Season
First Division

No.	Date	Opponent	F	A	Scorers	Att.
1	18-Aug	Third Lanark	4	2	Ferguson (4)	6000
2	25-Aug	DUMBARTON	0	0		8000
3	1-Sep	Hamilton Accies	3	3	Ferguson, Gardiner, Morgan	8000
4	8-Sep	HEARTS	4	0	Rankin	6000
5	15-Sep	Clydebank	2	1	Ferguson (2)	8000
6	22-Sep	KILMARNOCK	1	1	Rankin	
7	29-Sep	Airdrieonians	1	3	Gray	
8	6-Oct	GREENOCK MORTON	1	3	Ferguson	
9	13-Oct	ST. MIRREN	2	1	Ferguson, McSkimming	6000
10	20-Oct	Queens Park	2	2	Kelly, Rankin	
11	27-Oct	FALKIRK	2	1	Rankin, Archibald	
12	3-Nov	Hibernian	2	2	Gardiner, Gray	5000
13	10-Nov	CLYDE	1	3	Ferguson	
14	17-Nov	Kilmarnock	0	4		
15	24-Nov	Dumbarton	3	4	Ferguson (2), Morgan	
16	1-Dec	AYR UNITED	5	1	Ferguson (3), Lennie, McSkimming	
17	8-Dec	PARTICK THISTLE	0	1		5000
18	15-Dec	CELTIC	3	4	Ferguson (2), Morgan	10000
19	22-Dec	Hearts	1	0	Ferguson	
20	29-Dec	THIRD LANARK	3	1	Ferguson (2), Gardiner	
21	1-Jan	HAMILTON ACCIES	3	0	Rankin (2), Gardiner	10000
22	5-Jan	Falkirk	1	1	Gardiner	3000
23	12-Jan	QUEENS PARK	6	3	Ferguson (3), Finlayson, Stewart, Rankin	3000
24	26-Jan	CLYDEBANK	4	1	Rankin (2), Ferguson, Lennie	
25	2-Feb	Cylde	2	0	Ferguson, Gardiner	
26	9-Feb	AIRDRIEONIANS	2	0	Ferguson (2)	8000
27	16-Feb	St. Mirren	1	1	Ferguson	
28	23-Feb	Rangers	0	0		12000
29	2-Mar	Ayr United	3	1	Ferguson (2), McSkimming	
30	12-Mar	Greenock Morton	0	2		
31	16-Mar	PARTICK THISTLE	4	1	Ferguson (2), Morgan, McIntosh	
32	30-Mar	HIBERNIAN	2	1	Gardiner, Morgan	
33	6-Apr	Rangers	1	2	Ferguson	
34	13-Apr	Celtic	1	1	Rankin	30000

Player Appearances

Player	(Total)
Rundell	33
Stewart	33
McIntosh	32
Murray	31
Ferguson	31
Morgan	31
McSkimming	30
Rankin	30
Gardiner	25
Finlayson	14
Lennie	14
Kelly	12
Gray	12
Lees	7
McStey	7
Archibald	7
Reid	3
Dunsmuir	1
Bennett	1
Robertson	1

1918 Div. 1

		Pl.	Home W.	D.	L.	F.	A.	Away W.	D.	L.	F.	A.	F. (Total)	A.	Pts.
1	Rangers	34	15	1	1	42	12	10	5	2	24	12	66	24	56
2	Celtic	34	11	4	2	34	13	13	3	1	32	13	66	26	55
3	Kilmarnock	34	12	2	3	45	16	7	3	7	24	25	69	41	43
3	Morton	34	9	6	2	27	17	8	3	6	26	25	53	42	43
5	MOTHERWELL	34	11	3	3	43	21	5	6	6	27	30	70	51	41
6	Partick Thistle	34	10	4	3	36	19	4	8	5	15	18	51	37	40
7	Queen's Park	34	11	4	2	41	15	3	2	12	23	48	64	63	34
7	Dumbarton	34	8	2	7	30	29	5	6	6	18	20	48	49	34
9	Clydebank (1)	34	7	4	6	30	26	7	1	9	25	30	55	56	33
10	Heart of Mid.	34	11	1	5	24	15	3	3	11	17	43	41	58	32
11	St. Mirren	34	9	6	2	27	12	2	1	14	15	38	42	50	29
12	Hamilton Acad.	34	8	5	4	33	22	3	1	13	19	41	52	63	28
13	Third Lanark	34	6	3	8	29	22	4	4	9	27	40	56	62	27
13	Falkirk	34	8	6	3	29	21	1	3	13	9	37	38	58	27
15	Airdrieonians	34	8	2	7	26	19	2	4	11	20	39	46	58	26
16	Hibernian	34	7	4	6	27	26	1	5	11	15	31	42	57	25
17	Clyde	34	5	2	10	20	32	4	0	13	17	40	37	72	20
18	Ayr United	34	3	4	10	20	28	2	5	10	12	33	32	61	19

1918 - 19 Season
First Division

No.	Date	Opponent	F	A	Scorers	Att.
1	17-Aug	KILMARNOCK	1	2	Lennie	
2	24-Aug	Dumbarton	0	2		
3	31-Aug	HAMILTON ACCIES	1	1	Ferguson	
4	7-Sep	Hearts	0	0		8000
5	14-Sep	HIBERNIAN	0	0		
6	21-Sep	Third Lanark	1	1	McIntosh	
7	28-Sep	ST. MIRREN	1	2	Ferguson	
8	5-Oct	Ayr United	2	1	Stewart, Rankin	
9	12-Oct	PARTICK THISTLE	1	1	Paton	
10	19-Oct	GREENOCK MORTON	2	0	Ferguson (2)	5000
11	26-Oct	Rangers	0	0		20000
12	2-Nov	Airdrieonians	1	1	Lennie	
13	9-Nov	CLYDEBANK	1	1	Ferguson	5000
14	23-Nov	FALKIRK	2	1	Lees, Gardiner	
15	30-Nov	Kilmarnock	2	0	Ferrier (2)	4000
16	7-Dec	CELTIC	3	1	Ferrier, Gardiner, Kelly	
17	14-Dec	CLYDE	3	2	Hart (2), Gardiner	5000
18	21-Dec	Hibernian	3	0	Lennie (2), Ferguson	5000
19	28-Dec	RANGERS	0	1		
20	1-Jan	Hamilton Accies	3	1	Ferguson (2), Ferrier	10000
21	4-Jan	QUEENS PARK	3	1	Ferguson (2), Rankin	
22	11-Jan	Greenock Morton	2	6	Rankin, Gardiner	
23	18-Jan	AYR UNITED	4	0	Ferguson (2), Young, Rankin	8000
24	25-Jan	Celtic	0	0		
25	1-Feb	AIRDRIEONIANS	1	3	Lennie	
26	8-Feb	Cylde	2	1	Ferguson (2)	8000
27	15-Feb	Clydebank	1	2	Ferguson	4000
28	22-Feb	THIRD LANARK	1	1	Lennie	
29	8-Mar	HEARTS	1	2	Ferguson	
30	22-Mar	Falkirk	3	2	Ferguson, Gardiner, Lennie	
31	5-Apr	St. Mirren	0	1		
32	12-Apr	Partick Thistle	0	2		
33	21-Apr	Queens Park	3	1	Brown, Kelly, ?	
34	26-Apr	DUMBARTON	3	0	Robertson (2), Gardiner	

Player Appearances

Player	(Total)
Gardiner	32
McIntosh	31
Stewart	31
Craig	30
Lennie	29
Rankin	29
Anderson	29
Ferguson	25
McSkimming	21
Bell	21
Ferrier	16
Craig Brown	14
Morgan	8
Paton	7
McStey	7
Bennett	5
Rundell	4
Lees	4
Kelly	3
Skelly	3
Kennedy	2
Landells	2
Young	2
McNeill	2
Robertson	2
Finlayson	1
Archibald	1
McDougall	1
Hart	1
Thom	1

1919 Div. 1

		Pl.	Home W.	D.	L.	F.	A.	Away W.	D.	L.	F.	A.	F. (Total)	A.	Pts.
1	Celtic	34	13	3	1	33	10	13	3	1	38	12	71	22	58
2	Rangers	34	15	2	0	51	7	11	3	3	35	9	86	16	57
3	Morton	34	10	7	0	49	20	8	4	5	27	20	76	40	47
4	Partick Thistle	34	11	1	5	38	21	6	6	5	24	22	62	43	41
5	MOTHERWELL	34	7	5	5	28	19	7	5	5	23	21	51	40	38
5	Ayr United	34	9	1	7	34	22	6	7	4	28	31	62	53	38
7	Heart of Mid.	34	8	5	4	31	20	6	4	7	28	32	59	52	37
8	Queen's Park	34	10	1	6	39	29	5	4	8	20	28	59	57	35
8	Kilmarnock	34	6	4	7	30	24	8	3	6	31	35	61	59	35
10	Clydebank (1)	34	7	4	6	31	35	5	4	8	23	30	54	65	32
10	St. Mirren	34	6	8	3	26	25	4	4	9	17	30	43	55	32
12	Third Lanark	34	4	4	9	27	34	7	5	5	33	28	60	62	31
13	Airdrieonians	34	4	7	6	21	27	5	4	8	24	27	45	54	29
14	Hamilton Acad.	34	6	2	9	23	31	5	3	9	26	44	49	75	27
15	Dumbarton	34	4	6	7	16	20	3	2	12	15	38	31	58	22
16	Falkirk	34	3	5	9	28	34	3	3	11	18	39	46	73	20
16	Clyde	34	4	4	9	23	33	3	2	12	22	42	45	75	20
18	Hibernian	34	5	0	12	16	35	0	3	14	14	56	30	91	13

1919 - 20 Season
First Division

No.	Date	Opponent	F	A	Scorers	Att.
1	16-Aug	DUNDEE	3	1	Ferguson (3)	10000
2	23-Aug	Cylde	1	4	Ferrier	4000
3	27-Aug	Falkirk	2	1	Ferguson, Robertson	4000
4	30-Aug	HIBERNIAN	3	2	Ferguson, Rankin, Robertson	9000
5	6-Sep	Queens Park	1	1	Ferguson	
6	10-Sep	Hamilton Accies	3	0	Ferguson (3)	10000
7	13-Sep	RAITH ROVERS	4	1	Ferguson (2), Rankin, Ferrier	
8	20-Sep	Greenock Morton	1	0	Ferguson	7000
9	27-Sep	RANGERS	1	0	Ferguson	22000
10	4-Oct	ABERDEEN	3	3	Ferguson (2), Ferrier	
11	6-Oct	Dundee	0	3		
12	11-Oct	AYR UNITED	1	1	Ferguson	
13	18-Oct	Albion Rovers	1	1	Gardiner	8000
14	25-Oct	KILMARNOCK	1	1	Ferguson	
15	1-Nov	Hearts	0	2		10000
16	8-Nov	DUMBARTON	1	1	Robertson	
17	22-Nov	FALKIRK	4	0	Robertson, Gardiner, Kelly, Lennie	
18	29-Nov	AIRDRIEONIANS	2	1	Brown J, Rankin	11000
19	6-Dec	Celtic	0	5		10000
20	13-Dec	Partick Thistle	1	2	Jackson	
21	20-Dec	CLYDEBANK	3	2	Ferguson, Rankin, Ferrier	
22	27-Dec	St. Mirren	1	2	Ferguson	
23	1-Jan	HAMILTON ACCIES	1	0	Ferguson	9000
24	3-Jan	HEARTS	4	1	Rankin (2), Ferguson, C Brown	5000
25	5-Jan	Airdrieonians	1	0	Ferguson	
26	10-Jan	Ayr United	0	0		
27	17-Jan	PARTICK THISTLE	1	0	Ferguson	
28	31-Jan	Dumbarton	3	2	Ferrier (2), Ferguson	
29	14-Feb	CLYDE	5	1	Ferguson (3), Gardiner, Rankin	8000
30	21-Feb	Clydebank	1	5	Ferguson	7000
31	28-Feb	ALBION ROVERS	2	0	Ferguson, Rankin	10000
32	6-Mar	Hibernian	1	0	Ferrier	
33	16-Mar	Rangers	0	0		19000
34	20-Mar	THIRD LANARK	3	3	Rabertson (2), Rankin	8000
35	27-Mar	Raith Rovers	2	0	Rankin (2)	
36	3-Apr	GREENOCK MORTON	4	3	Ferguson (2), Robertson, Gardiner	8000
37	10-Apr	QUEENS PARK	4	1	Ferguson (2), Kelly, OG	8000
38	14-Apr	Third Lanark	0	2		
39	17-Apr	CELTIC	0	0		20000
40	19-Apr	Kilmarnock	1	0	Rankin	
41	24-Apr	ST. MIRREN	3	0	Ferguson, Lennie, C Brown	7000
42	1-May	Aberdeen	1	1	Ferrier	11000
S c						
1	24-Jan	Partick Thistle	1	3	Ferguson	35000

Player Appearances

	(Total)
Rundell	43
Rankin	41
Ferrier	39
Stewart	38
Craig Brown	38
McGregor	37
Lennie	37
James Jackson	36
Ferguson	36
Paterson	34
Gardiner	32
Robertson	12
Kelly	9
Anderson	9
John Jackson	6
McDougal	4
Hunter	3
Lees	3
James Brown	2
Rutherford	1
Bowie	1

1920 Div. 1

		Pl.	Home					Away					F.	A.	Pts.
			W.	D.	L.	F.	A.	W.	D.	L.	F.	A.	(Total)		
1	Rangers	42	18	2	1	68	18	13	7	1	38	7	106	25	71
2	Celtic	42	15	6	0	54	14	14	4	3	35	17	89	31	68
3	MOTHERWELL	42	15	6	0	53	22	8	5	8	21	31	74	53	57
4	Dundee	42	16	2	3	48	24	6	4	11	31	41	79	65	50
5	Clydebank (1)	42	12	6	3	47	24	8	2	11	31	30	78	54	48
6	Morton	42	10	6	5	37	15	6	7	8	34	33	71	48	45
7	Airdrieonians	42	11	6	4	27	11	6	4	11	30	32	57	43	44
8	Third Lanark	42	11	4	6	35	28	5	7	9	21	34	56	62	43
8	Kilmarnock	42	15	0	6	40	31	5	3	13	19	43	59	74	43
10	Ayr United	42	11	7	3	44	19	4	3	14	28	50	72	69	40
11	Dumbarton	42	7	9	5	26	23	6	4	11	31	42	57	65	39
12	Queen's Park	42	11	5	5	41	28	3	5	13	26	45	67	73	38
12	Partick Thistle	42	12	5	4	36	24	1	7	13	15	38	51	62	38
12	St. Mirren	42	9	3	9	32	38	6	5	10	31	43	63	81	38
15	Clyde	42	11	4	6	44	31	3	5	13	20	40	64	71	37
15	Heart of Mid.	42	8	5	8	31	28	6	4	11	26	44	57	72	37
17	Aberdeen	42	8	7	6	23	19	3	6	12	23	45	46	64	35
18	Hibernian	42	11	3	7	38	27	2	4	15	22	52	60	79	33
19	Raith Rovers	42	10	3	8	33	29	1	7	13	28	54	61	83	32
20	Falkirk	42	10	6	5	36	27	0	5	16	9	47	45	74	31
21	Hamilton Acad.	42	10	5	6	40	34	1	2	18	16	52	56	86	29
22	Albion Rovers	42	7	4	10	27	37	3	4	14	16	40	43	77	28

1920 - 21 Season
First Division

No.	Date	Opponent	F	A	Scorers	Att.
1	16-Aug	HIBERNIAN	4	2	Dick (3), Ferguson	8000
2	21-Aug	Rangers	1	2	Ferguson	40000
3	28-Aug	HAMILTON ACCIES	2	0	Ferrier, Robertson	20000
4	1-Sep	RANGERS	0	2		22000
5	4-Sep	Raith Rovers	2	1	Stewart, Ferguson	
6	7-Sep	Celtic	0	1		
7	11-Sep	PARTICK THISTLE	0	4		
8	18-Sep	Queens Park	6	0	Ferguson (4), Stewart, Lennie	
9	21-Sep	St. Mirren	2	1	Ferguson (2)	
10	25-Sep	FALKIRK	4	2	Ferguson (3), Lennie	10000
11	2-Oct	Albion Rovers	1	1	Ferguson	
12	9-Oct	DUNDEE	1	2	Ferguson	12000
13	16-Oct	Hibernian	3	2	Ferrier (2), Rankin	
14	23-Oct	Kilmarnock	3	0	Ferguson (2), Ferrier	
15	30-Oct	ST. MIRREN	2	0	Ferguson, Rankin	8000
16	6-Nov	CLYDEBANK	0	0		
17	13-Nov	Greenock Morton	1	4	Rankin	
18	20-Nov	DUMBARTON	8	2	Ferguson (4), Lennie (2), Rankin, Robertson	8000
19	27-Nov	Ayr United	0	0		2000
20	4-Dec	HEARTS	2	2	Ferguson, Robertson	
21	11-Dec	Airdrieonians	1	1	Reid	22000
22	18-Dec	Aberdeen	1	1	Reid	10000
23	25-Dec	AYR UNITED	6	1	Ferguson (4), Ferrier, Lennie	
24	1-Jan	Hamilton Accies	4	1	Ferguson (2), Ferrier, Finlayson	20000
25	3-Jan	GREENOCK MORTON	2	2	Ferguson, Ferrier	12000
26	5-Jan	AIRDRIEONIANS	1	0	Ferguson	12000
27	8-Jan	ALBION ROVERS	1	1	Ferguson	12000
28	22-Jan	CELTIC	1	1	Rankin	15000
29	29-Jan	Third Lanark	1	3	Ferguson	
30	12-Feb	Hearts	0	1		
31	26-Feb	Dumbarton	0	2		
32	12-Mar	Falkirk	0	1		
33	19-Mar	Partick Thistle	0	0		
34	23-Mar	CLYDE	3	1	Ferguson (2), Ferrier	6000
35	26-Mar	RAITH ROVERS	2	1	Ferguson (2)	6000
36	2-Apr	Third Lanark	1	0	Lennie	10000
37	9-Apr	Dundee	1	2	Lennie	
38	11-Apr	Cylde	0	1		3000
39	16-Apr	ABERDEEN	4	0	Ferguson (4)	6000
40	20-Apr	QUEENS PARK	2	1	Ferguson (2)	5000
41	23-Apr	Clydebank	2	1	Rankin (2)	2000
42	30-Apr	KILMARNOCK	0	1		6000
S c						
1	5-Feb	RENTON	3	0	Reid (2), C Brown	
2	19-Feb	Ayr United	1	1	Ferguson	
2r	23-Feb	AYR UNITED	1	1	Reid	
2/2r	2-Mar	AYR UNITED*	3	1	Ferguson (2), Rankin	
3	5-Mar	PARTICK THISTLE	2	2	Ferguson (2)	
3r	8-Mar	Partick Thistle	0	0		
3/2r	15-Mar	PARTICK THISTLE#	1	2	Ferguson	

* Played at Parkhead # Played at Ibrox

Player Appearances

	(Total)
Craig Brown	46
Stewart	46
Ferguson	43
Ferrier	43
Lennie	42
McDougal	41
Rundell	39
Paterson	39
Rankin	36
McGregor	28
Reid	25
Gardiner	18
James Jackson	15
Robertson	15
Henderson	10
Wallace	10
Dr Finlayson	9
Dick	8
Bell	4
James Brown	1
Crosbie	1

1921 Div. 1

		Pl.	Home					Away					F.	A.	Pts.
			W.	D.	L.	F.	A.	W.	D.	L.	F.	A.	(Total)		
1	Rangers	42	19	1	1	50	11	16	5	0	41	13	91	24	76
2	Celtic	42	16	3	2	50	15	14	3	4	36	20	86	35	66
3	Heart of Mid.	42	15	2	4	48	16	5	8	8	26	33	74	49	50
4	Dundee	42	13	5	3	35	13	6	6	9	19	35	54	48	49
5	MOTHERWELL	42	11	5	5	46	28	8	5	8	29	23	75	51	48
6	Partick Thistle	42	10	9	2	34	16	7	3	11	19	23	53	39	46
7	Clyde	42	16	3	2	43	17	5	0	16	20	45	63	62	45
8	Third Lanark	42	10	3	8	45	27	9	3	9	29	34	74	61	44
8	Morton	42	10	8	3	44	21	5	6	10	22	37	66	58	44
10	Airdrieonians	42	9	5	7	46	32	8	4	9	25	32	71	64	43
11	Aberdeen	42	9	7	5	30	18	5	7	9	23	36	53	54	42
11	Kilmarnock	42	13	2	6	43	25	4	6	11	19	43	62	68	42
13	Hibernian	42	9	5	7	31	23	7	4	10	27	34	58	57	41
14	Ayr United	42	10	8	3	40	21	4	4	13	22	48	62	69	40
14	Hamilton Acad.	42	9	8	4	26	16	5	4	12	18	41	44	57	40
16	Raith Rovers	42	14	0	7	38	21	2	5	14	16	37	54	58	37
17	Albion Rovers	42	6	5	10	31	31	5	7	9	26	37	57	68	34
17	Falkirk	42	7	6	8	33	31	4	6	11	21	41	54	72	34
19	Queen's Park	42	6	8	7	24	28	5	3	13	21	52	45	80	33
20	Clydebank (1)	42	6	6	9	33	31	1	8	12	14	41	47	72	28
21	Dumbarton	42	9	1	11	25	27	1	3	17	16	62	41	89	24
22	St. Mirren	42	5	2	14	25	39	2	2	17	18	53	43	92	18

1921 - 22 Season
First Division

	Date	Opponent			Scorers	Att.
1	17-Aug	Greenock Morton	0	0		9500
2	20-Aug	RAITH ROVERS	2	1	Ferguson (2)	9000
3	27-Aug	Rangers	1	2	Reid	40000
4	3-Sep	GREENOCK MORTON	2	0	Ferguson (2)	12000
5	10-Sep	Hamilton Accies	1	3	Ferguson	
6	13-Sep	Cylde	0	1		
7	17-Sep	HIBERNIAN	4	1	Reid (2), Ferguson, Rankin	
8	21-Sep	DUNDEE	2	1	Ferguson (2)	8000
9	24-Sep	Albion Rovers	0	0		
10	1-Oct	CLYDE	2	0	Ferguson (2)	8000
11	3-Oct	Dundee	1	1	Ferguson	
12	8-Oct	Ayr United	1	2	Ferguson	7000
13	15-Oct	DUMBARTON	5	0	Ferguson (3), Reid, Lennie	6000
14	22-Oct	Third Lanark	3	4	Rankin (2), Ferrier	
15	29-Oct	ST. MIRREN	1	1	Reid	
16	5-Nov	Falkirk	0	1		
17	12-Nov	HEARTS	3	1	Ferguson, Tennant, Rankin	8000
18	19-Nov	Kilmarnock	0	4		
19	26-Nov	CELTIC	1	1	Tennant	17000
20	3-Dec	Partick Thistle	2	0	Ferguson (2)	
21	10-Dec	CLYDEBANK	5	2	Ferguson (5)	6000
22	17-Dec	Aberdeen	0	2		
23	24-Dec	AIRDRIEONIANS	1	2	Ferguson	10000
24	31-Dec	Queens Park	1	2	Hart	
25	2-Jan	HAMILTON ACCIES	2	1	Ferguson, Ferrier	
26	3-Jan	Clydebank	0	2		
27	7-Jan	Hibernian	0	2		
28	14-Jan	PARTICK THISTLE	2	1	Ferrier, Tennant	
29	4-Feb	RANGERS	2	0	Ferguson, Lennie	10000
30	18-Feb	THIRD LANARK	1	3	Ferguson	
31	1-Mar	KILMARNOCK	3	0	Ferguson, Hart, Ferrier	
32	4-Mar	Raith Rovers	1	4	Lennie	
33	15-Mar	Celtic	0	2		
34	18-Mar	QUEENS PARK	5	1	Rankin (3), Ferrier, Paterson	6000
35	25-Mar	St. Mirren	1	2	Hart	10000
36	29-Mar	Hearts	0	0		
37	8-Apr	Airdrieonians	0	2		6000
38	12-Apr	ABERDEEN	3	0	Ferguson (3)	
39	15-Apr	AYR UNITED	2	1	Ferguson (2)	4000
40	19-Apr	Dumbarton	2	3	Ferguson, Hart	
41	22-Apr	FALKIRK	0	1		
42	29-Apr	ALBION ROVERS	1	1	Ferguson	4500
S c						
1	28-Jan	East Fife	3	0	Ferguson (2), Tennant	6000
2	11-Feb	HIBERNIAN	3	1	Ferrier (2), Tennant	15000
3	25-Feb	ALLOA ATHLETIC	1	0	Ferguson	20000
4	11-Mar	GREENOCK MORTON	1	2	Hart	15000

Player Appearances

(Total)	
Rundell	46
Paterson	45
Stewart	45
Ferrier	44
Craig Brown	42
Rankin	40
Ferguson	37
McDougal	34
James Jackson	26
Reid	26
Lennie	24
Hart	20
Newbigging	20
Tennant	18
Allan	11
Hamilton	6
Henderson	5
Davidson	4
Martin	3
Landells	1

1922 Div. 1

	Pl.	Home W.	D.	L.	F.	A.	Away W.	D.	L.	F.	A.	F. (Total)	A.	Pts.
1 Celtic	42	19	2	0	51	4	8	11	2	32	16	83	20	67
2 Rangers	42	15	4	2	45	14	13	6	2	38	12	83	26	66
3 Raith Rovers	42	12	7	2	41	16	7	6	8	25	27	66	43	51
4 Dundee	42	13	8	0	33	8	6	3	12	24	32	57	40	49
5 Falkirk	42	13	6	2	35	11	3	11	7	13	27	48	38	49
6 Partick Thistle	42	12	6	3	32	17	8	2	11	25	36	57	53	48
7 Hibernian	42	11	7	3	31	12	5	7	9	24	32	55	44	46
8 St. Mirren	42	11	6	4	43	24	6	6	9	28	37	71	61	46
9 Third Lanark	42	10	7	4	34	22	7	5	9	24	30	58	52	46
10 Clyde	42	12	7	2	36	15	4	5	12	24	36	60	51	44
11 Albion Rovers	42	11	4	6	27	18	6	6	9	28	33	55	51	44
12 Morton	42	14	5	2	39	17	2	5	14	19	40	58	57	42
13 MOTHERWELL	42	15	3	3	49	19	1	4	16	14	39	63	58	39
14 Ayr United	42	11	6	4	30	20	2	6	13	25	43	55	63	38
15 Aberdeen	42	10	5	6	31	17	3	4	14	17	37	48	54	35
16 Airdrieonians	42	10	4	7	35	23	2	7	12	11	33	46	56	35
17 Kilmarnock	42	12	6	3	44	26	1	3	17	12	57	56	83	35
18 Hamilton Acad.	42	7	8	6	37	29	2	8	11	14	33	51	62	34
19 Heart of Mid.	42	9	6	6	34	21	2	4	15	16	39	50	60	32
20 Dumbarton	42	9	4	8	36	39	1	6	14	10	42	46	81	30
21 Queen's Park	42	5	5	11	22	46	4	5	12	16	36	38	82	28
22 Clydebank (1)	42	5	6	10	18	37	1	2	18	16	66	34	103	20

1922 - 23 Season
First Division

	Date	Opponent			Scorers	Att.
1	19-Aug	Greenock Morton	0	2		
2	26-Aug	RANGERS	0	4		18000
3	2-Sep	Hibernian	1	2	Ferguson	18000
4	9-Sep	DUNDEE	3	4	Ferguson (2), Hart,	8000
5	16-Sep	Alloa Athletic	1	1	Ferguson	500
6	23-Sep	AYR UNITED	4	0	Ferrier (2), Ferguson, Hart	5000
7	30-Sep	Raith Rovers	1	1	C Brown	8000
8	7-Oct	HAMILTON ACCIES	0	0		10000
9	14-Oct	Celtic	0	1		
10	21-Oct	ABERDEEN	3	1	Ferguson, Ferrier, C Brown	
11	28-Oct	THIRD LANARK	1	1	Lennie	6000
12	4-Nov	Kilmarnock	6	0	Ferguson (3), Rankin, Ferrier	
13	11-Nov	Albion Rovers	1	1	Ferrier	3000
14	18-Nov	PARTICK THISTLE	1	1	Rankin	
15	25-Nov	CLYDE	5	3	Ferguson (3), Ferrier, Rankin	3000
16	2-Dec	Falkirk	0	1		5000
17	9-Dec	HEARTS	4	1	Ferguson (3), Rankin	7000
18	16-Dec	HIBERNIAN	0	2		6000
19	23-Dec	St. Mirren	3	3	Little, Rennie, Rankin	
20	30-Dec	FALKIRK	3	2	Ferrier, Stewart, Tennant	6000
21	1-Jan	Hamilton Accies	0	3		12000
22	2-Jan	GREENOCK MORTON	4	3	Ferguson (3), Wardrope	7000
23	6-Jan	Rangers	1	2	Tennant	15000
24	20-Jan	AIRDRIEONIANS	0	0		7000
25	31-Jan	Ayr United	0	2		3000
26	3-Feb	ALLOA ATHLETIC	2	0	Greenshields, Ferrier	5000
27	13-Feb	Third Lanark	2	1	Ferguson, Rankin	7000
28	17-Feb	ST. MIRREN	1	1	Quinn	
29	28-Feb	Partick Thistle	0	3		
30	3-Mar	ALBION ROVERS	1	0	Ferguson	
31	14-Mar	Hearts	2	1	Ferguson (2)	
32	17-Mar	Airdrieonians	1	4	Ferguson	
33	24-Mar	RAITH ROVERS	2	0	Ferguson (2)	5500
34	31-Mar	Cylde	0	3		
35	7-Apr	KILMARNOCK	4	1	Reid (2), Ferguson, Ferrier	4500
36	14-Apr	Dundee	1	3	Ferguson	10000
37	21-Apr	CELTIC	0	0		
38	28-Apr	Aberdeen	1	2	Ferguson	
S c						
1	13-Jan	St. Johnstone	2	1	Ferguson, Lennie	12000
2	27-Jan	ST. MIRREN	2	1	Lennie, Little	17000
3	10-Feb	FALKIRK	3	0	Ferguson (3)	22000
4	24-Feb	BO'NESS	4	2	Ferguson (3), Reid	15000
Sf	10-Mar	CELTIC*	0	2		75000

* Played at Ibrox

Player Appearances

(Total)	
Rundell	39
Ferrier	38
Little	34
Stewart	32
Ferguson	32
Craig Brown	31
Reid	31
Rankin	29
Lennie	26
Newbigging	24
James Jackson	22
Wardrope	22
Martin	16
Greenshields	15
Tennant	8
Quinn	8
Hart	5
Wyper	2
McDougal	2

1923 Div. 1

	Pl.	Home W.	D.	L.	F.	A.	Away W.	D.	L.	F.	A.	F. (Total)	A.	Pts.
1 Rangers	38	15	4	0	43	11	8	5	6	24	18	67	29	55
2 Airdrieonians	38	14	4	1	41	16	6	6	7	17	22	58	38	50
3 Celtic	38	10	5	4	29	21	9	3	7	23	18	52	39	46
4 Falkirk	38	9	10	0	27	7	5	7	7	17	25	44	32	45
5 Aberdeen	38	10	6	3	28	12	5	6	8	18	22	46	34	42
6 St. Mirren	38	11	6	2	32	14	4	6	9	22	30	54	44	42
7 Dundee	38	13	2	4	28	11	4	5	10	23	34	51	45	41
8 Hibernian	38	14	2	3	31	13	3	5	11	14	27	45	40	41
9 Raith Rovers	38	9	8	2	18	14	4	5	10	13	29	31	43	39
10 Ayr United	38	11	6	2	31	15	2	6	11	12	29	43	44	38
11 Partick Thistle	38	11	4	4	33	14	3	5	11	18	34	51	48	37
12 Heart of Mid.	38	6	10	3	29	20	5	5	9	22	30	51	50	37
13 MOTHERWELL	38	10	6	3	38	24	3	4	12	21	36	59	60	36
14 Morton	38	9	3	7	28	20	3	8	8	16	27	44	47	35
15 Kilmarnock	38	11	1	7	37	26	3	6	10	20	40	57	66	35
16 Clyde	38	10	4	5	24	12	2	5	12	12	32	36	44	33
17 Third Lanark	38	8	5	6	29	22	3	3	13	11	37	40	59	30
18 Hamilton Acad.	38	8	6	5	29	18	3	1	15	14	41	43	59	29
19 Albion Rovers	38	7	3	9	25	22	1	7	11	13	42	38	64	26
20 Alloa	38	3	7	9	16	29	3	4	12	11	23	27	52	23

1920-21 Season
Back: Wallace, Muircroft (Vice-Pres), Marshall, McDonald, Smith
Middle: Kerr, Nelson, McGiviney, Brown, Henry, A.Mackie, Gibb, F.Moore
Front: J.Moore (Pres), Ferguson, J.Mackie, Armour, Barr (Sec), Anderson (Train)

1928-29 Season
Back: Mrs Hunter, Donaldson (Train), Frame, McNeil, Little, MacFadyen, Arnott Craig, McClory, Thackeray, Allan Craig, W.Tennant, Johnman, Walker (Train), Hunter (Man)
Front: Stevenson, Douglas, T.Tennant, Ferrier, Keenan, Cameron, McMurtrie, Master Hunter

1923 - 24 Season
First Division

No.	Date	Opponent	F	A	Scorers	Att.
1	18-Aug	RANGERS	0	3		20000
2	25-Aug	Hamilton Accies	1	2	Ferguson	12000
3	1-Sep	GREENOCK MORTON	3	1	Ferguson (2), Wardrope	
4	8-Sep	Partick Thistle	2	0	Ferguson, Ferrier	15000
5	15-Sep	CLYDE	1	1	Ferguson	3500
6	22-Sep	Hibernian	4	2	Ferguson (2), Ferrier (2)	10000
7	29-Sep	CLYDEBANK	3	2	Ferguson (2), Rankin	
8	6-Oct	Ayr United	0	0		
9	13-Oct	DUNDEE	4	2	Ferguson, Ferrier, Rankin, Little	8000
10	20-Oct	KILMARNOCK	4	0	Ferguson (2), Rankin, White	
11	27-Oct	Aberdeen	1	3	Ferrier	
12	3-Nov	HEARTS	3	2	Ferguson (2), Rankin	6000
13	10-Nov	Airdrieonians	0	2		
14	17-Nov	QUEENS PARK	2	1	Ferguson, McFadyen	5000
15	24-Nov	Falkirk	0	2		
16	1-Dec	ST. MIRREN	0	2		6500
17	8-Dec	Third Lanark	1	2	Ferguson	4000
18	15-Dec	Celtic	1	2	Ferrier	5000
19	22-Dec	RAITH ROVERS	1	3	Ferguson	
20	29-Dec	Queens Park	2	2	Ferrier (2)	6000
21	1-Jan	HAMILTON ACCIES	3	1	Ferguson (2), Stewart	10000
22	2-Jan	Greenock Morton	2	3	Ferguson, Rankin	
23	5-Jan	AIRDRIEONIANS	2	1	C Brown, White	10000
24	12-Jan	Cylde	3	2	Ferguson, Ferrier, Stewart	3500
25	19-Jan	FALKIRK	3	1	Ferguson (2), Rankin	3000
26	2-Feb	Rangers	0	3		20000
27	13-Feb	CELTIC	0	1		
28	16-Feb	St. Mirren	0	4		
29	27-Feb	Raith Rovers	1	1	Ferguson	
30	1-Mar	AYR UNITED	1	0	Ferguson	2500
31	8-Mar	Dundee	1	4	McFadyen	6000
32	15-Mar	HIBERNIAN	2	1	Ferrier, Stevenson	2500
33	22-Apr	ABERDEEN	1	1	Ferguson	3000
34	29-Apr	Hearts	1	2	Ferguson	10000
35	5-Apr	Clydebank	2	0	McFadyen, White	3500
36	12-Apr	PARTICK THISTLE	1	1	Rankin	3000
37	19-Apr	THIRD LANARK	2	2	Ferrier, Little	
38	26-Apr	Kilmarnock	0	1		4000
S c						
1	26-Jan	BREADALBANE	5	0	Ferguson (3), C Brown, Stewart	3000
2	9-Feb	Forfar Athletic	3	1	Ferguson, Rankin, C Brown	4000
3	23-Feb	AIRDRIEONIANS	0	5		28000

Player Appearances

(Total)	
Rundell	41
Little	41
Ferrier	39
Rankin	37
Ferguson	36
White	35
Johnman	35
Stewart	30
Reid	27
Newbigging	26
Craig Brown	20
McDougal	16
McFadyen	15
Martin	11
Stevenson	10
Winters	7
Findlay	4
Hamilton	3
Wardrope	3
Quinn	3
Greenshields	2
Taylor	1
Fowler	1

1924 Div. 1

		Pl.	Home W.	D.	L.	F.	A.	Away W.	D.	L.	F.	A.	F. (Total)	A.	Pts.
1	Rangers	38	14	4	1	38	7	11	5	3	34	15	72	22	59
2	Airdrieonians	38	13	6	0	48	17	7	4	8	24	29	72	46	50
3	Celtic	38	11	5	3	36	15	6	7	6	20	18	56	33	46
4	Raith Rovers	38	13	3	3	40	12	5	4	10	16	26	56	38	43
5	Dundee	38	12	6	1	48	22	3	7	9	22	35	70	57	43
6	St. Mirren	38	10	5	4	37	15	5	7	7	16	30	53	45	42
7	Hibernian	38	12	3	4	41	21	3	8	8	25	31	66	52	41
8	Partick Thistle	38	9	4	6	32	23	6	5	8	26	32	58	55	39
9	Heart of Mid.	38	12	4	3	43	17	2	6	11	18	33	61	50	38
10	MOTHERWELL	38	11	4	4	36	26	4	3	12	22	37	58	63	37
11	Morton	38	12	3	4	31	16	4	2	13	17	38	48	54	37
12	Hamilton Acad.	38	11	2	6	37	26	4	4	11	15	31	52	57	36
13	Aberdeen	38	11	5	3	27	14	2	5	12	10	27	37	41	36
14	Ayr United	38	11	7	1	32	16	1	3	15	6	44	38	60	34
15	Falkirk	38	10	4	5	28	15	3	2	14	18	38	46	53	32
16	Kilmarnock	38	9	4	6	28	25	3	4	12	20	40	48	65	32
17	Queen's Park	38	7	7	5	22	21	4	2	13	21	39	43	60	31
18	Third Lanark	38	9	3	7	32	33	2	5	12	22	45	54	78	30
19	Clyde	38	8	6	5	26	21	2	3	14	14	49	40	70	29
20	Clydebank (1)	38	8	3	8	21	25	2	2	15	21	46	42	71	25

1924 - 25 Season
First Division

No.	Date	Opponent	F	A	Scorers	Att.
1	16-Aug	Queens Park	1	2	Stevenson	7000
2	23-Aug	GREENOCK MORTON	3	0	Ferguson (2), Ferrier	
3	29-Aug	Hibernian	0	1		
4	6-Sep	AYR UNITED	1	1	Ferguson	
5	13-Sep	Third Lanark	1	1	Tennant	10000
6	20-Sep	DUNDEE	4	1	Ferguson, Ferrier, Reid, Little	
7	27-Sep	Celtic	0	4		
8	4-Oct	Hearts	2	2	Ferguson, Cringan	
9	11-Oct	ABERDEEN	1	2	Ferguson	7000
10	18-Oct	HAMILTON ACCIES	3	3	Ferguson (3)	11000
11	25-Oct	Falkirk	1	2	Ferguson	6000
12	1-Nov	COWDENBEATH	0	3		6500
13	8-Nov	Partick Thistle	2	2	Ferguson, Stevenson	
14	15-Nov	ST. JOHNSTONE	4	1	Ferguson (2), Ferrier, Tennant	6000
15	22-Nov	St. Mirren	1	4	Tennant	
16	29-Nov	AIRDRIEONIANS	1	5	Ferrier	8000
17	6-Dec	Kilmarnock	2	0	Ferguson (2)	
18	13-Dec	RAITH ROVERS	2	1	Ferguson, Ferrier	3000
19	20-Dec	HEARTS	0	0		5000
20	27-Dec	RANGERS	0	1		15000
21	3-Jan	QUEENS PARK	4	1	Ferguson (2), McGrath, Tennant	8000
22	5-Jan	FALKIRK	4	1	Ferguson,Stevenson,Tennant,Greenshields	4000
23	7-Jan	Hamilton Accies	1	1	Ferrier	9000
24	10-Jan	St. Johnstone	1	2	Ferguson	
25	17-Jan	CELTIC	1	0	Ferguson	12000
26	31-Jan	Greenock Morton	0	0		
27	11-Feb	HIBERNIAN	1	1	Ferguson	5000
28	14-Feb	Raith Rovers	0	1		
29	28-Feb	PARTICK THISTLE	1	3	Ferguson	5000
30	4-Mar	Cowdenbeath	0	4		
31	14-Mar	Dundee	0	1		
32	21-Mar	THIRD LANARK	8	0	Ferg'n(2),Stev'n(2),McGrath(2),Tennant,Ferrier	4000
33	28-Mar	Airdrieonians	0	5		
34	1-Apr	ST. MIRREN	1	2	Ferguson	
35	4-Apr	KILMARNOCK	2	1	Ferguson (2)	
36	11-Apr	Ayr United	0	1		
37	18-Apr	RANGERS	1	1	Tennant	
38	25-Apr	Aberdeen	0	2		15000
S c						
1	24-Jan	GALSTON	6	3	Ferguson (5), McGrath	4500
2	7-Feb	ARTHURLIE	2	0	Stevenson, McGrath	8000
3	21-Feb	Aberdeen	0	0		25000
3r	25-Feb	ABERDEEN	1	2	Ferguson	13000

Player Appearances

(League)	
Ferguson	35
Ferrier	35
Stevenson	33
McClory	32
Frame	27
Little	26
Johnman	24
Tennant	21
Greenshields	20
Coyle	20
McGrath	20
Alan Craig	19
White	18
Cringan	14
Paterson	9
Reid	9
Martin	8
McCafferty	7
Rundell	5
McDonald	4
McFadyen	2
Healey	2
Newbigging	1
Craig Brown	1

1925 Div. 1

		Pl.	Home W.	D.	L.	F.	A.	Away W.	D.	L.	F.	A.	F. (Total)	A.	Pts.
1	Rangers	38	16	3	0	46	10	9	7	3	30	16	76	26	60
2	Airdrieonians	38	15	4	0	51	10	10	3	6	34	21	85	31	57
3	Hibernian	38	16	1	2	56	16	6	7	6	22	27	78	43	52
4	Celtic	38	13	3	3	51	13	5	5	9	26	31	77	44	44
5	Cowdenbeath	38	13	3	3	52	21	3	7	9	24	44	76	65	42
6	St. Mirren	38	12	2	5	36	22	6	2	11	29	41	65	63	40
7	Partick Thistle	38	8	6	5	35	27	6	4	9	25	34	60	61	38
8	Dundee	38	11	4	4	30	14	3	4	12	17	40	47	54	36
9	Raith Rovers	38	11	4	4	34	22	3	4	12	19	39	53	61	36
10	Heart of Mid.	38	10	6	3	44	28	2	5	12	20	40	64	68	35
11	St. Johnstone	38	8	7	4	38	29	4	4	11	19	43	57	72	35
12	Kilmarnock	38	10	4	5	35	21	2	5	12	18	43	53	64	33
13	Hamilton Acad.	38	10	2	7	29	26	5	1	13	21	37	50	63	33
14	Morton	38	8	7	4	29	23	4	2	13	17	46	46	69	33
15	Aberdeen	38	7	4	8	23	20	4	6	9	23	36	46	56	32
16	Falkirk	38	10	4	5	33	18	2	4	13	11	36	44	54	32
17	Queen's Park	38	9	4	6	30	22	3	4	12	20	49	50	71	32
18	MOTHERWELL	38	9	5	5	42	27	1	5	13	12	36	54	63	30
19	Ayr United	38	7	6	6	28	25	4	2	13	15	40	43	65	30
20	Third Lanark	38	5	5	9	29	32	6	3	10	24	52	53	84	30

1925 - 26 Season
First Division

	Date	Opponent	F	A	Scorers	Att.
1	15-Aug	CLYDEBANK	2	1	Ferguson (2)	8000
2	22-Aug	Rangers	0	1		28000
3	29-Aug	QUEENS PARK	1	0	McGrath	7000
4	5-Sep	Dundee United	1	1	Ferguson	12000
5	12-Sep	HIBERNIAN	2	1	Ferguson (2)	8000
6	19-Sep	Greenock Morton	1	1	Ferguson	
7	26-Sep	AIRDRIEONIANS	2	1	McFadyen, Tennant	
8	3-Oct	Cowdenbeath	2	2	Stevenson, Ferrier	
9	5-Oct	Dundee	2	1	Ferguson, Tennant	
10	10-Oct	FALKIRK	3	0	Ferguson (3)	8000
11	17-Oct	Hamilton Accies	2	0	Ferguson (2)	
12	24-Oct	ABERDEEN	1	1	Ferrier	10000
13	31-Oct	St. Johnstone	2	2	Tennant (2)	8000
14	7-Nov	RAITH ROVERS	5	0	Ferrier (2), Ferrier (2), McGrath	
15	14-Nov	Hearts	1	3	Little	18000
Aban.	25-Nov	Rangers	1	3	Little	6000
17	28-Nov	Partick Thistle	1	2	Tennant (2)	7000
18	5-Dec	ST. MIRREN	0	1		7000
19	12-Dec	Raith Rovers	1	2	McFadyen	
20	19-Dec	HEARTS	3	1	McFadyen (2), Ferrier	
21	26-Dec	Queens Park	3	0	Murphy, McFadyen, Ferrier	
22	1-Jan	HAMILTON ACCIES	1	0	Tenant	15000
23	2-Jan	Falkirk	3	3	Stevenson, Ferrier, Murphy	10000
24	4-Jan	Greenock Morton	4	1	McFadyen (3), Ferrier	
25	9-Jan	Clydebank	1	1	Thackery	3500
26	16-Jan	ST. JOHNSTONE	4	1	Tennant (2), Stevenson, Murphy	6000
27	30-Jan	Celtic	1	3	Ferrier	
28	6-Feb	DUNDEE UNITED	4	0	McFadyen (2), Ferrier, Tennant	
29	13-Feb	Hibernian	1	3	Stevenson	
30	20-Feb	COWDENBEATH	2	0	Ferrier, Banks	5000
31	23-Feb	St. Mirren	2	2	McFadyen (2)	5000
32	27-Feb	KILMARNOCK	1	2	Stevenson	
33	10-Mar	Airdrieonians	0	2		5000
34	13-Mar	Aberdeen	0	1		10000
35	20-Mar	DUNDEE	2	0	Ferrier, Little	4000
36	27-Mar	CELTIC	2	1	Little, Tennant	
37	3-Apr	PARTICK THISTLE	1	0	McFadyen	
38	10-Apr	Kilmarnock	2	1	McFadyen, Tennant	
Sc						
1	23-Jan	Partick Thistle	0	3		23000

Player Appearances (Total)

Player	
McClory	39
Frame	39
Craig	39
Ferrier	39
Thackery	38
Stevenson	38
Little	37
McFadyen	37
Tennant	32
Johnman	28
Murphy	14
McGrath	13
Ferguson	13
McCafferty	12
Gardiner	5
Livingston	2
Banks	2
Reid	1

1926 Div. 1

	Pl.	Home W.	D.	L.	F.	A.	Away W.	D.	L.	F.	A.	F. (Total)	A.	Pts.
1 Celtic	38	15	4	0	59	15	10	4	5	38	25	97	40	58
2 Airdrieonians	38	13	3	3	53	22	10	1	8	42	32	95	54	50
3 Heart of Mid.	38	14	2	3	52	21	7	6	6	35	35	87	56	50
4 St. Mirren	38	12	4	3	37	23	8	3	8	25	29	62	52	47
5 MOTHERWELL	38	15	1	3	41	15	4	7	8	26	31	67	46	46
6 Rangers	38	12	1	6	39	21	7	5	7	40	34	79	55	44
7 Cowdenbeath	38	14	3	2	54	20	4	3	12	33	48	87	68	42
8 Falkirk	38	8	10	1	35	21	6	4	9	26	36	61	57	42
9 Kilmarnock	38	11	4	4	49	30	6	3	10	30	47	79	77	41
10 Dundee	38	9	4	6	29	27	5	5	9	18	32	47	59	37
11 Aberdeen	38	10	4	5	35	23	3	6	10	14	31	49	54	36
12 Hamilton Acad.	38	10	5	4	40	29	3	4	12	28	50	68	79	35
13 Queen's Park	38	10	1	8	43	39	5	3	11	27	42	70	81	34
14 Partick Thistle	38	8	6	5	39	35	2	7	10	25	38	64	73	33
15 Morton	38	9	5	5	35	30	3	2	14	22	54	57	84	31
16 Hibernian	38	8	3	8	48	37	4	3	12	24	40	72	77	30
17 Dundee United	38	7	4	8	31	27	4	2	13	21	47	52	74	28
18 St. Johnstone	38	5	8	6	22	31	4	2	13	21	47	43	78	28
19 Raith Rovers	38	9	2	8	30	30	2	2	15	16	51	46	81	26
20 Clydebank (1)	38	7	3	9	37	33	0	5	14	18	59	55	92	22

1926 - 27 Season
First Division

	Date	Opponent	F	A	Scorers	Att.
1	14-Aug	Queens Park	2	1	McFadyen, Stevenson	
2	21-Aug	KILMARNOCK	1	0	McFadyen	6000
3	28-Aug	Falkirk	1	1	Ferrier	8000
4	4-Sep	CLYDE	2	0	Ferrier (2)	
5	11-Sep	Rangers	0	2		18000
6	18-Sep	DUNDEE	2	5	Tennant, McMurtrie	
7	25-Sep	Cowdenbeath	1	1	Tennant	
8	2-Oct	GREENOCK MORTON	6	0	Tennant (4), Ferrier, McMurtrie	
9	9-Oct	Hibernian	1	1	Tennant	10000
10	16-Oct	Airdrieonians	3	1	Ferrier (2), Tennant	3000
11	23-Oct	HEARTS	5	1	Tennant (3), Stevenson, Ferrier	
12	30-Oct	HAMILTON ACCIES	3	1	Stevenson, McMurtrie, Hutchieson	6000
13	6-Nov	Dunfermline	4	0	Tennant (4)	3000
14	13-Nov	ST. JOHNSTONE	5	2	Tennant (2), McMurtrie (2), Little	
15	20-Nov	Dundee United	1	0	Tennant	8000
16	27-Nov	PARTICK THISTLE	3	1	Stevenson (2), Thackery	10000
17	4-Dec	CELTIC	0	1		20000
18	11-Dec	St. Mirren	1	5	Ferrier	
19	18-Dec	ABERDEEN	1	0	McFadyen	7000
20	25-Dec	QUEENS PARK	2	1	Hutchieson (2)	8000
21	1-Jan	Hamilton Accies	3	0	McFadyen, Stevenson, Ferrier	16000
22	3-Jan	FALKIRK	3	3	McFadyen, Hutchieson, Wilson	15000
23	8-Jan	Cylde	4	1	McFadyen (3), Stevenson	
24	15-Jan	RANGERS	1	4	Stevenson	31000
25	29-Jan	Dundee	1	3	Stevenson	8000
26	5-Feb	Hearts	3	1	Stevenson, McFadyen, Ferrier	
27	9-Feb	COWDENBEATH	0	0		
28	12-Feb	Greenock Morton	3	0	McFadyen, McMurtrie, Ferrier	
29	19-Feb	HIBERNIAN	2	1	McNeil, McMurtrie	
30	26-Feb	AIRDRIEONIANS	1	5	Stevenson	
31	12-Mar	Kilmarnock	4	1	Ferrier (3), McMurtrie	6000
32	19-Mar	DUNFERMLINE	2	1	Ferrier, Little	
33	26-Mar	St. Johnstone	1	0	Thackery	
34	2-Apr	DUNDEE UNITED	6	0	Cameron (3), Ferrier (3)	
35	9-Apr	Partick Thistle	0	3		20000
36	20-Apr	Celtic	2	3	McFadyen, Ferrier	
37	23-Apr	ST. MIRREN	1	0	McFadyen	4000
38	30-Apr	Aberdeen	0	2		7000
Sc						
1	22-Jan	Dundee	0	3		22100

Spanish Tour 11th May - 14th June 1927: P 8, W 6, D 1, L 1, F 23, A 10.

Player Appearances (League)

Player	
Stevenson	37
Johnman	37
McClory	36
Frame	36
Ferrier	35
Craig	35
Thackery	35
McNeil	30
Hutchison	28
McMurtrie	27
McFadyen	21
Tennant	17
Little	11
Wilson	7
Cameron	6
Murphy	5
Keenan	4
Bryers	3
Banks	2
Arnot Craig	2
Connell	2

1927 Div. 1

	Pl.	Home W.	D.	L.	F.	A.	Away W.	D.	L.	F.	A.	F. (Total)	A.	Pts.
1 Rangers	38	15	2	2	41	15	8	8	3	44	26	85	41	56
2 MOTHERWELL	38	13	2	4	46	26	10	3	6	35	26	81	52	51
3 Celtic	38	14	2	3	58	21	7	5	7	43	34	101	55	49
4 Airdrieonians	38	13	5	1	64	23	5	4	10	33	41	97	64	45
5 Dundee	38	11	3	5	45	21	6	6	7	32	30	77	51	43
6 Falkirk	38	11	7	1	56	23	5	3	11	21	37	77	60	42
7 Cowdenbeath	38	12	3	4	41	18	6	3	10	33	42	74	60	42
8 Aberdeen	38	11	6	2	49	29	2	8	9	24	43	73	72	40
9 Hibernian	38	11	5	3	40	27	5	2	12	22	44	62	71	39
10 St. Mirren	38	13	1	5	54	32	3	4	12	24	44	78	76	37
11 Partick Thistle	38	10	3	6	58	39	5	3	11	31	35	89	74	36
12 Queen's Park	38	11	2	6	47	35	4	4	11	27	49	74	84	36
13 Heart of Mid.	38	7	7	5	34	25	5	4	10	31	39	65	64	35
14 St. Johnstone	38	8	7	4	29	19	5	2	12	26	50	55	69	35
15 Hamilton Acad.	38	7	5	7	34	38	6	4	9	26	47	60	85	35
16 Kilmarnock	38	8	5	6	36	29	4	3	12	18	42	54	71	32
17 Clyde	38	7	7	5	34	26	3	2	14	20	59	54	85	29
18 Dunfermline Ath.	38	7	3	9	29	37	3	5	11	24	48	53	85	28
19 Morton	38	11	0	8	40	38	1	4	14	16	63	56	101	28
20 Dundee United	38	6	5	8	31	34	1	3	15	25	67	56	101	22

1927 - 28 Season
First Division

	Date	Opponent	F	A	Scorers	Att.
1	13-Aug	DUNFERMLINE	4	0	Ferrier (3), Stevenson	7500
2	20-Aug	Dundee	3	0	Cameron (2), Stevenson	
3	27-Aug	HIBERNIAN	2	1	Stevenson, OG	
4	3-Sep	Cylde	2	1	Ferrier, Cameron	
5	10-Sep	FALKIRK	2	3	Hutchieson, Cameron	10000
6	17-Sep	Kilmarnock	3	1	Ferrier, Cameron, Keenan	
7	24-Sep	RANGERS	1	1	Ferrier	30000
8	1-Oct	Raith Rovers	4	2	Stevenson (2), Cameron, Ferrier	
9	8-Oct	QUEENS PARK	4	1	Little, McFadyen, Keenan, Stevenson	
10	15-Oct	HAMILTON ACCIES	3	1	Ferrier, McFadyen, Stevenson	
11	22-Oct	Hearts	0	0		18000
12	29-Oct	AIRDRIEONIANS	1	1	Keenan	8000
13	5-Nov	COWDENBEATH	2	1	Ferrier, Keenan	5000
14	12-Nov	St. Johnstone	4	1	Ferrier (3), Cameron	8000
15	19-Nov	BO'NESS	3	2	Ferrier (2), Cameron	
16	26-Nov	Partick Thistle	1	1	Stevenson	15000
17	3-Dec	Celtic	2	1	Cameron, Ferrier	20000
18	10-Dec	ST. MIRREN	4	0	Cameron (2), Stevenson, Keenan	
19	17-Dec	Aberdeen	0	2		
20	24-Dec	Dunfermline	5	0	Ferrier (2), Stevenson, Cameron, Craig	500
21	31-Dec	CLYDE	5	0	Ferrier (3), Stevenson, Cameron	
22	2-Jan	HAMILTON ACCIES	5	1	Cameron (2), Stevenson, Ferrier, McFadyen	12000
23	3-Jan	Falkirk	1	2	Cameron	12000
24	7-Dec	Hibernian	2	2	Keenan, Cameron	
25	14-Jan	KILMARNOCK	3	3	Keenan, Ferrier, Stevenson	
26	28-Jan	Queens Park	1	3	Ferrier	15000
27	11-Feb	Rangers	2	0	Ferrier, Stevenson	50000
28	15-Feb	RAITH ROVERS	6	0	Ferrier (2), Stevenson, Tennant, Douglas, McMurtrie	
29	22-Feb	Airdrieonians	2	0	Ferrier, Stevenson	
30	25-Feb	HEARTS	0	3		7000
31	7-Mar	DUNDEE	2	2	Stevenson, Keenan	
32	17-Mar	ST. JOHNSTONE	1	0	Tennant	4000
33	21-Mar	Cowdenbeath	4	3	Stevenson (2), Tennant (2)	
34	24-Mar	bo'ness	1	1	McMurtrie	
35	31-Mar	PARTICK THISTLE	1	3	Tennant	
36	7-Apr	CELTIC	3	1	Tennant (2), Stevenson	24000
37	14-Apr	St. Mirren	1	1	Tennant	4000
38	16-Apr	ABERDEEN	2	1	Tennant, Stevenson	
S c						
1	21-Jan	Huntley	3	0	Cameron (2), Keenan	3000
2	4-Feb	RAITH ROVERS	2	2	Cameron, Stevenson	5300
2r	8-Feb	Raith Rovers	2	1	Cameron, Keenan	7000
3	18-Feb	Hearts	2	1	Stevenson (2)	40000
4	3-Mar	CELTIC	0	2		23000

Argentina Tour 13th May - 24th June 1927: P 11, W 6, D 1, L 4, F 22, A 18.

Player Appearances

(Total)	
Thackery	43
Ferrier	43
McClory	42
Johnman	40
Stevenson	40
Cameron	40
Alan Craig	39
McMurtrie	32
Keenan	32
Frame	21
McNeill	12
W Tennant	7
Hutchieson	6
Wilson	6
Gerrard	4
Bryers	3
Arnot Craig	3
T Tennant	2
Reid	1
Douglas	1

1928 Div. 1

		Pl.	Home W.	D.	L.	F.	A.	Away W.	D.	L.	F.	A.	F. (Total)	A.	Pts.
1	Rangers	38	17	1	1	67	16	9	7	3	42	20	109	36	60
2	Celtic	38	14	3	2	56	13	9	6	4	37	26	93	39	55
3	MOTHERWELL	38	12	4	3	51	24	11	5	3	41	22	92	46	55
4	Heart of Mid.	38	10	5	4	47	20	10	2	7	42	30	89	50	47
5	St. Mirren	38	11	6	2	46	26	7	2	10	31	50	77	76	44
6	Partick Thistle	38	10	5	4	48	31	8	2	9	37	36	85	67	43
7	Aberdeen	38	15	1	3	47	15	4	4	11	24	46	71	61	43
8	Kilmarnock	38	10	5	4	41	30	5	5	9	27	48	68	78	40
9	Cowdenbeath	38	8	4	7	32	32	8	3	8	34	36	66	68	39
10	Falkirk	38	12	1	6	55	29	4	4	11	21	40	76	69	37
11	St. Johnstone	38	9	4	6	38	27	5	4	10	28	40	66	67	36
12	Hibernian	38	11	6	2	50	24	2	3	14	23	51	73	75	35
13	Airdrieonians	38	8	3	8	31	31	4	8	7	28	38	59	69	35
14	Dundee	38	12	0	7	46	37	2	7	10	19	43	65	80	35
15	Clyde	38	7	6	6	28	25	3	5	11	18	47	46	72	31
16	Queen's Park	38	10	4	5	52	31	2	2	15	17	49	69	80	30
17	Raith Rovers	38	7	5	7	35	32	4	2	13	25	57	60	89	29
18	Hamilton Acad.	38	9	4	6	46	32	2	2	15	21	54	67	86	28
19	Bo'Ness	38	6	8	5	27	27	3	0	16	21	59	48	86	26
20	Dunfermline Ath.	38	4	1	14	22	53	0	3	16	19	73	41	126	12

1928 - 29 Season
First Division

	Date	Opponent	F	A	Scorers	Att.
1	11-Aug	Airdrieonians	1	0	McMurtrie	7000
2	18-Aug	RAITH ROVERS	3	1	Ferrier (3)	
3	25-Aug	Queens Park	3	2	W Tennant (2), Ferrier	
4	1-Sep	CLYDE	1	0	Ferrier	
5	8-Sep	Ayr United	0	2		
6	15-Sep	PARTICK THISTLE	5	4	Ferrier (2), T Tennant, Stevenson, McMurtrie	
7	22-Sep	Hibernian	1	1	T Tennant	
8	29-Sep	Rangers	0	0		40000
9	6-Oct	ABERDEEN	1	0	Cameron	
10	13-Oct	CELTIC	3	3	McFadyen, Ferrier, Cameron	
11	20-Oct	HAMILTON ACCIES	4	3	Watson (2), Ferrier, McFadyen	
12	27-Oct	Falkirk	7	0	Watson (6), Ferrier	
13	3-Nov	KILMARNOCK	2	3	Ferrier (2)	
14	10-Nov	Hearts	1	5	Ferrier	
15	17-Nov	ST. JOHNSTONE	1	1	McMenemy	4000
16	24-Nov	St. Mirren	3	2	Murdoch, Cameron, Stevenson	8000
17	1-Dec	COWDENBEATH	5	1	Stevenson (2), Ferrier, McMenemy, Murdoch	
18	8-Dec	Dundee	0	3		8000
19	15-Dec	THIRD LANARK	3	2	Murdoch, McMenemy, Ferrier	
20	22-Dec	Raith Rovers	2	2	Watson, Ferrier	
21	29-Dec	AIRDRIEONIANS	4	2	Ferrier (2), Watson, Stevenson	4000
22	1-Jan	Hamilton Accies	3	0	Ferrier (2), Watson	10000
23	2-Jan	FALKIRK	2	1	Cameron, Watson	8000
24	5-Jan	QUEENS PARK	0	5		9000
25	12-Jan	Cylde	1	1	Ferrier	
26	26-Jan	Third Lanark	2	2	Stevenson, Ferrier	
27	6-Feb	Partick Thistle	3	1	Cameron (2), Bone	2000
28	9-Feb	HIBERNIAN	3	1	Cameron, Stevenson, Ferrier	
29	23-Feb	Aberdeen	1	1	Stevenson	
30	9-Mar	Kilmarnock	2	4	Douglas, Ferrier	7000
31	16-Mar	HEARTS	3	2	Murdoch, Ferrier	
32	20-Mar	Celtic	0	2		
33	23-Mar	St. Johnstone	3	2	W Tennant (2), Murdoch, McMenemy	5000
34	30-Mar	ST. MIRREN	1	1	Murdoch	
35	6-Apr	Cowdenbeath	3	1	W Tennant, McMenemy, Ferrier	
36	17-Apr	RANGERS	2	4	W Tennant, McMenemy	6500
37	20-Apr	DUNDEE	1	1	Ferrier	3000
38	27-Apr	AYR UNITED	5	0	Ferrier (3), W Tennant, Johnman	2300
S c						
1	19-Jan	LEITH ATHLETIC	4	1	Cameron (2), Murdoch, Stevenson	3500
2	2-Feb	St. Johnstone	3	2	Cameron (2), Ferrier	15700
3	16-Feb	Airdrieonians	1	1	Cameron	11500
3r	20-Feb	AIRDRIEONIANS	3	1	Cameron (2), Murdoch	
4	6-Mar	Celtic	0	0		
4r	13-Mar	CELTIC	1	2	Ferrier	

Player Appearances

(League)	
Johnman	38
McClory	37
Alan Craig	36
Ferrier	36
Frame	35
McFadyen	34
Stevenson	33
McNeil	32
Murdoch	26
McMenemy	25
Cameron	21
Alex Hunter	15
Watson	13
W Tennant	12
McMurtrie	7
T Tennant	5
Bone	4
Douglas	2
Arnot Craig	2
Little	1
Gerrand	1
Bryers	1

1929 Div. 1

		Pl.	Home W.	D.	L.	F.	A.	Away W.	D.	L.	F.	A.	F. (Total)	A.	Pts.
1	Rangers	38	14	5	0	51	8	16	2	1	56	24	107	32	67
2	Celtic	38	13	2	4	38	17	9	5	5	29	27	67	44	51
3	MOTHERWELL	38	12	4	3	49	35	8	6	5	36	31	85	66	50
4	Heart of Mid.	38	13	4	2	56	23	6	5	8	35	34	91	57	47
5	Queen's Park	38	13	1	5	69	31	5	6	8	31	38	100	69	43
6	Partick Thistle	38	12	3	4	60	34	5	4	10	31	36	91	70	41
7	Aberdeen	38	14	3	2	55	20	2	5	12	26	48	81	68	40
8	St. Mirren	38	9	3	7	46	35	7	5	7	32	40	78	75	40
9	St. Johnstone	38	11	4	4	35	22	3	6	10	22	48	57	70	38
10	Kilmarnock	38	9	4	6	45	32	5	4	10	34	42	79	74	36
11	Falkirk	38	11	5	3	41	32	3	3	13	27	54	68	86	36
12	Hamilton Acad.	38	9	6	4	38	31	4	3	12	20	52	58	83	35
13	Cowdenbeath	38	10	3	6	28	18	4	2	13	27	51	55	69	33
14	Hibernian	38	9	5	5	39	25	4	1	14	15	37	54	62	32
15	Airdrieonians	38	10	4	5	38	24	2	3	14	18	41	56	65	31
16	Ayr United	38	8	3	8	36	33	4	4	11	29	51	65	84	31
17	Clyde	38	9	4	6	32	27	3	2	14	15	44	47	71	30
18	Dundee	38	4	5	10	27	31	5	6	8	32	38	59	69	29
19	Third Lanark	38	8	3	8	46	41	2	3	14	25	61	71	102	26
20	Raith Rovers	38	7	5	7	34	39	2	1	16	18	66	52	105	24

1929 - 30 Season
First Division

No.	Date	Opponent	F	A	Scorers	Att.
1	10-Aug	RANGERS	0	2		27000
2	17-Aug	Aberdeen	2	2	Cameron, Murdoch	14000
3	24-Aug	DUNDEE	3	0	Cameron (2), Ferrier	7000
4	31-Aug	Cylde	2	1	Stevenson, Ferrier	
5	7-Sep	HEARTS	0	2		8000
6	14-Sep	Ayr United	2	3	Cameron, Stevenson	
7	21-Sep	AIRDRIEONIANS	2	0	Ferrier, McMenemy	5000
8	28-Sep	Queens Park	3	0	McMenemy (2), Stevenson	
9	5-Oct	HIBERNIAN	3	0	Ferrier (2), Cameron	3500
10	12-Oct	Cowdenbeath	0	0		
11	19-Oct	FALKIRK	4	3	McMenemy (2), Murdoch, Ferrier	
12	26-Oct	Hamilton Accies	3	2	Ferrier (2), Cameron	8000
13	2-Nov	DUNDEE UNITED	6	1	Cameron (3), Dowall (2), McMenemy	
14	9-Nov	CELTIC	2	1	Dowall (2)	
15	16-Nov	St. Johnstone	1	1	Dowall (2)	
16	23-Nov	Partick Thistle	1	6	Ferrier	
17	30-Nov	ST. MIRREN	3	0	Murdoch, Dowall, Ferrier	
18	7-Dec	KILMARNOCK	2	0	Ferrier (2), Cameron	
19	14-Dec	Greenock Morton	3	1	Cameron, Ferrier, Murdoch	
20	21-Dec	Rangers	2	4	Cameron, Stevenson	22200
21	28-Dec	ABERDEEN	4	1	Stevenson (2), Murdoch, Ferrier	
22	1-Jan	HAMILTON ACCIES	5	1	Murdoch (2), Dowall (2), Stevenson	8000
23	2-Jan	Falkirk	1	4	Stevenson	
24	4-Jan	Dundee	3	0	McMenemy, Dowall, Ferrier	12000
25	11-Jan	CLYDE	2	1	McMenemy, Stevenson	3000
26	25-Jan	Hearts	2	3	McMenemy, Dowall	20000
27	8-Feb	Airdrieonians	0	2		8000
28	22-Feb	Hibernian	1	1	Ferrier	5000
29	1-Mar	COWDENBEATH	7	2	Dowall (3), Ferrier (3), Stevenson	
30	8-Mar	Dundee United	1	1	Stevenson	4500
31	15-Mar	Celtic	4	0	McMenemy (2), Dowall, Ferrier	
32	22-Mar	ST. JOHNSTONE	5	0	McFadyen (2), Dowall (2), Ferrier	2000
33	29-Mar	PARTICK THISTLE	4	0	Murdoch, Ferrier, Stevenson, Dowall	
34	5-Apr	St. Mirren	2	0	Dowall, McFadyen	
35	12-Apr	Kilmarnock	3	2	Dowall, Stevenson, Ferrier	
36	19-Apr	GREENOCK MORTON	3	0	Ferrier (2), Dowall	
37	21-Apr	AYR UNITED	4	1	McMenemy (2), Stevenson, Ferrier	
38	26-Apr	QUEENS PARK	9	0	Ferrier (4), Dowall (3), Murdoch (2)	
Sc						
1	18-Jan	EAST STIRLING	6	0	Dowall (3), Stevenson (2), Murdoch	4000
2	1-Feb	CLYDE	3	0	Murdoch (2), Dowall	10000
3	15-Feb	RANGERS	2	5	McFadyen, Stevenson	27000

Player Appearances
(Total)

Player	Apps
McClory	41
Alan Craig	41
Murdoch	41
Ferrier	40
Stevenson	38
McMenemy	37
Hunter	36
McFadyen	31
Telfer	30
Dowall	25
Johnman	22
Frame	20
Cameron	16
McNeill	11
Nisbet	10
Wales	10
Watson	2
Bone	1

1930 Div. 1

	Team	Pl.	Home W.	D.	L.	F.	A.	Away W.	D.	L.	F.	A.	F. (Total)	A.	Pts.
1	Rangers	38	18	0	1	65	13	10	4	5	29	19	94	32	60
2	MOTHERWELL	38	17	0	2	68	15	8	5	6	36	33	104	48	55
3	Aberdeen	38	14	5	0	50	24	9	2	8	35	37	85	61	53
4	Celtic	38	12	1	6	52	21	10	4	5	36	25	88	46	49
5	St. Mirren	38	11	2	6	41	19	7	3	9	32	37	73	56	41
6	Partick Thistle	38	11	4	4	46	27	5	5	9	26	34	72	61	41
7	Falkirk	38	11	5	3	40	21	5	4	10	22	43	62	64	41
8	Kilmarnock	38	12	2	5	47	30	3	7	9	30	43	77	73	39
9	Ayr United	38	10	5	4	46	32	6	1	12	24	60	70	92	38
10	Heart of Mid.	38	8	6	5	35	26	6	3	10	34	43	69	69	37
11	Clyde	38	8	4	7	37	32	5	7	7	27	37	64	69	37
12	Airdrieonians	38	11	3	5	42	26	5	1	13	18	40	60	66	36
13	Hamilton Acad.	38	12	3	4	49	27	2	4	13	27	54	76	81	35
14	Dundee	38	9	3	7	32	26	5	3	11	19	32	51	58	34
15	Queen's Park	38	9	2	8	36	36	6	2	11	31	44	67	80	34
16	Cowdenbeath	38	10	3	6	38	19	3	4	12	26	55	64	74	33
17	Hibernian	38	7	6	6	27	20	2	5	12	18	42	45	62	29
18	Morton	38	7	5	7	46	40	3	2	14	21	55	67	95	27
19	Dundee United	38	5	6	8	33	38	2	2	15	23	71	56	109	22
20	St. Johnstone	38	5	5	9	33	37	1	2	16	15	59	48	96	19

1930 - 31 Season
First Division

No.	Date	Opponent	F	A	Scorers	Att.
1	9-Aug	EAST FIFE	4	1	Murdoch, McMenemy, Stevenson, Dowall	
2	16-Aug	Hibernian	2	2	McMenemy, McFadyen	12000
3	23-Aug	QUEENS PARK	2	1	Dowall, Ferrier	
4	30-Aug	Rangers	1	1	Ferrier	
5	6-Sep	KILMARNOCK	1	1	Dowall	
6	13-Sep	Aberdeen	4	2	Murdoch, McMenemy, Dowall, Stevenson	
7	20-Sep	HAMILTON ACCIES	3	0	Ferrier, Murdoch, Stevenson	10000
8	27-Sep	Falkirk	1	0	Wales	
9	4-Oct	CLYDE	4	4	Stevenson (2), Murdoch	
10	11-Oct	Greenock Morton	3	0	Dowall (2), Ferrier	
11	18-Oct	Airdrieonians	5	0	Murdoch (2), McMenemy (2), Ferrier	
12	25-Oct	CELTIC	3	3	Murdoch (2), Ferrier	30000
13	1-Nov	Dundee	1	2	Dowall	19000
14	8-Nov	LEITH	4	1	Dowall (3), Stevenson	
15	15-Nov	Hearts	1	5	Murdoch	20000
16	29-Nov	Ayr United	3	2	Dowall, Ferrier, McFadyen	
17	6-Dec	COWDENBEATH	3	1	Stevenson (2), McMenemy	5000
18	13-Dec	St. Mirren	1	2	Dowall	
19	20-Dec	East Fife	1	1	Murdoch	
20	25-Dec	Partick Thistle	3	0	McMenemy, Murdoch, McFadyen	25000
21	27-Dec	HIBERNIAN	6	0	Ferrier (3), McFadyen (2), Murdoch	3000
22	1-Jan	Hamilton Accies	0	1		
23	3-Jan	Queens Park	3	1	Dowall (2), Stevenson	12000
24	10-Jan	RANGERS	1	0	Dowall	
25	24-Jan	Kilmarnock	4	1	McFadyen (3), Murdoch	
26	7-Feb	Cylde	6	0	McFadyen (3), Murdoch (3)	12000
27	9-Feb	ABERDEEN	5	0	Stevenson (3), McFadyen (2)	
28	18-Feb	GREENOCK MORTON	3	0	Ferrier, Stevenson, McFadyen	
29	21-Feb	AIRDRIEONIANS	4	0	Douglas (2), McFadyen, ?	
30	4-Mar	Celtic	1	4	McFadyen	
31	7-Mar	DUNDEE	2	0	Ferrier (2)	5000
32	17-Mar	Leith Athletic	5	2	McFadyen (2), McMenemy, Stevenson, Murdoch	
33	21-Mar	HEARTS	2	0	McFadyen (2)	
34	30-Mar	FALKIRK	6	1	McMenemy (2), Murdoch, Stevenson, McFadyen	
35	4-Apr	PARTICK THISTLE	0	0		
36	18-Apr	Cowdenbeith	0	1		
37	22-Apr	AYR UNITED	1	1	McFadyen	1100
38	25-Apr	ST. MIRREN	3	1	McFadyen (2), McMenemy	2500
Sc						
1	17-Jan	BATHGATE	6	0	Stevenson (4), McMenemy, Wales	2500
2	31-Jan	ALBION ROVERS	4	1	Ferrier (2), Stevenson, McMenemy	3000
3	14-Feb	Hibernian	3	0	Murdoch (2), McFadyen	33300
4	28-Feb	Cowdenbeith	1	0	Murdoch	18673
Sf	14-Mar	St. Mirren*	1	0	Murdoch	
F	11-Apr	Celtic	2	2	McMenemy, Stevenson	105000
Fr	15-Apr	Celtic	2	4	Stevenson, Murdoch	98588

* Played at Ibrox

South African Tour 18th May - 3rd July 1931: P 15, W 14, D 0, L 1, F 57, A 10.

Player Appearances
(n.b. Scottish Cup line-ups are incomplete, and therefore have not been included in totals))

(League only)

Player	Apps
McClory	38
Wales	38
Craig	37
Telfer	37
McMenemy	36
Ferrier	35
Murdoch	35
Stevenson	35
Hunter	34
Johnman	34
Dowall	25
McFadyen	20
Ellis	7
Douglas	4
Nisbet	2
Reid	1
Watson	1

1931 Div. 1

	Team	Pl.	Home W.	D.	L.	F.	A.	Away W.	D.	L.	F.	A.	F. (Total)	A.	Pts.
1	Rangers	38	16	2	1	55	9	11	4	4	41	20	96	29	60
2	Celtic	38	16	2	1	64	14	8	8	3	37	20	101	34	58
3	MOTHERWELL	38	14	5	0	57	15	10	3	6	45	27	102	42	56
4	Partick Thistle	38	16	2	1	50	16	8	3	8	26	27	76	43	53
5	Heart of Mid.	38	12	2	5	58	33	7	4	8	32	30	90	63	44
6	Aberdeen	38	13	3	3	53	20	4	4	11	26	43	79	63	41
7	Cowdenbeath	38	12	3	4	40	21	5	4	10	18	44	58	65	41
8	Dundee	38	13	2	4	40	16	4	3	12	25	47	65	63	39
9	Airdrieonians	38	11	2	6	38	32	6	3	10	21	34	59	66	39
10	Hamilton Acad.	38	12	4	3	35	15	4	1	14	24	42	59	57	37
11	Kilmarnock	38	11	2	6	33	22	4	3	12	26	38	59	60	35
12	Clyde	38	7	3	9	31	44	8	1	10	29	43	60	87	34
13	Queen's Park	38	9	6	4	45	27	4	1	14	26	45	71	72	33
14	Falkirk	38	10	1	8	43	35	4	3	12	34	52	77	87	32
15	St. Mirren	38	8	5	6	28	29	3	3	13	21	43	49	72	30
16	Morton	38	8	3	8	38	33	3	4	12	20	50	58	83	29
17	Leith Athletic	38	5	6	8	30	33	3	5	11	21	52	51	85	27
18	Ayr United	38	8	5	6	37	37	0	6	13	16	55	53	92	27
19	Hibernian	38	8	4	7	32	28	1	3	15	17	53	49	81	25
20	East Fife	38	7	4	8	31	40	1	0	18	14	73	45	113	20

1931-32 Season

Back : McKenzie, Wales, Telfer, Mackrell, Ellis
Middle: Donaldson (Trainer), Johnman, Dowall, McClory, Craig, Blair. Wull Walker (Trainer)
Front : Murdoch, Moffat, McMenemy, Ferrier, McFadyen, Stevenson

1931 - 32 Season
First Division

	Date	Opponent	F	A	Scorers	Att.
1	8-Aug	Queens Park	5	1	McFadyen (4), Murdoch	10000
2	15-Aug	RANGERS	4	2	Murdoch (2), Stevenson, Dowall	25000
3	19-Aug	Ayr United	3	1	McFadyen, Dowall, OG	8000
4	22-Aug	Kilmarnock	0	1		12500
5	26-Aug	Airdrieonians	2	2	McFadyen, McMenemy	12000
6	29-Aug	ABERDEEN	3	0	McFadyen (3)	7000
7	1-Sep	St. Mirren	1	0	Dowall	8000
8	5-Sep	Hamilton Accies	2	2	Ferrier, McFadyen	12000
9	12-Sep	FALKIRK	4	1	Ferrier, Douglas, McFadyen, Stevenson	8000
10	16-Sep	THIRD LANARK	6	0	McFadyen (5), Ferrier	5000
11	19-Sep	Cylde	3	2	Douglas, Ferrier, Wylie	5000
12	26-Sep	LEITH ATHLETIC	7	1	McFadyen (4), Douglas (2), Stevenson	3000
13	3-Oct	Greenock Morton	2	2	McFadyen (2)	10000
14	10-Oct	DUNDEE UNITED	5	0	McFadyen (3), Douglas (2)	4000
15	17-Oct	HEARTS	2	0	McFadyen, Ferrier	8000
16	24-Oct	Cowdenbeith	5	1	McFadyen (3), Stevenson, Ferrier	3000
17	31-Oct	CELTIC	2	2	Dowall, Douglas	25000
18	14-Nov	Dundee	2	2	McFadyen (2)	5000
19	21-Nov	AYR UNITED	6	0	McFadyen (4), Craig, McMenemy	5000
20	28-Nov	AIRDRIEONIANS	3	0	Ferrier (2), McFadyen	6000
21	5-Dec	ST. MIRREN	4	1	Moffatt, Stevenson, McFadyen, McMenemy	7000
22	12-Dec	Third Lanark	2	0	McFadyen, McMenemy	22000
23	19-Dec	QUEENS PARK	4	1	Moffatt, Stevenson, McFadyen, McMenemy	8000
24	21-Dec	Rangers	0	1		55000
25	1-Jan	HAMILTON ACCIES	3	1	Ferrier, McFadyen, Stevenson	13000
26	2-Jan	Falkirk	3	2	Moffatt, Murdoch, McFadyen	10000
27	9-Jan	KILMARNOCK	4	0	Ferrier (3), Wylie	6000
28	23-Jan	Aberdeen	1	0	McFadyen	12000
29	6-Feb	Leith Athletic	5	0	Moffatt (3), Wylie (2)	3000
30	17-Feb	GREENOCK MORTON	4	2	McFadyen (2), Murdoch (2)	3000
31	20-Feb	Dundee United	6	1	McFadyen (4), Murdoch (2)	6000
32	27-Feb	Hearts	1	0	Stevenson	21000
33	12-Mar	Celtic	4	2	Murdoch (2), Stevenson, McFadyen	30000
34	19-Mar	PARTICK THISTLE	1	0	Stevenson	7000
35	26-Mar	DUNDEE	4	0	Moffatt (2), Stevenson, Wales	5000
36	2-Apr	Partick Thistle	0	0		32000
37	16-Apr	COWDENBEITH	3	0	Ferrier, McFadyen, McMenemy	2500
38	30-Apr	CLYDE	3	0	McFadyen (2), Ferrier	7000

S c

	Date	Opponent	F	A	Scorers	Att.
1	16-Jan	STENHOUSEMUIR	7	2	Murdoch(2),McFadyen(2),McMen',Steve'n,Ferr'r	3400
	30-Jan	Queens Park	2	0	Stevenson, Moffatt	58000
3	13-Feb	CELTIC	2	0	Ferrier, Murdoch	36000
4	5-Mar	Rangers	0	2		88000

Player Appearances (Total)

Player	Total
McClory	42
Ellis	42
Craig	41
Telfer	41
Wales	40
Ferrier	40
Stevenson	38
McFadyen	37
Dowall	36
McMenemy	34
Murdoch	30
Moffatt	13
Douglas	8
Johnman	7
Wylie	5
Blair	4
MacKrell	2
McKenzie	1
Hunter	1

1932 Div. 1

	Pl.	Home W.	D.	L.	F.	A.	Away W.	D.	L.	F.	A.	F. (Total)	A.	Pts.
1 MOTHERWELL	38	18	1	0	72	11	12	5	2	47	20	119	31	66
2 Rangers	38	16	2	1	67	14	12	3	4	51	28	118	42	61
3 Celtic	38	13	2	4	64	24	7	6	6	30	26	94	50	48
4 Third Lanark	38	15	1	3	61	29	6	3	10	31	52	92	81	46
5 St. Mirren	38	13	2	4	49	22	7	2	10	28	34	77	56	44
6 Partick Thistle	38	11	3	5	33	26	8	1	10	25	33	58	59	42
7 Aberdeen	38	10	6	3	33	15	6	3	10	24	34	57	49	41
8 Heart of Mid.	38	10	5	4	35	18	7	0	12	28	43	63	61	39
9 Kilmarnock	38	13	2	4	50	26	3	5	11	18	44	68	70	39
10 Hamilton Acad.	38	11	3	5	54	29	5	3	11	30	36	84	65	38
11 Dundee	38	9	7	3	38	26	5	3	11	23	46	61	72	38
12 Cowdenbeath	38	11	4	4	38	28	4	4	11	28	50	66	78	38
13 Clyde	38	10	5	4	37	24	3	4	12	21	46	58	70	35
14 Airdrieonians	38	10	5	4	45	28	3	1	15	29	53	74	81	32
15 Morton	38	10	4	5	54	31	2	3	14	24	56	78	87	31
16 Queen's Park	38	9	2	8	36	38	4	3	12	23	41	59	79	31
17 Ayr United	38	9	1	9	43	32	2	6	11	27	58	70	90	29
18 Falkirk	38	10	3	6	52	31	1	2	16	18	45	70	76	27
19 Dundee United	38	4	5	10	18	49	2	2	15	22	69	40	118	19
20 Leith Athletic	38	6	0	13	23	49	0	4	15	23	88	46	137	16

1932 - 33 Season
First Division

	Date	Opponent	F	A	Scorers	Att.
1	13-Aug	KILMARNOCK	3	3	Ferrier, Murdoch, McMenemy	12000
2	20-Aug	Aberdeen	1	1	Ferrier, Murdoch, McMenemy	21000
3	24-Aug	Dundee	3	0	McFadyen (2), McMenemy	8000
4	27-Aug	CLYDE	1	0	Ferrier	6000
5	3-Sep	St. Johnstone	1	0	McFadyen	10000
6	10-Sep	HAMILTON ACCIES	4	1	Ferrier, Murdoch, McFadyen, McMenemy	12000
7	14-Sep	AYR UNITED	3	1	Murdoch (2), Stevenson	3500
8	17-Sep	Falkirk	2	2	McFadyen, McMenemy	11000
9	24-Sep	GREENOCK MORTON	7	0	Ferr'r(3),Steve'n,McMen',Murdoch,McFadyen	4000
10	1-Oct	Rangers	2	2	Ferrier, Murdoch	47000
11	8-Oct	QUEENS PARK	7	2	Ferrier (3), McFadyen (2), Stevenson, Murdoch	6000
12	15-Oct	Hearts	0	2		36000
13	22-Oct	Celtic	1	4	McFadyen	20000
14	29-Oct	PARTICK THISTLE	1	2	Ferrier	4000
15	5-Nov	DUNDEE	6	1	McFadyen (3), Moffatt, O'Gilvie, McMenemy	4500
16	12-Nov	Ayr United	6	2	Ferrier (2), McFadyen (2), O'Gilvie, McMenemy	4000
17	19-Nov	Airdrieonians	4	1	Ferrier (2), McFadyen, O'Gilvie	6000
18	26-Nov	St. Mirren	5	2	McFadyen (3), Moffatt, O'Gilvie	6000
19	3-Dec	THIRD LANARK	6	3	McFadyen (5), Moffatt	4500
20	10-Dec	east stirling	4	1	McFadyen (2), Moffatt, Ferrier	4000
21	17-Dec	COWDENBEITH	2	0	Ferrier, McMenemy	3000
22	24-Dec	Kilmarnock	3	1	McFadyen, O'Gilvie, Moffatt	8000
23	31-Dec	ABERDEEN	2	3	Moffatt, OG	6000
24	2-Jan	Hamilton Accies	3	2	Stevenson (2), Wales	15000
25	3-Jan	FALKIRK	2	0	McFadyen, Stevenson	6000
26	7-Jan	Cylde	3	2	Ferrier, McFadyen, O'Gilvie	8500
27	14-Jan	ST. JOHNSTONE	1	0	McFadyen	4000
28	28-Jan	Greenock Morton	2	1	Ferrier, McFadyen, O'Gilvie	7000
29	11-Feb	RANGERS	1	3	Ferrier	30000
30	25-Feb	Queens Park	2	4	Blair, McFadyen	6000
31	11-Mar	CELTIC	4	2	McFadyen (4)	17000
32	25-Mar	AIRDRIEONIANS	4	1	McMenemy (2), Ferrier, McFadyen	3500
33	29-Mar	HEARTS	5	1	McFadyen (2), Stevenson, Ferrier, Murdoch	4500
34	3-Apr	Partick Thistle	1	0	McFadyen	20000
35	8-Apr	ST. MIRREN	3	0	Ferrier, Stevenson, McFadyen	4000
36	22-Apr	EAST STIRLING	4	1	Ogilvie (2),Ellis, McFadyen	2000
37	25-Apr	Third Lanark	1	1	Stevenson	2000
38	29-Apr	Cowdenbeith	4	1	McFadyen (3), Ferrier	2000

S c

	Date	Opponent	F	A	Scorers	Att.
1	21-Jan	Hamilton Accies	2	0	Stevenson, McFadyen	16500
2	4-Feb	MONTROSE	7	1	McFadyen (5), Wales, Ferrier	2967
3	18-Feb	DUNDEE	5	0	McFadyen (2), McMenemy, Ellis, Ferrier	8000
4	4-Mar	Kilmarnock	3	3	McFadyen (2), Ferrier	20685
4r	8-Apr	KILMARNOCK	8	3	McFadyen (4), Murdoch (2), Ellis, OG	23000
Sf	18-Mar	Clyde*	2	0	Ferrier, McFadyen	25000
F	15-Apr	Celtic	0	1		102000

* Played at Ibrox

Player Appearances (Total)

Player	Total
McClory	45
McFadyen	45
Ferrier	44
Wales	44
Ellis	40
Stevenson	36
McMenemy	35
Telfer	33
Blair	30
Dowall	25
Ogilvie	22
Murdoch	22
Crapnell	18
Moffatt	17
McKenzie	16
MacKrell	8
Johnston J	2
Wyllie	1

1933 Div. 1

	Pl.	Home W.	D.	L.	F.	A.	Away W.	D.	L.	F.	A.	F. (Total)	A.	Pts.
1 Rangers	38	14	5	0	67	22	12	5	2	46	21	113	43	62
2 MOTHERWELL	38	15	1	3	66	24	12	4	3	48	29	114	53	59
3 Heart of Mid.	38	15	3	1	49	16	6	5	8	35	35	84	51	50
4 Celtic	38	13	3	3	47	18	7	5	7	28	26	75	44	48
5 St. Johnstone	38	15	2	2	47	17	2	8	9	23	38	70	55	44
6 Aberdeen	38	13	4	2	63	19	5	2	12	22	39	85	58	42
7 St. Mirren	38	12	3	4	48	23	6	3	10	25	37	73	60	42
8 Hamilton Acad.	38	11	5	3	54	31	7	1	11	36	47	90	78	42
9 Queen's Park	38	11	5	3	46	24	6	2	11	32	55	78	79	41
10 Partick Thistle	38	9	3	7	47	28	8	3	8	28	27	75	55	40
11 Falkirk	38	9	5	5	46	25	6	1	12	24	45	70	70	36
12 Clyde	38	12	0	7	42	29	3	5	11	27	46	69	75	35
13 Third Lanark	38	12	3	4	47	27	2	4	13	23	53	70	80	35
14 Kilmarnock	38	8	5	6	45	39	5	4	10	27	47	72	86	35
15 Dundee	38	9	6	4	34	27	3	3	13	26	50	60	77	33
16 Ayr United	38	11	2	6	41	28	2	2	15	21	67	62	95	30
17 Cowdenbeath	38	9	3	7	44	38	1	2	16	21	73	65	111	25
18 Airdrieonians	38	9	2	8	37	34	1	1	17	18	68	55	102	23
19 Morton	38	4	3	12	29	42	2	6	11	20	55	49	97	21
20 East Stirling.	38	6	3	10	30	44	1	0	18	25	71	55	115	17

***1933 Season**: An unnamed team group*

1933-34 Season

Back: Wylie, Crapnell, Wales, Blair, McClory, Telfer, Johnstone, Ellis
Front: Dowall, McFadyen, Ferrier, Stevenson, Ogilvie, McKenzie

1933 - 34 Season
First Division

No.	Date	Opponent	F	A	Scorers	Att.
1	12-Aug	Cylde	1	0	Ferrier	10000
2	19-Aug	ST. JOHNSTONE	1	0	Stevenson	6000
3	23-Aug	DUNDEE	1	0	McFadyen	5000
4	26-Aug	queen of the south	5	0	McFadyen (5)	10000
5	2-Sep	RANGERS	2	1	McFadyen (2)	25000
6	9-Sep	Hamilton Accies	2	1	Ferrier, O'Gilvie	10000
7	13-Sep	Hibernian	2	0	Stevenson, McFadyen	20000
8	16-Sep	ABERDEEN	4	1	McFadyen (2), O'Gilvie, Stevenson	5000
9	23-Sep	Queens Park	5	1	Ogilvie (2), McFadyen (2), Ferrier	20000
10	25-Sep	Aberdeen	1	1	Stevenson	12000
11	30-Sep	FALKIRK	2	1	McFadyen, Stevenson	7000
12	7-Oct	Kilmarnock	3	1	Stevenson, O'Gilvie, McFadyen	20000
13	14-Oct	HEARTS	2	1	Ferrier, Stevenson	12000
14	21-Oct	CELTIC	1	1	McFadyen	18000
15	28-Oct	Partick Thistle	4	1	McFadyen (2), Stevenson, O'Gilvie	20000
16	4-Nov	Dundee	3	2	Ogilvie (2), McFadyen	20000
17	11-Nov	HIBERNIAN	2	1	Ferrier, McFadyen	7000
18	18-Nov	AIRDRIEONIANS	3	1	McFadyen (2), O'Gilvie	6000
19	25-Nov	ST. MIRREN	1	0	Ferrier	6000
20	2-Dec	Third Lanark	2	2	Ogilvie, McMenemy	8000
21	9-Dec	AYR UNITED	5	2	Ogilvie (2), McMenemy (2), Wales	11000
22	16-Dec	Cowdenbeith	4	0	McFadyen (3), Ferrier	1500
23	23-Dec	CLYDE	1	2	Blair	7000
24	30-Dec	St. Johnstone	2	1	Stevenson, McFadyen	10000
25	1-Jan	HAMILTON ACCIES	2	1	Dowall, McFadyen	12000
26	2-Jan	Falkirk	3	1	Wyllie, Johnstone C, McFadyen	20000
27	6-Jan	QUEEN OF THE SOUTH	1	2	Wyllie, Johnstone C, McFadyen	8000
28	13-Jan	Rangers	2	4	Stevenson (2)	65000
29	27-Jan	QUEENS PARK	3	0	McFadyen (2), McMenemy	9000
30	24-Feb	KILMARNOCK	2	0	Ogilvie, Ferrier	5000
31	10-Mar	Celtic	0	3		20000
32	17-Mar	PARTICK THISTLE	2	3	Stevenson, Crawley	6000
33	20-Mar	St. Mirren	3	1	McFadyen, Stewart, McGillivaray	8000
34	24-Mar	Airdrieonians	6	3	McFadyen (3), Stewart (3)	8000
35	7-Apr	THIRD LANARK	2	2	Ferrier, Stevenson	4000
36	11-Apr	COWDENBEITH	6	1	Crawley (3), O'Gilvie, Wyllie, McMenemy	1800
37	16-Apr	Hearts	3	1	McFadyen (2), Stevenson	14000
38	21-Apr	Ayr United	3	2	McFadyen (2), McMenemy	7000
S c						
1	20-Jan	GALA FAIRYDEAN	4	0	McFadyen (4)	3013
2	3-Feb	Partick Thistle	3	3	McMenemy (2), Telfer	33000
2r	7-Feb	PARTICK THISTLE	2	1	McFadyen, Stevenson	16000
3	17-Feb	EAST STIRLING	5	0	McFadyen (3), Ferrier, Stevenson	5200
4	3-Mar	Albion Rovers	1	1	McFadyen	16155
4r	7-Mar	ALBION ROVERS	6	0	McFadyen (3), O'Gilvie, Wales, McMenemy	11000
Sf	31-Mar	St. Mirren*	1	3	McFadyen	28000

* Played at Tynecastle

South African Tour 27th April - 23rd July 1934: P 16, W 16, D 0, L 0, F 81, A 12.

Player Appearances (Total)

Player	Total
Wales	45
McFadyen	44
McMenemy	44
Stevenson	44
Telfer	42
Blair	41
Ogilvie	35
Ferrier	35
Ellis	35
Crapnell	31
Robertson	29
McClory	13
Allan	13
Dowall	9
McKenzie	8
Wyllie	5
Johnstone C	3
Sinclair	3
Stewart W	3
Walker W	3
Crawley	2
McGillivray	2
Carlyle	2
Johnston J	1
Murray	1

1934 Div. 1

	Team	Pl.	Home W.	D.	L.	F.	A.	Away W.	D.	L.	F.	A.	F. (Total)	A. (Total)	Pts. (Total)
1	Rangers	38	16	3	0	65	18	14	3	2	53	23	118	41	66
2	MOTHERWELL	38	14	2	3	43	20	15	2	2	54	25	97	45	62
3	Celtic	38	12	5	2	47	20	6	6	7	31	33	78	53	47
4	Queen of the S.	38	11	2	6	44	36	10	1	8	31	42	75	78	45
5	Aberdeen	38	12	4	3	55	12	6	4	9	35	45	90	57	44
6	Heart of Mid.	38	11	5	3	52	23	6	5	8	34	36	86	59	44
7	Kilmarnock	38	11	3	5	45	28	6	6	7	28	36	73	64	43
8	Ayr United	38	10	4	5	48	37	6	6	7	39	55	87	92	42
9	St. Johnstone	38	11	3	5	43	19	6	3	10	31	34	74	53	40
10	Falkirk	38	12	3	4	49	31	4	3	12	24	37	73	68	38
11	Hamilton Acad.	38	9	5	5	35	30	6	3	10	30	49	65	79	38
12	Dundee	38	10	3	6	39	25	5	3	11	29	39	68	64	36
13	Partick Thistle	38	9	2	8	46	37	5	3	11	27	41	73	78	33
14	Clyde	38	8	5	6	36	29	2	6	11	20	41	56	70	31
15	Queen's Park	38	7	3	9	33	41	6	2	11	32	44	65	85	31
16	Hibernian	38	8	2	9	31	33	4	1	14	20	36	51	69	27
17	St. Mirren	38	5	4	10	29	35	4	5	10	17	40	46	75	27
18	Airdrieonians	38	7	3	9	37	46	3	3	13	22	57	59	103	26
19	Third Lanark	38	6	6	7	38	41	2	3	14	24	62	62	103	25
20	Cowdenbeath	38	4	3	12	33	45	1	2	16	25	73	58	118	15

1934 - 35 Season
First Division

No.	Date	Opponent	F	A	Scorers	Att.
1	11-Aug	QUEEN OF THE SOUTH	4	0	McFadyen (2), McMenemy (2)	15000
2	18-Aug	Rangers	0	1		50000
3	22-Aug	CELTIC	1	0	McMenemy	20000
4	25-Aug	QUEENS PARK	3	0	McFadyen (2), Ellis	10000
5	1-Sep	Albion Rovers	3	2	McFadyen, O'Gilvie, Ellis	10000
6	8-Sep	HAMILTON ACCIES	0	0		12000
7	12-Sep	Partick Thistle	1	1	McFadyen	
8	15-Sep	Aberdeen	2	2	McFadyen (2)	15000
9	22-Sep	KILMARNOCK	3	2	Ferrier, Stevenson, McMenemy	
10	29-Sep	St. Johnstone	1	2	McFadyen	8500
11	6-Oct	CLYDE	1	1	Stevenson	
12	13-Oct	Hearts	1	2	McMenemy	30000
13	20-Oct	DUNDEE	5	3	Crawley (2), McFadyen (2), Ferrier	6000
14	27-Oct	Hibernian	1	1	McFadyen	
15	3-Nov	Airdrieonians	0	2		5000
16	10-Nov	St. Mirren	0	1		
17	17-Nov	FALKIRK	5	2	Wyllie, Ferrier, Stevenson, Ellis, McFadyen	
18	24-Nov	Ayr United	0	1		
19	1-Dec	DUNFERMLINE	9	3	McFadyen (4), Stevenson (3), O'Gilvie, McMenemy	
20	8-Dec	Celtic	2	3	Ellis, McFadyen	30000
21	15-Dec	PARTICK THISTLE	4	1	Thomson, Ferrier, Telfer, Stevenson	6000
22	22-Dec	queen of the south	3	2	McFadyen, Ferrier, Ellis	
23	29-Dec	RANGERS	2	2	McMenemy, Stevenson	25000
24	1-Jan	Hamilton Accies	1	6	McFadyen	
25	2-Jan	ALBION ROVERS	5	2	McFadyen (3), O'Gilvie (2)	10000
26	5-Jan	Queens Park	1	1	Ogilvie	
27	12-Jan	ABERDEEN	1	2	Ellis, McFadyen	
28	19-Jan	Kilmarnock	3	3	McFadyen (2), Ferrier	
29	2-Feb	ST. JOHNSTONE	0	1		
30	16-Feb	Cylde	3	3	Crawley (3)	8000
31	23-Feb	Dundee	1	3	McFadyen	8000
32	2-Mar	HEARTS	2	2	Ferrier, McMenemy	
33	16-Mar	HIBERNIAN	4	1	McFadyen (3), Stevenson	3000
34	23-Mar	AIRDRIEONIANS	3	2	McFadyen (2), Stevenson	2000
35	30-Mar	ST. MIRREN	3	0	McFadyen, O'Gilvie, Ellis	2000
36	13-Apr	Falkirk	3	0	Clelland, McFadyen, Stevenson	5000
37	20-Apr	AYR UNITED	2	3	Stevenson, Clelland	3000
38	27-Apr	Dunfermline	0	1		
S c						
1	26-Jan	Dundee	2	1	McKenzie, Ferrier	22000
2	9-Feb	GREENOCK MORTON	7	1	Crawley (3), McMenemy, O'Gilvie, Wales, Ellis	6000
3		Awarded a bye				
4	9-Mar	RANGERS	1	4	Telfer	30000

Player Appearances (Total)

Player	Total
Blair	41
Ellis	41
McFadyen	41
Wales	39
McClory	38
McMenemy	34
Ferrier	30
Ogilvie	30
Stevenson	28
Telfer	26
McKenzie	24
Allan	22
Thomson	8
Crawley	7
McGillivray	7
Dowall	6
Stewart	5
Clelland	4
Crapnell	4
Johnston J	4
Sinclair	4
McArthur	3
Johnstone C	2
Wyllie	2
Rogers	1

1935 Div. 1

	Team	Pl.	Home W.	D.	L.	F.	A.	Away W.	D.	L.	F.	A.	F. (Total)	A. (Total)	Pts. (Total)
1	Rangers	38	14	3	2	50	19	11	2	6	46	27	96	46	55
2	Celtic	38	15	2	2	61	19	9	2	8	31	26	92	45	52
3	Heart of Mid.	38	11	5	3	42	19	9	5	5	45	32	87	51	50
4	Hamilton Acad.	38	14	4	1	58	24	5	6	8	29	43	87	67	48
5	St. Johnstone	38	13	4	2	45	14	5	6	8	21	32	66	46	46
6	Aberdeen	38	13	3	3	42	17	4	7	8	26	37	68	54	44
7	MOTHERWELL	38	12	4	3	57	27	3	6	10	26	37	83	64	40
8	Dundee	38	10	4	5	35	27	6	4	9	28	36	63	63	40
9	Kilmarnock	38	10	3	6	43	30	6	3	10	33	38	76	68	38
10	Clyde	38	9	6	4	45	29	5	4	10	26	40	71	69	38
11	Hibernian	38	10	7	2	38	20	4	1	14	21	50	59	70	36
12	Queen's Park	38	11	4	4	43	30	2	6	11	18	50	61	80	36
13	Partick Thistle	38	10	5	4	38	25	5	0	14	23	43	61	68	35
14	Airdrieonians	38	10	3	6	42	31	3	4	12	22	41	64	72	33
15	Dunfermline Ath.	38	8	4	7	35	39	5	1	13	21	57	56	96	31
16	Albion Rovers	38	8	4	7	38	30	2	5	12	24	47	62	77	29
17	Queen of the S.	38	9	2	8	33	27	2	5	12	19	45	52	72	29
18	Ayr United	38	10	2	7	32	29	2	3	14	29	83	61	112	29
19	St. Mirren	38	7	3	9	31	33	4	2	13	18	37	49	70	27
20	Falkirk	38	8	3	8	42	33	1	3	15	16	49	58	82	24

1934-35 Season

Back: Crapnell, Johnston, McKenzie, Crawley, Hemmings (South Africa Man), Stewart
Middle: Smithers, Stevenson, Wales, McClory, Blair, Telfer, Ellis, Walker
Front: McMenemy, Muirhead, Ferrier, Hunter, McFadyen
Seated: Allan, Ogilvie

1935-36 Season

Back: Wales, Blair, McClory, Ellis (Cap), McArthur, Johnston, McKenzie
Front: Ogilvie, Wylie, McMenemy, Stevenson, McFadyen, Ferrier, Crawley

1935 - 36 Season
First Division

	Date	Opponent			Scorers	Att.
1	10-Aug	Kilmarnock	3	2	Stevenson, Ferrier, McMenemy	12000
2	17-Aug	ABERDEEN	2	2	McFadyen, Stevenson	
3	24-Aug	Queens Park	2	2	McGillivray, Stevenson	
4	28-Aug	Ayr United	0	1		
5	31-Aug	ALBION ROVERS	2	0	McFadyen, Ferrier	
6	7-Sep	Cylde	2	1	Ferrier, McMenemy	
7	14-Sep	ST. JOHNSTONE	3	0	Ferrier, McFadyen, Ellis	
8	17-Sep	Partick Thistle	1	4	Stevenson, Ferrier, McMenemy	
9	21-Sep	Hamilton Accies	3	3	Wyllie (2), Bremner	12000
10	28-Sep	RANGERS	0	2		10000
11	5-Oct	queen of the south	1	1	Wales	
12	12-Oct	HEARTS	4	2	Stewart, Bremner, O'Gilvie, Stevenson	
13	19-Oct	Dunfermline	3	1	Stewart, Bremner, Wyllie	
14	26-Oct	CELTIC	1	2	Stevenson, Ferrier, McMenemy	20000
15	2-Nov	Third Lanark	1	2	Wyllie (2), Bremner	8000
16	9-Nov	ARBROATH	4	0	Bremner, O'Gilvie, McFadyen	4000
17	16-Nov	AIRDRIEONIANS	6	2	Ferrier (3), O'Gilvie (2), Wyllie	
18	23-Nov	Hibernian	3	2	Wyllie, Ferrier, Ellis	
19	30-Nov	Dundee	2	2	Wyllie (2)	4000
20	7-Dec	AYR UNITED	4	1	Bremner (2), O'Gilvie, Wyllie	
21	14-Dec	PARTICK THISTLE	5	3	Ferrier (2), Wyllie, O'Gilvie, Stevenson	2000
22	28-Dec	Aberdeen	1	1	Ogilvie	17000
23	1 Jan	HAMILTON ACCIES	2	1	Bremner, Ferrier	10000
24	2-Jan	Albion Rovers	2	0	Stewart, Bremner	
25	4-Jan	QUEENS PARK	1	0	Wales	8000
26	11-Jan	CLYDE	1	1	McMenemy	4000
27	18-Jan	St. Johnstone	3	2	Stevenson (2), McGillivray	
28	1-Feb	Rangers	0	0		
29	15-Feb	QUEEN OF THE SOUTH	0	2		
30	29-Feb	Hearts	2	2	Bremner, Wyllie	15000
31	14-Mar	Celtic	0	5		
32	21-Mar	THIRD LANARK	2	1	Stevenson, McGillivray	
33	28-Mar	arbroath	1	1	Ferrier	
34	4-Apr	KILMARNOCK	3	2	Ferrier, McFadyen, McGillivray	4000
35	11-Apr	Airdrieonians	1	1	Wales	
36	18-Apr	HIBERNIAN	1	1	McGillivray	4000
37	22-Apr	Dunfermline	2	3	Bremner, Stevenson	
38	25-Apr	DUNDEE	3	0	McFadyen (2), Ferrier	
S c						
1	29-Jan	arbroath	3	1	Wyllie (2), Ferrier	6000
2	8-Feb	ST. BERNARDS	3	0	Stevenson (3)	4782
3	22-Feb	Cowdenbeith	3	1	Wyllie, Ellis, Stevenson	11000
4	7-Mar	Cylde	2	3	Wyllie, O'Gilvie	25000

Player Appearances

	(Total)
Grant	42
McClory	42
Blair	41
Ellis	40
Wales	39
Stevenson	37
Bremner	36
Ogilvie	32
Ferrier	29
McFadyen	22
Wyllie	22
Telfer	20
McMenemy	15
McKenzie	14
Stewart	11
McGillivray	10
Hynds	2
Pollock	2
Cleland	1
Farmer	1
Rae	1
Stark	1

1936 Div. 1

		Pl.	Home W.	D.	L.	F.	A.	Away W.	D.	L.	F.	A.	F. (Total)	A.	Pts.
1	Celtic	38	17	1	1	71	16	15	1	3	44	17	115	33	66
2	Rangers	38	14	3	2	67	26	13	4	2	43	17	110	43	61
3	Aberdeen	38	15	3	1	52	19	11	6	2	44	31	96	50	61
4	MOTHERWELL	38	12	3	4	46	25	6	9	4	31	33	77	58	48
5	Heart of Mid.	38	14	4	1	56	20	6	3	10	32	35	88	55	47
6	Hamilton Acad.	38	11	4	4	56	31	4	3	12	21	43	77	74	37
7	St. Johnstone	38	10	4	5	43	27	5	3	11	27	54	70	81	37
8	Kilmarnock	38	10	4	5	46	30	4	3	12	23	34	69	64	35
9	Third Lanark	38	11	4	4	47	29	4	1	14	16	36	63	65	35
10	Partick Thistle	38	12	5	2	47	22	0	5	14	17	50	64	72	34
11	Arbroath	38	6	6	7	22	24	5	5	9	24	45	46	69	33
12	Dundee	38	9	5	5	42	34	2	5	12	25	46	67	80	32
13	Queen's Park	38	8	6	5	36	25	3	4	12	22	50	58	75	32
14	Dunfermline Ath.	38	6	6	7	31	36	6	2	11	36	56	67	92	32
15	Queen of the S.	38	9	6	4	34	26	2	3	14	20	46	54	72	31
16	Albion Rovers	38	8	2	9	41	33	5	2	12	28	59	69	92	30
17	Hibernian	38	7	3	9	29	31	4	4	11	27	51	56	82	29
18	Clyde	38	10	1	8	35	33	0	7	12	28	51	63	84	28
19	Airdrieonians	38	8	4	7	44	37	1	5	13	24	54	68	91	27
20	Ayr United	38	8	2	9	30	31	3	1	15	23	67	53	98	25

1936 - 37 Season
First Division

	Date	Opponent			Scorers	Att.
1	8-Aug	QUEENS PARK	3	1	Stevenson, Graham, Grant	
2	15-Aug	Hearts	4	3	McFadyen (2), Stevenson, Stewart W	30000
3	18-Aug	Queens Park	0	0		8000
4	22-Aug	CLYDE	4	1	Stevenson (2), McFadyen, Graham	8000
5	29-Aug	St. Johnstone	3	1	McFadyen (2), Bremner	9000
6	5-Sep	QUEEN OF THE SOUTH	4	1	McFadyen (2), Bremner, Stevenson	
7	9-Sep	HEARTS	1	3	Graham	15000
8	12-Sep	Rangers	2	3	Bremner, McGillivray	43000
9	19-Sep	HAMILTON ACCIES	5	2	Ellis, McGillivray, Ferguson, Bremner, McFadyen	11000
10	26-Sep	Aberdeen	0	2		20000
11	3-Oct	KILMARNOCK	2	1	Stewart W, McFadyen	
12	10-Oct	Albion Rovers	4	1	McFadyen (2), McGillivray (2)	4000
13	17-Oct	THIRD LANARK	1	2	McFadyen	
14	24-Oct	arbroath	0	0		3000
15	31-Oct	Falkirk	1	1	McFadyen	8000
16	7-Nov	HIBERNIAN	3	4	Stevenson (3)	5000
17	14-Nov	DUNDEE	2	1	Wales, Stewart	
18	21-Nov	St. Mirren	0	3		8000
19	28-Nov	Partick Thistle	0	1		
20	12-Dec	Celtic	2	3	Stewart (2)	20000
21	19-Dec	Cylde	2	1	Ferrier (2)	
22	26-Dec	ST. JOHNSTONE	2	2	Stewart (2)	7000
23	1-Jan	Hamilton Accies	3	2	Stewart (2), O'Gilvie	
24	2-Jan	ALBION ROVERS	9	1	McGillivray(3),Stewart (3),Stevenson (2),O'Gilvie	4000
25	4-Jan	Dunfermline	2	2	McGillivray, McCulloch	2000
26	9-Jan	queen of the south	2	0	Ogilvie, Stewart	
27	16-Jan	RANGERS	1	4	McGillivray	20000
28	23-Jan	Kilmarnock	1	0	McGillivray	
29	6-Feb	ABERDEEN	1	0	Stewart	10000
30	20-Feb	Third Lanark	1	1	Ferrier	
31	20-Mar	Hibernian	2	1	Stewart, O'Gilvie	
32	27-Mar	Dundee	0	0		8000
33	31-Mar	ARBROATH	3	1	Ferrier, Main, O'Gilvie	
34	3-Apr	ST. MIRREN	4	1	Stewart (3), Main	2000
35	10-Apr	PARTICK THISTLE	4	2	Stewart (2), Wales, O'Gilvie	3500
36	14-Apr	DUNFERMLINE	6	0	Stewart (3), Ferrier (2), O'Gilvie	
37	19-Apr	FALKIRK	4	2	Ogilvie (3), Stewart	
38	30-Apr	CELTIC	8	0	Stewart (6), Stevenson, McCulloch	
S c						
1	30-Jan	GALSTON	3	1	Ogilvie, Ellis, Graham	1070
2	13-Feb	Falkirk	3	0	Stewart (2), Bremner	19700
3	10-Mar	duns (tynecastle)	5	2	Ogilvie (2), Bremner (2), McCulloch	6525
4	17-Mar	Celtic	4	4	Stewart (2), Stevenson (2)	36159
4r	24-Mar	CELTIC	1	2	Wales	36800

Player Appearances

	(Total)
Blair	43
Ellis	42
Stevenson	35
McArthur	35
Wales	32
Grant	30
Stewart A	29
McKenzie	27
Bremner	27
Telfer	25
Ogilvie	22
McFadyen	20
McGillivray	16
Hynds	15
Ferguson	13
McCulloch	13
Stewart W	12
Ferrier	10
Graham	9
McClory	8
Main	7
McMenemy	1
Pattison	1

1937 Div. 1

		Pl.	Home W.	D.	L.	F.	A.	Away W.	D.	L.	F.	A.	F. (Total)	A.	Pts.
1	Rangers	38	15	3	1	50	11	11	6	2	38	21	88	32	61
2	Aberdeen	38	15	4	0	53	16	8	4	7	36	28	89	44	54
3	Celtic	38	14	3	2	59	26	8	5	6	30	32	89	58	52
4	MOTHERWELL	38	14	1	4	67	29	8	6	5	29	25	96	54	51
5	Heart of Mid.	38	17	0	2	67	22	7	3	9	32	38	99	60	51
6	Third Lanark	38	12	4	3	42	20	8	2	9	37	41	79	61	46
7	Falkirk	38	13	1	5	60	26	6	5	8	38	40	98	66	44
8	Hamilton Acad.	38	12	2	5	54	38	6	3	10	37	58	91	96	41
9	Dundee	38	7	10	2	36	23	5	5	9	22	46	58	69	39
10	Clyde	38	10	4	5	35	28	6	2	11	24	42	59	70	38
11	Kilmarnock	38	10	5	4	36	26	4	4	11	24	44	60	70	37
12	St. Johnstone	38	13	1	5	50	25	1	7	11	24	43	74	68	36
13	Partick Thistle	38	8	6	5	43	26	3	6	10	30	42	73	68	34
14	Arbroath	38	9	5	5	33	23	4	0	15	24	61	57	84	31
15	Queen's Park	38	3	7	9	24	36	6	5	8	27	41	51	77	30
16	St. Mirren	38	9	2	8	43	35	2	5	12	25	46	68	81	29
17	Hibernian	38	2	11	6	29	34	4	2	13	25	49	54	83	25
18	Queen of the S.	38	6	4	9	28	35	2	4	13	21	60	49	95	24
19	Dunfermline Ath.	38	3	7	9	34	45	2	4	13	31	53	65	98	21
20	Albion Rovers	38	4	2	13	32	51	1	4	14	21	65	53	116	16

1937 - 38 Season
First Division

No.	Date	Opponent	F	A	Scorers	Att.
1	14-Aug	Cylde	2	2	Ogilvie, McCulloch	
2	18-Aug	Rangers	1	2	McCulloch	20000
3	21-Aug	ARBROATH	5	1	Stevenson (3), Stark, O'Gilvie	4000
4	25-Aug	CLYDE	1	0	Stewart	
5	28-Aug	queen of the south	3	0	Ogilvie, Stevenson, McCulloch	10000
6	4-Sep	RANGERS	1	1	McCulloch	25000
7	11-Sep	Hamilton Accies	3	1	Stewart (2), Stevenson	10000
8	15-Sep	arbroath	1	2	McCulloch	
9	18-Sep	ABERDEEN	2	1	Ogilvie (2)	8000
10	25-Sep	Kilmarnock	2	0	Ogilvie, Bremner	
11	2-Oct	HEARTS	3	3	Ogilvie, Bremner, Stewart	8000
12	9-Oct	Queens Park	3	1	Ogilvie, Bremner, Stewart	
13	16-Oct	GREENOCK MORTON	4	1	Ogilvie (2), Bremner, Stewart	
14	23-Oct	FALKIRK	3	2	Ogilvie, Stewart, Stevenson	
15	30-Oct	Hibernian	1	1	Ogilvie	12000
16	6-Nov	Dundee	2	2	Ogilvie, Ellis	
17	13-Nov	ST. MIRREN	3	2	Ogilvie (2), Stevenson	6000
18	20-Nov	PARTICK THISTLE	1	1	Wales	6000
19	27-Nov	Ayr United	3	3	Ellis, Stewart, Stevenson	
20	4-Dec	CELTIC	1	2	Steenson	
21	11-Dec	Third Lanark	3	5	Stewart, Johnston J, OG	
22	25-Dec	QUEEN OF THE SOUTH	5	1	Stevenson (2), Hastie (2)	
23	1-Jan	HAMILTON ACCIES	0	1		
24	3-Jan	Greenock Morton	1	4	McKenzie	
25	8-Jan	Aberdeen	0	4		18000
26	15-Jan	KILMARNOCK	4	3	McGillivray (4)	3000
27	29-Jan	Hearts	0	2		15000
28	5-Feb	QUEENS PARK	3	0	Bremner (2), Ellis	
29	19-Feb	Falkirk	1	0	Stewart	
30	26-Feb	HIBERNIAN	1	0	Stewart	
31	12-Mar	DUNDEE	1	1	Stewart	6000
32	23-Mar	ST. JOHNSTONE	3	1	Ogilvie, Stewart, Main	
33	26-Mar	Partick Thistle	0	3		5000
34	2-Apr	AYR UNITED	4	3	Bremner (2), O'Gilvie, McGillivray	
35	9-Apr	Celtic	1	4	Bremner	
36	12-Apr	St. Mirren	0	3		
37	16-Apr	THIRD LANARK	4	4	Stewart (3), Bremner	
38	30-Apr	St. Johnstone	2	2	Stewart, McCulloch	
S c						
1	22-Jan	Cylde	4	1	Ogilvie (2), Bremner, ?	
2	12-Feb	stenhousemuir	1	1	Ogilvie	4869
2r	16-Feb	STENHOUSEMUIR	6	1	Ogilvie (2), McGillivray (2), Bremner, OG	
3	5-Mar	HAMILTON ACCIES	2	0	Stewart (2), Stevenson	22500
4	19-Mar	St. Bernards	1	3	Hastie	3600

Player Appearances (League)

Bremner	36
Ogilvie	36
Blair	33
Ellis	33
Stewart	33
McKenzie	32
Stevenson	31
McCulloch	30
Wales	30
McArthur	29
Grant	26
Telfer	19
Hynds	11
McGillivray	10
Johnston	9
Murray	9
Hastie	8
Main	5
Brown	2
Graham	2
Martin	2
Stark	1

1938 Div. 1

	Pl.	Home W.	D.	L.	F.	A.	Away W.	D.	L.	F.	A.	F. (Total)	A.	Pts.
1 Celtic	38	16	3	0	70	15	11	4	4	44	27	114	42	61
2 Heart of Mid.	38	16	2	1	48	16	10	4	5	42	34	90	50	58
3 Rangers	38	11	5	3	44	23	7	8	4	31	26	75	49	49
4 Falkirk	38	9	4	6	43	27	10	5	4	39	25	82	52	47
5 MOTHERWELL	38	12	5	2	49	28	5	5	9	29	41	78	69	44
6 Aberdeen	38	12	3	4	47	18	3	6	10	27	41	74	59	39
7 Partick Thistle	38	12	2	5	45	32	3	7	9	23	38	68	70	39
8 St. Johnstone	38	11	4	4	47	29	5	3	11	31	52	78	81	39
9 Third Lanark	38	7	8	4	34	30	4	5	10	34	43	68	73	35
10 Hibernian	38	8	8	3	38	27	3	5	11	19	38	57	65	35
11 Arbroath	38	8	7	4	37	30	3	6	10	21	49	58	79	35
12 Queen's Park	38	6	8	5	33	32	5	4	10	26	42	59	74	34
13 Hamilton Acad.	38	9	3	7	48	30	4	4	11	33	46	81	76	33
14 St. Mirren	38	11	2	6	42	25	3	3	13	16	41	58	66	33
15 Clyde	38	6	9	4	41	31	4	4	11	27	47	68	78	33
16 Queen of the S.	38	6	4	9	26	32	5	7	7	32	39	58	71	33
17 Ayr United	38	6	9	4	42	31	3	6	10	24	54	66	85	33
18 Kilmarnock	38	9	5	5	35	33	3	4	12	30	58	65	91	33
19 Dundee	38	10	3	6	47	27	3	3	13	23	47	70	74	32
20 Morton	38	5	1	13	44	55	1	2	16	20	72	64	127	15

1938 - 39 Season
First Division

No.	Date	Opponent	F	A	Scorers	Att.
1	13-Aug	QUEEN OF THE SOUTH	8	5	Bremner(3),Stewart(2),McCulloch,Telfer, O'Gilvie	8000
2	20-Aug	Rangers	2	2	Bremner, Stewart	40000
3	24-Aug	queen of the south	3	4	McCulloch, Hastie, Stewart	11000
4	27-Aug	KILMARNOCK	5	2	Ellis (3 X Pens), Stewart, Bremner	6000
5	3-Sep	Aberdeen	0	0		
6	10-Sep	HAMILTON ACCIES	2	3	Stewart, Ellis	12000
7	14-Sep	RANGERS	0	5		
8	17-Sep	Hearts	0	4		
9	24-Sep	QUEENS PARK	2	0	Mathie (2)	
10	1-Oct	Raith Rovers	1	0	Mathie	
11	8-Oct	CLYDE	3	2	Mathie (2), McCulloch	7000
12	15-Oct	Albion Rovers	4	3	Stevenson (2), Ellis, Bremner	
13	22-Oct	ARBROATH	4	0	Mathie (2), Bremner, Stevenson	
14	29-Oct	St. Mirren	2	2	Mathie, McCulloch	10000
15	5-Nov	Partick Thistle	2	4	Ogilvie, Stevenson	
16	12-Nov	AYR UNITED	1	2	Stevenson (2), Ellis, Bremner	
17	19-Nov	Celtic	3	1	Bremner (2), Johnston	
18	26-Nov	THIRD LANARK	5	1	Ogilvie (2), McCulloch, Stevenson, Bremner	
19	3-Dec	St. Johnstone	1	2	Mathie	
20	10-Dec	Falkirk	1	2	Stevenson	
21	17-Dec	HIBERNIAN	3	2	Mathie (2), O'Gilvie	
22	28-Dec	Kilmarnock	3	1	Mathie (2), Bremner	
23	31-Dec	ABERDEEN	2	2	McCulloch (2)	
24	2-Jan	Hamilton Accies	1	2	Ogilvie	
25	3-Jan	ALBION ROVERS	3	1	Wales, McKenzie, Mathie	
26	11-Jan	Queens Park	0	0		
27	14-Jan	RAITH ROVERS	2	4	Mathie, Bremner	
28	28-Jan	Cylde	0	4		
29	11-Feb	HEARTS	4	2	Mathie (2), Bremner, Stevenson	11500
30	25-Feb	arbroath	0	2		
31	8-Mar	ST. MIRREN	2	1	Stevenson, Johnston	
32	11-Mar	PARTICK THISTLE	4	3	McCulloch (2), O'Gilvie, Bremner	
33	18-Mar	Ayr United	1	6	Mathie	
34	1-Apr	Third Lanark	1	3	Ellis	
35	5-Apr	CELTIC	2	3	Ogilvie (2)	
36	8-Apr	ST. JOHNSTONE	3	1	Mathie (2), Stevenson	
37	14-Apr	FALKIRK	1	3	McCulloch	
38	29-Apr	Hibernian	1	2	McCulloch	
S c						
1	21-Jan	Huntly	8	1	Ogilvie (4), Mathie (2), Bremner, McCulloch	3200
2	4-Feb	Dundee United	5	1	Ogilvie (2), McCulloch (2), Mathie	11346
3	18-Feb	ST. MIRREN	4	2	Ogilvie (2), Stevenson (2)	17000
4	4-Mar	CELTIC **	3	1	McCulloch (2), Stevenson	31000
Sf	25-Mar	Aberdeen*	1	1	Mathie	81000
Sfr	29-Mar	Aberdeen*	3	1	Mathie, McCulloch, Bremner	41000
F	22-Apr	Cylde	0	4		94799

* Played at Ibrox **1st All Ticket Match At Fir Park*

Player Appearances (Total)

Ellis	43
Ogilvie D	43
Blair	42
McKenzie	42
Telfer	42
Bremner	40
McCulloch	39
Stevenson	38
Mathie	37
Wales	37
Murray	35
Frame	10
Turnbull	8
Grant	6
Johnston	6
Main	3
Ogilvie J	3
Brown	2
Evans	2
McLeod	2
Martin	2
Young	2
Ferguson	1
Hastie	1
McGillivray	1

1939 Div. 1

	Pl.	Home W.	D.	L.	F.	A.	Away W.	D.	L.	F.	A.	F. (Total)	A.	Pts.
1 Rangers	38	16	3	0	62	19	9	6	4	50	36	112	55	59
2 Celtic	38	11	3	5	62	31	9	5	5	37	22	99	53	48
3 Aberdeen	38	16	1	2	64	23	4	5	10	27	38	91	61	46
4 Heart of Mid.	38	13	1	5	61	30	7	4	8	37	40	98	70	45
5 Falkirk	38	11	4	4	42	24	8	3	8	31	39	73	63	45
6 Queen of the S.	38	11	6	2	40	21	6	3	10	29	43	69	64	43
7 Hamilton Acad.	38	13	1	5	39	23	5	4	10	28	48	67	71	41
8 St. Johnstone	38	12	2	5	53	32	5	4	10	32	50	85	82	40
9 Clyde	38	10	4	5	46	31	7	1	11	32	39	78	70	39
10 Kilmarnock	38	9	6	4	40	30	6	3	10	33	56	73	86	39
11 Partick Thistle	38	12	2	5	45	30	5	2	12	29	57	74	87	38
12 MOTHERWELL	38	12	1	6	56	42	4	4	11	26	44	82	86	37
13 Hibernian	38	9	5	5	43	23	5	2	12	25	46	68	69	35
14 Ayr United	38	8	6	5	46	33	5	3	11	30	50	76	83	35
15 Third Lanark	38	8	5	6	44	32	4	3	12	36	64	80	96	32
16 Albion Rovers	38	9	1	9	41	44	3	5	11	24	46	65	90	30
17 Arbroath	38	10	3	6	39	31	1	5	13	15	44	54	75	30
18 St. Mirren	38	8	5	6	31	30	3	2	14	26	50	57	80	29
19 Queen's Park	38	7	4	8	31	32	4	1	14	26	51	57	83	27
20 Raith Rovers	38	4	2	13	33	44	6	0	13	32	55	65	99	22

1939 - 40 Season
First Division

1	12-Aug	Kilmarnock	3	3	McCulloch (2), Mathie
2	19-Aug	ABREDEEN	3	0	Turnbull, Mathie, Bremner
3	23-Aug	KILMARNOCK	4	2	Turnbull, Wales, McCulloch, Bremner
4	26-Aug	Alloa Athletic	2	3	Ogilvie, Ellis
5	2-Sep	HEARTS	2	4	Wales, McCulloch

Due to the outbreak of war, the Scottish Football League was suspended after 2nd September fixtures. On 21st October the leagues were resumed on a regional basis, with a west & south section and an east & north section. These fixtures were not officially recorded and no championship was awarded

1939 - 40 Season
Western District League

	League	Emergency Cup	Other Cups & Friendlies
Played	30	6	4
Won	15	4	3
Drew	8	1	0
Lost	7	1	1
Goals F	64	16	8
Goals A	56	16	4

League Position: 4th, Lanarkshire Cup Winners, S.E. Cup Semi Final

1940 - 41 Season
Southern District League

	League	South. Lge. Cup	Other Cups & Friendlies
Played	30	6	2
Won	13	2	0
Drew	4	1	1
Lost	13	3	1
Goals F	73	19	2
Goals A	65	13	5

1941 - 42 Season
Southern District League

	League	South. Lge. Cup	Other Cups & Friendlies
Played	30	6	5
Won	16	2	3
Drew	3	0	0
Lost	11	4	2
Goals F	76	7	9
Goals A	62	15	8

1942 - 43 Season
Southern District League

	League	Southern Lge. Cup	Other Cups & Friendlies
Played	30	6	2
Won	15	1	0
Drew	4	1	1
Lost	11	4	1
Goals F	60	8	4
Goals A	54	18	5

Reserve LGE. Cup Winners, Glasgow & Dist. Reserve LGE. Champs.

1943 - 44 Season
Southern District League

	League	Southern Lge. Cup	Other Cups & Friendlies
Played	30	6	6
Won	12	3	5
Drew	8	1	0
Lost	10	2	1
Goals F	69	11	20
Goals A	53	12	1

League Position 5th, Summer Cup Winners

1944 - 45 Season
Southern District League

	League	Southern Lge. Cup	Other Cups & Friendlies
Played	30	6	0
Won	18	3	
Drew	5	1	
Lost	7	2	
Goals F	83	11	
Goals A	54	12	

League Position 3rd, Southern League Cup Finalists

1945 - 46 Season
Southern District League (Victory Season)

	Lge.	Lge. Cup	Other Cups & Friendlies
P	30	6	2
W	11	2	1
D	9	1	0
L	10	3	1
F	54	9	3
A	55	13	6

1946 Div. 1 (Interim Season)

		Pl.	Home W.	D.	L.	F.	A.	Away W.	D.	L.	F.	A.	F. (Total)	A.	Pts.
1	Rangers	30	12	2	1	45	23	10	2	3	40	18	85	41	48
2	Hibernian	30	11	3	1	42	13	6	3	6	25	24	67	37	40
3	Aberdeen	30	13	1	1	49	10	3	5	7	24	31	73	41	38
4	Celtic	30	7	5	3	30	21	5	6	4	25	23	55	44	35
5	Clyde	30	6	5	4	36	27	5	4	6	28	27	64	54	31
6	MOTHERWELL	30	6	4	5	27	26	5	5	5	27	29	54	55	31
7	Heart of Mid.	30	6	5	4	32	23	5	3	7	31	34	63	57	30
8	Queen's Park	30	6	2	7	29	24	5	6	4	31	36	60	60	30
9	Third Lanark	30	9	0	6	36	30	5	2	8	27	38	63	68	30
10	Morton	30	6	7	2	43	26	3	4	8	29	43	72	69	29
11	Falkirk	30	9	2	4	42	30	2	3	10	20	40	62	70	27
12	Partick Thistle	30	8	2	5	34	30	3	2	10	20	35	54	65	26
13	Queen of the S.	30	7	3	5	40	32	2	3	10	22	50	62	82	24
14	St. Mirren	30	5	3	7	29	28	4	2	9	25	42	54	70	23
15	Kilmarnock	30	4	5	6	29	39	3	3	9	27	48	56	87	22
16	Hamilton Acc.	30	2	5	8	26	37	3	1	11	18	51	44	88	16

Pre-War Foreign Tours & Other Matches

(Motherwell played many pre-war Friendlies against other Scottish teams. Many of these were not necessarily first team matches, therefore these games have been omitted)

Pre-War Friendlies (versus Non Scottish Opposition)

1895

23-Apr	PRESTON N E	2	2	Goldie, Edgar	

1896

27-Apr	BURNLEY	0	2		1000

1908

27-Apr	WOOLICH ARSENAL	1	1	Reid	1500

1914

18-Apr	Barrow	1	1	Whitehead	

1926

6-Mar	Burnley	4	1	Tennant (2), Ferrier, McFadyen	
17-Apr	Halifax town	3	0	Ferrier (2), Tennant	
19-Apr	Blackpool	2	1	Stevenson, McMurtrie	

1927

5-Mar	Carlisle	9	4	Keenan (3),McFadyen(2),Ferrier(2),McMurtrie,Craig	
27-Apr	Manchester United	1	5	Hutchieson	

1927 Tour Of Spain

15-May	Swansea	4	3	McFadyen (2), Thackery, McMurtrie	
19-May	Real Madrid	3	1	Hutchieson, Ferrier, Thackery	10000
22-May	Barcelona	2	2	A Craig, Hutchieson	22000
26-May	Swansea	1	0	Ferrier	
29-May	Bilbao Select	1	3	McMurtrie	12000
5-Jun	Vigo Celta	3	1	Ferrier (2), McFadyen	
7-Jun	Vigo Celta	4	0	Keenan, Stevenson, Thackery, Ferrier	
12-May	Red Star Olympique	5	0	Ferrier (3), McFadyen, Stevenson	

1928 Tour Of South America

13-May	Buenos Aires Select	0	1		
17-May	Provinces	1	2	Ferrier	
20-May	Capitol	2	3	McFadyen (2)	
25-May	Rosaria	4	3	McFadyen (3), Stevenson	
2-Jun	Argentine Assoc	3	0	McFadyen (2), Ferrier	
3-Jun	Argentina & Uruguay	3	0	McFadyen (2), Tennant	
5-Jun	Provinces	4	1	McFadyen (2), Ferrier (2)	
7-Jun	Rosaria	3	2	McFadyen, Stevenson, McMurtrie	
10-Jun	Penerole (uruguay)	1	0	Tennent	
21-Jun	Brazil	1	1	Ferrier	
24-Jun	Brazil Select	0	5		

1928-29

18-Sep	Huddersfield	2	0	T Tennant (2)	10000
1-Apr	Everton	4	1	W Tennant (2), McMenemy, Ferrier	
3-Apr	Blackpool	0	2		
13-Apr	Doncaster Rovers	2	1	W Tennant, McMenemy	

1929-30

30-Sep	HUDDERSFIELD TOWN	2	4	Ferrier (2)	
30-Apr	SWANSEA	2	2	Dowall, Ferrier	

1931 Tour Of South Africa

20-May	Griqualand West	4	0	McFadyen (2), McMenemy, Ferrier	
23-May	Witwatersrand	1	0	McFadyen (2), McMenemy, Ferrier	28000
25-May	Natal	6	0	McFadyen (4), Stevenson, Murdoch	10000
27-May	Natal Northern District	3	0	McFadyen, Finlayson, Dowall	
30-May	Transval	4	0	McFadyen (4)	25000
1-Jun	Orange Free State	2	1	Finlayson, Dowall	
3-Jun	East Rand	3	0	McFadyen, McMenemy, Dowall	6000
6-Jun	South Africa (Durban)	2	1	Craig, Dowall	
10-Jun	Natal	1	3	McFadyen	7000
13-Jun	South Africa (Jo'burg)	8	0	McFadyen (6), McMenemy, Murdoch	29000
17-Jun	Pretoria	2	0	McFadyen, Murdoch	
20-Jun	Eastern Frontier X1	3	2	Ferrier (2), McMenemy	5000
23-Jun	Eastern Province	6	1	McFadyen(2),Ferrier(2),Stevenson,McMenemy	8000
27-Jun	Western Province	7	0	McFadyen (4), Stevenson (2), Ferrier	7000
1-Jul	South Africa (Cape Town)	5	2	McFadyen (3), Stevenson, Ferrier	10000

1931-32

25-Apr	Leinster Select (Dublin)	2	1	Murdoch, Ferrier	

1932 Tour Of France

5-May	Beerschot A C (Antwerp)	5	0	McFadyen (2), Murdoch (2), Telfer	
8-May	Standard Liege(Brussels)	4	2	Murdoch (2), Wyllie (2)	
15-May	Red Star Olympique(Paris)	3	1	Murdoch (2), Stevenson	
16-May	Racing Club de Paris	5	0	McFadyen (2), Moffett, Ferrier, Stevenson	

1933-34

26-Apr	Clapton Orient	6	4	McFadyen (4), McMenemy, O'Gilvie	15000

1934 Tour Of South Africa & Rhodesia

17-May	Eastern Province	10	1	McFadyen (6), Stevenson (3), McMenemy	3000
19-May	Frontier X1	6	2	McFadyen (3), McMenemy (2), Stevenson	
23-May	Griqualand West	9	0	Craig (3),Johnston(2),McMenemy(2),O'Gilvie(2)	
26-May	Southern Transvaal	7	1	McFadyen (4), O'Gilvie (2), Stevenson	25000
28-May	Orange Free State	3	1	McFadyen, O'Gilvie (2)	
31-May	Natal (Durban)	7	1	McFadyen (3), Ferrier (3), O'Gilvie	10000
2-Jun	Transvaal	2	1	McFadyen, McMenemy	
7-Jun	Matabeleland	3	0	Crawley (3)	
9-Jun	Mashonaland	6	0	McFadyen (5), O'Gilvie	
13-Jun	Northern Transvaal	2	1	McFadyen, Stewart	6000
16-Jun	South Africa (Durban)	5	2	McFadyen (2), McMenemy (2), Stevenson	20000
20-Jun	Natal (Maritzburg)	5	0	McFadyen (2), Crawley (2), Stevenson	
23-Jun	South Africa (Jo'burg)	3	0	Stevenson (2), O'Gilvie	25000
27-Jun	Eastern Transvaal	1	0	McFadyen	
30-Jun	Western Province	7	0	McFadyen (4), O'Gilvie (2), Crawley	
2-Jul	South Africa (Cape Town)	5	2	McFadyen (3), McMenemy, O'Gilvie	

1934-35

28-Mar	Red Star Olympique (Paris)	4	3	McFadyen, O'Gilvie	
25-Apr	Clapton Orient	1	2	McFadyen	

1935-36

26-Apr	Leinster (Dublin)	5	3	Stevenson (2), Ferrier, McFadyen, Bremner	
30-Apr	Clapton Orient	0	1		

1936-37

21-Sep	Huddersfield town	3	1	Bremner, Graham, Ellis	
21-Apr	HUDDERSFIELD TOWN	2	2	Stevenson, Ferrier	
23-Apr	Leinster F A (Dublin)	1	2	Ferrier	
25-Apr	Munster F A (Cork)	3	2	Stewart (2), O'Gilvie	

1937-38

24-Apr	Leinster F A (Dublin)	2	2	Ogilvie, Stewart	5000

1938-39

30-Apr	Leinster F A (Dublin)	0	5		

1946-47: "A" Division

No.	Date	Opponent	Score	Scorers	Johnman John	Kilmarnock	Shaw	McLeod	Paton	Russell	Henderson	Redpath	Brown	Bremner	Barclay	Gibson	Humphries	Irving	Kerr	Watson	Robertson	Buchanan	Slavin	Johnstone Joe	Reid Joe	Leitch	Mc Roberts
1	10-Aug	RANGERS	2 - 4	Brown (2)	x	x	x	x	x	x	x	x	x	x	x												
2	14-Aug	Morton	1 - 3	Brown	x	x	x	x	x	x	x	x	x	x	x												
3	17-Aug	Queen of the South	6 - 1	Brown (3), Humphries (2), Barclay	x	x	x	x	x	x			x	x	x	x	x										
4	21-Aug	ABERDEEN	2 - 2	Humphries, Barclay	x	x	x	x	x	x			x	x	x	x	x										
5	24-Aug	HEARTS	0 - 2		x	x	x	x	x	x				x	x	x	x	x									
6	28-Aug	Queens Park	1 - 1	Gibson	x	x	x	x		x		x		x	x	x	x	x									
7	31-Aug	HIBERNIAN	2 - 1	Humphries, Brown	x	x	x	x		x			x		x	x	x		x	x							
8	04-Sep	Falkirk	2 - 5	Gibson, Kilmarnock	x	x	x	x		x			x		x	x	x		x	x							
9	07-Sep	HAMILTON ACADEMICAL	4 - 0	Brown (2), Robertson (2)	x	x	x	x	x	x			x		x	x				x	x						
10	14-Sep	Clyde	1 - 3	OG	x	x	x	x	x	x			x		x	x				x	x						
11	02-Nov	ST MIRREN	4 - 2	Brown (2), Watson, Bremner	x	x	x	x	x	x			x	x	x		x			x							
12	09-Nov	Partick Thistle	2 - 0	Kilmarnock, Bremner	x	x	x	x	x			x	x	x	x		x			x							
13	16-Nov	KILMARNOCK	2 - 1	Brown (2)	x	x	x	x	x			x	x	x	x		x			x							
14	23-Nov	CELTIC	1 - 2	Brown	x	x	x	x	x			x	x	x	x		x			x							
15	30-Nov	Third Lanark	1 - 2	Bremner	x	x	x	x	x			x	x	x	x		x			x							
16	07-Dec	Rangers	1 - 2	Bremner	x	x	x	x	x			x	x	x	x		x			x							
17	14-Dec	MORTON	0 - 1		x	x	x	x	x			x	x	x	x		x			x							
18	21-Dec	Aberdeen	1 - 3	Johnstone	x	x	x	x	x			x		x			x			x				x	x		
19	28-Dec	QUEENS PARK	1 - 0	Bremner	x	x	x	x	x			x		x			x			x				x		x	
20	01-Jan	Hamilton Academical	2 - 2	Leitch, OG	x	x	x	x	x			x		x	x		x			x						x	
21	02-Jan	QUEEN OF THE SOUTH	5 - 1	Bremner (2), Barclay (2), Leitch	x	x	x	x	x			x		x	x		x			x						x	
22	04-Jan	CLYDE	3 - 3	Barclay, Leitch, Johnstone	x	x	x	x	x			x		x	x		x			x						x	
23	11-Jan	Hearts	1 - 2	Bremner	x	x	x	x	x			x	x	x	x		x			x							
24	18-Jan	FALKIRK	2 - 0	Barclay, Brown	x	x	x	x	x			x	x	x	x		x			x							
25	01-Feb	Hibernian	2 - 1	Redpath, Robertson	x	x	x	x	x			x	x		x		x			x	x						
26	22-Mar	Kilmarnock	0 - 2		x	x	x	x	x			x	x		x		x			x	x						
27	19-Apr	THIRD LANARK	2 - 1	McRoberts, Bremner	x	x	x	x	x			x		x	x		x			x							x
28	21-Apr	St. Mirren	2 - 1	Johnstone, Watson	x	x	x	x	x			x		x	x		x			x							x
29	26-Apr	PARTICK THISTLE	3 - 3	McRoberts, Kilmarnock, Redpath	x	x	x	x	x			x		x	x		x			x							x
30	03-May	Celtic	2 - 3	Watson, Humphries	x	x	x	x	x			x		x	x		x			x							x

LEAGUE CUP

Date	Opponent	Score	Scorers	Johnman John	Kilmarnock	Shaw	McLeod	Paton	Russell	Henderson	Redpath	Brown	Bremner	Barclay	Gibson	Humphries	Irving	Kerr	Watson	Robertson	Buchanan	Slavin	Johnstone Joe	Reid Joe	Leitch	Mc Roberts
21-Sep	QUEEN OF THE SOUTH	0 - 1		x	x	x		x	x		x	x		x	x				x	x						
28-Sep	Falkirk	1 - 1	Watson	x	x	x	x	x	x			x		x		x			x	x						
05-Oct	Aberdeen	3 - 2	Robertson (2), Brown	x	x	x	x	x	x			x		x		x			x	x						
12-Oct	Queen of the South	3 - 4	OG, Brown, Humphries	x	x	x	x	x	x			x		x		x			x	x						
19-Oct	FALKIRK	5 - 3	Brown (2), Humphries (2), Slaven	x	x		x	x	x			x	x	x		x					x	x				
26-Oct	ABERDEEN	3 - 0	Brown (2), Kilmarnock	x	x	x	x	x	x			x	x	x		x			x							

SCOTTISH CUP

Round	Date	Opponent	Score	Scorers	Att.	Johnman John	Kilmarnock	Shaw	McLeod	Paton	Russell	Henderson	Redpath	Brown	Bremner	Barclay	Gibson	Humphries	Irving	Kerr	Watson	Robertson	Buchanan	Slavin	Johnstone Joe	Reid Joe	Leitch	Mc Roberts
	25-Jan	FORFAR	3 - 0	Humphries, Johnstone, Brown	6000	x	x	x	x	x			x	x	x			x			x				x			
	22-Feb	Falkirk	0 - 0		15000	x	x	x	x	x			x	x	x	x		x			x							
	08-Mar	FALKIRK	1 - 0	Watson	23000	x	x	x	x	x			x	x	x	x		x			x							
	15-Mar	East Fife	2 - 0	Brown, Shaw	14500	x	x	x	x	x			x	x	x	x		x			x							
S/F	29-Mar	HIBERNIAN	1 - 2	Kilmarnock	48000	x	x	x	x	x			x	x	x	x		x			x							

1947 'A' Division

		Pl.	Home W.	D.	L.	F.	A.	Away W.	D.	L.	F.	A.	F. (Total)	A.	Pts.
1	Rangers	30	12	1	2	42	13	9	3	3	34	13	76	26	46
2	Hibernian	30	9	4	2	40	14	10	2	3	29	19	69	33	44
3	Aberdeen	30	11	3	1	32	17	5	4	6	26	24	58	41	39
4	Heart of Mid.	30	8	3	4	30	24	8	3	4	22	19	52	43	38
5	Partick Thistle	30	10	0	5	40	20	6	3	6	34	39	74	59	35
6	Morton	30	7	4	4	33	21	5	6	4	25	24	58	45	34
7	Celtic	30	8	2	5	30	27	5	4	6	23	28	53	55	32
8	MOTHERWELL	30	8	3	4	33	23	4	2	9	25	31	58	54	29
9	Third Lanark	30	7	3	5	33	29	4	3	8	23	35	56	64	28
10	Clyde	30	4	5	6	27	33	5	4	6	28	32	55	65	27
11	Falkirk	30	5	4	6	39	33	3	6	6	23	28	62	61	26
12	Queen of the S.	30	4	4	7	23	33	5	4	6	21	36	44	69	26
13	Queen's Park	30	3	5	7	18	25	5	1	9	29	35	47	60	22
14	St. Mirren	30	6	2	7	21	24	3	2	10	26	41	47	65	22
15	Kilmarnock	30	4	4	7	22	30	2	5	8	22	36	44	66	21
16	Hamilton Acad.	30	1	6	8	22	40	1	1	13	16	45	38	85	11

1947-48: "A" Division

No.	Date	Opponent	Score	Scorers	Att.	Johnston John	Kilmarnock	Shaw	McLeod	Paton A	Redpath	Russell	Humphries	Watters	Watters	Brenner G H	Barclay	Johnston Joe	Sinclair	Paton W J	Reid	Kerr	Mathie	McRoberts	Anderson	Robertson	Porteous
1	13-Aug	Queens Park	5 - 2	Humphries (3), Watters, Kilmarnock		x	x	x	x	x	x		x	x	x	x	x										
2	27-Aug	HEARTS	3 - 1	Humphries (2), Watters		x	x	x	x	x	x		x	x	x	x	x										
3	20-Sep	Aidrie	5 - 1	Humphries (3), Watters (2)		x	x	x	x	x	x		x	x	x	x	x										
4	27-Sep	Celtic	1 - 0	Humphries		x	x	x	x	x	x		x	x	x	x	x										
5	04-Oct	Queen of the South	0 - 3			x	x	x	x	x	x		x	x		x	x				x						
6	11-Oct	THIRD LANARK	2 - 1	Humphries, Watters		x	x	x	x	x	x		x	x	x	x		x									
7	18-Oct	Morton	3 - 2	Johnstone (3)		x	x	x	x	x	x		x	x	x	x		x									
8	25-Oct	CLYDE	4 - 1	Humphries (3), Johnstone		x	x	x	x	x	x		x	x	x	x		x									
9	01-Nov	HIBERNIAN	0 - 2		14000	x	x	x	x	x	x		x	x	x	x		x									
10	08-Nov	Partick Thistle	1 - 2	Watson	20000	x	x	x	x	x		x	x	x	x	x		x									
11	15-Nov	Third Lanark	3 - 0	Humphries (2), Watson		x	x	x	x		x		x	x	x	x		x				x					
12	22-Nov	DUNDEE	0 - 2			x	x	x	x		x		x	x	x	x		x				x					
13	06-Dec	St. Mirren	2 - 4	Watson, Watters		x	x	x	x	x	x		x	x	x	x		x									
14	13-Dec	FALKIRK	0 - 0			x	x	x	x	x	x		x	x	x			x			x						
15	20-Dec	QUEENS PARK	0 - 2			x	x	x	x	x	x		x	x	x			x			x						
16	27-Dec	Hearts	1 - 0	Watson		x	x	x	x	x	x		x	x	x				x		x						
17	01-Jan	AIRDRIE	2 - 0	Humphries, Sneddon		x	x		x	x	x		x	x	x	x	x		x								
18	03-Jan	Aberdeen	1 - 2	Watson		x	x		x	x	x		x	x	x	x	x				x						
19	10-Jan	QUEEN OF THE SOUTH	3 - 1	Humphries, Redpath, Watson		x	x		x	x	x		x		x	x	x		x					x			
20	17-Jan	Rangers	0 - 2			x	x	x	x	x	x		x	x		x	x		x								
21	14-Feb	Clyde	2 - 3	Bremner, Humphries		x	x	x	x	x	x		x	x		x	x									x	
22	28-Feb	PARTICK THISTLE	2 - 0	Paton, Humphries		x	x	x		x	x	x	x	x		x	x			x							
23	13-Mar	Dundee	0 - 2			x	x	x	x	x	x		x	x		x	x			x							
24	20-Mar	CELTIC	0 - 3			x	x	x	x	x	x		x	x		x	x			x							
25	27-Mar	ST MIRREN	0 - 1			x	x	x	x	x	x		x	x		x	x			x							
26	03-Apr	Falkirk	2 - 2	Robertson, McRoberts		x	x	x	x	x	x		x	x		x	x			x							
27	09-Apr	MORTON	0 - 1			x	x	x	x	x	x			x		x	x			x							x
28	17-Apr	ABERDEEN	2 - 1	Watters, Kilmarnock		x	x	x	x	x	x		x	x		x		x					x				
29	19-Apr	Hibernian	0 - 5			x	x	x	x	x	x		x	x		x	x			x							
30	24-Apr	Rangers	1 - 1	Humphries		x		x	x	x		x	x	x		x	x		x						x		

LEAGUE CUP

	Date	Opponent	Score	Scorers	Att.	Johnston John	Kilmarnock	Shaw	McLeod	Paton A	Redpath	Russell	Humphries	Watters	Watters	Brenner G H	Barclay	Johnston Joe	Sinclair	Paton W J	Reid	Kerr	Mathie	McRoberts	Anderson	Robertson	Porteous
	09-Aug	QUEEN OF THE SOUTH	4 - 0	Humphries (2), Redpath, Bremner		x	x	x	x	x	x		x	x	x	x	x										
	16-Aug	Aberdeen	0 - 2			x	x	x	x	x	x		x	x	x	x	x										
	23-Aug	ST MIRREN	3 - 1	Bremner, Watters, Humphries		x	x	x	x	x	x		x	x	x	x	x										
	30-Aug	Queen of the South	1 - 0	Watson		x	x	x	x	x	x		x	x	x	x	x										
	06-Sep	ABERDEEN	2 - 0	Kilmarnock, Bremner		x	x	x	x	x	x		x	x	x	x	x										
	13-Sep	St. Mirren	3 - 0	Humphries (2), McLeod		x	x	x	x	x	x		x	x	x	x	x										

SCOTTISH CUP

	Date	Opponent	Score	Scorers	Att.	Johnston John	Kilmarnock	Shaw	McLeod	Paton A	Redpath	Russell	Humphries	Watters	Watters	Brenner G H	Barclay	Johnston Joe	Sinclair	Paton W J	Reid	Kerr	Mathie	McRoberts	Anderson	Robertson	Porteous
aet	24-Jan	HAMILTON ACADEMICAL	2 - 2	Humphries (2)	21000	x	x	x	x	x	x		x	x	x	x	x										
	31-Jan	Hamilton Academical	2 - 0	Reid, Barclay	22000	x	x	x	x	x	x		x	x	x		x				x						
	07-Feb	THIRD LANARK	1 - 0	Humphries	12059	x	x	x	x	x	x		x	x		x	x				x						
	21-Feb	Celtic	0 - 1		55231	x	x	x	x	x	x		x	x		x	x									x	

FRIENDLIES

	Date	Opponent	Score	Scorers	
	29-Nov	Celtic	1 - 3	Watson	
	06-Mar	Bolton Wands.	4 - 3	Bremner, Watters, Shaw, Wm Paton	

1948 'A' Division

		Pl.	Home W.	D.	L.	F.	A.	Away W.	D.	L.	F.	A.	F. (Total)	A.	Pts.
1	Hibernian	30	13	2	0	52	6	9	2	4	34	21	86	27	48
2	Rangers	30	10	2	3	33	17	11	2	2	31	11	64	28	46
3	Partick Thistle	30	7	3	5	39	24	9	1	5	22	18	61	42	36
4	Dundee	30	10	2	3	43	18	5	1	9	24	33	67	51	33
5	St. Mirren	30	9	2	4	31	20	4	3	8	23	38	54	58	31
6	Clyde	30	8	3	4	34	27	4	4	7	18	30	52	57	31
7	Falkirk	30	6	5	4	31	21	4	5	6	24	27	55	48	30
8	MOTHERWELL	30	7	2	6	19	17	6	1	8	26	30	45	47	29
9	Heart of Mid.	30	7	3	5	21	18	3	5	7	16	24	37	42	28
10	Aberdeen	30	8	4	3	33	16	2	3	10	12	29	45	45	27
11	Third Lanark	30	8	1	6	33	29	2	5	8	23	44	56	73	26
12	Celtic	30	5	4	6	21	25	5	1	9	20	31	41	56	25
13	Queen of the S.	30	7	3	5	33	27	3	2	10	16	47	49	74	25
14	Morton	30	3	4	8	18	19	6	2	7	29	24	47	43	24
15	Airdrieonians	30	7	1	7	26	32	0	6	9	14	46	40	78	21
16	Queen's Park	30	5	2	8	29	32	4	0	11	16	43	45	75	20

1947-48 Season
Back : Kilmarnock, McLeod, Johnson, Paton, Redpath, Higgins
Front : Humphries, Forrest, Kelly, Watson, Joe Johnson

1948-49 Season
Back: Redpath, Bremner, Paton, Johnston, Shaw, Kilmarnock
Front: McLeod, Watson, Mathie, Humphries, Barclay

1948-49: "A" Division

No.	Date	Opponent	Score	Scorers	Att.	Johnston John	Kilmarnock	Shaw	McLeod	Paton A	Redpath	Russell	Goodall	Watson	Humphries	Mathie	Brenner G H	McCall	Aitkenhead	Johnston Joe	Barclay	Sinclair	Robertson	Paton W J	Watters
1	14-Aug	RANGERS	1 - 1	Mathie		x	x	x	x	x	x			x	x	x	x				x				
2	18-Aug	East Fife	1 - 0	Mathie		x	x	x	x	x	x			x	x	x	x				x				
3	21-Aug	ALBION ROVERS	5 - 1	Watson (3), Kilmarnock, Redpath		x	x	x	x	x	x			x	x	x	x				x				
4	28-Aug	Aberdeen	0 - 2			x	x	x	x	x	x			x	x	x	x				x				
5	01-Sep	HEARTS	3 - 0	Bremner, Mathie, Watson		x	x	x	x	x	x			x		x	x				x			x	
6	04-Sep	Queen of the South	1 - 2	Bremner		x	x	x	x	x	x	x		x		x	x			x					
7	23-Oct	St. Mirren	0 - 0			x	x	x	x	x	x		x	x	x		x			x					
8	30-Oct	FALKIRK	0 - 3			x	x	x	x	x	x		x	x	x		x			x					
9	06-Nov	Morton	1 - 1	Mathie		x	x		x	x		x		x	x	x	x			x		x			
10	13-Nov	CLYDE	2 - 3	Bremner (2)		x	x	x	x	x	x		x	x		x	x			x					
11	20-Nov	HIBERNIAN	5 - 1	Johnstone, Mathie, Goodall, Watson (2)		x	x	x	x	x		x	x	x		x	x			x					
12	27-Nov	Partick Thistle	1 - 1	Mathie		x	x	x	x	x	x		x	x		x				x	x				
13	04-Dec	Third Lanark	3 - 1	Watson, Mathie, Bremner		x	x	x	x	x	x		x	x		x	x			x					
14	11-Dec	DUNDEE	0 - 2			x	x	x		x	x	x	x			x	x			x					x
15	18-Dec	Celtic	2 - 3	Mathie, Bremner		x	x	x		x	x	x	x	x		x	x				x				
16	25-Dec	EAST FIFE	1 - 2	Mathie		x	x	x		x	x	x	x	x		x	x			x					
17	01-Jan	Albion Rovers	3 - 1	Aitkenhead (2), McCall		x	x	x		x	x	x	x	x		x	x						x		
p 30/4	03-Jan	ABERDEEN	1 - 1	Watson		x	x			x	x	x		x	x	x		x				x	x		
19	08-Jan	Rangers	0 - 2			x	x	x		x	x	x		x		x	x	x				x			
20	15-Jan	QUEEN OF THE SOUTH	2 - 3	Russell, Aitkenhead		x	x	x			x	x		x		x	x	x	x			x			
21	29-Jan	Hearts	1 - 5	Mathie		x	x	x		x	x	x		x		x	x	x				x			
p 9/4	05-Feb	ST MIRREN	4 - 1	Mathie, Bremner, McCall, Goodall		x	x	x		x	x	x	x	x		x	x	x							
23	12-Feb	Falkirk	0 - 3			x	x	x		x	x	x		x	x	x	x	x							
p 23/4	19-Feb	MORTON	1 - 0	McCall		x	x	x	x	x		x		x	x	x		x					x		
25	26-Feb	Clyde	0 - 1			x	x	x		x	x	x		x	x	x		x					x		
p 16/4	05-Mar	Hibernian	1 - 5	Mathie		x	x	x		x	x	x	x	x		x	x	x							
27	12-Mar	PARTICK THISTLE	3 - 1	Bremner (2), McCall		x	x	x		x	x	x	x	x		x	x	x							
28	19-Mar	THIRD LANARK	1 - 0	Goodall		x	x	x		x	x	x	x	x		x	x	x							
p 27/4	26-Mar	Dundee	1 - 2	Mathie		x	x	x		x	x	x	x	x		x	x	x							
30	02-Apr	CELTIC	0 - 1			x	x	x	x	x		x	x	x			x	x	x						

LEAGUE CUP

No.	Date	Opponent	Score	Scorers	Att.	Johnston John	Kilmarnock	Shaw	McLeod	Paton A	Redpath	Russell	Goodall	Watson	Humphries	Mathie	Brenner G H	McCall	Aitkenhead	Johnston Joe	Barclay	Sinclair	Robertson	Paton W J	Watters
	11-Sep	FALKIRK	1 - 0	Watson		x	x	x	x	x	x			x	x	x	x				x				
	18-Sep	Albion Rovers	1 - 0	Watson		x	x	x	x	x	x	x		x		x	x				x				
	25-Sep	DUNDEE	0 - 1			x	x	x	x	x	x	x		x		x	x			x					
	02-Oct	Falkirk	0 - 1			x	x	x	x	x	x		x	x		x	x			x					
	09-Oct	ALBION ROVERS	8 - 3	Humphries (4), Watson (2), Redpath, Johnstone		x	x	x	x	x	x		x	x	x		x			x					
	16-Oct	Dundee	1 - 0	Mathie		x	x	x	x	x	x		x	x		x	x			x					

SCOTTISH CUP

No.	Date	Opponent	Score	Scorers	Att.	Johnston John	Kilmarnock	Shaw	McLeod	Paton A	Redpath	Russell	Goodall	Watson	Humphries	Mathie	Brenner G H	McCall	Aitkenhead	Johnston Joe	Barclay	Sinclair	Robertson	Paton W J	Watters
	22-Jan	STRANRAER	3 - 0	Humphries, Watson, Goodall	9800	x	x	x		x	x	x	x	x	x	x	x								
	05-Feb	RANGERS	0 - 3		31000	x	x	x		x	x	x	x	x		x		x	x						

LANARKSHIRE CUP

	Date	Opponent	Score
	02-May	AIRDRIE	1 - 2
	06-May	Aidrie	0 - 0

FRIENDLIES

	Date	Opponent	Score
	05-Mar	Arbroath	4 - 2

1949 'A' Division

		Pl.	Home W.	D.	L.	F.	A.	Away W.	D.	L.	F.	A.	F. (Total)	A.	Pts.
1	Rangers	30	11	3	1	39	18	9	3	3	24	14	63	32	46
2	Dundee	30	13	1	1	41	20	7	4	4	30	28	71	48	45
3	Hibernian	30	9	3	3	37	20	8	2	5	38	32	75	52	39
4	East Fife	30	9	1	5	38	19	7	2	6	26	27	64	46	35
5	Falkirk	30	9	3	3	44	23	3	5	7	26	31	70	54	32
6	Celtic	30	7	3	5	26	17	5	4	6	22	23	48	40	31
7	Third Lanark	30	9	2	4	33	22	4	3	8	23	30	56	52	31
8	Heart of Mid.	30	8	2	5	37	22	4	4	7	27	32	64	54	30
9	St. Mirren	30	9	3	3	30	16	4	1	10	21	31	51	47	30
10	Queen of the S.	30	8	3	4	28	19	3	5	7	19	34	47	53	30
11	Partick Thistle	30	4	8	3	25	24	5	1	9	25	39	50	63	27
12	MOTHERWELL	30	7	2	6	29	20	3	3	9	15	29	44	49	25
13	Aberdeen	30	5	4	6	26	26	2	7	6	13	22	39	48	25
14	Clyde	30	5	4	6	27	30	4	2	9	23	37	50	67	24
15	Morton	30	4	6	5	21	22	3	2	10	18	29	39	51	22
16	Albion Rovers	30	3	1	11	18	44	0	1	14	12	61	30	105	8

1949-50: "A" Division

No	Date	Opponent	Score	Scorers	Att	Hamilton	Kilmarnock	Shaw	Higgins	McLeod	Paton A	Aitkenhead John	Redpath	Watters	Watson	Humphries	Kelly	Brenner G H	McCall	Robertson	Telford	Paton W J	Russell	Forrest	Mathie	Johnston John	Hunter	Anderson
1	10-Sep	FALKIRK	2 - 2	Robertson, Aitkenhead			x		x		x	x	x	x	x					x			x		x	x		
2	17-Sep	Third Lanark	3 - 3	McCall (2), Watters			x		x		x	x	x	x	x				x	x	x					x		
3	24-Sep	ST MIRREN	2 - 2	Watters, Aitkenhead		x	x	x			x	x	x	x	x					x	x		x					
4	01-Oct	Dundee	1 - 3	Redpath		x	x	x			x	x	x	x	x				x	x	x							
5	08-Oct	CELTIC	1 - 2	Watters		x	x		x		x	x	x	x	x				x			x			x			
6	15-Oct	Partick Thistle	2 - 0	McCall, Humphries		x	x		x		x	x	x	x	x	x				x		x						
7	22-Oct	RAITH ROVERS	1 - 1	Aitkenhead		x	x		x		x	x	x	x	x	x				x		x						
8	29-Oct	Queen of the South	0 - 2			x	x		x		x	x	x	x	x	x				x								x
9	05-Nov	East Fife	1 - 2	Aitkenhead		x	x	x			x	x	x	x	x	x		x	x									
10	12-Nov	HIBERNIAN	1 - 3	Humphries		x	x	x			x	x	x	x	x	x		x	x									
11	19-Nov	CLYDE	5 - 2	Humphries (2), Kelly, Watson, Aitkenhead		x	x	x			x	x	x	x	x	x	x		x									
12	26-Nov	Hearts	0 - 2			x	x				x	x	x	x	x	x	x	x	x									
13	03-Dec	STIRLING ALB	2 - 1	Aitkenhead, Watson		x	x	x		x	x	x		x	x		x	x	x									
14	10-Dec	RANGERS	4 - 0	Kelly (2), McCall, Watson	29000	x	x		x	x	x	x	x		x		x	x	x									
15	17-Dec	Aberdeen	0 - 5			x	x		x	x	x	x	x		x		x	x	x									
16	24-Dec	Falkirk	4 - 2	Kelly (3), McCall		x	x		x	x	x	x	x		x		x	x	x									
17	31-Dec	THIRD LANARK	4 - 0	Bremner, McCall (2), Watson		x	x		x	x	x	x	x		x		x	x	x									
18	02-Jan	St. Mirren	1 - 1			x	x		x	x	x	x	x		x		x	x	x									
19	03-Jan	DUNDEE	0 - 2			x	x		x	x	x	x	x		x		x	x	x									
20	07-Jan	Celtic	1 - 3			x	x		x	x	x	x	x		x		x	x	x									
21	14-Jan	PARTICK THISTLE	0 - 2			x	x		x	x	x	x	x		x		x	x	x									
22	21-Jan	Raith Rovers	2 - 0	Watson (2)		x	x		x	x	x	x	x		x		x	x	x									
23	04-Feb	QUEEN OF THE SOUTH	1 - 0	Kelly		x	x	x	x	x	x	x	x	x	x		x											
p 17/4	11-Feb	EAST FIFE	3 - 4	Aitkenhead (2), Kelly		x	x	x		x	x	x	x	x			x	x						x				
25	18-Feb	Hibernian	1 - 6			x	x	x		x	x	x	x		x		x	x						x				
26	25-Feb	Clyde	0 - 1			x	x	x		x	x	x			x		x		x		x	x						
27	04-Mar	HEARTS	2 - 3	Kelly, Bremner		x	x	x		x	x	x			x		x	x			x						x	
P 8/4	11-Mar	Stirling Albion	4 - 1			x	x	x		x	x	x	x	x			x	x						x			x	
29	18-Mar	Rangers	0 - 2			x	x	x		x	x	x	x	x			x	x						x				
30	25-Mar	ABERDEEN	5 - 1	Watters, Kelly (3), Aitkenhead		x	x	x		x	x	x	x	x			x	x						x				

LEAGUE CUP

No	Date	Opponent	Score	Scorers	Att	Hamilton	Kilmarnock	Shaw	Higgins	McLeod	Paton A	Aitkenhead John	Redpath	Watters	Watson	Humphries	Kelly	Brenner G H	McCall	Robertson	Telford	Paton W J	Russell	Forrest	Mathie	Johnston John	Hunter	Anderson
	13-Aug	Partick Thistle	0 - 2				x		x		x	x	x	x	x					x			x		x	x		
	17-Aug	DUNDEE	2 - 0	Aitkenhead, Kelly			x		x		x	x	x	x	x		x			x	x					x		
	20-Aug	Clyde	2 - 2	Bremner, Watson			x		x		x	x	x	x	x			x		x					x	x		
	27-Aug	PARTICK THISTLE	1 - 1	Aitkenhead			x		x		x	x	x	x	x					x			x		x	x		
	31-Aug	Dundee	1 - 0	Kelly			x		x		x	x	x	x	x		x			x					x	x		
	03-Sep	CLYDE	1 - 1	Watters			x		x		x	x	x	x	x					x			x		x	x		

SCOTTISH CUP

No	Date	Opponent	Score	Scorers	Att	Hamilton	Kilmarnock	Shaw	Higgins	McLeod	Paton A	Aitkenhead John	Redpath	Watters	Watson	Humphries	Kelly	Brenner G H	McCall	Robertson	Telford	Paton W J	Russell	Forrest	Mathie	Johnston John	Hunter	Anderson
	28-Jan	RANGERS	2 - 4	Aitkenhead, Kelly	32000	x	x		x	x	x	x	x		x		x	x	x									

LANARKSHIRE CUP

		Opponent	Score
		Aidrie	2 - 2
		AIRDRIE	6 - 3
		ALBION ROVERS	4 - 0

FRIENDLIES

	Date	Opponent	Score
	11-Feb	Sunderland	1 - 1
	01-Apr	Hearts	0 - 4
	19-Apr	Morton	1 - 2
	26-Apr	Kilbirnie Sel	2 - 1

1950 'A' Division

		Pl.	Home W.	Home D.	Home L.	Home F.	Home A.	Away W.	Away D.	Away L.	Away F.	Away A.	F. (Total)	A. (Total)	Pts.
1	Rangers	30	11	4	0	32	12	11	2	2	26	14	58	26	50
2	Hibernian	30	13	0	2	50	15	9	5	1	36	19	86	34	49
3	Heart of Mid.	30	12	1	2	55	16	8	2	5	31	24	86	40	43
4	East Fife	30	8	3	4	31	18	7	4	4	27	25	58	43	37
5	Celtic	30	11	4	0	37	17	3	3	9	14	33	51	50	35
6	Dundee	30	10	1	4	29	15	2	6	7	20	31	49	46	31
7	Partick Thistle	30	8	1	6	30	20	5	2	8	25	25	55	45	29
8	Aberdeen	30	7	2	6	33	25	4	2	9	15	31	48	56	26
9	Raith Rovers	30	7	3	5	34	29	2	5	8	11	25	45	54	26
10	MOTHERWELL	30	6	3	6	33	25	4	2	9	20	33	53	58	25
11	St. Mirren	30	6	4	5	26	15	2	5	8	16	34	42	49	25
12	Third Lanark	30	7	2	6	26	28	4	1	10	18	34	44	62	25
13	Clyde	30	6	3	6	26	19	4	1	10	30	54	56	73	24
14	Falkirk	30	3	7	5	24	29	4	3	8	24	43	48	72	24
15	Queen of the S.	30	5	5	5	22	25	0	1	14	9	38	31	63	16
16	Stirling Albion	30	4	2	9	20	32	2	1	12	18	45	38	77	15

1949-50 Season

Back: Kilmarnock, McLeod, Hamilton, Paton, Redpath, Shaw
Front : Watters, Forrest, Kelly, Watson, Aitkenhead

1950-51 Season

Back : J Collins, A Hepburn, T Baird, J Kerr, M Muirhead
Middle : J Marshall, W Walker, Kilmarnock, McLeod, Johnston, Shaw, Redpath, B Ellis, J Hunter
Front : G Stevenson, Watters, Forrest, Paton, Kelly, Watson, Aitkenhead, A McNay

1950-51: "A" Division

						Johnston John	Hamilton	Kilmarnock	Shaw	McLeod	Paton	Redpath	Forrest	Humphries	Kelly	Watson	Aitkenhead John	Aitkenhead Jack	Hunter	Aitken	Muir	Higgins	Cumming	Brenner	Johnston Joe	Watters	Sneddon	Cleland
1	09-Sep	Third Lanark	0 - 2				x	x	x	x	x	x	x			x		x							x	x		
p 11/4	16-Sep	PARTICK THISTLE	4 - 1				x	x	x	x	x	x	x			x		x							x	x		
3	23-Sep	Aidrie	3 - 2	Hunter, Kelly, Forrset		x		x	x	x	x	x	x		x	x									x		x	
4	30-Sep	EAST FIFE	4 - 2	Watson, Kelly, Forrest, Aitkenhead			x	x	x	x	x	x	x		x	x	x		x									
p 25/4	07-Oct	Celtic	1 - 3	Forrest		x		x		x		x	x			x		x	x	x		x			x			
6	14-Oct	HIBERNIAN	2 - 6	Forrest, Aitkenhead	25000		x	x	x	x	x	x	x		x	x	x		x									
7	21-Oct	Falkirk	4 - 0	Kelly (2), Aitkenhead, Watters		x		x	x	x	x	x	x		x	x	x									x		
p 1/11	28-Oct	Morton	0 - 5			x		x		x	x	x	x			x		x	x				x		x			
9	04-Nov	ST MIRREN	4 - 0	Aitkenhead (2), Kelly (2)		x		x	x	x	x	x	x		x	x	x									x		
10	11-Nov	Dundee	0 - 0			x		x	x	x	x	x	x		x	x	x									x		
11	19-Nov	Hearts	3 - 3	Forrest (2), Watters		x		x	x	x	x	x	x		x	x	x									x		
12	25-Nov	CLYDE	1 - 1	Watters		x		x	x	x	x	x	x		x	x	x									x		
13	02-Dec	Raith Rovers	4 - 3	Kelly (2), Watson, Forrest		x		x	x	x	x	x	x	x		x	x									x		
14	09-Dec	Aberdeen	2 - 4	Humphries, Johnston Joe		x		x	x	x	x	x	x	x		x	x								x			
p 7/3	16-Dec	RANGERS	2 - 3	Forrest, Humphries		x		x		x		x	x	x	x	x				x	x			x				
16	23-Dec	THIRD LANARK	4 - 1	Forrest (2), Watters, Kelly		x		x	x	x	x	x	x		x	x	x									x		
p 14/4	30-Dec	Partick Thistle	1 - 1	Kelly		x		x		x		x	x		x	x		x		x					x			x
18	02-Jan	AIRDRIE	1 - 2	Aitkenhead		x		x	x	x	x	x	x		x	x	x									x		
p 8/5	02-Jan	East Fife	2 - 3	Forrest, Sneddon		x		x		x		x	x	x		x						x	x		x		x	
20	06-Jan	CELTIC	2 - 1	Watson, Forrest		x		x	x	x	x	x	x		x	x	x									x		
21	13-Jan	Hibernian	1 - 3	Forrest	15000		x	x	x	x	x	x	x		x	x	x									x		
22	20-Jan	Falkirk	4 - 2	Forrest (2), Kelly, Watson			x	x	x	x	x	x	x		x	x	x									x		
23	03-Feb	MORTON	1 - 1	Redpath		x		x	x	x	x	x	x		x	x	x						x					
p 17/4	10-Feb	St. Mirren	0 - 3			x		x	x	x	x		A		x	x			x			x			x			
25	17-Feb	DUNDEE	0 - 2				x	x	x	x	x	x	x		x	x	x									x		
p 5/5	24-Feb	HEARTS	2 - 4	Humphries, Forrest		x		x	x	x	x		x	x	x	x					x				x			
27	03-Mar	Clyde	2 - 1	Kelly, Watson		x		x	x	x	x	x	x	x	x	x	x											
p 2/5	10-Mar	RAITH ROVERS	3 - 2	Watson, Aitkenhead, Humphries		x		x	x	x	x	x	x	x	x	x	x											
29	17-Mar	ABERDEEN	1 - 1	Redpath		x		x	x	x	x	x	x	x	x	x	x											
30	24-Mar	Rangers	0 - 3			x		x	x		x	x		x	x				x	x		x				x		

LEAGUE CUP

						Johnston John	Hamilton	Kilmarnock	Shaw	McLeod	Paton	Redpath	Forrest	Humphries	Kelly	Watson	Aitkenhead John	Aitkenhead Jack	Hunter	Aitken	Muir	Higgins	Cumming	Brenner	Johnston Joe	Watters	Sneddon	Cleland
	12-Aug	AIRDRIE	3 - 1	Watson, Aitkenhead, Forrest			x	x	x	x	x	x	x	x	x	x	x											
	16-Aug	Hearts	1 - 4	Kelly		x		x	x	x	x	x	x		x	x	x									x		
	19-Aug	PARTICK THISTLE	2 - 1	Forrest, Kelly		x		x	x	x	x	x	x	x	x	x	x											
	26-Aug	Aidrie	6 - 2	Forrest (3), Watson, Humphries, Kelly		x		x	x	x	x	x	x	x	x	x	x											
	30-Aug	HEARTS	3 - 2	Kelly (2), Aitkenhead		x		x	x	x	x	x	x		x	x	x									x		
	02-Sep	Partick Thistle	3 - 2	Forrest (2), Kelly	22000	x		x	x	x	x	x	x		x	x	x									x		
	16-Sep	Celtic	4 - 1	Watson, Forrest, Hunter, OG		x		x	x	x	x	x	x		x	x	x									x		
	20-Sep	CELTIC	0 - 1			x		x	x	x	x	x	x		x	x	x									x		
S/F	07-Oct	AYR UNITED	4 - 3	Watson (2), Aitkenhead (2)			x	x	x	x	x	x	x		x	x	x		x									
F	28-Oct	HIBERNIAN	3 - 0	Kelly, Forrest, Watters	64000	x	x	x	x	x	x	x	x		x	x	x									x		

SCOTTISH CUP

						Johnston John	Hamilton	Kilmarnock	Shaw	McLeod	Paton	Redpath	Forrest	Humphries	Kelly	Watson	Aitkenhead John	Aitkenhead Jack	Hunter	Aitken	Muir	Higgins	Cumming	Brenner	Johnston Joe	Watters	Sneddon	Cleland
	27-Jan	Peterhead	4 - 0	Forrest (2), Watson, Aitkenhead	5200		x	x	x	x	x	x	x		x	x	x									x		
	10-Feb	HAMILTON ACADEMICAL	4 - 1	Kelly (2), Forrest, Watters	18000		x	x	x	x	x	x	x		x	x	x									x		
	10-Mar	Ayr United	2 - 2	Watson, Forrest	22152	x		x	x	x	x	x	x		x	x	x									x		
rep.	14-Mar	AYR UNITED	2 - 1	Kelly, McLeod	26625	x		x	x	x	x	x	x		x	x	x									x		
S/F	31-Mar	HIBERNIAN	3 - 2	Kelly (2), McLeod	46000	x		x		x	x	x	x	x	x	x	x					x						
F	21-Apr	CELTIC	0 - 1		131943	x		x	x	x	x	x	x	x	x	x	x											

LANARKSHIRE CUP

	12-May	Aidrie	1 - 1
	16-May	AIRDRIE	2 - 1
	19-May	Albion Rovers	1 - 2

1951 'A' Division

		Pl.	Home					Away					F.	A.	Pts.
			W.	D.	L.	F.	A.	W.	D.	L.	F.	A.	(Total)		
1	Hibernian	30	13	1	1	44	9	9	3	3	34	17	78	26	48
2	Rangers	30	10	3	2	36	13	7	1	7	28	24	64	37	38
3	Dundee	30	11	3	1	32	12	4	5	6	15	18	47	30	38
4	Heart of Mid.	30	10	3	2	46	17	6	2	7	26	28	72	45	37
5	Aberdeen	30	9	2	4	35	21	6	3	6	26	29	61	50	35
6	Partick Thistle	30	9	4	2	30	15	4	3	8	27	33	57	48	33
7	Celtic	30	6	3	6	29	25	6	2	7	19	21	48	46	29
8	Raith Rovers	30	8	2	5	30	16	5	0	10	22	36	52	52	28
9	MOTHERWELL	30	7	3	5	35	27	4	3	8	23	38	58	65	28
10	East Fife	30	7	4	4	28	24	3	4	8	20	42	48	66	28
11	St. Mirren	30	7	3	5	22	20	2	4	9	13	31	35	51	25
12	Morton	30	6	0	9	30	29	4	4	7	17	30	47	59	24
13	Third Lanark	30	7	1	7	22	21	4	1	10	18	30	40	51	24
14	Airdrieonians	30	7	2	6	39	31	3	2	10	13	36	52	67	24
15	Clyde	30	6	4	5	19	23	2	3	10	18	34	37	57	23
16	Falkirk	30	6	3	6	24	27	1	1	13	11	54	35	81	18

1951-52: " A" Division

	Date	Opponent	Score	Scorers	Att	Johnston John	Kilmarnock	Shaw	Cox	Paton	Redpath	Sloan	Humphries	Forrest	Kelly	Aitkenhead John	Hunter	Muir	Aitkenhead Jack	Aitken	Grozier	Higgins	Hamilton	Johnston Joe	Robinson	Watson	McLeod
1	08-Sep	CELTIC	2 - 2	Kelly (2)		x	x	x		x	x		x	x	x	x										x	x
p 21/4	15-Sep	Hibernian	1 - 3	Robinson		x	x	x	x	x	x	x	x		x	x										x	
3	22-Sep	AIRDRIE	4 - 1	Watson, Kelly, Aitkenhead, Forrest		x	x	x		x	x		x	x	x	x										x	x
4	29-Sep	Partick Thistle	1 - 2	Kelly		x	x			x	x		x	x	x	x		x								x	x
5	06-Oct	QUEEN OF THE SOUTH	4 - 0	Kelly (2), Humphries, Grozier		x	x	x		x			x	x	x	x					x			x			x
p 26/4	13-Oct	East Fife	1 - 6	Aitkenhead		x	x	x	x	x	x		x	x	x	x											x
7	20-Oct	Stirling Albion	1 - 2	Forrest		x	x	x		x	x		x	x	x	x					x						x
8	27-Oct	MORTON	1 - 2	Aitkenhead		x	x			x	x		x	x	x	x		x			x						x
9	03-Nov	St. Mirren	0 - 3			x	x	x		x	x			x	x	x	x									x	x
10	10-Nov	DUNDEE	2 - 1	Watson, Aitkenhead		x	x	x		x	x			x	x	x	x									x	x
11	17-Nov	HEARTS	0 - 5			x	x	x		x	x		x	x	x				x							x	x
12	24-Nov	Third Lanark	1 - 0	Kelly		x	x			x	x		x	x	x	x						x				x	x
13	01-Dec	RAITH ROVERS	1 - 3	Aitkenhead		x	x			x	x			x	x	x	x					x				x	x
14	08-Dec	ABERDEEN	3 - 3	Kelly, Humphries		x	x			x	x		x	x	x	x										x	x
15	15-Dec	Rangers	0 - 3			x	x	x		x	x		x	x	x	x										x	x
16	22-Dec	Celtic	2 - 2	Kelly, McLeod	30000	x	x	x		x	x		x	x	x	x										x	x
17	29-Dec	HIBERNIAN	3 - 1	Aitkenhead (3)		x	x	x	x	x	x	x			x	x	x									x	
p 23/4	01-Jan	Aidrie	2 - 1	Humphries, Kelly		x	x	x	x	x	x	x	x		x	x										x	
19	02-Jan	PARTICK THISTLE	1 - 1	Aitkenhead	15000	x	x	x	x	x	x	x	x		x				x							x	
20	05-Jan	Queen of the South	1 - 4	Watson		x	x	x		x	x	x	x		x	x										x	x
21	12-Jan	EAST FIFE	2 - 1	Kelly (2)			x	x		x	x	x	x		x	x							x			x	x
22	19-Jan	STIRLING ALBION	5 - 2	Aitkenhead (2), Sloan, Humphries, Watson		x	x	x		x	x	x	x		x	x		x								x	
p 12/4	02-Feb	Morton	2 - 0	Kelly, Sloan	8000	x	x	x	x	x	x	x	x		x	x		x									
24	09-Feb	ST MIRREN	2 - 0	Aitkenhead, Kelly		x	x	x	x	x	x			x	x	x	x										x
25	16-Feb	Dundee	2 - 1	Watson, Kelly		x	x		x		x	x	x		x	x				x						x	x
p 30/4	23-Feb	Hearts	2 - 2	Kelly, Sloan		x	x	x	x	x	x	x			x	x										x	x
27	01-Mar	THIRD LANARK	1 - 1	Sloan	9000	x	x	x	x	x	x	x		x	x				x							x	
p 28/4	08-Mar	Raith Rovers	0 - 2			x	x	x	x		x		x		x					x					x	x	x
29	15-Mar	Aberdeen	2 - 2	Kelly, Sloan		x	x	x	x	x	x	x	x		x	x										x	
30	22-Mar	RANGERS	2 - 1	Watson, Sloan		x	x	x	x		x	x	x		x	x				x						x	

LEAGUE CUP

	Date	Opponent	Score	Scorers	Att	Johnston John	Kilmarnock	Shaw	Cox	Paton	Redpath	Sloan	Humphries	Forrest	Kelly	Aitkenhead John	Hunter	Muir	Aitkenhead Jack	Aitken	Grozier	Higgins	Hamilton	Johnston Joe	Robinson	Watson	McLeod
	11-Aug	STIRLING ALBION	6 - 4	Watson (2), Aitkenhead (2), Forrest, Kelly	8000	x	x	x		x	x		x	x	x	x										x	x
	15-Aug	Hibernian	4 - 0	Kelly (2), Forrest (2)	35000	x	x	x		x	x		x	x	x	x										x	x
	18-Aug	Partick Thistle	0 - 0			x	x	x		x	x		x	x	x	x										x	x
	25-Aug	Stirling Albion	2 - 3	Kelly, Humphries		x	x	x		x	x		x	x	x	x										x	x
	29-Aug	HIBERNIAN	1 - 0	Aitkenhead		x	x	x		x	x		x	x	x	x										x	x
	01-Sep	PARTICK THISTLE	3 - 2	Watson, Kelly, Forrest		x	x	x		x	x		x	x	x	x										x	x
	15-Sep	St. Johnstone	4 - 0	Watson, Forrest, Kelly, Aitkenhead		x	x	x		x	x		x	x	x	x										x	x
	19-Sep	ST. JOHNSTONE	3 - 0	Watson, Kelly, Redpath		x	x	x		x	x		x	x	x	x										x	x
S/F	13-Oct	DUNDEE	1 - 5	Watson		x	x	x		x	x		x	x	x	x										x	x

SCOTTISH CUP

	Date	Opponent	Score	Scorers	Att	Johnston John	Kilmarnock	Shaw	Cox	Paton	Redpath	Sloan	Humphries	Forrest	Kelly	Aitkenhead John	Hunter	Muir	Aitkenhead Jack	Aitken	Grozier	Higgins	Hamilton	Johnston Joe	Robinson	Watson	McLeod
	26-Jan	Forfar Athletic	4 - 2	McLeod, Watson, Sloan, Kelly	4000	x	x	x		x	x	x	x	x	x	x											x
	09-Feb	St. Mirren	3 - 2	Watson (2), Humphries	29651	x	x	x		x	x	x	x	x	x	x											x
	23-Feb	Dunfermline	1 - 1	Watson	22295	x	x	x	x	x	x	x	x		x	x										x	
	27-Feb	DUNFERMLINE	4 - 0	Humphries (2), Aitkenhead, Watson	16500	x	x		x	x	x	x	x	x	x	x										x	
	08-Mar	Rangers	1 - 1	Sloan	82000	x	x		x	x	x	x	x	x	x	x										x	
	12-Mar	RANGERS	2 - 1	Aitkenhead, Humphries	37000	x	x	x	x	x	x	x	x		x	x										x	
S/F	29-Mar	HEARTS	1 - 1	Watson	98547	x	x	x	x	x	x	x	x		x	x										x	
S/F R	07-Apr	HEARTS	1 - 1	Watson	80000	x	x	x	x	x	x	x	x		x	x										x	
S/F R2	09-Apr	HEARTS	3 - 1	Kelly, Humphries, Redpath	59468	x	x	x	x	x	x	x	x		x	x										x	
F	19-Apr	DUNDEE	4 - 0	Watson, Redpath, Kelly, Humphries	136274	x	x	x	x	x	x	x	x		x	x										x	

1952 'A' Division

		Pl.	Home					Away					F.	A.	Pts.
			W.	D.	L.	F.	A.	W.	D.	L.	F.	A.	(Total)		
1	Hibernian	30	12	2	1	58	15	8	3	4	34	21	92	36	45
2	Rangers	30	10	4	1	32	13	6	5	4	29	18	61	31	41
3	East Fife	30	11	2	2	44	19	6	1	8	27	30	71	49	37
4	Heart of Mid.	30	9	5	1	44	25	5	2	8	25	28	69	53	35
5	Raith Rovers	30	9	2	4	23	14	5	3	7	20	28	43	42	33
6	Partick Thistle	30	7	3	5	28	24	5	4	6	20	27	48	51	31
7	MOTHERWELL	30	8	4	3	33	24	4	3	8	18	33	51	57	31
8	Dundee	30	7	3	5	31	22	4	3	8	22	30	53	52	28
9	Celtic	30	7	5	3	30	22	3	3	9	22	33	52	55	28
10	Queen of the S.	30	10	3	2	38	18	0	5	10	12	42	50	60	28
11	Aberdeen	30	7	4	4	37	24	3	3	9	28	34	65	58	27
12	Third Lanark	30	7	3	5	28	23	2	5	8	23	39	51	62	26
13	Airdrieonians	30	7	3	5	31	26	4	1	10	23	43	54	69	26
14	St. Mirren	30	9	2	4	28	19	1	3	11	15	39	43	58	25
15	Morton	30	7	1	7	30	23	2	5	8	19	33	49	56	24
16	Stirling Albion	30	4	4	7	22	40	1	1	13	14	59	36	99	15

1951-52 Season

Back : J Collins, A Hepburn, A McNay, T Baird, J Marshall, M Muirhead
Middle : W Walker (Trainer), Kilmarnock, Cow, Paton, Johnston, Redpath, Shaw, B Ellis (Coach).
Front : G Stevenson (Manager), Sloan, Humphries, Kelly, Watson, Aitkenhead, J ('Sailor') Hunter (Sec.)

1952-53 Season

As Cup Winners Motherwell played Hibs (League Winners) in the Lord Provest of Glasgow Cup, this was an attempt at introducing a Scottish style Charity Shield. This was the only time the Cup was played for with Motherwell winning convincingly. The proceeds from this match went to the Police Benevolent fund.

1952-53: "A" Division

	Date	Opponent	Score	Scorers	Att.	Johnston John	Kilmarnock	Shaw	Cox	Paton	Redpath	Sloan	Humphries	Forrest	Kelly	Aitkenhead John	Hunter	Muir	Dawson	Brown	Higgins	Bryers	Reid	Robinson	Williams
1	06-Sep	Dundee	0 - 0		24000	x	x	x	x	x	x	x	x	x	x	x									
2	13-Sep	EAST FIFE	3 - 3	Sloan, Kelly, Aitkenhead		x	x	x	x	x	x	x	x	x	x	x									
3	20-Sep	Aidrie	2 - 1	Kelly, Forrest	12000	x	x	x	x	x	x	x	x	x	x	x									
4	27-Sep	HIBERNIAN	3 - 7	Aitkenhead, Sloan, Humphries	18000	x	x	x	x	x	x	x	x	x	x	x									
5	04-Oct	Celtic	0 - 3			x	x	x	x	x	x	x	x	x	x	x									
6	11-Oct	ST. MIRREN	1 - 1	Forrest	8000	x	x	x	x	x	x	x	x	x	x	x									
7	18-Oct	Third Lanark	2 - 1	Kelly, Aitkenhead		x	x	x	x	x	x	x		x	x	x			x						
8	25-Oct	PARTICK THISTLE	1 - 2	Dawson		x	x	x	x	x		x		x	x	x			x	x					
9	01-Nov	Aberdeen	1 - 5	Kelly		x	x	x	x	x		x	x	x	x	x			x						
10	08-Nov	CLYDE	3 - 6	Kelly (2), Dawson		x	x	x	x	x		x	x	x	x	x			x						
11	15-Nov	Raith Rovers	1 - 1	Aitkenhead		x	x	x	x	x		x	x		x	x	x		x						
12	22-Nov	Hearts	1 - 3	Aitkenhead		x	x				x	x	x	x	x	x			x		x	x			
p 20/4	29-Nov	RANGERS	0 - 3			x	x		x	x	x	x	x	x	x	x		x							
14	06-Dec	Queen of the South	1 - 3	Kelly		x		x	x	x		x	x	x	x	x			x				x		
15	13-Dec	FALKIRK	2 - 1	Kelly (2)	7000	x	x	x	x	x		x	x	x	x	x			x						
16	20-Dec	DUNDEE	2 - 1	Kelly (2)		x	x	x	x	x		x	x	x	x	x			x						
17	27-Dec	East Fife	2 - 2	Forrest (2)		x	x	x	x	x		x	x	x	x	x			x						
18	01-Jan	AIRDRIE	4 - 1	Aitkenhead, Kelly, Humphries, Robinson		x	x	x	x	x		x	x	x	x	x								x	
19	03-Jan	Hibernian	2 - 7	Sloan (2)		x	x	x	x	x		x	x	x	x	x								x	
20	10-Jan	CELTIC	4 - 2	Robinson, Humphries (2), Aitkenhead		x	x	x	x	x		x	x	x	x	x								x	
21	17-Jan	St. Mirren	5 - 2	Johnston (2), Paton (2), Sloan		x	x	x	x	x		x	x	x	x	x								x	
22	31-Jan	THIRD LANARK	1 - 5	Kelly		x	x	x	x	x		x	x	x	x	x			x						
23	14-Feb	Partick Thistle	2 - 4	Aitkenhead (2)		x	x	x			x	x	x	x	x	x				x				x	
p 18/4	21-Feb	ABERDEEN	4 - 1	OG, Kelly (2), Redpath		x	x	x	x	x	x	x	x	x	x	x									
25	28-Feb	Clyde	2 - 3	Cox, Humphries		x	x	x	x		x	x	x	x	x	x								x	
26	07-Mar	RAITH ROVERS	2 - 1	Williams, Humphries		x	x	x	x	x		x	x		x	x								x	x
p 24/1	14-Mar	HEARTS	1 3	Sloan		x	x	x	x	x		x	x	x	x	x								x	
28	21-Mar	Rangers	1 - 4	Forrest		x		x	x	x	x	x	x	x	x	x							x		
29	28-Mar	QUEEN OF THE SOUTH	3 - 2	Kilmarnock, Sloan, Kelly		x	x		x	x	x	x	x	x	x	x					x				
30	04-Apr	Falkirk	1 - 2	Kilmarnock		x	x		x	x	x	x	x	x	x	x		x							

LEAGUE CUP

	Date	Opponent	Score	Scorers	Att.	Johnston John	Kilmarnock	Shaw	Cox	Paton	Redpath	Sloan	Humphries	Forrest	Kelly	Aitkenhead John	Hunter	Muir	Dawson	Brown	Higgins	Bryers	Reid	Robinson	Williams
	09-Aug	ABERDEEN	5 - 2	Humphries (2), Cox, Kelly, Aitkenhead	8000	x	x	x	x	x	x	x	x	x	x	x									
	13-Aug	Rangers	0 - 2			x	x	x	x	x	x	x	x	x	x	x									
	16-Aug	Hearts	1 - 0	Sloan	35000	x	x	x	x	x	x	x	x	x	x	x									
	23-Aug	Aberdeen	1 - 0	Aitkenhead		x	x	x	x	x	x	x	x	x	x	x									
	27-Aug	RANGERS	3 - 3	Humphries, Forrest, Paton		x	x	x	x	x	x	x	x	x	x	x									
	30-Aug	HEARTS	1 - 2	Aitkenhead	18000	x	x	x	x	x	x	x	x	x	x	x									

SCOTTISH CUP

	Date	Opponent	Score	Scorers	Att.	Johnston John	Kilmarnock	Shaw	Cox	Paton	Redpath	Sloan	Humphries	Forrest	Kelly	Aitkenhead John	Hunter	Muir	Dawson	Brown	Higgins	Bryers	Reid	Robinson	Williams
	07-Feb	Alloa Athletic	2 - 0	Aitkenhead, Redpath	8500	x	x	x	x	x		x	x	x	x	x			x						
	21-Feb	Aberdeen	5 - 5	Kelly, Aitkenhead (2), Shaw, Cox	28000	x	x	x	x			x	x	x	x	x				x				x	
rep.	25-Feb	ABERDEEN	1 - 5	Robinson	18900	x	x	x	x	x		x	x	x	x	x				x					

LORD PROVEST OF GLASGOW CHARITY CUP

	Date	Opponent	Score
firhill	23-Sep	HIBERNIAN	5 - 1

LANARKSHIRE CUP

	Date	Opponent	Score
		HAMILTON ACADEMICAL	2 - 1
		ALBION ROVERS	3 - 0

1953 'A' Division

		Pl.	Home W.	Home D.	Home L.	Home F.	Home A.	Away W.	Away D.	Away L.	Away F.	Away A.	F. (Total)	A. (Total)	Pts.
1	Rangers	30	12	1	2	49	14	6	6	3	31	25	80	39	43
2	Hibernian	30	10	3	2	45	18	9	2	4	48	33	93	51	43
3	East Fife	30	11	2	2	49	21	5	5	5	23	27	72	48	39
4	Heart of Mid.	30	8	3	4	36	18	4	3	8	23	32	59	50	30
5	Clyde	30	8	2	5	43	30	5	2	8	35	48	78	78	30
6	St. Mirren	30	6	6	3	29	21	5	2	8	23	37	52	58	30
7	Dundee	30	8	5	2	30	11	1	6	8	14	26	44	37	29
8	Celtic	30	7	3	5	33	26	4	4	7	18	28	51	54	29
9	Partick Thistle	30	6	4	5	32	33	4	5	6	23	30	55	63	29
10	Queen of the S.	30	8	3	4	31	24	2	5	8	12	37	43	61	28
11	Aberdeen	30	8	4	3	45	26	3	1	11	19	42	64	68	27
12	Raith Rovers	30	5	7	3	25	20	4	1	10	22	33	47	53	26
13	Falkirk	30	7	1	7	29	28	4	3	8	24	35	53	63	26
14	Airdrieonians	30	6	4	5	33	33	4	2	9	20	42	53	75	26
15	MOTHERWELL	30	7	2	6	34	39	3	3	9	23	41	57	80	25
16	Third Lanark	30	6	2	7	24	24	2	2	11	28	51	52	75	20

1953-54: "B" Division

						Johnston John	Kilmarnock	Shaw	Cox	Paton	Redpath	Sloan	Humphries	Kelly	Forrest	Aitkenhead	Hunter J	Dawson	Hunter R	Williams	McSeveney	Aitken	Geddes	Bryden	Higgins	Kerr
1	05-Sep	Forfar Athletic	5 - 0	Sloan (2), Hunter, Forrest, Dawson	2800	x	x	x	x	x	x	x			x	x	x	x								
2	12-Sep	ALLOA	6 - 0	Humphries (3), Forrest (2), Hunter	8600	x	x	x	x	x	x	x	x		x	x	x									
3	19-Sep	Albion Rovers	3 - 2	Forrest, Humphries, Sloan	6000	x	x	x		x	x	x	x		x		x			x			x			
4	26-Sep	AYR UNITED	3 - 4	Forrest (2), Williams		x	x	x	x	x	x	x	x		x		x			x						
5	03-Oct	Dumbarton	3 - 4	Hunter (2), Redpath		x	x	x	x	x	x	x	x		x		x			x						
6	10-Oct	QUEENS PARK	4 - 0	Redpath, Hunter, Humphries, Sloan		x	x		x	x	x	x	x		x	x	x							x		
7	13-Oct	Dundee United	0 - 1		9000	x	x	x	x	x	x	x	x		x	x	x									
8	24-Oct	MORTON	3 - 2	Redpath, Forrest, Hunter	8000	x	x	x	x	x	x	x	x		x	x	x									
9	31-Oct	Stenhousemuir	4 - 0	Hunter (2), Aitkenhead, Forrest	8500	x	x	x	x	x	x	x	x		x	x	x									
10	07-Nov	DUMBARTON	4 - 1	Forrest (3), Redpath	3000	x	x		x	x	x		x	x	x	x	x			x						
11	14-Nov	ST. JOHNSTONE	3 - 1	Hunter (2), Sloan	8000	x	x	x	x	x	x	x	x		x	x	x									
12	21-Nov	Third Lanark	2 - 1	Forrest, Aitkenhead	12000	x	x	x	x	x	x	x	x		x	x	x									
13	28-Nov	Cowdenbeath	5 - 1	Humphries, Forrest (2), Hunter, Sloan	5000	x	x	x	x	x	x	x	x		x	x	x									
14	05-Dec	KILMARNOCK	0 - 2		14000	x	x	x	x	x		x	x		x	x	x					x				
15	12-Dec	Arbroath	4 - 0	Forrest (2), Humphries, Hunter	2800	x	x	x	x	x	x	x	x		x	x	x									
16	19-Dec	FORFAR ATHLETIC	5 - 1	Hunter (2), Cox, Forrest, Aitkenhead		x	x	x	x	x	x	x	x		x	x	x									
17	26-Dec	Alloa Athletic	3 - 2	Redpath, Forrest, Sloan		x	x	x	x	x	x	x	x		x	x	x									
18	01-Jan	ALBION ROVERS	6 - 0	Humphries, Sloan (2), Forrest, Hunter, Aitkenhead		x	x	x	x	x	x	x	x		x	x	x									
19	02-Jan	Ayr United	3 - 0	Aitkenhead, Humphries, Hunter		x	x		x	x	x	x	x	x	x	x	x									
20	09-Jan	DUNFERMLINE	3 - 0	Humphries, Forrest, Hunter		x	x	x	x	x	x	x	x		x	x	x									
21	16-Jan	Queens Park	0 - 0			x	x	x	x		x	x	x		x	x	x							x		
22	23-Jan	DUNDEE UNITED	12 - 1	Humphries (6), Hunter (4), Redpath (2)		x	x		x	x	x	x	x		x	x	x							x		
23	06-Feb	Morton	5 - 2	Forrest (3), Hunter (2)		x	x	x	x	x	x	x			x	x	x		x							
24	20-Feb	Stenhousemuir	1 - 2	Redpath		x	x	x		x	x	x	x		x	x			x			x				
p 10/4	27-Feb	DUMBARTON	6 - 6	Williams (3), Humphries, McSeveney, Forrest		x	x		x	x	x		x		x					x	x				x	x
26	06-Mar	St. Johnstone	6 - 2	Hunter (3), Forrest, Kilmarnock, Humphries		x	x	x		x	x	x	x		x	x	x					x				
p 24/3	13-Mar	THIRD LANARK	1 - 1	McSeveney		x	x	x	x	x	x		x		x	x		x			x					
28	20-Mar	COWDENBEATH	5 - 2	Humphries (2), Hunter, Sloan, Redpath		x	x	x	x	x	x	x	x		x	x	x									
p 31/3	27-Mar	Kilmarnock	2 - 4	Hunter, McSeveney		x	x	x	x	x	x	x	x				x		x		x					
p 7/4	03-Apr	ARBROATH	2 - 1	McSeveney, Redpath		x	x	x	x	x	x	x	x		x				x		x					

LEAGUE CUP

						Johnston John	Kilmarnock	Shaw	Cox	Paton	Redpath	Sloan	Humphries	Kelly	Forrest	Aitkenhead	Hunter J	Dawson	Hunter R	Williams	McSeveney	Aitken	Geddes	Bryden	Higgins	Kerr
	08-Aug	KILMARNOCK	3 - 0	Redpath (2), Cox		x	x	x	x	x	x	x			x	x	x			x						
	12-Aug	Dundee United	5 - 0	Cox (2), Sloan (2), Forrest		x	x	x	x	x	x	x			x	x	x			x						
	15-Aug	MORTON	2 - 0	Kelly, Cox		x	x	x	x	x	x	x		x	x		x			x						
	22-Aug	Kilmarnock	1 - 4	Kelly		x	x	x	x	x	x	x		x	x					x			x			
	26-Aug	DUNDEE UNITED	3 - 1	Kelly, Redpath, Sloan		x	x	x	x	x	x	x		x	x		x			x						
	29-Aug	Morton	3 - 2	Hunter (2), Forrest		x	x	x	x		x	x			x			x	x	x				x		

SCOTTISH CUP

						Johnston John	Kilmarnock	Shaw	Cox	Paton	Redpath	Sloan	Humphries	Kelly	Forrest	Aitkenhead	Hunter J	Dawson	Hunter R	Williams	McSeveney	Aitken	Geddes	Bryden	Higgins	Kerr
	30-Jan	St. Mirren	2 - 1	Aitkenhead, Sloan	22382	x	x	x	x	x	x	x	x		x	x	x									
	13-Feb	DUNFERMLINE	5 - 2	Forrest (3), Aitkenhead (2)	10000	x	x	x	x	x	x	x	x		x	x	x									
	27-Feb	RAITH ROVERS	4 - 1	OG, Humphries, Hunter, Forrest	20000	x	x		x	x	x	x	x	x	x	x	x									
	13-Mar	Partick Thistle	1 - 1	Hunter	23000	x	x		x	x	x	x	x	x	x	x	x									
	15-Mar	PARTICK THISTLE	2 - 1	Hunter, Humphries	36000	x	x	x	x	x	x	x	x		x	x	x									
S/F	27-Mar	CELTIC	2 - 2	Humphries, Aitken	27600	x	x	x	x	x	x	x	x		x	x						x				
S/F R	29-Mar	CELTIC	1 - 3	Hunter	92621	x	x		x	x	x	x	x		x	x	x								x	

LANAKSHIRE CUP

		ALBION ROVERS	1 - 1
		Albion Rovers	1 - 1
		ALBION ROVERS	4 - 1
		Hamilton Academical	3 - 0

1954 'B' Division

		Pl.	Home					Away					F.	A.	Pts.
			W.	D.	L.	F.	A.	W.	D.	L.	F.	A.	(Total)		
1	MOTHERWELL	30	11	2	2	63	20	10	1	4	46	23	109	43	45
2	Kilmarnock	30	11	2	2	45	17	8	2	5	26	22	71	39	42
3	Third Lanark	30	7	5	3	43	24	6	5	4	35	24	78	48	36
4	Stenhousemuir	30	10	3	2	44	22	4	5	6	22	36	66	58	36
5	Morton	30	7	3	5	47	32	8	0	7	38	33	85	65	33
6	St. Johnstone	30	8	3	4	47	24	6	0	9	33	47	80	71	31
7	Albion Rovers	30	9	3	3	33	23	3	4	8	22	40	55	63	31
8	Dunfermline Ath.	30	9	2	4	30	23	2	7	6	18	34	48	57	31
9	Ayr United	30	6	3	6	24	26	5	5	5	26	30	50	56	30
10	Queen's Park	30	7	5	3	45	23	2	4	9	11	28	56	51	27
11	Alloa	30	4	5	6	31	31	3	5	7	19	41	50	72	24
12	Forfar Athletic	30	5	1	9	19	30	5	3	7	19	39	38	69	24
13	Cowdenbeath	30	8	3	4	46	29	1	2	12	21	52	67	81	23
14	Arbroath	30	6	3	6	32	29	2	4	9	21	38	53	67	23
15	Dundee United	30	6	4	5	27	21	2	2	11	27	58	54	79	22
16	Dumbarton	30	5	5	5	30	31	2	3	10	21	61	51	92	22

1953-54 Season
Back: Kilmarnock, Cox, Paton, Johnstone, Redpath, Shaw
Front: Sloan, Humphries, Kelly, Hunter, Aitkenhead

1954-55 Season
Back: McIntyre, Kilmarnock, Shaw, Cox, Mason, Redpath
Front: Hunter, Aitken, McSeveney, Humphries, Williams

1954-55: "A" Division

No.	Date	Opponent	Score	Scorers		Johnston John	Weir Hastie	Kilmarnock	Shaw	Cox	Paton	Redpath	Sloan	Humphries	Hunter J	Forrest	Aitkenhead	Dawson	Williams	Aitken	McSeveney	McFadyen	Kerr	Bain	Weir B	McNeil	Cameron	Reid	Harper	Mason	McIntyre
1	11-Sep	Falkirk	1 - 1	Cox			X	X	X	X	X	X	X		X	X	X			X											
2	18-Sep	QUEEN OF THE SOUTH	2 - 1	Bain, Aitken			X	X	X	X	X	X		X		X			X	X				X							
p 30/4	25-Sep	Rangers	0 - 2				X	X	X	X		X		X	X	X			X	X				X							
4	02-Oct	ABERDEEN	1 - 3	Bain			X	X	X	X	X	X		X	X				X	X				X							
p 18/4	09-Oct	Hearts	2 - 3	Aitken (2)			X	X	X	X	X	X		X	X				X	X										X	
6	16-Oct	CLYDE	2 - 0	Bain (2)			X	X	X	X	X	X		X	X				X	X				X							
p 13/4	23-Oct	Kilmarnock	2 - 1	Hunter, Williams			X	X	X		X			X	X				X	X			X				X			X	
8	30-Oct	RAITH ROVERS	3 - 2	Hunter, Aitken, Williams			X	X		X	X	X		X	X				X	X	X			X							
9	06-Nov	PARTICK THISTLE	1 - 2	Hunter			X	X	X		X	X		X	X				X	X				X						X	
10	13-Nov	Hibernian	1 - 4	Aitken		X		X	X	X		X		X	X				X	X				X						X	
11	20-Nov	EAST FIFE	3 - 5	Hunter (2), Sloan			X	X	X	X			X	X	X		X		X	X				X							
12	27-Nov	CELTIC	2 - 2	Hunter, Forrest			X	X	X	X				X	X	X	X		X	X				X							
13	04-Dec	Dundee	1 - 4	Forrest				X	X	X	X	X		X	X	X	X			X											X
14	11-Dec	ST. MIRREN	2 - 3	Aitken, Sloan				X	X	X	X	X	X		X	X			X	X											X
15	18-Dec	Stirling Albion	3 - 1	Williams (2), Kilmarnock				X	X	X		X	X	X		X			X					X						X	X
16	25-Dec	FALKIRK	0 - 3					X	X	X		X	X	X	X	X			X	X											X
17	01-Jan	Queen of the South	0 - 1					X	X	X		X	X	X	X	X			X	X											X
18	03-Jan	RANGERS	2 - 0	McSeveney, Williams				X	X	X		X	X	X					X	X	X									X	X
19	08-Jan	Aberdeen	1 - 4	McSeveney			X	X	X	X		X	X	X	X				X	X	X										
p 16/4	15-Jan	HEARTS	1 - 1	Aitken				X	X	X		X	X	X	X				X	X	X										X
21	22-Jan	Clyde	2 - 2	McSeveney, Humphries				X	X	X		X		X	X				X	X	X									X	X
22	29-Jan	KILMARNOCK	0 - 1					X	X	X		X		X	X				X	X	X									X	X
23	12-Feb	Raith Rovers	2 - 3	McSeveney, Redpath				X	X	X		X	X	X					X	X	X									X	X
24	26-Feb	Partick Thistle	1 - 0	Bain				X	X			X	X				X			X	X			X		X				X	X
25	?	HIBERNIAN	1 - 5	Bain				X	X				X		X		X				X		X	X		X	X				X
26	12-Mar	East Fife	2 - 4	Hunter, Bain				X	X				X		X		X				X		X	X		X	X				X
27	19-Mar	Celtic	0 - 1					X	X		X	X		X	X				X	X	X									X	X
28	26-Mar	DUNDEE	0 - 2					X	X	X				X	X					X	X			X		X	X				X
29	02-Apr	St. Mirren	1 - 0	Hunter				X	X	X		X		X	X				X	X	X									X	X
30	09-Apr	STIRLING ALBION	3 - 1	Humphries (2), Aitken				X	X			X		X						X	X	X				X	X	X			X

LEAGUE CUP

	Date	Opponent	Score	Scorers		Johnston John	Weir Hastie	Kilmarnock	Shaw	Cox	Paton	Redpath	Sloan	Humphries	Hunter J	Forrest	Aitkenhead	Dawson	Williams	Aitken	McSeveney	McFadyen	Kerr	Bain	Weir B	McNeil	Cameron	Reid	Harper	Mason	McIntyre
	14-Aug	St. Mirren	4 - 4	Humphries (2), Redpath, Hunter			X	X	X	X	X	X	X	X	X	X	X														
	18-Aug	KILMARNOCK	3 - 0	Hunter, Aitken, Forrest			X	X	X	X	X	X			X	X	X			X			X								
	21-Aug	RAITH ROVERS	1 - 1	Aitken			X	X	X	X	X	X			X	X	X			X			X								
	28-Aug	ST. MIRREN	3 - 1	Aitken (2), Humphries			X	X	X	X	X	X		X	X	X	X			X											
	01-Sep	Kilmarnock	1 - 0	Sloan			X	X	X	X	X	X	X		X			X		X					X						
	04-Sep	Raith Rovers	0 - 3				X	X	X	X	X	X			X	X	X			X									X		
	22-Sep	RANGERS	2 - 1	Aitken, Hunter			X	X	X	X	X	X			X	X			X	X				X							
	25-Sep	Rangers	1 - 1	Bain			X	X	X	X	X	X			X		X		X	X				X							
S/F	09-Oct	EAST FIFE	2 - 1	Kilmarnock, Bain			X	X	X	X	X	X		X	X	X			X					X							
F	23-Oct	HEARTS	1-4	Redpath			X	X		X	X	X		X	X				X	X	X			X							

SCOTTISH CUP

	Date	Opponent	Score	Scorers	Att.	Johnston John	Weir Hastie	Kilmarnock	Shaw	Cox	Paton	Redpath	Sloan	Humphries	Hunter J	Forrest	Aitkenhead	Dawson	Williams	Aitken	McSeveney	McFadyen	Kerr	Bain	Weir B	McNeil	Cameron	Reid	Harper	Mason	McIntyre
	05-Feb	Forres Mechanics	4 - 3	McSeveney, Williams, SLOAN, Aitken	6500			X	X	X		X	X	X					X	X	X									X	X
	19-Feb	Third Lanark	3 - 1	Aitken, Sloan, Redpath	21000			X	X			X	X				X			X	X			X		X				X	X
	05-Mar	Aidrie	1 - 4	Hunter	25000			X	X			X	X		X		X			X	X			X						X	X

LANARKSHIRE CUP

aet		AIRDRIE	3 - 0

1955 'A' Division

		Pl.	Home W.	D.	L.	F.	A.	Away W.	D.	L.	F.	A.	F. (Total)	A.	Pts.
1	Aberdeen	30	14	0	1	41	9	10	1	4	32	17	73	26	49
2	Celtic	30	10	4	1	42	16	9	4	2	34	21	76	37	46
3	Rangers	30	13	2	0	40	8	6	1	8	27	25	67	33	41
4	Heart of Mid.	30	10	2	3	40	25	6	5	4	34	20	74	45	39
5	Hibernian	30	8	2	5	28	23	7	2	6	36	31	64	54	34
6	St. Mirren	30	8	3	4	31	23	4	5	6	24	31	55	54	32
7	Clyde	30	6	7	2	33	20	5	2	8	26	30	59	50	31
8	Dundee	30	9	2	4	32	21	4	2	9	16	27	48	48	30
9	Partick Thistle	30	5	5	5	24	29	6	2	7	25	32	49	61	29
10	Kilmarnock	30	5	3	7	18	24	5	3	7	28	34	46	58	26
11	East Fife	30	6	1	8	32	35	3	5	7	19	27	51	62	24
12	Falkirk	30	6	6	3	28	23	2	2	11	14	31	42	54	24
13	Queen of the S.	30	7	2	6	22	29	2	4	9	16	27	38	56	24
14	Raith Rovers	30	9	1	5	34	23	1	2	12	15	34	49	57	23
15	MOTHERWELL	30	5	2	8	23	31	4	2	9	19	31	42	62	22
16	Stirling Albion	30	2	1	12	15	40	0	1	14	14	65	29	105	6

1955-56: "A" Division

						Weir Hastie	Kilmarnock	Shaw	Redpath	Sloan	Humphries	Hunter J	Forrest	Aitkenhead	Williams	Aitken	McSeveney	McFadyen	Kerr	Bain	Reid	Paton	Gardiner	Quinn	Rea	Mason	Brown S	Hunter R	Pollock	Cox	Cameron	Nelson	Toner
1	10-Sep	EAST FIFE	5 - 2	Aitkenhead (3), W Reid, Bain		x	x	x	x	x			x	x		x				x	x	x											
p11/4	17-Sep	Stirling Albion	1 - 0	Sloan		x	x	x		x			x	x		x			x			x	x	x									
3	24-Sep	AIRDRIE	0 - 2			x	x	x	x	x	x			x		x		x		x		x											
p 9/4	01-Oct	St. Mirren	1 - 1	Sloan		x	x	x		x			x	x		x			x			x	x	x									
p 16/4	08-Oct	HIBERNIAN	1 - 1	Quinn		x	x						x			x	x		x	x		x	x	x					x				
6	15-Oct	Celtic	2 - 2	Gardiner, Aitken		x	x	x		x					x	x		x			x	x	x										x
7	22-Oct	QUEEN OF THE SOUTH	1 - 2	Gardiner		x	x	x		x			x		x	x		x			x	x	x										
8	29-Oct	KILMARNOCK	2 - 1	W Reid, Hunter		x	x	x				x	x	x		x		x			x	x	x										
9	05-Nov	Dunfermline Ath.	0 - 1			x	x	x				x	x	x		x		x			x	x	x										
10	12-Nov	FALKIRK	0 - 0			x	x	x			x		x			x	x	x				x	x									x	
11	19-Nov	Aberdeen	1 - 1	McSeveney		x	x	x		x	x			x		x	x	x				x	x										
12	26-Nov	Rangers	2 - 2	Aitkenhead, Gardiner		x	x	x		x	x			x		x	x	x				x	x										
13	03-Dec	PARTICK THISTLE	3 - 1	Aitken (2), McSeveney		x	x	x		x	x			x		x	x	x				x	x										
14	10-Dec	CLYDE	2 - 2	McSeveney (2)		x	x	x		x	x			x		x	x	x				x	x										
15	17-Dec	Hearts	1 - 7	Gardiner		x	x	x			x	x		x		x	x	x				x	x										
16	24-Dec	RAITH ROVERS	5 - 1	Bain (2), Humphries, W Reid, Gardiner		x	x	x			x			x		x		x		x	x	x	x										
17	31-Dec	Dundee	1 - 2	Gardiner		x	x	x			x			x		x		x		x	x	x	x										
18	02-Jan	Aidrie	0 - 3			x	x	x			x		x	x		x		x			x	x	x										
19	07-Jan	STIRLING ALBION	2 - 0	Aitken, Bain		x	x	x			x			x		x		x		x		x	x		x								
20	14-Jan	East Fife	2 - 0	W Reid (2)		x	x	x						x		x		x	x	x	x	x			x								
21	21-Jan	ST. MIRREN	1 - 1	W Reid		x	x	x						x		x		x	x	x	x	x			x								
22	28-Jan	Hibernian	0 - 7			x	x	x		x						x		x	x	x	x	x	x										
23	11-Feb	CELTIC	2 - 2	Gardiner, Forrest		x	x						x	x		x	x	x	x		x	x	x										
24	25-Feb	Queen of the South	0 - 0			x	x						x		x	x	x		x		x	x	x				x						
25	03-Mar	Kilmarnock	1 - 2	Kerr		x	x						x				x	x	x			x	x	x	x		x						
26	10-Mar	DUNFERMLINE	2 - 1	Kerr, Gardiner		x	x						x				x	x	x			x	x	x	x						x		
27	17-Mar	Falkirk	4 - 3	Forrest, Gardiner, Cox, Kerr		x	x						x				x		x			x	x	x	x	x				x			
28	24-Mar	ABERDEEN	1 - 1	Quinn		x	x						x				x		x			x	x	x	x	x	x						
29	31-Mar	RANGERS	1 - 2	Quinn		x	x						x			x	x		x			x	x	x	x	x							
30	07-Apr	Partick Thistle	1 - 2	Aitken		x	x						x			x	x		x			x	x	x	x	x							
p 18/4	14-Apr	Clyde	3 - 1			x	x			x			x			x	x		x			x	x	x		x							
p 23/4	21-Apr	HEARTS	1 - 0	Sloan		x	x			x			x	x		x	x		x			x	x	x									
33	25-Apr	Raith Rovers	3 - 4	Kerr, Quinn, Aitkenhead		x	x						x	x		x			x			x	x	x			x	x					
34	28-Apr	DUNDEE	1 - 2	Sloan		x	x			x			x		x	x						x				x	x	x	x				

LEAGUE CUP

						Weir Hastie	Kilmarnock	Shaw	Redpath	Sloan	Humphries	Hunter J	Forrest	Aitkenhead	Williams	Aitken	McSeveney	McFadyen	Kerr	Bain	Reid	Paton	Gardiner	Quinn	Rea	Mason	Brown S	Hunter R	Pollock	Cox	Cameron	Nelson	Toner
	13-Aug	Forfar Athletic	6 - 1	Bain (2), Sloan (2), Humphries, Forrest		x	x	x	x	x	x		x	x			x			x		x											
	17-Aug	DUNDEE UNITED	7 - 1																														
	20-Aug	Albion Rovers	2 - 0	Forrest (2)		x	x	x	x	x	x		x	x						x	x	x											
	27-Aug	FORFAR ATHLETIC	2 - 1	Bain, Sloan		x	x	x	x	x			x	x						x	x	x								x			
	31-Aug	Dundee United	2 - 0																														
	03-Sep	ALBION ROVERS	4 - 0	W Reid (2), Bain, Sloan		x	x	x	x	x			x	x		x				x	x	x											
	14-Sep	St. Johnstone	2 - 1	Aitkenhead, Cox		x	x	x	x				x	x		x				x	x	x								x			
aet	17-Sep	ST. JOHNSTONE	0 - 1			x	x	x	x				x	x					x	x	x	x								x			
	21-Sep	ST. JOHNSTONE	2 - 0	Aitkenhead, Hunter		x	x	x	x	x	x	x	x	x		x						x											
S/F	01-Oct	ST. MIRREN	3 - 3	aet		x	x		x	x	x			x		x	x				x	x					x						
S/F R	08-Oct	ST. MIRREN	0 - 2			x	x		x	x	x			x		x	x				x	x					x						

SCOTTISH CUP

						Weir Hastie	Kilmarnock	Shaw	Redpath	Sloan	Humphries	Hunter J	Forrest	Aitkenhead	Williams	Aitken	McSeveney	McFadyen	Kerr	Bain	Reid	Paton	Gardiner	Quinn	Rea	Mason	Brown S	Hunter R	Pollock	Cox	Cameron	Nelson	Toner
	08-Feb	QUEENS PARK	0 - 2		12000	x	x						x	x		x	x	x	x		x	x	x										

FRIENDLIES

	29-Feb	PRESTON N. E.	2 - 3

1956 'A' Division

		Pl.	Home					Away					F.	A.	Pts.
			W.	D.	L.	F.	A.	W.	D.	L.	F.	A.	(Total)		
1	Rangers	34	12	4	1	51	13	10	4	3	34	14	85	27	52
2	Aberdeen	34	11	3	3	52	29	7	7	3	35	21	87	50	46
3	Heart of Mid.	34	13	2	2	65	17	6	5	6	34	30	99	47	45
4	Hibernian	34	11	4	2	57	24	8	3	6	29	26	86	50	45
5	Celtic	34	9	4	4	31	18	7	5	5	24	21	55	39	41
6	Queen of the S.	34	12	2	3	46	23	4	3	10	23	50	69	73	37
7	Airdrieonians	34	8	4	5	41	41	6	4	7	44	55	85	96	36
8	Kilmarnock	34	7	6	4	26	20	5	4	8	26	25	52	45	34
9	Partick Thistle	34	8	4	5	36	22	5	3	9	26	38	62	60	33
10	MOTHERWELL	34	7	6	4	30	21	4	5	8	23	38	53	59	33
11	Raith Rovers	34	6	7	4	30	30	6	2	9	28	45	58	75	33
12	East Fife	34	11	3	3	43	21	2	2	13	18	48	61	69	31
13	Dundee	34	10	2	5	35	24	2	4	11	21	41	56	65	30
14	Falkirk	34	9	2	6	37	28	2	4	11	21	47	58	75	28
15	St. Mirren	34	9	2	6	39	23	1	5	11	18	47	57	70	27
16	Dunfermline Ath.	34	6	4	7	26	36	4	2	11	16	46	42	82	26
17	Clyde	34	2	4	11	21	40	6	2	9	29	34	50	74	22
18	Stirling Albion	34	4	3	10	15	27	0	2	15	8	55	23	82	13

1956-57: 1st Division

No.	Date	Opponent	Score	Scorers	Att.	Weir Hastie	Kilmarnock	McSeveney	Aitken	Forrest	Kerr	Sloan	Quinn	Gardiner	Bain	Hunter J	Reid W	McCann	Rea	Aitkenhead	Brown S	Reid S	Baker	Holton	Paton	Brims	Cowie	Gilchrist	McFadyen
1	08-Sep	Partick Thistle	3 - 2	Gardiner (2), Quinn		x		x	x	x		x	x	x				x		x				x	x				
2	15-Sep	EAST FIFE	2 - 2	Quinn, Gardiner		x		x	x	x		x	x	x				x		x				x	x				
3	22-Sep	Aidrie	4 - 1	Gardiner (2), McCann (2)		x		x	x	x		x	x	x				x	x					x	x				
4	29-Sep	CELTIC	1 - 0	Quinn, Gardiner		x		x	x	x			x	x		x		x	x					x	x				
p 8/4	06-Oct	Dundee	1 - 3	Sloan		x			x			x	x	x				x					x	x		x	x	x	
6	13-Oct	DUNFERMLINE	3 - 2	Hunter (2), Aitken		x		x	x	x			x	x		x		x			x			x	x				
7	20-Oct	Hibernian	1 - 1	J Hunter		x		x	x	x			x	x		x		x			x			x	x				
8	27-Oct	QUEEN OF THE SOUTH	7 - 0	Gardiner (3), Quinn (3), Hunter		x		x	x	x			x	x		x		x		x				x	x				
9	03-Nov	AYR UNITED	4 - 2	Sloan (2), Quinn, Hunter		x		x	x	x		x	x	x		x		x						x	x				
10	10-Nov	Rangers	3 - 2	Aitkenhead, Gardiner, Quinn		x		x	x	x			x	x		x				x				x	x				x
11	17-Nov	RAITH ROVERS	0 - 2			x		x	x	x		x	x	x		x				x				x	x				x
12	24-Nov	ST. MIRREN	3 - 0	Gardiner, Hunter, Quinn		x		x	x	x		x	x	x		x	x							x	x				
13	01-Dec	Kilmarnock	2 - 2	Sloan, Hunter		x		x	x	x		x	x	x		x	x							x	x				
14	08-Dec	Hearts	2 - 3	Hunter, W Reid		x		x	x	x			x	x		x	x							x	x				
15	15-Dec	QUEENS PARK	4 - 2	McCann (2), W Reid, Quinn		x		x	x	x			x	x		x	x	x						x	x				
16	22-Dec	Aberdeen	3 - 2	Hunter (2), Quinn		x		x	x	x			x	x		x	x	x						x	x				
17	29-Dec	FALKIRK	1 - 3	Hunter		x		x	x	x			x	x		x	x	x						x	x				
18	01-Jan	AIRDRIE	2 - 0	McCann (2)		x		x	x	x			x	x		x	x	x						x	x				
19	02-Jan	East Fife	2 - 1	Gardiner (2)		x		x	x	x			x	x	x	x		x						x	x				
20	05-Jan	PARTICK THISTLE	2 - 2	Quinn, Aitken		x		x	x	x			x	x	x	x		x						x	x				
21	12-Jan	Celtic	1 - 2	Gardiner		x		x	x	x			x	x		x	x	x						x	x				
22	19-Jan	DUNDEE	4 - 2	S REID, McCann, Hunter, Gardiner		x		x	x	x			x	x		x	x	x						x	x				
23	26-Jan	Dunfermline Ath.	1 - 3	W Reid		x		x	x	x				x		x	x	x				x		x	x				
24	09 Feb	HIBERNIAN	3 - 0	S Reid, Bain, Gardiner		x		x	x	x				x	x	x		x				x		x	x				
p 24/4	23-Feb	Queen of the South	2 - 2	Gardiner, Hunter		x		x	x	x			x	x		x		x				x		x	x				
26	02-Mar	Ayr United	2 - 1	Quinn, McCann		x		x	x	x			x	x			x	x				x		x	x				
27	09-Mar	RANGERS	2 - 5	Gardiner, Sloan		x		x		x		x	x	x				x				x		x	x	x			
28	16-Mar	Raith Rovers	2 - 3	Hunter (2)		x		x	x	x				x				x				x		x		x			x
29	23-Mar	St. Mirren	0 - 4			x			x	x				x				x				x			x	x	x	x	
30	30-Mar	KILMARNOCK	0 - 2			x		x	x	x				x				x				x		x	x	x		x	
31	06-Apr	HEARTS	1 - 3	Quinn		x			x			x	x		x		x	x						x	x	x		x	
32	13-Apr	Queens Park	0 - 1			x		x	x			x	x	x				x			x	x		x			x		
33	20-Apr	ABERDEEN	2 - 5	Hunter, Forrest		x		x	x	x			x	x		x		x			x			x	x				
34	27-Apr	Falkirk	2 - 1	Quinn, Hunter		x		x	x	x		x	x	x		x		x						x					

LEAGUE CUP

No.	Date	Opponent	Score	Scorers	Att.	Weir Hastie	Kilmarnock	McSeveney	Aitken	Forrest	Kerr	Sloan	Quinn	Gardiner	Bain	Hunter J	Reid W	McCann	Rea	Aitkenhead	Brown S	Reid S	Baker	Holton	Paton	Brims	Cowie	Gilchrist	McFadyen
	11-Aug	DUNDEE	0 - 1			x	x	x	x	x	x		x	x			x			x						x			
	15-Aug	Aidrie	3 - 1			x	x	x	x	x	x		x	x			x									x			
	18-Aug	Raith Rovers	2 - 4			x	x	x	x	x			x	x		x		x		x						x			
	25-Aug	Dundee	1 - 2	Aitkenhead		x	x		x	x			x	x		x		x		x					x	x			
	29-Aug	AIRDRIE	6 - 1	Gardiner (4), Quinn (2)		x			x	x		x	x	x		x		x		x					x	x			
	01-Sep	RAITH ROVERS	0 - 1			x		x	x	x		x	x	x				x		x					x	x			

SCOTTISH CUP

No.	Date	Opponent	Score	Scorers	Att.	Weir Hastie	Kilmarnock	McSeveney	Aitken	Forrest	Kerr	Sloan	Quinn	Gardiner	Bain	Hunter J	Reid W	McCann	Rea	Aitkenhead	Brown S	Reid S	Baker	Holton	Paton	Brims	Cowie	Gilchrist	McFadyen
	02-Feb	Stirling Albion	2 - 1	Hunter, Brown	8912	x		x	x	x				x		x		x				x	x		x	x			
	16-Feb	DUMBARTON	1 - 3	Gardiner	16000	x		x	x	x				x	x	x		x					x		x	x			

FRIENDLIES

Date	Opponent	Score
27-Jul	HAMILTON ACADEMICAL	2 - 0

1957 Div. 1

		Pl.	Home W.	D.	L.	F.	A.	Away W.	D.	L.	F.	A.	F. (Total)	A.	Pts.
1	Rangers	34	13	2	2	51	22	13	1	3	45	26	96	48	55
2	Heart of Mid.	34	11	3	3	40	23	13	2	2	41	25	81	48	53
3	Kilmarnock	34	9	6	2	35	20	7	4	6	22	19	57	39	42
4	Raith Rovers	34	10	2	5	52	32	6	5	6	32	26	84	58	39
5	Celtic	34	9	6	2	33	14	6	2	9	25	29	58	43	38
6	Aberdeen	34	10	1	6	36	24	8	1	8	43	35	79	59	38
7	MOTHERWELL	34	9	2	6	41	32	7	3	7	31	34	72	66	37
8	Partick Thistle	34	11	3	3	37	18	2	5	10	16	33	53	51	34
9	Hibernian	34	6	8	3	38	20	6	1	10	31	36	69	56	33
10	Dundee	34	10	2	5	38	23	3	4	10	17	38	55	61	32
11	Airdrieonians	34	8	2	7	45	40	5	2	10	32	49	77	89	30
12	St. Mirren	34	8	3	6	37	25	4	3	10	21	47	58	72	30
13	Queen's Park	34	9	2	6	33	19	2	5	10	22	40	55	59	29
14	Falkirk	34	5	2	10	28	35	5	6	6	23	35	51	70	28
15	East Fife	34	7	3	7	33	34	3	3	11	26	48	59	82	26
16	Queen of the S.	34	8	3	6	36	37	2	2	13	18	59	54	96	25
17	Dunfermline Ath.	34	6	3	8	31	36	3	3	11	23	38	54	74	24
18	Ayr United	34	5	2	10	27	35	2	3	12	21	54	48	89	19

1956-57 Season
Back row : Gilchrist, Holton, H Weir, Aitken, Cowie, Forrest.
Front row : Hunter, McCann, Gardiner, McPhee, S Reid.

***1957-58 Season**:*
Back : McSeveney, Holton, McFadyen, Gardiner, Brown, Cowie, Martis, Forrest, Aitken.
Middle : B Ancell, A Weir, McCann, Campbell, Shaw, H Weir, Stenhouse, McCallum, McPhee, St John, J Hunter.
Front : Ellis, Quinn, Hunter, Reid, Baker, Rea, Newman, Kerr. Kneeling : Reid.

1957-58: 1st Division

	Date	Opponent	Score	Scorers	Weir Hastie	Wyllie	McSeveney	Brown J	Campbell	Shaw	Gilchrist	Holton	Weir A	Martis	Hunter W	Aitken	Brims	Paton	Forrest	McFadyen	Kerr	Rea	Baker	Reid S	Quinn	McCann	Stenhouse	Hunter J	Gardiner	St John	Brown S	McPhee	Cowie
1	07-Sep	ST. MIRREN	4 - 2	Gardiner (2), Hunter (2)	x						x	x				x	x	x	x		x							x	x			x	
2	14-Sep	Hibernian	1 - 2	McPhee	x		x				x					x		x	x		x				x			x	x			x	
3	21-Sep	AIRDRIE	1 - 2	McCann	x		x				x					x		x	x		x					x		x	x			x	
p 21/4	28-Sep	Celtic	2 - 2	Hunter, Quinn	x							x			x	x		x				x	x		x		x		x				x
5	05-Oct	PARTICK THISTLE	4 - 1	Rea (2), Gardiner, Kerr	x					x						x	x		x	x	x	x				x			x			x	
6	12-Oct	Dundee	0 - 3			x	x			x		x			x	x		x								x	x		x				x
p 23/4	19-Oct	Queens Park	7 - 0			x	x					x			x	x							x			x	x		x		x	x	
8	26-Oct	FALKIRK	2 - 5	Stenhouse, Baker		x	x					x			x	x					x		x			x	x		x	x			
9	02-Nov	Hearts	2 - 2	St John (2)		x	x			x		x				x			x				x		x	x			x	x			
10	09-Nov	RAITH ROVERS	0 - 2			x	x		x	x		x				x			x				x		x	x			x	x			
11	16-Nov	Kilmarnock	1 - 0	OG		x				x		x				x	x		x	x			x					x	x	x			
12	23-Nov	QUEEN OF THE SOUTH	4 - 2	St John (3), McSeveney		x	x			x		x				x	x		x	x				x				x		x			
13	30-Nov	Clyde	1 - 4	McSeveney		x	x			x		x				x			x	x				x				x	x	x			
14	07-Dec	RANGERS	2 - 2	Gardiner (2)		x	x			x		x				x			x	x						x		x	x	x			
15	14-Dec	ABERDEEN	4 - 1	Quinn (2), Gardiner, Baker		x	x			x		x				x			x	x			x		x			x	x				
16	21-Dec	East Fife	1 - 2	Gardiner		x	x					x				x	x		x	x			x			x		x	x				
17	28-Dec	Third Lanark	2 - 4	Hunter, McSeveney		x	x					x				x			x	x			x		x			x	x	x			
18	01-Jan	Aidrie	1 - 4		x		x					x	x		x	x			x	x						x			x	x			
19	02-Jan	HIBERNIAN	3 - 1	Weir, Kerr, St John		x						x	x	x		x					x				x	x			x	x		x	
20	04-Jan	St. Mirren	3 - 1	Gardiner, McPhee, Weir	x		x					x	x	x		x					x				x	x			x			x	
21	11-Jan	CELTIC	1 - 3	Quinn	x		x					x	x	x		x					x				x	x			x			x	
22	18-Jan	Partick Thistle	2 - 3	St John (2)	x		x				x		x	x		x					x					x			x	x		x	
p 28/4	25-Jan	DUNDEE	1 - 0	Gardiner	x		x		x				x	x		x		x	x							x			x		x		
p 16/4	08-Feb	QUEENS PARK	4 - 1	Gardiner (2), St John, Hunter	x		x				x		x	x	x	x				x								x	x	x			
p 30/4	15-Feb	Falkirk	1 - 1		x		x				x		x	x	x	x			x	x								x		x			
26	22-Feb	HEARTS	0 - 4		x		x					x	x	x		x			x						x	x			x	x			
27	01-Mar	Raith Rovers	1 - 1		x		x						x	x	x	x	x		x	x								x		x			
28	08-Mar	KILMARNOCK	2 - 2	St John, Gardiner	x		x					x	x	x		x			x						x	x			x	x			
p 3/5	15-Mar	Queen of the South	2 - 1	St.John, McCann	x		x	x					x	x	x	x			x							x		x		x			
30	22-Mar	CLYDE	1 - 1	Hunter	x		x					x	x	x		x			x						x	x		x		x			
31	29-Mar	Rangers	2 - 2	St John (2)	x		x		x				x	x		x			x			x			x	x				x			
32	05-Apr	Aberdeen	3 - 4		x		x						x	x	x	x			x	x						x		x		x			
33	12-Apr	EAST FIFE	2 - 0	Hunter (2)	x		x					x	x	x		x			x							x		x	x	x			
34	26-Apr	THIRD LANARK	1 - 2	Aitken	x		x					x	x	x	x	x			x									x	x	x			

LEAGUE CUP

	Date	Opponent	Score	Scorers	Weir Hastie	Wyllie	McSeveney	Brown J	Campbell	Shaw	Gilchrist	Holton	Weir A	Martis	Hunter W	Aitken	Brims	Paton	Forrest	McFadyen	Kerr	Rea	Baker	Reid S	Quinn	McCann	Stenhouse	Hunter J	Gardiner	St John	Brown S	McPhee	Cowie
	10-Aug	FALKIRK	1 - 4	Gardiner	x						x	x				x			x				x		x			x	x			x	x
	14-Aug	Queen of the South	0 - 3		x						x	x				x			x				x		x			x	x			x	x
	17-Aug	ABERDEEN	2 - 3	Gardiner, Forrest	x						x	x				x			x				x		x	x			x			x	x
	24-Aug	Falkirk	3 - 1	Aitken, McPhee, OG	x						x	x				x			x					x		x		x	x			x	x
	28-Aug	QUEEN OF THE SOUTH	2 - 1	Hunter (2)	x						x	x				x			x					x		x		x	x			x	x
	30-Aug	Aberdeen	3 - 5	McCann, McPhee, Forrest	x						x	x				x			x					x		x		x	x			x	x

SCOTTISH CUP

	Date	Opponent	Score	Scorers	Att.	Weir Hastie	Wyllie	McSeveney	Brown J	Campbell	Shaw	Gilchrist	Holton	Weir A	Martis	Hunter W	Aitken	Brims	Paton	Forrest	McFadyen	Kerr	Rea	Baker	Reid S	Quinn	McCann	Stenhouse	Hunter J	Gardiner	St John	Brown S	McPhee	Cowie
	01-Feb	East Stirling	7 - 3	Gardiner (4), Weir (2), Kerr	3500	x		x			x		x	x			x					x					x			x	x		x	
	15-Feb	PARTICK THISTLE	2 - 2	Kerr, St John	17560	x		x					x	x	x		x					x					x			x	x		x	
rep.	19-Feb	Partick Thistle	4 - 0		30000	x		x					x	x	x		x					x					x			x	x		x	
	01 Mar	Inverness Caly	7 - 0	Forrest (2), Kerr (2), Gardiner, Weir, St John	9375	x		x						x	x		x			x		x					x			x	x		x	
	15-Mar	ABERDEEN	2 - 1	McSeveney, St John	19000	x		x					x	x	x		x			x	x					x	x				x			
S/F	05-Apr	CLYDE	2 - 3	Quinn, St John	41000	x		x					x	x	x		x			x			x			x	x				x			

1958 Div. 1

		Pl.	Home W.	D.	L.	F.	A.	Away W.	D.	L.	F.	A.	F. (Total)	A.	Pts.
1	Heart of Mid.	34	15	2	0	79	17	14	2	1	53	12	132	29	62
2	Rangers	34	10	2	5	47	26	12	3	2	42	23	89	49	49
3	Celtic	34	7	6	4	42	22	12	2	3	42	25	84	47	46
4	Clyde	34	13	1	3	53	27	5	5	7	31	34	84	61	42
5	Kilmarnock	34	8	6	3	36	24	6	3	8	24	31	60	55	37
6	Partick Thistle	34	11	1	5	37	25	6	2	9	32	46	69	71	37
7	Raith Rovers	34	10	2	5	37	20	4	5	8	29	36	66	56	35
8	MOTHERWELL	34	8	3	6	36	31	4	5	8	32	36	68	67	32
9	Hibernian	34	6	4	7	34	26	7	1	9	25	34	59	60	31
10	Falkirk	34	6	5	6	30	32	5	4	8	34	50	64	82	31
11	Dundee	34	10	1	6	32	22	3	4	10	17	43	49	65	31
12	Aberdeen	34	8	0	9	40	35	6	2	9	28	41	68	76	30
13	St. Mirren	34	7	4	6	31	27	4	4	9	28	39	59	66	30
14	Third Lanark	34	6	2	9	32	39	7	2	8	37	49	69	88	30
15	Queen of the S.	34	6	4	7	33	32	6	1	10	28	40	61	72	29
16	Airdrieonians	34	8	2	7	47	45	5	0	12	24	47	71	92	28
17	East Fife	34	5	2	10	24	40	5	1	11	21	48	45	88	23
18	Queen's Park	34	1	0	16	18	60	3	1	13	23	54	41	114	9

1958-59: 1st Division

						Weir Hastie	Wyllie	McSeveney	Holton	McCallum R	Aitken	Cowie	Martis	McCann	Reid S	Weir A	Quinn	Stenhouse	Strachan	Gardiner	St John	Forrest	Brown S	McPhee	Hunter W	Reid W	Stewart	Roberts	Campbell	McFadyen	Baker
1	20-Aug	PARTICK THISTLE	3 - 1	St John (2), Forrest		X		X			X		X	X		X				X	X	X	X		X						
2	06-Sep	Aidrie	5 - 1	St John (3), Quinn, OG		X		X			X		X	X		X				X	X		X		X						
3	13-Sep	HIBERNIAN	2 - 3	St John, Gardiner		X		X			X		X	X		X				X	X		X		X						
4	20-Sep	Dunfermline Ath.	4 - 0	St John (2), Gardiner, Hunter		X		X			X		X	X	X	X				X	X		X		X						
5	27-Sep	ST. MIRREN	2 - 2	S Reid, Hunter		X		X			X		X	X	X	X				X	X		X		X						
6	04-Oct	Dundee	1 - 1	Weir		X		X			X		X	X	X	X	X				X		X		X						
7	11-Oct	THIRD LANARK	8 - 1	Weir (2), S Reid, Aitken, Quinn (2), St John (2)		X		X			X		X	X	X	X	X				X		X		X						
8	18-Oct	Falkirk	1 - 1	S Reid		X		X			X		X	X	X	X	X				X		X		X						
9	25-Oct	CLYDE	1 - 0	St John		X		X			X		X	X	X	X	X				X		X		X						
10	01-Nov	Hearts	2 - 0	Hunter, Quinn		X		X			X		X	X	X	X	X				X		X		X						
11	08-Nov	RAITH ROVERS	3 - 3	St John, Weir, Aitken		X		X			X		X	X	X	X	X				X		X		X						
12	15-Nov	KILMARNOCK	1 - 1	OG		X		X			X		X	X	X	X	X				X		X		X						
13	22-Nov	Stirling Albion	5 - 2	Hunter (2), W Reid (2), St John		X		X			X		X	X		X	X				X		X		X	X					
14	29-Nov	RANGERS	2 - 2	Quinn, W Reid		X		X			X		X	X		X	X				X		X		X	X					
p 2/1	06-Dec	Celtic	3 - 3	Quinn (2), St John		X		X		X			X	X	X	X	X	X			X	X									
16	13-Dec	Aberdeen	4 - 0	St John (2), S REID, Weir			X	X	X		X		X	X	X	X	X				X					X					
17	20-Dec	QUEEN OF THE SOUTH	6 - 1	S Reid (2), Weir (2), St John (2)			X	X	X		X	X		X	X	X	X				X				X						
18	27-Dec	Partick Thistle	0 - 4				X	X	X		X		X	X	X	X	X				X				X						
19	01-Jan	AIRDRIE	5 - 2	OG, Forrest, St John, Hunter, Quinn		X		X	X		X		X	X		X	X				X	X			X						
20	03-Jan	Hibernian	2 - 2	Hunter, Quinn		X		X	X		X		X	X	X	X	X				X				X						
21	10-Jan	DUNFERMLINE	1 0			X		X	X		X		X	X	X	X	X				X				X						
p 23/2	17-Jan	St. Mirren	1 - 4			X		X	X		X		X	X	X	X	X				X				X						
23	24-Jan	DUNDEE	2 - 0	Strachan (2)		X		X	X		X		X	X	X	X	X		X						X						
24	07-Feb	Third Lanark	2 - 5	Hunter, Quinn		X		X	X		X			X	X	X	X		X			X			X						
25	14-Feb	FALKIRK	1 - 0	Strachan		X		X	X		X		X	X	X	X	X		X						X						
26	21-Feb	Clyde	0 - 2			X		X	X		X		X	X	X	X	X				X				X						
27	18-Mar?	HEARTS	0 - 1			X		X	X		X		X	X	X	X	X				X				X						
28	07-Mar	Raith Rovers	0 - 3			X		X	X		X		X	X	X	X	X				X				X						
29	14-Mar	Kilmarnock	3 - 1			X		X			X			X	X	X	X				X			X	X						
30	21-Mar	STIRLING ALBION	3 - 0	Quinn (3)		X		X	X		X		X	X	X	X	X				X				X						
31	28-Mar	Rangers	1 - 2	St John		X		X	X		X		X	X	X	X	X				X				X						
32	04-Apr	CELTIC	2 - 0			X		X			X		X			X	X				X	X			X		X				
33	11-Apr	ABERDEEN	2 - 0	S Reid, Hunter		X		X			X		X	X	X	X	X				X	X			X						
34	18-Apr	Queen of the South	5 - 0	Weir (3), S Reid (2)		X		X			X		X	X	X	X	X				X	X						X			

LEAGUE CUP

						Weir Hastie	Wyllie	McSeveney	Holton	McCallum R	Aitken	Cowie	Martis	McCann	Reid S	Weir A	Quinn	Stenhouse	Strachan	Gardiner	St John	Forrest	Brown S	McPhee	Hunter W	Reid W	Stewart	Roberts	Campbell	McFadyen	Baker
	09-Aug	Queen of the South	2 - 1	Quinn, Gardiner		X					X		X	X		X	X			X	X	X							X	X	
	13-Aug	DUNDEE	1 - 2	St John		X		X			X		X	X		X	X			X	X				X					X	
	16-Aug	PARTICK THISTLE	2 - 5	Hunter, St John		X					X		X	X			X			X	X				X				X	X	X
	23-Aug	QUEEN OF THE SOUTH	4 - 0	Gardiner (2), Weir, St John		X		X			X		X	X		X				X	X	X	X		X						
	27-Aug	Dundee	3 - 2	St John, Hunter, Weir		X		X			X		X	X		X				X	X	X	X		X						
	30-Aug	Partick Thistle	1 - 1	Hunter		X		X			X		X	X		X	X				X	X	X		X						

SCOTTISH CUP

						Weir Hastie	Wyllie	McSeveney	Holton	McCallum R	Aitken	Cowie	Martis	McCann	Reid S	Weir A	Quinn	Stenhouse	Strachan	Gardiner	St John	Forrest	Brown S	McPhee	Hunter W	Reid W	Stewart	Roberts	Campbell	McFadyen	Baker
	31-Jan	Aidrie	7 - 2	St John (4), Weir (2), Hunter	14000	X		X	X		X		X	X	X	X	X				X				X						
	28-Feb	St. Mirren	2 - 3	Quinn (2)	26956	X		X	X		X		X	X	X	X	X				X				X						

FRIENDLIES

	20-Oct	LEEDS UNITED	7 - 0
	10-Nov	DJUGARDENS	2 - 1
	??	CELTIC	1 - 1
	??	Glentoran	4 - 1

1959 Div. 1

		Pl.	Home					Away					F.	A.	Pts.
			W.	D.	L.	F.	A.	W.	D.	L.	F.	A.	(Total)		
1	Rangers	34	13	2	2	41	17	8	6	3	51	34	92	51	50
2	Heart of Mid.	34	12	2	3	49	25	9	4	4	43	26	92	51	48
3	MOTHERWELL	34	11	4	2	44	19	7	4	6	39	31	83	50	44
4	Dundee	34	10	5	2	36	25	6	4	7	25	26	61	51	41
5	Airdrieonians	34	8	3	6	35	32	7	4	6	29	30	64	62	37
6	Celtic	34	11	4	2	48	24	3	4	10	22	29	70	53	36
7	St. Mirren	34	8	4	5	38	33	6	3	8	33	41	71	74	35
8	Kilmarnock	34	10	3	4	38	23	3	5	9	20	28	58	51	34
9	Partick Thistle	34	8	4	5	34	27	6	2	9	25	39	59	66	34
10	Hibernian	34	8	3	6	38	31	5	3	9	30	39	68	70	32
11	Third Lanark	34	6	5	6	40	31	5	5	7	34	52	74	83	32
12	Stirling Albion	34	6	5	6	27	25	5	3	9	27	39	54	64	30
13	Aberdeen	34	7	4	6	42	29	5	1	11	21	37	63	66	29
14	Raith Rovers	34	9	3	5	33	25	1	6	10	27	45	60	70	29
15	Clyde	34	8	2	7	37	34	4	2	11	25	32	62	66	28
16	Dunfermline Ath.	34	7	3	7	41	41	3	5	9	27	46	68	87	28
17	Falkirk	34	6	4	7	32	33	4	3	10	26	46	58	79	27
18	Queen of the S.	34	4	5	8	24	44	2	1	14	14	57	38	101	18

1958-59 Season
Back: McSeveney, Holton, MacFadyen, Gardiner, Brown, Cowie, Martis, Forrest, Aitken
Middle: A.Weir, McCann, Campbell, Shaw, H.Weir, Stenhouse, McCallum, McPhee, St.John
Front: Reid, Quinn, Hunter, Reid, Baker, Rea, Newman, Kerr

1959-60 Season
Back: Forest, McCallum, Cattenach, H.Weir, Wylie, Martis, Delaney
Middle: St.John, McCann, Stewart, McSeveney, McCallum, Roberts, Martin, Aitken
Front: Young, Quinn, W.Reid, S.Reid, Stevenson, A.Weir, Lindsay, Hunter, Kerr

1959-60: 1st Division

No	Date	Opponent	Score	Scorers	Att	Weir Hastie	Wyllie	McSeveney	McCallum R	Aitken	Martis	Delaney	McCann	Reid S	Quinn	Stenhouse	Strachan	St John	Young	Forrest	McPhee	Hunter W	Reid W	Weir A	Roberts	Mackin	Paterson
1	19-Aug	Dunfermline Ath.	0 - 6			x			x	x	x		x	x	x			x		x		x		x			
2	05-Sep	AIRDRIE	4 - 1	Quinn (3), St John	13423	x			x	x	x		x	x	x			x		x		x		x			
3	12-Sep	Ayr United	2 - 5	Roberts, Hunter		x			x	x	x		x	x	x			x		x		x			x		
4	19-Sep	ST. MIRREN	1 - 4	Quinn	17465	x		x		x		x	x	x	x			x		x		x			x		
5	26-Sep	Dundee	1 - 1	S Reid		x		x			x		x	x	x			x		x		x			x		x
6	03-Oct	PARTICK THISTLE	4 - 0	Reid (2), Quinn, Roberts	10356	x		x		x	x			x	x					x	x	x	x		x		
7	10-Oct	Hibernian	3 - 1	S Reid, St John, Quinn		x		x		x	x		x	x	x			x		x		x	x				
8	17-Oct	STIRLING ALBION	2 - 1	McCallum, St John	9058	x		x	x	x	x		x	x	x			x		x		x					
9	24-Oct	Celtic	1 - 5	St John		x		x	x	x	x		x	x	x			x		x		x					
10	31-Oct	Kilmarnock	0 - 2				x			x	x	x	x	x	x			x		x		x		x			
11	07-Nov	ABERDEEN	3 - 1	St John, Quinn, McCann	8769			x		x	x		x		x		x	x		x		x		x		x	
12	14-Nov	CLYDE	3 - 2	Quinn, Weir, St John	7778			x		x	x		x		x			x		x	x	x		x		x	
13	21-Nov	Third Lanark	4 - 1	Quinn (2), Hunter, St John				x		x	x		x	x	x			x				x	x	x		x	
14	28-Nov	RANGERS	2 - 1	St John, Weir	21343			x		x	x		x	x	x			x				x	x	x		x	
15	05-Dec	Raith Rovers	1 - 1	OG				x		x	x	x	x	x	x			x				x	x	x		x	
16	12-Dec	HEARTS	3 - 0	S Reid, Hunter, St John	18900			x		x	x		x	x	x			x				x	x	x		x	
17	19-Dec	Arbroath	1 - 3	Quinn				x		x	x		x	x	x			x				x	x	x		x	
18	26-Dec	DUNFERMLINE	1 - 1	Quinn	7092			x		x	x		x	x	x			x				x	x	x		x	
19	01-Jan	Aidrie	1 - 0	Weir				x		x	x		x	x	x		x	x				x		x		x	
20	02-Jan	AYR UNITED	3 - 3	Hunter, St John, OG	12940					x	x		x	x	x		x	x				x	x	x		x	
21	09-Jan	St. Mirren	1 - 5	Quinn							x				x			x				x				x	
22	16-Jan	DUNDEE	0 - 0		9669						x				x	x		x				x				x	
23	23-Jan	Partick Thistle	2 - 1	Quinn, Delaney							x				x			x				x				x	
24	06-Feb	HIBERNIAN	3 - 4	Weir (2), St John	12599						x				x			x				x				x	
25	20-Feb	Stirling Albion	3 - 0	OG, McPhee, St John				x		x	x		x	x	x			x			x	x		x		x	
p 21/3	27-Feb	CELTIC	1 - 2	Hunter	11808	x				x	x		x		x		x	x			x	x	x	x			
27	05-Mar	KILMARNOCK	1 - 2	McPhee	15934			x		x	x		x		x			x			x	x	x		x	x	
28	12-Mar	Aberdeen	2 - 2	McPhee, St John		x		x		x	x		x		x			x			x	x	x	x			
29	19-Mar	Clyde	4 - 1	St John (2), Quinn, Weir		x				x	x		x		x		x	x			x	x	x	x			
30	26-Mar	THIRD LANARK	3 - 3	St John (2), Strachan	7204						x	x			x			x			x	x				x	
p 18/4	02-Apr	Rangers	2 - 0	Aitken, Hunter							x	x			x			x	x		x	x				x	
32	16-Apr	RAITH ROVERS	2 - 1	St John, Young	8057	x				x	x		x		x		x	x	x			x	x	x			
33	23-Apr	Hearts	1 - 1	Quinn							x				x			x	x			x				x	
34	30-Apr	ARBROATH	6 - 0	St John (3), Quinn (3)	5490						x				x			x	x			x				x	

LEAGUE CUP

Date	Opponent	Score	Scorers	Att	Weir Hastie	Wyllie	McSeveney	McCallum R	Aitken	Martis	Delaney	McCann	Reid S	Quinn	Stenhouse	Strachan	St John	Young	Forrest	McPhee	Hunter W	Reid W	Weir A	Roberts	Mackin	Paterson
08-Aug	DUNDEE	4 - 2	Quinn (2), St John, S Reid		x		x		x	x		x	x	x			x		x		x		x			
12-Aug	Rangers	2 - 1	St John, Quinn	34000	x		x		x	x		x	x	x			x		x		x		x			
15-Aug	Hibernian	3 - 1	St John (3)		x		x		x	x		x	x	x			x		x		x		x			
22-Aug	Dundee	4 - 1	Reid (2), Quinn (2)	18000	x		x		x	x		x	x	x			x		x		x		x			
26-Aug	RANGERS	2 - 1	St John, Hunter		x		x		x	x		x	x	x			x		x		x		x			
29-Aug	HIBERNIAN	4 - 2	S Reid (2), Weir, Quinn		x		x		x	x		x	x	x			x		x		x		x			
09-Sep	HEARTS	1 - 1	St John		x		x		x	x		x	x	x			x		x		x		x			
16-Sep	Hearts	2 - 6			x		x		x	x		x	x	x			x		x		x		x			

SCOTTISH CUP

Date	Opponent	Score	Scorers	Att	Weir Hastie	Wyllie	McSeveney	McCallum R	Aitken	Martis	Delaney	McCann	Reid S	Quinn	Stenhouse	Strachan	St John	Young	Forrest	McPhee	Hunter W	Reid W	Weir A	Roberts	Mackin	Paterson
13-Feb	KEITH	6 - 0	McPhee (2), Quinn (2), St John, OG	9003			x		x	x		x	x	x			x			x		x	x		x	
27-Feb	Kilmarnock	0 - 2		28329			x		x	x		x		x			x			x	x	x	x		x	

FRIENDLIES

Date	Opponent	Score	Scorers
05-Oct	WINTERTHUR	3 - 0	S Reid, W Reid, St John
30-Mar	GOTHENBURG	2 - 1	
13-Apr	ATH BILBAO	3 - 2	OG, Hunter, St John
26-Apr	FLAMENCO	9 - 2	St John (6), Hunter (2), Quinn
02-Apr	Hearts		

1960 Div. 1

		Pl.	Home W.	D.	L.	F.	A.	Away W.	D.	L.	F.	A.	F. (Total)	A.	Pts.
1	Heart of Mid.	34	14	2	1	56	22	9	6	2	46	29	102	51	54
2	Kilmarnock	34	13	2	2	34	20	11	0	6	33	25	67	45	50
3	Rangers	34	5	6	6	30	22	12	2	3	42	16	72	38	42
4	Dundee	34	11	1	5	41	25	5	9	3	29	24	70	49	42
5	MOTHERWELL	34	9	4	4	42	26	7	4	6	29	35	71	61	40
6	Clyde	34	7	5	5	41	30	8	4	5	36	39	77	69	39
7	Hibernian	34	8	4	5	52	39	6	3	8	54	46	106	85	35
8	Ayr United	34	9	4	4	36	26	5	2	10	29	47	65	73	34
9	Celtic	34	7	5	5	36	24	5	4	8	37	35	73	59	33
10	Partick Thistle	34	10	0	7	26	32	4	4	9	28	46	54	78	32
11	Raith Rovers	34	7	3	7	38	27	7	0	10	26	35	64	62	31
12	Third Lanark	34	7	3	7	45	38	6	1	10	30	45	75	83	30
13	Dunfermline Ath.	34	7	5	5	39	34	3	4	10	33	46	72	80	29
14	St. Mirren	34	5	3	9	38	44	6	3	8	40	42	78	86	28
15	Aberdeen	34	8	4	5	35	32	3	2	12	19	40	54	72	28
16	Airdrieonians	34	5	1	11	31	54	6	5	6	25	26	56	80	28
17	Stirling Albion	34	4	3	10	28	36	3	5	9	27	36	55	72	22
18	Arbroath	34	4	5	8	29	41	0	2	15	9	65	38	106	15

1960-61: 1st Division

	Date	Opponent	Score	Scorers	Weir H	McSeveney	Weir L	Reid	Martis	McCann	Young	Quinn	St John	Hunter	Weir A	Roberts	McPhee	Lindsay	Delaney	Aitken	Strachan	Stevenson	Wyllie	McCallum
1	24-Aug	AYR UNITED	2 - 2	St John, McCann	x	x	x		x	x	x	x		x	x	x			x					
2	10-Sep	Aidrie	2 - 4	St John, Weir	x		x		x	x		x	x	x	x	x				x	x			
3	17-Sep	PARTICK THISTLE	2 - 0	St John (2)	x	x	x	x	x	x	x	x	x	x	x									
4	24-Sep	Dunfermline Ath.	6 - 1	St John (3), Quinn (2), Weir	x	x	x	x	x	x	x	x	x	x	x									
5	01-Oct	Clyde	0 - 1		x	x	x	x	x	x	x	x	x	x	x									
6	08-Oct	RAITH	2 - 1	McCann, Quinn	x	x	x	x	x	x		x	x	x	x	x								
7	15-Oct	THIRD LANARK	4 - 5	Quinn (2), St John, Lindsay	x	x	x	x	x	x		x	x	x	x	x								
8	22-Oct	Dundee United	1 - 0	Roberts	x	x	x	x		x		x				x	x	x			x			x
9	29-Oct	HEARTS	1 - 1	Weir	x	x	x		x	x		x		x	x	x	x	x						
10	05-Nov	St. Mirren	3 - 2	Quinn (2), McSeveney	x	x	x		x	x		x		x	x	x	x	x						
11	12-Nov	Aberdeen	3 - 3	Weir (2), McSeveney	x	x	x		x	x		x		x	x	x	x	x						
12	26-Nov	HIBERNIAN	4 - 1	Quinn (3), Weir	x	x	x		x	x		x	x	x	x	x	x							
13	03-Dec	Kilmarnock	3 - 5	McCann, Weir, St John	x	x	x		x	x		x	x	x	x		x	x						
14	10-Dec	ST. JOHNSTONE	2 - 0	Quinn (2)	x	x	x		x	x		x	x	x	x		x	x						
15	17-Dec	DUNDEE	2 - 0	St John, Quinn	x		x		x	x		x	x	x	x		x	x	x					
16	24-Dec	Celtic	0 - 1		x		x		x	x		x	x	x	x		x	x	x					
17	26-Dec	RANGERS	1 - 2	Lindsay	x	x	x	x	x	x	x			x	x	x		x						
18	31-Dec	Ayr	0 - 0		x		x		x	x		x	x	x	x		x	x	x					
19	02-Jan	AIRDRIE	2 - 0	Quinn, St John	x		x		x	x		x	x	x	x		x	x	x					
20	07-Jan	thistle	3 - 1	Quinn, Hunter, Weir	x		x		x	x		x	x	x	x		x	x	x					
21	14-Jan	DUNFERMLINE	2 - 4	St John, Weir	x		x		x	x		x	x	x	x		x	x	x					
22	21-Jan	CLYDE	2 - 1	Hunter, McCann	x		x		x	x		x	x	x	x			x	x	x				
23	04-Feb	Raith Rovers	3 - 1	Weir, St John, Quinn	x	x			x	x		x	x	x	x			x	x	x				
24	18-Feb	Third Lanark	1 - 1	Roberts	x	x			x	x		x	x	x	x			x	x	x				
25	04-Mar	Hearts	5 - 1	Aitken (2), St John, Hunter, McPhee	x	x			x	x		x	x	x		x	x		x	x				
26	07-Mar	DUNDEE UNITED	4 - 3	St John (2), McSeveney (2)	x	x			x	x		x	x	x		x	x		x	x				
27	15-Mar	ST. MIRREN	0 - 3		x	x			x	x		x	x	x		x	x		x	x				
28	18-Mar	ABERDEEN	1 - 0	Quinn	x	x			x	x		x	x	x		x	x		x	x				
29	25-Mar	Rangers	2 - 2	St John, Quinn	x				x	x		x	x	x		x			x	x	x	x		
30	01-Apr	Hibernian	1 - 2	Roberts	x				x	x		x	x	x		x			x	x	x	x		
31	08-Apr	KILMARNOCK	1 - 3	Hunter					x	x		x	x	x		x	x		x	x	x		x	
32	19-Apr	St. Johnstone	1 - 2	Quinn					x	x		x	x	x		x	x		x	x	x		x	
33	22-Apr	Dundee	2 - 2	St John, Quinn					x	x		x	x	x		x	x		x	x	x		x	
34	29-Apr	CELTIC	2 - 2	Roberts (2)					x	x		x	x	x		x	x		x	x	x		x	

LEAGUE CUP

	Date	Opponent	Score	Scorers	Weir H	McSeveney	Weir L	Reid	Martis	McCann	Young	Quinn	St John	Hunter	Weir A	Roberts	McPhee	Lindsay	Delaney	Aitken	Strachan	Stevenson	Wyllie	McCallum
	13-Aug	CLYDE	4 - 4	Quinn, McSeveney, Hunter, Roberts	x	x			x	x	x	x		x	x	x				x	x			
	17-Aug	St. Mirren	4 - 0	Quinn (2), Hunter (2)	x	x	x	x	x	x		x	x	x	x	x								
	20-Aug	HEARTS	2 - 3	McPhee, Hunter	x	x	x		x	x	x	x		x	x	x				x				
	27-Aug	Clyde	1 - 1	Roberts	x	x	x		x	x	x	x		x	x	x				x				
	31-Aug	ST. MIRREN	5 - 2	Roberts (2), Hunter, Quinn, McCann	x	x	x	x	x	x		x	x	x	x	x								
	03-Sep	Hearts	1 - 2	Quinn	x	x	x	x	x	x		x	x	x	x	x								

SCOTTISH CUP

	Date	Opponent	Score	Scorers	Weir H	McSeveney	Weir L	Reid	Martis	McCann	Young	Quinn	St John	Hunter	Weir A	Roberts	McPhee	Lindsay	Delaney	Aitken	Strachan	Stevenson	Wyllie	McCallum
	11-Feb	Cowdenbeath	4 - 1	McSeveney, Weir, St John, Quinn	x	x			x	x		x	x	x	x			x	x	x				
	25-Feb	RANGERS	2 - 2	St John, McCann	x	x			x	x		x	x	x	x	x			x	x				
rep.	01-Mar	Rangers	5 - 2	Roberts (2), St John, Delaney, McPhee	x	x			x	x		x	x	x		x	x		x	x				
	11-Mar	AIRDRIE	0 - 1		x	x			x	x		x	x	x		x	x		x	x				

LANARKSHIRE CUP

Date	Opponent	Score
01-May	HAMILTON ACADEMICAL	7 - 0

FRIENDLIES

Date	Opponent	Score	Scorers
07-Aug	Toulouse	2 - 1	
26-Sep	BAHIA	3 - 0	Young, St John, Hunter
19-Oct	TOULOUSE	4 - 1	
17-Apr	Norwich City	0 - 2	
24-Oct	Dunfermline Ath.	2 - 4	Quinn, Roberts

1961 Div. 1

		Pl.	Home W.	D.	L.	F.	A.	Away W.	D.	L.	F.	A.	F. (Total)	A.	Pts.
1	Rangers	34	14	1	2	52	19	9	4	4	36	27	88	46	51
2	Kilmarnock	34	12	4	1	45	19	9	4	4	32	26	77	45	50
3	Third Lanark	34	11	2	4	55	33	9	0	8	45	47	100	80	42
4	Celtic	34	9	4	4	33	22	6	5	6	31	24	64	46	39
5	MOTHERWELL	34	9	3	5	34	28	6	5	6	36	29	70	57	38
6	Aberdeen	34	9	2	6	38	34	5	6	6	34	38	72	72	36
7	Heart of Mid.	34	8	3	6	26	25	5	5	7	25	28	51	53	34
8	Hibernian	34	10	3	4	41	30	5	1	11	25	39	66	69	34
9	Dundee United	34	9	3	5	36	21	4	4	9	24	37	60	58	33
10	Dundee	34	9	3	5	38	23	4	3	10	23	30	61	53	32
11	Partick Thistle	34	8	4	5	36	30	5	2	10	23	39	59	69	32
12	Dunfermline Ath.	34	8	4	5	43	42	4	3	10	22	39	65	81	31
13	Airdrieonians	34	9	4	4	39	28	1	6	10	22	43	61	71	30
14	St. Mirren	34	6	5	6	25	22	5	2	10	28	36	53	58	29
15	St. Johnstone	34	7	5	5	30	29	3	4	10	17	34	47	63	29
16	Raith Rovers	34	5	4	8	26	34	5	3	9	20	33	46	67	27
17	Clyde	34	5	7	5	31	29	1	4	12	24	48	55	77	23
18	Ayr United	34	5	6	6	24	26	0	6	11	27	55	51	81	22

1960-61 Season
Back: McSeveney, Strachan, H.Weir, Aitken, Martis, Roberts
Front: Young, Quinn, McCann, Hunter, A.Weir

1961-62 Season
McCann, Weir, Quinn, Hunter, Thompson, Aitken, McPhee, McCallum, Thomson, Roberts, McCallum, McSeveney, Murray, Wylie, Delaney and Martis, are only sixteen of the above squad.

1961-62: 1st Division

No.	Date	Opponent	Score	Scorers	Att.	Weir H	McSeveney	Thomson	McCann	Martis	McPhee	Hunter	Roberts	Aitken	Quinn	Weir A	Lindsay	Stevenson	McCallum	Young	Delaney	Wyllie	Strachan	Main	Goldie
1	23-Aug	PARTICK THISTLE	1 - 3		7676	x	x	x	x	x	x		x	x	x	x							x		
2	09-Sep	Stirling Albion	4 - 2	Roberts (2), Quinn, OG		x	x	x	x	x	x		x	x	x	x							x		
3	16-Sep	AIRDRIE	5 - 2	Aitken (2), Lindsay (2), Weir	7384	x	x	x	x	x	x	x	x	x	x	x									
4	23-Sep	St. Johnstone	1 - 1	McPhee		x	x	x	x	x	x	x	x	x	x	x									
5	30-Sep	DUNFERMLINE	1 - 1	Roberts	9325	x	x	x	x	x	x	x	x	x	x		x								
6	07-Oct	Raith Rovers	3 - 0			x	x	x	x			x	x	x	x	x	x	x							
7	14-Oct	DUNDEE	2 - 4	Hunter (2)	11036	x	x	x	x	x		x	x	x	x		x	x							
8	21-Oct	RANGERS	2 - 2	Quinn, McPhee	24334	x	x	x	x		x	x	x	x	x	x			x						
9	28-Oct	Aberdeen	0 - 3			x	x	x	x		x	x	x	x	x	x			x						
10	04-Nov	St. Mirren	1 - 2	McPhee		x	x	x	x		x	x	x	x	x	x			x						
11	11-Nov	HIBERNIAN	5 - 1	Delaney (3), McPhee, Roberts	5470	x	x	x	x		x	x		x	x				x	x	x				
12	18-Nov	DUNDEE UNITED	2 - 1	Delaney , Roberts	7665	x	x	x			x	x	x	x	x				x	x	x				
13	25-Nov	Third Lanark	1 - 2	OG		x	x	x			x	x	x	x	x				x	x	x				
14	02-Dec	Hearts	6 - 2	Delaney (3), Quinn (2), Roberts		x	x	x		x	x	x	x	x	x					x	x				
15	16-Dec	FALKIRK	3 - 0	McPhee, Hunter, Quinn	6689	x	x	x		x	x	x	x	x	x					x	x				
16	23-Dec	Kilmarnock	2 - 1	Quinn, Hunter		x	x	x		x	x	x	x	x	x					x	x				
17	06-Jan	Partick Thistle	0 - 1			x	x	x		x	x	x	x	x	x					x	x				
18	10-Jan	STIRLING ALBION	5 - 3		5432	x	x	x		x	x	x	x	x	x					x	x				
19	13-Jan	ST. JOHNSTONE	2 - 2	Quinn (2)	7087	x	x	x		x	x	x	x	x	x					x	x				
20	17-Jan	Aidrie	1 - 2			x	x	x	x	x	x	x	x	x	x					x					
21	20-Jan	Dunfermline Ath.	1 - 2	McPhee		x		x	x	x	x		x	x	x	x					x			x	
22	22-Jan	Celtic	1 - 1	Young		x			x	x	x	x	x	x	x				x	x	x				
23	03-Feb	RAITH	3 - 0	Roberts, Young, Aitken	5003	x			x	x	x	x	x	x	x				x	x	x				
24	10-Feb	Dundee	3 - 1	Quinn, Roberts, Young					x	x	x	x	x	x	x				x	x	x	x			
25	24-Feb	ABERDEEN	1 - 3	Weir	7876				x	x	x	x		x	x	x			x	x	x	x			
26	28-Feb	Rangers	1 - 2						x	x	x	x	x	x	x				x	x	x	x			
27	03-Mar	ST. MIRREN	2 - 1	Quinn (2)	8233				x	x	x	x	x	x	x	x			x		x	x			
28	14-Mar	Hibernian	2 - 1	Young, Delaney						x	x	x	x	x	x	x			x	x	x	x			
29	17-Mar	Dundee United	1 - 1	Quinn			x	x		x	x	x	x	x	x			x			x	x			
30	24-Mar	THIRD LANARK	0 - 3		7074		x	x		x	x	x	x	x	x			x			x	x			
31	02-Apr	HEARTS	1 - 2	Hunter	2320			x		x	x	x	x	x	x	x				x	x	x			
32	07-Apr	Falkirk	2 - 4	Hunter, Stevenson				x		x	x	x	x		x		x	x			x	x			x
33	21-Apr	KILMARNOCK	0 - 2		4236			x		x	x	x	x	x	x		x	x			x	x			
34	23-Apr	CELTIC	0 - 4		8351			x		x	x	x	x	x	x		x	x			x	x			

LEAGUE CUP

	Date	Opponent	Score	Scorers	Att.	Weir H	McSeveney	Thomson	McCann	Martis	McPhee	Hunter	Roberts	Aitken	Quinn	Weir A	Lindsay	Stevenson	McCallum	Young	Delaney	Wyllie	Strachan	Main	Goldie
	12-Aug	DUNDEE UNITED	5 - 3	Stevenson (3), Quinn (2)	11241				x	x		x	x	x	x		x	x			x	x	x		
	16-Aug	Aberdeen	4 - 3	Quinn (2), Roberts, Hunter					x	x		x	x	x	x		x	x			x	x	x		
	19-Aug	DUNFERMLINE	1 - 1	Quinn	11757				x	x		x	x	x	x		x	x			x	x	x		
	26-Aug	Dundee United	2 - 0						x	x		x	x	x	x		x	x			x	x	x		
	30-Aug	ABERDEEN	2 - 1	Quinn, Strachan	9932	x	x	x	x	x		x	x		x	x	x						x		
	02-Sep	Dunfermline Ath.	0 - 2			x	x	x	x	x		x	x		x	x	x						x		
	13-Sep	ST. JOHNSTONE	2 - 3		12215	x	x	x	x	x	x	x	x	x	x	x									
	20-Sep	St. Johnstone	1 - 1			x	x	x	x	x	x	x	x	x	x	x									

SCOTTISH CUP

	Date	Opponent	Score	Scorers	Att.	Weir H	McSeveney	Thomson	McCann	Martis	McPhee	Hunter	Roberts	Aitken	Quinn	Weir A	Lindsay	Stevenson	McCallum	Young	Delaney	Wyllie	Strachan	Main	Goldie
	13-Dec	DUNDEE UNITED	4 - 0	McPhee (2), Young, Hunter	8537	x	x	x		x	x	x	x	x	x					x	x				
	27-Jan	ST. JOHNSTONE	4 - 0	Hunter (2), Young, Roberts	10624	x			x	x	x	x	x	x	x				x	x	x				
	17-Feb	Stranraer	3 - 1	McSeveney (2), Hunter					x	x	x	x	x	x	x				x	x	x	x			
	10-Mar	Stirling Albion	6 - 0	Delaney (3), Stevenson, Quinn, OG			x	x	x	x	x	x		x	x			x			x	x			
semi	31-Mar	Rangers	1 - 3	Roberts			x	x		x	x	x	x	x	x			x			x	x			

FRIENDLIES

Date	Opponent	Score	Scorers
20-Nov	ELFSBORG	2 - 1	Young, Aitken
04-Apr	OLYMPIC NIMES	1 - 2	Jones
07-May	Olympic Nimes	0 - 0	
13-May	Marseilles	4 - 1	

1962 Div. 1

		Pl.	Home					Away					F.	A.	Pts.
			W.	D.	L.	F.	A.	W.	D.	L.	F.	A.	(Total)		
1	Dundee	34	13	2	2	41	23	12	2	3	39	23	80	46	54
2	Rangers	34	12	2	3	43	18	10	5	2	41	13	84	31	51
3	Celtic	34	12	4	1	46	16	7	4	6	35	21	81	37	46
4	Dunfermline Ath.	34	13	1	3	46	15	6	4	7	31	31	77	46	43
5	Kilmarnock	34	10	4	3	41	27	6	6	5	33	31	74	58	42
6	Heart of Mid.	34	7	5	5	30	28	9	1	7	24	21	54	49	38
7	Partick Thistle	34	12	0	5	36	21	4	3	10	24	34	60	55	35
8	Hibernian	34	7	5	5	31	30	7	0	10	27	42	58	72	33
9	MOTHERWELL	34	7	3	7	35	34	6	3	8	30	28	65	62	32
10	Dundee United	34	8	3	6	43	30	5	3	9	27	41	70	71	32
11	Third Lanark	34	8	3	6	37	31	5	2	10	22	29	59	60	31
12	Aberdeen	34	6	6	5	33	27	4	3	10	27	46	60	73	29
13	Raith Rovers	34	5	5	7	24	29	5	2	10	27	44	51	73	27
14	Falkirk	34	6	2	9	23	30	5	2	10	22	38	45	68	26
15	Airdrieonians	34	7	2	8	35	33	2	5	10	22	45	57	78	25
16	St. Mirren	34	7	3	7	29	29	3	2	12	23	51	52	80	25
17	St. Johnstone	34	4	2	11	14	34	5	5	7	21	27	35	61	25
18	Stirling Albion	34	5	3	9	22	32	1	3	13	12	44	34	76	18

1962-63: 1st Division

No.	Date	Opponent	Score	Scorers	Wyllie	Delaney	McCallum R	Aitken	Martis	McCann	Lindsay	Roberts	Strachan	Hunter	Goldie	Quinn	Russell	McCallum W	Jones	McSeveney	Stewart	Thomson L	Weir	McBride	Thomson M	Wallace	Murray	Ramsay	Goodwin
1	22-Aug	QUEEN OF THE SOUTH	1 - 2	McCallum	x	x	x		x	x	x	x			x	x	x						x						
2	08-Sep	Aidrie	4 - 1	Quinn, Goodwin, Goldie, Lindsay	x	x	x		x	x	x	x			x	x	x												x
3	15-Sep	HIBERNIAN	2 - 2	Roberts, Lindsay	x	x	x	x	x	x	x	x	x	x	x														
4	22-Sep	St. Mirren	0 - 2		x	x	x			x	x	x			x		x	x	x										x
5	29-Sep	PARTICK THISTLE	1 - 1	Aitken	x	x	x	x			x	x		x	x	x		x	x										
6	06-Oct	Third Lanark	2 - 2	Roberts, Hunter	x		x	x	x		x	x		x	x	x		x	x										
7	13-Oct	CELTIC	0 - 2		x		x	x	x	x	x	x		x		x				x	x								
8	20-Oct	Hearts	1 - 2	Roberts, Lindsay	x		x		x	x	x	x			x	x				x		x			x				
9	31-Oct	Kilmarnock	1 - 7	Roberts	x	x	x	x	x	x	x	x			x	x						x							
10	03-Nov	DUNDEE UNITED	0 - 0		x	x	x	x	x	x	x	x			x	x						x							
11	10-Nov	Falkirk	2 - 3	Quinn (2)	x	x	x	x	x	x	x	x			x	x						x							
p 17/11	21-Nov	ABERDEEN	0 - 2		x	x	x	x	x	x	x	x				x							x	x					
13	24-Nov	Dunfermline Ath.	3 - 4	Russell (2), McBride	x	x	x	x	x	x	x	x					x						x	x					
14	01-Dec	RANGERS	1 - 1	McBride	x	x	x	x	x	x	x	x					x						x	x					
15	08-Dec	Raith Rovers	5 - 2	Russell(3), McBride, Lindsay	x		x	x	x	x	x						x						x	x	x				
16	15-Dec	Dundee	2 - 2	Roberts (2)	x		x	x	x	x	x	x					x						x	x	x				
17	22-Dec	CLYDE	6 - 2	McBride (2), Russell (2), McCallum, McCann	x		x	x	x	x	x	x					x						x	x	x				
18	29-Dec	Queen of the South	2 - 0	McCann, McBride	x		x	x	x	x	x	x					x						x	x	x				
19	01-Jan	AIRDRIE	3 - 0	Roberts, Aitken, McBride	x		x	x	x	x	x	x					x						x	x	x				
20	05-Jan	ST. MIRREN	1 - 1	Russell	x		x	x	x	x	x	x					x						x	x	x				
21	09-Feb	Dundee United	1 - 2	McCann	x	x	x	x		x	x	x						x					x	x	x				
22	16-Feb	FALKIRK	4 - 1	McBride (2), Wallace, Russell	x		x	x	x	x	x	x					x							x	x	x			
23	20-Feb	THIRD LANARK	3 - 3	McBride (2), Russell	x		x	x	x	x	x	x					x						x	x	x				
24	23-Feb	Aberdeen	1 - 1	McBride	x		x	x	x	x	x	x					x						x	x	x				
p 30/3	01-Feb	DUNFERMLINE	0 - 0		x		x		x		x	x					x						x	x	x	x	x		
26	13-Mar	KILMARNOCK	2 - 1	Delaney, Murray	x	x	x	x	x		x	x											x	x	x		x		
27	17-Mar	Hibernian	0 - 1		x	x	x	x	x		x	x											x	x	x		x		
p 20/4	20-Mar	DUNDEE	2 - 1	McCann, Lindsay	x	x	x	x	x	x	x	x												x	x		x		
29	24-Mar	Partick Thistle	0 - 2		x	x	x	x	x	x	x	x												x	x		x		
30	27-Mar	Clyde	3 - 2	Weir, Aitken, McBride	x	x	x	x	x	x	x							x					x	x					
31	29-Mar	Rangers	1 - 1	McBride	x	x		x		x	x							x				x	x	x	x		x		
p 11/5	11-Apr	HEARTS	1 - 3	Lindsay	x	x		x		x	x							x				x	x	x	x		x		
33	13-Apr	Celtic	0 - 6		x	x		x			x	x						x				x	x	x	x		x		
34	15-Apr	RAITH	5 - 1		x	x		x			x	x						x					x	x	x		x	x	

LEAGUE CUP

No.	Date	Opponent	Score	Scorers	Wyllie	Delaney	McCallum R	Aitken	Martis	McCann	Lindsay	Roberts	Strachan	Hunter	Goldie	Quinn	Russell	McCallum W	Jones	McSeveney	Stewart	Thomson L	Weir	McBride	Thomson M	Wallace	Murray	Ramsay	Goodwin
	11-Aug	FALKIRK	9 - 1	Russell (5), Quinn (4)	x	x	x	x	x	x	x	x		x		x	x												
	15-Aug	Aberdeen	0 - 4		x	x	x	x	x		x	x				x	x						x					x	x
	18-Aug	Partick Thistle	1 - 1	Hunter	x	x	x	x	x		x	x		x	x	x	x												
	25-Aug	Falkirk	1 - 0	Lindsay	x	x	x	x	x		x	x		x	x	x	x												
	29-Aug	ABERDEEN	4 - 0	Roberts (2), Delaney, Hunter	x	x	x	x	x	x	x	x		x		x				x									
	01-Sep	PARTICK THISTLE	0 - 1		x	x	x	x	x	x	x	x		x		x				x									

SCOTTISH CUP

No.	Date	Opponent	Score	Scorers	Wyllie	Delaney	McCallum R	Aitken	Martis	McCann	Lindsay	Roberts	Strachan	Hunter	Goldie	Quinn	Russell	McCallum W	Jones	McSeveney	Stewart	Thomson L	Weir	McBride	Thomson M	Wallace	Murray	Ramsay	Goodwin
	06-Feb	East Stirling	0 - 1		x	x	x	x		x	x	x						x					x	x	x				

1963 Div. 1

		Pl.	Home					Away					F.	A.	Pts.
			W.	D.	L.	F.	A.	W.	D.	L.	F.	A.	(Total)		
1	Rangers	34	13	4	0	53	15	12	3	2	41	13	94	28	57
2	Kilmarnock	34	12	4	1	55	16	8	4	5	37	24	92	40	48
3	Partick Thistle	34	11	1	5	39	26	9	5	3	27	18	66	44	46
4	Celtic	34	10	3	4	33	16	9	3	5	43	28	76	44	44
5	Heart of Mid.	34	10	4	3	45	26	7	5	5	40	33	85	59	43
6	Aberdeen	34	10	2	5	38	19	7	5	5	32	28	70	47	41
7	Dundee United	34	10	6	1	41	20	5	5	7	26	32	67	52	41
8	Dunfermline Ath. 349	5	3	37	20	4	3	10	13	27	50	47	34		
9	Dundee	34	9	6	2	39	20	3	3	11	21	29	60	49	33
10	MOTHERWELL	34	6	7	4	32	23	4	4	9	28	40	60	63	31
11	Airdrieonians	34	10	0	7	36	33	4	2	11	16	43	52	76	30
12	St. Mirren	34	6	4	7	32	36	4	4	9	20	36	52	72	28
13	Falkirk	34	8	1	8	35	35	4	2	11	19	34	54	69	27
14	Third Lanark	34	6	4	7	28	29	3	4	10	28	39	56	68	26
15	Queen of the S.	34	6	3	8	20	30	4	3	10	16	45	36	75	26
16	Hibernian	34	4	5	8	17	30	4	4	9	30	37	47	67	25
17	Clyde	34	6	1	10	25	38	3	4	10	24	45	49	83	23
18	Raith Rovers	34	0	4	13	16	48	2	1	14	19	70	35	118	9

1962-63 Season
Back: Aitken, McCallum, Delaney, Wyllie, Martis, MaCann
Front: Lindsay, Quinn, Russell, Hunter, Roberts

1963-64 Season

Back : Aitken, McCloy, McCallum, McBride, Delaney (with cup), M. Thomson, Martis, Murray

Front : I. Thomson, Hunter, Weir

1963-64 1st Division

No.	Date	Opponent	Score	Scorers	Att.	Wyllie	Delaney	Thomson M	Aitken	Martis	McCann	Lindsay	Roberts	McBride	Robertson	Weir A	Murray	Hunter	Carlyle	McCallum R	Moore	Thomson I	Coakley	Baillie	Murdoch	Goodwin	McCallum W	Weir L
1	21-Aug	Dunfermline Ath.	0 - 2			x	x	x	x	x	x	x	x	x	x	x												
2	07-Sep	AIRDRIE	3 - 0	Roberts, Lindsay, McBride	7001	x	x	x	x	x	x	x	x	x	x	x												
3	14-Sep	St. Mirren	1 - 2	Roberts		x	x	x	x	x	x	x	x	x	x	x												
4	21-Sep	ST. JOHNSTONE	1 - 3	Murray	5860	x	x	x	x	x	x		x	x	x	x	x											
5	28-Sep	PartickThistle	0 - 0			x	x	x	x	x	x			x	x	x	x											x
6	05-Oct	HIBERNIAN	4 - 3	McBride (3), Weir	6449	x	x	x	x	x	x	x		x	x	x		x										
7	12-Oct	Dundee	3 - 1	Weir (2), Robertson		x	x	x	x	x	x	x		x	x	x		x										
8	19-Oct	Queen of the South	2 - 2	McBride, Lindsay		x	x	x		x	x	x		x	x	x	x	x										
9	26-Oct	DUNDEE UNITED	0 - 3		5061	x	x	x	x	x	x	x		x	x	x		x										
10	02-Nov	Third Lanark	1 - 3	Lindsay		x	x	x	x	x	x	x		x	x	x		x										
11	09-Nov	EAST STIRLING	4 - 1	McBride (2), Carlyle, McCann	4856	x	x	x	x	x	x	x		x		x		x	x									
12	16-Nov	Aberdeen	2 - 6	Carlyle, Weir		x	x		x	x	x	x		x	x	x			x	x								
13	23-Nov	FALKIRK	3 - 0	McBride (2), Lindsay	3384	x		x	x	x	x	x		x		x	x		x	x								
14	30-Nov	Kilmarnock	2 - 5	Aitken, McBride		x	x	x	x	x	x	x		x		x	x		x									
15	07-Dec	Hearts	1 - 1	McCann		x	x	x	x	x	x	x		x		x	x		x									
16	14-Dec	RANGERS	3 - 3	McCann (2), Hunter	16501	x	x	x	x		x	x		x			x	x	x	x								
17	21-Dec	Celtic	1 - 2	McBride		x	x	x	x		x	x		x	x		x		x	x								
18	28-Dec	DUNFERMLINE	1 - 1	Lindsay	5680	x	x	x	x		x	x		x		x	x		x	x								
19	01-Jan	Aidrie	1 - 1	Lindsay		x		x	x	x	x	x		x		x	x		x	x								
20	02-Jan	ST. MIRREN	3 - 0	McBride (2), Carlyle	6462	x	x	x	x		x	x		x		x	x		x	x								
21	04-Jan	St. Johnstone	1 - 1	McBride		x	x	x	x		x	x		x	x		x		x	x								
22	11-Jan	QUEEN OF THE SOUTH	0 - 0		4718	x	x	x			x	x		x	x		x		x	x	x							
23	18-Jan	PARTICK THISTLE	2 - 1	Martis, OG		x	x	x		x	x	x		x	x				x	x		x						
24	01-Feb	Hibernian	1 - 3	Carlyle		x	x	x		x	x	x		x	x				x	x								
25	08-Feb	DUNDEE	2 - 2	McBride (2)		x	x	x			x	x		x	x	x	x		x	x								
26	22-Feb	Dundee United	1 - 4	McCann			x	x		x	x	x		x		x	x		x	x					x			
27	01-Feb	THIRD LANARK	1 - 1	McBride		x				x	x			x		x	x		x	x		x				x	x	
28	14-Mar	ABERDEEN	0 - 1			x	x	x	x	x	x	x		x		x	x			x								
29	17-Mar	East Stirling	0 - 0			x	x	x	x	x	x			x		x	x			x		x						
30	21-Mar	Falkirk	4 - 0	Lindsay, Weir, McBride, Robertson		x	x	x	x	x	x	x		x	x	x				x								
31	28-Mar	CELTIC	0 - 4			x	x			x	x	x		x	x	x	x			x		x						
32	01-Apr	KILMARNOCK	2 - 0	Delaney, Baillie		x	x			x	x	x		x	x	x	x						x	x				
33	04-Apr	HEARTS	0 - 1			x	x		x	x	x	x		x			x			x			x	x				
34	18-Apr	Rangers	1 - 5	McBride			x			x	x			x		x	x			x	x		x	x	x			

LEAGUE CUP

	Date	Opponent	Score	Scorers	Att.	Wyllie	Delaney	Thomson M	Aitken	Martis	McCann	Lindsay	Roberts	McBride	Robertson	Weir A	Murray	Hunter	Carlyle	McCallum R	Moore	Thomson I	Coakley	Baillie	Murdoch	Goodwin	McCallum W	Weir L
	10-Aug	Partick Thistle	2 - 0	McCann, Lindsay		x		x	x	x	x	x	x	x	x	x				x								
	14-Aug	HEARTS	3 - 0	Robertson, McBride, Roberts		x	x	x	x	x	x	x	x	x	x	x												
	17-Aug	Falkirk	6 - 0	McBride (3), Roberts (2), Aitken		x	x	x	x	x	x	x	x	x	x	x												
	24-Aug	PARTICK THISTLE	2 - 0	McBride, Robertson		x	x	x	x	x	x	x	x	x	x	x												
	28-Aug	Hearts	0 - 0			x	x	x	x	x	x	x	x	x	x	x												
	31-Aug	FALKIRK	4 - 0	McCann, Lindsay, McBride, Roberts		x	x	x	x	x	x	x	x	x	x	x												
	11-Sep	MORTON	0 - 0			x	x	x	x	x	x	x	x	x	x	x												
	18-Sep	Morton	0 - 2			x	x	x	x	x	x	x	x	x	x	x												

SCOTTISH CUP

	Date	Opponent	Score	Scorers	Att.	Wyllie	Delaney	Thomson M	Aitken	Martis	McCann	Lindsay	Roberts	McBride	Robertson	Weir A	Murray	Hunter	Carlyle	McCallum R	Moore	Thomson I	Coakley	Baillie	Murdoch	Goodwin	McCallum W	Weir L
	25-Jan	DUMBARTON	4 - 1	McBride (3), Robertson		x	x	x		x	x	x		x	x	x	x			x								
	15-Feb	HEARTS	3 - 3	McBride (3)		x	x	x	x		x	x		x	x	x	x			x								
rep.	19-Feb	Hearts	2 - 1	Aitken, McBride		x	x	x	x		x	x		x	x	x	x			x								
	07-Mar	Dundee	1 - 1	McBride		x	x	x	x	x	x	x		x		x	x			x								
rep.	11-Mar	DUNDEE	2 - 4	McBride, Murray		x	x	x	x	x	x	x		x		x	x			x								

SUMMER CUP

Date	Opponent	Score
02-May	Kilmarnock	2 - 2
06-May	AIRDRIE	1 - 2
09-May	QUEEN OF THE SOUTH	2 - 0
13-May	KILMARNOCK	1 - 4
16-May	Aidrie	2 - 1
20-May	Queen of the South	2 - 1

FRIENDLIES

Date	Opponent	Score
27-Apr	Nimes	

1964 Div. 1

		Pl.	Home					Away					F.	A.	Pts.
			W.	D.	L.	F.	A.	W.	D.	L.	F.	A.	(Total)		
1	Rangers	34	13	1	3	43	19	12	4	1	42	12	85	31	55
2	Kilmarnock	34	14	2	1	50	15	8	3	6	27	25	77	40	49
3	Celtic	34	13	3	1	61	16	6	6	5	28	18	89	34	47
4	Heart of Mid.	34	8	5	4	39	23	11	4	2	35	17	74	40	47
5	Dunfermline Ath.	34	11	3	3	41	16	7	6	4	23	17	64	33	45
6	Dundee	34	11	3	3	53	27	9	2	6	41	23	94	50	45
7	Partick Thistle	34	11	3	3	30	16	4	2	11	25	38	55	54	35
8	Dundee United	34	10	2	5	43	23	3	6	8	22	26	65	49	34
9	Aberdeen	34	5	5	7	26	26	7	3	7	27	27	53	53	32
10	Hibernian	34	9	4	4	33	22	3	2	12	26	44	59	66	30
11	MOTHERWELL	34	7	5	5	29	24	2	6	9	22	38	51	62	29
12	St. Mirren	34	9	4	4	24	23	3	1	13	20	51	44	74	29
13	St. Johnstone	34	6	3	8	27	32	5	3	9	27	38	54	70	28
14	Falkirk	34	7	4	6	24	26	4	2	11	30	58	54	84	28
15	Airdrieonians	34	7	3	7	34	41	4	1	12	18	56	52	97	26
16	Third Lanark	34	5	3	9	27	36	4	4	9	20	38	47	74	25
17	Queen of the S.	34	3	3	11	23	47	2	3	12	17	45	40	92	16
18	East Stirling.	34	4	2	11	19	36	1	0	16	18	55	37	91	12

1964-65: 1st Division

	Date	Opponent	Score	Scorers	Wyllie	Delaney	McCallum R	McCann	Martis	Murray	Coakley	Lindsay	McBride	Weir A	Hunter	Thomson M	Carlyle	Aitken	Bailey	Robertson	McCallum W	Gallacher	Donnachie	Hume	Ramsay	McCloy	Thompson I
1	19-Aug	CELTIC	1 - 3	Lindsay	x	x	x	x		x		x	x	x	x	x	x										
2	05-Sep	Aidrie	3 - 0	Weir, Lindsay, McBride	x	x	x	x		x		x	x	x	x	x	x										
3	12-Sep	THIRD LANARK	3 - 3	Murray, Hunter, McBride	x	x	x	x		x	x	x	x	x	x	x											
4	19-Sep	St. Mirren	4 - 1	Aitken (2), Weir, McBride	x	x	x	x		x	x		x	x	x	x		x									
5	26-Sep	DUNDEE	2 - 1	Baillie (2)	x	x	x	x		x	x		x	x		x		x	x								
6	03-Oct	Dunfermline Ath.	0 - 3		x	x	x	x		x	x	x	x	x		x			x								
7	10-Oct	ST. JOHNSTONE	2 - 2	Weir, McBride	x	x	x	x		x	x	x	x	x		x			x								
8	17-Oct	Aberdeen	1 - 0	McBride	x	x	x	x		x	x	x	x	x		x			x								
9	24-Oct	Partick Thistle	2 - 1	Weir, Hunter	x	x	x	x		x		x	x	x	x	x				x							
10	31-Oct	HIBERNIAN	0 - 2		x	x	x	x		x		x	x	x	x	x				x							
11	07-Nov	Kilmarnock	1 - 1	Lindsay	x		x	x	x	x		x	x	x		x				x	x						
12	14-Nov	HEARTS	1 - 3	Hunter	x	x	x	x		x		x	x	x	x	x					x						
13	21-Nov	Rangers	0 - 1		x	x	x	x		x		x	x	x	x	x					x						
14	28-Nov	MORTON	4 - 1	Carlyle (2), McBride, McCann	x	x	x	x		x			x	x	x	x	x				x						
p 22/3	05-Dec	CLYDE	0 - 1		x	x	x	x		x			x	x	x	x	x				x						
16	12-Dec	Falkirk	1 - 1	Carlyle	x	x	x	x		x			x	x	x	x	x				x						
17	19-Dec	DUNDEE UNITED	2 - 4	McBride (2)	x	x	x	x		x			x	x	x	x	x				x						
18	26-Dec	Celtic	0 - 2		x	x	x	x		x	x		x		x	x					x				x		
19	01-Jan	AIRDRIE	1 - 2	McBride	x	x	x	x		x			x	x	x	x	x				x						
20	09-Jan	ST. MIRREN	4 - 0	Gallacher (2), McBride (2)	x	x	x	x		x			x	x	x	x	x					x					
21	16-Jan	Dundee	2 - 4	McBride (2)	x	x	x	x		x			x	x	x	x	x					x					
22	23-Jan	DUNFERMLINE	1 - 3	Weir	x	x	x	x		x			x	x	x	x	x					x					
23	10-Feb	St. Johnstone	1 - 1	Aitken	x	x	x	x		x			x	x	x	x		x				x					
24	27-Feb	PARTICK THISTLE	0 - 2		x	x	x	x		x	x		x	x	x	x		x									
25	10-Mar	Hibernian	0 - 2		x	x	x	x		x		x	x	x	x	x	x										
26	13-Mar	KILMARNOCK	0 - 2		x	x	x	x		x		x	x	x	x	x	x										
27	20-Mar	Hearts	0 - 2		x	x	x		x		x		x	x				x			x		x	x			
28	03-Apr	Morton	2 - 0	McBride (2)		x	x		x		x		x	x				x			x		x	x		x	
29	07-Apr	Clyde	1 - 1	McBride		x	x		x		x		x	x				x			x		x	x		x	
30	14-Apr	ABERDEEN	2 - 2	McBride (2)	x	x	x		x		x		x	x				x			x		x	x			
31	17-Apr	FALKIRK	1 - 0	McBride	x	x	x		x		x		x	x				x			x		x	x			
32	21-Apr	RANGERS	1 - 3	Hunter	x	x	x	x	x		x		x		x			x					x	x			
33	24-Apr	Dundee United	1 - 3	Donnachie		x	x				x		x	x	x	x		x			x		x			x	
34	28-Apr	Third Lanark	2 - 0	McBride (2)		x	x			x		x	x	x		x		x					x			x	x

LEAGUE CUP

	Date	Opponent	Score	Scorers	Wyllie	Delaney	McCallum R	McCann	Martis	Murray	Coakley	Lindsay	McBride	Weir A	Hunter	Thomson M	Carlyle	Aitken	Bailey	Robertson	McCallum W	Gallacher	Donnachie	Hume	Ramsay	McCloy	Thompson I
	08-Aug	Falkirk	1 - 1	Lindsay	x	x	x	x	x	x	x	x	x	x	x												
	12-Aug	DUNDEE	3 - 0		x	x	x	x	x	x	x	x	x	x	x												
	15-Aug	DUNDEE UNITED	0 - 1		x	x	x	x		x		x	x	x	x	x	x										
	22-Aug	FALKIRK	3 - 0	McBride (3)	x	x	x	x		x		x	x	x	x	x	x										
	26-Aug	Dundee	0 - 6		x	x	x	x		x		x	x	x	x	x	x										
	29-Aug	Dundee United	1 - 2	Lindsay	x	x	x	x		x	x	x	x	x	x	x											

SCOTTISH CUP

	Date	Opponent	Score	Scorers	Wyllie	Delaney	McCallum R	McCann	Martis	Murray	Coakley	Lindsay	McBride	Weir A	Hunter	Thomson M	Carlyle	Aitken	Bailey	Robertson	McCallum W	Gallacher	Donnachie	Hume	Ramsay	McCloy	Thompson I
	13-Feb	STENHOUSEMUIR	3 - 2	Weir (2), McBride	x	x	x	x		x			x	x	x	x	x					x					
	20-Feb	ST. JOHNSTONE	1 - 0	McBride	x	x	x	x		x	x		x	x	x	x		x									
	06-Mar	HEARTS	1 - 0	Carlyle	x	x	x	x		x		x	x	x	x	x	x										
S/F	27-Mar	CELTIC	2 - 2	McBride (2)	x	x	x	x		x		x	x	x	x	x					x						
S/F R	31-Mar	CELTIC	0 - 3		x	x	x	x		x		x	x	x	x	x					x						

SUMMER CUP

	Date	Opponent	Score
		THIRD LANARK	5 - 1
		Aidrie	1 - 0
		Kilmarnock	1 - 1
		Third Lanark	3 - 1
		KILMARNOCK	3 - 0
		AIRDRIE	3 - 0
S/F1	22-May	Hibernian	0 - 2
S/F2	28-May	HIBERNIAN	6 - 2
F 1	29-May	DUNDEE UNITED	3 - 1
F 2	02-Jun	Dundee United	0 - 1

1965 Div. 1

		Pl.	Home					Away					F.	A.	Pts.
			W.	D.	L.	F.	A.	W.	D.	L.	F.	A.	(Total)		
1	Kilmarnock	34	12	4	1	38	17	10	2	5	24	16	62	33	50
2	Heart of Mid.	34	11	3	3	46	24	11	3	3	44	25	90	49	50
3	Dunfermline Ath.	34	14	2	1	55	14	8	3	6	28	22	83	36	49
4	Hibernian	34	11	2	4	44	26	10	2	5	31	21	75	47	46
5	Rangers	34	9	5	3	42	16	9	3	5	36	19	78	35	44
6	Dundee	34	9	4	4	47	32	6	6	5	39	31	86	63	40
7	Clyde	34	10	3	4	35	22	7	3	7	29	36	64	58	40
8	Celtic	34	9	2	6	33	18	7	3	7	43	39	76	57	37
9	Dundee United	34	10	1	6	38	24	5	5	7	21	27	59	51	36
10	Morton	34	9	4	4	38	21	4	3	10	16	33	54	54	33
11	Partick Thistle	34	5	5	7	28	30	6	5	6	29	28	57	58	32
12	Aberdeen	34	8	5	4	33	27	4	3	10	26	48	59	75	32
13	St. Johnstone	34	6	5	6	31	24	3	6	8	26	38	57	62	29
14	MOTHERWELL	34	4	4	9	24	31	6	4	7	21	23	45	54	28
15	St. Mirren	34	8	2	7	27	32	1	4	12	11	38	38	70	24
16	Falkirk	34	6	5	6	27	26	1	2	14	16	59	43	85	21
17	Airdrieonians	34	3	3	11	26	48	2	1	14	22	62	48	110	14
18	Third Lanark	34	2	0	15	11	41	1	1	15	11	58	22	99	7

1964-65 Season

Back: McCann, Aitken, Hope, McCloy, Goodwin, Wylie, McCallum, H.Weir, Brown, Martis, Delaney, Murray
Middle: Coakley, Unknown, Lindsay, Unknown, A.Weir, Robertson, Hunter, Unknown, Bailey
Front: M.Thomson, Unknown, Unknown, McBride, Unknown, I.Thomson, Unknown, McCallum

1965-66 Season

Back: Thomson, B.McCallum, Wyllie, Delaney, Martis, W.McCallum
Front: Coakley, Curry, McBride, Hunter, Lindsay

1965-66: 1st Division

No.	Date	Opponent	Score	Scorers	McCloy	Thomson M	McCallum R	Aitken	Martis	Murray	Hunter	Thomson L	Delaney	McLaughlin	Weir A	Moffat	Campbell	Lindsay	McCallum W	Cairney	Logan	Coakley	Howieson	Wyllie
1	25-Aug	DUNFERMLINE	1 - 3	McCallum		x	x	x	x	x		x	x			x		x					x	x
2	11-Sep	Stirling Albion	0 - 1		x	x	x	x	x	x		x	x	x								x	x	
3	18-Sep	HAMILTON ACADEMICAL	4 - 2	McLaughlin, Delaney, Murray, McCallum	x	x	x	x	x	x	x	x	x	x	x									
4	25-Sep	Partick Thistle	1 - 1	McLaughlin	x	x	x	x	x	x		x	x	x			x	x						
5	09-Oct	Hibernian	2 - 2	Thomson, Delaney	x	x	x	x	x	x		x	x	x		x	x							
6	16-Oct	ST. JOHNSTONE	5 - 3	Aitken (2), McCallum, THOMSON, Murray	x	x	x	x	x	x		x	x	x		x	x							
7	23-Oct	Hearts	2 - 5	Delaney, McLaughlin	x	x	x	x	x	x		x	x	x			x	x						
8	30-Oct	Falkirk	0 - 2		x	x	x	x	x	x		x		x		x							x	
9	06-Nov	CLYDE	0 - 1		x	x	x	x	x	x		x		x		x	x		x					
10	13-Nov	Kilmarnock	0 - 5		x	x	x	x	x	x	x	x		x		x	x							
11	20-Nov	DUNDEE UNITED	0 - 3		x	x	x	x	x	x		x		x		x	x	x						
12	27-Nov	RANGERS	0 - 3		x	x	x	x	x	x		x	x	x		x	x							
13	11-Dec	ST. MIRREN	4 - 1	Campbell, Delaney, Moffat, Murray	x	x	x		x	x	x	x	x			x	x		x					
14	18-Dec	ABERDEEN	1 - 0	McLaughlin	x	x	x	x	x	x	x	x	x			x	x							
15	25-Dec	Dundee	0 - 4		x	x	x	x	x	x	x	x	x				x	x						
16	01-Jan	Hamilton Academical	4 - 1	Delaney, Murray, Hunter, I Thomson	x	x	x	x	x	x	x	x	x				x	x						
17	03-Jan	STIRLING ALBION	0 - 1		x	x	x	x	x	x	x	x	x				x	x						
18	08-Jan	Dunfermline Ath.	1 - 6	Lindsay	x	x	x		x	x	x	x	x	x			x	x						
19	15-Jan	PARTICK THISTLE	0 - 3		x	x	x		x	x	x	x	x	x			x	x						
20	22-Jan	Celtic	0 - 1		x	x	x		x	x	x	x	x	x			x	x						
21	29-Jan	HIBERNIAN	4 - 0	Campbell (2), Lindsay, Cairney	x		x		x	x		x	x	x	x		x		x	x				
22	12-Feb	St. Johnstone	3 - 3	Thomson (2), Cairney	x		x		x	x	x	x	x				x	x	x	x				
23	26-Feb	FALKIRK	3 - 0	I Thomson (2), McLaughlin	x		x		x	x	x		x	x			x			x	x	x		
24	05-Mar	Clyde	3 - 1	I Thomson (2), Coakley	x		x		x	x	x	x	x	x			x			x		x		
25	09-Mar	Morton	1 - 3	Thomson	x	x	x			x	x	x	x	x			x			x		x		
26	12-Mar	KILMARNOCK	0 - 3		x	x	x			x	x	x	x	x			x			x		x		
27	19-Mar	Dundee United	1 - 5	Cairney	x		x		x	x	x	x	x	x			x		x	x				
28	23-Mar	HEARTS	4 - 2	Murray, Cairney, McCallum, Delaney	x		x		x	x	x	x	x	x			x		x	x				
29	09-Apr	MORTON	3 - 0	Lindsay, McCallum, Murray	x	x	x		x	x	x		x				x	x	x	x				
30	16-Apr	St. Mirren	0 - 0		x	x	x		x	x	x	x	x				x		x	x				
31	19-Apr	Rangers	1 - 2	Campbell	x	x	x		x	x	x		x				x		x	x		x		
32	23-Apr	Aberdeen	2 - 1	Cairney (2)	x	x	x		x	x	x		x				x		x	x		x		
33	30-Apr	DUNDEE	2 - 0	Cairney, Lindsay	x	x	x			x	x		x				x	x	x	x				
34	07-May	CELTIC	0 - 1		x	x	x		x	x	x		x				x	x	x	x				

LEAGUE CUP

	Date	Opponent	Score	Scorers	McCloy	Thomson M	McCallum R	Aitken	Martis	Murray	Hunter	Thomson L	Delaney	McLaughlin	Weir A	Moffat	Campbell	Lindsay	McCallum W	Cairney	Logan	Coakley	Howieson	Wyllie
	14-Aug	DUNDEE	1 - 0	Delaney	x	x	x	x	x	x	x	x	x		x			x						
	18-Aug	Celtic	0 - 1		x	x	x	x	x	x	x	x	x					x					x	
	21-Aug	Dundee United	1 - 4	Howieson	x	x	x	x	x	x		x	x		x			x					x	
	28-Aug	Dundee	2 - 1	Howieson, OG		x	x	x	x	x		x	x			x		x					x	x
	01-Sep	CELTIC	2 - 3	Delaney, Murray	x	x	x	x	x	x	x	x	x	x									x	
	04-Sep	DUNDEE UNITED	3 - 2	Delaney (2), OG	x	x	x	x	x	x	x	x	x	x									x	

SCOTTISH CUP

	Date	Opponent	Score	Scorers	McCloy	Thomson M	McCallum R	Aitken	Martis	Murray	Hunter	Thomson L	Delaney	McLaughlin	Weir A	Moffat	Campbell	Lindsay	McCallum W	Cairney	Logan	Coakley	Howieson	Wyllie
	09-Feb	East Stirling	0 - 0		x		x		x	x		x	x	x			x	x	x	x				
rep.	14-Feb	EAST STIRLING	4 - 1	Cairney (2), L Thomson (2)	x		x		x	x		x	x	x			x	x	x	x				
	21-Feb	Kilmarnock	0 - 5		x		x		x	x		x	x	x			x	x	x	x				

FRIENDLIES

	Date	Opponent	Score	Scorers
	28-Jul	CELTIC	1 - 1	Thomson

(On Isle of Man)

1966 Div. 1

		Pl.	Home W.	D.	L.	F.	A.	Away W.	D.	L.	F.	A.	F. (Total)	A.	Pts.
1	Celtic	34	16	1	0	66	12	11	2	4	40	18	106	30	57
2	Rangers	34	15	1	1	49	10	10	4	3	42	19	91	29	55
3	Kilmarnock	34	12	2	3	36	18	8	3	6	37	28	73	46	45
4	Dunfermline Ath.	34	11	2	4	52	29	8	4	5	42	26	94	55	44
5	Dundee United	34	10	3	4	45	27	9	2	6	34	24	79	51	43
6	Hibernian	34	8	6	3	45	22	8	0	9	36	33	81	55	38
7	Heart of Mid.	34	7	5	5	28	21	6	7	4	28	27	56	48	38
8	Aberdeen	34	8	3	6	35	26	7	3	7	26	28	61	54	36
9	Dundee	34	9	2	6	35	29	5	4	8	26	32	61	61	34
10	Falkirk	34	10	1	6	32	26	5	0	12	16	46	48	72	31
11	Clyde	34	7	2	8	33	29	6	2	9	29	35	62	64	30
12	Partick Thistle	34	9	5	3	34	25	1	5	11	21	39	55	64	30
13	MOTHERWELL	34	9	0	8	31	26	3	4	10	21	43	52	69	28
14	St. Johnstone	34	6	6	5	34	36	3	2	12	24	45	58	81	26
15	Stirling Albion	34	7	2	8	25	29	2	6	9	15	39	40	68	26
16	St. Mirren	34	6	3	8	27	34	3	1	13	17	48	44	82	22
17	Morton	34	4	5	8	18	31	4	0	13	24	53	42	84	21
18	Hamilton Acad.	34	3	1	13	19	56	0	1	16	8	61	27	117	8

1966-67: 1st Division

No.	Date	Opponent	Score	Scorers	McCloy	Thomson M	McCallum R	McCallum W	Martis	Campbell	Moffat	Hunter	Deans	Cairney	Weir A	Lindsay	Murray	McDaid	Whiteford	Donnachie	McCall	Wyllie	Thomson L	Reid
1	10-Sep	Aidrie	1 - 2	Hogg	x	x	x	x	x	x	x	x	x	x	x									
2	17-Sep	STIRLING ALBION	1 - 1	Deans	x	x	x	x	x	x	x	x	x	x	x	s								
p 15/12	24-Sep	St. Mirren	5 - 0	Campbell (5)	x	x	x	x	x	x	x	x	x	x	s		x							
4	01-Oct	HIBERNIAN	1 - 2	Campbell	x	x	x	x	x	x	x	x	x	x		s	x							
5	08-Oct	Clyde	1 - 3	Moffat	x	x	x	x	x	x	x	x	x	x	s		x							
6	15-Oct	ST. JOHNSTONE	3 - 3	McCallum, Hunter, W McCallum	x	x	x	x	x	x	x	x		x			x		s				x	
7	22-Oct	Dundee	0 - 3		x	x	x	x	x	x	x	x		x				x	x	s				
8	29-Oct	AYR	0 - 0		x	x	x	x	x	x	x	x	x	x	s			x						
9	05-Nov	Rangers	1 - 5	Moffat	x		x	x	x	x	x	x	x	x			x		x					
10	12-Nov	Partick Thistle	2 - 2	Deans, Campbell	x		x	x	x	x	x		x	x		x	x		x					
11	19-Nov	DUNDEE UNITED	1 - 1	Deans	x	s	x	x	x	x	x		x	x		x	x		x					
12	26-Nov	DUNFERMLINE	6 - 2	Deans (3), Hunter (2), Murray	x	s	x	x	x	x		x	x	x		x	x		x					
13	03-Dec	Aberdeen	1 - 2	Hunter	x	s	x	x	x	x		x	x	x		x	x		x					
14	10-Dec	Celtic	2 - 4	Murray, Lindsay	x		x	x	x	x		x	x	x		x	x		x					
15	17-Dec	KILMARNOCK	2 - 0	Murray, Lindsay	x	x	x	x	x	x	x	x				x	x		x					
16	31-Dec	Hearts	2 - 1	Campbell (2)	x	x	x	x	x	x	x	x				x	x		x	s				
17	02-Jan	AIRDRIE	2 - 2	Campbell (2)	x	x	x	x	x	x	x	x				x	x		x	s				
18	03-Jan	Stirling Albion	0 - 0		x	x	x	x	x	x	x				x	x			x	x			s	
19	14-Jan	Hibernian	1 - 2	Lindsay	x	x	x	x	x	x	x				x	x	x		x	s				
20	21-Jan	CLYDE	1 - 1	Moffat	x	x	x	x	x	x	x	x				x	x		x					
21	04-Feb	St. Johnstone	1 - 1	Campbell	x	x	x	x		x	s	x		x		x	x		x		x			
22	11-Feb	DUNDEE	5 - 3	Murray, McCall, Lindsay, Hunter, Campbell	x	x	x	x		x	s	x		x		x	x		x		x			
23	01-Mar	Ayr United	3 - 3	Hunter (2), Deans			x	x	x	x		x	x	x		x	x		x			x		
24	04-Mar	RANGERS	1 - 5	McCallum	x	s	x	x	x	x		x	x	x		x	x		x					
25	11-Mar	PARTICK THISTLE	5 - 0	Campbell (2), Martis, Moffat, Lindsay			x	x	x	x	x	x	x			x	x		x			x		
26	18-Mar	Dundee United	1 - 1	Lindsay	x	x	x	x	x	x	x	x		x		x			x		s			
27	25-Mar	Dunfermline Ath.	1 - 2	Moffat	x	x	x	x	x	x	x	x		x		x	s		x					
28	01-Apr	FALKIRK	1 - 2	Murray	x	x	x	x	x	x	x	x				x	x		x	s				
29	04-Apr	ABERDEEN	3 - 2	Deans, Campbell, Hunter	x	x		x	x	x	x	x	x		x		s		x				x	
30	08-Apr	CELTIC	0 - 2		x	x		x	x	x	x	x	x		x		s		x				x	
31	12-Apr	Kilmarnock	0 - 3		x	x		x	x	x	x	x	x		x		s		x				x	
32	19-Apr	ST. MIRREN	4 - 0	Deans (2), Campbell, I Thomson	x	x		x	x	x	x	x	x		x				x				x	
33	22-Apr	Falkirk	1 - 0	Campbell	x	x		x	x	x	x	x	x		x				x				x	
34	29-Apr	HEARTS	1 - 0	Deans	x	x		x	x	x	x	x	x		x		s		x				x	

LEAGUE CUP

Date	Opponent	Score	Scorers	McCloy	Thomson M	McCallum R	McCallum W	Martis	Campbell	Moffat	Hunter	Deans	Cairney	Weir A	Lindsay	Murray	McDaid	Whiteford	Donnachie	McCall	Wyllie	Thomson L	Reid
13-Aug	Dunfermline Ath.	1 - 2	Moffat	x	x	x			x	s			x	x	x	x			x			x	x
17-Aug	FALKIRK	2 - 2	Deans, Campbell	x	x	x		x	x	x		x	x	x	x	x							
20-Aug	PARTICK THISTLE	4 - 0	Deans (2), McCallum, Campbell	x	x	x	x	x	x	x	x	x	x	x	s								
27-Aug	DUNFERMLINE	4 - 3	Deans (2), Cairney, McCallum	x	x	x	x	x	x	x	x	x	x	x	s								
31-Aug	Falkirk	2 - 0	Cairney (2)	x	x	x	x	x	x	x	x	x	x	x	s								
03-Sep	Partick Thistle	0 - 0		x	x	x	x	x	x	x	x	x	x	x	s								

SCOTTISH CUP

Date	Opponent	Score	Scorers	McCloy	Thomson M	McCallum R	McCallum W	Martis	Campbell	Moffat	Hunter	Deans	Cairney	Weir A	Lindsay	Murray	McDaid	Whiteford	Donnachie	McCall	Wyllie	Thomson L	Reid
28-Jan	EAST FIFE	0 - 1		x		x	x	x	x	x	x	x			x	x		x	s				

FRIENDLIES

Date	Opponent	Score
20-Feb	Hull City	0 - 4

1967 Div. 1

		Pl.	Home W.	D.	L.	F.	A.	Away W.	D.	L.	F.	A.	F. (Total)	A.	Pts.
1	Celtic	34	14	2	1	61	17	12	4	1	50	16	111	33	58
2	Rangers	34	13	3	1	54	13	11	4	2	38	18	92	31	55
3	Clyde	34	10	2	5	29	20	10	4	3	35	28	64	48	46
4	Aberdeen	34	11	3	3	44	17	6	5	6	28	21	72	38	42
5	Hibernian	34	10	3	4	43	24	9	1	7	29	25	72	49	42
6	Dundee	34	9	5	3	34	16	7	4	6	40	35	74	51	41
7	Kilmarnock	34	9	5	3	33	18	7	3	7	26	28	59	46	40
8	Dunfermline Ath.	34	9	4	4	46	27	5	6	6	26	25	72	52	38
9	Dundee United	34	7	5	5	36	33	7	4	6	32	29	68	62	37
10	MOTHERWELL	34	7	6	4	37	26	3	5	9	22	34	59	60	31
11	Heart of Mid.	34	7	6	4	22	16	4	2	11	17	32	39	48	30
12	Partick Thistle	34	5	8	4	25	21	4	4	9	24	47	49	68	30
13	Airdrieonians	34	7	1	9	27	27	4	5	8	14	26	41	53	28
14	Falkirk	34	8	1	8	18	24	3	3	11	15	46	33	70	26
15	St. Johnstone	34	8	3	6	31	30	2	2	13	22	43	53	73	25
16	Stirling Albion	34	3	6	8	18	34	2	3	12	13	51	31	85	19
17	St. Mirren	34	4	1	12	18	47	0	6	11	7	34	25	81	15
18	Ayr United	34	1	4	12	11	37	0	3	14	9	49	20	86	9

1966-67 Season
Front : Coakley, Lindsay, McBride, Weir, Hunter, Bailey
Back : McCann, Delaney, Wylie, R McCallum, Martis, Murray

1967-68 Season
Back : Jim Muir, Whiteford, Wark, Donnelly, McCloy, McCallum, Murray
Front : R Howitt (Manager), Wilson, McInally, R Campbell, Deans, Goldthorpe, W Humphries (Coach)

1967-68: 1st Division

No.	Date	Opponent	Score	Scorers	Att.	McCloy	Whiteford	McCallum R	Thomson L	Martis	McCallum W	Lindsay	Campbell	Deans	Cairney	Weir A	Hogg	Murray	Goldthorpe	McKay	Thomson M	Forsyth	Moffat	McCall	Wilson	McInally	Murray J	Beaton	Muir	Gray
1	09-Sep	AIRDRIE	1 - 2	Hogg		x	x	x	x	x	x	x	x	x	x	x	s													
2	16-Sep	Morton	1 - 2	Campbell		x	x		x	x	x		x	x		x	x	x		x										s
3	23-Sep	DUNFERMLINE	1 - 1	Deans		x	x	x	x	x	x	x	x	x	x	x														
4	30-Sep	Dundee	1 - 2	Goldthorpe		x	x			x	x	x	x	x		s	x	x	x	x										
5	07-Oct	RANGERS	0 - 2		20500	x	x			x	x	x	x	x	s			x	x	x	x									
6	14-Oct	STIRLING A	3 - 1	Campbell (2), Goldthorpe	2400	x	x			x	x	x	x	x				x	x	x	x	s								
7	21-Oct	Celtic	2 - 4	Campbell (2)		x	x			x	x	x	x	x				x	x	x	x	s								
8	28-Oct	HEARTS	2 - 5	Deans, Whiteford	5300	x	x			x	x	x	x	x				x	x	x	x	s								
9	04-Nov	Dundee United	1 - 1	Deans	5000	x	x			x	x	s	x	x	x			x	x	x	x									
10	11-Nov	Falkirk	0 - 1		4000	x	x			x	x		x	x	x			x	s	x	x		x							
11	18-Nov	KILMARNOCK	1 - 2	Whiteford	3000	x	x		s	x		x	x	x	x			x		x	x		x							
12	25-Nov	Aberdeen	1 - 2	Murray		x	x			x	s	x	x	x				x		x		x	x	x						
13	02-Dec	RAITH ROVERS	2 - 2	Hogg, Campbell	2131	x	x			x		x	x	x			x	x		x		x		x						
14	09-Dec	Partick Thistle	2 - 2	Deans, McCall	7000	x	x			x		x	x	x			x	x		x		x		x						
15	16-Dec	HIBERNIAN	0 - 1			x	x			x	x		x	x	x					x		x		x	x					
16	28-Dec	Clyde	3 - 2	Wilson, McCall, Deans		x	x			x	x		x	x	s					x		x		x	x	x				
17	30-Dec	ST. JOHNSTONE	2 - 1	Wilson, McInally		x	x			x	x		x	x						x		x		x	x	x				
18	01-Jan	Aidrie	2 - 2	Deans, McInally		x	x			x	x		s	x	x					x		x		x	x	x				
19	02-Jan	MORTON	2 - 1	Deans (2)		x	x			x	x		x	x	s					x		x		x	x	x				
20	06-Jan	Dunfermline Ath.	0 - 3		5000	x	x			x	x		x	x						x		x		x	x	x				
21	13-Jan	DUNDEE	2 - 4	Deans (2)		x	x			x	x		x	x						x		x		x	x	x				
22	20-Jan	Rangers	0 - 2		35000	x	x			x	x		x	x						x		x		x	x	x				
23	03-Feb	Stirling Albion	2 - 1	McInally (2)	1000	x	x			x	x		x	x			x	x		x		s		x		x				
24	10-Feb	CELTIC	0 - 1		18000	x	x			x	x		x	x						x				x	x	x	x			
25	17-Feb	Hearts	2 - 3	Campbell, Murray	10000	x	x			x	x	s	x	x				x		x		x		x	x					
26	02-Mar	DUNDEE UNITED	1 - 3	Wilson	3200	x	x			x	x		x		x					x		x		x	x		x			
27	09-Mar	FALKIRK	1 - 1	Goldthorpe	3400	x	x			x	x		x		x				s	x		x		x	x		x			
28	16-Mar	Kilmarnock	1 - 1	Deans		x	x			x	x		x	x					x	x				s	x	x		x		
29	23-Mar	ABERDEEN	0 - 3			x	x			x	x		x	x					x	x					x	x		x		
30	30-Mar	Raith Rovers	1 - 3	McInally		x	x			x	x		x		x					x	x			s	x	x		x		
31	06-Apr	PARTICK THISTLE	2 - 1	Whiteford, McInally		x	x			x	x		x	x						x	x			x	x	x				
32	13-Apr	Hibernian	1 - 2	Wilson		x	x			x	x	x	s							x	x			x	x	x			x	
33	20-Apr	CLYDE	0 - 1		2000	x	x			x	x	x								x	x			x	x	x			x	
34	27-Apr	St. Johnstone	0 - 1		3000	x	x			x	x	x								x	x			x	x	x			x	

LEAGUE CUP

	Date	Opponent	Score	Scorers	Att.	McCloy	Whiteford	McCallum R	Thomson L	Martis	McCallum W	Lindsay	Campbell	Deans	Cairney	Weir A	Hogg	Murray	Goldthorpe	McKay	Thomson M	Forsyth	Moffat	McCall	Wilson	McInally	Murray J	Beaton	Muir	Gray
	12-Aug	CLYDE	2 - 2	Thomson, Campbell	4000	x	x	x	x		x		x	x	x	x	x			x				s						
	16-Aug	Hibernian	0 - 1			x	x	x	x		x		x	x	x		x				x		x	s						
	19-Aug	Dundee	1 - 2	Campbell		x	x	x	x		x		x	x	x	s	x				x			x						
	26-Aug	Clyde	1 - 2	Cairney	4050	x	x	x	s	x	x		x	x	x		x	x						x						
	30-Aug	HIBERNIAN	2 - 1	Campbell, Lindsay	4200	x	x	s	x	x	x	x	x	x		x		x			x									
	02-Sep	DUNDEE	2 - 5	Deans, Campbell		x	x		x	x	x	x	x	x		x		x			x									

SCOTTISH CUP

	Date	Opponent	Score	Scorers	Att.	McCloy	Whiteford	McCallum R	Thomson L	Martis	McCallum W	Lindsay	Campbell	Deans	Cairney	Weir A	Hogg	Murray	Goldthorpe	McKay	Thomson M	Forsyth	Moffat	McCall	Wilson	McInally	Murray J	Beaton	Muir	Gray
	27-Jan	AIRDRIE	1 - 1	McCall	6094	x	x			x	x	s	x	x						x		x		x	x	x				
rep.	31-Jan	Aidrie	0 - 1		5637	x	x			x	x		x	x	s					x		x		x	x	x				

FRIENDLIES

	Date	Opponent	Score	Scorers
	03-Aug	Ipswich Town	0 - 4	
	05-Aug	Tranmere Rovers	2 - 2	Deans, Clairney
		Aalborg	1 - 1	Deans

1968 Div. 1

		Pl.	Home W.	D.	L.	F.	A.	Away W.	D.	L.	F.	A.	F. (Total)	A.	Pts.
1	Celtic	34	14	3	0	53	14	16	0	1	53	10	106	24	63
2	Rangers	34	14	2	1	50	13	14	3	0	43	21	93	34	61
3	Hibernian	34	12	2	3	40	17	8	3	6	27	32	67	49	45
4	Dunfermline Ath.	34	9	1	7	38	18	8	4	5	26	23	64	41	39
5	Aberdeen	34	11	1	5	36	17	5	4	8	27	31	63	48	37
6	Morton	34	10	4	3	35	25	5	2	10	22	28	57	53	36
7	Kilmarnock	34	9	4	4	34	23	4	4	9	25	34	59	57	34
8	Clyde	34	9	3	5	39	25	6	1	10	16	30	55	55	34
9	Dundee	34	8	2	7	44	39	5	5	7	18	20	62	59	33
10	Partick Thistle	34	6	5	6	25	28	6	2	9	26	39	51	67	31
11	Dundee United	34	7	7	3	36	30	3	4	10	17	42	53	72	31
12	Heart of Mid.	34	9	1	7	24	23	4	3	10	32	38	56	61	30
13	Airdrieonians	34	7	5	5	26	20	3	4	10	19	38	45	58	29
14	St. Johnstone	34	6	2	9	19	26	4	5	8	24	26	43	52	27
15	Falkirk	34	3	6	8	19	25	4	6	7	17	25	36	50	26
16	Raith Rovers	34	5	4	8	32	30	4	3	10	26	56	58	86	25
17	MOTHERWELL	34	4	3	10	20	32	2	4	11	20	34	40	66	19
18	Stirling Albion	34	4	3	10	18	44	0	1	16	11	61	29	105	12

1968-69: 2nd Division

No.	Date	Opponent	Score	Scorers	Att.	MacRae	Whiteford	Wark	Donnelly	McCallum	Campbell	Muir	Forsyth	Deans	Goldthorpe	Wilson	MacKay	McCloy	McInally	Murray	Bryson	Murphy	Martis	McFarlane	Clark
1	21-Aug	ALBION ROVERS	7 - 0	McInally (2), Wilson (2), Campbell, Deans, Muir	4000	x	x	x	x	x	x	x	x	x		x	s		x						
2	07-Sep	Forfar Athletic	0 - 1			x		x	x	x	x	x	s	x	x	x	x		x						
3	14-Sep	HAMILTON ACADEMICAL	2 - 1	Campbell, Whiteford		x	x	x	x	x	x	x	x	x	s	x	x								
4	18-Sep	AYR UNITED	4 - 1	Deans (2), Whiteford, Wark		x	x	x	x	x	x	x	x	x			x		x	s					
5	21-Sep	Stenhousemuir	6 - 1	McInally, Deans (2), Forsyth, Donnelly, Wark		x	x	x	x	x	x	s	x	x			x		x	x					
6	28-Sep	Queens Park	2 - 1	McInally (2)			x	x	x	x	x		s	x		x	x	x	x	x					
7	05-Oct	COWDENBEATH	4 - 1	Deans (3), Muir			x	x	x	x	x	x		x		x	x	x	x	s					
8	12-Oct	Alloa Athletic	2 - 0	McInally, Deans			x	x	x	x	x		x	x		x	s	x	x	x					
9	19-Oct	EAST FIFE	4 - 0	Deans (2), Campbell, Forsyth			x	x	x	x	x		x	x		x			x	x					
10	26-Oct	Stirling Albion	4 - 0	Deans (2), Campbell, Wark			x	x	x		x		x	x		x	s	x	x	x			x		
11	09-Nov	BERWICK RANGERS	7 - 0	Deans (3), Forsyth (2), McInally, Whiteford			x	x	x	x	x	s	x	x		x		x	x	x					
12	16-Nov	Clydebank	4 - 0	McInally, Deans, Forsyth, Whiteford			x	x	x	x	x		x	x		x	s	x	x	x					
13	23-Nov	Montrose	2 - 0	McInally, Deans	1000		x	x	x	x	x	s	x	x		x		x	x	x					
14	30-Nov	BRECHIN CITY	2 - 0	McInally, Muir			x	x	x	x	x	x	x	x		x		x	x	s					
15	07-Dec	QUEEN OF THE SOUTH	2 - 2	Deans, Muir			x	x	x	x	x	s	x	x		x		x	x	x					
16	14-Dec	Stranraer	2 - 0	Murray, McInally			x	x	x	x	x	x	x	x	s			x	x	x					
17	21-Dec	DUMBARTON	1 - 1	Deans			x	x	x	x	x	s	x	x		x		x	x	x					
18	28-Dec	East Stirling	4 - 0	Wilson, Deans, Bryson, Forsyth			x	x	x	x	x		x	x		x		x	x	s	x				
19	01-Jan	FORFAR ATHLETIC	3 - 1	Deans, Wilson, Whiteford			x	x	x	x	x	x	x	x		x		x	x	s					
20	02-Jan	Hamilton Academical	1 - 0	Whiteford			x	x	x	x	x		x	x		x		x	x	s	x				
21	11-Jan	QUEENS PARK	5 - 1	Deans (2), Forsyth, McInally, Murray			x	x	x	x	x		x	x		x		x	x	x					
22	18-Jan	Cowdenbeath	5 - 0	Forsyth (2), Campbell, Deans, McInally			x	x	x	x	x		x	x		x		x	x	x	s				
23	01-Feb	ALLOA	4 - 0	Forsyth (2), McRae, Muir		x	x	x	x	x	x	x	x					x	x		x				
24	08-Feb	East Fife	1 - 3	McInally		s	x	x	x	x	x	x	x					x	x	x	x				
25	01-Mar	Berwick Rangers	3 - 1	Murphy, Forsyth, Wilson		x	x	x	x	x	x		x	x		x			x			x			
26	08-Mar	CLYDEBANK	2 - 1	Forsyth, Wilson		x	x	x	x	x	x	s	x	x		x			x			x			
27	15-Mar	MONTROSE	4 - 1	Wark (3), Donnelly			x	x	x	x	x		x	x		x		x	x			x			
28	22-Mar	Brechin City	0 - 0		500		x	x	x	x	x		x	x		x		x	x			x			
29	29-Mar	Queen of the South	2 - 1	Goldthorpe, Wark			x	x	x	x	x		x	x	x	x		x				x			
30	05-Apr	STRANRAER	3 - 0	Goldthorpe, Muir, Wark		x	x	x	x	x	x	x	x	x	x	s			x						
31	12-Apr	Dumbarton	4 - 2	Donnelly, Deans, Muir, Goldthorpe		x	x	x	x	x	x	x	x	x	x	x						s			
32	14-Apr	STENHOUSEMUIR	7 - 1	Deans,Goldthorpe(2),Muir(2),Donnelly,Campbell		x	x	x	x	x	x	x	x	x	x	x						s			
33	19-Apr	EAST STIRLING	4 - 0	Deans (3), Donnelly	3300	x	x	x	x	x	x	x	x	x	x	x			s						
34	23-Apr	Ayr United	1 - 1	Muir		x	x	x	x	x	x	x	x	x	x	x						s			
35	26-Apr	STIRLING ALBION	3 - 0	Goldthorpe (3)		x	x	x	x	x	x	x	x	x	x	x			s						
36	29-Apr	Albion Rovers	1 - 0	Goldthorpe		x	x	x	x	x	x	x	x		x	x						x			s

LEAGUE CUP

Date	Opponent	Score	Scorers	Att.	MacRae	Whiteford	Wark	Donnelly	McCallum	Campbell	Muir	Forsyth	Deans	Goldthorpe	Wilson	MacKay	McCloy	McInally	Murray	Bryson	Murphy	Martis	McFarlane	Clark
10-Aug	Hamilton Academical	1 - 2	Muir		x		x	x	s	x	x		x		x	x		x				x	x	
14-Aug	MONTROSE	1 - 2	Campbell		x		x	x	x	x	x		x	s	x	x		x				x		
17-Aug	ST. MIRREN	6 - 0	Forsyth (2), Wilson, Deans, McInally, Muir	3600	x	x	x	x	x	x	x		x		x			x				x		
24-Aug	HAMILTON ACADEMICAL	0 - 0		6000	x	x	x	x	x	x	x	x	x		x	s		x						
28-Aug	Montrose	1 - 2	McRae		x	x	x	x	x	x	x	x	x		x			x						
31-Aug	St. Mirren	0 - 2			x	x	x	x	x	x	s	x	x		x		x	x						

SCOTTISH CUP

Date	Opponent	Score	Scorers	Att.	MacRae	Whiteford	Wark	Donnelly	McCallum	Campbell	Muir	Forsyth	Deans	Goldthorpe	Wilson	MacKay	McCloy	McInally	Murray	Bryson	Murphy	Martis	McFarlane	Clark
25-Jan	CLYDE	1 - 1	Deans	10243		x	x	x	x	x		x	x		x		x	x	x					
28-Jan	Clyde	1 - 2	Bryson	8250		x	x	x	x	x		x	x		x		x	x	x					

FRIENDLIES

Date	Opponent	Score	Scorers
02-Aug	TRANMERE ROVERS	2 - 0	Muir (2)

1969 Div. 2

		Pl.	Home					Away					F.	A.	Pts.
			W.	D.	L.	F.	A.	W.	D.	L.	F.	A.	(Total)		
1	MOTHERWELL	36	16	2	0	68	12	14	2	2	44	11	112	23	64
2	Ayr United	36	13	3	2	54	15	10	4	4	28	16	82	31	53
3	East Fife	36	13	4	1	51	14	8	2	8	31	31	82	45	48
4	Stirling Albion	36	11	4	3	41	19	10	2	6	26	21	67	40	48
5	Queen of the S.	36	11	2	5	43	20	9	5	4	32	21	75	41	47
6	Forfar Athletic	36	10	4	4	42	26	8	3	7	29	30	71	56	43
7	Albion Rovers	36	13	2	3	37	18	6	3	9	23	38	60	56	43
8	Stranraer	36	10	3	5	28	15	7	4	7	29	30	57	45	41
9	East Stirling.	36	12	1	5	42	21	5	4	9	28	41	70	62	39
10	Montrose	36	11	2	5	35	20	4	2	12	24	51	59	71	34
11	Queen's Park	36	8	3	7	25	26	5	4	9	25	33	50	59	33
12	Cowdenbeath	36	5	3	10	32	37	7	2	9	22	30	54	67	29
13	Clydebank	36	4	7	7	28	30	2	8	8	24	37	52	67	27
14	Dumbarton	36	7	2	9	33	35	4	3	11	13	34	46	69	27
15	Hamilton Acad.	36	4	6	8	24	33	4	2	12	13	39	37	72	24
16	Berwick Rangers	36	6	6	6	24	24	1	3	14	18	46	42	70	23
17	Brechin City	36	6	3	9	25	33	2	3	13	15	45	40	78	22
18	Alloa	36	4	3	11	23	31	3	4	11	22	48	45	79	21
19	Stenhousemuir	36	5	3	10	30	42	1	3	14	25	83	55	125	18

1968-69 Season
Back: Wark, Goldthorpe, Currie, MacRae, Forsyth, McCloy, McCallum, Campbell, Murray
Front: Whiteford, Wilson, Donnelly, Deans, McInally, Muir

1969-70 Season
Back : Whiteford, Wark, Forsyth, McCloy, McCallum, R Campbell
Front : Wilson, Donelly, Deans, McInally, Jim Muir, Murray

1969-70: 1st Division

	Date	Opponent	Score	Scorers	Att.	McCloy	Whiteford	Wark	Forsyth	McCallum	Campbell	Wilson	Donnelly	Deans	Muir Jim	McInally	Muir John	Murray	Goldthorpe	Murphy	MacRae	Watson	Heron	Murdoch	McCabe	Phillips	McIllwraith
1	30-Aug	KILMARNOCK	1 - 0	Deans		x	x	x	x	x	x	x	x	x	x	x		s									
2	03-Sep	Dundee	3 - 1	Donnelly, McInally, Deans	4800	x	x	x	x	x	x	x	x	x	x	x		s									
3	06-Sep	Clyde	2 - 0	Deans, Donnelly	3000	x	x	x	x	x	x	x	x	x	x	x		s									
4	14-Sep	ST. JOHNSTONE	4 - 1	Deans (2), Muir, McInally	10000	x	x	x	x	x	x	x	x	x	x	x		s									
5	20-Sep	Morton	0 - 1			x	x	x	x	x			x	x	x	x		x	x								
6	27-Sep	AIRDRIE	2 - 2	Deans (2)		x	x	x	x	x	x	x	x	x	x	x		s									
7	04-Oct	DUNDEE UNITED	0 - 2			x		x	x	x		x	x	x	x	x		s	x		x						
8	11-Oct	Hearts	2 - 2	Muir, McInally		x	x	x	x	x	x	x	x	x	x	x					s						
p 29/10	18-Oct	RANGERS	2 - 2	McInally, Donnelly		x	x	x	x	x	x	x	x		x	x		x	s								
10	25-Oct	Raith Rovers	2 - 2	Murray, Murphy		x		x	x	x	x	x	x		x	x		x		x						s	
11	01-Nov	ST. MIRREN	3 - 0	Murphy (2), Goldthorpe		x	x	x	x	x	x	x	x		x	s			x	x							
12	08-Nov	Partick Thistle	2 - 2	Muir (2)		x		x	x	x	x	x	x	s	x	x			x	x							
13	15-Nov	CELTIC	1 - 2	Deans		x		x	x	x	x	x	x	s	x	x			x	x							
14	22-Nov	Aberdeen	1 - 4	Muir		x		x	x		x	x	x	x	x	x			x	x	s						
15	29-Nov	Hibernian	1 - 1	Goldthorpe		x		x	x	x	x	x		x	x	x			x	x	s						
16	06-Dec	DUNFERMLINE	0 - 0			x		x	x	x	x	x		x	x	x	s		x	x							
17	13-Dec	Kilmarnock	2 - 2	Deans (2)	3500			x	x	x	x	x		x	x	x			x	x	x						
18	20-Dec	DUNDEE	1 - 1	Muir	4500			x	x	x	x	x	s	x	x	x			x	x	x						
19	27-Dec	Ayr United	0 - 1		8000			x	x	x	x	x	s	x	x	x			x	x	x						
p 11/3	01-Jan	Aidrie	0 - 1					x	x	x	x	x	x	x	x	x		s	x		x						
p 2/3	03-Jan	MORTON	1 - 0	Goldthorpe				x	x	x	x	x	x	x		x		s	x	x	x						
p 13/4	10-Jan	AYR UNITED	3 - 0	Deans, Heron, Wark			x	x	x	x		x		x	x	x				s	x	x	x				
23	17-Jan	St. Johnstone	3 - 4	McInally (2), Wilson	4200		x	x	x		x	x	s	x	x	x			x	x	x						
24	31-Jan	CLYDE	1 - 0	Goldthorpe			x	x	x	x	x	x	x	x					x	s	x						x
p 25/3	07-Feb	Dunfermline Ath.	1 - 2	Heron				x	x	x	x	x	s	x	x					x	x	x	x				
p 1/4	14-Feb	HIBERNIAN	2 - 1	McInally, Muir				x	x	x	x	x		x	x	x				s	x	x	x				
27	21-Feb	Dundee United	0 - 0				x	x	x	x	x	x	x	x	x	x					x						
28	28-Feb	HEARTS	0 - 2		7900			x	x	x	x	x	x	x	x	x			x	s	x						
29	07-Mar	Rangers	1 - 2	Wilson				x	x	x	x	x	x	x		x	x		x		x						
30	14-Mar	RAITH ROVERS	1 - 2	Muir				x	x	x	x	x	x		x	x					x	x	x				
31	21-Mar	St. Mirren	3 - 2	Deans (2), Campbell	6060			x	x	x	x	x		x	x	x				s	x	x	x				
32	28-Mar	PARTICK THISTLE	3 - 1	Deans (2), McInally				x	x	x	x	x		x	x	x			s		x	x	x				
33	04-Apr	Celtic	1 - 6	Deans				x	x	x		x	x	x	x	x				x	x		x		s		
34	18-Apr	ABERDEEN	0 - 2		6100		x	x	x	x		x		x	x	x				s		x	x	x			

LEAGUE CUP

	Date	Opponent	Score	Scorers	Att.	McCloy	Whiteford	Wark	Forsyth	McCallum	Campbell	Wilson	Donnelly	Deans	Muir Jim	McInally	Muir John	Murray	Goldthorpe	Murphy	MacRae	Watson	Heron	Murdoch	McCabe	Phillips	McIllwraith
	09-Aug	EAST FIFE	2 - 0	Wilson (2)	5000	x	x	x	x	x	x	x	x	x	x	x		s									
	13-Aug	Montrose	4 - 1	McInally (3), Campbell		x	x	x	x	x	x	x	x	x	x	x		s									
	16-Aug	ALBION ROVERS	5 - 1	McInally (3), Campbell, Donnelly		x	x	x	x	x	x	x	x	x	x	x		s									
	20-Aug	MONTROSE	3 - 2	Wilson, Murray, Campbell		x	x	x	x	x	x	x	x	x	x	x		s									
	23-Aug	East Fife	0 - 0			x	x	x	x	x	x	x	x			x		s							x	x	
	27-Aug	Albion Rovers	4 - 2	Muir (3), McInally		x	x	x		x	s	x	x		x	x			x		x					x	
	10-Sep	Morton	0 - 3			x	x	x	x	x	x	x	x	x	x	x		s									
	24-Sep	MORTON	3 - 0	Forsyth, Muir, McInally		x	x	x	x	x		x	x	x	x	x		s	x								
P/O	30-Sep	MORTON	1 - 0	Muir		x		x	x	x		x	x	x	x	x		s	x		x						
S/F	06-Nov	ST. JOHNSTONE	0-2			x	x	x	x	x		x	x	x	x	x			x		s						

SCOTTISH CUP

	Date	Opponent	Score	Scorers	Att.	McCloy	Whiteford	Wark	Forsyth	McCallum	Campbell	Wilson	Donnelly	Deans	Muir Jim	McInally	Muir John	Murray	Goldthorpe	Murphy	MacRae	Watson	Heron	Murdoch	McCabe	Phillips	McIllwraith
	24-Jan	ST. JOHNSTONE	2 - 1	Deans, McInally	8834		x	x	x		x	x	s	x	x	x			x	x	x						
	07-Feb	INVERNESS C.	3 - 1	Deans (2), McInally	7761			x	x	x	x	x	x	x	x	x			x	s	x						
	21-Feb	KILMARNOCK	0 - 1		16574			x	x	x	x	x	x	x	x	x			x	s	x						

LANARKSHIRE CUP

	Date	Opponent	Score
	20-Oct	HAMILTON ACADEMICAL	
rep.	24-Nov	HAMILTON ACADEMICAL	

FRIENDLIES

	Date	Opponent	Score	Scorers
	29-Jul	Carlisle United	1 - 0	Muir
	02-Aug	Bradford	1 - 1	Murphy

1970 Div. 1

		Pl.	Home W.	D.	L.	F.	A.	Away W.	D.	L.	F.	A.	F. (Total)	A.	Pts.
1	Celtic	34	12	2	3	54	18	15	1	1	42	15	96	33	57
2	Rangers	34	13	1	3	38	17	6	6	5	29	23	67	40	45
3	Hibernian	34	12	3	2	40	17	7	3	7	25	23	65	40	44
4	Heart of Mid.	34	6	7	4	28	19	7	5	5	22	17	50	36	38
5	Dundee United	34	10	3	4	36	23	6	3	8	26	41	62	64	38
6	Dundee	34	11	2	4	29	15	4	4	9	20	29	49	44	36
7	Kilmarnock	34	10	5	2	37	21	3	5	9	25	36	62	57	36
8	Aberdeen	34	6	6	5	30	19	8	1	8	25	26	55	45	35
9	Morton	34	9	5	3	33	21	4	4	9	19	31	52	52	35
10	Dunfermline Ath.	34	12	2	3	32	17	3	3	11	13	28	45	45	35
11	MOTHERWELL	34	8	4	5	25	18	3	6	8	24	33	49	51	32
12	Airdrieonians	34	8	3	6	33	26	4	5	8	26	38	59	64	32
13	St. Johnstone	34	9	4	4	35	28	2	5	10	15	34	50	62	31
14	Ayr United	34	10	3	4	26	20	2	3	12	11	32	37	52	30
15	St. Mirren	34	6	5	6	28	28	2	4	11	11	26	39	54	25
16	Clyde	34	8	4	5	21	18	1	3	13	13	38	34	56	25
17	Raith Rovers	34	4	6	7	15	24	1	5	11	17	43	32	67	21
18	Partick Thistle	34	4	4	9	22	33	1	3	13	19	49	41	82	17

1970-71: 1st Division

	Date	Opponent	Score	Scorers	Att.	MacRae	Whiteford	Wark	Forsyth	McCallum	Watson	Campbell	McInally	Muir Jim	Goldthorpe	Heron	Lawson	Main	Deans	Martin	Donnelly	Fallon	McCabe	Ritchie	Burns	Hamilton W
1	29-Aug	KILMARNOCK	4 - 1	Goldthorpe, Deans, Main, Heron	6500	x	x	x	x	x	x	x		s	x	x		x	x							
2	05-Sep	Aidrie	0 - 3		6300	x	x	x	x	x	x	x	s		x	x		x	x							
3	12-Sep	CLYDE	2 - 1	Main, McInally	5100	x	x	x	x	x	x		x	x	x	x		s	x							
4	19-Sep	St. Johnstone	1 - 2	Heron	4800	x	x	x	x	x	x	s	x	x	x	x			x							
5	26-Sep	MORTON	2 - 0	Deans, Muir	6000	x	x	x	x	x	x		x	x	x	x			x	s						
6	03-Oct	Rangers	1 - 3	Deans	25000	x	x	x	x	x	x		x		x	x	x		x							
7	10-Oct	HIBERNIAN	4 - 0	McInally (3), Muir	7650	x	x	x	x	x	x		x		x	x		x	x							
8	17-Oct	Dunfermline Ath.	1 - 0	McInally	4000	x	x	x	x	x			x	x		x	x		x		x					
9	24-Oct	Cowdenbeath	1 - 0	Muir	3000	x	x	x	x	x			x	x		x	x		x		x					
10	31-Oct	CELTIC	0 - 5		20000	x	x	x	x	x				x	x	x	x		x		x					
11	07-Nov	Falkirk	0 - 1		6000	x	x	x	x	x	x	x	x	x		x	s				x					
12	14-Nov	ST. MIRREN	2 - 1	Donnelly, Deans	7000	x	x	x	x	x	x	x		x		x	s		x		x					
13	21-Nov	Dundee United	2 - 2	Deans, Whiteford	5000	x	x	x	x		x	x		x		x	x		x		x					
14	28-Nov	ABERDEEN	0 - 2		10000	x	x	x	x	x	x	x		x		x	s		x		x					
15	05-Dec	Ayr United	0 - 0		7000	x	x	x	x	x	x	x	s	x		x			x		x					
16	12-Dec	HEARTS	1 - 2	Deans	8000	x	x	x	x	x	x			x	x	x	s		x		x					
17	19-Dec	DUNDEE	1 - 1	Forsyth	7000	x	x	x	x	x	x			x	x	x	s		x		x					
18	26-Dec	Kilmarnock	0 - 0		7500	x	x	x		x	x	x				x	x	x	x		x					
19	01-Jan	AIRDRIE	1 - 1	Lawson	8000	x	x	x	x	x	x	x		s		x	x		x		x					
p 21/4	02-Jan	Clyde	2 - 1	Deans, McInally	1700	x	x	x	x	x	x		x	x	x	x			x							
21	09-Jan	ST. JOHNSTONE	4 - 1	Heron, Whiteford, Campbell, Deans	5500	x	x	x	x	x	x	x				x	x	s	x		x					
p 5/4	16-Jan	Morton	2 - 0	Deans, Muir	5300		x		x	x		x	x	x	x	x			x	s		x	x			
23	30-Jan	RANGERS	1 - 2	Muir	17500	x	x	x	x	x	x	x		x		x	s		x		x					
24	06-Feb	Hibernian	0 - 1		7092	x	x	x	x	x	x		s	x		x	x		x		x					
25	20-Feb	DUNFERMLINE	4 - 3	McInally, Deans, Martin, Whiteford	5000	x	x	x	x	x	x		x			x	x	x	x	s						
26	27-Feb	COWDENBEATH	1 - 3	Forsyth	4000	x	x	x	x	x	x		x				x	x	x	x						
p 12/4	06-Mar	Celtic	0 - 3		23000	x	x	x	x	x	x			x	x	x			x	x						
28	13-Mar	FALKIRK	1 - 1	Forsyth	4600	x	x	x	x	x	x		x				x	x	x	x						
29	20-Mar	St. Mirren	2 - 0	Muir, Heron	4800	x	x	x	x	x	x			x		x	x	x	x							
30	27-Mar	DUNDEE UNITED	1 - 2	Goldthorpe	6500	x	x	x	x	x	x			x	x		x		x	x						
31	03-Apr	Aberdeen	0 - 0		13000	x	x	x	x	x	x			x	x	x	x		x							
32	10-Apr	AYR UNITED	1 - 1	Heron	4200	x	x	x	x	x	x			x	x	x	x		x							
33	17-Apr	Hearts	1 - 0	Wark	5500	x	x	x	x	x	x		x	x	x	x			x							
34	24-Apr	Dundee	0 - 4		4000	x	x	x	x	x	x		x	x	x	x			x							s

LEAGUE CUP

	Date	Opponent	Score	Scorers	Att.	MacRae	Whiteford	Wark	Forsyth	McCallum	Watson	Campbell	McInally	Muir Jim	Goldthorpe	Heron	Lawson	Main	Deans	Martin	Donnelly	Fallon	McCabe	Ritchie	Burns	Hamilton W
	08-Aug	Morton	4 - 1	Forsyth, Campbell, Heron, Goldthorpe			x	x	x	x	x	x	x	x	x	x					s			x		
	12-Aug	RANGERS	0 - 2				x	x	x	x	x	x	x	x	x	x					s			x		
	15-Aug	DUNFERMLINE	3 - 0	Whiteford, Forsyth, Heron	4576		x	x	x	x	x	x	x	x	x	x								x		
	19-Aug	Rangers	0 - 2				x	x	x	x	x	x	x		x	x	x							x		
	22-Aug	MORTON	0 - 2				x	x	x	x	x	x	x	x	x	x	s							x		
	26-Aug	Dunfermline Ath.	1 - 1	Heron			x	x	x	x	x	x	x	s	x	x	x							x		

SCOTTISH CUP

	Date	Opponent	Score	Scorers	Att.	MacRae	Whiteford	Wark	Forsyth	McCallum	Watson	Campbell	McInally	Muir Jim	Goldthorpe	Heron	Lawson	Main	Deans	Martin	Donnelly	Fallon	McCabe	Ritchie	Burns	Hamilton W
	23-Jan	Stirling Albion	1 - 3	Whiteford	4156	x	x	x	x	x	x	x	s	x		x			x		x					

TEXACO CUP

	Date	Opponent	Score	Scorers	Att.	MacRae	Whiteford	Wark	Forsyth	McCallum	Watson	Campbell	McInally	Muir Jim	Goldthorpe	Heron	Lawson	Main	Deans	Martin	Donnelly	Fallon	McCabe	Ritchie	Burns	Hamilton W
	14-Sep	STOKE CITY	1 - 0	Goldthorpe	14450	x	x	x	x	x	x		x	x	x	x			x							
	30-Sep	Stoke City	1 - 2	McInally	15779	x	x	x	x	x	x		x		x	x	x		x	s				s		
	21-Oct	Tottenham Hot.	2 - 3	Donnelly, McInally	17350	x	x	x	x	x			x	x	s	x	x		x		x					
	03-Nov	TOTTENHAM HOT.	3 - 1	Donnelly, Heron, Watson	22450	x	x	x	x	x	x	x		x		x	s		x		x			s		
S/F 1	16-Dec	Hearts	1 - 1	Muir	21220	x	x	x	x	x	x	s		x		x	x		x		x			s		
S/F 2	03-Mar	HEARTS	1 - 2	Heron	25300		x	x	x	x	x		x			x	x	x	x	s				x	s	

FRIENDLIES

Date	Opponent	Score	Scorers
01-Aug	ASTON VILLA	2 - 1	Muir, McInally
12-Feb	Millwall	0 - 1	

1971 Div. 1

		Pl.	Home W.	D.	L.	F.	A.	Away W.	D.	L.	F.	A.	F. (Total)	A.	Pts.
1	Celtic	34	15	1	1	43	7	10	5	2	46	16	89	23	56
2	Aberdeen	34	11	6	0	38	7	13	0	4	30	11	68	18	54
3	St. Johnstone	34	10	3	4	33	20	9	3	5	26	24	59	44	44
4	Rangers	34	10	5	2	33	10	6	4	7	25	24	58	34	41
5	Dundee	34	9	2	6	30	23	5	8	4	23	22	53	45	38
6	Dundee United	34	8	4	5	34	29	6	4	7	19	25	53	54	36
7	Falkirk	34	8	5	4	24	20	5	4	8	22	33	46	53	35
8	Morton	34	9	4	4	25	17	4	4	9	19	27	44	44	34
9	MOTHERWELL	34	7	4	6	30	27	6	4	7	13	20	43	47	34
10	Airdrieonians	34	8	3	6	33	26	5	5	7	27	39	60	65	34
11	Heart of Mid.	34	8	5	4	24	16	5	2	10	17	24	41	40	33
12	Hibernian	34	8	4	5	33	24	2	6	9	14	29	47	53	30
13	Kilmarnock	34	5	6	6	26	31	5	2	10	17	36	43	67	28
14	Ayr United	34	7	5	5	22	15	2	3	12	15	39	37	54	26
15	Clyde	34	5	5	7	19	23	3	5	9	14	36	33	59	26
16	Dunfermline Ath.	34	6	5	6	26	19	0	6	11	18	37	44	56	23
17	St. Mirren	34	4	3	10	20	30	3	6	8	18	26	38	56	23
18	Cowdenbeath	34	1	2	14	13	39	6	1	10	20	38	33	77	17

1970-71 Season
Back: MacRae, Lawson, Whiteford, Donnelly, McCallum, Ritchie, Forsyth
Front: Goldthorpe, Martin, Deans, Muir, Wark, Heron, Watson

1971-72 Season
Back: Wark, Whiteford, Goldthorpe, MacRae, Gillespie, McInally, McCallum, Burns, Watson, Heron, Martin
Front: McKenzie (Train), Campbell, McCabe, Forsyth, Howitt (Man), Lawson, Brown, Deans, Ritchie (Coach)

1971-72: 1st Division

No.	Date	Opponent	Score	Scorers	Att.	MacCrae	Whiteford	Wark	Forsyth	McCallum	Goldthorpe	Martin	Watson	Deans	McInally	Heron	Brown	Campbell	Gillespie	Lawson	McClymont	Muir Jim	Main	Muir John	McCabe	Burns	Ritchie	Fallon
1	04-Sep	AIRDRIE	0 - 1		5763	x	x	x	x	x	x	x	x	x	x	x												
2	11-Sep	Clyde	0 - 2		2500	x	x	x	x	x	s	x	x	x	x	x	x											
3	18-Sep	KILMARNOCK	3 - 0	Goldthorpe (2), Heron	3774	x	x	x	x	x	x	x	x	x		x	x	s										
4	25-Sep	Dunfermline Ath.	1 - 1	Goldthorpe	6000	x		x	x	x	x	x	x	x		x	x		x	s								
5	02-Oct	HIBERNIAN	1 - 1	Deans	5757	x		x	x	x	x	x	x	x	s	x	x		x									
6	09-Oct	St. Johnstone	1 - 5	Deans	5000	x	x	x	x	x	x	s	x	x		x	x	x										
7	16-Oct	MORTON	3 - 1	Lawson (2), McClymont	4232	x	x	x	x	x	x	s	x					x		x	x	x						
8	23-Oct	Rangers	0 - 4		20000	x	x	x	x	x	x		x		x			s		x	x	x						
9	30-Oct	DUNDEE	1 - 3	Muir	3812	x		x	x	x	x				x	x		x	x	s	x	x						
10	06-Nov	HEARTS	5 - 3	Heron (3), Goldthorpe, Muir	5449	x		x	x	x	x				x	x		x	x	x		x						
11	13-Nov	Ayr United	1 - 1	Goldthorpe	4800	x		x	x	x	x					x		x	x			x	x	x				
12	20-Nov	ABERDEEN	0 - 4		6251	x		x	x	x	x					x		x	x			x	x	x				
13	27-Nov	Dundee United	0 - 2		3000	x			x	x	x	x					x	x	x		s		x	x	x			
14	04-Dec	FALKIRK	2 - 1	Heron, McCabe	3827	x		x	x	x	x					x	x	x	x					x	x			
15	11-Dec	Partick Thistle	3 - 8	Brown, Heron, McCabe	7500	x		x	x	x	x					x	x	x	x			x			x			
16	18-Dec	CELTIC	1 - 5	McInally	19000			x	x	x	x		x		x	x		x	x						x	x		
17	25-Dec	East Fife	1 - 1	Heron	4100		x	x	x		x		x		x	x		x				x		x			x	
18	01-Jan	Aidrie	2 - 0	Muir, Heron	7000		x	x	x		x		x		x	x		x				x		x			x	
19	03-Jan	CLYDE	4 - 1	Campbell, Heron, McCabe, OG	6664		x	x	x		x		x		x	x		x				x		x	s		x	
20	08-Jan	Kilmarnock	0 - 1		5000		x	x	x		x	x				x		x		x				x	x		x	
21	15-Jan	DUNFERMLINE	4 - 1	McCabe (2), Goldthorpe, Lawson	4603		x	x	x	x	x	x				x		x		s				x	x		x	
22	22-Jan	Hibernian	2 - 1	Muir, McInally	8000		x	x	x			x			x	x		x		x				x	x			
23	29-Jan	ST. JOHNSTONE	2 - 0	Campbell, Lawson	4900		x	x	x	x					x	x		x		x				x	x		x	
p 5/4	12-Feb	Morton	2 - 3	Lawson, Heron	2500		x		x	x			x		x	x		x		x		x		x		x		
25	19-Feb	RANGERS	2 - 0	Lawson, Heron	16192	x		x	x	x		s	x		x	x		x		x				x	x			
26	04-Mar	Dundee	0 - 2		5000			x	x	x	s		x		x	x		x		x				x	x			x
p 21/3	11-Mar	Hearts	0 - 0		9000			x	x	x			x		x	x		x		x				x	x	x		
28	18-Mar	AYR UNITED	2 - 2	McCabe, Watson	4093		x		x	x			x		x	x		x		x				x	x	x		
29	25-Mar	Aberdeen	1 - 4	McInally	10000		x		x	x			x		x	x		x		x				x	x			x
30	01-Apr	DUNDEE UNITED	0 - 1		2234		x		x	x			x		x	x		x		x				x	x			x
31	08-Apr	Falkirk	0 - 3		4500		x		x	x	x				x	x		x		x		x	x			x		
32	15-Apr	PARTICK THISTLE	2 - 1	Lawson, Heron	5000		x	x	x	x			x		x	x		x		s				x	x			x
33	22-Apr	Celtic	2 - 5	McInally, Muir	20000		x	x	x	x		s	x		x	x		x		x					x			x
34	29-Apr	EAST FIFE	1 - 1	McCabe	4315		x		x	x			x		x	x		x		x				x	x			x

LEAGUE CUP

	Date	Opponent	Score	Scorers	Att.	MacCrae	Whiteford	Wark	Forsyth	McCallum	Goldthorpe	Martin	Watson	Deans	McInally	Heron	Brown	Campbell	Gillespie	Lawson	McClymont	Muir Jim	Main	Muir John	McCabe	Burns	Ritchie	Fallon
	14-Aug	HIBERNIAN	0 - 3		6840	x	x	x	x	x	x		x	x		x		x				x						
	18-Aug	Kilmarnock	0 - 1		5000	x	x	x		x	x		x		x	x	x	x		x								
	21-Aug	Dundee United	2 - 2	Martin, Heron	6050	x	x	x		x		x	x	x		x	x	x					x					
	25-Aug	KILMARNOCK	2 - 0	Watson (2)	5000	x	x	x	x	x		x	x	x		x				x			x					
	28-Aug	Hibernian	1 - 2	McInally	14252		x	x	x	x		x	x	x	x	x							x			x		
	01-Sep	DUNDEE UNITED	1 - 3	Whiteford	2760		x	x	x	x		x	x	x	x	x				s			x			x		

SCOTTISH CUP

	Date	Opponent	Score	Scorers	Att.	MacCrae	Whiteford	Wark	Forsyth	McCallum	Goldthorpe	Martin	Watson	Deans	McInally	Heron	Brown	Campbell	Gillespie	Lawson	McClymont	Muir Jim	Main	Muir John	McCabe	Burns	Ritchie	Fallon
	05-Feb	MONTROSE	2 - 0	Lawson, McCabe	5034	x		x	x	x		s	x		x	x		x		x				x	x			
	26-Feb	Ayr United	0 - 0		11500	x		x	x	x			x		x	x		x		x				x	x			
rep.	01-Mar	AYR UNITED	2 - 1	Heron, Lawson	11648			x	x	x			x		x	x		x		x				x	x	x		
	18-Mar	RANGERS	2 - 2	Heron, Campbell	28500		x		x	x			x		x	x		x		x				x	x			x
rep.	27-Mar	Rangers	2 - 4	Lawson (2)	44800		x		x	x	s		x		x	x		x		x				x	x			x

TEXACO CUP

	Date	Opponent	Score	Scorers	Att.	MacCrae	Whiteford	Wark	Forsyth	McCallum	Goldthorpe	Martin	Watson	Deans	McInally	Heron	Brown	Campbell	Gillespie	Lawson	McClymont	Muir Jim	Main	Muir John	McCabe	Burns	Ritchie	Fallon
	15-Sep	STOKE CITY	0 - 1		8300	x	x	x	x	x	x	x	x	x		x	x	s								s		
	29-Sep	Stoke City	1 - 4	Heron	13600	x	s	x	x	x	x		x		x	x	x		x			x				s		

LANARKSHIRE CUP

	Opponent	
	AIRDRIE	

FRIENDLIES

Date	Opponent	Score
31-Jul	STOKE CITY	0 - 0
03-Aug	Chesterfield	1 - 2
04-Aug	Scunthorpe United	1 - 2
09-Aug	Castelnuova	8 - 0
11-Aug	Ancona	0 - 0

1972 Div. 1

		Pl.	Home W.	Home D.	Home L.	Home F.	Home A.	Away W.	Away D.	Away L.	Away F.	Away A.	F. (Total)	A. (Total)	Pts.
1	Celtic	34	15	1	1	48	14	13	3	1	48	14	96	28	60
2	Aberdeen	34	13	3	1	54	13	8	5	4	26	13	80	26	50
3	Rangers	34	11	0	6	41	21	10	2	5	30	17	71	38	44
4	Hibernian	34	11	2	4	34	13	8	4	5	28	21	62	34	44
5	Dundee	34	8	6	3	30	14	6	7	4	29	24	59	38	41
6	Heart of Mid.	34	10	5	2	29	17	3	8	6	24	32	53	49	39
7	Partick Thistle	34	9	5	3	35	23	3	5	9	18	31	53	54	34
8	St. Johnstone	34	7	5	5	26	21	5	3	9	26	37	52	58	32
9	Dundee United	34	7	5	5	36	37	5	2	10	19	33	55	70	31
10	MOTHERWELL	34	9	3	5	33	26	2	4	11	16	43	49	69	29
11	Kilmarnock	34	7	3	7	27	28	4	3	10	22	36	49	64	28
12	Ayr United	34	5	6	6	20	19	4	4	9	20	39	40	58	28
13	Morton	34	5	7	5	23	20	5	0	12	23	32	46	52	27
14	Falkirk	34	7	4	6	26	23	3	3	11	18	37	44	60	27
15	Airdrieonians	34	4	6	7	25	37	3	6	8	19	39	44	76	26
16	East Fife	34	2	7	8	19	34	3	8	6	15	27	34	61	25
17	Clyde	34	5	4	8	16	26	2	6	9	17	40	33	66	24
18	Dunfermline Ath.	34	5	5	7	19	24	2	4	11	12	26	31	50	23

1972-73: 1st Division

No.	Date	Opponent	Score	Scorers	Att.	Ritchie	Whiteford	Wark	Forsyth	McCallum	Muir John	Gray	Murray	Lawson	McClymont	Martin	Goldthorpe	MacRae	Heron	Muir Jim	Watson	Campbell	Goodwin	McCabe	McInally	Millar P	Brown	Main	Burns	Leishman	Murray	Lindsay
1	02-Sep	DUNDEE	2 - 2	Lawson, Forsyth	4050	x		x	x		x			x					x	s		x		x	x	x	x					
2	09-Sep	Aidrie	2 - 1	Lawson, McClymont	4000	x	x	x	x	x	x	x	x	x	x	x	s															
3	16-Sep	KILMARNOCK	2 - 0	Wark, McClymont	4550	x	x	x	x	x	x	x	x	x	x	x	s															
4	23-Sep	St. Johnstone	2 - 2	McClymont, Murray	3700		x	x	x	x	x	x	x	x	x	x		x														
5	30-Sep	Aberdeen	2 - 7	Gray, McClymont	10000		x	x	x	x	x	x	x	x	x	x	s	x														
6	07-Oct	DUNDEE UNITED	1 - 4	Lawson	3947		x	x	x	x	x	x		x	x		x	x	x	s												
7	14-Oct	RANGERS	0 - 2		17621		x	x		x	x	x		x	x	x		x	x	s	x											
8	21-Oct	Hearts	0 - 0		8000		x	x	x	x		x						x		x	x	x		x	x							
9	28-Oct	FALKIRK	1 - 1	Campbell	4651		x	x		x		x		s				x		x	x	x	x	x	x							
10	04-Nov	Ayr United	2 - 3	McClymont, Watson	4800		x	x		x					x			x		x	x	x	x	x	x							
11	11-Nov	CELTIC	0 - 5		12439		x	x		x		s			x			x		x	x	x	x	x	x							
12	18-Nov	Partick Thistle	3 - 0	Campbell, McCabe, McClymont	5000		x	x		x		x			x			x			x	x	x	x	x							
13	25-Nov	EAST FIFE	0 - 1		3433		x	x		x		x		s	x			x			x	x	x	x	x							
14	02-Dec	Morton	0 - 1		3500		x	x		x		x		s	x			x			x	x	x	x	x							
p 10/4	09-Dec	HIBERNIAN	1 - 1	Goldthorpe	4405		x	x		x	s					x	x	x			x		x	x	x	x						
16	16-Dec	Dumbarton	0 - 0		3000		x	x		x							x	x	x	x	x	x	x	x	s							
17	23-Dec	ARBROATH	2 - 0	Muir, Heron	2330		x	x		x							x	x	s	x	x	x	x	x		x						
18	30-Dec	Dundee	0 - 2		3000		x			x						s		x	x	x	x	x	x	x	x	x						
19	02-Jan	AIRDRIE	2 - 0	Martin, OG	6167		x	x		x						s		x	x	x		x	x	x	x	x						
20	06-Jan	Kilmarnock	0 - 1		4000		x	x		x				x	s	x		x	x		x		x		x	x						
21	13-Jan	ST. JOHNSTONE	2 - 1	Goldthorpe	3365		x	x		x				x			x	x	s		x	x	x	x		x						
22	20-Jan	ABERDEEN	2 - 0	Campbell, Lawson	4500		x	x		x				x			x	x			x	x	x	x	s	x						
23	27-Jan	Dundee United	2 - 1	Lawson, McCabe	4020		x	x		x				x			x	x			x	x	x	x		x						
24	10-Feb	Rangers	1 - 2	Miller	22000		x	x		x				x			x	x			x	x	x	x	s	x						
25	17-Feb	HEARTS	2 - 2	Miller, McCabe	4770		x	x		x				x		s	x	x			x	x	x	x		x						
26	03-Mar	Falkirk	1 - 0	Whiteford	3500		x	x		x				x			x	x			x	x	x	x		x					s	
27	10-Mar	AYR UNITED	1 - 2	Miller	3845		x	x		x				x		s	x	x			x	x	x	x		x						
p 3/4	17-Mar	Celtic	0 - 2		22000		x	x		x	x					x	x	x			x		x		x	x						
29	24-Mar	PARTICK THISTLE	0 - 0		3080		x	x		x				x				x		x	x	x	x	x	x	s						
30	31-Mar	East Fife	1 - 3	Miller	2755		x	x		x		x					s	x		x	x	x	x	x		x						
31	07-Apr	MORTON	3 - 0	Goldthorpe, McCabe, OG	2750		x	x		x		x					x	x		x	x	s	x	x		x						
32	14-Apr	Hibernian	1 - 0	Miller	8405		x	x		x							x	x		x	x	s	x		x	x						x
33	21-Apr	DUMBARTON	0 - 2		3557		x	x		x	x						x	x		s	x		x	x	x	x						
34	28-Apr	Arbroath	0 - 1		2519		x	x		x					s		x	x		x	x	x	x	x	x							

LEAGUE CUP

	Date	Opponent	Score	Scorers	Att.	Ritchie	Whiteford	Wark	Forsyth	McCallum	Muir John	Gray	Murray	Lawson	McClymont	Martin	Goldthorpe	MacRae	Heron	Muir Jim	Watson	Campbell	Goodwin	McCabe	McInally	Millar P	Brown	Main	Burns	Leishman	Murray	Lindsay
	12-Aug	Clyde	2 - 2	Lawson (2)		x	x	x			x			x		x	x		x	x						x		x					
	16-Aug	EAST STIRLING	1 - 0	Wark		x	x	x	x		x			x			x		x	x		x			x		s					
	19-Aug	DUNDEE	1 - 3	Heron		x	x	x	x		x			x			x		x	x		x			x		s					
	23-Aug	East Stirling	5 - 1	Lawson, OG, Gray, McInally, Wark		x	x	x	x		x	x		x			s		x	x		x			x					x		
	26-Aug	CLYDE	1 - 1	McCabe		x		x	x		x			x					x	s		x		x		x	x	x				
	30-Aug	Dundee	1 - 2	Muir		x		x	x		x	x		x	x							x		x	x		s	x				
	04-Sep	ALBION ROVERS	4 - 1	McClymont, Murray, Martin, Forsyth		x	x	x	x	x	x	x	x	x	x	x	s															
	06-Sep	Albion Rovers	4 - 1	Goldthorpe, Martin, Murray, McCabe		x	x	x	x	x	x		x	x	x	x	s							x								
	20-Sep	AIRDRIE	0 - 1			x	x	x	x	x	x	x	x	x	x	x	s															
	04-Oct	Aidrie	1 - 1	Whiteford		x	x	x	x	x	x	x	x	x	x	x	s															

SCOTTISH CUP

	Date	Opponent	Score	Scorers	Att.	Ritchie	Whiteford	Wark	Forsyth	McCallum	Muir John	Gray	Murray	Lawson	McClymont	Martin	Goldthorpe	MacRae	Heron	Muir Jim	Watson	Campbell	Goodwin	McCabe	McInally	Millar P	Brown	Main	Burns	Leishman	Murray	Lindsay
	03-Feb	RAITH	2 - 1	Goldthorpe, Campbell	5621	x	x	x		x				x			x				x	x	x	x	s	x						
	24-Feb	CELTIC	0 - 4		24672		x	x		x				x		s	x	x			x	x	x	x		x						

TEXACO CUP

	Date	Opponent	Score	Scorers	Att.	Ritchie	Whiteford	Wark	Forsyth	McCallum	Muir John	Gray	Murray	Lawson	McClymont	Martin	Goldthorpe	MacRae	Heron	Muir Jim	Watson	Campbell	Goodwin	McCabe	McInally	Millar P	Brown	Main	Burns	Leishman	Murray	Lindsay
	12-Sep	Coventry City	3 - 3	Lawson (2), McInally	7370	x	x	x	x	x	x	x	x	x	x	x									s				s			
	27-Sep	COVENTRY CITY	1 - 0	McClymont	9812	s	x	x	x	x	x	x	x	x	x	x	s	x														
	18-Oct	Hearts	0 - 0		13623	s	x	x		x				x				x	s	x	x	x	x	x	x							
	11-Aug	HEARTS	4 - 2	McCabe, Campbell, Wark, McClymont	14600	s	x	x			x	x		x	x	s		x				x	x	x								
	14-Mar	Norwich City	0 - 2		19000		x	x		x				x				x		x	x	x	x	x	x	s			s			
	21-Mar	NORWICH CITY	3 - 2	McCabe (3)	12066		x	x		x	x				x			x			x	x	x	x	x	s			s			

FRIENDLIES

	Date	Opponent	Score	Scorers
	29-Jul	Warkington	2 - 2	Muir, Heron
	03-Aug	SCUNTHORPE UNITED	0 - 2	
	05-Aug	Stevenage	0 - 4	
	07-Aug	Peterborough United	0 - 2	

1973 Div. 1

		Pl.	Home W.	D.	L.	F.	A.	Away W.	D.	L.	F.	A.	F. (Total)	A.	Pts.
1	Celtic	34	14	3	0	47	10	12	2	3	46	18	93	28	57
2	Rangers	34	14	2	1	36	10	12	2	3	38	20	74	30	56
3	Hibernian	34	12	2	3	43	17	7	5	5	31	16	74	33	45
4	Aberdeen	34	10	6	1	42	15	6	5	6	19	19	61	34	43
5	Dundee	34	13	4	0	45	10	4	5	8	23	33	68	43	43
6	Ayr United	34	11	4	2	33	21	5	4	8	17	30	50	51	40
7	Dundee United	34	11	3	3	32	24	6	2	9	24	27	56	51	39
8	MOTHERWELL	34	5	6	6	20	23	6	3	8	18	25	38	48	31
9	East Fife	34	8	3	6	26	21	3	5	9	20	33	46	54	30
10	Heart of Mid.	34	7	4	6	15	17	5	2	10	24	33	39	50	30
11	St. Johnstone	34	8	3	6	35	30	2	6	9	17	37	52	67	29
12	Morton	34	8	4	5	33	21	2	4	11	14	32	47	53	28
13	Partick Thistle	34	4	5	8	17	25	6	3	8	23	28	40	53	28
14	Falkirk	34	6	4	7	24	26	1	8	8	14	30	38	56	26
15	Arbroath	34	8	3	6	31	23	1	5	11	8	40	39	63	26
16	Dumbarton	34	3	9	5	26	30	3	2	12	17	42	43	72	23
17	Kilmarnock	34	6	3	8	23	30	1	5	11	17	41	40	71	22
18	Airdrieonians	34	2	4	11	16	35	2	4	11	18	40	34	75	16

1972-73 Season
Back: Wark, Whiteford, Ritchie, Watson, Heron
Middle: Struthers, McCallum, McInally, Jim Muir, Goldthorp, John Muir, Millar, Forsyth, French
Front: Howitt (Man), Campbell, Martin, Lawson, Brown, McCabe, McKenzie (Train)

1973-74 Season
Back: Wark, Watson, Jim Muir, Ritchie, McCallum, Goodwin, John Muir, Whiteford
Front: Campbell, McClymont, McCabe, Martin, Millar, Lawson, Goldthorp, McKenzie (Train)

1973-74: 1st Division

No.	Date	Opponent	Score	Scorers	Att.	MacRae	Rennie	Wark	Watson	Muir Jim	Muir John	McCallum	Goodwin	Campbell	Martin	Lawson	Goldthorpe	McClymont	Millar	McCabe	Graham	Watson W	Pettigrew	Gray	Whiteford	Joyce J	Kennedy	McGuiness	Leishman	Taylor	Burns
1	01-Sep	ABERDEEN	0 - 0		6083	x		x	x	x			x	x	s	x	s	x	x	x					x						
2	08-Sep	Arbroath	2 - 0	McCabe, Goldthorpe	2821	x		x	x	x	x		s	x		s	x	x	x	x	x										
3	15-Sep	HEARTS	2 - 2	Martin, Goldthorpe	9815	x		x	x	x			x	x	x	s	x		x	x	x										
4	22-Sep	Falkirk	1 - 1	Goldthorpe	5500	x		x	x	x			x	x	x		x	x	x		x										
5	29-Sep	DUNDEE UNITED	4 - 0	Graham (2), Martin, Goldthorpe	4973	x		x	x	x	s		x	x	x	s	x	x	x		x										
6	06-Oct	Celtic	0 - 2		32000	x		x	x	x	s		x		x	s	x	x	x	x	x										
7	13-Oct	PARTICK THISTLE	1 - 2	Lawson	7164	x		x	x	x						x	x	x	x	x	x	x									
8	20-Oct	Ayr United	0 - 1		5000		x	x	x	x			x				x	x	x	x	x	x									
9	27-Oct	ST. JOHNSTONE	0 - 1		4955		x	x	x	x				x	x		x	x	x		x	x	s			s					
10	03-Nov	Dumbarton	0 - 3		6000		x	x	x	x				x	x		x	x	x		x	x		s							
11	10-Nov	HIBERNIAN	1 - 1	McClymont	6583		x	x	x	x				s			s	x	x	x	x	x	x	x							
12	17-Nov	Dunfermline Ath.	4 - 2	Goldthorpe (2), Muir, Watson	5000		x	x	x	x				x	x		x	x	x		x	x									
13	24-Nov	MORTON	1 - 0	Graham	3690		x	x	x	x				x	x		x	x	x		x	x					s				
p 24/4	01-Dec	Rangers	1 - 2	Goldthorpe	10000		x	x	x	x				x	x		x	x	x		x	x									
15	08-Dec	CLYDE	0 - 0		2596		x	x	x	x				x	x		x	x	x		x	x		s			s				
16	15-Dec	EAST FIFE	3 - 1	Martin, Goldthorpe, Graham	2043		x	x	x	x					x		x	x	x		x	x		x				s			
17	22-Dec	Dundee	1 - 0	Goldthorpe	6009		x	x	x	x					x		x	x	x		x	x		x							
18	29-Dec	Aberdeen	0 - 0		8000		x	x	x	x	x			x	x		x	x		x	x										
19	01-Jan	ARBROATH	3 - 4	Graham (2), Muir	7029		x	x	x	x					x		x	x		x	x	x		x							
20	05-Jan	Hearts	0 - 2		10000		x	x		x			x		x		x	x		x	x	x		x			s				
p 17/4	12-Jan	FALKIRK	2 - 1	Martin, Pettigrew	3479		x	x	x	x			x		x				x	x	x	x	x								
22	19-Jan	Dundee United	1 - 0	Graham	3500		x	x	x	x			x		x		x	s	x		x	x					x				
23	02-Feb	CELTIC	3 - 2	Martin, Goldthorpe, Graham	16669		x	x	x	x					x		x		x	x	x	x					x				
24	09-Feb	Partick Thistle	0 - 1		6000		x	x	x	x				s	x		x		x	x	x	x					x				
25	23-Feb	AYR UNITED	2 - 0	Miller, Graham	7630		x	x	x	x					x		x	x	x		x	x		x							
26	02-Mar	St. Johnstone	1 - 0	Miller	3000		x	x	x	x	x				x		x	x	x		x			x			s				
27	?	DUMBARTON	2 - 0	Pettigrew (2)	3337		x	x	x		x		x					x	x	x	x	x	x								
p 15/4	16-Mar	Hibernian	0 - 1		10700		x	x	x		x		x		x				x	x	x	x	x				s				
29	23-Mar	DUNFERMLINE	1 - 0	Gray	4069		x	x	x	x					x			x	x		x		x	x			s	s	x		
30	30-Mar	Morton	3 - 4	Graham (2), Pettigrew	2500		x	x	x	x					x			x	x		x		x					x	x		
31	06-Apr	RANGERS	1 - 4	OG	13346		x	x	x	x					x			x	x		x	x	x	x				s			
32	13-Apr	Clyde	3 - 0	Graham, Goodwin, Martin	3000		x	x	x		x		x		x				x	x	x	x	x								
33	20-Apr	East Fife	0 - 1		2400		x	x	x		x		x		x				s	x	x	x	x				x				
34	27-Apr	DUNDEE	2 - 2	Graham, Muir	4000		x	x	x		x				s		x		x		x		x	x						x	x

LEAGUE CUP

	Date	Opponent	Score	Scorers	Att.	MacRae	Rennie	Wark	Watson	Muir Jim	Muir John	McCallum	Goodwin	Campbell	Martin	Lawson	Goldthorpe	McClymont	Millar	McCabe	Graham	Watson W	Pettigrew	Gray	Whiteford	Joyce J	Kennedy	McGuiness	Leishman	Taylor	Burns
	11-Aug	Aberdeen	1 - 3	Lawson	11000	x		x	x	x	x	x		x		x		x	x	x											
	15-Aug	EAST FIFE	5 - 0	Miller (2), Campbell, Muir, McCabe		x		x	x	x	x		x	x	s	x	s	x	x	x			s								
	18-Aug	DUNDEE UNITED	4 - 0	Campbell, Miller, McCabe, McClymont	5000	x		x	x	x	x		x	x		x		x	x	x			s								
	22-Aug	East Fife	0 - 3			x		x	x	x	x		x	x		x		x	x	x			s								
	25-Aug	Dundee United	3 - 0	Miller, Lawson, McCabe	4500	x		x	x	x	x		x	x		x		x	x	x			s								
	29-Aug	ABERDEEN	0 - 0		9808	x		x	x	x	x		x	x		x		x	x	x			s								
	12-Sep	CELTIC	1 - 2	Goldthorpe	20072	x		x	x	x			x	x	s		x	x	x	x	x										
	10-Oct	Celtic	1 - 0	Goldthorpe	28065	x		x	x	x			x	x		x		x	x	x		x									
rep.	29-Oct	Celtic	2 - 3	McClymont, Graham	21000	x		x	x	x			x	x		x		x	x	s	x	x									

SCOTTISH CUP

	Date	Opponent	Score	Scorers	Att.	MacRae	Rennie	Wark	Watson	Muir Jim	Muir John	McCallum	Goodwin	Campbell	Martin	Lawson	Goldthorpe	McClymont	Millar	McCabe	Graham	Watson W	Pettigrew	Gray	Whiteford	Joyce J	Kennedy	McGuiness	Leishman	Taylor	Burns
	27-Jan	BRECHIN	2 - 0	Martin (2)	5791		x	x	x	x			x		x		x		x		x	x		s			x				
	16-Feb	Arbroath	3 - 1	Goldthorpe (3)	4444		x	x	x	x			s		x		x		x		x	x		x			x				
	10-Mar	Celtic	2 - 2	Graham, Kennedy	48000		x	x	x	x					x		x		x		x	x		x			x				
rep.	13-Mar	CELTIC	0 - 1		24875		x	x	x	x	s				x		x	x	x		x	x		s			x				

TEXACO CUP

	Date	Opponent	Score	Scorers	Att.	MacRae	Rennie	Wark	Watson	Muir Jim	Muir John	McCallum	Goodwin	Campbell	Martin	Lawson	Goldthorpe	McClymont	Millar	McCabe	Graham	Watson W	Pettigrew	Gray	Whiteford	Joyce J	Kennedy	McGuiness	Leishman	Taylor	Burns
	25-Sep	Coventry City	1 - 0	Campbell	9714	x		x	x	x			x	x	x	s	x	x	x		x										s
	03-Oct	COVENTRY CITY	3 - 2	Campbell, Lawson, Goldthorpe	13034	x		x	x	x			x	x	x	s	x	x	x		x										s
	23-Oct	Norwich City	0 - 2		10670		x	x	x	x			x				x	x	x	x	x	x	s								s
	06-Nov	NORWICH CITY	0 - 1		7018		x	x	x	x							s	x	x	x	x	x	x	x							s

LANARKSHIRE CUP

	Date	Opponent	Score
	03-Aug	Hamilton Academical	

FRIENDLIES

	Date	Opponent	Score
	30-Jul	Inverness C.	0 - 0
	01-Aug	Golspie	6 - 0
	07-Aug	TRANMERE ROVERS	1 - 1

1974 Div. 1

		Pl.	Home W.	D.	L.	F.	A.	Away W.	D.	L.	F.	A.	F. (Total)	A.	Pts.
1	Celtic	34	12	4	1	51	12	11	3	3	31	15	82	27	53
2	Hibernian	34	14	2	1	46	18	6	7	4	29	24	75	42	49
3	Rangers	34	9	3	5	32	17	12	3	2	35	17	67	34	48
4	Aberdeen	34	7	9	1	26	9	6	7	4	20	17	46	26	42
5	Dundee	34	7	3	7	32	25	9	4	4	35	23	67	48	39
6	Heart of Mid.	34	6	6	5	26	20	8	4	5	28	23	54	43	38
7	Ayr United	34	9	4	4	23	16	6	4	7	21	24	44	40	38
8	Dundee United	34	7	3	7	30	25	8	4	5	25	26	55	51	37
9	MOTHERWELL	34	8	5	4	28	20	6	2	9	17	20	45	40	35
10	Dumbarton	34	7	3	7	23	23	4	4	9	20	35	43	58	29
11	Partick Thistle	34	7	4	6	19	16	2	6	9	14	30	33	46	28
12	St. Johnstone	34	3	6	8	20	31	6	4	7	21	29	41	60	28
13	Arbroath	34	5	2	10	24	32	5	5	7	28	37	52	69	27
14	Morton	34	4	5	8	20	27	4	5	8	17	22	37	49	26
15	Clyde	34	5	2	10	13	26	3	7	7	16	39	29	65	25
16	Dunfermline Ath.	34	3	5	9	28	37	5	3	9	15	28	43	65	24
17	East Fife	34	3	2	12	9	30	6	4	7	17	21	26	51	24
18	Falkirk	34	1	11	5	17	21	3	3	11	16	37	33	58	22

1974-75: 1st Division

No.	Date	Opponent	Score	Scorers	Att.	Rennie	Lloyd	Watson W	Dickson	Wark	Watson R	Muir	MacLaren	Miller	Stevens	Goodwin	Graham	McIlwraith	Martin	Pettigrew	Goldthorpe	Taylor	Gardner	Kennedy	McClymont	McGuiness	McCabe	Leishman	Joyce	Hamilton
1	31-Aug	Dundee United	0 - 5		4000	x		x	x	x				x			x		x	x		x		x	s	s				
2	07-Sep	AIRDRIE	1 - 3	Graham	4707	x		x	x		x	x		x			x			x	s	x		x	s		x			
3	14-Sep	Ayr United	4 - 0	Goldthorpe (2), Stevens, McCabe	4001		x	x	x	x	x	s			x		x			s	x	x				x	x			
4	21-Sep	CELTIC	1 - 2	Taylor	13113		x	x	x	x	x	s			x		x			s	x	x				x	x			
5	28-Sep	DUNDEE	0 - 1		3939	x		x	x	x	x	s					x		x	s	x	x		x			x			
6	05-Oct	Arbroath	1 - 1	Graham	2000	x		x	x	x	x	s			x		x		s		x	x		x			x			
7	12-Oct	Hibernian	2 - 6	Graham, Goldthorpe	12389	x		x	x		x	x		x	x	s	x				x	x		x			s			
8	19-Oct	KILMARNOCK	2 - 0	Graham, McIllwraith	3628	x		x	s	x	x	x		x		x	x	x		s	x		x							
9	26-Oct	Morton	3 - 0	Goldthorpe (2), McIllwraith	3000	x		x	s	x	x	x		x		x	x	x		s	x		x							
10	02-Nov	DUNFERMLINE	1 - 2	McIllwraith	3793	x			x	x	x	x		x		x	x	x		s	x		x					s		
11	09-Nov	Clyde	0 - 0		2000	x		x	s	x	x	x		x		x	x	x			x	s	x							
12	16-Nov	RANGERS	0 - 5		19000	x		x	s	x	x	x		x		x	x	x		s	x		x							
13	23-Nov	St. Johnstone	1 - 0	Graham	2300		x	x		x	x		x	x		x	x	x			s		x				x	s		
14	30-Nov	ABERDEEN	2 - 1	Goodwin, McIllwraith	3472		x	x		x	x		x	x		x	x	x			s	x	x		s					
15	07-Dec	Partick Thistle	1 - 2	Goldthorpe	3000		x	x		x	x		x	x		x	x	x		s	x	x							s	
16	14-Dec	HEARTS	1 - 3	Miller	5142		x	x		x	x		x	x		x		x		x	x	x			s		s			
17	21-Dec	Dumbarton	1 - 0	Pettigrew	3050		x	x		x	x		x	x		s	s	x		x	x	x								x
18	28-Dec	DUNDEE UNITED	0 - 1		3516		x	x		x	x		x	x			s	x		x	x	x							s	x
19	01-Jan	Aidrie	0 - 2		8000		x	x		x	x		x	x		x	x	x		x	s	x			s					
20	04-Jan	AYR UNITED	5 - 1	Pettigrew (4), Graham	3468	x		x	s	x	x		x			x	x	x	s	x	x	x								
21	11-Jan	Celtic	3 - 2	Pettigrew (2), Graham	26000	x		x	s	x	x		x			x	x	x	s	x	x	x								
p 10/2		Dundee	1 - 4	Pettigrew	5300	x		x	s	x	x		x	x		x	x	x		x	s		x							
23	01-Feb	ARBROATH	3 - 1	Pettigrew (2), Miller	3767	x		x		x	x		x	x		x	x	x		x	x	s							s	
24	08-Feb	HIBERNIAN	4 - 1	Pettigrew (2), Graham, Watson	7452	x		x		x	x		x	x		x	x	s		x	s	x	x							
25	22-Feb	Kilmarnock	1 - 3	Gardner	5500	x		x	x	x	x		x			x	x	s		x	x	s	x							
26	01-Mar	MORTON	3 - 0	Pettigrew (3)	3738	x		x		x	x		x	x		s	x	x		x	x	s	x							
27	12-Mar	Dunfermline Ath.	1 - 0	Pettigrew	3009	x		x	s	x	x		x	x		s	x	x		x	x		x							
28	15-Mar	CLYDE	1 - 1	Pettigrew	4487	x		x	s	x	x		x	x			x	x		x	x	s	x							
29	22-Mar	Rangers	0 - 3		40000	x		x	s	x	x		x	x			x		x	x	x	s	x							
30	29-Mar	ST. JOHNSTONE	3 - 0	Pettigrew (2), Miller	4643	x		x	s	x	x		x	x			x		x	x	x	s	x							
p 23/4		Aberdeen	2 - 2	Pettigrew, Graham	8030	x		x	s	x	x		x	x			x		x	x	x		x							s
32	12-Apr	PARTICK THISTLE	0 - 0		5104	x			x	x	x		x	x		s	x			x	x	x	x							s
33	19-Apr	Hearts	1 - 4	Pettigrew	8000	x		x	s	x	x		x	x			x			x	s	x	x							x
34	26-Apr	DUMBARTON	3 - 1	Miller, Graham, McIllwraith	6072	x		x	s	x	x		x	x		x	x	s		x			x							x

LEAGUE CUP

	Date	Opponent	Score	Scorers	Att.	Rennie	Lloyd	Watson W	Dickson	Wark	Watson R	Muir	MacLaren	Miller	Stevens	Goodwin	Graham	McIlwraith	Martin	Pettigrew	Goldthorpe	Taylor	Gardner	Kennedy	McClymont	McGuiness	McCabe	Leishman	Joyce	Hamilton
	10-Aug	Celtic	1 - 2	Martin	19972	x		x	s	x	x	x		x			x		x		x	x		x	s					
	14-Aug	DUNDEE UNITED	4 - 0	Goldthorpe (2), Stevens, McCabe	3833	x		x	x	x	x	s		x			x		x		x	x		x		s				
	17-Aug	Ayr United	3 - 0	Goldthorpe, Taylor, Kennedy	7000	x		x	x	x	x	s		x			x		x		x	x		x		s				
	21-Aug	Dundee United	0 - 1		4000	x		x	x	x	x	s		x			x		x		x	x			x			s		
	24-Aug	AYR UNITED	5 - 0	Pettigrew (2), Taylor, Kennedy, Graham	3886	x		x	x	x	x			x			x		x	x		x		x	s			s		
	28-Aug	CELTIC	2 - 2	Pettigrew, Graham	14097	x		x	x	x	x			x			x		x	x		x		x	s			s		

SCOTTISH CUP

	Date	Opponent	Score	Scorers	Att.	Rennie	Lloyd	Watson W	Dickson	Wark	Watson R	Muir	MacLaren	Miller	Stevens	Goodwin	Graham	McIlwraith	Martin	Pettigrew	Goldthorpe	Taylor	Gardner	Kennedy	McClymont	McGuiness	McCabe	Leishman	Joyce	Hamilton
	25-Jan	PARTICK THISTLE	0 - 0		9288	x		x	s	x	x		x	s		x	x	x		x	x	x								
rep.	03-Feb	Partick Thistle	1 - 0	W Watson	10290	x		x	s	x	x		x			x	x	x		x		x	s							
	15-Feb	QUEENS PARK	4 - 0	McIllwraith, Graham, Pettigrew, Goldthorpe	7901	x			x	x	x					s	x	x		x	x	x	x						s	
	08-Mar	Aberdeen	1 - 0	Graham	23400	x		x	s	x	x		x	x		s	x	x		x	x		x							
S/F	05-Apr	AIRDRIE	1 - 1	Pettigrew	20574	x		x	s	x	x		x	x			x	x		x		s	x							x
S/F R	09-Apr	AIRDRIE	0 - 1		17605	x		x	s	x	x		x	x			x			x	x	s	x							x

FRIENDLIES

Date	Opponent	Score
20-Jul	O F S Gottingen	1 - 1
26-Jul	St. Pauli	2 - 0
28-Jul	Aarhus	1 - 0
23-Jul	Eintracht B'weig	1 - 1
30-Jul	Aalborg	2 - 0
10-Mar	AARHUS	3 - 0
05-Aug	AALBIONORG	3 - 0

1975 Div. 1

		Pl.	Home					Away					(Total)		
			W.	D.	L.	F.	A.	W.	D.	L.	F.	A.	F.	A.	Pts.
1	Rangers	34	14	1	2	39	15	11	5	1	47	18	86	33	56
2	Hibernian	34	12	2	3	41	16	8	7	2	28	21	69	37	49
3	Celtic	34	11	2	4	47	20	9	3	5	34	21	81	41	45
4	Dundee United	34	10	5	2	41	19	9	2	6	31	24	72	43	45
5	Aberdeen	34	9	6	2	42	20	7	3	7	24	23	66	43	41
6	Dundee	34	11	1	5	32	17	5	5	7	16	25	48	42	38
7	Ayr United	34	9	5	3	29	27	5	3	9	21	34	50	61	36
8	Heart of Mid.	34	8	6	3	24	16	3	7	7	23	36	47	52	35
9	St. Johnstone	34	8	4	5	27	20	3	8	6	14	24	41	44	34
10	MOTHERWELL	34	8	2	7	30	23	6	3	8	22	34	52	57	33
11	Airdrieonians	34	7	7	3	26	20	4	2	11	17	35	43	55	31
12	Kilmarnock	34	5	7	5	26	29	3	8	6	26	39	52	68	31
13	Partick Thistle	34	7	5	5	27	31	3	5	9	21	31	48	62	30
14	Dumbarton	34	3	5	9	19	24	4	5	8	25	31	44	55	24
15	Dunfermline Ath.	34	3	6	8	24	32	4	3	10	22	34	46	66	23
16	Clyde	34	4	6	7	25	30	2	4	11	15	33	40	63	22
17	Morton	34	4	5	8	17	28	2	5	10	14	34	31	62	22
18	Arbroath	34	4	5	8	20	27	1	2	14	14	39	34	66	17

1974-75 Season

Back: McGuiness, Mills, French, MacRae, Pettigrew, Burns, Main, Ross, Gray
Middle: Watson, Whiteford, Goldthorpe, Jim Muir, Goodwin, McCallum, Lawson, John Muir
Front: Leishman, Campbell, Martin, Millar, Wark, McClymont, McCabe, Kennedy

1975-76 Season

Back: B. Watson, Gardiner, Goodwin, McAdam, McVie, Goldthorpe, Rennie, Millar, McLaren, McIlwraith, McCabe, Kennedy, McManus
Front: McKenzie (Trainer), Graham, W.Watson, Pettigrew, McLean (Manager), Wark, Dickson, Taylor, Davidson, Ritchie (Coach)

1975-76: Premier League

No.	Date	Opponent	Score	Scorers	Att.	Rennie	Muir	Wark	McVie	Watson R	Watson W	Stevens	MacLaren	Millar P	MacAdam	Dickson	Kennedy	Davidson	Pettigrew	Graham	Taylor	Gardner	Marinello	Goldthorp	McIllwraith	Farrell	McManus	O'Neill
1	30-Aug	AYR UNITED	1 - 1	Stevens	5115	x		x	x	x	x	x			x			s	x	x	x	x						
2	06-Sep	Aberdeen	2 - 2	Pettigrew (2)	5500	x		x	x	x	x	x	s	s	x			x	x	x	x							
3	13-Sep	CELTIC	1 - 1	Davidson	18612	x		x	x	x	x	s	x	x	x			x	x	x				s				
4	20-Sep	Dundee United	1 - 1	Millar	5600	x		x	x	x	x	x	x	x				x	x	x	s	s						
5	27-Sep	HEARTS	1 - 1	Pettigrew	6073	x		x	x	x	x	x		x	s			x	x	x	x			s				
6	04-Oct	St. Johnstone	1 - 2	Pettigrew	2600	x		x	x	x		x	x	x	x		s	x	x	x	s							
7	11-Oct	HIBERNIAN	2 - 1	Pettigrew, Stevens	8207	x		x	x		x	x		x	x			x	x	x	x			s				
8	18-Oct	RANGERS	2 - 1	Pettigrew, Davidson	18925	x		x	x	x		x		x	x			x	x	x	x							
9	25-Oct	Dundee	6 - 3	Pettigrew (4), Taylor (2)	6853	x		x	x	x	s		x	x	x			x	x	x	x				s			
10	01-Nov	Ayr United	0 - 2		6400	x		x	x	x	x	x	s	x	x			s	x	x	x							
11	08-Nov	ABERDEEN	3 - 0	Taylor, Graham, Marinello	6294	x		x	x	x			x	x	x				x	x	x	s			x		s	
12	15-Nov	Celtic	2 - 0	Pettigrew (2)	33000	x		x	x	x		x		x	x			s	x	x	x				x			
13	22-Nov	DUNDEE UNITED	2 - 1	Pettigrew, Graham	6328	x		x	x	x		x		x	x			s	x	x	x				x			
14	29-Nov	Hearts	3 - 3	Pettigrew, Gardner (2)	15500	x		x	x			x	x	x				x	x	x	x	x			s			
15	06-Dec	ST. JOHNSTONE	2 - 1	Pettigrew, Miller	5632	x		x	x	s		x	x	x	s			x	x	x	x	x						
16	13-Dec	Hibernian	0 - 1		15991	x		x	x	s		x	x	x	s			x	x	x		x	x					
17	20-Dec	Rangers	2 - 3	Pettigrew, MacLaren	20000	x		x	x	x	s	x	x	x	s			x	x	x			x					
18	27-Dec	DUNDEE	3 - 2	Pettigrew, Graham (2)	7169	x		x	x		x	x	x		s			x	x	x		x	x					
19	01-Jan	AYR UNITED	1 - 0	MacLaren	7367	x		x	x	s	x	x	x					x	x	x		x	x					
20	03-Jan	Aberdeen	0 - 0		16177	x		x	x	x	x	x	x		x			x	x				x					
21	10-Jan	CELTIC	1 - 3	Davidson	18092	x		x	x	x	x	x	x		x			x	x		s		x					
22	17-Jan	Dundee United	4 - 1	Pettigrew, R Watson, Graham, Marinello	5200	x		x	x	x	x	x	x	s				x	x	x	s		x					
23	31-Jan	HEARTS	2 - 0	Pettigrew (2)	10054	x		x	x		x	x	x	s				x	x	x	x	s	x					
24	07-Feb	St. Johnstone	3 - 1	Pettigrew, Taylor, OG	3500	x		x	x	x	x		x	s				x	x	x	x	s	x					
25	21-Feb	HIBERNIAN	0 - 1		10578	x		x		x	x	x	x					x	x	x	x	s	x					
26	28-Feb	RANGERS	0 - 1		25241	x		x	x	x		x	x		x		s	x	x	x	s	x						
27	20-Mar	ABERDEEN	2 - 1	Pettigrew, Davidson	5908	x		x		x		x	x	x				s	x	x	x	x	x					
28	27-Mar	Celtic	0 - 4		29000	x		x		x	x	x	x	x	s			x	x	x			x					
29	03-Apr	DUNDEE UNITED	3 - 2	Miller, McVie, Stevens	3829	x		x	x	x	x	s	x	x	x			x	x	x								
30	10-Apr	Hearts	2 - 1	Graham, Gardner	11500	x		x	x	x	x	s		x			x	x	x	x		x						
31	14-Apr	ST. JOHNSTONE	2 - 0	Pettigrew, Marinello	4334	x		x	x	x		x	x	x				x	x	x			x					
32	17-Apr	Hibernian	0 - 2		9098	x		x	x	x		x	x	x		s		x	x	x			x					
33	21-Apr	Rangers	1 - 2	Stevens	27000	x		x	x	x		x	x	x	s			x	x	x	s		x					
34	24-Apr	DUNDEE	1 - 1	MacLaren	4675	x		x	x	x		x	x	x	s			x	x	x	s		x					
35	01-May	Dundee	0 - 1		7661	x		x	x	x		x	x	x	s			x	x	x	s		x					
36	03-May	Ayr United	1 - 2	Marinello	6500	x		x	x	x		x	x	x	s			x	x	x	s		x					

LEAGUE CUP

	Date	Opponent	Score	Scorers	Att.	Rennie	Muir	Wark	McVie	Watson R	Watson W	Stevens	MacLaren	Millar P	MacAdam	Dickson	Kennedy	Davidson	Pettigrew	Graham	Taylor	Gardner	Marinello	Goldthorp	McIllwraith	Farrell	McManus	O'Neill
	09-Aug	CLYDE	2 - 0	Miller, Pettigrew	4587	x		x	x	x		x		x			s	x	x	x	x	x				s		
	13-Aug	Aidrie	1 - 2	Davidson	4962	x		x	x	x		x		x				x	x	x	x	x		s		s		
	16-Aug	Rangers	1 - 1	Wark	24985	x		x	x	x		s	x	x	x			x	x	x	s	x						
	20-Aug	AIRDRIE	2 - 0	Pettigrew (2)	5122	x		x	x	x	x	x		x	x			x	x		x	s		x				
	23-Aug	RANGERS	2 - 2	Pettigrew, R Watson	16029	x		x	x	x	x	x		x				s	x	x	x	s						
	27-Aug	Clyde	2 - 1	Goldthorpe, Taylor	1500	x		x			x	x	x	x				x	x		x	x		x		s		s

SCOTTISH CUP

	Date	Opponent	Score	Scorers	Att.	Rennie	Muir	Wark	McVie	Watson R	Watson W	Stevens	MacLaren	Millar P	MacAdam	Dickson	Kennedy	Davidson	Pettigrew	Graham	Taylor	Gardner	Marinello	Goldthorp	McIllwraith	Farrell	McManus	O'Neill
	24-Jan	CELTIC	3 - 2	Pettigrew, Graham, Taylor		x		x	x	x	x	x	x					x	x	x	x		s					
	14-Feb	Cowdenbeath	2 - 0	Graham, Marinello		x		x	x	x	x	x	x					s	x	x	x		x					
	06-Mar	HIBERNIAN	2 - 2	Pettigrew, Marinello		x		x	x	x	x		x		s			x	x	x	s	x	x					
	10-Mar	Hibernian	1 - 1	Graham		x		x	x	x	x		x					x	x	x	s	x	x					
*	15-Mar	HIBERNIAN	2 - 1	Taylor, Marinello		x		x	x	x	x		x					x	x	x	x	x	s					
	31-Mar	RANGERS	2 - 3	Pettigrew, MacLaren		x		x	x	x	x		x					x	x	x	s	x	x					

* On neutral ground

ANGLO SCOTTISH

	Date	Opponent	Score	Scorers	Att.	Rennie	Muir	Wark	McVie	Watson R	Watson W	Stevens	MacLaren	Millar P	MacAdam	Dickson	Kennedy	Davidson	Pettigrew	Graham	Taylor	Gardner	Marinello	Goldthorp	McIllwraith	Farrell	McManus	O'Neill
	04-Aug	DUNDEE	1 - 1	McVie		x		x	x	x			x	x	x			x	x		x	x						
	06-Aug	Dundee	1 - 0	Graham		x		x	x	x			x	x	x			x	x	x	x							
	17-Sep	Blackburn Rovers	0 - 0			x		x	x	x	x	x			x				x	x	x	x						
	30-Sep	BlackBURN ROVERS	2 - 1	Pettigrew, Davidson		x		s	x			x	x	x	x			x	x	x	x	x						
	21-Oct	Fulham	1 - 1	Pettigrew		x	s	x	x		x	x		x	x			x	x	x	x							
	04-Nov	FULHAM	2 - 3	Graham, Davidson		x		x	x	x			x	x	x			x	x	x	x			s				

FRIENDLIES

Date	Opponent	Score	Scorers
26-Jul	Ross County	5 - 0	
28-Jul	Inverness Clach	1 - 1	
29-Jul	Brora	4 - 2	
01-Aug	SHEFFIELD WED.	2 - 0	MacAdam (2)
	Valur	0 - 0	

1976 Premier League

		Pl.	Home W.	Home D.	Home L.	Home F.	Home A.	Away W.	Away D.	Away L.	Away F.	Away A.	F. (Total)	A. (Total)	Pts.
1	Rangers	36	15	2	1	38	12	8	6	4	22	12	60	24	54
2	Celtic	36	10	5	3	35	18	11	1	6	36	24	71	42	48
3	Hibernian	36	13	2	3	37	15	5	5	8	18	28	55	43	43
4	MOTHERWELL	36	11	4	3	29	18	5	4	9	28	31	57	49	40
5	Heart of Mid.	36	7	5	6	23	20	6	4	8	16	25	39	45	35
6	Ayr United	36	10	3	5	29	24	4	2	12	17	35	46	59	33
7	Aberdeen	36	8	5	5	27	19	3	5	10	22	31	49	50	32
8	Dundee United	36	9	3	6	27	20	3	5	10	19	28	46	48	32
9	Dundee	36	8	5	5	31	26	3	5	10	18	36	49	62	32
10	St. Johnstone	36	3	4	11	19	34	0	1	17	10	45	29	79	11

1976-77: Premier League

						Rennie	Hunter	Kennedy	Wark	MacLaren	Watson	Stevens	MacAdam	McVie	Millar P	Graham	Pettigrew	Davidson	O'Rourke	Marinello	Miller J	Hood	Mungall	O'Neill	Farrell	Spark	Lindsay J	Muir
1	04-Sep	Kilmarnock	1 - 1	McVie	5500	x		x		x		x		x	x	x	x	x		s		x			x			
2	11-Sep	HIBERNIAN	2 - 2	Graham, Marinello	5696	x		x	x	x	s	x		x	x	x	x	x		s		x						
3	18-Sep	Partick Thistle	0 - 2		5500	x		x	x	x		x		x	x	x	x	x		s		x						
4	25-Sep	AYR UNITED	4 - 1	Pettigrew (2), O'Rourke (2)	4241	x		x	x	x	x	x	s		x	x	x		x	x								
5	02-Oct	Dundee United	0 - 2		6500	x		x	x	x	x	x	x		x	x	x	s	x	x								
p 2/11	09-Oct	Aberdeen	1 - 3		15207	x		x	x	x		x	s	x	x	x	x	x	s	x								
7	16-Oct	HEARTS	1 - 1	O'Rourke	7932	x		x	x	x		x	s	x	x	x	s	x	x	x								
8	23-Oct	RANGERS	3 - 1	Pettigrew (2), Wark	15857	x		x	x			x	x	x	x	x	x	x		x								
9	30-Oct	Celtic	0 - 2		31000	x		x	x	s		x	x	x	x	x	x	x	s	x								
10	06-Nov	KILMARNOCK	5 - 4	Pettigrew, O'Rourke (3), Davidson	4754	x		x	x			x	x	x	x	x	x	x	x	s								
p 24/11	13-Nov	Hibernian	2 - 0	Pettigrew, Graham	6600	x		x	x	x		x		x	x	s	x	x	x	x		s						
12	20-Nov	PARTICK THISTLE	3 - 0	Pettigrew (2), Davidson	5800	x		x	x	s		x		x	x	x	x	x	x	x		s						
13	27-Nov	Ayr United	1 - 4	Marinello	4800	x		x	x	x		x	s	x	x	x	x	x		x		s						
P 4/5	04-Dec	DUNDEE UNITED	1 - 1	Graham	2367			x	x			x	x	s		x	x	x			x		x				x	x
p 5/4	11-Dec	ABERDEEN	1 - 1	Pettigrew	4523		x		x	x	x	x			x	x	x	x	x		x							
16	18-Dec	Hearts	1 - 2	Stevens	10000	x		x	x		x	x			x	x	x	x	x	x		s						
17	25-Dec	Rangers	0 - 1		25000	x		x	x		x	x	x		x	x	x	x	s	x		s						
p10/5	01-Jan	CELTIC	2 - 2	Stevens, Marinello	8859			s	x			x	x	x	x	x	x	x		x	x							x
19	03-Jan	Kilmarnock	2 - 2	Pettigrew (2)	6500	x		x	x		x	x	x		x	x	x		x			x						
20	08-Jan	HIBERNIAN	1 - 1	O'Rourke	7626	x		x	x	x	x	x			x	s	x		x	x		x						
p 30/3	15-Jan	Partick Thistle	0 - 0		4819		x		x	x	x	x	x		x	x	x	x			x	s						
22	22-Jan	AYR UNITED	2 - 4	Pettigrew, O'Rourke	5455	x		x	x		x	x	x		x	s	x	x	x	s		x						
p 16/3	05-Feb	Dundee United	1 - 1	Pettigrew	6081	x		s	x	x	x	x	x		x		x	x	x	x		s						
24	19-Feb	HEARTS	2 - 1	Pettigrew, O'Rourke	6900	x		s	x	x	x	x	x		x		x	x	x	x		s						
25	05-Mar	RANGERS	0 - 2		15468	x		s	x	x	x	x	x		x		x	x	x	x		s						
26	16-Mar	Celtic	2 - 2	Graham, Davidson	23000	x			x	x	x	x	x		x	x	x	x	x		s							
27	19-Mar	KILMARNOCK	2 - 0	Graham (2)	4080	x			x	x	x	x	x		s	x	x	x	x		x			s				
28	23-Mar	Aberdeen	1 - 2	Wark	7489	x			x	x	x	x	x		x	x	x		x	s	x							
29	26-Mar	Hibernian	2 - 1	Pettigrew (2)	6451	x			x	x	x	x	x		x	x	x		x		x			s				
30	02-Apr	PARTICK THISTLE	1 - 1	Davidson	6000	x			x	x	x	x	x		x	x	x	x			x							
31	09-Apr	Ayr United	2 - 3	Pettigrew (2)	6157		x	s	x	x	x	x	x		x	x	x	x			x							
32	13-Apr	CELTIC	3 - 0	Kennedy, OG (2 - Lynch)	13820		x	x	x	x	x	x	x			x	x	x			x							
33	16-Apr	DUNDEE UNITED	4 - 0	Pettigrew, Graham (2), Davidson	5821		x	x	x	x	x	x	x			x	x	x			x							
34	20-Apr	Rangers	1 - 4	Pettigrew	5008		x	x	x	x		x	x		x	x	x	x			x							
35	23-Apr	ABERDEEN	1 - 3	Kennedy	4209		x	x	x	x		x	x			s	x	x			x		x	x				
36	30-Apr	Hearts	2 - 3	Pettigrew, OG	6500		x	x	x			x	x			s	x	x	x		x		x	x			x	

LEAGUE CUP

						Rennie	Hunter	Kennedy	Wark	MacLaren	Watson	Stevens	MacAdam	McVie	Millar P	Graham	Pettigrew	Davidson	O'Rourke	Marinello	Miller J	Hood	Mungall	O'Neill	Farrell	Spark	Lindsay J	Muir
	14-Aug	PARTICK THISTLE	1 - 1	Pettigrew	6232		x	x			x	x		x	x	x	x	x	x	s						x		
	18-Aug	Dundee	1 - 2	Pettigrew	6000	x		x			x	x		x	x	x	x	x	x	s			s			x		
	21-Aug	Hearts	1 - 2	Davidson	13000		x	s	x	x	x	x		x	x	x	x	x	s	x								
	25-Aug	DUNDEE	3 - 3	Davidson (2), Graham	4258		x		x	x		x		x	x	x	x	x		x		x						
	28-Aug	HEARTS	1 - 4	Hood	7874		x		x	x		x		x	x	x	x	s	s	x		x			x			
	01-Sep	Partick Thistle	0 - 2		4000	x		x	x	x	s	x			x	x	x	x	x			s			x			

SCOTTISH CUP

						Rennie	Hunter	Kennedy	Wark	MacLaren	Watson	Stevens	MacAdam	McVie	Millar P	Graham	Pettigrew	Davidson	O'Rourke	Marinello	Miller J	Hood	Mungall	O'Neill	Farrell	Spark	Lindsay J	Muir
	29-Jan	KILMARNOCK	3 - 0	Pettigrew (2), Davidson	8335	x			x	x	x		x	x	x	x	x	x										
	26-Feb	ST. MIRREN	2 - 1	Pettigrew, Davidson	26709	x			x	x	x	x	x		x		x	x	x	x								
	12-Mar	Rangers	0 - 2		35572	x		x	x	x	x	x	x			x	x	x	s	s		x						

ANGLO SCOTTISH

						Rennie	Hunter	Kennedy	Wark	MacLaren	Watson	Stevens	MacAdam	McVie	Millar P	Graham	Pettigrew	Davidson	O'Rourke	Marinello	Miller J	Hood	Mungall	O'Neill	Farrell	Spark	Lindsay J	Muir
	07-Aug	KILMARNOCK	1 - 1	Davidson		x				x	s	x		x	x	x	x	x	x	x						x		
	11-Aug	Kilmarnock	0 - 4			x				x	x	x		x	x	x	x	x	x	x								

FRIENDLIES

	31-Jul	Fraserburgh	4 - 1	Davidson (2), Pettigrew, O'Rourke
	02-Aug	Keith	0 - 1	
	29-May	AJAX	4 - 2	MacLaren, MacAdam, Davidson, Pettigrew
	11-Oct	SUNDERLAND	3 - 1	Graham, Stevens, Pettigrew

South American Tour

*	Toluca	1 - 2	Taylor
**	Violet	1 - 0	Farrell
**	Racing of Haiti	1 - 2	Kennedy
***	Santa Fe	1 - 2	Pettigrew

Matches played: * in Aztec Stadium, Mexico City. ** Haiti. *** Columbia

1977 Premier League

		Pl.	Home W.	Home D.	Home L.	Home F.	Home A.	Away W.	Away D.	Away L.	Away F.	Away A.	F. (Total)	A. (Total)	Pts.
1	Celtic	36	13	5	0	44	16	10	4	4	35	23	79	39	55
2	Rangers	36	12	4	2	36	16	6	6	6	26	21	62	37	46
3	Aberdeen	36	11	4	3	30	18	5	7	6	26	24	56	42	43
4	Dundee United	36	8	5	5	26	17	8	4	6	28	28	54	45	41
5	Partick Thistle	36	9	5	4	27	24	2	8	8	13	20	40	44	35
6	Hibernian	36	4	10	4	14	12	4	8	6	20	23	34	35	34
7	MOTHERWELL	36	8	7	3	38	25	2	5	11	19	35	57	60	32
8	Ayr United	36	4	5	9	23	36	7	3	8	21	32	44	68	30
9	Heart of Mid.	36	5	6	7	26	28	2	7	9	23	38	49	66	27
10	Kilmarnock	36	4	5	9	21	30	0	4	14	11	41	32	71	17

1976-77 Season
Back: Spark, Lindsay, Gray, Kennedy, Farrell, Mungall, Ross, McManus
Middle: McKenzie (Train), McLaren, Watson, McVie, A.Hunter, McAdam, Stevens, Miller, Gardiner, Barrowman, John Hunter (Asst. Train)
Front: McLean (Man), O'Rouke, Marinello, Davidson, Wark, Graham, Pettigrew, Brown (Asst. Man)

1977-78 Season
Back: McKenzie (Train), Kennedy, Davidson, Stevens, McVie, Hunter, McAdam, Millar, Gray, Pettigrew, Lindsay
Front: Miller, McLean (Man), Marinello, Watson, Wark, Graham, MacLaren, Brown (Asst. Man), Mungall

1977-78: Premier League

No	Date	Opponent	Score	Scorers	Att	Rennie	Muir	Wark	Watson	Stevens	MacLaren	McVie	Millar P	Miller J	MacAdam	Purdie	O'Rourke	Pettigrew	Marinello	Davidson	Mungall	Clinging	Robertson	O'Neill	Kennedy	McLeod	Lindsay	Somerville
1	13-Aug	Hibernian	0 - 0		8885		x	x	x	x	s	x		x	x	x		x	x	x								
2	20-Aug	PARTICK THISTLE	3 - 0	MacAdam, Davidson, Purdie	5110		x	x	x	x	x	x	s	x	x	x			x	x								
3	27-Aug	Celtic	1 - 0	Davidson	29000		x	x	x	x	x	x	s	x	x	x			x	x				s				
4	10-Sep	ST. MIRREN	0 - 3		7432	x		x	x	x	x	x		x	x	x		x	s	x				s				
5	17-Sep	AYR UNITED	5 - 0	MacAdam, Purdie, Miller, Davidson, O'Rourke	4585	x		x	x		x	x	x		x	x	s		x	x								
p 29/3	24-Sep	Dundee United	2 - 3	Purdie, Pettigrew	7813	x		x	x	x	x	x	x		x	x	s	x	x					s				
7	01-Oct	ABERDEEN	1 - 1	O'Neill	6466	x		x	x	x	x	x	x		x	x	s		s	x				x				
8	08-Oct	Clydebank	1 - 2	Marinello	4500	x		x	x	x	x	x	x	s		x	x		s	x				x				
9	15-Oct	RANGERS	1 - 4	O'Rourke	20050		x	x		x	x	x	x	x		x	s		s	x				x	x			
10	22-Oct	HIBERNIAN	1 - 0	Stevens	5045	x		x	x	x	x		x	x			s		x	x			x				x	
11	29-Oct	Partick Thistle	0 - 1		6000	x		x	x	x	x		x	x			s		x	x				s			x	
12	05-Nov	CELTIC	2 - 3	MacAdam, O'Rourke	16547	x		x	x	x	x		x	x	x	s	s		x	x			x					
13	12-Nov	St. Mirren	0 - 1		8259	x		x	x	x	x		x	x	x	s	s		x	x			x					
14	19-Nov	Ayr United	1 - 1	Pettigrew	3996	x		x	x	x		x	x	x			x	x	x				x					
15	26-Nov	DUNDEE UNITED	0 - 0		4841	x		x	x	x	x		x	x			x	x	x	x	s							
16	03-Dec	Aberdeen	1 - 4	Pettigrew	9500	x		x	x	x	x		x	x		s	x	x	x	x								
17	10-Dec	CLYDEBANK	2 - 1	Marinello, Davidson	3650	x		x	x	x	x	x	s			x	x	x	x	x								
18	17-Dec	Rangers	1 - 3	Miller	23000	x		x	s	x	x	x	x	x		x	x	x		x					s			
19	24-Dec	Hibernian	1 - 2	Pettigrew	8305	x		x	x	x	x	x	x	x		s	x	x	x						s			
20	31-Dec	PARTICK THISTLE	2 - 0	MacLaren, Stevens	7823	x		x	x	x	x	x	x	x			x	x	x		s							
21	02-Jan	Celtic	1 - 0	O'Rourke	23000	x		x	x	x	x	x	x				x	x	x		x							
22	07-Jan	ST. MIRREN	1 - 0	Stevens	8670	x		x	x	x	x	x	x	s			x	x	x	x	s							
23	14-Jan	AYR UNITED	3 - 0	Pettigrew, Marinello, Stevens	6982	x			x	x	x	x	x	x			x	x	x						x			
24	21-Jan	Dundee United	1 - 1	Stevens	4054	x		x	x	x	s	x						x	x	x	x	x			s	x		
25	04-Feb	ABERDEEN	0 - 0		8845	x		x	x	x		x	x	x			x	x	x	x		s						
26	25-Feb	RANGERS	3 - 5	Davidson (2), O'Rourke	20387	x		x	x	x	x	x	x		s		x	x	x	x		s						
27	11-Mar	Clydebank	2 - 0	MacLaren, Davidson	2000	x		x	x	x	x	x	x				x	x	x	x								
28	15-Mar	HIBERNIAN	2 - 4	Stevens, Davidson	4536	x		x	x	x	x	x	x				x	x	x	x								
29	18-Mar	Partick Thistle	3 - 2	Pettigrew, Clinging (2)	5500	x		x	s	x		x	x					x	x	x	x	x			x	s		
30	22-Mar	CELTIC	2 - 1	Marinello (2)	9613	x		x	x	x		x	x					x	x	x	x	x						
31	25-Mar	St. Mirren	1 - 1	Clinging	10000	x		x	x	x		x				s		x	x	x	x	x			s	x		
32	01-Apr	Ayr United	1 - 0	Pettigrew	2759	x		x	x	x	x		x					x	x	x	x	x						
33	08-Apr	DUNDEE UNITED	0 - 1		4907	x		x	x	x	x		x					x	x	x	x	x			s			
34	15-Apr	Aberdeen	0 - 5		16240	x		x	x	x	x	s	x					x	x	x	x	x			s			
35	22-Apr	CLYDEBANK	0 - 1		3068	x		x	x		x		x					x	x	x	x	x			s	x	s	
36	29-Apr	Rangers	0 - 2		40000	x		x	x	x	x		x					x	x			x				x	x	s

LEAGUE CUP

Date	Opponent	Score	Scorers	Att	Rennie	Muir	Wark	Watson	Stevens	MacLaren	McVie	Millar P	Miller J	MacAdam	Purdie	O'Rourke	Pettigrew	Marinello	Davidson	Mungall	Clinging	Robertson	O'Neill	Kennedy	McLeod	Lindsay	Somerville
31-Aug	Celtic	0 - 0		23000		x	x	x	x	x	x		x	x	x				x				s	x			
03-Sep	CELTIC	2 - 4	Davidson (2)	20494		x	x	x	x	x	x		x	x	x			x	x				s	s			

SCOTTISH CUP

Date	Opponent	Score	Scorers	Att	Rennie	Muir	Wark	Watson	Stevens	MacLaren	McVie	Millar P	Miller J	MacAdam	Purdie	O'Rourke	Pettigrew	Marinello	Davidson	Mungall	Clinging	Robertson	O'Neill	Kennedy	McLeod	Lindsay	Somerville
28-Jan	Arbroath	4 - 0	Marinello (2), O'Rourke, MacLaren	4439	x		x	x	x	x	x	x	x			x	x	x									
27-Feb	QUEENS PARK	1 - 3	O'Rourke	5185	x		x	x	x	x	x		x	s		x	x	x	x		s						

ANGLO SCOTTISH

Date	Opponent	Score	Scorers
06-Aug	ALLOA	7 - 0	Davidson (5), Pettigrew, Purdie
10-Aug	Alloa Athletic	4 - 1	O'Neill (2), Marinello, Kennedy
13-Sep	NOTTS COUNTY	1 - 1	J Miller
27-Sep	Notts County	0 - 1	

FRIENDLIES

Date	Opponent	Score
01-Aug	Peterhead	2 - 1
02-Aug	Buckie	4 - 3

1978 Premier League

		Pl.	Home W.	Home D.	Home L.	Home F.	Home A.	Away W.	Away D.	Away L.	Away F.	Away A.	F. (Total)	A. (Total)	Pts.
1	Rangers	36	12	4	2	35	18	12	3	3	41	21	76	39	55
2	Aberdeen	36	14	3	1	43	13	8	6	4	25	16	68	29	53
3	Dundee United	36	9	4	5	28	17	7	4	7	14	15	42	32	40
4	Hibernian	36	10	5	3	35	16	5	2	11	16	27	51	43	37
5	Celtic	36	11	3	4	36	19	4	3	11	27	35	63	54	36
6	MOTHERWELL	36	8	3	7	28	24	5	4	9	17	28	45	52	33
7	Partick Thistle	36	10	2	6	25	23	4	3	11	27	41	52	64	33
8	St. Mirren	36	7	5	6	29	25	4	3	11	23	38	52	63	30
9	Ayr United	36	5	3	10	17	28	4	3	11	19	40	36	68	24
10	Clydebank	36	5	3	10	16	33	1	4	13	7	31	23	64	19

1978-79: Premier League

	Date	Opponent	Score	Scorers	Att.	Latchford	Rennie	Miller	Wark	Boyd	Makin	Stevens	McLeod	Pettigrew	Larnach	Lindsay	MacLaren	Shanks	Clinging	Marinello	Somerville	McVie	Capaldi	Wilson	Carr	Mungall	Smith	Leonard	Donnelly	Kennedy	Raffarty	Dempsey	Meikle	Kane	Carberry	Irvine	Hare
p 2/5	12-Aug	PARTICK THISTLE	0 - 1		3919	x		x	x	x	x	x	x	x	x	x	x	s	s																		
2	19-Aug	St. Mirren	1 - 0	Stevens	7861	x		x	x	x	x	x	s		x	x	x		x	x	s																
3	26-Aug	CELTIC	1 - 5	OG	19710	x		x	x	x	x	x	s	x	x	x	x			x	s																
4	09-Sep	Aberdeen	0 - 4		13200	x		x	x	x		x	s	x	x	s	x		x	x		x															
5	16-Sep	DUNDEE UNITED	0 - 1		3372	x			x	s		x	x	x	x		x	x	s	x		x	x														
6	23-Sep	HEARTS	0 - 1		5219	x			x	s		x		x	x	s	x	x	x			x	x	x													
7	30-Sep	Rangers	1 - 4	Clinging	25000	x			x		s	x		x	x		x	x	x	x		x	s														
8	07-Oct	HIBERNIAN	2 - 3	Larnach, Clinging	5516	x				x		x	s	x	x	s		x	x	x		x		x	x												
9	14-Oct	Morton	2 - 1	Pettigrew, Lindsay	6000		x		x			x	s	x	x	s	x	x	x	x		x		x													
10	21-Oct	Partick Thistle	0 - 2		6010		x	x	x			x	s		x	s		x	x	x		x		x	x												
11	28-Oct	ST. MIRREN	1 - 2	Pettigrew	6007		x		x			x		x	s		x	x	x	x		x		x	x	s											
12	04-Nov	Celtic	2 - 1	MacLaren, Stevens	21000		x		x			x		x	x	s	x	s	x	x		x		x	x												
13	11-Nov	ABERDEEN	1 - 1	Wilson	5448		x	x	x			x		x	x	s	x		s	x		x		x	x												
14	18-Nov	Dundee United	1 - 2	Larnach	5876		x	x	x			x		x	x	s	x	s		x		x		x	x												
15	25-Nov	Hearts	2 - 3	Larnach, Marinello	8984		x		x			x	x		x	x		x	x	x		x	s	x	s												
p 2/5	02-Dec	RANGERS	1 - 2	Irvine	13052		x		x		x	x	x	x	x				x								x		s		s				x	x	
p 4/4	09-Dec	Hibernian	2 - 2	Pettigrew (2)	6000		x	x	x				x	x	x	s		x	x			x	x	x	s												
18	16-Dec	MORTON	1 - 1	Pettigrew	5347		x	x	x	x		x	x	x	x	s			x	x			s	x													
19	23-Dec	PARTICK THISTLE	1 - 1	Miller	5729		x	x	x			x	x	x	s	x			x		s	x		x			x										
p 17/2	30-Dec	St. Mirren	0 - 1		7600		x	x	x	x		x		x	x				x			x		x			x	s	s								
p 4/4	01-Jan	CELTIC	3 - 4	Larnach, Clinging, Stevens	8744		x		x			x	x	x	s				x								x		x		s	x			x	x	
22	20-Jan	HEARTS	3 - 2	Pettigrew, Stevens, Clinging	3881		x	x	x	x		x	x	x		x			x				s	x			x	s									
23	10-Feb	HIBERNIAN	0 - 3		5105		x	x	x	x		x	s	x		x			x			x	s				x	x									
24	03-Mar	Partick Thistle	0 - 0		5500		x					x	x	x	s				x		x							s	x	x	x	x	x				
p 18/4	07-Mar	DUNDEE UNITED	0 - 4		2653		x		x				x	x	s				x		x						x	s	x	x	x	x					
26	10-Mar	ST. MIRREN	0 - 3		4795		x					x	x	x	s				x		x			s			x		x	x	x	x					
27	14-Mar	Morton	0 - 6		3000		x		x			x	x	x	x				s							x	x	x	x		s	x					
28	17-Mar	Celtic	1 - 2	Donnelly	16000		x		x				x		x				x		s			x		s			x	x	x	x		x			
29	24-Mar	ABERDEEN	1 - 1	Stevens	2800		x		x		x	x		x	x				x					s					x			s			x	x	x
30	26-Mar	Aberdeen	0 - 8		7672		x		x				x		x				x		s			x		s	x		x	x		x		x			
31	31-Mar	Dundee United	1 - 2	Irvine	5655		x		x			x	x		x				s					x			x		x			x	s		x	x	
32	07-Apr	Hearts	0 - 3		7000		x		x			x	x	x	s				x					s			x		x			x			x	x	
33	11-Apr	Rangers	0 - 3		8000		x		x			x	x	x	s				x					s			x		x			x			x	x	
34	14-Apr	RANGERS	2 - 0	Clinging, Donnelly	14612		x		x		x		x	x	x				x					s			x		x		s				x	x	
35	21-Apr	Hibernian	0 - 4		7000		x		x		x	x	x	x	x				x					s					x		s				x	x	
36	28-Apr	MORTON	3 - 3	Irvine (2), Stevens	3546				x		x	x	x	x	x				x								x		s		s				x	x	

LEAGUE CUP

	Date	Opponent	Score	Scorers	Att.	Latchford	Rennie	Miller	Wark	Boyd	Makin	Stevens	McLeod	Pettigrew	Larnach	Lindsay	MacLaren	Shanks	Clinging	Marinello	Somerville	McVie	Capaldi	Wilson	Carr	Mungall	Smith	Leonard	Donnelly	Kennedy	Raffarty	Dempsey	Meikle	Kane	Carberry	Irvine	Hare
	30-Aug	Clyde	1 - 3	Marinello	4000	x		x	x	x	x	x	s	x	x	x	x			x	s																
	02-Sep	CLYDE	3 - 0	Pettigrew, Marinello, Clinging	3803	x		x	x	x		x	s	x	x		x		x	x	s	x															
	04-Oct	Celtic	1 - 0	Pettigrew	19000	x				x		x	s	x	s	x	x		x	x		x	x				x										
	11-Oct	CELTIC	1 - 4	Marinello	17911	x			x			x	s	x	x	x	x		x	x		x			x					s							

SCOTTISH CUP

	Date	Opponent	Score	Scorers	Att.	Latchford	Rennie	Miller	Wark	Boyd	Makin	Stevens	McLeod	Pettigrew	Larnach	Lindsay	MacLaren	Shanks	Clinging	Marinello	Somerville	McVie	Capaldi	Wilson	Carr	Mungall	Smith	Leonard	Donnelly	Kennedy	Raffarty	Dempsey	Meikle	Kane	Carberry	Irvine	Hare
	12-Feb	Rangers	1 - 3	Clinging	12000		x	x	x	x		x	s	x	x	s			x			x		x			x										

ANGLO SCOTTISH

	Date	Opponent	Score	Scorers	Att.	Latchford	Rennie	Miller	Wark	Boyd	Makin	Stevens	McLeod	Pettigrew	Larnach	Lindsay	MacLaren	Shanks	Clinging	Marinello	Somerville	McVie	Capaldi	Wilson	Carr	Mungall	Smith	Leonard	Donnelly	Kennedy	Raffarty	Dempsey	Meikle	Kane	Carberry	Irvine	Hare
	06-Aug	ST. MIRREN	1 - 0	Lindsay		x		x	x		x	x		x		x	x	x	x	x	s									s							
	09-Aug	St. Mirren	0 - 3			x		x	x		x	x	s	s	x	x	x	x	x	x																	

FRIENDLIES

Date	Opponent	Score	Scorers
24-Jul	Frederickshavn	1-0	
26-Jul	Viborg	1-0	
27-Jul	Aalborg	4-1	
30-Jul	Vildborg	2-0	
31-Jul	Nibe Select	2-0	
03-Aug	West Bromwich A.	1-8	Stevens

1979 Premier League

		Pl.	Home W.	D.	L.	F.	A.	Away W.	D.	L.	F.	A.	F. (Total)	A.	Pts.
1	Celtic	36	13	3	2	32	12	8	3	7	29	25	61	37	48
2	Rangers	36	12	5	1	32	10	6	4	8	20	25	52	35	45
3	Dundee United	36	12	4	2	33	16	6	4	8	23	21	56	37	44
4	Aberdeen	36	9	5	4	39	16	4	9	5	20	20	59	36	40
5	Hibernian	36	7	9	2	23	16	5	4	9	21	32	44	48	37
6	St. Mirren	36	8	3	7	23	20	7	3	8	22	21	45	41	36
7	Morton	36	9	4	5	34	23	3	8	7	18	30	52	53	36
8	Partick Thistle	36	10	2	6	31	21	3	6	9	11	18	42	39	34
9	Heart of Mid.	36	5	5	8	19	25	3	2	13	20	46	39	71	23
10	MOTHERWELL	36	2	5	11	20	38	3	2	13	13	48	33	86	17

1978-79 Season
Back: Stevens, McVie, Rennie, Mackin, Latchford, McLeod, Mungall
Middle: Hynd (Man), McKenzie (Train), Pettigrew, Marinello, Larnach, Kennedy, Boyd, Hagart (Asst. Man)
Front: Capaldi, Lindsasy, McLaren, Miller, Wark, Shanks, Clinging

1979-80 Season
Larnach, Pettigrew, Mackin, Wark, MacLeod (Man), McLeod, Rafferty, Kane, Dempsey,
Donnelly, Carberry, Irvine, Hare

1979-80: 1st Division

No.	Date	Opponent	Score	Scorers	Att.	Sproat	Wark	McLeod	Souter	Carson	Makin	Kane	Carberry	Smith	Kidd	Clinging	Irvine	McClelland	McLaughlin	Larnach	Cleland	Gahagan	O'Rourke	Dempsey	Donnelly	Meikle	Rafferty	Kelly	Ruane	Capaldi
1	11-Aug	Clydebank	1 - 1	Irvine	2000	x		x			x		x	x		x	x	x		s	x				x	x			s	
2	18-Aug	ARBROATH	1 - 1	OG	2895	x		x			x		x	x		x	x	x		s	x		x		s				x	
3	25-Aug	Stirling Albion	0 - 2		2100	x	s		x		x		x	x		x	x	x			x		x			x		s		
4	05-Sep	Dunfermline Ath.	0 - 2		2617	x	x		x					x		x	x	x		x	x			x		x				
5	09-Sep	BERWICK RANGERS	1 - 1	Rafferty	1781	x	x		x			s	x			x		x		x	x		s	x		x	x			
6	11-Sep	Hamilton Academical	2 - 3	McLaughlin, Wark	6000	x	x		x				x	x		x	x	x	x	x	x									
7	15-Sep	Raith Rovers	2 - 5	McLaughlin, Cleland	3097	x	x		x				x	x		x	x	x	x	x	x					s				
8	19-Sep	HEARTS	4 - 2	Souter, McLaughlin, Clinging, Larnach	3551	x	x		x				x			x	x	x	x	x	x			x						
9	22-Sep	Clyde	1 - 0	Souter	1800	x	x						x			x	x	x	x	x	x			x		s				
10	29-Sep	DUMBARTON	3 - 0	Irvine, Clinging, McLaughlin	3501	x	x		x				x			x	x	x	x	x	x			x						
11	06-Oct	St. Johnstone	3 - 1	Larnach, Irvine, Clinging	3634	x	x						x	x		x	x	x	x	x	x			x						
12	13-Oct	AYR UNITED	0 - 2		4139	x	x		s				x	x		x	x	x	x	x	x			x			s			
13	20-Oct	Aidrie	0 - 4		5600	x		x	x				x	s		x	x	x	x	x	x			x			s			
14	27-Oct	Arbroath	2 - 3	Clinging, Rafferty	1373	x		x	x				x			x	x	x	x	x	x			x			s			
15	03-Nov	STIRLING ALBION	1 - 0	McLaughlin	2096	x		x	x		x	s		x		x	x	x	x	x							x			
16	10-Nov	Berwick Rangers	2 - 2	Irvine (2)	1422	x		x	x		x	x		x		x	x	x	x	x	s									
17	17-Nov	RAITH ROVERS	1 - 2	McLaughlin	2200	x		x	x		x	x		x		x	x	x	x	x					s					
18	24-Nov	Hearts	1 - 2	Carberry	4800	x	x	x				x	x	x		x	x	x	x						x					
19	01-Dec	Dumbarton	1 - 1	McLaughlin	2000	x	x	x				x	x	x		x	x	x	x						x					
20	08-Dec	ST. JOHNSTONE	3 - 0	McClelland, Irvine, Clinging	2064	x	x	x	x				x	x		x	x	x	x						x		s			
21	15-Dec	Ayr United	0 - 0		4080	x	x	x	x			x	x	x		x	x	x	x											s
22	22-Dec	AIRDRIE	2 - 1	Irvine, Clinging	3686	x	x	x	x	x		x			x	x	x	x	x			s								
23	29-Dec	ARBROATH	0 - 0		3231	x	x	x	x	x		s			x	x	x		x			x	x							s
P 19/3	01-Jan	Stirling Albion	1 - 0	Irvine	1010	x		x	x	x					x	x	x	x	x			x	x							
25	05-Jan	BERWICK RANGERS	1 - 1	Kidd	2792	x	x	x	x	x	s	x			x	x		x	x			x								s
26	12-Jan	Raith Rovers	1 - 0	Kidd	2259	x	x	x	x	x				x	x		x	x	x			x								
p 19/2	19-Jan	HEARTS	0 - 0		4971	x	x	x	x	x		x			x	s	x	x	x			x								
p 15/3	02-Feb	HAMILTON ACADEMICAL	4 - 0	Clinging, McLaughlin, Gahagan, Irvine	3202	x	x	x		x					x	x	x	x	x			x	x							
29	09-Feb	ST. JOHNSTONE	1 - 2	Clinging	2061	x	x		x	x		s	x			x	x	x	x			x		x						
30	23-Feb	Ayr United	5 - 0	McLaughlin (2), Souter, Kidd, Irvine	4302	x	x		x	x				x	x	x	x	x	x				s		x					
p 25/3	01-Mar	Clydebank	2 - 1	Souter (2)	2000	x	x		x	x					x		x	x	x		x	s	x		x					
32	03-Mar	HAMILTON ACADEMICAL	2 - 1	Irvine, Kidd	3616	x	x	x	x	x					x	x	x		x			s	x		x					
33	08-Mar	DUNFERMLINE	1 - 1	Kidd	3114	x	x	x		x					x	x	x	x	x			x	x							
p 16/4	22-Mar	Clyde	2 - 0		900	x	x			x					x	x	x	x	x			x	x		x					
35	29-Mar	CLYDEBANK	3 - 2	Gahagan, Clinging, OG	2145	x	x	x	x	x		s		s	x	x	x	x	x			x								
36	05-Apr	CLYDE	3 - 0	Irvine (2), Carson	2516	x	x		x	x					x	x	x	x	x			x			x					
p 23/4	12-Apr	Dumbarton	0 - 1		800	x	x		x	x					x	x	x	x	x			x	x							
38	19-Apr	Aidrie	1 - 3	Irvine	7000	x	x		x		x		s	x	x		x		x	x		x	x							
39	26-Apr	DUMFERMLINE	1 - 1	McLaughlin	1942	x		x	x		x		x	x	x		x		x			x	x							

LEAGUE CUP

	Date	Opponent	Score	Scorers	Att.	Sproat	Wark	McLeod	Souter	Carson	Makin	Kane	Carberry	Smith	Kidd	Clinging	Irvine	McClelland	McLaughlin	Larnach	Cleland	Gahagan	O'Rourke	Dempsey	Donnelly	Meikle	Rafferty	Kelly	Ruane	Capaldi
	29-Aug	QUEENS PARK	1 - 4	Irvine	2017	x	s				x		x	x		x		x		x	x		x	x			x	s		
	01-Sep	Queens Park	2 - 0	Clinging, Irvine	1011	x	x		s		x		x	x		x	x	x		x	x				x	s				

SCOTTISH CUP

	Date	Opponent	Score	Scorers	Att.	Sproat	Wark	McLeod	Souter	Carson	Makin	Kane	Carberry	Smith	Kidd	Clinging	Irvine	McClelland	McLaughlin	Larnach	Cleland	Gahagan	O'Rourke	Dempsey	Donnelly	Meikle	Rafferty	Kelly	Ruane	Capaldi
	26-Jan	Queen of the South	0 - 2		5210	x	x	x	x	x		x				x	x	x	x		x		s							

LANARKSHIRE CUP

	Date	Opponent	Score
	04-Aug	AIRDRIE	
	05-Aug	ALBION ROVERS	

FRIENDLIES

	Date	Opponent	Score
	07-Aug	Alloa Athletic	1 - 1
	08-Aug	Falkirk	0 - 0

1980 Div. 1

		Pl.	Home W.	D.	L.	F.	A.	Away W.	D.	L.	F.	A.	F. (Total)	A.	Pts.
1	Heart of Mid.	39	13	7	1	33	18	7	6	5	25	21	58	39	53
2	Airdrieonians	39	14	2	4	46	21	7	7	5	32	26	78	47	51
3	Ayr United	39	11	5	4	37	22	5	7	7	27	29	64	51	44
4	Dumbarton	39	10	4	5	34	22	9	2	9	25	29	59	51	44
5	Raith Rovers	39	8	7	5	30	22	6	8	5	29	24	59	46	43
6	MOTHERWELL	39	9	7	3	32	17	7	4	9	27	31	59	48	43
7	Hamilton Acad.	39	11	5	3	39	20	4	5	11	21	39	60	59	40
8	Stirling Albion	39	7	6	7	23	19	6	7	6	17	21	40	40	39
9	Clydebank	39	9	6	5	32	21	5	2	12	26	36	58	57	36
10	Dunfermline Ath.	39	7	7	5	23	24	4	6	10	16	33	39	57	35
11	St. Johnstone	39	5	5	9	28	32	7	5	8	29	42	57	74	34
12	Berwick Rangers	39	5	7	7	36	31	3	8	9	21	33	57	64	31
13	Arbroath	39	7	5	7	31	32	2	5	13	19	47	50	79	28
14	Clyde	39	3	6	10	22	34	3	7	10	21	35	43	69	25

1980-81: 1st Division

No.	Date	Opponent	Score	Scorers	Att.	Sproat	Carson	MacLeod	Wark	Kidd	McLaughlin	Forbes	Gahagan	Smith	Souter	McClelland S	Irvine	McClelland C	Clinging	O'Rourke	McKeever	Cleland	Larnach	Carberry	Williams L	McKay	Rafferty	Coyne	McLean	Kane	Williams D	Mills
1	09-Aug	Ayr United	0 - 5		3782	x	x	x		x	x		x			x	s	x	x	x	s		x									
2	16-Aug	FALKIRK	3 - 0	McClelland, McKeever, Kidd	2531	x	x			x	x	s	s	x		x		x	x	x	x		x									
3	23-Aug	Hamilton Academical	2 - 4	McClelland, Kidd	3936	x	x			x	s	x	s	x		x	x	x	x	x			x									
4	06-Sep	Hibernian	0 - 1		4390	x	x			x	x	s	s			x		x	x	x	x		x	x								
5	09-Sep	Clydebank	2 - 2	Clinging, Carson	1500	x	x			x	x					x		x	x	x	x		x	x								
6	13-Sep	RAITH ROVERS	1 - 1	Kidd	2230	x	x			x	x		x		s	x	s	x	x	x			x	x								
7	17-Sep	DUNDEE	3 - 2	Kidd, Irvine, McKeever	2300	x	x			x	x				x	x	s	x	x	x	x			x								
8	20-Sep	Berwick Rangers	2 - 3	Clinging, Kidd	1191	x	x	x		x		x	s		x	x	x	x	x		s			x								
9	27-Sep	Dumbarton	2 - 1	Kidd, McKeever	1000	x	x	x	x	x			x	x		x	x	s	x	x												
10	01-Oct	DUNFERMLINE	2 - 0	McLaughlin, McKeever	1848	x	x	x	x	x	x		x	x			x		x		x											
11	04-Oct	ST. JOHNSTONE	2 - 2	Kidd, OG	2470	x	x	x	x	x	x		x	x	s		x		x		x											
12	11-Oct	East Stirling	1 - 1	Kidd	1200		x	x	x	x	x		x	x	x		x		x								s		x			
13	18-Oct	STIRLING ALBION	2 - 1	Carson, Rafferty	1990		x	x	x	x	s		x	x	x		x		x						x		x					
14	25-Oct	Raith Rovers	0 - 2		2000		x	x	x	x	s		x	x	x		x		x						x		x					
15	01-Nov	HIBERNIAN	2 - 0	Kidd, Irvine	3855		x	x	x	x	x	x		x			x	x	x						x							s
16	08-Nov	Dundee	1 - 2	Carson	5112		x	x	x	x	x	x		x			x	x	x						x							
17	15-Nov	BERWICK RANGERS	2 - 1	Irvine, McLeod	1980	x	x	x	x	x	x	x	s	x			x	x	x			s										
18	22-Nov	DUMBARTON	4 - 2	Forbes, Cleland, McClelland, Souter	2223	x	x	x	x	x		x	s	x	x		x	x				x										
19	29-Nov	St. Johnstone	2 - 2	Kidd, Irvine	2135	x	x	x	x	x	s	x	s	x	x		x	x				x										
20	06-Dec	EAST STIRLING	1 - 1	Cleland	1999	x	x	x	x	x	x	x	s	x	x			x			x	s										
21	13-Dec	Stirling Albion	0 - 2		1000	x	x	x	x	x	x	x	s	x				x			x	s								x		
22	20-Dec	CLYDEBANK	3 - 0	Cleland (2), Forbes	1671	x	x	x		x	x	x	x			x	x					x				x				s		
p 18/3	27-Dec	Falkirk	1 - 0	Irvine	1500	x	x	x	x	x	x	x	x		x	x	x															
24	01-Jan	HAMILTON ACADEMICAL	1 - 3	McLaughlin	3250	x	x	x		x	x	x	x			x	x	s				x				x				s		
p 28/3	03-Jan	Dunfermline Ath.	3 - 1	Gahagan, Irvine, Kidd	2658	x	x		x	x	x	x	x			x	x			x		s						x				
26	10-Jan	AYR UNITED	3 - 2	Irvine (2), McLaughlin	2554	x	x	x	x	x	x	x	x			x	x					x										
p 2/5	17-Jan	Stirling Albion	3 - 0	Souter (2), McLaughlin	505	x	x		x	x	x	x	x		x	x	x									x						
28	31-Jan	RAITH ROVERS	0 - 0		2953	x	x	x	x	x	x	x	x			x	x					x										
29	07-Feb	Berwick Rangers	2 - 2	McLaughlin, Irvine	950	x		x	x	x	x	x	x	x	x	x	x															
30	21-Feb	DUNDEE	4 - 1	McClelland (2), Irvine, McLaughlin	2072	x		x	x		x	x	x	x	x	x	x					x										
31	28-Feb	ST. JOHNSTONE	3 - 2	Forbes (2), Cleland	2646	x		x	x		x	x	x	x	x	x	x					x										
p 8/4	07-Mar	Dumbarton	0 - 0		1432																											
33	14-Mar	EAST STIRLING	2 - 1	Souter, Rafferty	1800	x	x	x	x	x	x		x		x	x	x					x					s					
34	21-Mar	Clydebank	0 - 0		902	x	x	x	x	x	x	x	x	x		x	x										s	s				
35	04-Apr	FALKIRK	1 - 0	Kidd	2045	x	x		x	x	x	x	x			x	x			x	s					s		x				
36	11-Apr	AYR UNITED	1 - 0	Kidd	2068	x	x		x	x	x	x	x		x	x	x				s					x						
37	18-Apr	Hamilton Academical	2 - 1	Souter, Cleland	2601	x	x		x	x	x	x	x		x	x	x				s	s				x						
38	25-Apr	HIBERNIAN	1 - 1	Irvine	3478	x	x		x	x	x	x	x		x	x	x				s	s				x						

LEAGUE CUP

Date	Opponent	Score	Scorers	Att.	Sproat	Carson	MacLeod	Wark	Kidd	McLaughlin	Forbes	Gahagan	Smith	Souter	McClelland S	Irvine	McClelland C	Clinging	O'Rourke	McKeever	Cleland	Larnach	Carberry	Williams L	McKay	Rafferty	Coyne	McLean	Kane	Williams D	Mills
27-Aug	Stenhousemuir	0 - 0		800	x	x			x	x		x	x		s	x	x	x	x			x									
30-Aug	STENHOUSEMUIR	6 - 1	McLaughlin (3), Clinging (2), Kidd	1839	x	x	x		x	x		s			x	s	x	x	x	x		x									
03-Sep	DUNDEE UNITED	2 - 1	McKeever, Clinging	3327	x	x			x	x		s			x		x	x	x	x		x	x								
24-Sep	Dundee United	2 - 4	Irvine, Clinging	5628	x	x	x		x			x	x	x	x	s		x	x	x											

SCOTTISH CUP

Date	Opponent	Score	Scorers	Att.	Sproat	Carson	MacLeod	Wark	Kidd	McLaughlin	Forbes	Gahagan	Smith	Souter	McClelland S	Irvine	McClelland C	Clinging	O'Rourke	McKeever	Cleland	Larnach	Carberry	Williams L	McKay	Rafferty	Coyne	McLean	Kane	Williams D	Mills
24-Jan	Stenhousemuir	1 - 1	Forbes	2250	x	x	x	x	x	x	x	x			x	x					x										
28-Jan	STENHOUSEMUIR	2 - 1	McClelland, Gahagan	2735	x	x	x	x	x	x	x	x			x	x					x										
14-Feb	DUMBARTON	2 - 1	Larnach, Clinging	4370	x		x	x	x	x	x	x	x	x	x	x															
07-Mar	Dundee United	1 - 6	Souter	10236	x		x	x		x	x	x	x	x	x	x					x										

LANARKSHIRE CUP

Date	Opponent	
02-Aug	Albion Rovers	
03-Aug	Aidrie	

FRIENDLIES

Date	Opponent	Score	Scorers
06-Aug	COVENTRY CITY	2 - 0	Larnach, Clinging

1981 Div. 1

		Pl.	Home W.	D.	L.	F.	A.	Away W.	D.	L.	F.	A.	F. (Total)	A.	Pts.
1	Hibernian	39	14	4	2	38	9	10	5	4	29	15	67	24	57
2	Dundee	39	14	4	2	42	18	8	4	7	22	22	64	40	52
3	St. Johnstone	39	12	3	5	31	21	8	8	3	33	24	64	45	51
4	Raith Rovers	39	11	7	1	26	11	9	3	8	23	21	49	32	50
5	MOTHERWELL	39	14	5	1	41	20	5	6	8	24	31	65	51	49
6	Ayr United	39	11	5	3	34	17	6	6	8	25	25	59	42	45
7	Hamilton Acad.	39	9	5	6	39	27	6	2	11	22	30	61	57	37
8	Dumbarton	39	8	5	6	23	22	5	6	9	26	28	49	50	37
9	Falkirk	39	7	4	8	24	29	6	4	10	15	23	39	52	34
10	Clydebank	39	8	6	5	31	25	2	7	11	17	34	48	59	33
11	East Stirling.	39	4	10	6	20	24	2	7	10	21	32	41	56	29
12	Dunfermline Ath.	39	6	3	11	17	28	4	4	11	24	30	41	58	27
13	Stirling Albion	39	4	6	9	13	21	2	5	13	5	27	18	48	23
14	Berwick Rangers	39	5	6	8	18	27	0	6	14	13	55	31	82	22

1980-81 Season
Back: Rafferty, Wark, MacLeod, MacLean, Smith, Carson, Soutar, McLelland
Front: Gahagan, Irvine, Kidd, McLaughlin, Clinging

1981 -82 Season
Back : Clelland, McLean, Carson, Sproat, Mills, Sameroff, McLaughlin
Middle: Wark, McKay, Conn, I McLeod, Irvine, Forbes, McClair, Williams
Front: S McClelland, Gahagan, Clinging, Souter, Raffarty, McKeever, Healey

1981-82: 1st Division

No.	Date	Opponent	Score	Scorers	Att.	Sproat	McLeod	McClelland	Wark	Rafferty	McKay	O'Hara	Carson	Coyne	McLaughlin	Irvine	Cleland	Gahagan	Conn	McClair	Forbes	McKeever	Sameroff	Clinging	Mills	Souter	McAllister G
1	29-Aug	Kilmarnock	0 - 2		2700	x	x		x				x		x	x	x	x		x	x			s	s	x	
2	05-Sep	QUEENS PARK	1 - 0	Irvine	1966	x	x	x	x				x		x	x	x	x	s		x			x			
3	08-Sep	HAMILTON ACADEMICAL	2 - 2	McLaughlin, Forbes	2130	x	x	x	x				x		x	x	x	s	x		x			x			
4	12-Sep	St. Johnstone	3 - 1	McLaughlin, Cleland, Irvine	2518	x	x	x	x				x		x	x	x	x	x		x				s		
5	16-Sep	FALKIRK	3 - 2	McLaughlin (2), Irvine	1914	x	x	x	x				x		x	x	x	x	x		x				s		
6	19-Sep	Dumbarton	6 - 0	Cleland (3), McLaughlin (2), Clinging	1200	x	x	x	x				x		x	x	x	x	x		x			s			
7	23-Sep	RAITH ROVERS	3 - 0	McLaughlin (2), Irvine	2100	x	x	x	x				x		x	x	x	x	x		x				s		
8	26-Sep	Dunfermline Ath.	2 - 1	Irvine, Mills	3500	x	x	x	x				x		x	x	x	x	x		x				s		
9	03-Oct	EAST STIRLING	3 - 0	McLaughlin, Conn, Cleland	2528	x		x	x		x		x		x	x	x	s	x					x	x		
10	10-Oct	AYR UNITED	1 - 1	Gahagan	5354	x		x	x		x		x		x	x	x	x	x		x			s			
11	17-Oct	Clydebank	7 - 1	Rafferty (2), McClelland, OG, Gahagan, Irvine (2)	1600	x		x	x	x	x		x		x	x		x	x		x						
12	24-Oct	HEARTS	2 - 2	McKeever (2)	7662	x	x	x			x		x		x	x		x	x		x	x			s		
13	31-Oct	Queen of the South	2 - 0	Irvine, McKeever	2500		x	x	s	s	x		x		x	x		x	x		x	x	x				
14	07-Nov	Queens Park	1 - 0	McLaughlin	2640		x	x	x	s			x	x	x	x		x	x	s		x	x				
15	14-Nov	KILMARNOCK	2 - 0	Cleland, Irvine	5068		x	x	x	x			x	x	x	x	s	x				x	x				
16	21-Nov	Falkirk	1 - 1	Gahagan	3000		x	x	x	x			x	x	x	x	x	x	s				x	s			
17	28-Nov	DUMFERMLINE	6 - 1	Irvine (2), Forbes, Rafferty, Gahagan, McLaughlin	3581	x	x	x	x	x			x	x	x	x		x			x						
18	05-Dec	East Stirling	6 - 0	Carson, Forbes, Rafferty, Irvine, McClelland, McLaughlin	2000	x	x	x	x	x			x	x	x	x		x			x			s			
p 17/2	26-Dec	ST. JOHNSTONE	2 - 2	Gahagan, McLaughlin	4205	x	x	x	x			s	x	x	x	x		x			x	x					
p 13/2	03-Jan	Hamilton Academical	0 - 1		4049	x		x	x		x	s	x	x	x	x	x	x			x	s					
p 19/1	16-Jan	CLYDEBANK	3 - 1	Rafferty, Gahagan, McLaughlin	2925	x	x	x	x	x		s	x	x	x	x	s	x			x						
22	30-Jan	Hearts	3 - 0	Irvine, Coyne, Clinging	11054	x	x	x	x			x	x	x		x	x	x			x			s			
23	06-Feb	QUEEN OF THE SOUTH	2 - 1	Carson, Cleland	2946	x		x	x		x		x	x		x	x	x		s	x			x			
24	20-Feb	Raith Rovers	2 - 0	Irvine, Clelland	2000	x	x	x	x			x	x		x	x	s	x			x	x					
25	27-Feb	QUEENS PARK	3 - 0	McLaughlin, Cleland, Irvine	3325	x	x	x	x	s		x	x		x	x	x	x			x						
26	03-Mar	DUMBARTON	1 - 1	Carson	3202	x	x	x	s	x		x	x	x	x	x		x			x	s					
27	06-Mar	St. Johnstone	2 - 3	Irvine, Coyne	2914	x	x		s	x		x	x	x	x	x	x	x			x						
28	13-Mar	Ayr United	1 - 1	Clelland	3185	x	x	x	x			x	x		x	x	x	x			x						
29	20-Mar	HAMILTON ACADEMICAL	3 - 2	McLaughlin, Cleland, Irvine	4030	x	x	x	x	s		x	x	x	x	x	x	x									
30	27-Mar	KILMARNOCK	1 - 0	McLaughlin	4816	x	x	x	x			x		x	x	x	x	x	s		x						
31	03-Apr	East Stirling	2 - 1	Forbes, Cleland	1000	x	x	x	x			x			x	x	x	x	x	s	x						
32	10-Apr	DUMBARTON	1 - 0	Cleland	2742	x	x	x				x	x		x	x	x	x	x		x						
33	14-Apr	Ayr United	3 - 4	Clelland (2), Irvine	2317	x	x	x				x	x		x	x	x	x	x	s	x						
34	17-Apr	Falkirk	3 - 1	Forbes (2), McClair	3000	x	x	x	x			x	x	x	s	x		x		x	x						
35	20-Apr	Raith Rovers	1 - 0	McLaughlin	1568	x	x	x				x	x	x	x	x		x		x	x						
36	24-Apr	CLYDEBANK	0 - 0		3689	x	x	x				x	x	x	x	x	s	x	s	x	x						
37	01-May	Queen of the South	5 - 2	McClair (2), Irvine, Gahagan, Cleland	500	x	x	x			x	x		x	x	x	x	x	s	x							s
38	08-May	DUNFERMLINE	2 - 2	McLaughlin, McClair	2492	x	x	x			x	x		s	x	x	x	x	x	x							
39	15-May	Hearts	1 - 0	Irvine	14709	x	x	x		x		x		x	x	x	x	x	x	x							

LEAGUE CUP

Date	Opponent	Score	Scorers	Att.	Sproat	McLeod	McClelland	Wark	Rafferty	McKay	O'Hara	Carson	Coyne	McLaughlin	Irvine	Cleland	Gahagan	Conn	McClair	Forbes	McKeever	Sameroff	Clinging	Mills	Souter	McAllister G
08-Aug	Partick Thistle	0 - 2		3172	x	x	x	x				x		x	x	s	x			x			x		x	
12-Aug	AYR UNITED	2 - 3	Cleland, Clinging	1970	x	x	x	x				x			x	x	x	s	x	x			x	s		
15-Aug	DUNDEE UNITED	1 - 2	McLaughlin	2884	x	x	x	x				x		x	s	x	x	x		x			x		s	
19-Aug	Ayr United	0 - 1		2202	x	x	x	x				x		x	s	x	x	x	x				x			
22-Aug	PARTICK THISTLE	0 - 1		2098	x	x	x	x				x		x	s	x	x	x	x				x			
26-Aug	Dundee United	1 - 1	Forbes	4484	x	x	x	x				x		x	x				x	x			x		x	

SCOTTISH CUP

Date	Opponent	Score	Scorers	Att.	Sproat	McLeod	McClelland	Wark	Rafferty	McKay	O'Hara	Carson	Coyne	McLaughlin	Irvine	Cleland	Gahagan	Conn	McClair	Forbes	McKeever	Sameroff	Clinging	Mills	Souter	McAllister G
23-Jan	ABERDEEN	0 - 1	(J.Hewitt, fastest ever Scottish Cup goal-8.5 Secs)	12679	x	x	x	x	x		x	x	s	x	x	s	x			x						

LANARKSHIRE CUP

Date	Opponent	Score	Scorers
01-Aug	Aidrie		
02-Aug	Albion Rovers		

FRIENDLIES

Date	Opponent	Score	Scorers
29-Jul	MORTON	1 - 2	Souter
09-Jan	Hibernian	0-2	
11-Jan	Estoril	0-1	
13-Jan	Amoril	0-2	
11-Oct	SAN JOSE EARTHQUAKES	5 - 2	Carson,Clinging,Conn,McKeever,Gahagan
10-May	Carluke		

1982 Div. 1

		Pl.	Home W.	D.	L.	F.	A.	Away W.	D.	L.	F.	A.	F. (Total)	A.	Pts.
1	MOTHERWELL	39	12	7	0	41	17	14	2	4	51	19	92	36	61
2	Kilmarnock	39	6	12	2	25	11	11	5	3	35	18	60	29	51
3	Heart of Mid.	39	12	2	5	33	19	9	6	5	32	18	65	37	50
4	Clydebank	39	12	3	5	33	27	7	5	7	28	26	61	53	46
5	St. Johnstone	39	12	3	4	44	29	5	5	10	25	31	69	60	42
6	Ayr United	39	12	6	1	39	20	3	6	11	17	30	56	50	42
7	Hamilton Acad.	39	10	3	6	20	16	6	5	9	32	33	52	49	40
8	Queen's Park	39	11	5	4	32	17	2	5	12	9	24	41	41	36
9	Falkirk	39	8	8	4	26	19	3	6	10	23	33	49	52	36
10	Dunfermline Ath.	39	3	9	7	24	31	8	5	7	22	25	46	56	36
11	Dumbarton	39	10	1	9	25	30	3	8	8	24	31	49	61	35
12	Raith Rovers	39	5	2	13	13	32	6	5	8	18	27	31	59	29
13	East Stirling.	39	4	6	9	20	35	3	4	13	18	42	38	77	24
14	Queen of the S.	39	2	5	13	25	50	2	5	12	19	43	44	93	18

1982-83: Premier League

	Date	Opponent	Score	Scorers	Att.	Sproat	Forsyth	McLeod	McClelland	Carson	McLaughlin	Gahagan	Clinging	Irvine	Conn	O'Hara	Forbes	Coyne	Wark	McClair	Cleland	Rafferty	Edvaldsson	Flavell	Mauchline	Burns	Graham	Dornan	Harrow	Walker	Cormack
1	04-Sep	RANGERS	2 - 2	Carson, Cleland	19159	x	x	x	x	x	x	x	s	x			x				s	x	x								
2	11-Sep	Dundee	1 - 3	Rafferty	4621	x	x	x	x		x	x	s		s		x			x	x	x	x								
3	18-Sep	CELTIC	0 - 7		17092	x			x	x		x			x	x	x		x	x		x	x								
4	25-Sep	Morton	1 - 3	OG	2200	x	x	x			s	x			x	s	x	x		x	x	x	x								
5	02-Oct	Aberdeen	1 - 2	Edvaldsson	9000	x	x	x	x	x			x		x	x		s			s	x	x	x							
6	09-Oct	ST. MIRREN	2 - 0	Mauchline, McLeod	4292	x	x	x	x	x			x		x	x						s	x	x	x	s					
7	16-Oct	Hibernian	0 - 1		4500	x	x	x	x	x		s				x		s				x	x	x	x	x					
8	23-Oct	DUNDEE UNITED	0 - 2		4555	x	x	x	x	x	x	s				x						s	x	x	x	x					
9	30-Oct	KILMARNOCK	4 - 1	Mauchline (2), McClair, McLaughlin	3016	x	x	x	x	x	x	x				x				s			x	x	x						
10	06-Nov	Rangers	0 - 4		17000	x	x	x	x	x		x				x	s			x			x	x	x	s					
11	13-Nov	DUNDEE	1 - 0	Flavell	3502	x	x	x	x	x		x				x	s			x	s	x	x	x							
12	20-Nov	Celtic	1 - 3	Flavell	14963	x	x	x	x	x		x				x				x		x	x	x							
13	27-Nov	MORTON	3 - 1	McClelland, Mauchline, OG	3124	x	x	x	x	x		x				x	s					x	x	x	x						
14	04-Dec	ABERDEEN	0 - 2		4929	x	x	x	x			x				x	s					x	x	x	x						
15	11-Dec	St. Mirren	0 - 3		3563	x	x	x	x			x				x	x			s		x	x	x	x						
16	18-Dec	HIBERNIAN	0 - 1		3818	x	x	x			x	x				x	x			s		x	x	x	x		s				
17	27-Dec	Dundee United	0 - 5		7682	x	x	x	s		x	x	s			x	x			x			x	x	x						
18	01-Jan	Kilmarnock	2 - 0	Flavell, Mauchlin	3300	x		x		x	s					x	s			x		x	x	x	x			x	x		
19	03-Jan	RANGERS	3 - 0	McClair (3)	11383	x	x			x						x	s			x		x	x	x	x			x	x		
20	08-Jan	Dundee	1 - 3	Edvaldsson	5313	x	x			x	s					x	s			x		x	x	x	x			x	x		
21	15-Jan	CELTIC	2 - 1	McClair (2)	15290			x		x						x	x	s		x		x	x		x			x	x	x	
22	22-Jan	Morton	1 - 0	McClair	3000			x		x						x	s			x		x	x	x	x			x	x	x	
23	08-Feb	Aberdeen	1 - 5	Rafferty	13500					x						x	x			x		x	x	x	x			x	x	x	
24	26-Feb	Hibernian	1 - 1	Harrow	4300			x				x	x			x	x	s		x		x	x		x			x	x	x	
25	01-Mar	ST. MIRREN	0 - 0		2905			x				x	s			x	x	x		x		x	x					x	x	x	
26	05-Mar	DUNDEE UNITED	1 - 4	McLaughlin	3589			x				x				x	x			x		x	x		x			x	x	x	
27	12-Mar	KILMARNOCK	3 - 1	Rafferty, McClair, MAUCHLIN	2895			x				x	s			x	x	s		x		x	x		x			x	x	x	
28	19-Mar	Rangers	0 - 1		17500			x				x	s			x	x	s		x		x	x		x			x	x	x	
29	26-Mar	DUNDEE	1 - 1	Forbes	3222			x		x		x					x	x		x		x		s	x			x	x	x	
30	02-Apr	Celtic	0 - 3		15454			x				x				x		x	x	x		s		x	x			x	x	x	
31	09-Apr	MORTON	4 - 1	Gahagan (2), Harrow, McClair	3764							x				x			x	x		x	x	x	x			x	x	x	s
32	23-Apr	St. Mirren	0 - 4		3257							x				x		x	x	x		x	x	x				x	x	x	
33	27-Apr	ABERDEEN	0 - 3		6187							x				x			x	x		x	x	x	x			x	x	x	s
34	30-Apr	HIBERNIAN	2 - 0	Gahagan, McClair	3532							x				x		x	x	x		x	x	x	s			x	x	x	
35	07-May	Dundee United	0 - 4		11933							x				x			x	x		x	x	x	x			x	x	x	s
36	14-May	Kilmarnock	1 - 1	McClair	1203							x				x		x	x	x		x	x	x				x	x	x	

LEAGUE CUP

	Date	Opponent	Score	Scorers	Att.	Sproat	Forsyth	McLeod	McClelland	Carson	McLaughlin	Gahagan	Clinging	Irvine	Conn	O'Hara	Forbes	Coyne	Wark	McClair	Cleland	Rafferty	Edvaldsson	Flavell	Mauchline	Burns	Graham	Dornan	Harrow	Walker	Cormack
	14-Aug	HEARTS	2 - 1	Coyne, Conn	4947	x	x	x	x	x		s		x	x	x	x	x		x		s									
	18-Aug	Clyde	3 - 3	Conn, McClair, McClelland	1945	x	x	x	x	x				x	x	x	x	x		x											
	21-Aug	FORFAR ATHLETIC	1 - 1	Forbes	2277	x	x	x	x	x		s		x	x	x	x	x		x		s									
	25-Aug	CLYDE	3 - 1	McClair (3)	2389	x		x	x	x		x	x		x	x	x	s	x	s	x										
	28-Aug	Hearts	0 - 1		9022	x	x	x	x	x		x	s		x	x		x		x	x	s									
	01-Sep	Forfar Athletic	1 - 0	McClair	1402	x	x	x	x		x	x				x				x	x	x	x								

SCOTTISH CUP

	Date	Opponent	Score	Scorers	Att.	Sproat	Forsyth	McLeod	McClelland	Carson	McLaughlin	Gahagan	Clinging	Irvine	Conn	O'Hara	Forbes	Coyne	Wark	McClair	Cleland	Rafferty	Edvaldsson	Flavell	Mauchline	Burns	Graham	Dornan	Harrow	Walker	Cormack
	29-Jan	Clyde	0 - 0		3831		s	x		x		s				x	x			x		x	x	x				x	x	x	
	02-Feb	CLYDE	3 - 4	Harrow, McClair, Coyne	4676		s	x		x						x	x			x		x	x	x			s	x	x	x	

LANARKSHIRE CUP

Date	Opponent	Score	Scorers
07-Aug	Albion Rovers	2 - 0	Conn, Forsyth
08-Aug	Hamilton Academical	5 - 1	Forbes (2), Irvine, Conn, Coyne

FRIENDLIES

Date	Opponent	Score	Scorers
02-Aug	Falkirk	3 - 1	Irvine, Conn, O'Hara
04-Aug	Cowdenbeath	1 - 1	O'Hara
05-Aug	Queens Park	0 - 0	
11-Aug	LEEDS UNITED	0 - 4	
18-Feb	HAMILTON ACADEMICAL	1 - 0	Edvaldsson
22-Feb	Raith Rovers	3 - 2	Gahagan (2), Mauchline
08-Mar	Alloa Athletic	2 - 2	McClair, O'HARA
28-Sep	Ballymena	1 - 2	O'Hara
04-Oct	Buckie	3 - 0	
	Islandur	0 - 0	

1983 Premier League

		Pl.	Home W.	D.	L.	F.	A.	Away W.	D.	L.	F.	A.	F. (Total)	A.	Pts.
1	Dundee United	36	13	4	1	57	18	11	4	3	33	17	90	35	56
2	Celtic	36	12	3	3	44	18	13	2	3	46	18	90	36	55
3	Aberdeen	36	14	0	4	46	12	11	5	2	30	12	76	24	55
4	Rangers	36	9	6	3	32	16	4	6	8	20	25	52	41	38
5	St. Mirren	36	8	5	5	30	18	3	7	8	17	33	47	51	34
6	Dundee	36	8	3	7	29	28	1	8	9	13	25	42	53	29
7	Hibernian	36	3	11	4	21	17	4	4	10	14	34	35	51	29
8	MOTHERWELL	36	9	3	6	28	27	2	2	14	11	46	39	73	27
9	Morton	36	4	4	10	14	26	2	4	12	16	48	30	74	20
10	Kilmarnock	36	3	7	8	17	31	0	4	14	11	60	28	91	17

1982-83 Season

Back : Irvine, Clelland, B Coyne, Sproat, Forbes, Burns, Healey
Middle : O'Hara, Clinging, Conn, A Forsyth, Carson, McClair, McAllister, McClelland
Front : McKay, Gahagan, McKenzie (Trainer), Wallace (Manager), Connor (Assist.Man.), Wylie (Physio), Rafferty, McLaughlin

1983-84 Season

Back : Burns, McFadden, Walker, Innes, Maxwell, Sproat, Shaw, McStay
Middle : Wallace (Manager), Cormack, Kennedy, Forbes, Carson, Edvaldsson, McLeod, McAllister, Rafferty
Front : Flavell, Mauchlin, Dornan, Wark, Campbell , Gillespie, Harrow, Gahagan

1983-84: Premier League

						Sproat	Walker	Dorman	McLeod	Wark	Black	Carson	Edvaldsson	Forbes	Mauchline	Cormack	Gahagan	Rafferty	Gillespie	Ritchie	Flavell	Harrow	McFadden	Burns	Alexander	McAllister	Fryer	Lyall	Boyd	Grant	McBride	Kennedy	Weldon	Dobbin	Maxwell	Wishart	Tracey
p 28/3	20-Aug	Dundee United	0 - 4		9465	x		x	x			x	x		x		x	x	x		x	x															
p 10/3	03-Sep	St. Mirren	1 - 1	Edvaldsson	3610		x	x		x		x	x	x		x	x	x	x	x																	
3	10-Sep	ABERDEEN	1 - 1	Gahagan	3061		x	x		x		x	x	x	x		x	x	x	x																	
4	17-Sep	CELTIC	0 - 3		8640		x	x		x		x	x	x	x		x	x	x	x																	
5	24-Sep	Hibernian	1 - 2	Irvine	4700		x	x	x			x	x		x	x	x	x	x	x																	
6	01-Oct	DUNDEE	1 - 3	Edvaldsson	2931		x	x	x			x	x	x	x		x	x			x		x														
p 18/4	08-Oct	Hearts	0 - 0		7886		x	x	x			x	x		x		x	x	x	x		x															
8	15-Oct	ST. JOHNSTONE	0 - 1		2434		x	x	x			x	x		x		x	x	x	x		x															
9	22-Oct	Rangers	2 - 1	Ritchie, Burns	15000		x	x	x			x	x	x	x	x	x			x		x	x	x													
10	29-Oct	DUNDEE UNITED	2 - 2	Alexander, Gahagan	4398		x	x	x			x	x	x	x		x					x		x	x												
11	05-Nov	ST. MIRREN	0 - 0		3914		x	x	x			x	x	x			x					x		x	x	x											
12	12-Nov	Celtic	0 - 4		13408		x	x		x		x	x	x		x	x					x			x		x										
13	19-Nov	Dundee	0 - 2		4638		x	x		x		x	x	x		x	x					x			x	x											
14	26-Nov	HIBERNIAN	1 - 2	Harrow	3965		x	x	x			x	x	x	x		x					x		s	x	x	s										
15	03-Dec	Aberdeen	1 - 3	Gahagan	18000		x	x	x	x		x		x	x	s	x						x		x	x											
16	10-Dec	RANGERS	0 - 3		13586		x	x	x	x		x		x	x		x		s				x		x	x											
17	17-Dec	St. Johnstone	1 - 3	Gahagan	3101	x		x	x		x	x		x	x		x			s		x	s		x			x									
18	26-Dec	HEARTS	1 - 1	Edvaldsson	7589	x		x	s		x		x	x	x		x	x	x						s	x		x									
19	31-Dec	Dundee United	1 - 2	Edvaldsson	6967	x		x	s		x		x	x	x		x	x	s						x	x		x									
20	02-Jan	St. Mirren	1 - 2	Harrow	3912	x		x	x		x		x	x	x			x	x			s	s			x		x									
21	07-Jan	CELTIC	2 - 2	Dornan, Rafferty	11268	x		x	x		x		x	x	x		s	x	x			x				s		x									
p 28/3	14-Jan	DUNDEE	2 - 4	Rafferty, Dornan	1828	x		x	x					x				x				x	x		x			x	x	x	s	s					
p 10/3	21-Jan	Hibernian	2 - 1	McFadden, Rafferty	4500	x			x				x	x			s	x				x	x					x		x		s	x	x			
24	04-Feb	Rangers	1 - 2	Harrow	16000	x		x	x		x		x				x	x	x			x	s			x		x			s						
25	11-Feb	ABERDEEN	0 - 4		6081	x		x	x		x	x			x			x				x	x			x			x		s	s					
26	25-Feb	ST. JOHNSTONE	1 - 0	Harrow	2537	x			x		x	x		x	x		s	x	x			x				x			x			s					
27	03-Mar	Hearts	1 - 2	Gahagan	6000	x		x	x		x	x		x			x	x	s			x				x		s	x								
p 18/4	17-Mar	Dundee	2 - 4	Harrow, Rafferty	1897	x		x	x					x				x				x	x		x			x	x	x	s	s					
29	24-Mar	HIBERNIAN	2 - 3	McFadden, Harrow	2587	x		x	x					x				x				x	x		x	s		x	x	x	s						
30	31-Mar	RANGERS	0 - 3		8574	x		x	x					x				x				x	x		x	s		x	x	x	s						
31	07-Apr	Aberdeen	1 - 2	Rafferty	16550				x		x			x			s	x				x	x		s	x		x	x			x			x		
32	14-Apr	Celtic	2 - 4	Gahagan, Forbes	5673	x		x	x					x				x				x	x		x	s		x	x	x	s						
33	21-Apr	ST. MIRREN	1 - 0	Lyall	1866	x			x		x			x			x	x				x				x		x	x			x				s	s
34	28-Apr	DUNDEE UNITED	1 - 3	Gahagan	1870	x			x		x						x	x				x				x		x	x	s		x				x	s
35	05-May	St. Johnstone	1 - 3	Lyall	1407						x			s	x		x					x				x		x	x	x		x			x	x	s
36	12-May	HEARTS	0 - 1		3751						x			s	x		x					x				x		x	x	x		x			x	x	s

LEAGUE CUP

						Sproat	Walker	Dorman	McLeod	Wark	Black	Carson	Edvaldsson	Forbes	Mauchline	Cormack	Gahagan	Rafferty	Gillespie	Ritchie	Flavell	Harrow	McFadden	Burns	Alexander	McAllister	Fryer	Lyall	Boyd	Grant	McBride	Kennedy	Weldon	Dobbin	Maxwell	Wishart	Tracey
	24-Aug	BERWICK RANGERS	2 - 0	Edvaldsson, Gahagan	2061		x	x	x			x	x	x	x		x			x	x	x															
	27-Aug	Berwick Rangers	2 - 0	Ritchie, Gillespie	1151		x	x	x			x	x	x	x		x		x	x				x													
	31-Aug	MORTON	3 - 0	Edvaldsson, Gillespie, Ritchie	2836		x	x		x		x	x	x	x		x	x	x	x																	
	07-Sep	Alloa Athletic	2 - 1	Gillespie (2)	1015		x	x	x	x		x		x		x	x	x	x	x																	
	05-Oct	Dundee United	2 - 4	Mauchlin, Gahagan	5100		x	x	x			x	x		x	x	x	x	x	x																	
	26-Oct	ALLOA	2 - 2	Alexander, Carson	1551		x	x		x		x	x	x	x	x		x				x			x												
	09-Nov	Morton	2 - 4	Ritchie, Harrow	2008		x	x	x			x	x			x	x			x		x			x	x											
	30-Nov	DUNDEE UNITED	0 - 3		1391	x		x	x	s		x	x	x	x				s	x		x			x	x											

SCOTTISH CUP

						Sproat	Walker	Dorman	McLeod	Wark	Black	Carson	Edvaldsson	Forbes	Mauchline	Cormack	Gahagan	Rafferty	Gillespie	Ritchie	Flavell	Harrow	McFadden	Burns	Alexander	McAllister	Fryer	Lyall	Boyd	Grant	McBride	Kennedy	Weldon	Dobbin	Maxwell	Wishart	Tracey
	06-Feb	QUEENS PARK	3 - 0	Harrow (3)	2067	x		x	x		x	x					x	x	s			x	x			x		x									
	18-Feb	CLYDEBANK	3 - 1	Harrow, Rafferty, Gillespie	3435	x		x	x		x	x			x		s	x	x			x				x			x		s						
	17-Mar	CELTIC	0 - 6		14700	x		s	x				x	x				x	s			x	x			x		x		x			x				

FRIENDLIES

	15-Aug	Sheffield United	1 - 0	Harrow
	01-Aug	Ross County	4 - 0	Gillespie (2), Mauchline, Gahagan
	02-Aug	Brora	1 - 0	Ritchie
	03-Aug	Nairn	1 - 0	Gillespie
	05-Aug	SHREWSBURY T.	2 - 1	Cormack, Forbes
	08-Aug	QUEENS P. RANGERS	1 - 1	Forbes
	09-Aug	Coleraine	1 - 1	Burns
	10-Aug	Glentoran	2 - 1	Gillespie, Harrow

1984 Premier League

		Pl.	Home					Away					F.	A.	Pts.
			W.	D.	L.	F.	A.	W.	D.	L.	F.	A.	(Total)		
1	Aberdeen	36	14	3	1	46	12	11	4	3	32	9	78	21	57
2	Celtic	36	13	5	0	46	15	8	3	7	34	26	80	41	50
3	Dundee United	36	11	3	4	38	14	7	8	3	29	25	67	39	47
4	Rangers	36	7	8	3	26	18	8	4	6	27	23	53	41	42
5	Heart of Mid.	36	5	9	4	23	23	5	7	6	15	24	38	47	36
6	St. Mirren	36	8	6	4	34	23	1	8	9	21	36	55	59	32
7	Hibernian	36	7	4	7	21	21	5	3	10	24	34	45	55	31
8	Dundee	36	6	1	11	28	42	5	4	9	22	32	50	74	27
9	St. Johnstone	36	6	1	11	19	33	4	2	12	17	48	36	81	23
10	MOTHERWELL	36	2	5	11	15	36	2	2	14	16	39	31	75	15

1984-85: 1st Division

No.	Date	Opponent	Score	Scorers	Att.	Maxwell	Dornan	Murray	Forbes	Stevens	MacLeod	McDonald	McAllister	Stewart	Alexander	Harrow	Lyall	McFadden	Boyd	Gahagan	Cormack	Mauchline	Blair	Clark R	Gardner	Kennedy	Doyle	Walker	McStay
1	11-Aug	KILMARNOCK	2 - 0	McAllister, Harrow	2384	x	x	x	x	x	x	x	x	x	s	x	x	s											
2	18-Aug	Hamilton Academical	0 - 2		4014	x	x	x	x	x	x	x	x		x	x	x	s	s										
3	25-Aug	PARTICK THISTLE	2 - 1	McAllister (2)	2579	x	x	x		x	x	x	x	x		x			x	x	s	s							
4	01-Sep	Forfar Athletic	2 - 1	Harrow, Gahagan	1383	x	x	x	x	x	x		x		s	x			x	x	s	x							
5	08-Sep	AYR UNITED	1 - 1	Cormack	2427	x	x	x	s	x	x	x	x			x		s	x	x	x								
6	15-Sep	Falkirk	3 - 0	Harrow, Forbes, McFadden	2409	x	x	x	x	x	x	s	x			x		s	x	x		x							
7	22-Sep	CLYDEBANK	0 - 1		2401	x	x	x	x	x	x	s	x			x			x	x		x	s						
8	29-Sep	MEADOWBANK	3 - 1	Alexander, Blair, Clark	2853	x	x		x		x	x	x		x	s			x	x		x	x	s					
9	06-Oct	Aidrie	0 - 2		5000	x	x	x	x	x	x		x		x	x			x	s			x	s					
10	13-Oct	BRECHIN	2 - 0	Harrow, Blair	1715	x	x	x	x		x		x		x	x			x			x	x						
11	20-Oct	Clyde	3 - 3	McDonald (2), Harrow	1907	x	x	x	x		x	s	x		x	x			x	s		x	x						
12	27-Oct	East Fife	2 - 1	Forbes, OG	1837	x	x		x		x	x	x	s		x			x	x		x	x	s					
13	03-Nov	ST. JOHNSTONE	0 - 2		1743	x			x		x	x	x	s		x			x	x		x	x	x					
14	10-Nov	Ayr United	3 - 1	Stewart, McDonald, Harrow	1945	x	x		x		x	x	x	x		x			x			x	s	x					
15	17-Nov	FALKIRK	2 - 3	Dornan, Mauchlin	2012	x	x		x		x	x	x	x		x			x	s		x	s	x					
16	24-Nov	Clydebank	1 - 2	Gahagan	1248		x	x	s		x	x		x		x			x	x			s	x	x	x			
17	01-Dec	Meadowbank	2 - 4	Stewart, Gahagan	1337		x	x	x		x			x		x				x			x		x	x	x	s	
18	08-Dec	AIRDRIE	1 - 1	McFadden	2838			x	x		x		x			x		x	x	x			s		x	x	x		
19	15-Dec	FORFAR ATHLETIC	2 - 0	Forbes, McAllister	1591			x	x		x		x	s		x			x	x				x	x	x			
20	22-Dec	Partick Thistle	1 - 2	OG	2012			x	x		x		x	x		x			x	x		x			x	x			
21	29-Dec	Kilmarnock	0 - 0		2050			x	x		x					x			x	x		x		x	x		x	x	
22	02-Jan	HAMILTON ACADEMICAL	3 - 0	McAllister, Stewart, Harrow	3878			x	x		x		x	x		x			x			x	x		x		x		
23	05-Jan	CLYDE	0 - 0		2729			x	x		x		x	x		x			x			x	x		x		x	s	
24	19-Jan	East Fife	2 - 1	Harrow, Stewart	1546			x	x		x			x	s	x			x	s		x	x		x		x		x
25	02-Feb	St. Johnstone	1 - 0	Blair	1657		x	x	x		x			x		x			x	s		x	x	x	x				s
26	09-Feb	Falkirk	2 - 0	Blair, Stewart	1700			x	x		x		x	x		x			x	s		x	x		x	x			
27	23-Feb	KILMARNOCK	2 - 2	Murray, Stewart	2288			x	x		x		x	x		x			x	x		x	s		x	s	x		
28	26-Feb	Brechin City	2 - 0	Kennedy, Blair	682			x	x		x		x	x		x			x			x	x		x	x		s	
29	02-Mar	Ayr United	2 - 1	Kennedy, Stewart	1837		s	x	x		x		x	x		x			x			x	x		x	x			
p 20/3	09-Mar	AIRDRIE	2 - 0	Murray, Walker	4483			x	x		x		x	x		x			x	s		x	x		x	x			
31	16-Mar	CLYDEBANK	1 - 0	Murray	2076		s	x	x		x		x	x					x	s		x	x		x	x		x	
32	23-Mar	Clyde	0 - 1		1816		s	x	x		x		x	x					x	s		x	x		x	x		x	
33	30-Mar	MEADOWBANK	0 - 1		2010			x	x		x		x	x		x			x	x		x	s		x	x		s	
34	06-Apr	EAST FIFE	5 - 0	Murray (2), Blair, Walker, Gahagan	1930		x	x	x				x	x		x				s			x	x	x	x	x	s	
p 24/4	13-Apr	ST. JOHNSTONE	4 - 0	Forbes, Stewart, McAllister, Gahagan	2376			x	x		x		x	x		x			x	s		x	x		x		x	s	
36	20-Apr	Partick Thistle	1 - 0	McStay	2500			x	x		x		x			x		s	x	s		x	x		x		x		x
37	27-Apr	Hamilton Academical	1 - 1	Harrow	2926			x	x		x		x	x		x			x	s		x	s		x		x		x
38	04-May	BRECHIN	2 - 1	Stewart, Walker	3007			x	x		x		x	x		x			x	s		x	s		x		x	x	
39	11-May	Forfar Athletic	0 - 0		1700			x	x		x		x	s		x			x			x	s		x		x	x	x

LEAGUE CUP

	Date	Opponent	Score	Scorers	Att.	Maxwell	Dornan	Murray	Forbes	Stevens	MacLeod	McDonald	McAllister	Stewart	Alexander	Harrow	Lyall	McFadden	Boyd	Gahagan	Cormack	Mauchline	Blair	Clark R	Gardner	Kennedy	Doyle	Walker	McStay
	22-Aug	Ayr United	0 - 1		3076	x	x	x	x	x	x		x			x		x	x	x								x	

SCOTTISH CUP

	Date	Opponent	Score	Scorers	Att.	Maxwell	Dornan	Murray	Forbes	Stevens	MacLeod	McDonald	McAllister	Stewart	Alexander	Harrow	Lyall	McFadden	Boyd	Gahagan	Cormack	Mauchline	Blair	Clark R	Gardner	Kennedy	Doyle	Walker	McStay
	26-Jan	DUMBARTON	4 - 0	Murray (2), Stewart, Blair	3084		x	x	x		x			x		x			x	s		x	x	x	x				s
	20-Feb	Meadowbank Th.	2 - 0	Harrow (2)	2095		x	x	x		x			x		x			x	s		x	x		x	x			s
	09-Mar	FORFAR ATHLETIC	4 - 1	Blair (2), McAllister, Gahagan	4062			x	x		x		x	x		x			x	s		x	x		x	x			s
S/F	13-Apr	CELTIC	0 - 0		30563			x	x		x		x	x		x			x	s		x	x		x		x	s	
S/F R	17-Apr	CELTIC	0 - 3		25677			x	x		x		x			x			x	s		x	x		x		x	x	

LANARKSHIRE CUP

Date	Opponent	Score	Scorers
04-Aug	ALBION ROVERS	2 - 1	Harrow (2)
07-Aug	AIRDRIE	3 - 1	MacLeod, Stewart, McFadden

FRIENDLIES

Date	Opponent	Score	Scorers
13-Jan	RANGERS/ CELTIC SEL.	1 - 3	Joe Jordan
31-Jul	DONCASTER ROVERS	1 - 1	McAllister
02-Aug	MIDDLESBROUGH	0 - 2	

1985 Div. 1

		Pl.	Home W.	D.	L.	F.	A.	Away W.	D.	L.	F.	A.	F. (Total)	A.	Pts.
1	MOTHERWELL	39	11	4	4	34	14	10	4	6	28	22	62	36	50
2	Clydebank	39	11	4	4	31	16	6	10	4	26	21	57	37	48
3	Falkirk	39	9	3	7	36	31	10	4	6	29	23	65	54	45
4	Hamilton Acad.	39	8	5	7	23	24	8	6	5	25	25	48	49	43
5	Airdrieonians	39	11	1	7	43	33	6	7	7	27	26	70	59	42
6	Forfar Athletic	39	9	7	4	27	18	5	6	8	27	31	54	49	41
7	Ayr United	39	9	6	5	31	25	6	3	10	26	27	57	52	39
8	Clyde	39	9	5	6	31	26	5	6	8	16	22	47	48	39
9	Brechin City	39	7	5	8	25	28	7	4	8	24	29	49	57	37
10	East Fife	39	6	6	8	26	25	6	6	7	29	31	55	56	36
11	Partick Thistle	39	8	5	6	28	22	5	4	11	22	33	50	55	35
12	Kilmarnock	39	8	8	4	23	23	4	2	13	19	38	42	61	34
13	Meadowbank T.	39	5	5	9	25	33	6	5	9	25	33	50	66	32
14	St. Johnstone	39	4	4	11	23	33	6	1	13	28	45	51	78	25

1984-85 Season

Back : Alexander, McAllister, McGoldrick, Maxwell, Stevens, McKeown, Kennedy, MacLeod, McLean
Middle : Forsyth, Walker, Dornan, McCart, Boyd, McBride, Layll, McStay, Forbes, Cormack, Hogg
Front : O'Hare, Gahagan, Wishart, Mauchline, McLean, Murray, Weldon, Harrow, Grant

1985-86 Season

Back: McCart, Clark, Kennedy, McAlister, McKeown, Gardiner, Maxwell, Forbes, McLeod, McStay, Allan
Middle: Blair, Dornan, Griffen, Boyd, Diver, McLean, McBride, McFadden, Stewart, Doyle, Findlay
Front: McKenzie (Physio), Wishart, Gahagan, Harrow, McLean (Man), Forsyth (Coach), Mauchlen, Walker, Murray, O'Hare, Murray (Youth Coach)

1985-86: Premier League

No.	Date	Opponent	Score	Scorers	Att.	Maxwell	Gardner	MacLeod	Wishart	Dorman	Kennedy	Murray	Doyle	Forbes	McCart	Boyd	McBride	Reilly	Stewart	McAllister	Baptie	Weir	Harrow	Mauchline	Wright	Blair	Clark J	Gahagan	Walker	McStay	Clark R	Mulvane	Griffin	McFadden
1	10-Aug	CLYDEBANK	0 - 0		2791		x	x			x	x				x			s	x			x	x		x	x		x					
p 15/1	17-Aug	Celtic	1 - 2	Blair	20189		x	x		x	x	x	x		s	x							x			x	x		s	x				
p 9/4	24-Aug	Aberdeen	1 - 1	Blair	14000		x	x		x	x	x		x		x							x			x	x			x				
p 12/3	31-Aug	DUNDEE UNITED	0 - 1		3327		x	x		x		x		x		x			x			s	x			x	x			x				
5	07-Sep	DUNDEE	1 - 3	Stewart	2607		x	x		x	x	x		x		x			x				x			x	x			s				
6	14-Sep	St. Mirren	1 - 4	Wright	3520		x	x				x			x	x		x	x			x			x	x		s	s	x				
7	21-Sep	HEARTS	2 - 1	Gahagan, Harrow	4806		x		x	x			x	x	x			x					x		x	x		x			s			
8	28-Sep	Hibernian	0 - 1		7000		x		x	x			x	x	x	x		s					x		x	x		x						
9	05-Oct	RANGERS	0 - 3		12711		x		x	x	x		x	x	x							x	x		x	s		s	x					
p 5/4	12-Oct	Clydebank	1 - 1	Walker	1941		x		x	x	x		x	x		x		x							x	x			x	s				
p 30/4	19-Oct	CELTIC	1 - 2	Walker	13902		x	x	x	x	x			x		x		s							x	x		x	x					
12	26-Oct	Dundee	1 - 3	Reilly	4628		x	x	x	x	x				x	x		x							x	x		s	x	s				
13	02-Nov	ST. MIRREN	3 - 1	Gahagan (2), Wright	3327		x	x	x	x	x			x		x		x					s		x	s		x	x					
14	09-Nov	Dundee United	0 - 3		5494		x	x	x	x		x		x	x			x					x		x			x						
15	16-Nov	ABERDEEN	1 - 1	Wright	4960		x	x	x	x		x		x	x			s					x		x	x		x		s				
16	23-Nov	Hearts	0 - 3		10119		x	x	x	x	s	x		x	x			s					x		x	x		x						
17	07-Dec	Rangers	0 - 1		12872		x		x	x	x	x		x	x	x		x	s				s		x							x		
18	14-Dec	CLYDEBANK	3 - 0	Reilly (2), Wright	1995		x	x	x	x	x			x		x		x	s				s		x			x				x		
p 15/1	21-Dec	Celtic	2 - 3	Reilly, Doyle	12002		x	x		x		x	x	x		x		x			x				x	x								
p 9/4	28-Dec	Aberdeen	2 - 3	Reilly, Kennedy	10300		x	x	x	x	x	x		x		x		x							x				x					
p 12/3	01-Jan	DUNDEE UNITED	2 - 0	Reilly (2)	5710		x	x	x			x	x	x		x		x			x				x				x					
22	04-Jan	HEARTS	1 - 3	Reilly	9850		x	x	x	x			x		x	x		x							x	s				x		x		
23	11-Jan	St. Mirren	0 - 1		3080		x	x	x		x		x	x		x		x	s				x		x			x		s				
24	18-Jan	DUNDEE	2 - 2	Baptie (2)	2204		x	x		x	s		x	x		x		x			x				x			x				x		
25	01-Feb	Hibernian	0 - 4		5002		x	x				x	x	x		x		x			x					x			x				x	s
26	08-Feb	RANGERS	1 - 0	Walker	11619		x	x		x		s	x	x	x	x		x			x		x					s	x					
p 5/4	22-Feb	Clydebank	1 - 1	Wright	1164		x	x	x			x		x		x		x			x				x			x	x					
p 30/4	01-Mar	CELTIC	0 - 2		12968	x		x	x	x	x	x				x		x			s				x			s	x		x			
29	15-Mar	Hearts	0 - 2		12071		x	x	x			x	x	x		x		x			x		s		x	s			x					
30	18-Mar	HIBERNIAN	2 - 0	Harrow, McLeod	3266		x	x	x			x	x	x		x					x		x			x		s	x			s		
31	22-Mar	Dundee United	0 - 4		5710		x	x	x			x	x	x		x		s			x		x		x	x			s					
32	29-Mar	ABERDEEN	0 - 1		4597		x	x	x	s		x	x	x		x		x			x				x				x					
33	12-Apr	ST. MIRREN	1 - 2	Walker	2294		x	s	x		x	x		x		x		x			x				x			x	x					
34	19-Apr	Dundee	0 - 4		3763	x		x	x	x	x	x				x		x			s				x				x		x			
35	26-Apr	HIBERNIAN	3 - 1	Reilly, Wright, Griffin	4061	x		x	x	s			x	x		x		x			x				x				x				x	
36	03-May	Rangers	0 - 2		9138	x		x	x				x	x		x		x			x				x			s	x				x	

LEAGUE CUP

No.	Date	Opponent	Score	Scorers	Att.	Maxwell	Gardner	MacLeod	Wishart	Dorman	Kennedy	Murray	Doyle	Forbes	McCart	Boyd	McBride	Reilly	Stewart	McAllister	Baptie	Weir	Harrow	Mauchline	Wright	Blair	Clark J	Gahagan	Walker	McStay	Clark R	Mulvane	Griffin	McFadden
	21-Aug	PARTICK THISTLE	1 - 0	Kennedy	2996		x	x			x	x	x	x		x		x				x	x			s			x	s				
	28-Aug	Hibernian	1 - 6	Harrow	5369		x			x		x	x	x		x					x		x				x			x				

SCOTTISH CUP

No.	Date	Opponent	Score	Scorers	Att.	Maxwell	Gardner	MacLeod	Wishart	Dorman	Kennedy	Murray	Doyle	Forbes	McCart	Boyd	McBride	Reilly	Stewart	McAllister	Baptie	Weir	Harrow	Mauchline	Wright	Blair	Clark J	Gahagan	Walker	McStay	Clark R	Mulvane	Griffin	McFadden
	25-Jan	BRECHIN	1 - 1	Kennedy	2648		x	x		x	x	s	x	x		x		x				x						x	s			x		
	11-Feb	Brechin City	1 - 1	Reilly	1056		x	x		x		x	x	x	x	x		x					x					s	x					
*	14-Feb	BRECHIN	2 - 0	Doyle, Wright	1156		x	s		x	x	x	x	x		x		x					s		x			x	x					
	05-Mar	Alloa Athletic	2 - 1	Harrow, Blair	1498		x		x	x		x		x	s	x		x					x		x	s			x				x	
	08-Mar	DUNDEE UNITED	0 - 1		2815		x	x	x			x	x	x		x					x		x		x	x			s					

* On neutral ground.

LANARKSHIRE CUP

	Date	Opponent	Score	Scorers
	03-Aug	Albion Rovers	1 - 1	Harrow
	03-Aug	Hamilton Academical	0 - 1	

FRIENDLIES

	Date	Opponent	Score	Scorers
	27-Jul	Inverness Clach	3 - 1	McAllister, Harrow, Divers
	29-Jul	Forres Mech	2 - 1	Harrow (2)
	31-Jul	Clyde	2 - 1	Stewart (2)

1986 Premier League

		Pl.	Home W.	Home D.	Home L.	Home F.	Home A.	Away W.	Away D.	Away L.	Away F.	Away A.	F. (Total)	A. (Total)	Pts.
1	Celtic	36	10	6	2	27	15	10	4	4	40	23	67	38	50
2	Heart of Mid.	36	13	5	0	38	10	7	5	6	21	23	59	33	50
3	Dundee United	36	10	6	2	38	15	8	5	5	21	16	59	31	47
4	Aberdeen	36	11	4	3	38	15	5	8	5	24	16	62	31	44
5	Rangers	36	10	4	4	34	18	3	5	10	19	27	53	45	35
6	Dundee	36	11	2	5	32	20	3	5	10	13	31	45	51	35
7	St. Mirren	36	9	2	7	26	24	4	3	11	16	39	42	63	31
8	Hibernian	36	6	4	8	27	25	5	2	11	22	38	49	63	28
9	MOTHERWELL	36	7	3	8	23	23	0	3	15	10	43	33	66	20
10	Clydebank	36	4	6	8	18	32	2	2	14	11	45	29	77	20

1986-87: Premier League

No.	Date	Opponent	Score	Scorers	Att.	Gardiner	Wishart	Murray	Philliben	Paterson	MacAdam	Kennedy	Boyd	Kirk	Smith	Walker	Wright	Farningham	Gahagan	Reilly	Mair	Candlish	Baptie	Maxwell	McKeown	Forbes	McStay	Doyle	Fraser	McCart	Arnott
1	09-Aug	Falkirk	1 - 1	Walker	3250	x	x	x				x	x		x	x	x			x	x					x	s		s		
2	13-Aug	CELTIC	0 - 4		13325	x	x	x				x	x		x	x				x	x					x	x		s		
3	16-Aug	ST. MIRREN	1 - 1	Walker	2844	x	x	x				x	x		x	x			s	x	x					x	s	x			
4	23-Aug	Hibernian	0 - 0		4461	x	x	s				x	x	x	x	x				s	x					x	x	x			
5	30-Aug	Hamilton Academical	3 - 0	Kirk (2), Smith	4333	x	x	s				x	x	x	x	x	x		x	s						x		x			
6	06-Sep	RANGERS	0 - 2		17013	x	x	x	x			x	x	x	x	x	x		s	x									s		
7	13-Sep	DUNDEE	0 - 0		2880	x	x	s	x			x	x	x	x	x	x		s	x	x										
8	20-Sep	Hearts	0 - 4		11119	x	x	s	x			x	x	x	x	x	x	x	s	x											
9	27-Sep	CLYDEBANK	0 - 1		2294		x	s	x			x	x	x	x	x	x	x	x	s				x							
10	04-Oct	Aberdeen	2 - 2	Kennedy, Walker	8751	x	x	x	x			x	x	x	x	x	x	x		s			s								
11	08-Oct	Dundee United	0 - 4		5740	x	x	x	x			x	x		x	x	x	x		x	s		s								
12	11-Oct	FALKIRK	2 - 2	Walker, Smith	2743	x	x	s	x			x	x	x	x	x	x			x	x		s								
13	18-Oct	Celtic	1 - 3	Kirk	19395	x	x		x		x	x	x	x	s	x	x	x		s	x										
14	25-Oct	HIBERNIAN	4 - 1	Walker, Reilly, Farningham, MacAdam	4007		x	x	s		x		x	x	x	x	x	x		x	s			x							
15	29-Oct	St. Mirren	0 - 1		2184		x	x	x		x			x	x	x	x	x		x	s			x				s			
16	01-Nov	HAMILTON ACADEMICAL	1 - 1	Smith	3349		x	x	x		x				x	x	x	x	s	x			s	x				x			
17	08-Nov	Rangers	1 - 0	Farningham	30994		x	x	x		x	x			x	x	x	x	s	x			s	x							
18	15-Nov	Dundee	1 - 1	Wishart	4167		x	x	x		x	x		x	x	x	x	x	s				s	x							
19	19-Nov	HEARTS	2 - 3	Walker, Farningham	6341		x	s	x		x	x		x	x	x	x	x	s				x	x							
20	22-Nov	Clydebank	3 - 2	Smith (2), OG	1326		x	s	x		x	x		x	x	x	x	x	x				s	x							
21	29-Nov	ABERDEEN	0 - 1		4479		x	x	x		x	x		x	x	x	x	x			s		s	x							
22	03-Dec	DUNDEE UNITED	0 - 2		2312		x	x	x		x	s		x	x	x	x	x	s		x			x							
23	06-Dec	Falkirk	0 - 1		2500	x	x		x		x	x		x	x	x	x				x	s	x					s			
24	13-Dec	CELTIC	1 - 1	Smith	11760	x	x		x		x	x		x	x	x	x				x		x					s			
25	20-Dec	Hibernian	1 - 0	Smith	4500	x	x		x		x	x		x	x	x	x	s		s	x		x								
26	27-Dec	ST. MIRREN	1 - 2	Reilly	3804	x	x		x		x	x		s	x	x	x	x		x	s		x								
27	01-Jan	Hamilton Academical	2 - 4	Smith, Kirk	3487		x			x	x		x	x	x	x	x	x	s	x			s	x							
28	06-Jan	RANGERS	0 - 1		19658		x		x	x	x		x	x	x	s	x	x		x			s	x							
p 27/1	10-Jan	DUNDEE	2 - 0	Walker, Reilly	2340	x	x		x	x	x		x		x	x	x			s	x								x		
p 25/2	17-Jan	Hearts	1 - 1	Kirk	9639	x	x		x	x		x	x	x	x	x	x	x			s		s								
31	24-Jan	CLYDEBANK	3 - 2	Wishart, Smith, Walker	2202		x		x	x	x		x		x	x	x		s		x		x	x							
32	07-Feb	Aberdeen	0 - 1		10000	x	x		x	x	x		x	x	s	x	x	x	s	x											
33	14-Feb	Dundee United	0 - 2		9904	x	x		x	x	x		x	x	x	x	x	s		x									s		
34	28-Feb	FALKIRK	1 - 0	Paterson	2958	x	x		x	x	x		x	x	x	x	s		s	x	x										
35	07-Mar	Celtic	1 - 3	Kirk	14840	x	x		x	x	x	s	x	x	x	x	x			x	s										
p 24/3	14-Mar	HIBERNIAN	2 - 1	Walker (2)	3469		x		x	x	x		x	x	x	x	x		s	x				x					s		
37	21-Mar	St. Mirren	1 - 1	OG	2624	x	x		x	x	x			x	x		x		s	x		x	x						s		
38	28-Mar	Rangers	0 - 1		37305		x			x	x	x	x	x	x	x	x	x			s			x					s		
39	04-Apr	HAMILTON ACADEMICAL	3 - 0	Kirk (2), Wishart	2356		x		x	x	x		x	x	x	x	x	x	s		s			x							
40	11-Apr	HEARTS	0 - 1		3907		x		x	x	x		x	x	x	x	x	x	s					x							
41	18-Apr	Dundee	1 - 4	Kirk	3080		x		x	x	x		x	x	x	x	x	x						x							s
42	25-Apr	ABERDEEN	0 - 2		2886		x		x	x	x		x	x	x	x	x		s		x				x						
43	02-May	Clydebank	0 - 0		1354		x		x	x	x		x	x	x	x	x				x			x					s		
44	09-May	DUNDEE UNITED	1 - 0	Mair	2340		x		x	x	x		x	x	x	x	x		s		x			x					s		

LEAGUE CUP

Rd	Date	Opponent	Score	Scorers	Att.	Gardiner	Wishart	Murray	Philliben	Paterson	MacAdam	Kennedy	Boyd	Kirk	Smith	Walker	Wright	Farningham	Gahagan	Reilly	Mair	Candlish	Baptie	Maxwell	McKeown	Forbes	McStay	Doyle	Fraser	McCart	Arnott
	20-Aug	ARBROATH	4 - 0	Smith (2), Reilly, Mair	2334	x	x	x				s	x	x	x	x			s	x	x					x	x				
	27-Aug	CLYDEBANK	2 - 0	Doyle, Gahagan	2013	x	x	s				x	x	x	x	x			x	x						x		x			
	03-Sep	FORFAR ATHLETIC	2 - 1	Wishart, Reilly	3010	x	x	x					x	x	x	x			x	x								x		x	
S/F	23-Sep	CELTIC *	2 - 2	Smith , Walker	26541	x	x	x	x			x	x	x	x	s	x	x	s	x											

* Lost on pens.

SCOTTISH CUP

Rd	Date	Opponent	Score	Scorers	Att.	Gardiner	Wishart	Murray	Philliben	Paterson	MacAdam	Kennedy	Boyd	Kirk	Smith	Walker	Wright	Farningham	Gahagan	Reilly	Mair	Candlish	Baptie	Maxwell	McKeown	Forbes	McStay	Doyle	Fraser	McCart	Arnott
	31-Jan	PARTICK THISTLE	3 - 1	Smith, Reilly, Kirk	5177	x	x		x	x	x		x	x	x	x	x		s										x		
	21-Feb	Hamilton Academical	2 - 1	Kirk, Walker	7074	x	x		x	x	x		x	x	x	x	x	x	s	s											
	10-Mar	Hearts	1 - 1	Walker	22045	x	x		x	x	x	s	x	x	x	x	x	x			s										
rep.	17-Mar	HEARTS	0 - 1		15275	x	x		x	x	x		x	x	x	x	s	x	s		x										

FRIENDLIES

Date	Opponent	Score	Scorers
03-Nov	LIVERPOOL	1 - 1	Kirk
25-Jul	Elgin	2 - 1	Gahagan, Baptie
26-Jul	Inverness Clach	3 - 0	Kirk, Smith, Fraser
27-Jul	Cove Rangers	2 - 1	Walker (2)
02-Aug	Southport	3 - 0	McLeod, Reilly, Smith
03-Aug	Fleetwood	3 - 1	Boyd, Reilly, Mair

1987 Premier League

		Pl.	Home					Away					F.	A.	Pts.
			W.	D.	L.	F.	A.	W.	D.	L.	F.	A.	(Total)		
1	Rangers	44	18	2	2	45	6	13	5	4	40	17	85	23	69
2	Celtic	44	16	5	1	57	17	11	4	7	33	24	90	41	63
3	Dundee United	44	15	5	2	38	15	9	7	6	28	21	66	36	60
4	Aberdeen	44	13	6	3	32	11	8	10	4	31	18	63	29	58
5	Heart of Mid.	44	13	7	2	42	19	8	7	7	22	24	64	43	56
6	Dundee	44	11	6	5	49	31	7	6	9	25	26	74	57	48
7	St. Mirren	44	9	5	8	23	20	3	7	12	13	31	36	51	36
8	MOTHERWELL	44	7	5	10	24	28	4	7	11	19	36	43	64	34
9	Hibernian	44	6	8	8	24	30	4	5	13	20	40	44	70	33
10	Falkirk	44	4	9	9	17	28	4	1	17	14	42	31	70	26
11	Clydebank	44	3	7	12	19	40	3	5	14	16	53	35	93	24
12	Hamilton Acad.	44	2	4	16	15	40	4	5	13	24	53	39	93	21

1986-87 Season

Back ; Dornan, McStay, McCart, Allan, Kennedy, Kirk, Smith, Wright, Gahagan
Middle : Candlish, McBride, Wishart, Maxwell, Gardiner, McKeown, Mair, Murray, Reilly, Hart (Physio)
Front : Jenks, Murray, Fraser, Walker, Boyd, Reilly, Doyle, Forsyth, McLean

1987-88 Season

Back : Wright, Cadden, Melvin, T McAdam, McCart, Paterson, Kennedy, Kirk, Clinton, Philliben, Mair.
Middle: Murray, McBride, Griffin, Gahagan, Farningham, P Smith, Duncan, Maxwell, McKeown, McKinstry, Dolan, M Reilly, Leitch, Bryce, Hart.
Front : T McLean, Fraser, Fairlie, Russell, Wishart, Boyd, Murray, J Reilly, Arnott, Candlish, T Forsyth.

1987-88: Premier League

	Date	Opponent	Score	Scorers	Att.	Duncan	MacAdam	Wishart	Murray	Philliben	Paterson	Boyd	Griffin	Fairlie	Russell	Smith	Farningham	Cowan	Kirk	Mair	Candlish	Gahagan	Caughey	Maxwell	Kennedy	Fraser	McBride	Shanks	Kinnaird	Wright	Arnott
1	08-Aug	ST. MIRREN	2 - 1	Fairlie, Russell	4134	x	x	x	x		x	x		x	x	x	s		x	x		s									
2	12-Aug	Dundee United	1 - 1	Boyd	6663	x	x	x	x		x	x		x	x	x	s		x	x										s	
3	15-Aug	Celtic	1 - 4	Kirk	24478	x	x	x	x		x	x		x	x	x	s		x	x										s	
4	22-Aug	ABERDEEN	0 - 1		4858	x	x	x	x		x	x		x	x	x			x	x					s					s	
5	29-Aug	FALKIRK	1 - 2	Mair	3132	x	x	x		x	x	x		x	x	x			x	x		s								s	
6	05-Sep	Dunfermline	1 - 0	Paterson	5500	x	x	x	x		x	x		s	x	x	x		s	x		x									
7	12-Sep	Hearts	0 - 1		11488	x	x	x		x	x	x		s	x	x	x		x	x										s	
8	19-Sep	RANGERS	0 - 1		19480	x	x	x		x	x	x		s	s	x	x		x	x	s	x								s	
9	26-Sep	DUNDEE	0 - 2		2656	x	x	x		x	x	x		x	x	x	x			s		x				s					
10	03-Oct	Morton	1 - 1	Philliben	2554	x	x	x		x	x	x		x	x	x			x	s		x				s					
11	06-Oct	HIBERNIAN	1 - 0	Wishart	4879	x	x	x		x	x	x			x	x			x	s	x	s				x					
12	10-Oct	St. Mirren	0 - 1		4232		x	x		x	x	x		s	x	x		x	x	s				x		x					
13	17-Oct	Falkirk	0 - 3		3000	x	x	x		x	x	x		x	x		x	x	s			x				s					
14	24-Oct	DUMFERMLINE	3 - 2	Farningham (2), Candlish	3685	x	x	x	x		x	x			x		x	x			x	s				x	s				
15	27-Oct	HEARTS	0 - 3		6699	x	x	x	x	s	x	x					x	x			x	x	s			x					
16	31-Oct	Rangers	0 - 1		36583	x	x	x	x	x	x						x	x	s		s	x	x			x					
17	07-Nov	DUNDEE UNITED	2 - 1	Boyd, Cowan	2927	x	x	x	x	x	x	x					x	x	s		x	x	s								
18	14-Nov	Hibernian	0 - 1		7000	x	x	x	x	x	x	x						x	x			x	x			s					s
19	17-Nov	CELTIC	0 - 2		17261	x		x	x	x	x	x						x	s		x	x	s		x	x					
20	21-Nov	Aberdeen	0 - 1		9700	x		x	x	x	x	x			x			x	x		x	s	s			x					
21	24-Nov	Dundee	0 - 2		3695	x		x		x	x	x	x		x		x	x	s	x			x								s
22	28-Nov	MORTON	1 - 0	Cowan	3008	x		x	x	x	x	x			x		x	x	x		x		s			s					
23	05-Dec	ST. MIRREN	2 - 1	Philliben, Farningham	2928	x		x	x	x	x	x					x	x	s		s		x			x	x				
24	12-Dec	Dundee United	1 - 3	Cowan	5792	x		x	x	x	x	x			x		x	x			s		x			s	x				
25	16-Dec	Hearts	1 - 1	Cowan	9047	x		x	x	x	x	x	s		x		x	x	x				x				s				
26	19-Dec	RANGERS	0 - 2		15346	x		x	x	x	x	x			x	s	x	x	s				x				x				
27	26-Dec	Dunfermline	1 - 1	Kirk	5506	x		x	x	x	x	x				x	x	x	x				x			s	s				
28	01-Jan	FALKIRK	0 - 0		4168	x		x	x	x	x	x	s			x	x	x	x				x				s				
29	09-Jan	DUNDEE	3 - 3	Smith, Farningham, Cowan	2785	x	s	x	x	x	x		x			x	x	x	x	x		s									
30	16-Jan	Morton	2 - 0	Smith (2)	3000	x	x	x		x	x	x	s			x	x	x	x	x		s									
31	23-Jan	ABERDEEN	2 - 1	Paterson, Farningham	6584	x	x	x		x	x	x			s	x	x	x	x	x		s									
32	06-Feb	Celtic	0 - 1		25035	x	x	x	x	s	x	x			x	x	x	x		x							s				
33	13-Feb	HIBERNIAN	0 - 2		5421	x	x	x	x	s	x	x			x	x	x	x					s				x				
34	27-Feb	St. Mirren	0 - 0		5419	x	x	x			x	x	x		x	x		x	x	x						s	s				
35	08-Mar	HEARTS	0 - 2		5831	x	x	x		s	x	x	x			x		x	x	s								x	x		
36	12-Mar	Rangers	0 - 1		39650	x	x	x			x	x	s			x		x	x			s						x	x		
37	19-Mar	Falkirk	0 - 0		5500	x	x	x		x	x	x			s	x		x	x			s						x	x		
38	26-Mar	DUNFERMLINE	3 - 2	Cowan (2), Russell	8958	x	x	x		x	x	x			x	x		x	x			s						s	x		
39	02-Apr	MORTON	1 - 0	Russell	4764	x	x	x		x	x	x			x	x		x	x			s						s	x		
40	09-Apr	Dundee	2 - 1	Cowan, Kirk	3732	x	x	x		x	x	x			x			x	s	x		s						x	x		
41	16-Apr	DUNDEE UNITED	4 - 2	Kirk (2), MacAdam, Russell	3922	x	x	x		x	x	x			x	s	s	x	x	x									x		
42	23-Apr	Hibernian	1 - 1	Farningham	5500	x	x	x		x	x	x			x	s	x	x	x			s							x		
43	30-Apr	CELTIC	0 - 1		13874	x	x	x		x	x	x			x	s		x	x	x		s							x		
44	07-May	Aberdeen	0 - 0		5550	x	x	x		x	x	x			x	s	x	x	x			s							x		

LEAGUE CUP

	Date	Opponent	Score	Scorers	Att.	Duncan	MacAdam	Wishart	Murray	Philliben	Paterson	Boyd	Griffin	Fairlie	Russell	Smith	Farningham	Cowan	Kirk	Mair	Candlish	Gahagan	Caughey	Maxwell	Kennedy	Fraser	McBride	Shanks	Kinnaird	Wright	Arnott
	19-Aug	AIRDRIE	3 - 1	Boyd, Fairlie, Mair	3716	x	x	x	x			x		x	x	x			x	x		s			x					s	
	26-Aug	ALBION ROVERS	4 - 0	Russell (2), Kirk, OG	2744	x		x	x		x	x		x	x	x			x	x		s			x					s	
	01-Sep	HIBERNIAN	1 - 0	Fairlie	8974	x	x	x	x		x	x		x	s	x	x		x	x										s	
S/F	23-Sep	RANGERS	1 - 3	Smith	45938	x	x	x		x	x	x		s	x	x	x		x	s		x									

SCOTTISH CUP

	Date	Opponent	Score	Scorers	Att.	Duncan	MacAdam	Wishart	Murray	Philliben	Paterson	Boyd	Griffin	Fairlie	Russell	Smith	Farningham	Cowan	Kirk	Mair	Candlish	Gahagan	Caughey	Maxwell	Kennedy	Fraser	McBride	Shanks	Kinnaird	Wright	Arnott
	30-Jan	KILMARNOCK	0 - 0		6488	x	x	x		x	x	x				x	x	x	x	x	s	s									
rep.	03-Feb	Kilmarnock	3 - 1	Mair, Farningham, McBride	7591	x	x	x		x	x	x			x	x	x	x	s	x							s				
	20-Feb	Dundee	0 - 2		7243	x	x	x			x	x	x		s	x	x	x	x	x							s				

FRIENDLIES

Date	Opponent	Score	Scorers
30-Jul	Queen of the South	0 - 0	
01-Aug	Arbroath	4 - 3	Kirk (4)
25-Jul	Elgin City	1 - 1	Farningham
26-Jul	Inverness Clach	3 - 0	Kirk, Smith, Fraser
27-Jul	Fort William	4 - 0	Boyd (2), Kirk, OG

1988 Premier League

		Pl.	Home W.	D.	L.	F.	A.	Away W.	D.	L.	F.	A.	F. (Total)	A.	Pts.
1	Celtic	44	16	5	1	42	11	15	5	2	37	12	79	23	72
2	Heart of Mid.	44	13	8	1	37	17	10	8	4	37	15	74	32	62
3	Rangers	44	14	4	4	49	17	12	4	6	36	17	85	34	60
4	Aberdeen	44	11	7	4	27	11	10	10	2	29	14	56	25	59
5	Dundee United	44	8	7	7	29	24	8	8	6	25	23	54	47	47
6	Hibernian	44	8	8	6	18	17	4	11	7	23	25	41	42	43
7	Dundee	44	9	5	8	31	25	8	2	12	39	39	70	64	41
8	MOTHERWELL	44	10	2	10	25	31	3	8	11	12	25	37	56	36
9	St. Mirren	44	5	11	6	22	28	5	4	13	19	36	41	64	35
10	Falkirk	44	8	4	10	26	35	2	7	13	15	40	41	75	31
11	Dunfermline Ath.	44	6	6	10	23	35	2	4	16	18	49	41	84	26
12	Morton	44	3	7	12	19	47	0	3	19	8	53	27	100	16

1988-89: Premier League

	Date	Opponent	Score	Scorers	Att.	Duncan	Maxwell	Wishart	Boyd	Philliben	Paterson	McCart	MacAdam	Farningham	McBride	Russell	Smith	Cowan	MacCabe	Kirk	Kinnaird	Gahagan	Arnott	O'Neill	McKeown	Griffin	Mair	Kennedy	Shanks	Bryce	Dolan
1	13-Aug	Hibernian	0 - 1		10010	x		x	x	x	x	x		x		x	x	s		x	x						s				
2	20-Aug	DUNDEE	1 - 1	McBride	3803			x	x	x	x	x		x	x	x	s	x		s	x				x						
3	27-Aug	Hamilton Academical	0 - 1		4336	x		x	x	x	x		x		x	x	x	x		x			s						s		
4	03-Sep	RANGERS	0 - 2		20112	x			x	x	x		x	x		x	x			x	x	s				x			s		
5	17-Sep	St. Mirren	0 - 1		4045	x		x	x	s	x		x	x	x	x			x	x	x		s								
6	24-Sep	DUNDEE UNITED	1 - 2	Kirk	3559	x		x	x	x	x		x	x	s	s		x	x	x	x										
7	28-Sep	Celtic	1 - 3	Kirk	20187	x		x	x	x	x		x	x		s		s	x	x	x	x									
8	01-Oct	ABERDEEN	1 - 1	Farningham	4225	x		x	x	x	x	x		x		x			x	x	x	s	s								
9	08-Oct	Hearts	2 - 2	Farningham, Paterson	8809	x		x	x	x	x	x		x		x		s	x	x	x	s									
10	12-Oct	Dundee	1 - 1	Boyd	4161			x	x	x	x	x		x	s	s		x	x	x	x				x						
11	22-Oct	HIBERNIAN	1 - 1	Cowan	5904	x		x	x	x	x	x		x		s		x	x	x	x	s									
12	29-Oct	Dundee United	1 - 1	Farningham	6266	x		x	x	x	x	x		x		x		x		x	x		s				s				
13	01-Nov	ST. MIRREN	1 - 2	Kirk	3773	x		x	x	x	x		s	x		x		x		x	x		x							s	
14	05-Nov	Rangers	1 - 2	Russell	35060	x		x	x	x			x	x		x		s		x	x	x					s	x			
15	12-Nov	HAMILTON ACADEMICAL	1 - 1	MacAdam	5659	x		x	s	x	x		x	x		x		x			x			x			x			s	
16	19-Nov	Aberdeen	1 - 2	Russell	10028	x		x	s	x	x		x	x		x		x	x			s		x					x		
17	26-Nov	HEARTS	2 - 0	Cowan, Kirk	6208	x		x	s	x	x		x		x	x		x	s	x	x			x							
18	03-Dec	CELTIC	1 - 3	Kirk	16392	x		x	s	x		x	x	x	x	s		x		x	x			x							
19	10-Dec	St. Mirren	1 - 2	Russell	4496	x		x	x	s		x	x	s	x	x		x		x	x			x							s
20	17-Dec	DUNDEE	1 - 0	Kirk	4560		x	x	x		x	x	x	x	x				s	x	x	x									
21	31-Dec	Hibernian	0 - 2		9000		x	x	x		x	x	x		x	x		s		x	x	s		x							
22	03-Jan	Hamilton Academical	0 - 2		5704		x	x	x		x	x	x		s	x		s	x	x	x			x							
23	07-Jan	RANGERS	2 - 1	Wishart, Kirk	19275		x	x	x		x	x	x		s	x		s	x		x			x					x		
24	14-Jan	Hearts	0 - 0		13283		x	x	x		x	x	x		s	x			x	x	x			x					s		
25	21-Jan	ABERDEEN	0 - 2		5906		x	x	x		x	x	x		x			x		x	x	s		x						s	
26	11-Feb	Celtic	2 - 1	Gahagan, Russell	21445		x	x	x		x	x	x			x				x	x	x		x			s			s	
p 14/3	25-Feb	DUNDEE UNITED	1 - 2	O'Neill	3545		x	x	s		x	x	x		x	x				x			x	x			x			s	
28	11-Mar	HIBERNIAN	0 - 0		5072		x	x	x		x	x	x			x				x			s	x			x			x	s
29	25-Mar	Dundee	1 - 2	Kirk	3718		x	x	x		x	x	x		s	x				x			s	x			x			x	
30	01-Apr	HAMILTON ACADEMICAL	1 - 0	Kirk	4683		x	x	x		x	s	x		x					x			s	x			x			x	x
31	06-Apr	Rangers	0 - 1		37782		x	x	x		x	x	x		s	x				x		x	x	x						s	
32	11-Apr	CELTIC	2 - 2	Gahagan, Arnott	10507		x	x	x		x	x	x		s	x				x		x	x	x						s	
33	22-Apr	Dundee United	1 - 1	Kirk	6301		x	x	x		x	x	x			x				x		x	x				s			s	x
34	29-Apr	ST. MIRREN	4 - 0	Kirk (4)	2703		x	x	x		x	x	x			x				x		x	x				s			s	x
35	06-May	Aberdeen	0 - 0		6500		x	x	x		x	x	x			x				x		x	x	x			s				s
36	13-May	HEARTS	1 - 1	O'Neill	4587		x	x	x		x	x	x			x				x		x	x	x			s				s

LEAGUE CUP

	Date	Opponent	Score	Scorers	Att.	Duncan	Maxwell	Wishart	Boyd	Philliben	Paterson	McCart	MacAdam	Farningham	McBride	Russell	Smith	Cowan	MacCabe	Kirk	Kinnaird	Gahagan	Arnott	O'Neill	McKeown	Griffin	Mair	Kennedy	Shanks	Bryce	Dolan
	17-Aug	Aidrie	1 - 0	Kirk	4500	x		x	x	s	x	x		x		x	x	x		x	x						s				
	24-Aug	Dunfermline Ath.	1 - 2	Kirk	6500	x		x	x	x	x				x	x	x	x		x	x		s						s		

SCOTTISH CUP

	Date	Opponent	Score	Scorers	Att.	Duncan	Maxwell	Wishart	Boyd	Philliben	Paterson	McCart	MacAdam	Farningham	McBride	Russell	Smith	Cowan	MacCabe	Kirk	Kinnaird	Gahagan	Arnott	O'Neill	McKeown	Griffin	Mair	Kennedy	Shanks	Bryce	Dolan
	28-Jan	Falkirk	1 - 1	Russell	7500		x	x	x		x	x	x			x			x	x	x			x			s			s	
rep.	01-Feb	FALKIRK	2 - 1	Kirk (2)	7029		x	x	x		x	x	x						x	x	x			x			s		x	s	
	18-Feb	Hibernian	1 - 2	Bryce	12000		x	x	x		x	x	x						x	x	x			x			s		x	s	

LANARKSHIRE CUP

	Date	Opponent	Score	Scorers
	26-Apr	Hamilton Academical		

FRIENDLIES

	Date	Opponent	Score	Scorers
	02-Aug	Raith Rovers	1 - 0	Smith
	04-Aug	Selkirk	4 - 0	
	05-Mar	ST. PATS	3 - 3	Kirk, McCart, Russell
	30-Jul	Elgin City	0 - 0	
	30-Jul	Fraserburgh		
	31-Jul	Deverondale		
	31-Jul	Peterhead	0 - 0	
	09-Aug	Nijmegan	0 - 1	
	??	Fortuna Sitard	1 - 2	

1989 Premier League

		Pl.	Home W.	D.	L.	F.	A.	Away W.	D.	L.	F.	A.	F. (Total)	A.	Pts.
1	Rangers	36	15	1	2	39	11	11	3	4	23	15	62	26	56
2	Aberdeen	36	10	7	1	26	10	8	7	3	25	15	51	25	50
3	Celtic	36	13	1	4	35	18	8	3	7	31	26	66	44	46
4	Dundee United	36	6	8	4	20	16	10	4	4	24	10	44	26	44
5	Hibernian	36	8	4	6	20	16	5	5	8	17	20	37	36	35
6	Heart of Mid.	36	7	6	5	22	17	2	7	9	13	25	35	42	31
7	St. Mirren	36	5	6	7	17	19	6	1	11	22	36	39	55	29
8	Dundee	36	8	4	6	22	21	1	6	11	12	27	34	48	28
9	MOTHERWELL	36	5	7	6	21	21	2	6	10	14	23	35	44	27
10	Hamilton Acad.	36	5	0	13	9	42	1	2	15	10	34	19	76	14

1988-89 Season

Back :Griffin, Smith, McAdam, Kennedy, Paterson, McCart, Kirk, Shanks, Philliben, Thomson, Gardner
Middle: Reilly, Mair, Farningham, Cowan, Maxwell, Duncan, McKeown, Wishart, Gahagan, McAnenay, Candlish
Front: Jenks (Coach), Bryce, Dolan, Fraser, Boyd, McLean (Man.), Kinnaird, McBride, Arnott, Russell, Forsyth (Coach)

1989-90 Season

Back: Dolan, McLean,Burley, Philliben, McKeown, Maxwell, Duncan, Shanks, Mair, Griffin, O'Neill
Middle: Wishart, Tannock, Cowan, Kirk, Paterson, McCart, McAdam,Cusack, Gardner, Reilly
Front: Forsyth (Asst.Man.), Bryce, Gahagan, Russell, Boyd, McLean (Manager), MacCabe, Candlish, Arnott, McBride, Jenks (Chief Scout.Youth Dev.)

1989-90: Premier League

	Date	Opponent	Score	Scorers	Att.	Maxwell	Burley	Boyd	Dolan	Philliben	McCart	Russell	O'Neill	Arnott	Mair	Cusack	MacCabe	MacAdam	Kirk	Paterson	McBride	Cooper	Reilly	Griffin	Gardner	Gahagan	McNair	McLean	Bryce
1	12-Aug	Dundee United	1 - 1	Cusack	8596	x	x	x	x	x	x	x	x	s	x	x			x									s	
2	19-Aug	ABERDEEN	0 - 0		6491	x	x	x	x	x	x	x	x	s		x			x									s	
3	26-Aug	ST. MIRREN	3 - 1	Cusack (2), Kirk	4703	x	x	x	s	x		x	x			x			x	x	x	x				s			
4	09-Sep	Dunfermline Ath.	1 - 1	OG	8537	x	x	x		s	x	x	x	x		x			x	x		x				s			
5	16-Sep	HEARTS	1 - 3	McCart	8948	x	x	x	s		x	x	x	x		x			x	x		x				s			
6	23-Sep	Celtic	1 - 1	Paterson	29207	x	x	x		s	x	x	x	x				x	x	x		x				s			
7	30-Sep	DUNDEE	3 - 0	O'Neill, Kirk, Cooper	4463	x	x	x			x	x	x	s		x		x	x	x		x				s			
8	03-Oct	RANGERS	1 - 0	Russell	17667	x	x	x			x	x	x	s		x		x	x	x		x				s			
9	14-Oct	Hibernian	2 - 3	Cusack (2)	11001	x	x		s		x	x	x	s		x		x	x	x		x	x	s					s
10	21-Oct	DUNDEE UNITED	3 - 2	Boyd, Arnott, Cooper	8184	x	x	x	s	x	x			x		s			x	x		x	x			x			
11	28-Oct	Aberdeen	0 - 1		13500	x	x	x	s		x	x		x				x	x	x		x	x			s			
12	04-Nov	St. Mirren	2 - 2	Cusack, Cooper	4584	x	x	x	s		x	x	x			x		x	x	x		x				s			
13	11-Nov	DUNFERMLINE	1 - 1	Cusack	9138	x	x	x	s		x	x	x	x		x			x	x		x				s			
14	18-Nov	Hearts	0 - 3		12035	x	x	x	x	x	x	x	x	x		x				x		x				s			
15	25-Nov	CELTIC	0 - 0		16029	x		x		x	x	x	x	s		x				x		x	s	x		x			
16	02-Dec	Dundee	1 - 2	Kirk	4049	x		x	x	x	x	x		s		x			x	x		x				s			
17	09-Dec	Rangers	0 - 3		33584	x	x	x		x	x	x		s		x			x	x		x				x			
p 9/1	16-Dec	HIBERNIAN	0 - 2		6447	x	x	x		x	x		x			x	s		x	x		x		s		x			
19	23-Dec	Dundee United	1 - 1	Russell	6651	x	x	x		x	x	x		x	x	s			x	x		x		s					
20	30-Dec	ABERDEEN	2 - 2	Cooper (2)	7267	x	x	x		x	x	s	x	x		x			x	x		x				s			
21	02-Jan	ST. MIRREN	2 - 0	Russell, Kirk	8253	x	x	x		s	x	x	x	x	s				x	x		x				x			
22	06-Jan	Dunfermline Ath.	5 - 0	Cusack (2), Gahagan (2), Kirk	8525	x	x	x		s	x	x	x			x			x	x		x				x			s
23	13-Jan	HEARTS	0 - 3		8822	x	x	x			x	x	x	x	x		s		x	x		x		s					
24	27-Jan	Celtic	1 - 0	Cusack	22500	x	x	x		s	x	x	x	x		x			x	x		x				s			
25	03-Feb	Hibernian	2 - 1	OG, Paterson	6001	x	x	x		s	x	x	x	x		x			x	x		x				s			
26	10-Feb	RANGERS	1 - 1	Arnott	17647	x	x	x		s	x	x	x	x		x			x	x		x				s			
27	17-Feb	DUNDEE	3 - 1	Kirk (2), Gahagan	5508	x	x	x		x		x	x	x		x			x	x		x		s		s			
28	03-Mar	Hearts	0 - 2		9205	x	x	x	s	x	x	x	x		x	x			x	x									s
29	10-Mar	DUNDEE UNITED	0 - 1		4697	x	x	x			x	x	x	x	x				x	x						x	s		s
30	24-Mar	Aberdeen	0 - 2		11200	x	x		x		x	x		x	x	x			x						x	s	x	s	
31	31-Mar	St. Mirren	0 - 0		5448	x	x		s	x	x	x		x		x			x	x		x		x		s			
32	07-Apr	DUNFERMLINE	1 - 3	OG	6351	x	x	x		x	x	x		x		x			x	x		x		s		s			
33	14-Apr	Rangers	1 - 2	Cusack	39305	x	x	x		x	x	x		x		x			s	x		x		x		s			
34	21-Apr	HIBERNIAN	1 - 0	Arnott	4435	x	x	x		x	x			x	s	x			x	x		x	s	x					
35	28-Apr	CELTIC	1 - 1	Cooper	13594	x	x	x		x	x			x	s	x			x	x		x		x		s			
36	05-May	Dundee	2 - 1	Russell, Kirk	5136	x	x	x		x	x	x		x		x			x	x		x	s			s			

LEAGUE CUP

	Date	Opponent	Score	Scorers	Att.	Maxwell	Burley	Boyd	Dolan	Philliben	McCart	Russell	O'Neill	Arnott	Mair	Cusack	MacCabe	MacAdam	Kirk	Paterson	McBride	Cooper	Reilly	Griffin	Gardner	Gahagan	McNair	McLean	Bryce
	15-Aug	Kilmarnock	4 - 1	Cusack (2), Kirk, Dolan	3903	x	x	x	s	x	x	x	x	x	s	x			x			x							
	23-Aug	St. Mirren	0 - 1		4750	x	x	x	s	x	x	x	x	x	x				x	x	s								

SCOTTISH CUP

	Date	Opponent	Score	Scorers	Att.	Maxwell	Burley	Boyd	Dolan	Philliben	McCart	Russell	O'Neill	Arnott	Mair	Cusack	MacCabe	MacAdam	Kirk	Paterson	McBride	Cooper	Reilly	Griffin	Gardner	Gahagan	McNair	McLean	Bryce
	20-Jan	CLYDE	7 - 0	McCart,Gahagan,Russell,Arnott,Kirk,Cooper,Bryce	4077	x	x	x		s	x	x	x	x					x	x		x				x			s
	24-Feb	Hearts	0 - 4		19161	x	x	x	s	x		x	x		s	x	x		x	x						x			

LANARKSHIRE CUP

	Date	Opponent	Score
	26-Apr	Albion Rovers	

ISLE OF MAN TOURNAMENT

	Date	Opponent	Score	Scorers
	24-Jul	Bolton Wands.	1 - 0	Arnott
	26-Jul	Dundalk	4 - 1	Cusack,O'Neil,Bryce,Kirk
F	29-Jul	St. Mirren	2 - 1	Arnott, Russell

FRIENDLIES

	Date	Opponent	Score	Scorers
	05-Aug	Wick Thistle	7 - 2	
	06-May	ALL STARS	2 - 2	Russell, Gahagan
	04-Aug	REAL SOCIADAD	4 - 0	Cusack (2), Dolan, McCart
	14-Jan	Saltcoats Victoria	4 - 1	

1990 Premier League

		Pl.	Home W.	D.	L.	F.	A.	Away W.	D.	L.	F.	A.	F. (Total)	A.	Pts.
1	Rangers	36	14	2	2	32	7	6	9	3	16	12	48	19	51
2	Aberdeen	36	12	4	2	33	13	5	6	7	23	20	56	33	44
3	Heart of Mid.	36	8	6	4	28	17	8	6	4	26	18	54	35	44
4	Dundee United	36	8	8	2	21	12	3	5	10	15	27	36	39	35
5	Celtic	36	6	6	6	21	20	4	8	6	16	17	37	37	34
6	MOTHERWELL	36	7	6	5	23	21	4	6	8	20	26	43	47	34
7	Hibernian	36	8	5	5	25	23	4	5	9	9	18	34	41	34
8	Dunfermline Ath.	36	5	6	7	17	23	6	2	10	20	27	37	50	30
9	St. Mirren	36	6	6	6	14	15	4	4	10	14	33	28	48	30
10	Dundee	36	4	8	6	23	26	1	6	11	18	39	41	65	24

1990-91: Premier League

No.	Date	Opponent	Score	Scorers	Att.	Maxwell	Burley	Boyd	Paterson	Nijholt	McCart	Russell	O'Neill	Arnott	Kirk	Gahagan	Cusack	Griffin	Philiben	Cooper	Angus	McLeod	Bryce	Dolan	O' Donnell	Mair	McLean	McGrillen	Ferguson
1	25-Aug	CELTIC	2 - 0	Russell, Arnott	17652	x	x	x	x	x	x	x	x	x	x	x	s	s											
2	01-Sep	Dundee United	0 - 1		7636	x	x	x		x	x	x	x	x	x		s		x	x	s								
3	08-Sep	ST. JOHNSTONE	3 - 0	O'Neill, Cusack, Kirk	5069	x	x	x	x	s	x	x	x	x	x		x			x		s							
4	15-Sep	St. Mirren	0 - 1		4678	x	x	x	x	s	x	x	x	x	x		x			x		s							
5	22-Sep	DUNFERMLINE	2 - 0	Arnott, Cooper	5354	x	x	x	s	x	x	x	x	x	x		x			x		s							
6	29-Sep	Rangers	0 - 1		34863	x	x	x	x	x	x	x	x	x	x		s			x		s							
7	06-Oct	HEARTS	1 - 1	Cusack	6780	x	x	x	s	x	x	x	x	x	x		x			x	s								
8	13-Oct	ABERDEEN	0 - 0		6602	x	x	x	s	x	x		x	x	x		x			x	x	s							
9	20-Oct	Hibernian	0 - 1		8500	x	x	x	s	x	x	x	x	s			x			x	x	x							
10	03-Nov	DUNDEE UNITED	0 - 2		8117	x	x	x	s	x	x	x		x	x		x	x		x		s							
11	06-Nov	Celtic	1 - 2	Russell	20317	x	x	x	x	x	x	s	x		s		x	x		x		x							
12	10-Nov	Dunfermline Ath.	3 - 3	Cusack, Arnott, Cooper	7200	x	x	x	x		x	x		x	x		x	x		x	s	s							
13	17-Nov	RANGERS	2 - 4	Cooper, Bryce	16457	x	x	x	x		x	x			x		x			x	x	x	s	s					
14	24-Nov	ST. MIRREN	1 - 1	Dolan	4720	x	x	x	x		x						x			x		x	s	x	x	x	s		
15	01-Dec	St. Johnstone	1 - 2	Griffen	6784	x	x	x	x		x						x	s	x	x			x	x		x		s	
16	11-Dec	HIBERNIAN	4 - 1	Griffen (2), Boyd, Arnott	4121	x	x	x	x		x	x	x	x			x	x		x	s	s							
17	15-Dec	Aberdeen	1 - 1	Arnott	9800	x	x	x	x		x	x	x	x			x	x		x		s		s					
18	22-Dec	Hearts	2 - 3	Arnott (2)	8625	x	x	x	x		x	x	x	x			x	x		x		s		s					
19	02-Jan	St. Mirren	2 - 2	Paterson, Cusack	6653	x	x	x	x		x	s	x	x			x	x		x	s								x
20	05-Jan	ST. JOHNSTONE	2 - 2	Arnott, Cooper	5338	x	x	x	x		x	s	x	x	s		x	x		x									x
21	19-Jan	Dundee United	0 - 3		6740	x		x	x		x	s	x	x	s		x	x		x	x								x
22	30-Jan	CELTIC	1 - 1	Angus	13542	x		x	x	s	x		x	x	x		s		x	x	x								x
23	02-Feb	Hibernian	1 - 1	Ferguson	6000	x		x	x	x	x			s	s		x	x	x	x	x								x
24	16-Feb	Rangers	0 - 2		32192	x		x	x		x			x	s		x	x	x	x	x	s			x				
25	27-Feb	DUNFERMLINE	1 - 0	Cooper	3203	x		x	x	x	x	s			x			x		x		x	s		x				x
26	02-Mar	HEARTS	1 - 3	Griffin	5212	x		x	x	x	x	s	x		x			x		x	s	x							x
p 19/2	05-Mar	ABERDEEN	0 - 2		5567	x		x	x	x	x	s	x		s		x	x		x	x	x							
28	09-Mar	St. Johnstone	4 - 1	Arnott (2), McLeod, Ferguson	5079	x		x	x	x	x			x	s			x		x	x	x			x				s
29	23-Mar	ST. MIRREN	3 - 1	Ferguson, Arnott, Cooper	6207	x		x	x	x	x	x		x	s		s		x	x					x				x
30	30-Mar	Celtic	2 - 1	Coyne, Ferguson	21252	x		x		x	x		x	x	s			x	x		x	s			x				x
31	13-Apr	HIBERNIAN	1 - 0	Arnott	5012	x			x	x	x		x	x	x		x	x	x	x					s			s	
32	16-Apr	DUNDEE UNITED	1 - 0	Ferguson	3531	x			x	x	x			s	x			x		x	x	x		s	x				x
33	20-Apr	Aberdeen	0 - 3		14200	x			x	x	x			x	s			x	x	x	x	x			x				s
34	27-Apr	Dunfermline Ath.	5 - 2	Ferguson (3), Kirk, Paterson	3552	x			x	x	x			x	x			x		x	s		s	x	x				x
35	04-May	RANGERS	3 - 0	Arnott (2), Philliben	12021	x			x	x	x			x	s			x	x	x	x	x			x				s
36	11-May	Hearts	1 - 2	Angus	8932	x		x	x	x	x			x	s		s	x		x	x				x				x

LEAGUE CUP

	Date	Opponent	Score	Scorers	Att.	Maxwell	Burley	Boyd	Paterson	Nijholt	McCart	Russell	O'Neill	Arnott	Kirk	Gahagan	Cusack	Griffin	Philiben	Cooper	Angus	McLeod	Bryce	Dolan	O' Donnell	Mair	McLean	McGrillen	Ferguson
	21-Aug	MORTON	4 - 3	O'Neill (2), Burley, Arnott	3198	x	x	x	x	x	x	x	x	x	x		x		s							s			
	28-Aug	CLYDE	2 - 0	Russell, Arnott	3535	x	x	x		x	x	x	x	x	x	s	x	s		x									
	04-Sep	Dundee United	0 - 2		8475	x	x	x	x	x	x	s	x	x	x		x			x	s								

SCOTTISH CUP

	Date	Opponent	Score	Scorers	Att.	Maxwell	Burley	Boyd	Paterson	Nijholt	McCart	Russell	O'Neill	Arnott	Kirk	Gahagan	Cusack	Griffin	Philiben	Cooper	Angus	McLeod	Bryce	Dolan	O' Donnell	Mair	McLean	McGrillen	Ferguson
	26-Jan	Aberdeen	1 - 0	Kirk	14170	x		x	x		x	s	x	x	s				x	x	x			x					x
	23-Feb	FALKIRK	4 - 2	Cusack (2), McLeod, KIRK	10271	x		x	x		x	s			s		x		x	x	x	x			x				x
	16-Mar	MORTON	0 - 0		9005	x		x	x	x	x			x	s			x		x	x	x			x				s
rep.	19-Mar	Morton	1 - 1	Boyd	7319	x		x	x	x	x	x	x	x	x		x			x					s				s
	03-Apr	CELTIC	0 - 0		41765	x		x		x	x	s	x	x	s			x	x		x				x				x
rep.	09-Apr	CELTIC	4 - 2	Arnott (2), O'Neill, Kirk	34589	x		x		x	x	s	x	x	s			x	x		x				x				x
	18-May	DUNDEE UNITED	4 - 3	Ferguson, O' Donnell, Angus, Kirk	52475	x		x	x	x	x		s	x	s			x			x				x				x

ISLE OF MAN TOUR

	Date	Opponent	Score	Scorers
	July	Stoke City	1 - 1	Cusack
	July	Wrexham	3 - 1	Cusack, Arnott, Griffin
	July	Oxford United	3 - 1	Bryce (2), McCart,

FRIENDLIES

	Date	Opponent	Score	Scorers
	04-Aug	Elgin	0 - 0	
	04-Aug	Portadown	1 - 0	Arnott
	07-Aug	Cliftonville	2 - 0	Arnott, McCart
	13-Aug	MOSCOW TORPEDO.	0 - 1	
	17-Aug	LEICESTER CITY	2 - 2	Kirk, Cusack
	29-Oct	Blackpool	3 - 2	Arnott (3)
	02-Aug	Stenhousemuir		
	05-Aug	Nairn		
	06-Aug	Ballymena	4 - 1	Cussack (2), Cooper, Arnott
	11-Aug	QUEEN OF THE SOUTH	2 - 0	Cusack, Arnott

1991 Premier League

		Pl.	Home W.	Home D.	Home L.	Home F.	Home A.	Away W.	Away D.	Away L.	Away F.	Away A.	F. (Total)	A. (Total)	Pts. (Total)
1	Rangers	36	14	3	1	40	8	10	4	4	22	15	62	23	55
2	Aberdeen	36	12	5	1	30	7	10	4	4	32	20	62	27	53
3	Celtic	36	10	4	4	30	14	7	3	8	22	24	52	38	41
4	Dundee United	36	11	3	4	28	16	6	4	8	13	13	41	29	41
5	Heart of Mid.	36	10	3	5	28	22	4	4	10	20	33	48	55	35
6	MOTHERWELL	36	9	5	4	28	18	3	4	11	23	32	51	50	33
7	St. Johnstone	36	6	4	8	23	25	5	5	8	18	29	41	54	31
8	Dunfermline Ath.	36	5	7	6	23	26	3	4	11	15	35	38	61	27
9	Hibernian	36	6	5	7	17	25	0	8	10	7	26	24	51	25
10	St. Mirren	36	4	5	9	14	25	1	4	13	14	34	28	59	19

1990-91 Season
Back : Ferguson, Cusack, Kirk, Paterson, Maxwell, McCart, Nijholt
Middle : Jenks, Philliben, McLeod, O'Donnell, Bryce, Angus, Griffin, Holmes (Physio)
Front : McLean, O'Neil, Arnott, Boyd, Dolan, Cooper, Forsyth

1991-92 Season
Back : Burke, Burns, Kinross, Brown, Ferguson, Russell, O'Neill, Dickson, Bryce
Middle : Dolan, Gardner, Philliben, Shepstone, Picken, Maaskant, Thomson, Nijholt, O'Donnell, Angus, Griffin
Front : T Forsyth, T McLean, Arnott, Verheul, Cooper, McCart, McGrillen, Shepherd, McLeod, ? , Jenks

1991-92: Premier League

	Date	Opponent	Score	Scorers	Att.	Thomson	Griffin	Nijholt	Maaskant	Philliben	McCart	Simpson	Dolan	Martin	Kirk	Arnott	McLeod	Russell	Ferguson	O' Donnell	Cooper	McGrillen	Angus	Shepherd	Verheul	Cusack	Gardner	McKinnon	Dykstra	Jones	Bryce	Gourlay
1	10-Aug	Falkirk	1 - 1	Nijholt	6000	x	x	x	x	x	x				x	x			s	x	x		x	s								
2	13-Aug	Rangers	0 - 2		35050	x	x	x	x	x	x				s		x		s	x	x		x		x							
3	17-Aug	HIBERNIAN	1 - 1	McCart	8018	x	x	x	x		x		x		x		s		x	x	x	s	x									
4	24-Aug	Aidrie	1 - 0	Nijholt	6000		x	x	x	x	x	x			x		s		x	x	x			s					x			
5	31-Aug	ST. MIRREN	1 - 0	Nijholt	5587	x	x	x	x	x	x	x			x				x	x	x	s	s									
6	07-Sep	Hearts	0 - 2		9003	x	x	x	x	x	x				x			s	s	x	x	x	x									
7	14-Sep	ABERDEEN	0 - 1		6452	x	x	x		x	x	x			s					x	x	x	x		s	x						
8	21-Sep	DUNFERMLINE	3 - 0	Philliben, Dolan, Russell	4541	x	x	x		x	x		x		x		x	s		x	x	s				x						
9	28-Sep	Dundee United	2 - 2	Ferguson, Dolan	6500	x	x	x		x	x	x	x				x	s		x	s		x			x						
10	05-Oct	St. Johnstone	1 - 0	Russell	5014	x	x	x		x		x	x		x		s	s		x	x					x	x					
11	08-Oct	CELTIC	0 - 2		1328	x		x		x	x	x	x		x		s	x	s	x	x					x						
12	12-Oct	FALKIRK	4 - 2	Cusack, Kirk, O' Donnell	5991	x	x	x		x	x	x	s		x	x			s	x	x					x						
13	19-Oct	Hibernian	0 - 0		8000	x	x	x		x	x	x	x		s	x			s	x	x					x						
14	26-Oct	HEARTS	0 - 1		5417	x	x			x	x	x	x		x	x			s	x	x				s	x						
15	30-Oct	Aberdeen	1 - 3	Arnott	9200	x	x			x	x	x	x		x	x			s	x	x					x	s					
16	02-Nov	St. Mirren	2 - 1	Cooper (2)	2654	x	x	x		s	x	x	x		x	x			s		x		x			x						
17	09-Nov	AIRDRIE	1 - 2	Cooper	5509	x	x		x	x		x	x		x				x	x	x	s				x	s					
18	16-Nov	ST. JOHNSTONE	1 - 1	Russell	4570	x	x	x		x		x		x	s	x		x		x	x	s				x						
19	20-Nov	Celtic	2 - 2	Arnott (2)	16215	x	x	x		x	x	x		x		x		s		x	x					x	s					
20	23-Nov	Dunfermline Ath.	0 - 0		4697	x	x	x		x			x	x	s	x		s		x	x					x	x					
21	30-Nov	RANGERS	0 - 2		15350	x	x	x	x	x			s	x				x	x	x	x	s					x					
22	03-Dec	DUNDEE UNITED	1 - 1	Kirk	4023	x	x	x	x	x			x	x	x	x		s		x	x	s										
23	07-Dec	Falkirk	1 - 0	Arnott	5200	x		x	x	x			x	x	s	x		x		x	x	s				x						
24	14-Dec	Hearts	1 - 3	McCart	10006	x		x	x		x		x	x		x	s	s		x			x			x	x					
p 14/1	21-Dec	ABERDEEN	3 - 3	Kirk, Nijholt, O' Donnell	5221	x		x		x			x	x	x	x				x	x	s	x	s				x				
26	28-Dec	Aidrie	0 - 2		5500	x		x	x	x			x	x		x		s	s	x	x		x			x						
27	01-Jan	ST. MIRREN	3 - 1	Nijholt, Kirk, Cooper	4380	x	x	x		x			x	x	x	x		s		x	x	x					s					
28	04-Jan	St. Johnstone	0 - 0		4956	x		x		x			x	x	s	x		s		x	x	x	x	x								
29	11-Jan	CELTIC	0 - 0		12115	x		x		x			x	x	x	x				x	x	s	x	s				x				
30	18-Jan	Rangers	0 - 2		38127	x		x		x			x	x	x	x		x		x	x			s			s	x				
31	01-Feb	HIBERNIAN	1 - 1	Angus	6105	x		x		x			x		x	x			s	x	x		x				s	x		x		
32	08-Feb	DUNFERMLINE	1 - 2	Arnott	6375	x		x		x		s	s		x	x			x	x	x		x					x		x		
33	22-Feb	Dundee United	2 - 2	Kirk, O' Donnell	4746	x		x				x	s	x	x				x	x	x	s	x					x		x		
34	29-Feb	ST. JOHNSTONE	3 - 1	Kirk, Cooper, McKinnon	4373	x		x				x	s	x	x				x	x	x	s	x					x		x		
p 17/3	07-Mar	Celtic	1 - 4	Arnott	15521	x		x					x	x		x	s	x		x			x	s			x	x		x		
36	14-Mar	AIRDRIE	0 - 3		5065	x		x				x	x	x	x	x				x	x	s	s					x		x		
37	21-Mar	St. Mirren	2 - 1	Jones, O' Donnell	2090	x		x				x	x	x	s	x				x	x	s	x					x		x		
38	28-Mar	FALKIRK	0 - 1		4395	x		x				x		x	s			x	x	x		x	x					x		x	s	
39	04-Apr	Hibernian	0 - 0		4337	x					x		x	x	x		x		s	x			x				s	x		x	x	
40	07-Apr	HEARTS	0 - 1		4502	x					x		x	x	x		x			x		s	x				s	x		x	x	
41	11-Apr	Aberdeen	0 - 2		6800	x		x			x		x	x	s		x				x		x				x	x		x	s	
42	18-Apr	Dunfermline Ath.	1 - 3	Arnott	2400	x		x					x	x	x	x	x			x	x							x		x	s	s
43	25-Apr	RANGERS	1 - 2	Arnott	12515	x		x		x	x		s	x	x	x	x	s		x	x							x				
44	02-May	DUNDEE UNITED	1 - 2	Angus	5989	x		x		s	x		s	x	x	x	x			x	x		x					x				

LEAGUE CUP

	Date	Opponent	Score	Scorers	Att.	Thomson	Griffin	Nijholt	Maaskant	Philliben	McCart	Simpson	Dolan	Martin	Kirk	Arnott	McLeod	Russell	Ferguson	O' Donnell	Cooper	McGrillen	Angus	Shepherd	Verheul	Cusack	Gardner	McKinnon	Dykstra	Jones	Bryce	Gourlay
	21-Aug	Raith Rovers	1 - 4	Kirk	3204		x	x	s		x		x		x			x	s	x	x		x			x			x			

SCOTTISH CUP

	Date	Opponent	Score	Scorers	Att.	Thomson	Griffin	Nijholt	Maaskant	Philliben	McCart	Simpson	Dolan	Martin	Kirk	Arnott	McLeod	Russell	Ferguson	O' Donnell	Cooper	McGrillen	Angus	Shepherd	Verheul	Cusack	Gardner	McKinnon	Dykstra	Jones	Bryce	Gourlay
	25-Jan	Ayr United	1 - 1	Martin	7894	x		x		x		s	x	x	x	x			s	x	x		x					x				
rep.	28-Jan	AYR UNITED	4 - 1	Nijholt, Ferguson, Kirk, Arnott	6507	x		x		x		s	x		x	x			x	x	x		x				s	x				
	15-Feb	Rangers	1 - 2	O' Donnell	38444	x		x				x	s	x	x	x			s	x	x		x					x		x		

E C W CUP

	Date	Opponent	Score	Scorers	Att.	Thomson	Griffin	Nijholt	Maaskant	Philliben	McCart	Simpson	Dolan	Martin	Kirk	Arnott	McLeod	Russell	Ferguson	O' Donnell	Cooper	McGrillen	Angus	Shepherd	Verheul	Cusack	Gardner	McKinnon	Dykstra	Jones	Bryce	Gourlay
	18-Sep	Katowice	0 - 2		8000	x	x	x		x	x		x		x		x	x	s	x	x					s						
	02-Oct	KATOWICE	3 - 1	Kirk (2), Cusack	10032	x	x	x		s	x		x		x			x	s	x	x		x			x						

FRIENDLIES

Date	Opponent	Score	Scorers
27-Jul	Elgin City		
28-Jul	Fort William		
05-Aug	Blantyre Vics		
03-Aug	Threave Rovers	0-0	
25-Jul	Schweinfurt	1-0	Angus
26-Jul	Schweinfurt X1	6-0	Kirk(2),O'Donnell,Arnott.Cooper,McLeod
28-Jul	V F L Yolkack	9-0	Ferguson (6), Arnott (2), Kirk
30-Jul	Kicker Offenback	3-2	O.Donnell (2), Griffin
03-Aug	QUEEN OF THE SOUTH	0-1	

1992 Premier League

		Pl.	Home W.	D.	L.	F.	A.	Away W.	D.	L.	F.	A.	F. (Total)	A.	Pts.
1	Rangers	44	14	5	3	50	14	19	1	2	51	17	101	31	72
2	Heart of Mid.	44	12	7	3	26	15	15	2	5	34	22	60	37	63
3	Celtic	44	15	3	4	47	20	11	7	4	41	22	88	42	62
4	Dundee United	44	10	7	5	37	25	9	6	7	29	25	66	50	51
5	Hibernian	44	7	8	7	28	25	9	9	4	25	20	53	45	49
6	Aberdeen	44	9	6	7	32	23	8	8	6	23	19	55	42	48
7	Airdrieonians	44	7	5	10	25	33	6	5	11	25	37	50	70	36
8	St. Johnstone	44	5	7	10	21	32	8	3	11	31	41	52	73	36
9	Falkirk	44	7	2	13	29	41	5	9	8	25	32	54	73	35
10	MOTHERWELL	44	5	6	11	25	29	5	8	9	18	32	43	61	34
11	St. Mirren	44	2	5	15	18	36	4	7	11	15	37	33	73	24
12	Dunfermline Ath.	44	2	7	13	11	35	2	3	17	11	45	22	80	18

1992-93: Premier League

No.	Date	Opponent	Score	Scorers	Att.	Thomson	Dykstra	Sneddon	Nijholt	Griffin	McKinnon	Simpson	Martin	Dolan	Kromheer	Philiben	McCart	Angus	Kirk	McLeod	Ferguson	Arnott	O' Donnell	Cooper	Baker	Shepherd	Shepstone	Gardner	Bryce	Gourley	Verheul	McGrillen	Graham
1	01-Aug	DUNDEE UNITED	0 - 1		5037	x		x	x		x	x	x		x			x	x		s	x		x			s						
2	04-Aug	HIBERNIAN	1 - 2	Kirk	5391	x		x	x		x	x	x		x				x	x		x		x		s		s					
3	08-Aug	Celtic	1 - 1	Kirk	24490	x		x	x		x	x	x		x			s	x	s		x	x	x									
4	15-Aug	ABERDEEN	2 - 1	Arnott, Angus	5561	x		x	x		x	x			x			x	x		x	x		x		s							
5	22-Aug	Partick Thistle	2 - 2	Ferguson, Arnott	5469	x		x	x		x	x	x		x						x	x	x	x	s	s							
6	29-Aug	Hearts	0 - 1		7600	x			x		x		x		x		x	s	s		x	x	x	x		x							
7	02-Sep	RANGERS	1 - 4	Arnott	10074	x		x	x		x		x				x	x	s		x	x	x	x	s								
8	12-Sep	Dundee	1 - 2	O' Donnell	3797	x			x		x		x		x		x	x	s		x	x	x	x			s						
9	19-Sep	ST. JOHNSTONE	3 - 3	Cooper, Baker, Kirk	4002		x		x	x	x		x	s				x	x	s			x	x	x				x				
10	26-Sep	Falkirk	0 - 1		4300		x			x	x		x	x			x		x	x	s		x	x	x	s							
11	03-Oct	AIRDRIE	2 - 0	Simpson, Kirk	4730		x		x		x	x	s	x		x	x		s	x	x		x	x									
12	10-Oct	Dundee United	1 - 1	McCart	5380		x	x	x		x	x	x	s		x	x		x			x		x	s								
13	17-Oct	CELTIC	1 - 3	McCart	10016		x	x	x		x		x			x	x	x	x			x		x	s					s			
14	24-Oct	HEARTS	1 - 3	Kirk	5171		x		x		x		x	x			x	x	x			x		x	s		x				s		
15	31-Oct	Rangers	2 - 4	Angus, Martin	38719		x	x	x		x		x	x			x	x						x	x			s				x	
16	07-Nov	PARTICK THISTLE	0 - 2		5379	x			x	x	x		x	s			x	x	x			x		x	x							s	
17	11-Nov	Aberdeen	0 - 2		8800		x	x	s	x	x	x	x		x	x		x		s		x		x									
18	21-Nov	St. Johnstone	A																														
19	24-Nov	St. Johnstone	0 - 2		3584		x	x			x	x	x			x		x	s	s		x	x	x	x								
20	28-Nov	DUNDEE	1 - 3	Arnott	3534		x	x					x	x		x	x	x	x		x		x	x						s		s	
21	01-Dec	Hibernian	2 - 2	Ferguson, Kirk	4750		x		x				x	x		x	x	x	s		x	x	x	x						s			
22	05-Dec	FALKIRK	3 - 1	Martin, Kirk, McGrillen	5018		x		x	x			x	s		x	x	x	x		x		x	x								s	
23	12-Dec	Aidrie	2 - 0	O' Donnell, Arnott	4500		x		s	x		x	x			x	x	x	x		x	x	x	s									
p 2/2	19-Dec	DUNDEE UNITED	2 - 0	Kirk, McGrillen	3783		x		x	x	x		x	x		x		s	x			x	x	x								s	
25	26-Dec	ABERDEEN	0 - 2		7907		x		x	x			x	x		x	x		s		x	x	x	x		s							
26	02-Jan	Partick Thistle	1 - 0	Martin	7156		x		x		x	x	x	x		x	x	s	x		s	x		x									
27	23-Jan	Hearts	0 - 0		6610		x		x				x	x	x	x	x	s	s			x	x	x				x					
28	30-Jan	Celtic	1 - 1	Angus	18513		x	x	x	x			x	x		x		x	s	s			x	x								x	
29	06-Feb	AIRDRIE	0 - 0		5382		x		x	x	x		x	x		x		s	x			x	x	x								s	
30	13-Feb	HIBERNIAN	0 - 0		5021		x		x	x	x		x	x		x		s	x			x	x	x								s	
31	20-Feb	Falkirk	3 - 1	OG, McGrillen, Dolan	4300		x	x	x		x		x	s		x		x	x	s			x	x								x	
p 16/1	23-Feb	RANGERS	0 - 4		14006		x	x	x	x	x		x	s		x			s				x	x								x	x
33	27-Feb	ST. JOHNSTONE	1 - 1	Dolan	4278		x			x	x		x	x	x	x			x		s			x		s						x	x
34	06-Mar	Dundee	1 - 1	Griffin	3370		x			x	x		x	x	x	x	s					s		x		x						x	x
35	09-Mar	Dundee United	0 - 0		5136		x	x		x			x	s		x	x	x	x			x	x	x								s	
p 3/4	13-Mar	CELTIC	2 - 0	Kirk, Cooper	10102		x		s	x	x		x			x	x	x	x			x	x	x								s	
37	20-Mar	PARTICK THISTLE	2 - 3	Kirk, McGrillen	6499		x		x	x	x		x	s		x	x		x			s	x	x								x	
38	27-Mar	Aberdeen	0 - 1		11200		x		x		x		x	s		x	x	x	x			x	x	x								s	
p 20/4	03-Apr	HEARTS	2 - 1	O' Donnell, McGrillen	4287		x		x	x	x		x			x	x	x	s				x	x								x	
40	10-Apr	Rangers	0 - 1		41353		x		s	x	x		x			x	x	x	x			x	x	x								s	
41	17-Apr	DUNDEE	1 - 2	McGrillen	4285		x		s	x	x		x			x	x	s	x			x	x	x								x	
42	24-Apr	St. Johnstone	0 - 0		4001		x		x	x	x		x			x	x	x	s				x	x								x	
43	01-May	Hibernian	0 - 1		5364		x		x	x	x		x			x	x	x	s			x	x	x								s	
44	08-May	FALKIRK	2 - 1	McCart, Arnott	5539		x		x	x	x		x			x	x	x	s			x	x	x								s	
45	15-May	Aidrie	2 - 0	O' Donnell, Graham	5988		x		x	x	x		x			x	x	x	s				x	x								s	x

LEAGUE CUP

Date	Opponent	Score	Scorers	Att.	Thomson	Dykstra	Sneddon	Nijholt	Griffin	McKinnon	Simpson	Martin	Dolan	Kromheer	Philiben	McCart	Angus	Kirk	McLeod	Ferguson	Arnott	O' Donnell	Cooper	Baker	Shepherd	Shepstone	Gardner	Bryce	Gourley	Verheul	McGrillen	Graham
12-Aug	CLYDE	4 - 2	Ferguson (3), Angus	3130	x		x	x		x	x	x					x	x	x	s	x		x			s						
19-Aug	FALKIRK	0 - 1		5510	x			x		x	x	x		x			s	x		s	x	x	x	x								

SCOTTISH CUP

Date	Opponent	Score	Scorers	Att.	Thomson	Dykstra	Sneddon	Nijholt	Griffin	McKinnon	Simpson	Martin	Dolan	Kromheer	Philiben	McCart	Angus	Kirk	McLeod	Ferguson	Arnott	O' Donnell	Cooper	Baker	Shepherd	Shepstone	Gardner	Bryce	Gourley	Verheul	McGrillen	Graham
09-Jan	RANGERS	0 - 2		14314		x		x		x	x	x		x	x	x	s	x		s	x		x									

FRIENDLIES

Date	Opponent	Score	Scorers
18-Jul	Inverness Th.	6 - 2	
23-Jul	Ayr United	2 - 1	Nijholt, Kirk
26-Apr	COVENTRY CITY	2 - 1	Graham, Kirk
21-Jul	Queen of the South	4 - 1	Jones (2), Baker, Shepherd
25-Jul	Stenhousemuir	3 - 2	
25-Jul	Hartlepool United	2 - 0	Kirk (2)

1993 Premier League

		Pl.	Home					Away					F.	A.	Pts.
			W.	D.	L.	F.	A.	W.	D.	L.	F.	A.	(Total)		
1	Rangers	44	20	2	0	52	11	13	5	4	45	24	97	35	73
2	Aberdeen	44	13	7	2	41	13	14	3	5	46	23	87	36	64
3	Celtic	44	13	5	4	37	18	11	7	4	31	23	68	41	60
4	Dundee United	44	8	7	7	25	27	11	2	9	31	22	56	49	47
5	Heart of Mid.	44	12	6	4	26	15	3	8	11	20	36	46	51	44
6	St. Johnstone	44	8	10	4	29	27	2	10	10	23	39	52	66	40
7	Hibernian	44	8	8	6	32	28	4	5	13	22	36	54	64	37
8	Partick Thistle	44	5	6	11	26	41	7	6	9	24	30	50	71	36
9	MOTHERWELL	44	7	4	11	27	37	4	9	9	19	25	46	62	35
10	Dundee	44	7	4	11	25	34	4	8	10	23	34	48	68	34
11	Falkirk	44	7	5	10	40	39	4	2	16	20	47	60	86	29
12	Airdrieonians	44	4	9	9	22	27	2	8	12	13	43	35	70	29

1992-93 Season

Back : Brown, Martin, Simpson, Kirk, Ritchie, Jones, Kromheer, McKinnon, O'Donnell, Nijholt, Angus, Cooper
Middle : Burke, Dickson, Shepherd, Philliben, Thomson, Picken, Dykstra, Gardner, Ferguson, Lavery, Bryce, Burns
Front : J Porteous (Physio), T McLean (Manager), McGrillen, McLeod, Gourlay, McCart, Verheul, Dolan, Griffin, Shepstone, Arnott, T Forsyth (Coach), W McLean (Youth)

1993-94 Season

Back: Gardner, Ritchie, Martin, Kirk, Kromheer, Graham, Krivokapic, Angus, O'Donnell, Cooper (Player/Coach)
Middle: Murray (Res. Coach), Dolan, Ross, Gourlay, Denham, Thomson, Dykstra, Philliben, McKinnon, Ferguson, McMillen, Forsyth (1st Team Coach)
Front: Porteous (Physio), Ferguson, Shepstone, Arnott, Burns, McLean (Man/Dir), McCart, Griffin, Shannon, McGrillen, McLean (SFA Community Officer)

1993-94: Premier League

No.	Date	Opponent	Score	Scorers	Att.	Dykstra	Shannon	Philliben	McKinnon	Krivokapic	Martin	McCart	Lambert	Angus	Arnott	Kirk	Dolan	Cooper	O' Donnell	Coyne	McGrillen	Burns	Shannon	Griffin	Burley	Graham	Ferguson	Davies	McMillan
1	07-Aug	CELTIC	2 - 2	Arnott, Burns	13569	x	x	s	x	x	x	x		x	x	x			x		s	x							
2	14-Aug	Dundee	2 - 1	McKinnon, McGrillen	4356	x	x	s	x	x	x	x		x	x	s			x		x	x							
3	21-Aug	Kilmarnock	1 - 0	McGrillen	7555	x	x		x	x	x	x		x	x	x		s	x		x					s			
4	28-Aug	RAITH ROVERS	4 - 1	McKinnon, Kirk, McGrillen, OG	5644	x	x		x	x	x	x		x	x	s		x	x		x					s			
5	04-Sep	St. Johnstone	0 - 3		4576	x	x		x	x	x	x				s	x	x	x		x					s	x		
6	11-Sep	HEARTS	2 - 0	O' Donnell, McGrillen	7662	x	x		x	x	x	x	x			s	x	s	x		x					x			
7	18-Sep	Partick Thistle	0 - 1		7224	x	x		x	x	x	x	x			s	x	s	x		x					x			
8	25-Sep	Dundee United	0 - 0		6633	x	x		x	x	x	x	x	s		x	x	s	x		x								
9	02-Oct	ABERDEEN	0 - 0		8594	x	x		x	x	x	x	x	s	x	x	x	s			x								
10	06-Oct	Rangers	2 - 1	Arnott (2)	39800	x	x	s	x	x	x	x	x	x	s	x	x				x								
11	09-Oct	HIBERNIAN	0 - 2		9090	x	x	s	x	x	x	x	x	s	x	x			x		x								
12	16-Oct	DUNDEE	1 - 0	Arnott	5126	x	x		x	x	x	x	x		x	x	x	s	x		s								
13	30-Oct	KILMARNOCK	2 - 2	Kirk, Martin	7384	x	x		x	x	x	x	x		x	x	x	s	x		s								
14	06-Nov	Raith Rovers	3 - 0	Arnott (2), O' Donnell	4473	x	x		x	x	x	x	x		x	x	s		x		x			s					
15	09-Nov	ST. JOHNSTONE	1 - 0	Lambert	4528	x	x	x	x	x	x		x		x	x	x		x		s			s					
16	13-Nov	Aberdeen	1 - 1	Kirk	11400	x	s	x	x	x	x	x	x		x	x	x		x		s		s						
17	20-Nov	DUNDEE UNITED	2 - 0	Kirk, Arnott	5807	x	x	s	x	x	x	x	x		x	x	x	s			x								
18	24-Nov	Celtic	0 - 2		17300	x	x	s	x	x	x	x	x	x		x		s	x		x								
19	30-Nov	PARTICK THISTLE	1 - 0	O' Donnell	5362	x	x		x	x	x	x	x		x	x	s		x	x	s								
20	04-Dec	RANGERS	0 - 2		14069	x	x			x	x	x	x		x	s	x		x	x	s			x					
21	11-Dec	Hibernian	2 - 3	Coyne (2)	7442	x	x	s	x	x	x	x	x			x	x		x	x	s								
22	15-Dec	Hearts	3 - 2	Coyne (2), McKinnon	5500	x	x	x	x		x	x	x			s	x	s	x	x	x								
23	18-Dec	Dundee	3 - 1	O' Donnell (2), Coyne	4700	x	x	x	x	x	x	x	x		s	x	s		x	x									
24	01-Jan	Kilmarnock	0 - 0		10500	x	x	s	x	x	x	x	x		s	x	x		x	x									
25	11-Jan	CELTIC	2 - 1	O' Donnell (2)	13159	x	x	x	x	x	x	x	x		x	s			x	x	s								
26	22-Jan	Partick Thistle	0 - 0		5500	x	x	x	x	x	x	x	x			x	s		x	x	s								
27	25-Jan	RAITH ROVERS	3 - 1	Kirk, Coyne, McGrillen	5067	x	x		x	x	x	x	s		x	x	x		x	x	s								
28	05-Feb	HEARTS	1 - 1	OG	7009	x	x	x	x	x	x	x		s	x	x	x			x	s								
29	08-Feb	St. Johnstone	1 - 2	Coyne	4300	x	x		x	x	x	x		x	s	x	s			x	x				x				
30	12-Feb	Dundee United	2 - 1	OG, OG	6573	x	x	x	x	x	x	x				x	x		x	x	s				s				
31	05-Mar	Rangers	1 - 2	Lambert	43669	x		x	x	x	x	x	x		x		x		x	x		s			s				
32	08-Mar	ABERDEEN	1 - 1	OG	7018	x	s	x	x	x	x	x	x		x		x		x	x	s		s						
33	12-Mar	HIBERNIAN	0 - 0		7126	x	x	s	x	x	x	x			x		x		x	x	s							x	
34	19-Mar	DUNDEE	3 - 1	Martin, Coyne, OG	6127	x	x	s	x	x	x	x			x		x		x	x	x							s	
35	26-Mar	Celtic	1 - 0	Arnott	36199	x	x	s	x	x	x	x			x		x		x	x	s							x	
36	30-Mar	Hearts	0 - 0		6200	x	x		x	x	x	x			x		x		x	x	x							s	
37	02-Apr	PARTICK THISTLE	2 - 2	Philliben, Coyne	6444	x	x	x	x	x		x	x		x		x		x	x	s							s	
p 3/5	09-Apr	DUNDEE UNITED	1 - 2	Kirk	5208	x	x		x	x	x	x	x	x		x				x	s				s			x	
39	16-Apr	Aberdeen	0 - 0		9600	x	x	x		x	x				x		x		x	x	s				x			x	s
40	23-Apr	Hibernian	2 - 0	Coyne, Krivokapic	6324	x	x	s	x	x	x	x	x			s	x			x	x							x	
41	26-Apr	RANGERS	2 - 1	Philliben, Coyne	11027	x	x	x	x	x	x		x			s	x			x	x							x	
42	30-Apr	KILMARNOCK	1 - 0	Coyne	8185	x	x	x	x	x	x		x			x	x		x	x	s							s	
43	07-May	Raith Rovers	3 - 3	Lambert, Kirk, McKinnon	3449	x	x	x	x	x	x		x			s	x			x	x							x	
44	14-May	ST. JOHNSTONE	0 - 1		5069	x	x	x	x	x	x		x			s	x			x	x							x	

LEAGUE CUP

	Date	Opponent	Score	Scorers	Att.	Dykstra	Shannon	Philliben	McKinnon	Krivokapic	Martin	McCart	Lambert	Angus	Arnott	Kirk	Dolan	Cooper	O' Donnell	Coyne	McGrillen	Burns	Shannon	Griffin	Burley	Graham	Ferguson	Davies	McMillan
	10-Aug	Ayr United	6 - 0	Arnott (2), McGrillen (2), Graham, Ferguson	3485	x	x	s	x	x	x	x		x	x		s		x		x					s	x		
	25-Aug	Aberdeen	2 - 5	Arnott, Shannon	12993	x	x	s	x	x	x	x		x	x		x	s	x		s	x							

SCOTTISH CUP

	Date	Opponent	Score	Scorers	Att.	Dykstra	Shannon	Philliben	McKinnon	Krivokapic	Martin	McCart	Lambert	Angus	Arnott	Kirk	Dolan	Cooper	O' Donnell	Coyne	McGrillen	Burns	Shannon	Griffin	Burley	Graham	Ferguson	Davies	McMillan
	29-Jan	CELTIC	1 - 0	Coyne	14061	x	x		x	x	x	x	x		x	s	x		x	x	s								
	19-Feb	Dundee United	2 - 2	Kirk, Philliben	12023	x	x	x	x	x	x	x	x			x	s		x	x	s								
rep.	01-Mar	DUNDEE UNITED	0 - 1		13002	x		x	x	x	x	x	x		x	x	s		x	x	s								

FRIENDLIES

	Date	Opponent	Score	Scorers
	24-Jul	Senior U.		
	27-Jul	Dunfermline Ath.		
	25-Jul	Durham City		
	29-Jul	Albion Rovers		
	29-Jul	Brechin City		
	31-Jul	BLACKBURN ROVERS	1 - 0	Arnott
	03-Aug	Stirling Albion		
	07-Apr	Inverness Th.		

1994 Premier League

		Pl.	Home					Away					F.	A.	Pts.
			W.	D.	L.	F.	A.	W.	D.	L.	F.	A.	(Total)		
1	Rangers	44	12	6	4	43	22	10	8	4	31	19	74	41	58
2	Aberdeen	44	11	9	2	33	12	6	12	4	25	24	58	36	55
3	MOTHERWELL	44	11	7	4	31	20	9	7	6	27	23	58	43	54
4	Celtic	44	8	11	3	25	17	7	9	6	26	21	51	38	50
5	Hibernian	44	11	7	4	29	15	5	8	9	24	33	53	48	47
6	Dundee United	44	5	11	6	26	25	6	9	7	21	23	47	48	42
7	Heart of Mid.	44	6	9	7	22	24	5	11	6	15	19	37	43	42
8	Kilmarnock	44	6	10	6	18	19	6	6	10	18	26	36	45	40
9	Partick Thistle	44	9	8	5	23	17	3	8	11	23	40	46	57	40
10	St. Johnstone	44	7	7	8	24	26	3	13	6	11	21	35	47	40
11	Raith Rovers	44	3	12	7	25	35	3	7	12	21	45	46	80	31
12	Dundee	44	6	7	9	26	26	2	6	14	16	31	42	57	29

1994-95: Premier League

No.	Date	Opponent	Score	Scorers	Att.	Woods	Howie	Shannon	Philliben	McKinnon	Krivokapic	Martin	McCart	Lambert	Dolan	Coyne	O' Donnell	Arnott	Davies	Burns	Kirk	McSkimming	May	McGrillen	Roddie	Allan	Ritchie	McLeish	McMillan	Van Der Gaag
1	13-Aug	Rangers	1 - 2	Coyne	43750	x		x	x	x		x	x	x		x	x		x	s	x			s		s				
2	20-Aug	HEARTS	1 - 1	Coyne	8249	x		x	x			x	x	x	x	x	x			s	x				x	s	s			
3	27-Aug	Kilmarnock	1 - 0	Coyne	7388	x		x	x			x	x	x	x	x	x		x	s	s				x	s				
4	10-Sep	Dundee United	1 - 1	Kirk	7501	x			x	x		x	x	x	x	x		x	x		x			s		s		s		
5	17-Sep	HIBERNIAN	1 - 1	Shannon	7005	x		x	x	x		x	x	x	x	x		x	x		s			s		s				
6	24-Sep	Partick Thistle	2 - 2	Coyne, Davies	5100	x		x	x	x		x	x	x	x	x		s	x		s				x	s				
7	01-Oct	CELTIC	1 - 1	Arnott	10869	x		x	x	x		x	x	x	x	x		x	x		s				s	s				
8	08-Oct	FALKIRK	5 - 3	Coyne (2), Arnott (2), Davies	6239	x		x	x	x		x		x	x	x		x	x		s					s		x		
9	15-Oct	Aberdeen	3 - 1	McKinnon, Kirk, Coyne	12505	x	s	x	x	x		x	x	x	x	x		x	x		s				s					
10	22-Oct	RANGERS	2 - 1	Arnott (2)	11160	x	s	x	x	x		x	x	x	x	x		x	x		s				s					
11	29-Oct	KILMARNOCK	3 - 2	Coyne (2), Martin	7436	x	s	x	x	x		x		x	x	x		x	x		s				s			x		
12	05-Nov	Hearts	2 - 1	Shannon, Coyne	8809	x	s	x	x	x		x	x	x	x	x		x	x		s				s					
13	08-Nov	DUNDEE UNITED	1 - 1	Martin	6145	x	s	x	x	x		x	x	x	x	x		x	x		s				s					
14	19-Nov	Hibernian	2 - 2	Coyne, Davies	9158	x	s	x	x	x		x	x	x	x	x			x		x	s			s					
15	26-Nov	PARTICK THISTLE	3 - 1	Coyne, Davies, Arnott	6893	x	s	x	x	x		x	x	x	x	x		x	x		s				s					
16	03-Dec	Celtic	2 - 2	Coyne (2)	21465	x	s	x	x	x		x	x	x	x	x		x	x		s				s					
17	10-Dec	ABERDEEN	0 - 1		7020	x	s	x	x	x		x	x	x		x		x	x		x	s			s					
18	26-Dec	Falkirk	1 - 0	Shannon	7838	x	s	x	x	x	x		x	x		x		x	x		s	x		s						
19	31-Dec	RANGERS	1 - 3	McGrillen	11269	x	s	x	x	x	x		x	x		x		x	x		s	x		s						
p 17/1	02-Jan	Kilmarnock	0 - 2		7500	s	x	x		x	x	x	x	x	x	x			x		x	s		s						
21	07-Jan	HEARTS	1 - 2	McGrillen	5117	x	s	x	x	x	x		x	x		x			x		s	x		x	s					
22	14-Jan	HIBERNIAN	0 - 0		6724	s	x	x		x	x	x	x	x	x	x			x		s	s		x						
23	21-Jan	Dundee United	1 - 6	Coyne	7306	s	x	x		x	x	x		x	x	x			x		x	x		s	s					
24	04-Feb	CELTIC	1 - 0	McKinnon	10771	x	s		x	x	x	x	x	x	x	x		x	x					s					s	
p 14/3	11-Feb	Partick Thistle	0 - 0		4327	x	s		s	x	x	x	x	x	x			x	x	x			x		s					
26	25-Feb	Aberdeen	2 - 0	McKinnon, Burns	8500	x	s	s	x	x	x		x	x	x			x		x		x	x		s					
27	04-Mar	FALKIRK	2 - 2	Lambert, May	6100	x	s	s	x	x	x	x	x	x	x			x		x			x		s					
28	18-Mar	DUNDEE UNITED	2 - 1	Burns, Arnott	4457	x	s	s	x		x	x		x	x			x	x	x			x		s				x	
29	21-Mar	Hibernian	0 - 2		5402	x	s	s	x		x	x		x	x	s		x	x	x			x						x	
30	01-Apr	Celtic	1 - 1	Coyne	24047	x	s			x	x	x		x	x	x		x	x	s		s	x							x
31	08-Apr	PARTICK THISTLE	1 - 2	Burns	9631	x	s		s	x	x	x		x	x	x			x	x		s			x					x
32	15-Apr	Falkirk	0 - 3		6200	x	s	x	x	x	x	x		x	x	x		x		s		x					s			
33	18-Apr	ABERDEEN	2 - 1	McSkimming, Arnott	7155	x	s		x	x	x	x		x	x	x		x		s		x	x		s					
34	29-Apr	Rangers	2 - 0	Arnott, McSkimming	43567	x	s		x	x		x		x	x	x		x	x	s		x	x		s					
35	06-May	KILMARNOCK	2 - 0	Lambert, May	7206	x	s		x	x		x		x	x	x		x	x	s		x	x		s					
36	13-May	Hearts	0 - 2		9031	x	s			x		x		x	x	x		x	x	s		x	x		s				x	

LEAGUE CUP

Date	Opponent	Score	Scorers	Att.	Woods	Howie	Shannon	Philliben	McKinnon	Krivokapic	Martin	McCart	Lambert	Dolan	Coyne	O' Donnell	Arnott	Davies	Burns	Kirk	McSkimming	May	McGrillen	Roddie	Allan	Ritchie	McLeish	McMillan	Van Der Gaag
16-Aug	CLYDEBANK	3 - 0	Burns, Coyne, Kirk	4172	s			x	x		x		x		x	x	x	x	x	s					x	s	x		
31-Aug	AIRDRIE	1 - 2	McCart	6010	x		x	x			x	x	x	x	x	x		s	x	s				x	s				

SCOTTISH CUP

Date	Opponent	Score	Scorers	Att.	Woods	Howie	Shannon	Philliben	McKinnon	Krivokapic	Martin	McCart	Lambert	Dolan	Coyne	O' Donnell	Arnott	Davies	Burns	Kirk	McSkimming	May	McGrillen	Roddie	Allan	Ritchie	McLeish	McMillan	Van Der Gaag
06-Feb	Falkirk	2 - 0	Burns (2)	8352	x	s		x	x	x	x	x	x	x				x	x				x	s				s	
18-Feb	Hibernian	0 - 2		10639	x	s	x	x	x	x	x		x	x			x	x	x	s			s						

U E F A CUP

Date	Opponent	Score	Scorers	Att.	Woods	Howie	Shannon	Philliben	McKinnon	Krivokapic	Martin	McCart	Lambert	Dolan	Coyne	O' Donnell	Arnott	Davies	Burns	Kirk	McSkimming	May	McGrillen	Roddie	Allan	Ritchie	McLeish	McMillan	Van Der Gaag
09-Aug	HAVNOR	3 - 0	McGrillen, Coyne, Kirk	7521	x		x	x	x		x	x	x	x	x	x		s		s			x		s				
23-Aug	Havnor	4 - 1	Kirk (2), Burns, Davies	480	x		x	x			x	x		x	s			x	x	x			x		s		x	s	
13-Sep	Dortmund	0 - 1		35420	x		x	x	x		x	x	x	x	x		x	x		s			s		s				
27-Sep	DORTMUND	0 - 2		9362	x		x	x	x		x	x	x	x	x		x	x	s	s					s				

FRIENDLIES

Date	Opponent	Score	Scorers
15-May	IPSWICH	3 - 2	Lambert (2), Coyne
July	Nijmegen		
July	Excelsior		
02-Aug	S D V B (away)		
July	Wrn Der Briec		
30-Jul	Persifino S V S	1 - 2	Burns

1995 Premier League

		Pl.	Home W.	Home D.	Home L.	Home F.	Home A.	Away W.	Away D.	Away L.	Away F.	Away A.	F. (Total)	A. (Total)	Pts. (Total)
1	Rangers	36	11	5	2	31	14	9	4	5	29	21	60	35	69
2	MOTHERWELL	36	8	6	4	29	23	6	6	6	21	27	50	50	54
3	Hibernian	36	9	7	2	37	19	3	10	5	12	18	49	37	53
4	Celtic	36	6	8	4	23	19	5	10	3	16	14	39	33	51
5	Falkirk	36	8	3	7	26	24	4	9	5	22	23	48	47	48
6	Heart of Mid.	36	9	4	5	26	14	3	3	12	18	37	44	51	43
7	Kilmarnock	36	8	4	6	22	16	3	6	9	18	32	40	48	43
8	Partick Thistle	36	4	9	5	23	23	6	4	8	17	27	40	50	43
9	Aberdeen	36	7	7	4	24	16	3	4	11	19	30	43	46	41
10	Dundee United	36	6	6	6	24	20	3	3	12	16	36	40	56	36

1994-95 Season

Back: Philliben, Coyne, Kirk, Martin, McKinnon, O'Donnell
Middle: Burns, McGrillen, Krivokapic, Woods, Dolan, Shannon, Davies
Front: Watson (Asst. Man), Arnott, McCart, Lambert, McLeish (Man)

1995-96 Season

Back : Lambert, Philliben, McSkimming, Essandoh, Van Der Gaag, Denholm, Ritchie, Krivokapic, Martin, Hendry.
Middle : J Porteous, Davies, Burns, McMillan, Woods, Howie, D Rae, McKinnon, Dolan, W McLean.
Front : J Griffin, Arnott, May , Coyne, McLeish, McCart, Roddie, P Ferguson, Watson.

1995-96: Premier League

No.	Date	Opponent	Result	Scorers	Att.	Howie	Woods	May	McKinnon	Phillben	Krivokapic	Van Der Gaag	Martin	McCart	Denham	Lambert	Dolan	Coyne	Arnott	Burns	Falconer	McSkimming	Davies	Roddie	Ritchie	McMillan	Hendry	Essandoh	Hicks	McLeish	Ferguson	McCulloch	Craigan	Sullivan
1	26-Aug	Hearts	1 - 1	Arnott	10971	x	s	x	x	s			x	x		x	x		x	x		s	x	x										
2	09-Sep	PARTICK THISTLE	1 - 1	OG	6155	x	s	x		x			x			x	x		x	x		x	s	x	x	s								
3	16-Sep	Celtic	1 - 1	Arnott	31000	x		x	x	x			x	x		x	x	x	x	s		x	s	s										
4	23-Sep	Falkirk	0 - 0		4246	x	s	x		x			x	x		x	x	x	x	s		x	s	x										
5	30-Sep	KILMARNOCK	3 - 0	Coyne (2), May	6356	x		x	x	x			x	x		x	s	x	x	s		x	x	s										
6	03-Oct	Rangers	1 - 2	McSkimming	37000	x		x	x	x			x	x		x	x	x	x	s		x	s	s										
7	07-Oct	RAITH	0 - 2		5727	x		x	x	x			x	x		x	s	x	x	s			x	x			s							
8	14-Oct	ABERDEEN	2 - 1	Coyne, Lambert	6842	x		x	x	x	x		x		s	x	x	x	x				x	s			s							
9	21-Oct	Hibernian	2 - 4	Hendry (2)	11500	x		x		x	x		x			x	x	x	x	s			x	x		s	s							
10	28-Oct	Partick Thistle	0 - 1		4500	x				x	x		x	x		x	x	x	s	s			x	s		x	x							
11	04-Nov	CELTIC	0 - 2		12077	x		x		x			x	x		x	x		x	s			x	s	s	x	x							
12	07-Nov	HEARTS	0 - 0		5595	x				x	x		x	x	s	x	x			x			x	x	s	x		s						
13	11-Nov	Raith Rovers	0 - 0		4300	x				x	x		x	x	s	x	x		s	x			x	x		x			s					
14	18-Nov	Kilmarnock	1 - 1	Burns	6608	x			x				x		x	x			x	x			x	s	s	x	s			x	x			
15	25-Nov	FALKIRK	1 - 1	Burns	5201	x			x		x		x		x	x	x		x	x			x	s	x	s	s							
16	02-Dec	HIBERNIAN	0 - 2		5362	x			x		x				x	x	x		x	x		x	s	x	x		s							
17	09-Dec	Aberdeen	0 - 1		13000	x		x	x		x		x		x	x	x		x	x			x	s	s		s							
18	19-Dec	RANGERS	0 - 0		10197	x		x	x		x		x		x	x	s			x		x	x	x	s			s						
p 10/1	26-Dec	Hearts	0 - 4		9288	x		x	x		x		x		x		x		x	x			x	s	x	s		s						
p 23/1	30-Dec	Falkirk	1 - 0	OG	4233	x		x	x	x	s		x		x	x			x	s	x		x			x	s							
p 16/1	01-Jan	KILMARNOCK	0 - 1		5781	x		x	x	x	x				x	x	x		x	s	x			x	s		s							
22	06-Jan	Celtic	0 - 1		35370	x	s	x	x		x		x		x	x	s		x	x		x	x		s									
23	13-Jan	PARTICK THISTLE	0 - 2		5226	x		x	x		x				x	x	x		x	x			s	s	x	x		s						
24	20-Jan	Hibernian	0 - 0		7676	x		x	x	x	s		x		x	x			s	s	x		x			x	x							
p 13/2	03-Feb	ABERDEEN	1 - 0	Burns	5090	x		x	x	s		x	x	x		x				s	x	x	s			x	x							
26	10-Feb	Rangers	2 - 3	Martin, Falconer	45566	x		x	x	s		x	x	x		x	s		x		x	x				x	s							
27	24-Feb	RAITH ROVERS	1 - 0	Falconer	5569	x		x	x			x	x	x		x	x	s		s	x	x	s				x							
28	02-Mar	FALKIRK	1 - 0	Falconer	5037	x		x	x	s		x	x	x		x	x	s		s	x		x				x							
29	16-Mar	Kilmarnock	1 - 0	Lambert	7035	x	s	x	x	s		x	x	x	s	x	x	x			x		x											
30	23-Mar	CELTIC	0 - 0		12397	x		x	x	x	s	x	x			x	x	s	s	x	x		x											
31	30-Mar	Partick Thistle	2 - 0	Davies, Van Der Gaag	5500	x		x	x	x		x	x	x		x		s	x	s	x		x		s									
32	06-Apr	HIBERNIAN	3 - 0	Falconer, Martin, Coyne	5964	x		x	x	s		x	x	x		x	x	x	s	s	x		x											
33	13-Apr	Aberdeen	1 - 2	Falconer	9500	x		x	x	s		x	x	x		x	x		x	s	x		x	s										
34	20-Apr	RANGERS	1 - 3	Arnott	13128	x		x	x	s		x	x	x		x	x		x	s	x	s	x											
35	27-Apr	Raith Rovers	0 - 2		3685	x				x		x	x	x		x					x	x	x	x	s		x					s	s	
36	04-May	HEARTS	1 - 1	Davies	6004	x				x		x	x	x		x		x			x	x	x	x			s					s	s	

LEAGUE CUP

Date	Opponent	Result	Scorers	Att.	Howie	Woods	May	McKinnon	Phillben	Krivokapic	Van Der Gaag	Martin	McCart	Denham	Lambert	Dolan	Coyne	Arnott	Burns	Falconer	McSkimming	Davies	Roddie	Ritchie	McMillan	Hendry	Essandoh	Hicks	McLeish	Ferguson	McCulloch	Craigan	Sullivan
19-Aug	Clydebank *	1 - 1	Arnott	2192	x	s	x	x			x	x			x	x	x	x			x	x	s										s
29-Aug	Dundee United	2 - 1	Lambert, Arnott	6839	x	s	x	x	x			x			x	x		x	x		x	s	x	s									
20-Sep	ABERDEEN	1 - 2	Arnott	9137	x		x	x	x			x	x		x	x	x	x	s		x	s	s										

* Won on pens.

SCOTTISH CUP

Date	Opponent	Result	Scorers	Att.	Howie	Woods	May	McKinnon	Phillben	Krivokapic	Van Der Gaag	Martin	McCart	Denham	Lambert	Dolan	Coyne	Arnott	Burns	Falconer	McSkimming	Davies	Roddie	Ritchie	McMillan	Hendry	Essandoh	Hicks	McLeish	Ferguson	McCulloch	Craigan	Sullivan
30-Jan	ABERDEEN	0 - 2		6035	x		x	x	x	s		x		x	x	x		x	x		x				s	s							

UEFA

Date	Opponent	Result	Scorers	Att.	Howie	Woods	May	McKinnon	Phillben	Krivokapic	Van Der Gaag	Martin	McCart	Denham	Lambert	Dolan	Coyne	Arnott	Burns	Falconer	McSkimming	Davies	Roddie	Ritchie	McMillan	Hendry	Essandoh	Hicks	McLeish	Ferguson	McCulloch	Craigan	Sullivan
08-Aug	MYPA	1 - 3	McSkimming	8280	s	x	x	x			x	x	x		x	x	x				x	s				x	s						
22-Aug	Mypa	2 - 0	Arnott, Burns	4158	x		x	x	s			x	x		x	x		x	x		s	x	x								s		

FRIENDLIES

Date	Opponent	Result	Scorers	Att.
12-Aug	MIDDLESBROUGH	1 - 4	Coyne	3157
15-Apr	WOLVERHAMPTON W.	1 - 2	OG	
25-Jul	Baldock Town	2 - 1	Dolan, Coyne	
08-Mar	Drogheda	0 - 0		550
	Caledonian Thistle			
21-Jul	Stirling Albion	1 - 1	Dolan	
29-Jul	Lommer			
04-Aug	Darlington			
28-Apr	Arthurlie			
27-Aug	Cumbernauld			
17-Feb	Northallerton	3 - 1	McKinnon, Burns, OG	453

1996 Premier League

		Pl.	Home W.	D.	L.	F.	A.	Away W.	D.	L.	F.	A.	F. (Total)	A.	Pts.
1	Rangers	36	13	3	2	47	16	14	3	1	38	9	85	25	87
2	Celtic	36	12	5	1	40	12	12	6	0	34	13	74	25	83
3	Aberdeen	36	11	1	6	31	17	5	6	7	21	28	52	45	55
4	Heart of Mid.	36	10	2	6	33	26	6	5	7	22	27	55	53	55
5	Hibernian	36	7	5	6	25	26	4	5	9	18	31	43	57	43
6	Raith Rovers	36	7	5	6	23	21	5	2	11	18	36	41	57	43
7	Kilmarnock	36	8	4	6	25	21	3	4	11	14	33	39	54	41
8	MOTHERWELL	36	6	6	6	15	16	3	6	9	13	23	28	39	39
9	Partick Thistle	36	3	5	10	12	28	5	1	12	17	34	29	62	30
10	Falkirk	36	4	4	10	17	26	2	2	14	14	34	31	60	24

1996-97: Premier League

No.	Date	Opponent	Score	Scorers	Att.	Howie	Woods	May	Philliben	McSkimming	Van Der Gaag	McMillan	Ross	Martin	Denham	McCart	Wishart	Burns	Dolan	Arnott	Coyne	Falconer	Coyle	Hendry	Davies	Christie	McCulloch	Roddie	Lehtonen	Craigan	McCallum	Valikari	Essandoh	Weir
1	10-Aug	Dundee United	1 - 1	Van Der Gaag	8157	x		x	s	x	x	s		x	x			s	x		x	x		x	x									
2	17-Aug	ABERDEEN	2 - 2	McSkimming (2)	6206	x		x	s	x	x	x	x	x			x	s	x	x		x					s							
3	24-Aug	Raith Rovers	3 - 0	Coyne, Arnott, Falconer	7800	x		x	s		x	x	x	x			x	x	x	x					x		s	s						
4	07-Sep	RANGERS	0 - 1		12288	x		x		x	x	x	s	x		s	x	x	x	x					x		s							
5	14-Sep	Dunfermline Ath.	1 - 1	May	5687	x		x		x	x		s	x		x	x	s	x	x		x			x			s						
6	21-Sep	Hearts	1 - 1	Arnott	10932	x		x		x	x		x	x		s	x	s	x	x		x			x		s							
7	28-Sep	KILMARNOCK	1 - 0	Arnott	5700	x		x	s		x		x	x		x	x	x	x	x				s	x		s							
8	12-Oct	Celtic	0 - 1		48500	x		x	x	x			s	x	x		x	x		x				x	x		s	s						
9	19-Oct	HIBERNIAN	1 - 1	McSkimming	6784	x		x	s	x	x		s	x		x	x	x	x	x				x			s							
10	26-Oct	Rangers	0 - 5		48160	x	s	x	s	x			x	x		x	x	x	x			x			x		s							
11	02-Nov	DUNDEE UNITED	1 - 3	Ross	5814	x		x	s	x			x	x		x	x	x		x	s	x			x		s							
12	16-Nov	Kilmarnock	4 - 2	Coyne (3), Philliben	7087	x		x	x	x				x		x		s	x	x	x				x		s	x	s					
13	23-Nov	HEARTS	0 - 2		5441	x		x	x	x			x	x	x	x		x		x	x				s		s	s						
14	30-Nov	Hibernian	0 - 2		7332	x		x	x	x		s	x	x		x			x		x				x			x		s	s			
15	07-Dec	CELTIC	2 - 1	Davies, Ross	11589	x		x	x	x		x	s	x		x		s	x		x				x			x	s					
16	11-Dec	RAITH ROVERS	0 - 1		4040		x	x	x	x		x	x	x		x		s	x		x						s	x	s					
17	14-Dec	Aberdeen	0 - 0		10036		x	x	x			x	s	x	s	x		x	x		x						s	x	x					
18	21-Dec	DUNFERMLINE	2 - 3	OG, Coyne	4529	x		x	s		x	x		x		x		x	x		x				x		s	x	s					
19	26-Dec	Dundee United	0 - 2		8072		x	x	s		x		s	x		x		s	x		x	x			x			x	x					
p 21/1	01-Jan	KILMARNOCK	2 - 0	Coyle (2)	5508	x		x	s	x	x		x	x			x	x			x	x	x		s		s							
21	04-Jan	Celtic	0 - 5		45374		x	x	x	x	x		s		s	x		s	x		x	x			x			x						
22	11-Jan	HIBERNIAN	2 - 1	McSkimming, OG	5855	x		x	s	x	x		x	x			x	s			x	x	x		s				x					
23	18-Jan	RANGERS	1 - 3	Coyle	13166	x		x	s	x	x		x	x			x	x			x	x	x		s		s							
24	01-Feb	Dunfermline Ath.	0 - 2		4796	x		x	x		x		x	x		s	x				x	x	x		x		s							
25	08-Feb	ABERDEEN	2 - 2	Falconer, Burns	5555	x		x	x	x		s		x	x			x			x	x	x		s		s					x		
p 18/2	11-Feb	Raith Rovers	5 - 1	Coyne (2), Coyle, Van Der Gaag, May	3062	x		x	s	x	x		x	x			s	x			x	x	x				s					x		
27	22-Feb	CELTIC	0 - 1		12131	x		x			x	x	x	x	s		x				x		x				x		s			x	s	
28	01-Mar	HIBERNIAN	1 - 1	Coyne	8800	x		x	s		x	x	x	x				x			x	x	x		s		s					x		
29	15-Mar	Kilmarnock	0 - 1		7616	x		x			x		x	x		s	s	x			x	x	x		s							x		x
30	22-Mar	HEARTS	0 - 1		6245	x			s		x		x	x		x		s			s	x	x	x	x	x						x		
31	05-Apr	Aberdeen	0 - 0		9500	x					x		x		x	x				s	s	x	x	x	x	x						x		s
32	12-Apr	RAITH ROVERS	5 - 0	Coyne(2), Falconer, Weir, Coyle	4691	x		x			x	x		x	s	s					x	x	x		x	s						x		x
33	19-Apr	DUNDEE UNITED	1 - 1	Coyne	5382	x		x			x	x	s	x	s					s	x	x	x			x						x		x
34	05-May	Rangers	2 - 0	Coyle (2)	50059	x		x	s	x	x	x	x	x				s		s	x		x									x		x
35	10-May	DUNFERMLINE	2 - 2	Weir, Van Der Gaag	6105	x		x			x	x	x	x		s				s	x	x	x		s							x		x

LEAGUE CUP

No.	Date	Opponent	Score	Scorers	Att.	Howie	Woods	May	Philliben	McSkimming	Van Der Gaag	McMillan	Ross	Martin	Denham	McCart	Wishart	Burns	Dolan	Arnott	Coyne	Falconer	Coyle	Hendry	Davies	Christie	McCulloch	Roddie	Lehtonen	Craigan	McCallum	Valikari	Essandoh	Weir
	13-Aug	ALLOA ATHLETIC *	0 - 0		3503	x		x	x	x		x		x	x		s	x	x	s		x			x		s							

* Lost on pens.

SCOTTISH CUP

No.	Date	Opponent	Score	Scorers	Att.	Howie	Woods	May	Philliben	McSkimming	Van Der Gaag	McMillan	Ross	Martin	Denham	McCart	Wishart	Burns	Dolan	Arnott	Coyne	Falconer	Coyle	Hendry	Davies	Christie	McCulloch	Roddie	Lehtonen	Craigan	McCallum	Valikari	Essandoh	Weir
	25-Jan	Partick Thistle	2 - 0	McSkimming, Davies	5502	x		x	x	x	x		x	x			s	x			x	x	x		s		s							
	15-Feb	HAMILTON ACADEMICAL	1 - 1	Coyle	8050	x		x		s	x	x	s	x	x			x			x	x	x		x		s							
rep.	26-Feb	Hamilton Academical	2 - 0	Coyle (2)	4825	x		x	x		x	x	x	x	s		s	s			x		x		x		x							
	08-Mar	Dundee United	1 - 4	Van Der Gaag	11054	x			s		x	x	x	x	s			x			x	x	x		s		x					x		

FRIENDLIES

No.	Date	Opponent	Score	Scorers	Att.
	27-Jul	Blyth Spartans	3 - 2	Hendry (2), Martin	
	03-Aug	F C PORTO	0 - 1		3610
	24-Jul	Southend United	0 - 1		
	23-Nov	Peterlee			
	29-Jul	Arbroath	6 - 0		
	05-Aug	Irvine Meadow			

1997 Premier League

		Pl.	Home					Away					F.	A.	Pts.
			W.	D.	L.	F.	A.	W.	D.	L.	F.	A.	(Total)		
1	Rangers	36	13	2	3	44	16	12	3	3	41	17	85	33	80
2	Celtic	36	14	2	2	48	9	9	4	5	30	23	78	32	75
3	Dundee United	36	10	4	4	21	10	7	5	6	25	23	46	33	60
4	Heart of Mid.	36	8	6	4	27	20	6	4	8	19	23	46	43	52
5	Dunfermline Ath.	36	8	4	6	32	30	4	5	9	20	35	52	65	45
6	Aberdeen	36	6	8	4	25	19	4	6	8	20	35	45	54	44
7	Kilmarnock	36	8	4	6	28	26	3	2	13	13	35	41	61	39
8	MOTHERWELL	36	5	5	8	24	25	4	6	8	20	30	44	55	38
9	Hibernian	36	6	4	8	18	25	3	7	8	20	30	38	55	38
10	Raith Rovers	36	3	5	10	18	39	3	2	13	11	34	29	73	25

1996-97 Season
Back : Essandoh, Denholm, Ritchie, Van Der Gaag, Falconer, Martin, Dolan
Middle : Davies, May, McMillan, Woods, Howie, McSkimming, Philliben, Hendry
Front : Burns, Arnott, Roddie, McLeish, McCart, McCulloch, Coyne

1997-98 Season
Back : J Porteous, Valakari, McCulloch, Christie, Denholm, Falconer, Craigan, Coyle, A Watson
Middle : J Griffin, McMillan, Shivute, Philliben, Woods, Gow, McSkimming, Hendry, Ross
Front : Arnott, May, Coyne, McLeish, Martin, Davies, Weir

1997-98: Premier League

No	Date	Opponent	Score	Scorers	Att	Woods	May	McMillan	Valikari	Martin	Denham	Philliben	Weir	Falconer	Ross	Craigan	Hendry	Coyne	McSkimming	Arnott	Davies	Dorner	Resch	Christie	Coyle	McCulloch	Shivute	Jonsonn	Garcin	Tuomelia	Newman	Lindqvist	Lundgren	Thomson
1	02-Aug	Dunfermline Ath.	2 - 0	Coyne (2)	5746	x	x	x	x	x	x		x	x	s			x			s	s	x		x									
2	16-Aug	ST. JOHNSTONE	0 - 1		5036	x	x	x	x			x	x	x	s	x		s			s	x	x		x									
3	23-Aug	Aberdeen	3 - 1	Weir (2), Coyne	11552	x	x	x	s	x	x		x	x	s			x				s	x	x	x									
4	13-Sep	CELTIC	2 - 3	Coyne (2)	11550	x	x	x	x	x	x		x	x	x			x						s	x	s	s							
5	20-Sep	HIBERNIAN	1 - 1	Coyne	7420	x	x	x	x	x		s	x	x		x		x						s	x	s	x							
6	27-Sep	Rangers	2 - 2	Coyne, Shivute	48672	x		x	x	x	x		x	x		s	s	x						x	x	s	x							
7	04-Oct	HEARTS	1 - 4	Coyne	8886	x	x	x	x	x	x		x	x				x							x		x							
8	08-Oct	Kilmarnock	0 - 1		6600	x	x	x			x		x	x	s	s	s	x						x	x	x	x							
9	18-Oct	Dundee United	0 - 4		7337	x		x	x	x		s	x	x	x	x	s	x						x	s		x							
10	25-Oct	ABERDEEN	1 - 2	Davies	6065	x		x	x		x	x	x			s	x				s			x	x	x	s	x						
11	01-Nov	St. Johnstone	3 - 4	Hendry, Davies, Coyle	4556	x		x	s		x				x		x	x			x			x	s	s	x	x	x					
12	08-Nov	KILMARNOCK	0 - 1		5346	x		x	x		x	s				x	s	x	x		x				x	x	s		x					
13	15-Nov	Celtic	2 - 0	Coyle , Weir	48010	x		x	x			x	s		x	x	x		x	s				x	x	x				s				
14	22-Nov	RANGERS	1 - 1	Coyne	12018	x	x	x	x			x			s	x	x	x	x	s				x	x	s								
15	29-Nov	Hibernian	1 - 1	Coyle	9999	x	x	x	x			x			s	x	x	x	x	s				x	x	s								
16	07-Dec	Hearts	0 - 0		12706	x	x	x			s	x			x	x	x	x	x	s				x	x		s							
17	13-Dec	DUNDEE UNITED	1 - 0	Coyne	4555	x	x	x		x	s	x	s		s		x	x	x						x		x				x			
18	20-Dec	DUNFERMLINE	2 - 0	Coyle (2)	4607	x	x	x		x	s	x	s				x	x	x		s				x		x				x			
19	27-Dec	Aberdeen	0 - 3		13038	x	x	x		x		x	s				x	x	x		s			s	x		x				x			
20	03-Jan	Kilmarnock	1 - 4	Coyle	8724	x	x	x		x		x	s				x	x	x		x			s	x		s				x			
21	10-Jan	CELTIC	1 - 1	Coyne	12350	x	x	x	s	x				x			s	x	x						x	x	s		x		x			
22	17-Jan	Rangers	0 - 1		49433	x	x		s	x			x	x	x			x	x						x	s	s		x		x			
23	31-Jan	HIBERNIAN	6 - 2	Arnott, Weir, Garcin, McCulloch (2), Coyne	6169	x				x		s	x	x	x			x	s	x				x	x	s			x		x			
24	07-Feb	Dundee United	0 - 1		6532	x	x	s				s	x	x	x			x		x				x	x	s			x		x			
25	21-Feb	HEARTS	2 - 4	Falconer, Coyle	8375	x	x	x	x	x				x	x			x			x			s	x	s			s		x			
26	25-Feb	ST. JOHNSTONE	2 - 1	Coyne (2)	4517	x	s	x	x	x				x	x			x			x			x	x	s			s		x			
27	28-Feb	Dunfermline Ath.	1 - 2	Coyne	4811	x	s	x	x	x				x	x			x			x			x	x	s			s		x			
28	14-Mar	RANGERS	2 - 1	Falconer, Coyle	11779	x	s	x	x	x	x			x	x			x			x			x	x	s	s							
29	21-Mar	Hibernian	0 - 1		10582	x	s	x	x	x	x			x	s			x			x			x	x	x			s					
30	28-Mar	DUNDEE UNITED	1 - 0	Coyle	5012	x		x	x	x	x	s		x				x			x			x	x	s	s					x		
31	04-Apr	Hearts	1 - 1	Coyne	14737	x		x	x	x	x	s			x			x			x			x	x	s	s					x		
32	11-Apr	KILMARNOCK	1 - 1	Lindqvist	6209	x		x	x	x	x	s			x			x						x	x	s	s		x			x		
33	18-Apr	Celtic	1 - 4	McMillan	49541	x	s	x	x	x	x			x				x						x	x	s	x					x	s	
34	25-Apr	DUNFERMLINE	1 - 3	Shivute	5745	x		x	x	x	x			x	s	x		x			s				x	s	x					x		
35	02-May	St. Johnstone	2 - 3	Martin, Coyne	6754	x	x	x	x	x	x			s	x			x		x	x				x		s					s		
36	09-May	ABERDEEN	1 - 2	Ross	6305		x	x	x	x	x			s	x			x		s	x			x	x	s								x

LEAGUE CUP

No	Date	Opponent	Score	Scorers	Att	Woods	May	McMillan	Valikari	Martin	Denham	Philliben	Weir	Falconer	Ross	Craigan	Hendry	Coyne	McSkimming	Arnott	Davies	Dorner	Resch	Christie	Coyle	McCulloch	Shivute	Jonsonn	Garcin	Tuomelia	Newman	Lindqvist	Lundgren	Thomson
	09-Aug	INVERNESS *	2 - 2	Falconer, Coyle	4247	x	x	x	s	x	x		x	x	s			x			x	s	x		x									
	20-Aug	MORTON	3 - 0	Coyle (3)	4576	x	x	x		x	x		x	x	s			x				s	x	x	x	s								
	09-Sep	Celtic	0 - 1		37006	x	x	x	x	x	x		x	x	s			x						x	x	s	s							

* Won on pens.

SCOTTISH CUP

No	Date	Opponent	Score	Scorers	Att	Woods	May	McMillan	Valikari	Martin	Denham	Philliben	Weir	Falconer	Ross	Craigan	Hendry	Coyne	McSkimming	Arnott	Davies	Dorner	Resch	Christie	Coyle	McCulloch	Shivute	Jonsonn	Garcin	Tuomelia	Newman	Lindqvist	Lundgren	Thomson
	24-Jan	Dumbarton	1 - 1	McSkimming	2412	x	x	x		x		s	x	x	s			x	x	s					x	x					x			
rep.	27-Jan	DUMBARTON	1 - 0	Coyle	4204	x	x	x		x		s	x	x				x	x	s	s				x	x					x			
	14-Feb	RANGERS	2 - 2	Coyle, Coyne	12602	x	x	x	s	x			x					x	s	x				x	x	s			x		x			
rep.	17-Feb	Rangers	0 - 3		42043	x	x	x	s	x			x		s			x	x					x	x	s			x		x			

FRIENDLIES

Date	Opponent	Score	Scorers
27-Jul	ASTON VILLA	0 - 3	
19-Jul	Ashington	0 - 0	
22-Jul	Carlisle United	3 - 3	Coyne, Burns, Denholm
24-Jul	Hartlepool United	1 - 1	Hendry
03-Apr	Partick Thistle	4 - 0	
28-Jul	Whitburn Juniors	3 - 1	
30-Jul	Huntly	2 - 1	

1998 Premier League

		Pl.	Home					Away					F.	A.	Pts.
			W.	D.	L.	F.	A.	W.	D.	L.	F.	A.	(Total)		
1	Celtic	36	12	4	2	41	9	10	4	4	23	15	64	24	74
2	Rangers	36	13	4	1	46	16	8	5	5	30	22	76	38	72
3	Hearts	36	10	5	3	36	24	9	5	4	34	22	70	46	67
4	Kilmarnock	36	9	4	5	24	21	4	7	7	16	31	40	52	50
5	St. Johnstone	36	7	5	6	20	21	6	4	8	18	21	38	42	48
6	Aberdeen	36	6	6	6	20	18	3	6	9	19	35	39	53	39
7	Dundee Utd.	36	5	7	6	23	18	3	6	9	20	33	43	51	37
8	Dunfermline Ath.	36	4	9	5	26	30	4	4	10	17	38	43	68	37
9	MOTHERWELL	36	6	4	8	26	28	3	3	12	20	36	46	64	34
10	Hibernian	36	6	4	8	26	24	0	8	10	12	35	38	59	30

1998-99: Premier League

No.	Date	Opponent	Score	Scorers	Att.	Kaven	Woods	Goram	McMillan	McGowan	Doesburg	May	Valikari	Brannan	McClair	McCulloch	Coyle	Teale	Gower	Michels	Matthaei	Stirling	Nevin	Thomas	Spencer	Adams	Goodman	Halliday	Shivute	Miller	Craigan	Nyyssonen	Ross	Christie	Ramsay	Bacque	Nicholas	Denham	Davies
1	01-Aug	ST. JOHNSTONE	1 - 0	Stirling	5686	x			x		x		x		x	s	x		x	x	x	x						s					x						
2	15-Aug	Rangers	1 - 2	Coyle	49275		x			x	x		x		x	s	x	x		x	x	x						s				x							
3	22-Aug	DUNFERMLINE	0 - 0		9859	x			x	x	x		x			s	x	x		x	x									s		x	x						
4	30-Aug	DUNDEE UNITED	1 - 0	Nyyssonen	11201	x			x	x	x		x		x		x	x			x								s			x	x						
5	12-Sep	Aberdeen	1 - 1	Coyle	11560	x			x	x	x		x		x	s	x	x		x	x	s	s										x						
6	19-Sep	KILMARNOCK	0 - 0		9063	x			x	x	x		x		x	s	x	x		x	x		s			s							x						
7	23-Sep	Hearts	0 - 3		12665	x			x	x	x		x				x	x		x	x		s			x							x						
8	26-Sep	Dundee	0 - 1		5655	x			x	x	x		x		x	s	x	x		s	x		x			x							s						
9	03-Oct	CELTIC	1 - 2	Adams	12103		x		x	x	x		x		x	s	x	x			x	x	s			s							x						
10	17-Oct	St. Johnstone	0 - 5		4062		x			x	x		x		x	s	x	x			s	x	x			x					s		x						
11	28-Oct	RANGERS	1 - 0	Spencer	11777	x			x	x	x		x	x		s	x	x					s		x	x								x					
12	31-Oct	ABERDEEN	2 - 2	Spencer, McGowan	8146	x			x	x	x		x	x		s	x	x					s		x	s		x						x					
13	07-Nov	Dundee United	2 - 2	Coyle (2)	6616	x			x	x	x	x	x	x		x	x	x					s		x	s					s								
14	14-Nov	HEARTS	3 - 2	Coyle (2), Brannan	8912	x			x	x	x	x	x	x			x	x					x		x	s							s						
15	21-Nov	Kilmarnock	0 - 0		10176	x			x	x	x	x	x	x	s		x	x					x		x	s													
16	28-Nov	Celtic	0 - 2		59889	x			x	x	x	x	x	x	s		x	x					s		x			x											
17	12-Dec	Dunfermline Ath.	1 - 1	Spencer	5182	x			x		x	x	x	x	s	x	x	x					s		x									x					
18	16-Dec	DUNDEE	2 - 1	Coyle, McMillan	4000	x			x	x			x	x		x	x	x		s			x	x	x	s													
19	19-Dec	ST. JOHNSTONE	1 - 2	Adams	5995	x			x	x	x	x	x	x		s	x			s			s	x	x	x													
20	26-Dec	DUNDEE UNITED	2 - 0	McMillan, Brannan	6001		x		x		x	s	x	x		x	x	x					x	x	x	s								s					
21	29-Dec	Aberdeen	1 - 1	McCulloch	15029		x		x		x	s	x	x		x	x	x					s	x	x	s								x					
22	01-Jan	KILMARNOCK	1 - 2	Brannan	8532		x			x	x		x	x		x	x			x	x		x	x		s													
23	30-Jan	Hearts	2 - 0	McCulloch, Adams	12821			x		x	x		x	x		x	x	x			x			x	x	s					s								
24	06-Feb	Dundee	0 - 1		4100			x		x	x		x	x		x	x	x					x			x					x				s	s			
25	21-Feb	CELTIC	1 - 7	Brannan	11963		x			x	x	x	x	x		x	x	x					s		x	s					x		s						
26	27-Feb	DUNFERMLINE	1 - 1	McCulloch	6094			x	x	x	x	x	x	x		x	x	x					x			s							s		s				
27	13-Mar	Rangers	1 - 2	Gower	49483			x	x	x	x	x	x	x		x		x	x		s		s			x				s									
28	20-Mar	ABERDEEN	1 - 1	Teale	6963			x	x		x	x	x	x				x	x		s		s	x	x					x							s		
29	03-Apr	Dundee United	3 - 0	Spencer (2), McCulloch	8110			x	x	x			x	x				x	x				x	x	x		x										s		
30	10-Apr	DUNDEE	1 - 2	Spencer	5717			x	x	x	s		x	x				x	x				x	x	x		x										s		
31	17-Apr	Celtic	0 - 1		59598			x	x	x	x		x	x		x		x	x						x	s	x				s						s		
32	24-Apr	HEARTS	0 - 4		8926			x	x	x	x		x	x		s		x	x		s		s	x	x		x												
33	01-May	Kilmarnock	1 - 0	Brannan	8867			x	x	x				x					x		x		x		x	x	x			s	x						s		
34	08-May	St. Johnstone	0 - 0		4599			x	x	x			x	x		s					x		x		x	x	x				x								
35	15-May	RANGERS	1 - 5	Nicholas	12036			x	x	x			x	x		s					x		x		x	x	x				x						s		
36	23-May	Dunfermline Ath.	2 - 1	Goodman, Ramsey	5313			x	x	x			x	x		x							x		x	x	x				x						s		

LEAGUE CUP

Date	Opponent	Score	Scorers	Att.	Kaven	Woods	Goram	McMillan	McGowan	Doesburg	May	Valikari	Brannan	McClair	McCulloch	Coyle	Teale	Gower	Michels	Matthaei	Stirling	Nevin	Thomas	Spencer	Adams	Goodman	Halliday	Shivute	Miller	Craigan	Nyyssonen	Ross	Christie	Ramsay	Bacque	Nicholas	Denham	Davies
08-Aug	East Fife	1 - 0	Halliday	1488	x				x	x		x		x	x		x			x	x						x	s	s		x							
18-Aug	AYR UNITED	0 - 2		4893		x					x			x	x	x	x		x		s						x		s	s			x				x	x

SCOTTISH CUP

Date	Opponent	Score	Scorers	Att.	Kaven	Woods	Goram	McMillan	McGowan	Doesburg	May	Valikari	Brannan	McClair	McCulloch	Coyle	Teale	Gower	Michels	Matthaei	Stirling	Nevin	Thomas	Spencer	Adams	Goodman	Halliday	Shivute	Miller	Craigan	Nyyssonen	Ross	Christie	Ramsay	Bacque	Nicholas	Denham	Davies
24-Jan	HEARTS	3 - 1	Brannan, Coyle, Thomas	9372			x	x		x		x	x		x	x	x			s		x	x	x	s													
13-Feb	STIRLING ALBION	2 - 0	McCulloch, OG	7244			x	x	x	x		x	x		x	x	x					x		x	s					s								
06-Mar	ST. JOHNSTONE	0 - 2		7660			x	x	x	x	s	x	x		x		x					s		x	x							x						

FRIENDLIES

Date	Opponent	Score	Scorers
25-Jul	WEST HAM UNITED	1 - 1	Coyle
28-Jul	LE HARVE	1 - 2	McMillan
04-Oct	Utrecht	1 - 4	Halliday
08-Jul	Finn Pa	0 - 3	
10-Jul	Lahti	0 - 2	
06-Jul	Rips	4 - 2	Stirling, Ross, Halliday, McMillan
18-Jul	Nairn	5 - 0	Coyle (3), Stirling, Trialist
20-Jul	Forres Mechanics	6 - 0	Coyle (3), Ross (2), McCulloch
25-Mar	Partick Thistle	1 - 0	Matthaei
22-Jul	East Stirling		

1999 Premier League

		Pl.	Home					Away					F.	A.	Pts.
			W.	D.	L.	F.	A.	W.	D.	L.	F.	A.	(Total)		
1	Rangers	36	12	5	1	32	11	11	3	4	46	20	78	31	77
2	Celtic	36	14	2	2	49	12	7	6	5	35	23	84	35	71
3	St. Johnstone	36	8	7	3	24	18	7	5	6	15	20	39	38	57
4	Kilmarnock	36	8	7	3	24	15	6	7	5	23	14	47	29	56
5	Dundee	36	7	4	7	18	23	6	3	9	18	33	36	56	46
6	Heart of Mid.	36	8	2	8	27	26	3	7	8	17	24	44	50	42
7	MOTHERWELL	36	6	5	7	20	31	4	6	8	15	23	35	54	41
8	Aberdeen	36	6	4	8	24	35	4	3	11	19	37	43	72	37
9	Dundee United	36	2	8	8	13	26	6	2	10	24	26	37	52	34
10	Dunfermline	36	4	7	7	18	29	0	9	9	10	30	28	59	28

1998-99 Season

Back : J Griffin, Miller, McGowan, Christie, Denholm, McCulloch, White, Striling, Craigan, Shivute, Ramsey, Petteri Jaatinen (fitness coach).
Middle : W McLean, Callaghan, ? , Thompson, ? , Brown, Woods, Kavin, Hodge, Dunn, ? , Hammill, J Porteous.
Front : Davies, Michels, Valikari, Coyle, McClair, Kampman, McMillan, Halliday, Ross, Matthaei, Kemp.

1999-2000 Season

Back : Halliday, Ramsey, Adams, Doesburg, Thomas, Woods, Townsley, Denholm, Brown, McGowan, McCulloch, Craigan, Valakari, Doherty.
Middle : M Weir, Hammell, Lasley, Fallon, Clarke, McLaughlin, Wilson, Dempsie , Miller, K McDonald, McFadden, Callaghan, McParland, Krivokapic.
Front : Hardy, Nevin, Nicholas, McMillan, Goodman, B Davies, Goram, J Griffin, Teale, Brannan, Spencer, Matthaei, J Porteous

1999-00: Premier League

No	Date	Opponent	Score	Scorers	Att	Goram	Woods	Doesburg	Kemble	Teale	Denham	Craigan	Strong	McMillan	McGowan	Townsley	Twaddle	Spencer	Goodman	Adams	Valakari	Brannan	McCulloch	Nicholas	Matthaei	Thomas	Nevin	Halliday	Harvey	Davies j	Corrigan	Curcic	Hammell	Ramsay
1	31-Jul	Hibernian	2 - 2	Nicholas, Nevin	13058	x				x		x			x	x			x	x	x	x	x	s		x	s							
2	07-Aug	DUNDEE UNITED	2 - 2	McCulloch (2)	6791	x		x		x				x		s		x	x		x	x	x	s	x	x								
3	15-Aug	Rangers	1 - 4	McCulloch	45464	x		x		x				x	s			x			x	x	x	x	x	x								
4	21-Aug	Kilmarnock	1 - 0	adams	7732	x		x		x		x		x	x			x	x	x		x	x					s						
5	28-Aug	DUNDEE	0 - 2		6382	x		x		x		x		x	x			x	x	x		x	x					s						
6	11-Sep	St. Johnstone	1 - 1	Spencer	5467		x	x		x				x		x		x		x	x	x	x	s		x	s	s						
p 23/11	20-Sep	HEARTS	1 - 0	Teale (Aband. Half Time)	6640	x		x		x				x		x		x			x	x	x			x	x							
8	16-Oct	HIBERNIAN	2 - 2	McCulloch, McMillan	7009	x		x		x				x		x	s	x	s		x	x	x	s		x	x							
9	20-Oct	ABERDEEN	5 - 6	Spencer (3), Goodman, Teale	5019	x		x		x		s		x		x	s	x	x		x	x				x	x	s						
10	23-Oct	Dundee United	2 - 0	Spencer, Teale	6213	x		x	x	x				x		s	x	x	s		x	x	x				x							
11	27-Oct	Celtic	1 - 0	Twaddle	58731	x		x	x	x				x	s		x	x	x		x	x	x	s			s							
12	30-Oct	ST. JOHNSTONE	1 - 0	Twaddle	6173	x		x	x		x				x	s	x	x	x		x	x	x				s							
13	06-Nov	Hearts	1 - 1	Spencer	12514		x	x	x	x				x		s	x	x			x	x	x				x		s					
14	20-Nov	Dundee	1 - 0	McCulloch	4340		x	x	x	x				x		s	x	x			x	x	x				x		s					
15	23-Nov	HEARTS	2 - 1	McCulloch, Nevin	7850		x	x	x	x				x		x	x	x	s		x	x	x	s			s							
16	28-Nov	CELTIC	3 - 2	Brannan, Townsley, Goodman	12775		x	x	x	x				x		x	x		x		x	x	x	s			s			s				
p 22/2	08-Dec	KILMARNOCK	0 - 4		5207	x			x		x			x	x	s	s	x			s	x	x						x	x	x			
19	11-Dec	Hibernian	2 - 2	Spencer (2)	9955		x	x	x	x				x		x		x			x	x		s			x	x	s					
20	18-Dec	RANGERS	1 - 5	Goodman	12640	x		x	x	x				x		x	x	x	x		x	x		s			s							
21	22-Jan	St. Johnstone	1 - 1	McMillan	4158	x		x	x		x			x		x	x	x	x		x	x		s			s				s			
22	26-Jan	Aberdeen	1 - 1	Spencer	10314	x			x		x			x		s	x	x	x		x	x	x	s			s				x			
23	05-Feb	DUNDEE	0 - 3		5865	x			x		x			x		x	x	x	s		x	x	x				s				x			
24	12-Feb	Kilmarnock	2 - 0	McMillan, Spencer	7057	x					x			x	x	s	s	x	x		x	x	x	s						x	x			
25	01-Mar	HEARTS	0 - 2		5588	x			x					x	x	x			x	x	x	x		s			s		s	x	x			
26	04-Mar	ABERDEEN	1 - 0	Goodman	6680	x			x			s		x	x	x		x	x	x	x			s			s		x		x			
27	18-Mar	Rangers	2 - 6	Kemble, McCulloch	49622	x			x					x	x		x			x	x	x	x	s			s		s		x	x		
28	25-Mar	Hearts	0 - 0		13102		x		x				x	x			x		x	x	x	x	x	s			s				x			
29	01-Apr	ST. JOHNSTONE	2 - 1	Brannan, Corrigan	5910		x						x	x	s		s		x	x	x	x	x	s						x	x	x		
30	05-Apr	Celtic	0 - 4		58353		x		x				x	x	x		x		x			x	x	x			x			x	x	x		
31	08-Apr	Dundee	1 - 4	Goodman	4701		x		x			s		x	x		x		x	x		x	x	s						x	x	s		
32	16-Apr	KILMARNOCK	2 - 0	Brannan, McCulloch	5813		x		x				x	x		x	x	s	x	s	x	x	x								x	s		
33	19-Apr	DUNDEE UNITED	1 - 3	McCulloch	4279	x			x				x	x		x	x	s	x		x	x	x								x	s		
34	22-Apr	Aberdeen	1 - 2	Brannan	8065		x						x			x		s	x	x	x	x	x	x			s				x		x	s
35	29-Apr	CELTIC	1 - 1	Brannan	10500		x		x				x			s		x	x	x		x	x	s			s		x		x		x	
36	06-May	HIBERNIAN	2 - 0	Twaddle (2)	5426		x		x				x	x		x	s	x	x	x		x		s					x		x			s
37	13-May	Dundee United	2 - 1	Goodman, Townsley	5908	x			x				x	x		s	x	x	x	x		x					s		x		x		s	
38	21-May	RANGERS	2 - 0	Twaddle, Spencer	49622	x			x				x				s	x	x	x	x	x					s		x		x		x	

LEAGUE CUP

Date	Opponent	Score	Scorers	Att	Goram	Woods	Doesburg	Kemble	Teale	Denham	Craigan	Strong	McMillan	McGowan	Townsley	Twaddle	Spencer	Goodman	Adams	Valakari	Brannan	McCulloch	Nicholas	Matthaei	Thomas	Nevin	Halliday	Harvey	Davies j	Corrigan	Curcic	Hammell	Ramsay
18-Aug	Raith Rovers *	2 - 2	Halliday, OG	2393	x		x						x	x	x		x	x	x		x				x	x	s						
13-Oct	Inverness Cale. Th..	1 - 0	McCulloch		x		x		x				x		x		x	s		x	x	x			x	x	s						
01-Dec	Dundee United	2 - 3	Townsley, Teale			x	x	x	x				x		x	x	x	x		x	x				s	s	x						

* Won on pens.

SCOTTISH CUP

	Date	Opponent	Score	Scorers	Att	Goram	Woods	Doesburg	Kemble	Teale	Denham	Craigan	Strong	McMillan	McGowan	Townsley	Twaddle	Spencer	Goodman	Adams	Valakari	Brannan	McCulloch	Nicholas	Matthaei	Thomas	Nevin	Halliday	Harvey	Davies j	Corrigan	Curcic	Hammell	Ramsay
	29-Jan	Arbroath *	1 - 0	Townsley	4101	x		x			x	x		x		x			x		x	x	x	x			s							
	01-Feb	Arbroath	1 - 1	Goodman	2019	x		x			x	x		x		x	x		x		x	x	x				s							
rep.	19-Feb	ARBROATH	2 - 0	Goodman, McCulloch	5311	x		x			x			x	x	s	s	x	x		x	x	x							x				
	26-Feb	AYR UNITED	3 - 4	McCulloch, Goodman, Brannan	5222	x		x			x			x	x	x	x		x		x	x	x	s			s			s				

* Abandoned

FRIENDLIES

	Date	Opponent	Score	Scorers
	21-Jul	Queens Park	4 - 0	McCulloch (2), Teale, Adams
	24-Jul	Carlisle United	4 - 1	Nyyssonen (2), Tensley, Goodman
	27-Jul	Tranmere Rovers	0 - 2	
	21-Mar	GOTHENBURG	0 - 0	
	16-Jul	Tord	9 - 0	Townsley(4),McCulloch(2),Goodman,Halliday,Teale
	14-Jul	Junkoping Sodra	3 - 0	McCulloch, Goodman, Halliday
	18-Jul	Huskavarna	5 - 0	McCulloch(2),Goodman,Halliday,Teale
	08-Oct	Airdrie	2 - 0	Townsley, Halliday
DL Park	22-Jul	NEWCASTLE UNITED	2 - 2	

2000 Premier League

		Pl.	Home W.	D.	L.	F.	A.	Away W.	D.	L.	F.	A.	F. (Total)	A.	Pts
1	Rangers	36	16	1	1	52	12	12	5	1	44	14	96	26	90
2	Celtic	36	12	3	3	58	17	9	3	6	32	21	90	38	69
3	Hearts	36	7	6	5	25	18	8	3	7	22	22	47	40	54
4	MOTHERWELL	36	8	3	7	27	34	6	7	5	22	29	49	63	52
5	St.Johnstone	36	5	7	6	16	18	5	5	8	20	26	36	44	42
6	Hibernian	36	7	6	5	30	27	3	5	10	19	34	49	61	41
7	Dundee	36	4	3	11	20	33	8	2	8	25	31	45	64	41
8	Dundee U	36	6	4	8	16	22	5	2	11	18	35	34	57	39
9	Kilmarnock	36	5	5	8	16	22	3	8	7	22	30	38	52	37
10	Aberdeen	36	6	4	8	28	37	3	2	13	16	46	44	83	33

2000-2001: Premier League

No.	Date	Opponent	Score	Scorers	Att.	Goram	Woods	Connolly	Corrigan	Kemble	Oueifio	McMillan	Strong	Hammell	Leitch	Strong	Twaddle	Townsley	Brannan	Adams	Harvey	Lasley	Elliot	Davies	Ramsey	Okoli	Goodman	Spencer	McCulloch	Chiba	McClen	Pearson	McFadden	Nicholas	Wood	Dempsie
1	29-Jul	DUNDEE	0 - 2		6160	x			x	x	s	x	x				x	x	x		x		s	x										x	s	
2	04-Aug	Celtic	0 - 1		58535	x			x	x		x	x	x				s	x		x		s	x					x					s	x	
3	12-Aug	Dundee United	1 - 1	Spencer	6201	x			x		x	x	x	x	s			x	x		x						s	x	x							
4	16-Aug	DUNFERMLINE	0 - 1		5257	x			x		x	x	x	x	x		x	s		s	x						s	x	x							
5	19-Aug	Kilmarnock	2 - 3	Elliot (2)	6533	x			x	x	x	x	x	x				x					x		s		x	x	x					s	s	
6	27-Aug	ABERDEEN	1 - 1	McCulloch	5541	x			x		x	x	x		x				x	x	s		s				x	x	x						s	
7	09-Sep	St. Mirren	1 - 0	McCulloch	5274	x			s	x	x	x		x	x		x	s	x				x				s	x	x							
8	16-Sep	Hibernian	0 - 2		9868	x			s	x	x	x	s	x			x	x	x	s			x				x		x							
9	23-Sep	RANGERS	0 - 1		11275	x				x	x	x	x	x	x		x		x	x			s				s	s	x							
10	01-Oct	Hearts	0 - 3		10460		x		s	x	x		x	x				s	x	x	x		x				s	x	x							
11	14-Oct	ST. JOHNSTONE	4 - 0	OG, McCulloch, Brannan, Elliot	4483		x		x	x			x	x				x	x	x			x				s	x	x		s			s		
12	21-Oct	Dundee	2 - 1	Elliot (2)	7344		x		x		x	x	x	x				s	x	x			x				s	x	x					s		
13	29-Oct	CELTIC	3 - 3	Adams, McCulloch, Brannan	10820		x		x	x		x	x	x	s			s	x	x			x				s	x	x							
14	04-Nov	DUNDEE UNITED	2 - 1	Brannan, McCulloch	6864		x		x	x		x	x	x	s			s	x	x			x				s	x	x							
15	11-Nov	Dunfermline Ath.	2 - 1	Townsley, Brannan	5280		x		x			x	x	x	x			s	x	x			x				x		x					s		
16	18-Nov	KILMARNOCK	1 - 2	Brannan	6571		x		x	x		x		x	x		s	x	x	s			x					x	x					s		
17	25-Nov	Aberdeen	3 - 3	McCulloch (2), Townsley	12324	x			x	x		x	x	x	x		s	x	x	s			s				x		x							
18	29-Nov	ST. MIRREN	2 - 0	Twaddle, Nicholas	5312		x		x	x	s		x	x	x		x	x	x				x		s				x					s		
19	03-Dec	HIBERNIAN	1 - 3	Elliot	5715		x		x	x		x	x	x	x		x	x	x				s		s				x					s		
20	10-Dec	Rangers	0 - 2		46519	x			x	x	s		x	x	x		x		x	s		x	x					s	x							
21	16-Dec	HEARTS	2 - 0	Townsley, Adams	5540	x			x		s	x	x	x	x		x	x	x	s			s					x	x							
22	23-Dec	St. Johnstone	3 - 2	Spencer, Adams, Townsley	3489	x			x		s	x	x	x	x		x	x		x			s					x	x		s					
23	26-Dec	DUNDEE	0 - 3			x			x	x	s	x	x	x	x							s	x					x			x		s	x		
24	02-Jan	Dundee United	0 - 2			x			x			x	x	x	x		x	x	x	s			s				s	x	x							
25	31-Jan	DUNFERMLINE	1 - 1	McCulloch	4601	x			x	x		x	x		x		s	x	x	x							s	x	x							
26	03-Feb	Kilmarnock	2 - 1	Brannan, Twaddle	6018	x			x		x	x	x	s	x			x	x	x		s						x	x							
27	10-Feb	ABERDEEN	0 - 1		6680	x			x		x	x	x	s	x			x	x	x			s					x	x							
28	21-Feb	Celtic	0 - 1			x			x	x		x	x	x	x			x		x		s	s	s				x	x							
29	24-Feb	St. Mirren	1 - 0	Townsley		x			x	x		x	x	x			x	x		x		x	s		s				x					s		
30	04-Mar	Hibernian	1 - 1	Strong		x			x				x	x	x		x	x		x		x	s		x		s	x				s				
31	17-Mar	RANGERS	1 - 2	Goodman		x			x				x		x							x	x		x	x	x			x		s	x	s	s	
32	31-Mar	Hearts	0 - 3				x		x				x	x	x		x	x		x		s	x		s	x				x				s		
33	07-Apr	ST. JOHNSTONE	1 - 0	Elliot			x		x				x	x	x		x			x		s	x			x				x			s	x	s	
34	21-Apr	ST. JOHNSTONE	0 - 1				x				x		x	x	x		x			s	x		x			x				x			s	x		
35	28-Apr	Dundee United	0 - 1					x	s		x			x			x			s	x	x	s			x				x		x			x	
36	05-May	ABERDEEN	0 - 2					x	x	x	x			x			x	x			x		x			s				x		s	s		x	
37	12-May	Dunfermline Ath.	2 - 1	Elliot (2)			x		x	x				x			x	x			x	s	x			s				x		x		x	s	
38	20-May	ST. MIRREN	3 - 3	Elliot (2), Ramsey			x		x	x				x			x	x			x	x	x		x							x	s	s		

LEAGUE CUP

Date	Opponent	Score	Scorers	Att.	Goram	Woods	Connolly	Corrigan	Kemble	Oueifio	McMillan	Strong	Hammell	Leitch	Strong	Twaddle	Townsley	Brannan	Adams	Harvey	Lasley	Elliot	Davies	Ramsey	Okoli	Goodman	Spencer	McCulloch	Chiba	McClen	Pearson	McFadden	Nicholas	Wood	Dempsie
22-Aug	Queens Park	3 - 0	Strong, McCulloch, Harvey	1845	x			x		x	x	x	x				x		x	s		x	s			x		x							
06-Sep	Dunfermline Ath.	0 - 2		3438	x			x		x	x		x	x			x	s				s	x			x	x	x					s		

SCOTTISH CUP

Date	Opponent	Score	Scorers	Att.	Goram	Woods	Connolly	Corrigan	Kemble	Oueifio	McMillan	Strong	Hammell	Leitch	Strong	Twaddle	Townsley	Brannan	Adams	Harvey	Lasley	Elliot	Davies	Ramsey	Okoli	Goodman	Spencer	McCulloch	Chiba	McClen	Pearson	McFadden	Nicholas	Wood	Dempsie
27-Jan	St. Mirren	2 - 1	McCulloch, Spencer	5002	x			x	x			x	x	x		s	x	x	x							x	s	x							
17-Feb	DUNDEE UNITED	0 - 2		6168	x			x		x			x	x		x	x		x		x	x					x				s	s			s

FRIENDLIES

Date	Opponent	Score	Scorers
22-Jul	HUDDERSFIELD	1 - 1	Brannan
25-Jul	LIVINGSTON	6 - 1	Harvey,Spencer,Brannan,Nicholas,Davies,Elliot
05-Apr	Dalziel F. P.	5 - 1	
19-May	10th ANNIVERSARY	6 - 6	
18-Jul	Balstra (Swe)	6 - 0	Adams(2),Townsley,Twaddle,Brannan,Davies
20-Jul	Enkopping	2 - 2	McCulloch, Townsley

2001 Premier League

		Pl.	Home W.	D.	L.	F.	A.	Away W.	D.	L.	F.	A.	F. (Total)	A.	Pts.
1	Celtic	38	17	1	1	49	11	14	3	2	41	18	90	29	97
2	Rangers	38	15	0	4	45	16	11	4	4	31	20	76	36	82
3	Hibernian	38	11	6	2	37	15	7	6	6	20	20	57	35	66
4	Kilmarnock	38	7	4	8	20	25	8	5	6	24	28	44	53	54
5	Hearts	38	11	2	6	36	21	3	8	8	20	29	56	50	52
6	Dundee	38	4	7	8	25	24	9	1	9	26	25	51	49	47
7	Aberdeen	38	6	6	7	24	24	5	6	8	21	28	45	52	45
8	MOTHERWELL	38	5	4	10	22	27	7	3	9	20	29	42	56	43
9	Dunfermline	38	8	6	5	20	17	3	3	13	14	37	34	54	42
10	St.Johnstone	38	4	6	9	22	31	5	7	7	18	25	40	56	40
11	Dundee U	38	5	6	8	21	28	4	2	13	17	35	38	63	35
12	St. Mirren	38	7	3	9	20	25	1	3	15	12	47	32	72	30

2000-01 Season
Back: A.MacDonald (Kit Controller), Pearson, K.MacDonald, McCulloch, Wilson, Townsley, Strong, Twaddle, Kemble, Dempsie, Miller, McFadden, Nicholas, Philliben (Coach)
Middle: Krivokapic (1st Team Coach), Crawley, Ramsay, Kinniburgh, Brannan, Ewing, Woods, Goram, Connolly, Corrigan, Constable, Clarke, Lasley, McParland (Yth Dev. Man)
Front: Weir (Coach), Brawley, Fallon, Spencer, Goodman, McMillan, B.Davies (Man), Adams, Elliott, Wood, J.Davies, Harvey, Portuous (Physio)

2001-02 Season
Back: Wood, Nicholas, Ramsay, Oueifio, Adams, Lasley, Hammell, Elliott
Middle: MacDonald, Pearson, Twaddle, Ready, Woods, Brown, Strong, Forest, Corrigan, Porteous (Physio)
Front: Philliben (Coach), Cosgrove, Martinez, Kelly, Davies, Leitch, Harvey, Dow, Krivokapic (Coach)

2001-2002: Premier League

No.	Date	Opponent	Score	Scorers	Att.	Brown	Corrigan	Hammell	Strong	Ready	Twaddle	Martinez	Dow	Elliot	Kelly	Adams	Tarrant	McFadden	Forrest	Lasley	Nicholas	Leitch	Deloumeaux	Soloy	Pearson	Lehmann	Woods	Dubordeau	Ramsey	Ferrere	Bernhard	Fagan	Cosgrove	Harvey	Kinniburgh	Quinn	Clark	McDonald K
1	28-Jul	Dunfermline	2 - 5	Kelly, Adams	4380	x	x	x	x	x	x	x	x	x	x	x	s			s	s																	
2	04-Aug	DUNDEE UNITED	0 - 0		5057	x	x	x	x	x	x	x	x	s	x		x					x											s	s				
3	12-Aug	KILMARNOCK	2 - 2	Dow, Elliot	5188	x	x	x	x	x	x	x	x	s	x	s	x		s			x																
4	18-Aug	Aberdeen	2 - 4	Ready, Kelly	10988	x	x	x	x	x	x	x	x	x	x	x			s						s								s					
5	25-Aug	LIVINGSTON	0 - 0		4328	x	x	x		x	s	s	x		x	x		x	x	x		x			s													
6	08-Sep	HIBERNIAN	1 - 3	Kelly	5784	x	x	s		x	x		x	x	x	x	s		x		s	x			x													
7	15-Sep	Rangers	0 - 3		47137	x	x	x	x	x		x		x	x	s			x	s		x			x									s				
8	22-Sep	HEARTS	2 - 0	Kelly, Elliot	4808	x	x	x		x	s		s	x	x	s			x	x	x	x			x													
9	29-Sep	St. Johnstone	3 - 2	Nicholas (2), Elliot	3209	x	x	x		x	x		s	x	x	s			x	x	s	x			x													
10	13-Oct	CELTIC	1 - 2	Strong	9922	x	s	x	x	x		s		x	x	s			x	x	x	x			x													
p 30/10	16-Oct	Dundee	1 - 3	Kelly	6836	x	x	x	x	x				x	x	x		s	x	s	x				x													
12	27-Oct	Dundee United	1 - 1	Kelly	6343	x	x	x	x	x		s		x	x	x			x		x				x								s					
13	03-Nov	DUNFERMLINE	1 - 0	Strong	4578	x	x	x	x	x	s			x	x	x			s	x	s	x			x													
14	17-Nov	Kilmarnock	0 - 2		6813	x	x	x	x	x	s			x		x				x	x	x	x		s													
15	24-Nov	ABERDEEN	3 - 2	Pearson, Elliot, McFadden	7320	x	x	x	x	x				x		x		s	s	x		x	x		x													
16	01-Dec	Livingston	1 - 3	McFadden	5426	x	x	x		x	s			x	x	x		s		x		x	x		x													
17	08-Dec	Hibernian	1 - 1	Elliot	11158	x	s	x	x	x				x	x	s		x		x		x	x	x														
18	15-Dec	RANGERS	2 - 2	Lasley, Kelly	9894	x	s	x	x	x				x	x			x		x		x	x	x	s													
19	22-Dec	Hearts	1 - 3	Elliot	10674		s	x	x	x				x	x			x		x		x	x	x	s		x											
20	26-Dec	ST. JOHNSTONE	1 - 2	McFadden	4659			x	x	x		s		x	x	x		s		x		x	x	x	s		x											
p 9/1	29-Dec	DUNDEE	4 - 2	McFadden (2), Elliot, Ready	5003			x	x	x				x				x		x	s	x	x	x	x		x		s									
22	02-Jan	Celtic	0 - 2		57695		x	x	x	x			x	s	x			x		x			x	x			x											
23	12-Jan	DUNDEE UNITED	2 - 0	McFadden, Hammil	6195		x	x	x			s	x		x	x		x		x	s		x	x			x											
24	19-Jan	Dunfermline Ath.	1 - 3	McFadden	4280			x	x	x				x				x		x	s	x	x	x	x	s	x											
25	23-Jan	KILMARNOCK	2 - 0	McFadden, Lehman	4342		s	x	x	x				x				x		x		x	x	x	s	x	x											
p 10/11	30-Jan	Aberdeen	0 - 1		11490	x	x	x	x	x	x			x		x				x	s	x	s		x													
27	02-Feb	LIVINGSTON	1 - 2	Soloy	4458			x	x	x				x		s		x			s	x	x	x	x	x	x											
28	09-Feb	HIBERNIAN	4 - 0	Ferrere (3), Lehman	5367		x	x	x	x				x		x				x	s	x	x			x	x			s								
29	16-Feb	Rangers	0 - 3		49284			x	x	x				x		x		x		x		x	x		s	x	x			s								
30	02-Mar	HEARTS	1 - 2	Lasley	7223		x	x	x	x				s		x		x		x		x				x	x			x								
31	09-Mar	St. Johnstone	2 - 0	Lehman, McFadden	3282		x	x	x	x		x		s				x		x			x		s	x	x			x								
32	16-Mar	Dundee	0 - 2		5785		x	x	x	x		x		s				x		x			x	s		x	x			x								
33	23-Mar	CELTIC	0 - 4		10134		x	x	x	x				x		s		x		x			x	x	x			x		s								
34	06-Apr	ST. JOHNSTONE	1 - 1	Elliot	3418		x	x	x	s		x		x		x		x			s		x					x		x	x							
35	13-Apr	Dundee United	0 - 1		5108		x	x		x		s		x		x		x					x			x	s	x		x	x							
36	21-Apr	Hibernian	0 - 4		7701		x	x	x	x		s		x		x		x					x		x			x		x		s						
37	27-Apr	Kilmarnock	4 - 1	Pearson, McFadden, Adams, Elliot	5642		x	x	x	x						x		x							x	x	x		x	x		s						
38	12-May	DUNDEE	2 - 1	Lehman, Elliot	5235			x						x		x		x		x			x		x	x	x		x						x	s	s	s

LEAGUE CUP

No.	Date	Opponent	Score	Scorers	Att.	Brown	Corrigan	Hammell	Strong	Ready	Twaddle	Martinez	Dow	Elliot	Kelly	Adams	Tarrant	McFadden	Forrest	Lasley	Nicholas	Leitch	Deloumeaux	Soloy	Pearson	Lehmann	Woods	Dubordeau	Ramsey	Ferrere	Bernhard	Fagan	Cosgrove	Harvey	Kinniburgh	Quinn	Clark	McDonald K
	25-Sep	Aidrie	1 - 2	Kelly	3309	x	x	x		x				x	x	s	s		x	x	x	x			x								s					

SCOTTISH CUP

No.	Date	Opponent	Score	Scorers	Att.	Brown	Corrigan	Hammell	Strong	Ready	Twaddle	Martinez	Dow	Elliot	Kelly	Adams	Tarrant	McFadden	Forrest	Lasley	Nicholas	Leitch	Deloumeaux	Soloy	Pearson	Lehmann	Woods	Dubordeau	Ramsey	Ferrere	Bernhard	Fagan	Cosgrove	Harvey	Kinniburgh	Quinn	Clark	McDonald K
	05-Jan	Dunfermline Ath.	0 - 3		5131		x	x	x				x	s	x	x		x	s	x			x	x	s		x											

FRIENDLIES

	Date	Opponent	Score	Scorers
	12-Jul	La Baule (Fra.)	1 - 4	Twaddle
	14-Jul	Noirt	0 - 2	
	15-Jul	Quatar Nat. team	2 - 2	Trialist (Bambuana), Strong
	17-Jul	Albion Rovers	2 - 0	Twaddle, Elliot
	21-Jul	NORWICH CITY	0 - 0	
	07-May	CHIEVO	1 - 1	McFadden
	13-May	Schweinfurt 05	3 - 1	Adams (2), Lasley

2002 Premier League

		Pl.	Home W.	Home D.	Home L.	Home F.	Home A.	Away W.	Away D.	Away L.	Away F.	Away A.	F. (Total)	A. (Total)	Pts. (Total)
1	Celtic	38	18	1	0	51	9	15	3	1	43	9	94	18	103
2	Rangers	38	14	4	1	42	11	11	6	2	40	16	82	27	85
3	Livingston	38	9	5	4	23	17	7	5	8	27	30	50	47	58
4	Aberdeen	38	12	2	5	31	19	4	5	10	20	30	51	49	55
5	Hearts	38	8	3	8	30	27	6	3	10	22	30	52	57	48
6	Dunfermline	38	9	4	6	25	24	3	5	11	16	40	41	64	45
7	Kilmarnock	38	7	6	6	24	26	6	4	9	20	28	44	54	49
8	Dundee U	38	6	5	8	18	30	6	5	8	20	29	38	59	46
9	Dundee	38	8	5	6	23	24	4	3	12	18	31	41	55	44
10	Hibernian	38	6	6	7	35	30	4	5	10	16	26	51	56	41
11	MOTHERWELL	38	8	5	6	30	25	3	2	14	19	44	49	69	40
12	St.Johnstone	38	2	3	15	11	32	3	3	12	13	30	24	62	21

2002-2003: Premier League

						Woods	Corrigan	Hammell	Lasley	Ramsey	Pearson	McDonald K	Leitch	Lehman	McFadden	Partridge	Adams	Sengewald	Fagan	Ferguson	Cowan	Khemas	Kinniburgh	Dubordeau	Dempsie	Quinn	Clarkson	Vaughan	Craig	Russell	Offiong	Wright	Scott	Ballantyne
1	03-Aug	Livingston	2 - 3	Leitch, Lehman	7124	x	x	x	x	x	x	x	x	x	x	x							s											
2	10-Aug	PARTICK THISTLE	1 - 1	Pearson	5788	x	x	x	x	x	x	x	x	x	x	x							s											
3	17-Aug	Kilmarnock	3 - 0	Pearson, Ramsey, McFadden	6164	x	x	x	x	x	x		x	x	x	x	x		s				s											
4	25-Aug	Dundee United	1 - 1	Pearson	5795	x	x	x	x	x	x		x	x	x	x	x			s			s											
5	31-Aug	HIBERNIAN	0 - 2		5888	x	x	x	x	x	x		x	x	x	x	x		s	s			s											
6	10-Sep	CELTIC	2 - 1	Fagan, McFadden	8448	x	x	x	x	s	x		x	x	x	x	x	x	s	s														
7	15-Sep	Hearts	2 - 4	McFadden, Lehman	8758	x	x	x	x	x		s		x	x	x	x	x	x	s														
8	21-Sep	Dunfermline Ath.	0 - 1		4987	x	x	x	x	s	x		x	x	x	x	x	x	s	s														
9	28-Sep	DUNDEE	1 - 1	McFadden	4025	x	x	x	x	x	x			x	x	x	x			x			s											
10	05-Oct	ABERDEEN	1 - 2	McFadden	6014	x	x	x	x	x			x	x	x	x	x			x										s				
11	19-Oct	Rangers	0 - 3		49376	x	x	x	x	x	x			x		x	x			x	x													
12	26-Oct	LIVINGSTON	1 - 5	Khemas	4342	x	x	x	x	x	x		x	x			x			s	x	x												
13	02-Nov	Partick Thistle	0 - 2		5404	x	x	x	s		x		x	s	x		x	x		s	x	x	x											
14	09-Nov	KILMARNOCK	0 - 1		5125		x	x		x	x	x		x		x	x			s	x	x	s	x						s				
15	16-Nov	DUNDEE UNITED	1 - 2	Lehman	5381		x	x		x	x			x		x	x		s	x	x	x		x						s				
16	23-Nov	Hibernian	1 - 3	Ferguson	8859		x	x			x			x	s	x	x	x	x	x	x			x										
17	30-Nov	Celtic	1 - 3	Lehman	56733		x	x				s	x	x	x		x		x	x		s	x	x	x	s								
18	04-Dec	HEARTS	6 - 1	McFadden(2),Adams,Pearson,Ferguson,Lehman	4114		x	x			x		x	x	x	x	x	x		s			x	x										
19	07-Dec	Aberdeen	1 - 1	Kinniburgh	9569		x	x				s	x	x	x		x		x	x			x	x		x	s							
20	14-Dec	Dundee	1 - 1	Lehman	5527		x	x				s	x	x	x		x		x	x			x	x		x	s							
p 19/2	21-Dec	DUNFERMLINE	2 - 1	Pearson, Craig	3741		x	x	s	s	x					x	x		x		x			x			x	x	x					
22	26-Dec	RANGERS	1 - 0	McFadden	11234		x	x			x		x	x	x	x	x				x		x	x										
23	29-Dec	Livingston	0 - 1		7216		x	x			x		x	x	x	x	x		s	s	x		x	x			s							
24	02-Jan	PARTICK THISTLE	2 - 2	Partridge, Clarkson	6262		x	x			x		x	x	x	x	x		s	s			x	x			x							
25	29-Jan	Kilmarnock	0 - 1		4457	s	x		x		x		x			x	x		s		x		x	x			x		x					
26	02-Feb	Dundee United	1 - 2	Adams	6672	x	x	x	s		x		x			x	x		s				x				x	x	x		s			
27	08-Feb	HIBERNIAN	2 - 1	Clarkson, Fagan	4999		x	x			x		x			x	x		s		x	s		x			x	x	x					
p 7/5	15-Feb	CELTIC	0 - 4		12037	x	x	x			x		x	s	x	x	x				x						x	x						
29	01-Mar	Hearts	1 - 2	Lasley	11704		x	x	x	x	x			s	x	x			x					x			x	x			s			
30	08-Mar	ABERDEEN	0 - 1		5636		x	x	x	x	x			s	x	x			x					x			x	x						
31	15-Mar	Rangers	0 - 2		49240		x	x	x	x				x	x	x	x							x			x	x						
32	05-Apr	Dunfermline Ath.	0 - 3		4066		x	x	x				x	x	x	x	x				x			x				x						
33	12-Apr	DUNDEE	1 - 2	McFadden	4693		x	x	x				x	x	x	x	x				x			x					x					
34	26-Apr	Partick Thistle	0 - 3		4870		x	x				s		x	x	x	x				x		s	x			x	x	x					
35	03-May	DUNDEE UNITED	2 - 2	Vaughan, Pearson	9056	x	x	x			x		x	s	x	x	x										x	x	x		s			
36	10-May	Hibernian	0 - 1		7809		x	x	x	x	x		x	x	x	x							s	x			s	x	s					
37	17-May	ABERDEEN	2 - 3	McFadden, Clarkson	4731		x	x	x	x	x		x	x	x	x								x				x	s					
38	24-May	LIVINGSTON	6 - 2	McFadden (3), Lasley (2), Craig	6003		x	x	x		x	x			x								x	x		x	x		x			s	s	s

LEAGUE CUP

						Woods	Corrigan	Hammell	Lasley	Ramsey	Pearson	McDonald K	Leitch	Lehman	McFadden	Partridge	Adams	Sengewald	Fagan	Ferguson	Cowan	Khemas	Kinniburgh	Dubordeau	Dempsie	Quinn	Clarkson	Vaughan	Craig	Russell	Offiong	Wright	Scott	Ballantyne
	24-Sep	East Fife	2 - 0	Lehman, McFadden	978	x	x	x	x	x		s	x	x	x	x	x			x	s									s				
	06-Nov	Aberdeen	1 - 3	Adams	6557	x	x	x	x	s	x		x	x		x	x			s	x	x	s											

SCOTTISH CUP

						Woods	Corrigan	Hammell	Lasley	Ramsey	Pearson	McDonald K	Leitch	Lehman	McFadden	Partridge	Adams	Sengewald	Fagan	Ferguson	Cowan	Khemas	Kinniburgh	Dubordeau	Dempsie	Quinn	Clarkson	Vaughan	Craig	Russell	Offiong	Wright	Scott	Ballantyne
	25-Jan	Kilmarnock	1 - 0	McFadden	6882		x	x	x		x		x		x	x	x		s		s		x	x			x							
	22-Feb	Clyde	2 - 0	McFadden (2)	5023		x	x	s	x	x			s	x	x	x		x					x			s	x	x					
	22-Mar	Stranraer	4 - 0	McFadden, OG, Adams, Lehman	4500		x	x	x		x		x	x	x	x	x							x				x						
S/F	19-Apr	Rangers	4 - 3	McFadden, Adams, Craig	29352		x	x			x		x		x	x	x							x			x	x	x					

FRIENDLIES

Date	Opponent	Result	Scorers
16-Jul	Stenhousemuir	3 - 0	Adams (2), Lehman
22-Jul	St. Mirren	2 - 0	Pearson, Adams
29-Jul	Arbroath	3 - 2	Russell (2), Mathie
24-Jul	BIRMINGHAM	2 - 1	Adams, McFadden
28-Jul	CARDIFF CITY	1 - 0	Adams
30-Jul	Bellshill Juniors	1 - 2	Clarkson

2003 Premier League

		Pl.	Home W.	D.	L.	F.	A.	Away W.	D.	L.	F.	A.	F. (Total)	A.	Pts.
1	Rangers	38	18	0	1	55	12	13	4	2	46	16	101	28	97
2	Celtic	38	18	1	0	56	12	13	3	3	42	14	98	26	97
3	Hearts	38	12	3	4	36	24	6	6	7	21	27	57	51	63
4	Kilmarnock	38	9	5	5	26	21	7	4	8	21	35	47	56	57
5	Dunfermline	38	9	3	7	32	30	4	4	11	22	41	54	71	46
6	Dundee	38	6	7	6	29	27	4	7	8	21	33	50	60	44
7	Hibernian	38	8	3	8	28	29	7	3	9	28	35	56	64	51
8	Aberdeen	38	5	7	7	19	21	8	3	8	22	33	41	54	49
9	Livingston	38	5	4	10	23	28	4	4	11	25	34	48	62	35
10	Partick Ths.	38	5	6	8	23	23	3	5	11	14	35	37	58	35
11	Dundee U	38	2	7	10	18	32	5	4	10	17	36	35	68	32
12	MOTHERWELL	38	6	4	9	31	34	1	3	15	14	37	45	71	28

2002-03 Season

Back : A McDonald, Mathie, K McDonald, Dempsie, Woods, Dubourdoux, Ewings, Jack, Lehmann, Partridge, P Salia.
Middle : G Diamond, Pearson, McFadden, Barkey, Russell, Kinniburgh, Cowan, Fitzpatrick, Clarke, Fagan, Corrigan, J Porteous.
Front : G Adams, D Adams, Ramsey, Sengewald, Butcher, Leitch, Hammell, Lasley, C McCart.

2003-04 Season

Back : Butcher, Quinn, Craigan, Clarkson, Partridge, Ewings, Marshall, Pearson, K McDonald, Mathie, Ballantyne, Malpas.
Front : Corrigan, Hammell, Lasley, McFadden, Fagan, Leitch, Adams, Burns, Cowan, Craig, Kinniburgh

2003-2004: Premier League

	Date	Opponent	Score	Scorers	Att.	Marshall	Corrigan	Hammell	Partridge	Craigan	McDonald K	Leitch	Pearson	Craig	Clarkson	Burns	Corr	Quinn	Kinniburgh	Wright	Lasley	Adams	McFadden	Dair	O' Donnell	Bollan	MacDonald S	Fagan	Fitzpatrick	Cowan
1	09-Aug	DUNDEE	0 - 3		6812	x	x	x	x	x	x	x	x	x	x	x							S							
2	16-Aug	Livingston	0 - 1		5316	x	x	x	x	x		x	x	s	x	x				x	x									
3	23-Aug	KILMARNOCK	2 - 1	Pearson, McFadden	5087	x	x	x	x			x	x	s	s	x		x			x	x	x							
4	30-Aug	PARTICK THISTLE	2 - 2	McFadden (2)	6193	x	x	x	x			x	x		s	x		x			x	x	x							
5	13-Sep	Hibernian	2 - 0	Clarkson (2)	8387	x	x	x	x	x		x	x	s	x	x					x	x		s						
6	20-Sep	Celtic	0 - 3		58013	x	x	x	x	x		x	x	x	x					s	x	x								
7	27-Sep	HEARTS	1 - 1	Adams	5880	x	x	x	x	x		x	x	x	x						x	x						s		
8	04-Oct	Dundee United	2 - 0	Adams (2)	6194	x	x	x	x	x		x	x	x	x						x	x		s						
9	19-Oct	RANGERS	1 - 1	Pearson	10824	x	x	x	x	x		x	x	x	x						x	x		s						
10	01-Nov	Aberdeen	3 - 0	Lasley, Pearson, Craig	9895	x	x	x	x	x		x	x	x	x						x	x		s						
11	08-Nov	Dundee	0 - 1		6374	x	x	x	x	x		x	x	x	x	s				s	x	x								
12	22-Nov	LIVINGSTON	1 - 1	Clarkson	6357	x	x	x	x	x		x	x	x	x	s					x	x								
13	25-Nov	DUNFERMLINE	2 - 2	Pearson, Corrigan	4220	x	x	x	x	x		x	x	x	x	s					x	x		s						
14	29-Nov	Kilmarnock	0 - 2		6320	x	x	x	x	x		x	x	x	x	s		s			x	x		s						
15	06-Dec	Partick Thistle	0 - 1		4124	x	x	x	x	x		x	x		x	x				s	x	x								
16	13-Dec	HIBERNIAN	0 - 1		4533	x	x	x		x		x	x		x	x		s			x	x		x						
17	21-Dec	CELTIC	0 - 2		10513	x	x	x		x		x	x		x	x		x			x	x		s						
18	27-Dec	Hearts	0 - 0		10046	x	x	x		x		x			x	x		x			x	x		x						
19	03-Jan	DUNDEE UNITED	3 - 1	Clarkson (3)	5549	x	x	x		x		x			x	x		x			x	x		x	s					
20	17-Jan	Rangers	0 - 1		48925	x	x	x		x		x			x	x		x			x	x		x		s	s			
21	24-Jan	Dunfermline Ath.	0 - 1		5270		x	x		x					x	x	x	x			x	x		x	x		s			
22	11-Feb	DUNDEE	5 - 3	Dairy (2), Lasley, Clarkson, Burns	4247	x	x	x		x	s				x	x		x			x	x		x	x	s	s			
23	14-Feb	Livingston	1 - 3	Adams	3492	x	x			x					x	x		x		s	x	x		x	x	x	s			
24	21-Feb	KILMARNOCK	1 - 0	Quinn	5163	x	x	x		x	x				x	x		x			x	x		x						
25	24-Feb	ABERDEEN	1 - 0	Wright	5220	x	x	x		x	s			s	x	x		x		s	x			x			x	x		
26	28-Feb	PARTICK THISTLE	3 - 0	Hammell, Clarkson, Adams	5790	x	x	x		x	s			s	x	x		x		s	x	x					x	x		
27	13-Mar	Celtic	1 - 1	Adams	47563	x	x	x						x	x	x		x		s	x	x		s			x	x		
p 7/4	20-Mar	HEARTS	1 - 1	Clarkson	5500	x	x	x		x				x	x	x		x		s		x		x	x					
29	24-Mar	Hibernian	3 - 3	Lasley, Adams, S McDonald	5670	x	x	x		x					x	x		x	s		x	x		s			x	x		
30	27-Mar	Dundee United	0 - 1		7585	x	x	x		x				s	x	x		x			x			x			x	x		
31	04-Apr	RANGERS	0 - 1		8967	x	x	x		x				x	s	x		x						x	x		x	x		
32	07-Apr	DUNFERMLINE	1 - 0	Adams	3920	x	x	x		x				x	s	x		x			x	x		x	x			s		
33	17-Apr	Aberdeen	2 - 0	Burns, Craig	7246		x	x		x				x	s	x	x	x			x	x		x	x					
34	24-Apr	Dunfermline Ath.	0 - 3		4290		x	x		x				x	s	x	x	x		x	x	x		x				s		
35	01-May	Rangers	0 - 4		47579	x	x	x		x				x	x	x		x				x		x				x		
36	08-May	DUNDEE UNITED	0 - 1		5722	x	x	x		x	s				x	x		x		s		x		x			x	x		
37	12-May	CELTIC	1 - 1	Clarkson	7799		x	x		x					x	x	x	x		s	x			x			x	x	s	
38	16-May	Hearts	2 - 3	Clarkson, McDonald	11974		x	x		x					x	x	x	x		s	x			x			x		x	s

LEAGUE CUP

	Date	Opponent	Score	Scorers	Att.	Marshall	Corrigan	Hammell	Partridge	Craigan	McDonald K	Leitch	Pearson	Craig	Clarkson	Burns	Corr	Quinn	Kinniburgh	Wright	Lasley	Adams	McFadden	Dair	O' Donnell	Bollan	MacDonald S	Fagan	Fitzpatrick	Cowan
	23-Sep	Forfar Athletic	3 - 3	Lasley, Pearson, Craig	1110	x	x	x	x	x		x	x	x	x					s	x	x	s							
		won on pens																												

SCOTTISH CUP

	Date	Opponent	Score	Scorers	Att.	Marshall	Corrigan	Hammell	Partridge	Craigan	McDonald K	Leitch	Pearson	Craig	Clarkson	Burns	Corr	Quinn	Kinniburgh	Wright	Lasley	Adams	McFadden	Dair	O' Donnell	Bollan	MacDonald S	Fagan	Fitzpatrick	Cowan
	10-Jan	St. Johnstone	3 - 0	Clarkson (2), S McDonald	4094	x	x	x		x		x			x	x		x			x	x		x	s		s	s		
	07-Feb	QUEEN OF THE SOUTH	3 - 2	Burns (2), Adams	8101	x	x	x		x					x	x		x			x	x		x	x	s	s			
	06-Mar	INVERNESS C T	0 - 1		7930	x	x	x						x	x	x		x		s	x	x			s		x	x		

FRIENDLIES

	Date	Opponent	Score	Scorers
	15-Jul	Aidrie	2 - 1	Adams (2)
	19-Jul	Hamilton Academical	1 - 1	Adams
	22-Jul	Stenhousemuir	0 - 0	
	26-Jul	Ayr United	4 - 1	Burns (3), Craig
	29-Jul	Carlisle United	2 - 0	Craig, Lasley
	30-Jul	Arbroath	3 - 0	Wright (2), Scott
	02-Aug	FULHAM	2 - 2	Burns (2)

2004 Premier League

		Pl.	Home					Away					F.	A.	Pts.
			W.	D.	L.	F.	A.	W.	D.	L.	F.	A.	(Total)		
1	Celtic	38	15	2	2	62	15	16	3	0	43	10	105	25	98
2	Rangers	38	16	0	3	48	11	9	6	4	28	22	76	33	81
3	Hearts	38	12	5	2	32	17	7	6	6	24	23	56	40	68
4	Dunfermline	38	9	7	3	28	19	5	4	10	17	33	45	52	53
5	Dundee U	38	8	6	5	28	27	5	4	10	19	33	47	60	49
6	MOTHERWELL	38	7	7	5	25	22	5	3	11	17	27	42	49	46
7	Dundee	38	8	3	8	21	20	4	7	8	27	37	48	57	46
8	Hibernian	38	6	5	8	25	28	5	6	8	16	32	41	60	44
9	Livingston	38	6	9	4	24	18	4	4	11	24	39	48	57	43
10	Kilmarnock	38	8	3	8	29	31	4	3	12	22	43	51	74	42
11	Aberdeen	38	5	3	11	22	29	4	4	11	17	34	39	63	34
12	Partick Ths.	38	5	4	10	24	32	1	4	14	15	35	39	67	26

2004-05 Season

Back : A McDonald, Fitzpatrick, Higgins, Kinniburgh, Fagan, Wright, Cowan, Quinn, Paterson, P Salia.
Middle : Porteous, O'Donnell, Foran, Corr, Marshall, Ewings, Clarkson, Partridge, C McCart.
Front : T Butcher, Burns, Bollan, S McDonald, Leitch, Craigan, Kerr, Hammell, Corrigan, M Malpas.

Advanced Subscribers

Alexander Brand, Motherwell
Ally Sim - Aberdeen
Anne Barnstaple - Motherwell
Arthur Richardson - Ampherlaw
Christopher MacRae
Colin Gilfillan - Kingston
Craig Burnside - North Carolina
Craig Scott - Motherwell
David L. Thomson - Motherwell
David MacGregor - Uddingston
David Tonner, Motherwell
Douglas McGregor
Duncan Buchanan
Ewan Clark - Motherwell
Ewan Thomson - Edinburgh
Geoff Baby - Kirkham, England
George Cliff
George H. Stewart - Motherwell
Gordon Richardson - Ampherlaw
Graeme A Wood
Graeme Thomson - Dundee
Graham Hamilton
Graham Harrison - Carluke
James Mitchell, Aberdeen
Janice Slamin - Motherwell
Jim Brown - Motherwell
Jim Tait - Craigneuk, Wishaw
John Leslie - Warrington, Cheshire
John McCulloch - Portswood, Southampton
Jordan Ross Brown - Bishopbriggs
Judith Tonner - Motherwell
Karen Barnstaple - Motherwell
Kathleen Gilmour, Motherwell
Keith Marr - Letchworth GC
Lee Dempster - Lanark
Lee Mitchell - Motherwell
Mark Robertson - Hawthorn Drive
Martin Cranstoun - Glasgow
Martin Milligan, Brodick, Arran
Martyn Brown - Motherwell
Michael Ross, Bradford, England
Neil Clark - Motherwell
Neil Grierson - Carluke
Nicolle Brown - Motherwell
Ricky Langford, Motherwell
Rob Clark
Robert Foster - Kirkfieldbank
Robin Burnside, North Carolina
Robin MacGregor, Uddingston
Sarah Phillips - Glassford, Strathaven
Steven Hunter - Motherwell
Steven Sherry - Motherwell
Stewart"Livi" Livingston - Law
Stewart Cliff
Stuart Harvey - Bearsden
Terry Willoughby - Leamington Spa
Tom Aitchison
Vic Graham - Dellburn Street
William Allan - Cambusnethan
William Barnstaple - Motherwell
William Law - Barnstapale, Devon
Alan "Kaney" Kane, Newarthill
David Earl, Wishaw, Scotland
Tony Hamilton, Motherwell
James Johnstone, Motherwell
Gary Preston, Netherton
Alen Slamin, Motherwell
Mike and Kenneth Angove
Andrew Smith - Law Village
Dave Windross, York City
Mick Grayson
David Jowett, Keighley
Steve Emms, Evesham
Mr. L.A. Zammit, Fareham
Leigh Edwards, Bransgore
Richard Shore
George Painter, Castle Cary
Chas Sumner, Kelsall
Moira & Frederick, Furness
Basil Godley & Margaret Alexander
Phil Hollow, Plymouth Argyle
Robert Smith, Stevenage Colts FC
David Brealey - Chesterfield
Geoff Allman
David Elwyn Griffiths
John Cowan
Jonny Stokkeland, Kvinesdal, Norway
Richard Wells
Fred Lee, Plymouth, Devon
Graham Spackman
John J. Byrne
Chris Marsh, Chesterfield
Stewart Davidson, Paisley
Bob Lilliman
Gareth A. Evans
John R. Orton
Richard Owen; Portsmouth FC Historian
Allan Grieve, Tillicoultry
George Mason
Stephen Kieran Byrne
Thomas Leleux
Colin Cresswell, Throckley
David Yates, Guiseley, Leeds
Steve Taylor, Bury
Simon Milne, Cheltenham
Jim Fisher
Keith & Kieron Coburn
Svein Borge Pettersen, Sandefjord
A and JA Waterman
Willy Østby - Proud Potter
Richard Lane, Norwell, Notts
David J. Godfrey
Robert J. Owen, Fauldhouse
Arran Matthews, Tylers Green
Nicholas Matthews, Tylers Green